Lecture Notes in Computer Science 5684

Commenced Publication in 1973
Founding and Former Series Editors:
Gerhard Goos, Juris Hartmanis, and Jan van Leeuwen

Martin Leucker   Carroll Morgan (Eds.)

Theoretical Aspects of Computing - ICTAC 2009

6th International Colloquium
Kuala Lumpur, Malaysia, August 16-20, 2009
Proceedings

 Springer

Volume Editors

Martin Leucker
TU München
Institut für Informatik
Garching, Germany
E-mail: leucker@in.tum.de

Carroll Morgan
University of New South Wales
School of Computer Science and Engineering
Sydney, Australia
E-mail: carrollm@cse.unsw.edu.au

Library of Congress Control Number: 2009931537

CR Subject Classification (1998): F.1, F.3, F.4, F.2, D.2

LNCS Sublibrary: SL 1 – Theoretical Computer Science and General Issues

ISSN   0302-9743
ISBN-10   3-642-03465-9 Springer Berlin Heidelberg New York
ISBN-13   978-3-642-03465-7 Springer Berlin Heidelberg New York

springer.com

© Springer-Verlag Berlin Heidelberg 2009
Printed in Germany

Typesetting: Camera-ready by author, data conversion by Scientific Publishing Services, Chennai, India
Printed on acid-free paper   SPIN: 12727575   06/3180   5 4 3 2 1 0

Preface

This volume contains the papers presented at ICTAC 2009: the 6th International Colloquium on Theoretical Aspects of Computing held August 18–20, 2009 in Kuala Lumpur, Malaysia, hosted by Universiti Kebangsaan Malaysia.

The ICTAC series was founded by the International Institute for Software Technology of the United Nations University (UNU-IIST). It brings together practitioners and researchers from academia, industry and government to present results and to exchange ideas and experience addressing challenges in both theoretical aspects of computing and in the exploitation of theory through methods and tools for system development. The series also promotes cooperation in research and education between participants and their institutions, from developing and industrial countries, in accordance with the mandate of the United Nations University. The previous ICTAC colloquia were held in Guiyang, China (2004, LNCS 3407), Hanoi, Vietnam (2005, LNCS 3722), Tunis, Tunisia (2006, LNCS 4281), Macao SAR, China (2007, LNCS 4711), and Istanbul, Turkey (2008, LNCS 5160).

This year, 81 submissions were received, distributed over 70 full research papers and 11 tool papers. Each submission was reviewed by at least three Program Committee members. We thank the members of the Program Committee and the other specialist referees for the effort and skill that they invested in the review and selection process, which was managed using EasyChair. The Committee decided to accept 20 papers: 17 full research papers and 3 tool papers. The program and the proceedings, moreover, contain keynote talks from four invited speakers: Zuohua Ding, Leslie Lamport, Annabelle McIver, and Sriram Rajamani. Each invited speaker also offered a tutorial on their work, and these were held before the conference.

ICTAC 2009 was accompanied by the Third International Workshop on Harnessing Theories for Tool Support in Software, chaired by Einar Broch Johnsen and Volker Stolz.

Events such as ICTAC are community efforts and cannot succeed without the generosity of sponsors. ICTAC 2009 was kindly supported by UNU-IIST, Universiti Kebangsaan Malaysia. Leslie Lamport's lecture was made possible by financial support from Formal Methods Europe.

We are grateful to our publisher, especially to Alfred Hofmann and Ursula Barth at Springer for their help in creating this volume. Finally, we would like to thank our fellow organizers of ICTAC 2009: the local organizers in Malaysia, our Workshop Chair Abhik Roychoudhury, and, at UNU-IIST, Kitty Chan. We were greatly helped by the advice, experience and enthusiasm of Zhiming Liu and the ICTAC Steering and Advisory Committees.

June 2009

Martin Leucker
Carroll Morgan

Conference Organization

Conference Committee

General Chairs	Abdullah Mohd Zin (Universiti Kebangsaan Malaysia)
	Jeff Sanders (UNU-IIST)
Program Chairs	Martin Leucker (TU München)
	Carroll Morgan (University of New South Wales)
Workshop Chair	Abhik Roychoudhury (National University of Singapore)
Local Organization	Zarina Shukur, Nazlia Omar, Syahanim Mohd Salleh,
	Mastura Sahak (Universiti Kebangsaan Malaysia)

ICTAC Steering Committee

John S. Fitzgerald	Newcastle University, UK
Martin Leucker	TU München, Germany
Zhiming Liu (Chair)	UNU-IIST, Macao, SAR
Tobias Nipkow	TU München, Germany
Augusto Sampaio	Universidade Federal de Pernambuco, Brazil
Natarajan Shankar	SRI, USA
Jim Woodcock	University of York, UK

Program Committee

Parosh Abdulla
Keijiro Araki
Farhad Arbab
Christel Baier
Mario Bravetti
Ana Cavalcanti
Deepak D'Souza
Van Hung Dang
David Deharbe
Wei Dong
Kokichi Futatsugi
John Fitzgerald
Wan Fokkink
Marcelo Frias
Paul Gastin
Susanne Graf
Lindsay Groves
Anne Haxthausen

Moonzoo Kim
Kim G. Larsen
Insup Lee
Kamal Lodaya
Larissa Meinicke
Ugo Montanari
Ahmed Patel
Pekka Pihlajasaari
Abhik Roychoudhury
Hassen Saidi
Augusto Sampaio
Cesar Sanchez
Marjan Sirjani
Sofiene Tahar
Serdar Tasiran
Helmut Veith
Mahesh Viswanathan
Tomas Vojnar

Ji Wang
Jim Woodcock
Husnu Yenigun

Naijun Zhan
Huibiao Zhu

External Reviewers

Naeem Abbasi
Nikola Benes
Chiranjib Bhattacharyya
Benedikt Bollig
Pontus Boström
Marius Bozga
Anne Brüggemann-Klein
Diego Caminha
Marco Carbone
Jonathan Cederberg
Rohit Chadha
Taolue Chen
Yuki Chiba
Vivien Chinnapongse
Vincenzo Ciancia
Wilhelm Dahlöf
Alexandre David
Anuj Dawar
Arnab De
Nikhil Dinesh
Simon Doherty
Harrison Duong
Rachid Echahed
Christian Eisentraut
Tayfun Elmas
Miguel Valero Espada
Pascal Fontaine
Martin Fränzle
Han Gao
Dinesh Garg
Nils Gesbert
Fatemeh Ghassemi
Ankit Goel
Navin Goyal
Susanne Graf
Hervé Grall
Alexander Gruler
Roberto Guanciale
Bjørn Haagensen

Yousra Ben Daly Hlaoui
Lukas Holik
Andreas Holzer
Hans Hüttel
Juliano Iyoda
Mohammad Javad Izadi
Naiyong Jin
Kalpesh Kapoor
Telikepalli Kavitha
Ramtin Khosravi
Sascha Klueppelholz
K Narayan Kumar
R Ravi Kumar
Shigeru Kusakabe
Anna Labella
Alberto Lluch Lafuente
Zdenek Letko
Qin Li
Xinxin Liu
Jaghoori Mohammad Mahdi
Nicolas Markey
Frederic Mesnard
Marius Mikucionis
Hiroshi Mochio
Laurent Mounier
Narasimha Murthy
Masaki Nakamura
Rajeev Narayanan
Martin Neuhäušer
Thomas Noll
Ulrik Nyman
Kazuhiro Ogata
Yoichi Omori
Adriano Peron
Paul Pettersson
Damien Pous
Pavithra Prabhakar
Vinayak Prabhu
M. Praveen

Adam Rogalewicz
Hamideh Sabouri
Jacques Sakarovitch
Sylvain Schmitz
Philippe Schnoebelen
Uwe Schöning
Maria Grazia Scutellà
Ali Sezgin
Simoni Shah
Zhiqiang Shi
Leila Silva
Pavel Smrz
Oleg Sokolsky

Daniel Thoma
Claus Thrane
Ninh Thuan Truong
Hoang Truong
Ing Ren Tsang
Shmuel Ur
Kapil Vaswani
Björn Victor
Ha Nguyen Viet
Ramesh Viswanathan
Pascal Weil
Andrew West

Table of Contents

Tool Papers

Static Analysis of Concurrent Programs Using Ordinary Differential Equations*

Zuohua Ding

Center of Math Computing and Software Engineering
Zhejiang Sci-Tech University
Hangzhou, Zhejiang, 310018, P.R. China
zouhuading@hotmail.com

Abstract. Static analysis may cause state space explosion problem. In this paper we demonstrate how ordinary differential equations can be used to check the deadlocks and boundedness of the programs. We hope that our method can avoid explosion of state space entirely. A concurrent program is represented by a family of differential equations of a restricted type, where each equation describes the program state change. This family of equations are shown analytically to have a unique solution. Each program state is measured by a time-dependent function that indicates the extent to which the state can be reached in execution. It is shown that 1) a program deadlocks iff every state measure converges to either 0 or 1 as time increases. Thus instead of exploring states, the solution of a family of differential equations is analyzed. 2) a program is bounded iff every state measure converges to a bounded nonnegative number.

Keywords: Concurrent program, State explosion, Ordinary differential equation, Deadlock detection, Boundedness checking.

1 Introduction

Static analysis is an approach to program behavior verification without execution. The approach is particularly useful in identifying program design errors prior to implementation. It has been demonstrated that detecting errors early in the lifecycle greatly reduces the cost of fixing those errors. A number of static concurrency analysis techniques have been proposed.

They span such approaches as reachability-based analysis techniques [22] [26] [38] [54] [69] [76], symbolic model checking [8] [47], flow equations [14], and dataflow analysis [23] [45] [60].

- Reachability analysis. Analysis using explicit state enumeration is conducted by constructing an equivalent state machine of the program against which properties can be checked. A major problem of reachability analysis is that the search space involved can expand exponentially with the increase in the number of concurrent processes. Reduction techniques have been proposed to alleviate the problem by not having to construct the entire state graph.

---

* Supported by NSF of China(No.90818013).

M. Leucker and C. Morgan (Eds.): ICTAC 2009, LNCS 5684, pp. 1–35, 2009.
© Springer-Verlag Berlin Heidelberg 2009

- Symbolic model checking. It has been widely used to verify designs of digital circuits against properties expressed in branching-time temporal logic CTL. The state space is represented symbolically by a logical formula captured using a Binary Decision Diagram (BDD). The technique works well for hardware designs with regular logical structures. For such systems, BDD representations can reduce the state space from exponential order of the number of state variables to linear. However, it is less likely to achieve similar reductions in software specifications whose logical structures are less regular.
- Flow equation. The necessary conditions for the existence of an execution trace that violates a specified property are expressed using a set of inequalities. These inequalities are then solved using standard integer linear programming packages. Nonexistence of solutions guarantees the satisfiability of the property while existence of solutions yields an inconclusive result. The technique has the advantage that the number of inequalities is essentially linear to the number of concurrent processes in a program. However, integer linear programming problems are generally NP-hard, and the standard techniques involved are potentially exponential.
- Data flow analysis. By approximating the execution model of a program, properties can be efficiently checked using a polynomial algorithm. However the conclusion thus obtained is usually either complete or sound but not both.

These techniques and approaches have been used in several analysis tools such as *Flow equation* in INCA [14], *data flow analysis* in FLAVERS [23], *Reachability Analysis* in SPIN [34], *Symbolic model checking* in SMV [12] and SMC [67].

In general all existing approaches appear to be very sensitive to the size of the program being analyzed in terms of the use of concurrency constructs and the number of asynchronous processes. While analysis may be partitioned in some cases, in other cases it suffers from combinatorial explosion: static concurrency analysis of arbitrary programs has been shown to be NP-hard [69]. Particularly, reachability analysis may cause state space explosion problem since it has to exhaustively explore all the reachable state space to detect concurrency errors. Although many techniques have been proposed to combat this explosion, such as state space reductions [27] [42] [71] [72], compositional techniques [75], abstraction [10], the state explosion problem still is the main technical obstacle to transition from research to practice.

Traditionally, concurrent systems are described as discrete event system models which are suited to model system concurrency. However, the discrete will lead to state explosion problem since model checkers build a finite state transition system and exhaustively explore the reachable state space searching for violations of the properties under investigation [11]. Hence, to thoroughly solve the state explosion problem, one solution is that the discrete event system models should be continunized to continuous system models, such that the systems can be described with analytic expressions. Therefore, instead of counting states, we can analyze the solutions of the analytic expressions.

Petri net seems a good candidate that bridges discrete event systems and continuous systems. On one hand, Petri nets have been used extensively as tools for the modeling, analysis and synthesis of discrete event systems. Petri nets offer advantages over finite automata, particularly when the issues of model complexity and concurrency of processes are of concern. On the other hand, a continuous system can be approximated by a Petri net [57] and a Petri net model is used as discrete event representation of the continuous variable system by Lunze et al. [43].

However, Petri nets also suffer from the state explosion problem while doing reachability analysis[49] even through there are some net reduction methods. One way to tackle that problem is to use some kind of relaxation by removing the integrality constraints. This relaxation leads to a continuous-time formalism: Continuous Petri Net (CPN) by David and Alla[15][16]. The price being paid is losing certain possibilities of analysis, but we can avoid the state explosion problem inherited from the discrete systems and take advantage of the extensive theory about continuous systems. A continuous Petri net, in fact, is an approximation of the timed (discrete) Petri net. The semantics of a continuous Petri net is defined by a set of ordinary differential equations (ODEs), where one equation describes the continuous changes over time on the marking value of a given place. Different firing styles in the CPN can lead to different semantics of CPN. In this paper, we consider a modified VCPNs in which the instantaneous firing speeds depend on the markings such that the markings are continuous without points of discontinuity.

Based on CPN, we will build differential equation model for concurrent programs. Each equation model consists of six types of ordinary differential equations. Each equation describes a state change of the program. A state can be measured by the time-dependent nonnegative number, called state measure, which indicates that the state can be reached to some extent when the program is in execution. Given a time instant, instead of displaying one state at a time as in the discrete event systems, a program will have all states shown up, with the state measure attached to each state. This information can help us to perform static analysis for the programs.

In this paper we focus on deadlock detection and boundedness checking.

Deadlock problem has been extensively studied in the in the literature [4] [7] [35] [39] [40] [53] [55] [61] [66] [74] [77]. There are several kinds of deadlock models [65], but we only consider two kinds of deadlock models in this paper: Communication(OR) model and Resource Sharing(AND) model. The first model comes from the situation that the processes of a concurrent program do not share the address spaces and the communication and synchronization are achieved through message passing. The second model comes from the situation that the processes of a concurrent program share the address space and the synchronization is achieved by the use of monitor and condition queues.

Boundedness is one of the most important properties of discrete Petri nets. It can be used to check if the system has congestion or resource leak. Determining the boundedness of a Petri net is usually through creating reachable graph or coverability tree [31] [25]. However, it is time consuming to create reachable graph or coverability tree, and sometime the state explosion problem may be hit. It is shown that the boundedness of Petri net is equivalent to the stability of the corresponding equation model.

Since it is hard to find explicit analytic solutions for nonlinear ordinary differential equations, we turn to find numerical solutions instead. With Matlab solver, we can get the numerical solutions. The computation error does not affect the performance.

This paper is organized as the following. Section 2 simply describes how to build Petri net model representation for concurrent programs. Section 3 defines a new type of continuous Petri net based on the discrete Petri net. Section 4 builds differential equation model for concurrent programs based on continuous Petri net. In Section 5, we prove the existence and uniqueness of the solutions of the differential equation model. In Section 6, we show how to compute state measures of a program in different situations. Section 7 gives sufficient and necessary conditions for a program to have deadlocks. Section 8 provides us an easy way to check the boundedness of a system. Section 9 explains why using Matlab to find the numerical solutions of the differential equation model. Section 10, Section 11 and section 12 are the case studies. Gas station problem, dinning philosophers and traffic network have been used as the examples. The last section, Section 13, is the discussion and conclusion of the paper.

2   Petri Net Representation of Concurrent Programs

Petri net models of concurrent programs have existed for some time. There are several ways to build (discrete) Petri net models from program languages such as from Ada [64] [44], CSP [70] [50] [59], and C [41].

The general principle to translate a program to a Petri net is that the resulting Petri net should capture essential details of the program's execution behavior that allow an analysis algorithm to distinguish between executions that are guaranteed to satisfy the property that is being evaluated from those that may fail to satisfy the property.

Although the languages are different, before translation, *Coarsening* step is always necessary: By removing all statements that do not affect program (static) behavior, we can get a 'skeleton' of the program. Here the 'affect' is kind of fuzzy, but it will be clear when applied to concrete languages.

While building a Petri net, we may obtain some 'valued-oriented' constructs such as parameters, variables that define the dynamic state of a program. We use special variables, called *state variables*, to record them at each place such that when the system is executed from one place to another place, *state variable*'s values will be changed. These variables are usually extracted from control constructs and concurrent constructs. Since we focus on static analysis, these variables are only used to define program state. We have the following definition.

Definition 1. *(Program State) A program state is defined as a family of variables whose values have changed.*

Definition 2. *An event is defined as an activity of the program and can change the state of the program.*

Definition 3. *A Petri net is a directed bipartite graph that can be written as a tuple (P, T, F, M_0), where P is the set of places, T is the set of transitions, $F \subset (P \times T) \cup (T \times P)$ is the set of arcs, and M_0 is the initial marking.*

In our Petri net model, a place is used to denote a program state and a transition is used to denote an event. The initial marking indicates the start state.

Events are regarded as instantaneous. If we wish to represent an activity with duration, we must introduce two events to represent its start and finish so that other events can occur between them. The semantics of the original language determines the boundaries between events. Typical events might be *send message, receive message, user defined event/action, read, write, system events*, etc.

In this paper, most of the events come from the synchronization [5]. In the case of disjoint address spaces, the synchronization for concurrent programs is through message passing between processes. Message passing are classified as Synchronous and Asynchronous. Synchronous message passing means that the sending operation needs to wait until an acknowledgment is received. Asynchronous message passing means that the sending operation can proceed without waiting for the message to arrive at its destination. In both cases, the receiving side is blocked. In the case of shared address spaces, the synchronization for concurrent systems is achieved by the use of monitor and condition queues. In general, processes are not independent. Often a process depends on the resource released by another process. If the process is not available, the process must wait until the process is available and at this moment the process is blocked. The process will be resumed after obtaining all the required resources.

Generally, the translation is on the control flow (such as if, loop, and select statements) and concurrent constructs. We are not going to give detailed translation rules for all programming languages, actually it is impossible and not necessary since different programming language may have different syntax, semantics and different concurrent constructs. We only focus on the rules to use Petri net to represent synchronization, which have been successfully implemented to Ada in our case study sections. For other rules on control flow, one may use Ada-Petri net rules[64] as a reference.

Rules For Message Passing

Asynchronous message passing mechanism can be translated to the Petri net as Fig. 1 shows. In the picture, $p_1 \to t_1 \to p_2$ represents process A, and $p_3 \to t_2 \to p_4$ represents process B. On the sending side, process A sends message to p from transition t_1, meanwhile it continues to execute to place p_2. On the receiving side, process B receives message from p at transition t_2, and t_2 is enabled. Hence both processes can continue the execution.

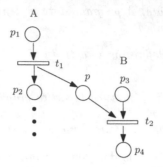

Fig. 1. Petri net for asynchronous message passing

Synchronous message passing mechanism can be translated to the Petri net as Fig. 2 shows. In the figure, $p_1 \rightarrow t_1 \rightarrow p(i) \rightarrow t_2 \rightarrow p_2$ represents process process A, and $p_3 \rightarrow t_3 \rightarrow p_4$ represents process B. First, process A sends message to $p(s)$ from transition t_1 and then waits for a response from process B. After getting request from $p(s)$, t_3 is enabled, and process B sends response back to $p(e)$, meanwhile it continues to execute to p_4. Finally, process A get response from $p(e)$ and thus t_2 is enabled. Hence A can continuou execution to p_2.

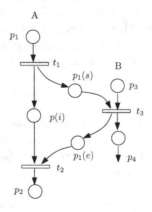

Fig. 2. Petri net for synchronous message passing (I)

Since an activity may cover a fragment of code, thus synchronous message passing may have more general Petri net translation as shown in Fig. 3. In the picture, $p_1 \rightarrow t_1 \rightarrow p_1(i) \rightarrow t_2 \rightarrow p_2$ represents process process A, $p_3 \rightarrow t_3 \rightarrow p_4 \rightarrow t_4 \rightarrow p_2(i) \rightarrow t_5 \rightarrow p_5 \rightarrow t_6 \rightarrow p_6$ represents process B, and $p_7 \rightarrow t_7 \rightarrow p_8$ represents process C. First, process A sends message to $p_1(s)$ from transition t_1 and then waits for a response from process B. After getting request from $p_1(s)$, t_3 is enabled. Thus, process B continues execution to t_4 and sends request to $p_2(s)$ to other process from t_4, and so on. Eventually process C will get request

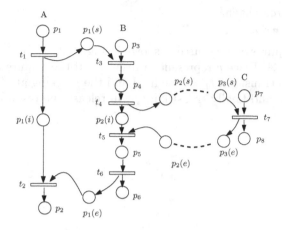

Fig. 3. Petri net for synchronous message passing (II)

from $p_3(s)$ and thus transition t_7 is enabled. Process c then sends response back to $p_3(e)$ to the sending process. Finally process A will get response from $p_1(e)$ which get response from B at transition t_2. At this moment, all processes can continue the execution.

In this way, we get Petri nets with the property: Each transition has at most two input arcs and at most two output arcs.

Definition 4. *A Place/Transition Chain is a net: All transitions are connected by a head place that has one output arc and no input arc, an end place that has one input arc and no output arc, and places that has one input arc and one output arc. If the head place and the end place are overlapping, then the chain is called* Place/Transition Cycle.

Definition 5. *A place/transition cycle is called* Process Cycle for Communication Model, *if every transition in the cycle is: 1) a transition that has one input arc and one output arc; this transition is called* Internal Transition *of the cycle, 2) a transition that has one input arc and two output arcs; this transition is called* Output Transition *of the cycle, here one output arc is to construct the cycle and the other is for the output of the cycle, 3) a transition that has two input arcs and one output arc; this transition is called* Input Transition *of the cycle, here one input arc is to construct the cycle and the other is for the input of the cycle, 4) a transition that has two input arcs and two output arcs; this transition is called* Input-Output Transition *of the cycle, here one input arc and one output arc are used to construct the cycle and the other two are used for the input and output of the cycle, respectively.*

Thus, each process in the communication model consists of one or many process cycles depending on if the process contains no or some select controls.

Rules For Resource Sharing
There are two cases.

1) A process requires one resource as shown in Fig, 4. $p_1 \rightarrow t_1 \rightarrow p_2 \rightarrow t_2 \rightarrow p_3$ represents process A. Place r represents a resource. If the required resource r is available, then the transition t_1 will be fired and the marking at place p_1 will be moved to place p_2, and finally transition t_2 will release the resource back.

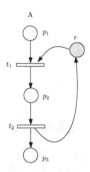

Fig. 4. One resource is required by the process

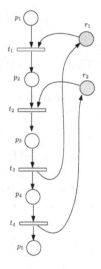

Fig. 5. Two resources are required by the process

2) A process requires two or more resources as shown in Fig. 5. $p_1 \rightarrow t_1 \rightarrow p_2 \rightarrow t_2 \rightarrow p_3 \rightarrow t_3 \rightarrow p_4 \rightarrow t_4 \rightarrow p_5$ represents process A. Places r_1 and r_2 represent two resources. If r_1 is available, then transition t_1 is fired, and the marking is moved from p_1 to p_2. If resource r_2 is also available, then transition t_2 is fired and the marking in p_2 is moved to p_3, otherwise, the process is waiting

at p_2. Thereafter, transition t_3 will release one resource, either r_1 or r_2, say r_1 in the picture. Finally, transition t_4 will release another resource r_2.

Definition 6. *A place/transition cycle is called* **Process Cycle for Resource Model,** *if every transition in the cycle is: 1) a transition that has one input arc and one output arc; this transition is called* **Internal Transition** *of the cycle, 2) a transition that has one input arc and two output arcs; this transition is called* **Output Transition** *of the cycle, here one output arc is to construct the cycle and the other is for the output of the cycle, 3) a transition that has two input arcs and one output arc; this transition is called* **Input Transition** *of the cycle, here one input arc is to construct the cycle and the other is for the input of the cycle.*

Thus, each process in the resource sharing model consists of one or many process cycles depending on if the process has alternative required resources.

3   From Discrete Petri Net to Continuous Petri Net

The Petri net obtained in the last section is discrete Petri net, in which the number of marks in the places are integers. A transition is enabled if each input place of the transition is marked with a token. An enabled transition fires by removing a token from each input place and adding a token to each output place. A transition that is never enabled is called dead. A marking of a Petri net is reachable if there exists a chain of transition firings that leads from initial marking to the marking. Thus, a Petri net, by successive firing of enabled transitions, generates a graph whose nodes are reachable markings and whose edges represent transition firings. Such Petri net can keep the properties consistent with the program, especially the deadlock.

After translation, a program can be represented as several process cycles that interact to each other through input/output places. We assume that each process cycle has one start state, meaning that only one place has a token from the start. While executing, if a place has a token, then the process is currently at the state of this place; otherwise, the process is not at the state of this place. Each input/output place may have big number of tokens, indicating that the data are waiting in the buffer to be processed.

Now check the following example to find out how the data is processed. As shown in Figure 6(a), a process cycle has places $p_1, p_2, \ldots$ and has an input place p_i at transition t_1. We assume that place p_1 has a token, meaning that the process is visiting this place, and p_i has 3 tokens, meaning that there are three data in the buffer.

The process has to visit place p_1 for 3 times to move away all 3 tokens in the place p_i. In other words, 3×1 tokens will be moved from place p_1 as shown in Figure 6(b)(c). Thus the tokens in the input place p_i can be regarded as an impact factor while tokens are moved from the process place p_1. If the number of data in the buffer is big, and a program has many such buffers, then we will get large number of reacheable markings which could limit the use of discrete Petri nets.

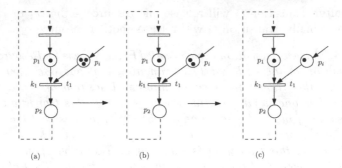

Fig. 6. Marking changes in discrete Petri net

Now we assume that the marking is moving as a continuous flow, then the marking moving rate can be regarded as the product of $k_1 \times m_1(t) \times m_i(t)$. In the product, k_1 is maximum firing speed of t_1, and $k_1 = \frac{1}{\delta_1}$, here δ_1 is the time delay for transition t_1 that can be obtained from program execution or from design phase; $m_1(t)$ and $m_i(t)$ are the markings of p_1 and p_i at time t, respectively. This can be pictured in Fig. 7.

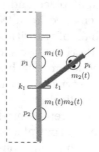

Fig. 7. Continuous flow in Petri net

Based on this idea, we propose a new continuous Petri net model. In this model, the instantaneous firing speed of a transition is proportional to the product of the markings of the input places.

Definition 7. *A Continuous Petri Net is a tuple $ConPN = < P, T, A_{pre}, A_{post}, v >$, where*

1. *$P = \{p_1, p_2, ..., p_n\}$ is a finite nonempty set of places,*
2. *$T = \{t_1, t_2, ..., t_m\}$ is a finite nonempty set of transitions,*
3. *$A_{pre} = \{p \to t\}$ is a set of directed arcs which connect places with transitions, $A_{post} = \{t \to p\}$ is a set of directed arcs which connect transitions to places,*
4. *$v : T \to (0, \infty)$ is a mapping to assign a firing constant to each transition.*

Definition 8. *Let $I = [0, \infty)$ be the time interval and let $m_i : I \to [0, \infty), i = 1, 2, \ldots, n$ be a set of mappings that associated with place p_i. A marking of a Continuous Petri Net $ConPN = < P, T, A_{pre}, A_{post}, v >$ is a mapping*

$$m : I \to [0, \infty)^n, m(\tau) = (m_1(\tau), m_2(\tau), \ldots, m_n(\tau)).$$

Definition 9. *A marked ConPN is a 2-tuple (N, M_0) where*
- *N is a ConPN,*
- *$M_0 = (m_1(0), m_2(0), \ldots, m_n(0))$ is its initial marking, where $m_i(0)$ takes value 1 or 0.*

A place holding initial marking 1 is called *start place*. The marking of a place can be used to measure how often this place has been visited. We have the definition:

Definition 10. *(State Measure) Given any time moment $t \in [0, \infty)$, the state can be reached to some degree. This degree is called State Measure, denoted as $m(t)$. State measures take nonnegative real numbers as their values.*

All the m_i defined above are the state measures. Note that state measure is different from probability since the state measures for the places between processes may exceed 1 in some cases. Later, we will prove that the state measures of each process cycle take values from [0,1]. For a state s in the process, if $m(t) = 1$, then we say that the program is completely in the state s, or simply in the state s. If $m(t) = 0$, then we say that the program is not in the state s.

A transition is enabled if all the input places have nonzero markings. Only enabled transitions can be fired. So, if new marking is moved into a place, we say that the state is increasing; if some marking is moved out from a place, we say that the state is decreasing. The change rate of state measure can be calculated as the following.

Let p_1 and p_2 be the input places of a transition t and their markings are $m_1(\tau)$ and $m_2(\tau)$, respectively. Let v be the firing constant associated with t, then the firing rate is defined as the product $v * m_1(\tau) * m_2(\tau)$, where $*$ represents the regular multiplication. This expression contains the enabling information: if one of m_1 and m_2 is zero, then the marking moving rate is 0, meaning the transition is not enabled.

Note: In the definition of Continuous Petri net defined by David and Alla, the firing rate is define by $v \min\{m_1(\tau), m_2(\tau)\}$. If both m_1 and m_2 are less than one, then

$$m_1(\tau) * m_2(\tau) < \min\{m_1(\tau), m_2(\tau)\}.$$

If at least one of m_1 and m_2 is bigger than one, then

$$m_1(\tau) * m_2(\tau) > \min\{m_1(\tau), m_2(\tau)\}.$$

Therefore, our definition magnifies the states, which is useful when we study the state trend. Our definition is to make the state marking differential, thus the state change is continuous without points of discontinuity.

Gilbert and Heiner [24] have successfully used the similar continuous Petri net model to study biochemical systems to explore in a general manner possible observable behaviors, where the firing rates of all the atomic actions is the product of the concentrations of the involved substances. Here concentrations are continuous functions, which are the state measure functions in our paper. It is worthy to mention that a tool, called Snoopy, developed by Scheibler [63], can be used to simulate Continuous Petri net. It can give the state measures at a given time.

We will use our new continuous Petri net model to study the program properties, particular the deadlock and boundedness, and find equivalent descriptions that can be easily used to check these two properties. Note that there are no changes for the net structure and initial markings while discrete Petri net is continunized.

Definition 11. *A stationary state of a marked ConPN is the state in which all transitions are firing.*

4   Building a Differential Equation Model

The net marking (state) changing depends on the program structures and the firing rates. Based on the semantics defined in the above section, the marking at each place can be represented by a differential equation. We have the following cases.

1) No inputs for the net as Fig. 8 shows.

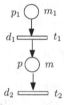

Fig. 8. Net without inputs

(a) Place has no choice. In (a), there are two internal transitions t_1 and t, and two places p_1 and p. Place p gets marking from place p_1. Let the marking at place p_1 and p be m_1 and m, respectively. Assume the firing constants at transition t_1 and t are d_1 and d, respectively. Then the marking m can be represented as

$$m'(\tau) = d_1 m_1(\tau) - dm(\tau).$$

(b) Place has choice. In (b), there are three internal transitions t_1, t_2 and t_3, and two places p_1 and p. Place p gets marking from place p_1 and then enables either transitions t_2 or t_3. Let the marking at place p_1 and p be m_1 and m, respectively. Assume the firing constants at transition t_1, t_2 and t_3 are d_1, d_2 and d_3, respectively. Then the marking m can be represented as

$$m'(\tau) = d_1 m_1(\tau) - (d_2 + d_3)m(\tau).$$

2) One input for the net as Fig. 9 shows.

(a) Input transition followed by internal transition. As Fig. 9(a) shows, transition t_1 is an input transition and t is an internal transition. Place p will get marking from place p_1 and p_2. Let the markings at places p_1, p_2 and p be m_1, m_2 and m, respectively. Assume that the firing constants at transition t_1 and t are d_1 and d, respectively. Then the marking m can be represented as

$$m'(\tau) = d_1 m_1(\tau) * m_2(\tau) - dm(\tau).$$

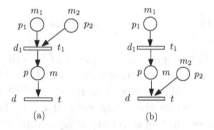

Fig. 9. Net with one input

(b) Internal transition followed by input transition. As Fig. 9(b) shows, transition t_1 is an internal transition and t is an input transition. Place p will get marking from place p_1, but will together with place p_2 send some marking out. Let the markings at places p_1, p_2 and p be m_1, m_2 and m, respectively. Assume the firing constants at transition t_1 and t are d_1 and d, respectively. Then the marking m can be represented as

$$m'(\tau) = d_1 m_1(\tau) - dm(\tau) * m_2(\tau).$$

3) Two inputs for the net as Fig. 10 shows.

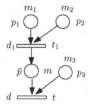

Fig. 10. Net with two inputs

Input transition t_1 has two input places m_1 and m_2 and input transition t_2 has two input places m and m_3. Assume the firing constants at transition t_1 and t are d_1 and d, respectively. Then the marking m can be represented as

$$m'(\tau) = d_1 m_1(\tau) * m_2(\tau) - dm(\tau) * m_3(\tau).$$

4) One sharing resource for two processes as shown in Fig. 11.

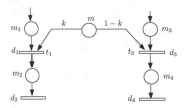

Fig. 11. Two processes sharing one resource

Let the resource be r. We assign a time-dependent function $k(t)$, called *control function*, to the resource to assist building equations. $k(t)$ takes value 0 or 1 and is piecewise continuous. In this picture, the firing rate of transition t_1 of the first process is $m_1 * k * r$, while the firing rate of t_3 of the second process is $m_3 * (1 - k) * r$. The corresponding differential equations are:

$$\begin{cases} m_1' = ()_1 - d_1 * m_1 * k * r, \\ m_2' = d_1 * m_1 * k * r - d_2 * m_2, \\ m_3' = ()_2 - d_3 * m_3(1 - k)r, \\ m_4' = d_3 m_3(1 - k)r - d_4 m_4. \end{cases}$$

Here we use () to represent some other state measures. If more than two processes are involved in sharing resource r, say 3 processes p_1, p_2 and p_3, then we will have two control functions: $k_1(t)$ and $k_2(t)$. Let t_1, t_3 and t_5 be the input transitions

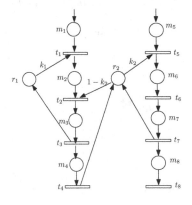

Fig. 12. Two processes sharing two resources

that need resource. The firing rates to the transitions are: $()_1 * k_1 * r$, $()_2 * (1 - k_1) * k_2 * r$, and $()_3 * (1 - k_1) * (1 - k_2) * r$, respectively.

5) Two sharing resource for two processes as Fig. 12 shows.

Let the two resources be r_1 and r_2. Two control functions $k_1(t)$ and $k_2(t)$ are assigned to r_1 and r_2, respectively. The corresponding differential equations are:

$$\begin{cases} m_1' = ()_1 - d_1 m_1 k_1 r_1, \\ m_2' = d_1 m_1 k_1 r_1 - d_2 m_2 (1 - k_2) r_2, \\ m_3' = d_2 m_2 (1 - k_2) r_2 - d_3 m_3, \\ m_4' = d_3 m_3 - d_4 m_4, \\ m_5' = ()_2 - d_5 k_2 r_2 m_5, \\ m_6' = d_5 m_5 k_2 r_2 - d_6 m_6, \\ m_7' = d_6 m_6 - d_7 m_7, \\ m_8' = d_7 m_7 - d_8 m_8, \\ r_1' = d_3 m_3 - d_1 k_1 r_1 m_1, \\ r_2' = d_4 m_4 + d_7 m_7 - d_2 (1 - k_2) r_2 m_2 - d_5 m_5 k_2 r_2. \end{cases}$$

Generally, if there are n resources, we will assign n control functions $k_1(t)$, $k_2(t), \ldots, k_n(t)$ to the resources. All the functions form a vector, $(k_1, k_2, \ldots, k_n)$, called *control vector*. Since $k_i(t)$ is piecewise continuous, on some fixed time intervals, we will have 2^n different differential equation groups. The control vector plays crucial role in the property analysis. Different property may require different technique to handle this vector since the values of the control functions are nondeterministic.

5 The Existence and Uniqueness of the Solutions for the Equation Model

From above section, we can model a system with a group of differential equations. But we still do not know if the group of equations have solutions. This requires a rigorous proof.

For a process cycle, let m be any state and assume its incoming transition is t_1 and the outgoing transition is t_2 as shown in Fig. 13(a), then we have the following 4 cases to compute the state measure of m: 1) t_1 and t_2 have no inputs, 2) t_1 has input m_{i_1} and t_2 does not have input, 3) t_1 has no input and t_2 has input m_{i_2}, 4) t_1 and t_2 have inputs m_{i_1} and m_{i_2}, respectively.

Hence, there are four equations corresponding to the cases:

$$m' = d_1 * m_1 - d_2 * m, \tag{1}$$

$$m' = d_1 * m_1 * m_{i_1} - d_2 * m, \tag{2}$$

$$m' = d_1 * m_1 - d_2 * m * m_{i_2}, \tag{3}$$

$$m' = d_1 * m_1 * m_{i_1} - d_2 * m * m_{i_2}. \tag{4}$$

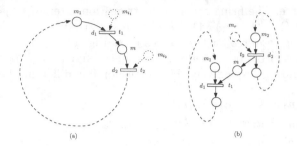

Fig. 13. (a) Process Cycle, (b) Interaction between two process cycles

For the input/output states between two processes as shown in Fig. 13(b), their state measures can be calculate as

$$m' = d_2 m_2 - d_1 m_1 m, \text{ or } m' = d_2 m_2 m_I - d_1 m_1 m.$$

Here m_1 and m_2 are the states in two different process cycles.

Generally, let x_i be the variables in the differential equation group. There are six types of equations.

- Type 1 [Internal]. $x'_i = d_{i-1} x_{i-1} - d_i x_i$. Here x_i and x_{i-1} are the states of the same process.
- Type 2 [Input-before]. $x'_i = d_{i-1} x_{i-1} x_k - d_i x_i$. Here x_i and x_{i-1} are the states of the same process. x_k is the input to this process.
- Type 3 [Input-after]. $x'_i = d_{i-1} x_{i-1} - d_i x_i x_k$. Here x_i and x_{i-1} are the states of the same process. x_k is the input to this process.
- Type 4 [Input-before-after]. $x'_i = d_{i-1} x_{i-1} x_k - d_i x_i x_l$. Here x_i and x_{i-1} are the states of the same process. x_k and x_l are the inputs to this process.
- Type 5 [Asynchronous]. $x'_k = d_i x_i - d_{i'} x_{i'} x_k$. Here x_i and $x_{i'}$ are the states of two different processes respectively. x_k is the message between these two processes.
- Type 6 [Synchronous]. $x'_k = d_i x_i x_l - d_{i'} x_{i'} x_k$. Here x_i and $x_{i'}$ are the states of two different processes respectively. x_k and x_l are the messages between these two processes, where x_l is usually indicates the request that can be calculated by Type 5 and x_k is the reply.

For each process cycle, we have a group of differential equations, each equation is one type of Type 1-Type 4. Formally, we have

Definition 12. *A differential equation group is called* **Process Equation Group** *if each equation of the group is one type of* **Type 1-Type 4**, $\sum x'_i = 0$, *and* $\sum x_i(0) = 1$.

For the messages between processes, they can be represented by Type 5 or Type 6. Formally, we have

Definition 13. *A differential equation is called* **Connection Equation** *if the equation is one of* **Type 5** *or* **Type 6** *and the equation contains states of other two* **Process Equation Groups**.

Note: 1) From the calculation point view, Type 3 is the same as Type 5 and Type 4 is the same as Type 6. 2) Notice that in the above six equations, the right hand side of each equation may have more than two items, but in that situation the extra items will be controlled by Control Functions. For the convenience, we only consider two items on the right side.

Consider a system described by a set of differential equations containing n variables $x_1, x_2, \ldots, x_n$, each equation is one of Type 1 - Type 6, and the equations can be further grouped as Process Equation Groups and Connection Equations. Without confusion, we use six types of equations to represent the whole equation group. Let the set of equations be the following:

$$
\begin{cases}
\vdots \\
x_i' = d_{i-1}x_{i-1} - d_i x_i \\
x_i' = d_{i-1}x_{i-1}x_k - d_i x_i \\
x_i' = d_{i-1}x_{i-1} - d_i x_i x_k \\
x_i' = d_{i-1}x_{i-1}x_k - d_i x_i x_l \\
x_k' = d_i x_i - d_{i'} x_{i'} x_k \\
x_k' = d_i x_i x_l - d_{i'} x_{i'} x_k \\
\vdots
\end{cases}
$$

where x_i can be any variables for the Process Equation Group and x_k can be any variables for the Connection Equations. The above equation group can also be rewritten as

$$
\begin{pmatrix}
\vdots \\
x_i \\
x_i \\
x_i \\
x_i \\
x_k \\
x_k \\
\vdots
\end{pmatrix}'
=
\begin{pmatrix}
\vdots \\
d_{i-1}x_{i-1} - d_i x_i \\
d_{i-1}x_{i-1}x_k - d_i x_i \\
d_{i-1}x_{i-1} - d_i x_i x_k \\
d_{i-1}x_{i-1}x_k - d_i x_i x_l \\
d_i x_i - d_{i'} x_{i'} x_k \\
d_i x_i x_l - d_{i'} x_{i'} x_k \\
\vdots
\end{pmatrix}.
$$

Let

$$
x =
\begin{pmatrix}
\vdots \\
x_i \\
x_i \\
x_i \\
x_i \\
x_k \\
x_k \\
\vdots
\end{pmatrix},
\quad
f(t, x) =
\begin{pmatrix}
\vdots \\
d_{i-1}x_{i-1} - d_i x_i \\
d_{i-1}x_{i-1}x_k - d_i x_i \\
d_{i-1}x_{i-1} - d_i x_i x_k \\
d_{i-1}x_{i-1}x_k - d_i x_i x_l \\
d_i x_i - d_{i'} x_{i'} x_k \\
d_i x_i x_l - d_{i'} x_{i'} x_k \\
\vdots
\end{pmatrix}.
$$

Then $x \in \mathbb{R}^n, f : [0, +\infty) \times \mathbb{R}^n \to \mathbb{R}^n$ and the above equation group can be represented as

$$x' = f(t, x).$$

Since the system has start states, thus x has initial value, for example $x(0) = x_0$. Hence the solution existence problem is transformed to the existence problem of *initial value problem*

$$x' = f(t, x), \quad t \geq 0, \quad x(0) = x_0.$$

Let $T > 0$ be any finite number and we consider the interval $[0, T] \subset [0, +\infty)$. Let

$$C([0, T], \mathbb{R}^n) = \{x : [0, T] \to \mathbb{R}^n \text{ such that } x \text{ is continuous on } [0, T]\},$$

and the mapping $f : [0, T] \times \mathbb{R}^n \to \mathbb{R}^n$ is continuous. The *initial value problem*:

$$x' = f(t, x), \quad t \in [0, T], \quad x(0) = x_0$$

is to find solution $x \in C([0, T], \mathbb{R}^n)$ such that

$$x'(t) = f(t, x(t)), \quad t \in [0, T].$$

We have the following equivalent description.

Proposition 14. *A function* $x \in C([0, T], \mathbb{R}^n)$ *with continuous derivative on* $[0, T]$ *is a solution of the initial value problem if and only if*

$$x(t) = x(0) + \int_0^t f(s, x(s))ds.$$

Based on this proposition, we may consider the map $F : C([0, T], \mathbb{R}^n) \to C([0, T], \mathbb{R}^n)$ define by

$$(Fx)(t) := x_0 + \int_0^t f(s, x(s))ds, \quad t \in [0, T].$$

Therefore, our initial problem is equivalent to finding a fixed point of F. We will use the following famous fixed point theorem to prove the existence of fixed point of F.

Theorem 15. *([68], p.29) Let* $\mathbb{E}$ *be a Banach space and let* $F : \mathbb{E} \to \mathbb{E}$ *be a continuous compact map. If the set*

$$\Omega := \{x \in \mathbb{E} : \lambda x = F(x) \text{ for some } \lambda > 1\}$$

is bounded, then F *has a fixed point.*

In this theorem, a Banach space $\mathbb{E}$ is a metric space $\mathbb{E}$ that is complete under the metric, i.e. all Cauchy sequences have limits in $\mathbb{E}$. For more information about Banach space, we refer to [28]. Let $\|.\|$ be the norm of space $\mathbb{R}^n$. Then $C([0, T], \mathbb{R}^n)$ is a Banach space with norm

$$\|x\|_\infty = sup\{\|x(t)\| : t \in [0, T]\}.$$

Theorem 16. *Mapping* F *has a unique fixed point in* $C([0, T], \mathbb{R}^n)$.

6   Computing Program States

Since the differential equation model contains nonlinear ordinary differential equations, it is in general hard to give analytic expressions to the solutions. Nevertheless, we may compute the solution trend and estimate the solution range. The proofs in this paper are omitted. The readers can get the details from us.

We need the following The Second Mean Value Theorem for integrals, which can be found in almost all calculus books, but could be in different forms. We choose it from [46], p.222.

Theorem 17. *Assume function f is integral in [a, b]. If function g is nonnegative and integrable, and increasing on [a, b], then there exists $\eta \in [a, b]$, such that*

$$\int_a^b f(x)g(x)dx = g(b)\int_\eta^b f(x)dx.$$

Sketch of the proof: Let

$$F(x) = \int_x^b f(t)dt, \ x \in [a,b].$$

Since f is integrable on $[a,b]$, F is continuous on $[a,b]$. Thus F has maximum M and minimum m. If $g(b) = 0$, then $g(x) \equiv 0$, $x \in [a, b]$. In this situation, the formula is true for all η. Now let $g(b) > 0$, then the formula is

$$F(\eta) = \int_\eta^b f(t)dt = \frac{1}{g(b)}\int_a^b f(x)g(x)dx.$$

It is equivalent to prove that

$$m \le \frac{1}{g(b)}\int_a^b f(x)g(x)dx \le M,$$

which is also equivalent to prove that

$$mg(b) \le \int_a^b f(x)g(x)dx \le Mg(b).$$

The rest is omitted.

We assume that each process has one start place. Each resource is a start place. Without specifying, t always represents time in the following results.

Proposition 18. *For any place/transition cycle, if it has at most one start place, then for any state measure m in the cycle, the limit as $t \to \infty$ of $m(t)$ exists and is in the set [0,1] no matter how the firing rates are chosen. Particularly, 1) If the cycle does not contain start place, then all state measures are 0. 2) If the cycle contains one start place, and all the inputs to the cycle have positive state measures, then for any state measure m in the cycle, the limit as $t \to \infty$ of $m(t)$ exists and is in the set (0, 1).*

Corollary 19. *If a state measure converges to zero in some firing constants, then it can not converge to zero no matter how to choose firing constants.*

Proposition 20. *If the ConPN of a program reaches stationary state, then for each process, its state measures converge to numbers in [0, 1] no matter how the firing constants are chosen.*

Note: We did not count the input places and the output places between processes. Their state measures may exceed 1, unless they also in some place/ transition cycle.

From this proposition, we may infer that the discrete state has been continunized.

Definition 21. *Two place/transition cycles are said in the same state measure class if both cycles satisfy the one of the following at the same time: 1) all state measures in the cycle converge to the numbers in (0, 1), 2) for any state measure m in the cycle, either m converges 0 or m converges to 1.*

Lemma 22. *Given a process cycle, we have the following results. 1) If we add an internal transition to the cycle, then the modified cycle is in the same state class as the old one. 2) If we add an internal transition as a choice to a chain that does not have input transitions, then the modified cycle is in the same state class as the old one.*

Theorem 23. *Given a process, if it has at least one input with state measure 0, then every state measure of the process either converges to 1 or converges to 0.*

Theorem 24. *Given a process cycle, if it does not have inputs, then every state measure of the process cycle converges to a number in (0, 1).*

7   Detecting Deadlock with Equations

This section shows that program deadlock has an equivalent description using the solutions of differential equations. The proofs are omitted.

Deadlock detection problem has been extensively studied in the literature [7] [39] [66] [74]. There are several deadlock models as listed in [65], but in this paper, we consider following two models.

Communication Model(OR). In this model, a concurrent system consists of a set of processes that communicate with one another via message passing. A process first sends requests (messages) to its dependents capable of servicing the request and waits for at least one response. This is because the request can be served by one of the dependents. So, the process waits for the first acknowledgment, and then proceeds with its computation on the acknowledged dependent. The above model is an abstract of a system of processes with CSP-like communication [32]. A process in CSP executing an alternative guarded command may wait for messages from several processes; a guard succeeds and execution continues when a message is received from any one of those processes. Communication deadlock has been studied by Huang [35], Zhou and Tai [77], Ng and Ravishankar [53], Rontogiannis et al. [61], etc.

Resource Model(AND). In this model, processes are permitted to request a set of resources or resources are sharable. A process is blocked until it is granted all the resources it has requested. A shared resource is not available for exclusive use until all its shared lock holders have released the lock. Deadlock situations may arise if and only if the following four resource competition conditions hold simultaneously [58] [74]: (1) mutual exclusion, (2) hold and wait, (3) no preemption, and (4) circular wait. We assume that when a process has exclusive access to a shared resource it releases it in finite time. Resource sharing deadlock has been studied by Obermarck [55],Badal [4], Lee [40], etc.

There are no commonly accepted definitions for deadlock, even through Lee [40] gave a formal definition. However, it seems all agree that the deadlock is a program state in which all processes (tasks) are blocked waiting for something that will never happen. Both models can be used a directed graph, known as the wait-for graph (WFG) [66] to describe the dependency relationship among processes.

For Communication model, WFG is used to describe the processes's wait-for situation. Detecting a cycle in the WFG is not a sufficient condition for deadlock. As pointed out by Holt [33], a knot is a sufficient condition for deadlock while a cycle is only a necessary condition. Algorithms proposed for this model can be found in [51] [48] [18] [9].

For Resource model, a resource deadlock involves a directed cycle instead of a knot in WFG. A cycle in a WFG is a necessary and sufficient condition for deadlock in the this model. Many non real-time algorithms have been proposed based on this model such as [9] [55].

We need the following definition to describe program deadlocks.

Definition 25. *Given a place / transition chain, if every output transition is directly followed by an input transition, then this chain is called require-provide chain. Further more, if the chain is closed, then it is called require-provide loop.*

The following theorem gives a sufficient and necessary condition for a program with communication model to have deadlocks. Note that in the following, the state measures of the program are actually the state measures of the corresponding ConPN.

Theorem 26. *[Communication Model] A program has a deadlock if and only if every state measure $m(t)$ of the program either converges to 1 (including identically to 1) or converges to 0 (including identically to 0) as $t \to \infty$ no matter how the firing constants are chosen.*

The next theorem gives a sufficient and necessary condition for a program with resource sharing model to have deadlocks.

Theorem 27. *[Resource Model] A program has a deadlock if and only if there exists a time moment t_0, such that from that moment, each control function $k(t)$*

will have a fixed value(0 or 1) and every state measure $m(t)$ of the program either converges to 1 or converges to 0 as $t \to \infty$ no matter how the firing constants are chosen.

Corollary 28. *[Resource Model] A program has a deadlock if and only if there exists a combination of $k(0)$'s such that every state measure $m(t)$ of the program either converges to 1 or converges to 0 as $t \to \infty$ no matter how the firing constants are chosen.*

Corollary 28 provides us an way to check the deadlocks of the program. However, the number of combinations of all $k(0)$ could increase exponentially as the number of control functions increases. Thus, we need to find a way to get rid of most of the combinations. A technique has been developed. The following is a simple description. Let k be the value of a control function at 0. A condition *cond* is associated with k: if $k = 1$, then $(k = 1) \simeq cond$; if $k = 0$, then $(k = 0) \simeq^{\neg} cond$. Let $k_1(t), k_2(t)$ be two control functions associated with resource r_1 and r_2. Process A requires r_1 and r_2 at the same time. Assume that $(k_1(0) = 1) \simeq cond_1$, and $(k_2(0) = 1) \simeq cond_2$. If the system deadlocks, then process A can not have resources r_1 and r_2 at the same time: we say that $cond_1$ and $cond_2$ are not compatible. This is equivalent to saying that $(k_1(0) = 1)$ and $(k_2(0) = 1)$ can not be true at the same time. Thus we can eliminate the combinations $k_1(0) + k_2(0) = 2$. In this way, we can eliminate most of the combinations of control functions at 0. This technique is the condition checking referred to above; it has been used in our previous work on test case generation [21].

8   Boundedness Checking

Boundedness is one of the most important properties of discrete Petri nets. The follows are some concepts for boundedness.

A marking of (P, T, F, M_0) is a mapping $M : P \to \mathcal{N}$. The expression $M \xrightarrow{t} M'$ denotes that the marking M enables transition t, and that M' is the marking reached by the occurence of t. The expression $M \xrightarrow{\sigma} M'$, where σ is a sequence $\sigma = t_1 t_2 \ldots t_n$ of transitions, denotes that there exist markings $M_1, M_2, \ldots, M_{n-1}$ such that $M \xrightarrow{t_1} M_1 \xrightarrow{t_2} M_2 \ldots M_{n-1} \xrightarrow{t_n} M'$. Such an expression is called *occurrence sequence*. We also say that a sequence σ of transitions is an occurence sequence of (P, T, F, M_0) if there exits a marking M such that $M_0 \xrightarrow{\sigma} M$.

A marking M' is reachable from M if there exists an occurence sequence $M \xrightarrow{\sigma} M'$. The reachable markings of a system (P, T, F, M_0) are the markings reachable from M_0.

A System is b-bounded if $M(p) \leq b$ for every place p and every reachable markings, and bounded if it is b-bounded for some number b.

Determining the boundedness of a Petri net is usually through creating coverability graph or coverability tree [31] [25]. However, creating coverability graph and coverability tree is time consuming, and sometime the state explosion problem may be hit. We define stability for the continuous Petri net and prove that the stability of continuous Petri net is equivalent to the boundedness of the corresponding discrete Petri net. Accordingly, we can check the boundedness of discrete Petri net by analyzing the solutions of differential equation group.

Definition 29. *(Stable State) Let m be the state measure of a state. If there exists a number $c > 0$ such that $m(t) \leq c$, $t \in [0, +\infty)$, then the state is stable.*

Definition 30. *(Stable System) If there exists a number $c > 0$ such that $m(t) \leq c$, $t \in [0, +\infty)$ for all states of the program, then the corresponding differential equation system is stable.*

Theorem 31. *A Petri net is bounded if and only if the corresponding differential equation system is stable.*

Corollary 32. *If if every state measure of the continuous Petri net converges to a nonnegative constant, then the corresponding discrete Petri net is bounded.*

From the proof of Theorem 31, we found that the if we set all $k(t) = \frac{1}{2}$, we will have the same equivalent result. Thus, in the practice, to save time, we may compute the equation model with $k(t) = \frac{1}{2}$ instead of the equation model with $k(t) = \{0, 1\}$. An explanation is that when the system is running, two processes have the same chance to get the resources. However, this method is only used for boundedness checking.

9   Numerical Solution

Generally speaking, it is hard to find explicit analytic solutions for nonlinear ordinary differential equations, thus most of the time, we turn to find numerical solutions instead. However, numerical solutions may give us computational errors due to the algorithm and the machine. Since Matlab is a standard solver for ordinary differential equations, we may use some functions in Matlab to solve our equations. In this situation, the computation error can come from two sources: truncation error (because a truncated Taylor Series is used in the computation), and rounding error (because a finite number of binary digits is used inside the machine). Since in our equation group, all coefficients d_i are set to 1, the equations exhibit non-stiffness [29]. Hence we have used the function *ode45* for non-stiffness to compute the solutions of our equation groups. *ode45* is designed to handle the following general problem

$$\frac{dx}{dt} = f(t, x), \ x(t_0) = x_0,$$

where t is the independent variable and x is a vector of dependent variables to be found.

For the truncation error, since *ode45* is the implementation of combined fourth and fifth-order Runge-Kutta method, and the fourth-order Runge-Kutta method has local truncation error $O(h^5)$ and the fifth-order Runge-Kutta method has local truncation error $O(h^6)$, where h is the step size, thus the global truncation error of $ode45$ is $O(h^5)$ [29]. Noticing that the fifth-order Runge-Kutta method can automatically adjust the step size, thus $ode45$ can approximate to the given accuracy by setting $opts$ with command $odeset$. Regarding the rounding error, since $ode45$ is absolute stable [2], the rounding error tends to zero during the iteration process.

Thus we check the system deadlocks by analyzing the behaviour of the numerical solution instead of that of original analytic solution.

10   Case Study (I): The Gas-Station Problem

The Gas-Station problem which models activities of an automated gas station was originally described in [30]. It was first modeled with an Ada tasking program for detecting deadlocks. Thereafter, this example has been widely studied for property analysis, specially deadlock analysis [22] [13] [52]. Generally, the automated gas station consists of a set of cashiers, a set of pumps and a set of customers. The scenario is as follows: customers arrive and pay the casher for gas. The cashier activates a pump, at which the customer then pumps gas. When the customer is finished, the pump reports the amount of gas actually pumped to the cashier, who then gives the customer the change.

We have checked for 3, 5, 7 and 10 customers, and the experimental data is displayed in Table 1. The experiments were conducted on a Dell computer with 2.33GHz Intel(R) Core(TM)2 CPU and 1.96G memory.

Table 1. Data of checking gas-station problem with equation model

# of Customers	3	5	7	10
Memory(M)	0.176	0.215	0.253	0.289
Time(second)	0.0568	0.0572	0.0578	0.0585

For comparison, we quote the data from TOTAL in the Table 2. This table shows the best cases when different optimization methods are applied. We have also used SPIN to check the gas-station problem and the experimental data is displayed in Table 3.

Based on the above experimental data, we find that as the number of customers increases, TOTAL needs the most time. We also noticed that there is a little difference between SPIN and ODE in this example: The increasing speeds

Table 2. Data of checking gas station problem with TOTAL

# of Customers	3	5	7	10
Method	nrt	nrt+sym	nrt+sym	nrt+sym
Time(second)	2	3	6	17

Table 3. Data of checking gas station problem with SPIN

# of Customers	3	5	7	10
state	66	78	90	108
Memory	2.501	2.501	2.501	2.501
Time(second)	0.0035	0.004	0.005	0.005

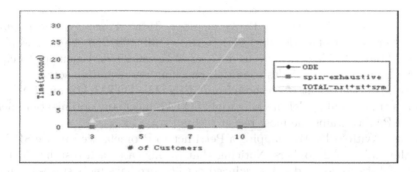

Fig. 14. Computing time for gas-station problem

of time and memory for SPIN are smaller than those for ODE. The reason is that in SPIN, although the number of customer process increases, the states being checked increase slowly since there are no communications among these customers, thus the customers does not affect much of the performance of SPIN. However, for ODE method, as the number of customer increases, the number of ODE will increases, hence, the time and the memory will increase accordingly. Fig. 14 displays the increasing trend of computing time when TOTAL, SPIN and ODE are applied.

11 Case Study (II): Dining Philosophers

Dijkstra's [17] dining philosopher problem is a very well-known example of a concurrent program. Although not a very realistic problem, it does contain a nontrivial deadlock and is probably the most commonly analyzed example [3] [22] [38]. A group of N philosophers is sitting around a table. The philosophers alternate between thinking and eating. Initially n forks are placed on the table between each pair of philosophers. In order to eat, a philosopher must first pick up both forks next to him. The forks are put down when the philosopher finishes eating and starts thinking. This problem is interesting because of the possibility of a circular deadlock. Deadlock may occur if all philosophers pick up their forks in the same order, say, the right fork followed by the left fork. In this case, there is one deadlock state corresponding to the situation in which all philosophers have picked up their right fork and are waiting for their left fork.

Table 4. Data of checking DP with equation model when condition checking is applied

# of Philosophers	5	10	20	30	100	200	400
# of combinations	2^5	2^{10}	2^{20}	2^{30}	2^{100}	2^{200}	2^{400}
Memory(M)	0.029	0.057	0.113	0.169	4.01	9.37	20.55
Total Time(second)	0.016	0.021	0.03	0.05	0.179	2.53	4.87

Our experiments were again conducted on a Dell computer with 2.33GHz Intel(R) Core(TM)2 CPU and 1.96G memory. Table 4 displays the required time and memory to find deadlocks for 5, 10, 20, 30, 100, 200, 400 philosophers with condition checking. It takes us 4.87 seconds and 20.55M memory to check 400 philosophers; that includes condition checking and equation solving.

We compare our results with those from SPIN [34], TOTAL [22] and PAT [56]. SPIN is a traditional model checking tool, TOTAL has many optimization methods, and PAT contains the most recent technology.

Checking With SPIN. By mapping a Petri net to Promela, we can use SPIN to check the dining philosophers. Noticing that in our case each task has 5 states instead of 3 states, as used in the reduced net [22], we have more states to check. For example, for 5 dining philosophers, our net has $5^5 = 3125$ states, while the reduced net has $3^5 = 243$ states. Table 5 shows the data of our experiment on the computer: Intel(R) Xeon(R) with E5410@2.33GHz CPU and 12GB memory. The search mode of SPIN is 'exhaustive'.

Table 5. Data of checking dining philosophers with SPIN in the search mode "exhaustive"

# of Philosophers	5	6	7	8	9	10
Memory(M)	2.696	4.454	16.856	106.114	776.583	9318.996
# of States	4201	2.7×10^4	1.7×10^5	1.2×10^6	7.7×10^6	9.24×10^7
Time(second)	0.009	0.053	0.37	2.78	87.8	1053.6

The states in the table are the generated states. By experimenting, we found that memory and time increase so quickly that we could not even complete 11 philosophers. Changing the search mode to 'supertrace/bitstate', we obtained the data in Table 6.

We found that the memory and the time used are almost double ours. We also noticed an interesting phenomenon: below number 13, SPIN seems to explore the complete state space, and above 14, SPIN tries a different search order.

Checking With TOTAL. In [22], the experiments with the 3-philosopher version show that each of the methods (net reduction, stubborn sets, sleep sets, net symmetry) can substantially reduce the size of the state space. However, the growth of the state space is still exponential in the number of philosophers when a single method is used. Their experiments stop at 3 philosophers without

Table 6. Data of checking dining philosophers with SPIN in the search mode "super-trace/bitstate"

# of Philosophers	Memory(M)	# of States	Time(second)
5	16.539	4201	0.0114
10	16.539	3×10^7	91.9
13	16.539	3.7×10^7	124
14	16.539	57	0.007
20	16.539	125	0.052
30	16.539	235	0.088
100	16.636	1005	0.363
200	18.437	2135	4.95
400	38.621	4225	9.63

optimization, at 20 with net reduction (nrt) only, at 5 with symmetry (sym) only, at 5 with sleep sets (sl) only, and at 10 with stubborn sets (st) only. The reason is that 'since either the computation has exhausted all resources or the computation time exceeds one hour'. The maximum number of philosophers they can check is 400 if all methods are combined, and then the computation time is 681 seconds. Table 7 displays the best results when different methods are applied or their combinations are applied.

Table 7. Data of checking dining philosophers with TOTAL

# of Philosophers	5	10	20	100	200	400
Method	sym/sl	st	nrt	nrt+sl	nrt+sl	nrt+st+sym
Time(second)	164/2	58	626	27	111	681

Checking With PAT. The PAT group provided us the data in Table 8. PAT, like SPIN, performs on-the-fly search and the search stops as soon as a counterexample is found. From the table we know that the time increases rapidly from 200 philosophers to 400 philosophers. As the PAT group mentioned, in this case PAT happens to pick up the right trace to start with and quickly find a deadlock state, and it is possible that if a different search order is chosen, it will take much more time to find such a state.

Table 8. Data of checking dining philosophers with PAT

# of Philosophers	5	10	20	100	200	400
Memory(M)	0.196	0.614	1.496	9.497	51.145	365.731
# of States	53	138	383	5943	21893	83794
Time(second)	0.001	0.002	0.01	1.07	9.11	113.7

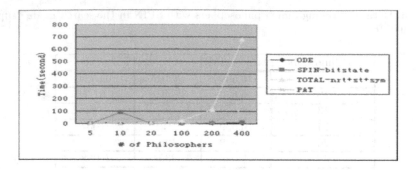

Fig. 15. Computing time for dining philosopher problem

Based on the above data, we conclude that our method can significantly reduce the computing time and memory usage. For example, for 400 philosophers,
TOTAL needs 681 seconds (memory is not given in [22]), PAT uses 113.7 seconds and 365.731M memory, and SPIN needs 9.63 seconds and 38.621M memory,
while our method uses only 4.87 seconds and 20.55M. Fig. 15 displays the increasing trend of computing time when different methods are applied.

12   Case Study (III): Traffic Network

We apply our technique to check the boundedness of a traffic network, and
thus analyze the impact of traffic light on the traffic network. Fig. 16 is a traffic
network that describes two road intersection, where m_1, m_2, m_3 and m_4 represent
4 phase green light states. m_5, m_6, m_7, m_8 are the interaction places between
traffic lights and the four road traffics. $m_9, m_{13}, m_{17}, m_{21}, m_{25}, m_{26}, m_{27}, m_{28}$
represent road traffics, $m_{11}, m_{15}, m_{19}, m_{23}$ represent traffic waiting for the left
turn, $m_{12}, m_{16}, m_{20}, m_{24}$ represent the traffic waiting for the right turn, and m_{29}
simply represents all other traffics surrounding this road intersection.

We assume that traffic rate is 1 car / second, thus all the firing rates related
to traffic are $d = 1$. Let d_1, d_2, d_3 and d_4 be the firing rates associated with traffic
lights. Thus the signal period of traffic lights are $\frac{1}{d_i}, i = 1, 2, 3, 4$. For example,
if $d_1 = 0.2$, then the traffic light changes every $\frac{1}{0.2} = 5$ seconds. The equation
model is represented in the following.

The initial values are $m_1(0) = m_9(0) = m_{13}(0) = m_{17}(0) = m_{21}(0) = 1$, all
others 0. If we set $d_1 = d_2 = d_3 = d_4 = 1$, the solution of the equation group by
Matlab is plotted in Fig. 17.

We see that $m_5, m_6, m_7, m_8 \to \infty$ as $t \to \infty$. Thus from Theorem 31, the
system is unbounded. This implies that the signal data can not be digested
and has been accumulated. Further analysis shows that the traffic lights keep
changing signaling, but the road traffics do not have enough time to follow,
which means that the road traffics can not digest the signals. Consequently, we
will have a heavy traffic on the road.

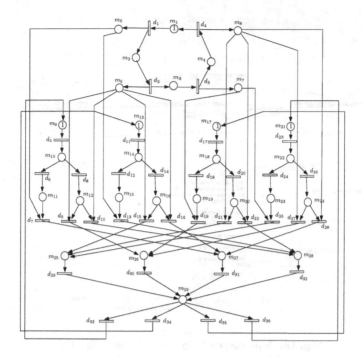

Fig. 16. Petri net model of traffic network

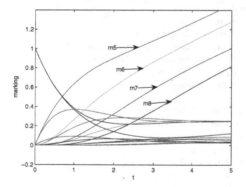

Fig. 17. State measures of traffic network

As a comparison, we have implemented an algorithm from [31] to generate coverability tree to check the boundedness. The interface to generate the tree is shown in Figure 18. It took 21607 seconds (almost 6 hours) to build the tree. However, it only took 0.015 seconds to calculate the solutions of the equation model.

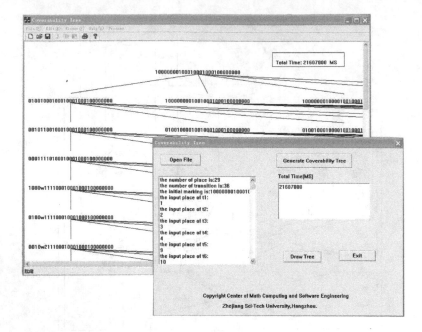

Fig. 18. A prototype to generate coverability tree

$$
\left\{
\begin{array}{l}
m'_1 = d_4 m_4 - d_1 m_1 \\
m'_2 = d_1 m_1 - d_2 m_2 \\
m'_3 = d_2 m_2 - d_3 m_3 \\
m'_4 = d_3 m_3 - d_4 m_4 \\
m'_5 = d_1 m_1 - 0.5 m_5 m_{11} - 0.5 m_5 m_{15} \\
m'_6 = d_2 m_2 - 0.25 m_6 m_{12} - 0.25 m_6 m_{16} \\
m'_7 = d_3 m_3 - 0.5 m_7 m_{19} - 0.5 m_7 m_{23} \\
m'_8 = d_4 m_4 - 0.25 m_8 m_{20} - 0.25 m_8 m_{24} \\
m'_9 = 0.25 m_{29} - m_9 \\
m'_{10} = m_9 - m_{10} \\
m'_{11} = 0.5 m_{10} - 0.5 m_5 m_{11} \\
m'_{12} = 0.5 m_{10} - 0.25 m_6 m_{12} \\
m'_{13} = 0.25 m_{29} - m_{13} \\
m'_{14} = m_{13} - m_{14} \\
m'_{15} = 0.5 m_{14} - 0.5 m_5 m_{15} \\
m'_{16} = 0.5 m_{14} - 0.25 m_6 m_{16} \\
m'_{17} = 0.25 m_{29} - m_{17} \\
m'_{18} = m_{17} - m_{18} \\
m'_{19} = 0.5 m_{18} - 0.5 m_7 m_{19} \\
m'_{20} = 0.5 m_{18} - 0.25 m_8 m_{20} \\
m'_{21} = 0.25 m_{29} - m_{21} \\
m'_{22} = m_{21} - m_{22} \\
m'_{23} = 0.5 m_{22} - 0.5 m_7 m_{23} \\
m'_{24} = 0.5 m_{22} - 0.25 m_8 m_{24} \\
m'_{25} = 0.5 m_7 m_{23} + 0.125 m_6 m_{16} + 0.125 m_8 m_{20} - m_{25} \\
m'_{26} = 0.5 m_7 m_{19} + 0.125 m_6 m_{12} + 0.125 m_8 m_{24} - m_{26} \\
m'_{27} = 0.5 m_5 m_{211} + 0.125 m_6 m_{16} + 0.125 m_8 m_{24} - m_{27} \\
m'_{28} = 0.5 m_5 m_{15} + 0.125 m_6 m_{12} + 0.125 m_8 m_{20} - m_{28} \\
m'_{29} = m_{25} + m_{26} + m_{27} + m_{28} - m_{29}
\end{array}
\right.
$$

13   Discussion and Conclusion

We have used six types of ordinary differential equations to describe concurrent programs, where each equation describes the state change of the program. By analyzing the solutions, we may check the deadlocks and boundedness of a program. With our method, the the complexity is determined by solving one equation group(for communication model) or by solving one equation group and the checking condition compatibility(for resource sharing model). While using the existing static analysis techniques, since model checkers build a finite state transition system and exhaustively explore the reachable state space searching for violations of the property [11], it is hard to avoid hitting state explosion problem even some state reduction techniques have been used.

There still exist a lot of issues to be solved before our technique offers improvement in real time over the state of the art. The follows are some examples:

- Computing. As one might concern, if the system is very large, particular the system has huge number of tasks, then the equation model will be very big. A single equation group may contain huge number of equations. For example to model a system with 10^{20} states that has been used for Symbolic Model Checking by Burch et al.[6], we need to solve 10^{20} equations. Matlab may not have enough power to perform such computing. A solution is to solve the equation group in parallel. Currently, we are developing a computing algorithm based on the work by Intievergelt[36].
- Property. Since Matlab can not give us analytic representations for the solutions of nonlinear ordinary differential equations, therefore, we are unable to further analyze the properties of the solutions. If the number of the equations is huge, we do require a tool to analyze the numerical solutions, not just to check the curves from Matlab.
- Performance. From equation model, we know that the program states are determined by the program structures and the firing constants. We have already investigated the role of concurrent structures in the computing of program states. For the firing constants, we have not come out of any results yet, however, we do experienced that the firing constants affect the state measures in the experiments. Hopefully, we will find some explicit formulas for firing constants in the performance analysis of the programs.

References

1. Allen, R., Garlan, D.: A formal basis for architectural connection. ACM Transactions on Software Engineering and Methodology 6(3), 213–249 (1997)
2. Ascher, U.M., Petzold, L.R.: Computer Methods for Ordinary Differential Equations and Differential-Algebraic Equations. Society for Industrial & Applied Mathematis, Philadelphia (1998)
3. Avrunin, G.S., Buy, U.A., Corbett, J.C., Dillon, L.K., Wileden, J.C.: Automated Analysis of Concurrent Systems with the Constrained Expression Toolset. IEEE Transactions on Software Engineering 17(11), 1204–1222 (1991)

4. Badal, D.Z.: The Distributed Deadlock Detection Algorithm. ACM Transactions on Computer Systems 4(4), 320–377 (1986)
5. Ben-Ari, M.: Principles of Concurrent and Distributed Programming, 2nd edn. Addison-Wesley, Reading (2006)
6. Burch, J.R., Clarke, E.M., Long, D.E.: Representing circuts more efficiently in symbolic model checking, In. In: Proceedings of the 28th Design Automation Conference, pp. 403–407. IEEE Computer Society Press, Los Alamltos (1991)
7. Boukerche, A., Tropper, C.: A Distributed Graph Algorithm for the Detection of Local Cycles and Knots. IEEE Trans. Parallel and Distributed Systems 9(8), 748–757 (1998)
8. Burch, J., Clarke, E., McMillan, K., Dill, D., Hwang, L.: Symbolic Model Checking: 10^{20} States and Beyond. Information and Computation 9(2), 142–170 (1992)
9. Chandy, K.M., Misra, J., Haas, L.M.: Distributed Deadlock Detection. ACM Transactions on Computer Systems 1(2), 144–156 (1983)
10. Clarke, E.M., Grumberg, O., Long, D.E.: Model Checking and Abstraction. ACM Transactions on Programming Language Systems 16(5), 1512–1542 (1994)
11. Clarke, E.M., Grumberg, O., Peled, D.: Model Checking. MIT Press, Cambridge (1999)
12. Clarke, E., McMillan, K., Campos, S., Hartonas-Garmhausen, V.: Symbolic Model Checking. In: Proceedings of 8th Computer Aided Verification Conference. Springer, Berlin (1996)
13. Corbett, J.C.: Evaluating Deadlock Detection Methods for Concurrent Software. IEEE Transactions on Software Engineering 22(3), 161–180 (1996)
14. Corbett, J.C., Avrunin, G.S.: Using integer programming to verify general safety and liveness properties. Formal Methods in System Desin 6, 97–123 (1995)
15. David, R., Alla, H.: Continuous Petri nets. In: Proceedings of 8th European Workshop on Application and Theory of Petri nets, Zaragoza, Spain, pp. 275–294 (1987)
16. David, R., Alla, H.: Autonomous and timed continuous Petri nets. In: Proceedings of 11th Int. Conf. on Application and Theory of Petri nets, Paris, France, pp. 367–381 (1990)
17. Dijkstra, E.W.: Hierarchical Ordering of Sequential Processes. Acta Informat 2, 115–138 (1971)
18. Dijkstra, E.W., Scholten, C.S.: Termination Detection for Diffusing Computations. Information Processing Letters 11(1), 1–4 (1980)
19. Ding, Z., Xiao, L., Hu, J.: Performance analysis of service composition using ordinary differential equations. In: Proceedings of FTDCS 2008, Kunming, China, October 21-23. IEEE Computer Society Press, Los Alamitos (2008)
20. Ding, Z., Zhang, K.: Performance analysis of concurrent programs using ordinary differential equations. In: COMPSAC 2008, Turku, Finland, July 28-August 1. IEEE Computer Society Press, Los Alamitos (2008)
21. Ding, Z., Zhang, K., Hua, J.: A Rigorous Approach Towards Test Case Generation. Information Sciences 178, 4057–4079 (2008)
22. Duri, S., Buy, U., Devarapalli, R., Shatz, S.M.: Application and Experimental Evaluation of State Space Reduction Methods for Deadlock Analysis in Ada. ACM Transactions on Software Engneering and Methodology 3(4), 340–380 (1994)
23. Dwyer, M.B., Clarke, L.A.: Data flow analysis for verifying properties of concurrent programs. In: Proc. Second Symp. Foundations of Software Enginemng, pp. 62–75 (1994)
24. Gilbert, D., Heiner, M.: From Petri nets to differential equations-an integrative approach for biochemical network analysis. In: Donatelli, S., Thiagarajan, P.S. (eds.) ICATPN 2006. LNCS, vol. 4024, pp. 181–200. Springer, Heidelberg (2006)

25. Goltz, U., Reisig, W.: Weighted Synchronic Distance. In: Application and Theory of Petri Nets, Informatik Fachberichte, vol. 52. Springer, Heidelberg (1982)
26. Dwyer, M.B., Clarke, L.A.: A compact Petri Net Representation and Its Implications for Analysis. IEEE Transactions on Software Engineering 22(11), 794–811 (1996)
27. Godefroid, P., Pirottin, D.: Refining Dependendes Improves Partial- Order verification Methods. In: Courcoubetis (ed.) Proc. Fifth lnt'l conf: Computer Aided Verfication, Elounda, Greece, pp. 438–449 (1993)
28. Hale, J.K.: Ordinary Differential Equations. Interscience, New York (1969)
29. Hairer, E., Nϕrsett, S.P., Wanner, G.: Solving Ordinary Differential Equations(I), Nonstiff Problems, 2nd edn. Springer, Heidelberg (1993)
30. Helmbold, D., Luckham, D.: Debugging Ada tasking programs. IEEE Software 2(2), 47–57 (1985)
31. Herrmann, J.W., Lin, E.: Petri Nets: Tutorial and Applications. In: The 32th Annual Symposium of the Washington Operations Research-Management Science Council, Washington, D.C., November 5 (1997)
32. Hoare, C.A.R.: Communicating sequential processes. Communication of ACM 21(8), 666–677 (1978)
33. Holt, R.C.: Some Deadlock Properties on Computer Systems. ACM Compuling Surveys 4(3), 179–196 (1972)
34. Holzmann, G.J.: Basic Spin Manual (1980), http://cm.bell-labs.com/netlib/spin/whatispin.html
35. Huang, S.T.: A Distributed Deadlock Detection Algorithm for CSP-Like Communication. ACM Transactions on Programming Languages and Systems 12(1), 102–122 (1990)
36. Intievergelt, J.: Parallel methods for integrating ordinary differential equations. Communications of the ACM 7(12), 731–733 (1964)
37. Juan, E., Tsai, J.J.P., Murata, T.: Compositional verification of concurrent systems using Petri-nets-based condensation rules. ACM Transactions on Programming Languages and Systems 20(3), 917–979 (1998)
38. Karam, G.M., Buhr, R.J.: Starvation and Critical Race Analyzers For Ada. IEEE Transactions on Software Engineering 16(8), 829–843 (1990)
39. Kim, Y.M., Lai, T.H., Soundarajan, N.: Efficient Distributed Deadlock Detection and Resolution Using Probes, Tokens, and Barriers. In: Proc. Int'l Conf. Parallel and Distributed Systems, pp. 584 591 (1997)
40. Lee, S.: Fast, Centralized Detection and Resolution of Distributed Deadlocks in the Generalized Model. IEEE Transactions on Software Engineering 30(9), 561–573 (2004)
41. Lin, B.: Efficient Compilation of Process-based Concurrent Programs Without Run-time Scheduling. In: Proceedings of Design, Automation, and Test in Europe (DATE), Paris, pp. 211–217 (1998)
42. Long, D.L., Clarke, L.A.: Task Interaction Graphs for Concurrency Analysis. In: Proc. 11th lntl. Conf. Software Eng, Pittsburgh, Penn, pp. 44–52 (1989)
43. Lunze, J., Nixdorf, B., Richter, H.: Hybrid modelling of continuous-variable systems with application to supervisory control. In: Proceedings of the European Control Conference 1997, Brussels, Belgium (1997)
44. Mandrioli, D., Zicari, R., Ghezzi, C., Tisato, F.: Modeling the Ada Task System by Petri nets. Computer Languages 10(1), 43–61 (1985)
45. Masticola, S.P., Ryder, E.G.: Static Infinite Wait Anomaly Detection in Polynomial Time. In: Proceedings of 1990 International Conference on Parallel Processing, vol. 2, pp. 78–87 (1990)

46. Math Department, East China Normal University: Mathematics Analysis (I)(II), 3rd edn. High education Press, China (2001)
47. McMillan, K.L.: Symbolic Model Checking. Kluwer Academic Publishers, Boston (1993)
48. Misra, J., Chandy, K.M.: A Distributed Graph Algorithm: Knot Detection. ACM Transactions on Programming Languages and Systems 4(4), 678–686 (1982)
49. Molloy, M.K.: Fast bounds for stochastic Petri nets. In: International Workshop on Timed Petri Nets, Torino, July 1985, pp. 244–249 (1985)
50. Morgan, E.T., Razouk, R.R.: Interactive State Space Analysis of Concurrent Systems. IEEE Transitions on Software Engineering 12(10), 1080–1091 (1987)
51. Natarajan, N.: A Distributed Scheme for Detecting Communication Deadlocks. IEEE Transactions on Software Engineering SE-12(4), 531–537 (1986)
52. Naumovich, G., Avrunin, G., Clarke, L.: Applying Static Analysis to Software Architectures. ACM SIGSOFT Notes 22(6), 77–93 (1997)
53. Ng, W.K., Ravishankar, C.V.: On-Line Detection and Resolution of Communication Deadlocks. In: Proc. 27th Ann. Hawaii Int'l Conf. System Science, pp. 524–533 (1994)
54. Notomi, M., Murata, T.: Hierarchical Reachability Graph of Bounded Petri Nets for Concurrent-Software Analysis. IEEE Transactions on Software Engineering 20(5), 325–336 (1994)
55. Obermarck, R.: Distributed Deadlock Detection Algorithm. ACM Trans. Database Syst. 7(2), 187–208 (1982)
56. PAT, http://www.comp.nus.edu.sg/~pat/
57. Peleties, P., DeCarlo, R.: Analysis of hybrid systems using symbolic dynamics and Petri nets. Automatica 30(9), 1421–1427 (1994)
58. Peterson, J.L., Silberschatz, A.: Operating System Concepts. Addison-Wesley, Reading (1983)
59. Pezzé, M., Taylor, R.N., Young, M.: Graph Models for Reachability Analysis. ACM Transactions on Software Engmeermg and Methodology 4(2), 171–213 (1995)
60. Reif, J.H., Smolka, S.A.: Data flow analysis of distributed communicating processes. Journal of Parallel Programming 19(1), 1–30 (1990)
61. Rontogiannis, P., Pavlides, G., Levy, A.: Distributed Algorithm for Communication Deadlock Detection. Information and Software Technology 33(7), 483–488 (1991)
62. Royden, H.L.: Real Analysis, 3rd edn. Macmillan Publishing Co., New York (1988)
63. Scheibler, D.: A Software Tool for Design and Simulation of Continuous Petri Nets (in German), Master Thesis, BTU Cottbus, Dep. of CS (2006)
64. Shatz, S.M., Mai, K., Black, C., Tu, S.: Design and Implementation of A Petri Net-based Toolkit for Ada Tasking analysis. IEEE Trans. Par. Dist. Syst. 1(4), 424–441 (1990)
65. Shih, C.-S., Stankovic, J.A.: Distributed Deadlock Detection in Ada Runtime Environments (1990)
66. Singhal, M.: Deadlock Detection in Distributed Systems. IEEE Computer 22, 37–48 (1989)
67. Sistla, A.P., Miliades, L., Gyuris, V.: SMC: A symmetry based model checker for verification of liveness properties. In: Proceedings of 9th Computer Aided Verification Conference, Haifa, Israel (1997)
68. Smart, D.R.: Fixed Point Theorems. Cambridge Univ. Press, Cambridge (1974)
69. Taylor, R.: A general purpose algorithm for analyzing concurrent programs. Communication of ACM 26(5), 362–376 (1983)
70. Tsai, J.P., Xu, K.: An empirical evaluation of deadlock detection in software architecture specifications. Annals of Software Engineering 7, 95–126 (1999)

71. Tu, S., Shatz, S.M., Murata, T.: Theory and Application of Petri Net Reduction for Ada-Tasking Deadlock Analysls. Tech. Report 91-15, EECS Dept., Univ. of Illinois, Chicago (1991)
72. Valmari, A.: A stubborn attack on state explosion. In: Clarke, E., Kurshan, R.P. (eds.) CAV 1990. LNCS, vol. 531, pp. 156–165. Springer, Heidelberg (1991)
73. Wang, X., Kwiatkowska, M.: Compositional state space reduction using untangled actions. Electronic Notes in Computer Science 175(3), 27–46 (2007)
74. Wojcik, B.E., Wojcik, Z.M.: Sufficient Condition for a Communication Deadlock and Distributed Deadlock Detection. IEEE Transactions on Software Engineering 5(12), 1587–1595 (1989)
75. Yeh, W.J., Young, M.: Compositional Reachabhty Analysls Uslng procesS Algebra. In: Roc. Symp. Testing, Analysis, and Verfication (TAV4), pp. 178–187. ACM SIGSOFT, New York (1991)
76. Young, M., Taylor, R.N., Forester, K., Brodbeck, D.: Integrated Concurrency Analysis In A Software Development Environment. In: Proceedings of the ACM SIGSOFT 1989 3rd Symposium on Software Testing, Analysis and Verification. Software Engineering Notes, vol. 14(8), pp. 200–209 (1989)
77. Zhou, J., Tai, K.C.: Deadlock Analysis of Synchronous Message-Passing Programs. In: Proceedings of the International Symposium on Software Engineering for Parallel and Distributed Systems, pp. 62–69 (1999)

The PlusCal Algorithm Language

Leslie Lamport

Microsoft Research

Abstract. Algorithms are different from programs and should not be
described with programming languages. The only simple alternative to
programming languages has been pseudo-code. PlusCal is an algorithm
language that can be used right now to replace pseudo-code, for both
sequential and concurrent algorithms. It is based on the TLA$^+$ specification language, and a PlusCal algorithm is automatically translated to
a TLA$^+$ specification that can be checked with the TLC model checker
and reasoned about formally.

1   Introduction

PlusCal is a language for writing algorithms, including concurrent algorithms.
While there is no formal distinction between an algorithm and a program, we
know that an algorithm like Newton's method for approximating the zeros of a
real-valued function is different from a program that implements it. The difference
is perhaps best described by paraphrasing the title of Wirth's classic book [1]: a
program is an algorithm plus an implementation of its data operations.

The data manipulated by algorithms are mathematical objects like numbers
and graphs. Programming languages can represent these mathematical objects
only by programming-language objects like bit strings and pointers, introducing
implementation details that are irrelevant to the algorithm. The customary way
to eliminate these irrelevant details is to use pseudo-code. There are two obvious
problems with pseudo-code: it has no precise meaning, and it can be checked
only by hand—a notoriously unreliable method of finding errors.

PlusCal is designed to replace pseudo-code for describing algorithms. A Plus-
Cal algorithm is translated to a TLA$^+$ specification [2]. That specification can
be debugged (and occasionally even completely verified) with the TLC model
checker [3]. A TLA$^+$ specification is a formula of TLA, a logic invented expressly
for proving properties of systems, so properties of an algorithm can be proved
by reasoning about its translation.

There are other languages that might be satisfactory replacements for pseudo-
code in a Utopian world where everyone has studied the language. A researcher
can use PlusCal in his next paper; a professor can use it in her next lecture.
PlusCal code is simple enough that explaining it is almost as easy as explaining
the pseudo-code that it replaces. I know of no other language that can plau-
sibly make this claim and has the expressive power to replace pseudo-code for

M. Leucker and C. Morgan (Eds.): ICTAC 2009, LNCS 5684, pp. 36–60, 2009.

both sequential and concurrent algorithms. Other languages used to describe algorithms are discussed in the conclusion.

PlusCal's simplicity comes from its simple, familiar programming language constructs that make it resemble a typical toy language. For example, here is the "Hello World" program:

> **--algorithm** *HelloWorld*
> **begin print** "Hello, world."
> **end algorithm**

PlusCal has the expressive power to replace pseudo-code because of its rich expression language. A PlusCal expression can be any expression of TLA$^+$, which means it can be anything expressible in set theory and first-order logic. This gives PlusCal's expression language all the power of ordinary mathematics, making it infinitely more powerful than the expression language of any programming language.

Programming languages have two other deficiencies that make them unsuitable as algorithm languages:

- They describe just one way to compute something. An algorithm might require that a certain operation be executed for all values of i from 1 to N; most programming languages must specify in which order those executions are performed. PlusCal provides two simple constructs for expressing nondeterminism.

- Execution of an algorithm consists of a sequence of steps. An algorithm's computational complexity is the number of steps it takes to compute the result, and defining a concurrent algorithm requires specifying what constitutes a single (atomic) step. Programming languages provide no well-defined notion of a program step. PlusCal uses labels to describe an algorithm's steps.

  Describing the grain of atomicity is crucial for concurrent algorithms, but is often unimportant for sequential algorithms. Labels can therefore be omitted and the translator instructed to choose the steps, which it makes as large possible to facilitate model checking.

PlusCal combines five important features: simple conventional program constructs, extremely powerful expressions, nondeterminism, a convenient way to describe the grain of atomicity, and model checking. The only novel aspect of any of these features is the particular method of using labels to indicate atomic actions. While the individual features are not new, their combination is. PlusCal is the only language I know of that has them all. This combination of features makes it ideal for writing algorithms.

PlusCal can be used not only in publications and in the classroom, but also in programming. Although most programming involves simple data manipulation, a program sometimes contains a nontrivial algorithm. It is more efficient to debug the algorithm by itself, rather than debugging it and its implementation at the same time. Writing the algorithm in PlusCal and debugging it with TLC before implementing it is a good way to do this.

Being easy to read does not necessarily make PlusCal easy to write. Like any powerful language, PlusCal has rules and restrictions that are not immediately obvious. Because of its inherent simplicity, the basic language should not be hard to learn. What many programmers and computer scientists will find hard is learning to take advantage of the power of the expression language. TLA$^+$ expressions use only basic math—that is, predicate logic, sets, and functions (which include tuples and records). However, many computer scientists would have difficulty describing even something as simple as a graph in terms of sets and functions. With PlusCal, the writer of an algorithm can reveal to the reader as much or as little of the underlying math as she wishes.

PlusCal's features imply its limitations. Programming languages are complex because of constructs like objects and variable scoping that are useful for writing large programs. PlusCal's simplicity limits the length of the algorithms it can conveniently describe. The largest algorithm I have written in it is about 500 lines. I expect that PlusCal would not work well for algorithms of more than one or two thousand lines. (However, a one-line PlusCal assignment statement can express what in a programming language requires a multi-line loop or the call of a complicated procedure.) Programming languages are inexpressive because they must yield efficient code. While it is possible to restrict PlusCal so it can be compiled into efficient code, any such restriction would reduce its utility for writing algorithms. PlusCal is for writing algorithms, not for writing large specifications or efficient programs.

The semantics of PlusCal is specified formally by its translation to TLA$^+$. A TLA$^+$ specification of the translation is included in the PlusCal distribution, which is available on the Web [4]. (The translator, which is written in Java, has the option of performing the translation by executing this specification with TLC.) The translation is described in Section 4. However, except for its expressions, PlusCal is so simple and most of its constructs so banal that there is no need to give a rigorous semantics here. Instead, the language is explained in Section 2 by a series of examples. Section 3 describes the few features not contained in the examples, and Section 5 completes the language description by explaining the constraints on where labels may and may not appear. To convince the reader that nothing is being hidden, a grammar of the full language (excluding its expressions) appears in the appendix. A language manual is available on the PlusCal Web site.

No attempt is made here to describe the complete language of TLA$^+$ expressions. The TLA$^+$ notation used in the examples is explained only where it does not correspond to standard mathematical usage. The PlusCal language manual briefly explains TLA$^+$ and its expressions. The semantics of TLA$^+$ expressions is trivial in the sense that a semantics consists of a translation to ordinary mathematics, and TLA$^+$ expressions are expressions of ordinary mathematics. A precise explanation of all the TLA$^+$ operators that can appear in a PlusCal expression is given in Section 16.1 of the TLA$^+$ manual [2].

2 Some Examples

A PlusCal algorithm can be written in either of two syntaxes—the clearer but longer p-syntax (p for *prolix*), or the more compact c-syntax that will look familiar to most programmers. The first two examples use the p-syntax; the next two use the c-syntax. The grammar given in the appendix is for the c-syntax.

2.1 Euclid's Algorithm

The first example is a simple version of Euclid's algorithm from Sedgewick's textbook [5, page 8]. The algorithm computes the GCD of two natural numbers m and n by setting u to m and v to n and executing the following pseudo-code.

> **while** $u \neq 0$ **do**
>   **if** $u < v$ **then** swap u and v **end if** ;
> $u := u - v$
> **end while** ;

Upon termination, v equals the GCD of m and n. The PlusCal version appears in Figure 1 on this page. (Symbols are actually typed as ASCII strings—for example, "$\in$" is typed "\in".) The variable declarations assert that the initial values of m and n are in the set $1 .. K$ of integers from 1 through K, and that u and v initially equal m and n, respectively. (We will see later where K is declared.) Assignment statements separated by $\parallel$ form a multi-assignment, executed by first evaluating all the right-hand expressions and then performing all the assignments. The **assert** statement checks the correctness of the algorithm, where $IsGCD(v, m, n)$ will be defined to be true iff v is the GCD of m and n, for natural numbers v, m, and n.

The algorithm appears in a comment in a TLA$^+$ module, as shown in Figure 2 on the next page. The module's EXTENDS statement imports the *Naturals* module, which defines arithmetic operators like subtraction and "$..$", and a special *TLC* module that is needed because of the algorithm's **assert** statement. The CONSTANT declaration declares the algorithm parameter K. The module next defines $Divides(i, j)$ to be true for natural numbers i and j iff i divides j, and it uses *Divides* to define *IsGCD*.

> **--algorithm** *EuclidSedgewick*
> **variables** $m \in 1 .. K,\ n \in 1 .. K,\ u = m,\ v = n$
> **begin while** $u \neq 0$ **do**
>   **if** $u < v$ **then** $u := v \parallel v := u$ **end if** ;
> $u := u - v$
>   **end while** ;
>   **assert** $IsGCD(v, m, n)$
> **end algorithm**

Fig. 1. Euclid's algorithm in PlusCal

```
┌──────────────────────── module Euclid ────────────────────────┐
  extends Naturals, TLC
  CONSTANT K
  Divides(i, j)   ≜  ∃ k ∈ 0..j : j = i * k
  IsGCD(i, j, k)  ≜      Divides(i, j)
                     ∧  Divides(i, k)
                     ∧  ∀ r ∈ 0..j ∪ 0..k :
                              Divides(r, j) ∧ Divides(r, k) ⇒ Divides(r, i)
  (* --algorithm EuclidSedgewick
     ...
     end algorithm *)
  \* BEGIN TRANSLATION
     Translator puts TLA⁺ specification here
  \* END TRANSLATION
└────────────────────────────────────────────────────────────────┘
```

Fig. 2. The module containing the PlusCal code for Euclid's algorithm

The translator inserts the algorithm's translation, which is a TLA$^+$ specification, between the BEGIN and END TRANSLATION comment lines, replacing any previous version. The translator also writes a configuration file that controls the TLC model checker. We must add to that file a command that specifies the value of K. TLC checks that the assertion is satisfied and that execution terminates for all K^2 possible choices of the variables' initial values. For $K = 50$, this takes about 25 seconds. (All execution times are for a 2.4 GHz personal computer.)

Remarks. The operation of swapping u and v can of course be expressed without a multiple assignment by declaring an additional variable t and writing:

$$t := u; \ u := v; \ v := t$$

It can also be written as follows.

   with $t = u$ **do** $u := v; \ v := t$ **end with**

The **with** statement declares t to be local to the **do** clause.

Instead of restricting m and n to lie in the range $1..K$, it would be more natural to allow them to be any positive integers. We do this by replacing $1..K$ with the set of positive integers; here are three ways to express that set in TLA$^+$, where *Nat* is defined in the *Naturals* module to be the set of all natural numbers:

$$Nat \setminus \{0\} \qquad \{i \in Nat : i > 0\} \qquad \{i + 1 : i \in Nat\}$$

To check the resulting algorithm, we would tell TLC to substitute a finite set of numbers for *Nat*.

As this example shows, PlusCal is untyped. Type correctness is an invariance property of an algorithm asserting that, throughout any execution, the values of the variables belong to certain sets. A type invariant for algorithm *EuclidSedgewick* is that the values of u and v are integers. For a type invariant like this whose proof is trivial, a typed language allows type correctness to be verified by type checking. If the proof is not completely trivial, as for the type invariant that u and v are natural numbers, type correctness cannot be verified by ordinary type checking. (If *natural number* is a type, then type checking is undecidable for a Turing complete language with subtraction.) These type invariants are easily checked by TLC.

2.2   The Quicksort Partition Operation

What most distinguishes the version of Euclid's algorithm given above from a program in an ordinary language is the expression $IsGCD(v, m, n)$. It hints at the expressive power that PlusCal obtains by using TLA$^+$ as its expression language. I now present a more compelling example of this: the *partition* operation of the quicksort algorithm [6].

Consider a version of quicksort that sorts an array $A[1], \ldots, A[N]$ of numbers. It uses the operation $Partition(lo, hi)$ that chooses a value *pivot* in $lo..(hi-1)$ and permutes the array elements $A[lo], \ldots, A[hi]$ to make $A[i] \leq A[j]$ for all i in $lo..pivot$ and j in $(pivot+1)..hi$. It is easy to describe a particular implementation of this operation with a programming language. The following PlusCal statement describes what the operation $Partition(lo, hi)$ is supposed to do, not how it is implemented. The code assumes that $Perms(A)$ is defined to be the set of permutations of A.

$$
\begin{aligned}
&\textbf{with } piv \in lo..(hi-1), \\
&\qquad B \in \{\, C \in Perms(A) : \\
&\qquad\qquad\qquad (\forall\, i \in 1..(lo-1) \cup (hi+1)..N : C[i] = A[i]) \\
&\qquad\qquad\quad \wedge (\forall\, i \in lo..piv,\ j \in (piv+1)..hi : C[i] \leq C[j])\,\} \\
&\quad \textbf{do } pivot := piv\,; \\
&\qquad\quad A := B \\
&\textbf{end with}
\end{aligned}
$$

This **with** statement is executed by nondeterministically choosing values of *piv* and B from the indicated sets and then executing the **do** clause. TLC will check the algorithm with all possible executions of this statement.

The operator *Perms* is defined in TLA$^+$ as follows, using local definitions of $Auto(S)$ to be the set of automorphisms of S, if S is a finite set, and of $\star$ to be function composition. (Arrays are what mathematicians call functions. In TLA$^+$, $[A \rightarrow B]$ is the set of functions with domain A and range a subset of B, and DOMAIN F is the domain of F if F is a function.)

$$
\begin{aligned}
&Perms(B) \;\triangleq \\
&\quad \textbf{let } Auto(S) \;\triangleq\; \{f \in [S \rightarrow S] : \forall\, y \in S : \exists\, x \in S : f[x] = y\} \\
&\qquad\quad f \star g \;\;\triangleq\; [x \in \text{DOMAIN } g \mapsto f[g[x]]] \\
&\quad \textbf{in } \{B \star f : f \in Auto(\text{DOMAIN } B)\}
\end{aligned}
$$

Using the description above of the *partition* operation and this definition of *Perms*, TLC will check partial correctness and termination of the usual recursive version of quicksort for all 4-element arrays A with values in a set of 4 numbers in about 100 seconds.

Remarks. This example is not typical. It was chosen to illustrate two things: how nondeterminism can be conveniently expressed by means of the **with** statement, and the enormous expressive power that PlusCal achieves by its use of ordinary mathematical expressions. The definition of *Perms* is the TLA$^+$ statement of one that many mathematicians would write, but few computer scientists would. Almost all computer scientists would define *Perms(B)* by recursion on the number of elements in B, the way it would be computed in most programming languages. (Such a definition can also be written in TLA$^+$.) To appreciate the power of ordinary mathematics, the reader should try to write a recursive definition of *Perms*.

A standard computer science education does not provide the familiarity with simple math needed to make the definition of *Perms* easy to understand. A textbook writer therefore might not want to include it in a description of quicksort. Because the definition is external to the PlusCal code, the writer has the option of omitting it and informally explaining the meaning of *Perms(B)*. On the other hand, a professor might want to take advantage of the opportunity it provides for teaching students some math.

2.3   The Fast Mutual Exclusion Algorithm

An example of a multiprocess algorithm is provided by the Fast Mutual Exclusion Algorithm [7]. The algorithm has N processes, numbered from 1 through N. Figure 3 on the next page is the original description of process number i, except with the noncritical section and the outer infinite loop made explicit. Angle brackets enclose atomic operations (steps). For example, the evaluation of the expression $y \neq 0$ in the first **if** statement is performed as a single step. If that expression equals *true*, then the next step of the process sets $b[i]$ to *false*. The process's next atomic operation is the execution of the **await** statement, which is performed only when y equals 0. (The step cannot be performed when y is not equal to 0.)

A PlusCal version of the algorithm appears in Figure 4 on the next page. The preceding examples use PlusCal's p-syntax; this example is written in PlusCal's alternative c-syntax. The PlusCal version differs from the original pseudo-code in the following nontrivial ways.

- It explicitly declares the global variables x, y, and b and their initial values, as well as the process-local variable j, whose initial value is not specified. (The TLA$^+$ expression $[v \in S \mapsto e]$ is the function F with domain S such that $F[v] = e$ for all v in S.)
- It declares a set of processes with identifiers in the set $1 .. N$ (one process for each identifier). Within the body of the **process** statement, *self* denotes the identifier of the process.

ncs: *noncritical section*;
start: ⟨b[i] := *true*⟩;
        ⟨x := i⟩;
        if ⟨y ≠ 0⟩ **then** ⟨b[i] := *false*⟩;
                           await ⟨y = 0⟩;
                           goto *start*   **fi**;
        ⟨y := i⟩;
        if ⟨x ≠ i⟩ **then** ⟨b[i] := *false*⟩;
                           for j := 1 **to** N **do await** ⟨¬b[j]⟩ **od**;
                           if ⟨y ≠ i⟩ **then await** ⟨y = 0⟩;
                                               goto *start*   **fi fi**;
        critical section;
        ⟨y := 0⟩;
        ⟨b[i] := *false*⟩;
        goto ncs

Fig. 3. Process i of the Fast Mutual Exclusion Algorithm, based on the original description. It assumes that initially $x = y = 0$ and $b[i] = false$ for all i in $1 .. N$.

--**algorithm** *FastMutex*
  { **variables** $x = 0$, $y = 0$, $b = [i \in 1 .. N \mapsto \text{FALSE}]$;
    process (*Proc* $\in 1 .. N$)
      variable j ;
      { ncs: **skip**; (∗ *The Noncritical Section* ∗)
      start: b[self] := TRUE ;
        l1: x := self ;
        l2: **if** (y ≠ 0) { l3: b[self] := FALSE ;
                             l4: **await** y = 0;
                                  goto *start* } ;
        l5: y := self ;
        l6: **if** (x ≠ self) { l7: b[self] := FALSE ;
                                j := 1;
                             l8: **while** (j ≤ N) { **await** ¬b[j] ;
                                                   j := j + 1   } ;
                             l9: **if** (y ≠ self) { l10: **await** y = 0;
                                                     goto *start*   }} ;
        cs: **skip**; (∗ *The Critical Section* ∗)
        l11: y := 0;
        l12: b[self] := FALSE ;
             goto ncs }}

Fig. 4. The Fast Mutual Exclusion Algorithm in PlusCal

- The critical and noncritical sections are represented by atomic **skip** instructions. (Because TLA specifications are closed under stuttering steps [8, 2], this algorithm actually describes nonatomic critical and noncritical sections that can do anything except modify the variables x, y, b, and j or jump to a different part of the process.)

- The grain of atomicity is expressed by labels. A single atomic step consists of an execution starting at a label and ending at the next label. For example, the execution of the test $y \neq 0$ at label $l2$ is atomic because a single step that begins at $l2$ ends when control reaches either $l3$ or $l4$.
- A **while** loop implements the original's **for** statement.

As this example shows, a PlusCal **await** statement can occur within a larger atomic action. A step containing the statement "**await** P" can be executed only when P evaluates to TRUE. This statement is equivalent to the dynamic logic statement "P?" [9].

For this algorithm, mutual exclusion means that no two processes are simultaneously at control point cs. The translation introduces a variable pc to represent the control state, where control in process p is at cs iff $cs[p]$ equals "cs". Mutual exclusion is therefore asserted by the invariance of:

$$\forall\, p, q \in 1 \,..\, N \; : \; (p \neq q) \Rightarrow \neg((pc[p] = \text{``cs''}) \wedge (pc[q] = \text{``cs''}))$$

TLC can check mutual exclusion and the absence of deadlock for all executions in about 15 seconds for $N = 3$ and 15 minutes for $N = 4$. It takes TLC about 5 times as long to check the absence of livelock as well, assuming weak fairness of each process's actions. (Fairness is discussed in Section 4.3.)

Remarks. Observe how similar the PlusCal version is to the pseudo-code, presented almost exactly as previously published. The 15 lines of pseudo-code are expressed in PlusCal with 17 lines of statements plus 4 lines of declarations. Those declarations include specifications of the initial values of variables, which are not present in the pseudo-code and are expressed by accompanying text. The extra two lines of PlusCal statements arise from converting a **for** to a **while**. (For simplicity, TLA$^+$ has no **for** or **until** statement.)

Readers who had never seen PlusCal would need the following explanation of the code in Figure 4.

> The **process** declaration asserts that there are N processes, numbered from 1 through N, and gives the code for process $self$. Execution from one label to the next is an atomic action, and an **await** P statement can be executed only when P is true. Variable declarations specify the initial value of variables, b being initially equal to an array with $b[i] = \text{FALSE}$ for each process i.

Compare this with the following explanation that would be needed by readers of the pseudo-code in Figure 3.

> The algorithm has N processes, numbered from 1 through N; the code of process i is given. Angle brackets enclose atomic operations, and an **await** P statement can be executed only when P is true. Variables x and y are initially equal to 0, and $b[i]$ is initially equal to *false* for each process i.

Instead of asserting mutual exclusion by a separate invariant, we can replace the critical section's **skip** statement by the following assertion that no other process is in its critical section.

assert $\forall\, p \in 1\,..\,N \setminus \{self\}\ :\ pc[p] \neq$ "cs"

Correctness of the algorithm does not depend on the order in which a process examines other processes' variables. The published version of the algorithm used a **for** loop to examine them in one particular order because there was no simple standard construct for examining them in an arbitrarily chosen order. To allow the iterations of the loop body to be performed in any order, we just replace the corresponding PlusCal code of Figure 4 with the following.

$$j\ :=\ 1\,..\,N\,;$$
$l8:$ **while** $(j \neq \{\})$ { **with** $(e \in j)$ { **await** $\neg b[e]$;
$$j\ :=\ j \setminus \{e\}\ \}\ \}\,;$$

Weak fairness of each process's actions prevents a process from remaining forever in its noncritical section—something that a mutual exclusion algorithm must allow. Absence of livelock should be checked under the assumption of weak fairness for each process's actions other than the noncritical section action. Section 4.3 explains how such a fairness assumption is asserted.

2.4   The Alternating Bit Protocol

Our final example is the alternating bit protocol, which is a distributed message-passing algorithm [10, Section 22.3]. A sender and a receiver process communicate over lossy FIFO channels, as pictured here.

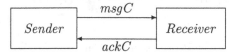

To send a message m, the sender repeatedly sends the pair $\langle m, sbit \rangle$ on channel $msgC$, where $sbit$ equals 0 or 1. The sender acknowledges receipt of the message by repeatedly sending $sbit$ on channel $ackC$. Upon receipt of the acknowledgement, the sender complements $sbit$ and begins sending the next message.

The PlusCal version of the algorithm appears in Figure 5 on the next page. To understand it, you must know how finite sequences are represented in TLA$^+$'s standard *Sequences* module. A sequence σ of length N is a function (array) whose domain (index set) is $1\,..\,N$, where $\sigma[i]$ is the ith element of the sequence. The *Head* and *Tail* operators are defined as usual, $Len(\sigma)$ is the length of sequence σ, and $Append(\sigma, e)$ is the sequence obtained by appending the element e to the tail of σ. Tuples are just finite sequences, so the pair $\langle a, b \rangle$ is a two-element sequence and $\langle a, b \rangle[2]$ equals b.

The algorithm assumes that the set *Msg* of possible messages is defined or declared and that $Remove(i, \sigma)$ is the sequence obtained by removing the ith element of σ if $1 \leq i \leq Len(\sigma)$. It can be defined in the TLA$^+$ module by

--algorithm *ABProtocol*

{ **variables** *input* = ⟨ ⟩; *output* = ⟨ ⟩; *msgC* = ⟨ ⟩; *ackC* = ⟨ ⟩;

  macro *Send*(*m*, *chan*) { *chan* := *Append*(*chan*, *m*) }

  macro *Rcv*(*v*, *chan*) { **await** *chan* ≠ ⟨ ⟩;
                            v := *Head*(*chan*);
                            chan := *Tail*(*chan*) }

  process (*Sender* = "S")
   variables *next* = 1; *sbit* = 0; *ack*;
   { *s*: **while** (TRUE) {
        either with (*m* ∈ *Msg*) { *input* := *Append*(*input*, *m*) }
        or   { **await** *next* ≤ *Len*(*input*);
                  Send(⟨*input*[*next*], *sbit*⟩, *msgC*) }
        or   { *Rcv*(*ack*, *ackC*);
                  if (*ack* = *sbit*) { *next* := *next* + 1;
                                    sbit := (*sbit* + 1) % 2 }}}}

  process (*Receiver* = "R")
   variables *rbit* = 1; *msg*;
   { *r*: **while** (TRUE) {
        either *Send*(*rbit*, *ackC*)
        or   { *Rcv*(*msg*, *msgC*);
                  if (*msg*[2] ≠ *rbit*) { *rbit* := (*rbit* + 1) % 2
                                output := *Append*(*output*, *msg*[1])}}}}

  process (*LoseMsg* = "L")
   { *l*: **while** (TRUE) {
        either with (*i* ∈ 1 .. *Len*(*msgC*)) { *msgC* := *Remove*(*i*, *msgC*)}
        or   **with** (*i* ∈ 1 .. *Len*(*ackC*)) { *ackC* := *Remove*(*i*, *ackC*) }}}
}

Fig. 5. The Alternating Bit Protocol in PlusCal

$$Remove(i, seq) \;\triangleq\; [\,j \in 1..(Len(seq) - 1) \mapsto$$
$$\textbf{if } j < i \textbf{ then } seq[j] \textbf{ else } seq[j + 1]\,]$$

The channels *msgC* and *ackC* are represented by variables whose values are finite sequences, initially equal to the empty sequence ⟨ ⟩. The variable *input* is the finite sequence of messages that the sender has decided to send and the variable *output* is the sequence of messages received by the receiver; initially both equal the empty sequence.

The operations of sending and receiving a message on a channel are represented by the macros *Send* and *Rcv*. Macros are expanded syntactically. For example, the statement *Send*(*rbit*, *ackC*) is replaced by

    ackC := *Append*(*ackC*, *rbit*)

which appends *rbit* to the sequence *ackC*. If *v* and *chan* are variables and *chan* equals a finite sequence, then the operation *Rcv*(*v*, *chan*) can be executed iff *chan* is non-empty, in which case it sets *v* to the first element of *chan* and removes that element from *chan*.

There are three processes: the sender, the receiver, and a *LoseMsg* process that models the lossiness of the channels by nondeterministically deleting messages from them. The process declaration *Sender* = "S" indicates that there is a single *Sender* process with identifier the string "S"; it is equivalent to the declaration *Sender* ∈ { "S" }. The only new PlusCal construct in the processes' code is

either S_1 **or** S_2 ... **or** S_n

which executes S_i for a nondeterministically chosen *i*.

The three processes run forever. The presence of just one label in each process means that the execution of one iteration of its **while** statement's body is a single atomic action. The sender can either choose a new message to send and append it to *input*, send the current message *input*[*next*], or receive an acknowledgement (if *ackC* is non-empty). The receiver can either receive a message and, if the message has not already been received, append it to *output*; or it can send an acknowledgement. A single step of the *LoseMsg* process removes an arbitrarily chosen message from either *msgC* or *ackC*. If *msgC* is the empty sequence, then 1 .. *Len*(*msgC*) is the empty set and only the **or** clause of the *LoseMsg* process can be executed. If both *msgC* and *ackC* equal the empty sequence, then the *LoseMsg* process is not enabled and can perform no step. (See Section 4.2 below for an explanation of why this is the meaning of the process's code.)

The important safety property satisfied by the algorithm is that the receiver never receives an incorrect message. This means that the sequence *output* of received messages is an initial subsequence of the sequence *input* of messages chosen to be sent. This condition is asserted by the predicate *output* ⊑ *input*, where ⊑ is defined by:

$$s \sqsubseteq t \;\stackrel{\Delta}{=}\; (Len(s) \le Len(t)) \wedge (\forall\, i \in 1..Len(s) \,:\, s[i] = t[i])$$

Section 4.3 discusses the desired liveness property, that every chosen message is eventually received.

Algorithm *ABProtocol* has an infinite number of reachable states. The sequence *input* can become arbitrarily long and, even if the sender puts only a single message in *input*, the sequences *msgC* and *argC* can become arbitrarily long. TLC will run forever on an algorithm with an infinite set of reachable states unless it finds an error. (TLC will eventually exceed the capacity of some data structure and halt with an error, but that could take many years because it keeps on disk the information about what states it has found.) We can bound the computation by telling TLC to stop any execution of the algorithm when it reaches a state not satisfying a specified constraint. For example, the constraint

$$(Len(input) < 4) \wedge (Len(msgC) < 5) \wedge (Len(ackC) < 5)$$

stops an execution when *input* has 4 messages or one of the channels has 5 messages. With this constraint and a set *Msg* containing 3 elements, TLC model checks the algorithm in 7.5 seconds.

Remarks. It may appear that, by introducing the *LoseMsg* process, we are forcing the channels to lose messages. This is not the case. As discussed in Section 4.3 below, an algorithm's code describes only what steps *may* be executed; it says nothing about what steps *must* be executed. Algorithm *ABProtocol*'s code does not require the *LoseMsg* process ever to delete a message, or the *Sender* process ever to send one. Section 4.3 explains how to specify what the algorithm must do.

Each process of the algorithm consists of an infinite loop whose body nondeterministically chooses one atomic action to execute. This structure is typical of high-level versions of distributed algorithms.

This example shows that PlusCal can easily describe a distributed message-passing algorithm, even though it has no special constructs for sending and receiving messages. Adding such constructs could eliminate the four lines of macros. However, what operations should they specify? Are messages broadcast or sent on point-to-point channels? Are they always delivered in order? Can they be lost? Can the same message be received twice? Different distributed algorithms make different assumptions about message passing, and I know of no simple construct that covers all possibilities. Any particular kind of message passing that is easy to explain should be easy to describe in PlusCal.

3   The Complete Language

We have seen almost all the PlusCal language constructs. The major omissions are the following (written in the p-syntax).

- TLA$^+$ has notation for records, where a record is a function whose domain is a finite set of strings and $a.b$ is syntactic sugar for $a[$"b"$]$. PlusCal allows the usual assignment to fields of a record, as in

  $v.a := 0; \ A[0].b := 42;$

  TLC will report an error if it tries to execute this code when v is not a record with an a component or A is not an array with $A[0]$ a record having a b component. This usually implies that v and A must be initialized to values of the correct "type".

- The **if** statement has optional **elsif** clauses (only in the p-syntax) followed by an optional **else** clause.

- PlusCal has procedure declarations and **call** and **return** statements. Since **call** is a statement, it does not return a value. The customary approach of making procedure calls part of expression evaluation would make specifying steps problematic, and allowing return values would complicate the translation. Procedures can easily return values by setting global variables (or process-local variables for multiprocess algorithms).

– PlusCal has an optional **define** statement for inserting TLA$^+$ definitions. It goes immediately after the declarations of the algorithm's global variables and permits operators defined in terms of those variables to be used in the algorithm's expressions.

The description of the language is completed in Section 5, which explains where labels are forbidden or required.

4   The TLA$^+$ Translation

4.1   An Example

A TLA$^+$ specification describes a set of possible behaviors, where a behavior is a sequence of states and a state is an assignment of values to variables. The heart of a TLA$^+$ specification consists of an initial predicate and a next-state action. The initial predicate specifies the possible initial states, and the next-state action specifies the possible state transitions. An action is a formula containing primed and unprimed variables, where unprimed variables refer to the old state and primed variables refer to the new state. For example, the action $x' = x + y'$ specifies all transitions in which the value of x in the new state equals the sum of its value in the old state and the value of y in the new state.

The translation from PlusCal to TLA$^+$ is illustrated with the version of Euclid's algorithm from Section 2.1. The algorithm is shown in Figure 6 on the next page with the two labels, $L1$ and $L2$, implicitly added by the translator. Also shown is the implicit label *Done* that represents the control point at the end of the algorithm.

The translation appears in Figure 7 on the next page. It uses the TLA$^+$ notation that a list of formulas bulleted with $\wedge$ or $\vee$ symbols denotes their conjunction or disjunction. Indentation is significant and is used to eliminate parentheses. (This notation makes large formulas easier to read, and engineers generally like it; but it confuses many computer scientists. The notation can be used in PlusCal expressions.)

The important parts of the translation are the definitions of the initial predicate *Init* and the next-state action *Next*. The predicate *Init* is obtained in the obvious way from the variable declaration, with the variable *pc* that represents the control state initialized to the initial control point—that is, to the string "L1".

Actions $L1$ and $L2$ specify the transitions representing execution steps starting at the corresponding control points. The conjunct $pc =$ "L1" of action $L1$ asserts that a transition can occur only in a starting state in which the value of the variable *pc* is "L1". (A conjunct containing no primed variables is an enabling condition.) The expression UNCHANGED f is an abbreviation for $f' = f$, so the conjunct UNCHANGED $\langle u, v \rangle$ asserts that the values of u and v are left unchanged by the transition. The imported *TLC* module defines $Assert(A, B)$ to equal A, but TLC halts and prints the value B and a trace of the current execution if it evaluates the expression when A equals FALSE.

```
--algorithm EuclidSedgewick
variables m ∈ 1..K, n ∈ 1..K, u = m, v = n
begin L1: while u ≠ 0 do
           if u < v then u := v || v := u end if;
    L2:  u := u − v
         end while;
         assert IsGCD(v, m, n)
    Done:
end algorithm
```

Fig. 6. Euclid's algorithm, showing labels $L1$ and $L2$ implicitly added by the translator and the implicit label $Done$

$Init \triangleq \land m \in 0..K$
$\qquad \land n \in 1..K$
$\qquad \land u = m$
$\qquad \land v = n$
$\qquad \land pc =$ "L1"

$L1 \triangleq \land pc =$ "L1"
$\qquad \land$ **if** $u \neq 0$ **then** $\land$ **if** $u < v$ **then** $\land u' = v$
$\qquad\qquad\qquad\qquad\qquad\qquad\qquad\qquad\qquad \land v' = u$
$\qquad\qquad\qquad\qquad\qquad\qquad$ **else** UNCHANGED $\langle u, v \rangle$
$\qquad\qquad\qquad\qquad \land pc' =$ "L2"
$\qquad\qquad\qquad$ **else** $\land Assert(IsGCD(v, m, n),$ "Failure of assertion at…")
$\qquad\qquad\qquad\qquad \land pc' =$ "Done"
$\qquad\qquad\qquad\qquad \land$ UNCHANGED $\langle u, v \rangle$
$\qquad \land$ UNCHANGED $\langle m, n \rangle$

$L2 \triangleq \land pc =$ "L2"
$\qquad \land u' = u - v$
$\qquad \land pc' =$ "L1"
$\qquad \land$ UNCHANGED $\langle m, n, v \rangle$

$vars \triangleq \langle m, n, u, v, pc \rangle$

$Next \triangleq L1 \lor L2 \lor (pc =$ "Done" $\land$ UNCHANGED $vars)$

$Spec \triangleq Init \land \Box[Next]_{vars}$

Fig. 7. The translation of Euclid's algorithm

The next-state action $Next$ allows all transitions that are allowed by $L1$ or $L2$, or that leave the tuple $vars$ of all the algorithm variables unchanged (are stuttering steps [8, 2]) when a terminated state has been reached. This last disjunct keeps TLC from reporting deadlock when the algorithm terminates. (An algorithm deadlocks when no further step is possible; termination is just deadlock we want to occur.) Since every TLA specification allows stuttering steps, this disjunct does not change the meaning of the specification, just the way TLC checks it.

Finally, *Spec* is defined to be the TLA formula that describes the safety part of the algorithm's complete specification. Proving that the algorithm satisfies a safety property expressed by a temporal formula P means proving $Spec \Rightarrow P$. Most PlusCal users can ignore *Spec*.

4.2   Translation as Semantics

A classic way of stating that a programming language is poorly defined is to say that its semantics is specified by the compiler. A goal of PlusCal was to make an algorithm's translation so easy to understand that it is a useful specification of the algorithm's meaning. To achieve this goal, the following principles were maintained:

T1. The only TLA$^+$ variables used in the translation are the ones declared in the algorithm plus *pc*. (Algorithms with procedures also use a variable *stack* for saving return locations and values of local procedure variables.)

T2. All identifiers declared or defined in the translation (including bound variables) are taken from the algorithm text, except for a few standard ones like *Init* and *Next*. ("Algorithm text" includes labels implicitly added by the translator.)

T3. There is a one-to-one correspondence between expressions in the translation and expressions in the algorithm. (The only exceptions are the expressions for pushing and popping items on the stack in the translation of procedure **call** and **return** statements.)

It may seem that PlusCal is so simple that its semantics is obvious. However, a naive user might be puzzled by what the following statement in a multiprocess algorithm does when x equals 0:

> *L1*: $x := x - 1$; **await** $x \geq 0$; $y := x$;
> *L2*: ...

Is x decremented but y left unchanged? Is the execution aborted and the original value of x restored? The statement's translation is:

$$L1 \; \triangleq \; \land \; pc = \text{``L1''}$$
$$\land \; x' = x - 1$$
$$\land \; x' \geq 0$$
$$\land \; y' = x'$$
$$\land \; \text{UNCHANGED} \; \ldots$$

Action $L1$ equals FALSE when $x = 0$, which is satisfied by no step, so the statement cannot be executed while x is less than 1. Statement $L1$ is equivalent to

> **await** $x > 0$; $x := x - 1$; $y := x$;

because the two statements' translations are mathematically equivalent. Realizing this might help users think in terms of what a computation does rather than how it does it.

Even a fairly sophisticated user may have trouble understanding this statement:

> $L1$: **with** $i \in \{1, 2\}$ **do await** $i = 2$
>   **end with**;
> $L2$: ...

Is it possible for an execution to deadlock because the **with** statement selects $i = 1$ and the **await** statement then waits forever for i to equal 2? The answer is probably not obvious to readers unfamiliar with dynamic logic. The translation of statement $L1$ is:

$$L1 \triangleq \land pc = \text{``L1''}$$
$$\land \exists i \in \{1, 2\} : i = 2$$
$$\land pc' = \text{``L2''}$$
$$\land \text{UNCHANGED} \langle \ldots \rangle$$

It should be clear to anyone who understands simple predicate logic that the second conjunct equals TRUE, so statement $L1$ is equivalent to **skip**.

These two examples are contrived. The first will not occur in practice because no one will put an **await** statement after an assignment within a single step, but the second abstracts a situation that occurs in real examples. Consider the *LoseMsg* process in the alternating bit protocol of Figure 5. It may not be clear what the **either/or** statement means if one or both channels are empty. Examining the TLA$^+$ translation reveals that the disjunct of the next-state action that describes steps of this process is:

$$\land pc[\text{``L''}] = \text{``l''}$$
$$\land \lor \land \exists i \in 1\,..\,Len(msgC) : msgC' = Remove(i, msgC)$$
$$\land \text{UNCHANGED } ackC$$
$$\lor \land \exists i \in 1\,..\,Len(ackC) : ackC' = Remove(i, ackC)$$
$$\land \text{UNCHANGED } msgC$$
$$\land pc' = [pc \text{ EXCEPT } ![\text{``L''}] = \text{``l''}]$$
$$\land \text{UNCHANGED } \langle input, output, next, sbit, ack, rbit, msg \rangle$$

(The reader should be able to deduce the meaning of the EXCEPT construct and, being smarter than the translator, should realize that the action's first conjunct implies that its third conjunct is a complicated way of asserting $pc' = pc$.) If $msgC$ is the empty sequence, then $Len(msgC) = 0$, so $1\,..\,Len(msgC)$ equals the empty set. Since $\exists i \in \{\} : \ldots$ equals FALSE, this action's second conjunct is equal to the conjunct's second disjunct. Hence, when $msgC$ equals the empty sequence, a step of the *LoseMsg* process can only be one that removes a message from $ackC$. If $ackC$ also equals the empty sequence, then the entire action equals FALSE, so in this case the process can do nothing.

It is not uncommon to specify the semantics of a programming language by a translation to another language. However, the TLA$^+$ translation can explain to ordinary users the meanings of their programs. The translation is written in the same module as the algorithm. The use of labels to name actions makes it easy to see the correspondence between the algorithm's code and disjuncts of the next-state action. (The translator can be directed to report the names and locations in the code of all labels that it adds.)

The semantics of PlusCal is defined formally by a TLA$^+$ specification of the translator as a mapping from an algorithm's abstract syntax tree to the sequence of tokens that form its TLA$^+$ specification [4]. The part of the specification that actually describes the translation is about 700 lines long (excluding comments). This specification is itself executable by TLC. The translator has a mode in which it parses the algorithm, writes a module containing the TLA$^+$ representation of the abstract syntax tree, calls TLC to execute the translation's specification for that syntax tree, and uses TLC's output to produce the algorithm's TLA$^+$ translation. (The abstract syntax tree does not preserve the formatting of expressions, so this translation may be incorrect for algorithms with expressions that use the TLA$^+$ bulleted conjunction/disjunction list notation.)

4.3   Liveness

An algorithm's code specifies the steps that may be taken; it does not require any steps to be taken. In other words, the code specifies the safety properties of the algorithm. To deduce liveness properties, which assert that something does eventually happen, we have to add liveness assumptions to assert when steps must be taken. These assumptions are usually specified as fairness assumptions about actions [11]. The two common types of fairness assumption are weak and strong fairness of an action. Weak fairness of action A asserts that an A step must occur if A remains continuously enabled. Strong fairness asserts that an A step must occur if A keeps being enabled, even if it is also repeatedly disabled.

For almost all sequential (uniprocess) algorithms, the only liveness requirement is termination. It must be satisfied under the assumption that the algorithm keeps taking steps as long as it can, which means under the assumption of weak fairness of the entire next-state action. (Since there is no other process to disable an action, weak fairness is equivalent to strong fairness for sequential algorithms.) The PlusCal translator can be directed to create the appropriate TLA$^+$ translation and TLC configuration file to check for termination.

For multiprocess algorithms, there is an endless variety of liveness requirements. Any requirement other than termination must be defined by the user in the TLA$^+$ module as a temporal-logic formula, and the TLC configuration file must be modified to direct TLC to check that it is satisfied. The three most common fairness assumptions are weak and strong fairness of each process's next-state action and weak fairness of the entire next-state action—the latter meaning that the algorithm does not halt if any process can take a step, but individual processes may be starved. The PlusCal translator can be directed to add one of these three fairness assumptions to the algorithm's TLA$^+$ translation. However, there is a wide variety of other fairness assumptions made by algorithms. These must be written by the user as temporal-logic formulas.

As an example, let us return to algorithm *ABProtocol* of Section 2.4. A liveness property we might want to require is that every message that is chosen is eventually delivered. Since the safety property implies that incorrect messages are not delivered, it suffices to check that enough message are delivered. This is expressed by the following temporal logic formula, which asserts that for any i, if *input* ever contains i elements then *output* will eventually contain i elements:

$$\forall\, i \in Nat\; : \; (Len(input) = i) \rightsquigarrow (Len(output) = i)$$

The algorithm satisfies this property under the assumption of strong fairness of the following operations:

- The sender's first **or** clause, which can send a message
- The sender's second **or** clause, which can receive an acknowledgement.
- The receiver's **either** clause, which can send an acknowledgement.
- The receiver's **or** clause, which can receive a message.

The translation defines the formula *Sender* to be the sender's next-state action. It is the disjunction of three formulas that describe the three clauses of the **either/or** statement. The first **or** clause is the only one that can modify $msgC$, so the action describing that clause is $Sender \wedge (msgC' \neq msgC)$. Similarly, the sender's last **or** clause is described by the action $Sender \wedge (ackC' \neq ackC)$. The relevant receiver actions are defined similarly. The complete TLA$^+$ specification of the algorithm, with these four strong fairness conditions, is the following formula:

$$
\begin{aligned}
&\wedge\; Spec\\
&\wedge\; \mathrm{SF}_{vars}(Sender \wedge (ackC' \neq ackC))\\
&\wedge\; \mathrm{SF}_{vars}(Sender \wedge (msgC' \neq msgC))\\
&\wedge\; \mathrm{SF}_{vars}(Receiver \wedge (ackC' \neq ackC))\\
&\wedge\; \mathrm{SF}_{vars}(Receiver \wedge (msgC' \neq msgC))
\end{aligned}
$$

This specification makes no fairness assumption on the sender's operation of choosing a message to send or on the *LoseMsg* process's operation of deleting a message. Those operations need never be executed.

To check the liveness property $\forall\, i \in Nat \ldots$, we must tell TLC to substitute a finite set for *Nat*. With the constraint described in Section 2.4, it suffices to substitute $0 \mathinner{.\,.} 4$ for *Nat*. It then takes TLC about 3.5 minutes to check that the algorithm satisfies the liveness property, about 30 times as long as the 7.5 seconds taken to check safety. This ratio of 30 is unusually large for such a small example; it arises because the liveness property being checked is essentially the conjunction of five formulas that are checked separately—one for each value of i. For a single value of i, the ratio of liveness to safety checking is about the same factor of 5 as for the Fast Mutual Exclusion Algorithm.

Fairness is subtle. Many readers may not understand why these four fairness assumptions are sufficient to ensure that all messages are received, or why strong fairness of the complete next-state actions of the sender and receiver are not. The ability to mechanically check liveness properties is quite useful. Unfortunately, checking liveness is inherently slower than checking safety and cannot be done on as large an instance of an algorithm. Fortunately, liveness errors tend to be less subtle than safety errors and can usually be caught on rather small instances.

5   Labeling Constraints

PlusCal puts a number of restrictions on where labels can and must appear. They are added to keep the TLA$^+$ translation simple—in particular, to achieve the principles T1–T3 described in Section 4.2. Here are the restrictions. (They can be stated more succinctly, but I have split apart some rules when different cases have different rationales.)

A **while** *statement must be labeled.*

Programming languages need loops to describe simple computations; PlusCal does not. For example, it is easy to write a single PlusCal assignment statement that sets $x[i]$ to the ith prime, for all i in the domain of x. In PlusCal, a loop is a sequence of repeated steps. Eliminating this restriction would require an impossibly complicated translation.

In any control path, there must be a label between two assignments to the same variable. However, a single multi-assignment statement may assign values to multiple components of the same (array- or record-valued) variable.

This is at worst a minor nuisance. Multiple assignments to a variable within a step can be eliminated by using a **with** statement—for example, replacing

$$x := f(x); \ \dots \ ; \ x := g(x, y)$$

by

with $temp = f(x)$ **do** $\dots$; $x := g(temp, y)$ **end with**

A translation could perform such a rewriting, but that would require violating T2.

A statement must be labeled if it is immediately preceded by an **if** *or* **either** *statement that contains a* **goto**, **call**, **return**, *or labeled statement within it.*

Without this restriction, the translation would have to either duplicate expressions, violating T3, or else avoid such duplication by giving expressions names, violating T2.

The first statement of a process or of a uniprocess algorithm must be labeled.

This is a natural requirement, since a step is an execution from one label to the next.

The **do** *clause of a* **with** *statement cannot contain any labeled statements.*

Allowing labels within a **with** statement would require the **with** variables to become TLA$^+$ variables, violating T1.

A statement other than a **return** *must be labeled if it is immediately preceded by a* **call** *; and a procedure's first statement must be labeled.*

This means that executing a procedure body requires at least one complete step. There is no need for intra-step procedure executions in PlusCal; anything they could compute can be described by operators defined in the TLA$^+$ module.

A statement that follows a **goto** *or* **return** *must be labeled.*

This just rules out unreachable statements.

A macro body cannot contain any labeled statements.

A macro can be used multiple times within a single process, where it makes no sense for the same label to appear more than once. Related to this constraint is the restriction that a macro body cannot contain a **while, call, return**, or **goto** statement.

6   Conclusion

PlusCal is a language for writing algorithms. It is designed not to replace programming languages, but to replace pseudo-code. Why replace pseudo-code? No formal language can be as powerful or easy to write. Nothing can beat the convenience of inventing new constructs as needed and letting the reader try to deduce their meaning from informal explanations.

The major problem with pseudo-code is that it cannot be tested, and untested code is usually incorrect. In August of 2004, I did a Google search for *quick sort* and tested the first ten actual algorithms on the pages it found. Of those ten, four were written in pseudo-code; they were all incorrect. The only correct versions were written in executable code; they were undoubtedly correct only because they had been debugged.

Algorithms written in PlusCal can be tested with TLC—either by complete model checking or by repeated execution, making nondeterministic choices randomly. It takes effort to write an incorrect sorting algorithm that correctly sorts all arrays of length at most 4 with elements in $1..4$. An example of an incorrect published concurrent algorithm and how its error could have been found by using PlusCal appears elsewhere [12].

Another advantage of an algorithm written in PlusCal is that it has a precise meaning that is specified by its TLA$^+$ translation. The translation can be a practical aid to understanding the meaning of the code. Since the translation is a formula of TLA, a logic with well-defined semantics and proof rules [13], it can be used to reason about the algorithm with any desired degree of rigor.

We can use anything when writing pseudo-code, including PlusCal. Pseudo-code is therefore, in principle, more expressive than PlusCal. In practice, it isn't. All pseudo-code I have encountered is easily translated to PlusCal. The Fast Mutual Exclusion Algorithm of Section 2.3 is typical. The PlusCal code looks very much like the pseudo-code and is just a little longer, mostly because of variable declarations. Those declarations specify the initial values of variables, which are usually missing from the pseudo-code and are explained in accompanying text. What is not typical about the Fast Mutual Exclusion example is that the pseudo-code describes the grain of atomicity. When multiprocess algorithms are described with pseudo-code, what constitutes an atomic action is usually either described in the text or else not mentioned, leaving the algorithm essentially unspecified. PlusCal forces the user to make explicit the grain of atomicity. She must explicitly tell the translator if she wants it to insert labels, which yields the largest atomic actions that PlusCal permits.

As dramatically illustrated by the quicksort *partition* example, PlusCal makes it easy to write algorithms not usually expressed in pseudo-code. The alternating bit protocol is another algorithm that is not easily written in ordinary pseudo-code. Of the first ten descriptions of the protocol found in January of 2008 by a Google search for *alternating bit protocol*, five were only in English, four were in different formal languages, and one described the processes in a pictorial finite-state machine language and the channels in English. None used pseudo-code. Of these five formal languages, all but finite-state machines were inscrutable to the casual reader. (Finite-state machines are simple, but too inexpressive to be used as an algorithm language.)

PlusCal is a language with simple program structures and arbitrary mathematical expressions. The existing programming language that most closely resembles it is SETL [14]. The SETL language provides many of the set-theoretic primitives of TLA$^+$, but it lacks the ability to define new operators mathematically; they must be described by procedures for computing them. Moreover, SETL cannot conveniently express concurrency or nondeterminism.

There are quite a few specification languages that can be used to describe and mechanically check algorithms. Many of them, including Alloy [15] and TLA$^+$ itself, lack simple programming-language constructs like semicolon and **while** that are invaluable for expressing algorithms clearly and simply. Some are more complicated than PlusCal because they are designed for system specifications that are larger and more complicated than algorithms. Others, such as Spin [16] and SMV [17], are primarily input languages for model checkers and are little better than programming languages at describing mathematical operators. Furthermore, many of these specification methods cannot express fairness, which is an important aspect of concurrent algorithms. I know of no specification language that combines the expressiveness and simplicity of PlusCal.

The one formal language I know of that has the replacement of pseudo-code as a stated goal is AsmL, the abstract state machine language of Gurevich et al. [18]. It is a reasonable language for writing sequential algorithms, though its use of types and objects make it more complicated and somewhat less expressive than PlusCal. However, while AsmL has ordinary control statements like **while**, they can appear only within an atomic step. This makes AsmL unsuitable for replacing pseudo-code for multiprocess algorithms. Also, it cannot be used to express fairness.

There are a number of toy programming languages that might be used for writing algorithms. All the ones I know of that can be compiled and executed allow only the simple expressions typical of programming languages. We could look to paper languages for better constructs than PlusCal's. Perhaps the most popular proposals for novel language constructs are Dijkstra's guarded commands [19], Hoare's CSP [20], and functional languages. Guarded command constructs are easily expressed with **either/or** and **with** statements, which provide more flexibility in specifying the grain of atomicity; the lack of shared variables and dependence on a particular interprocess communication mechanism make it difficult to write algorithms like Fast Mutual Exclusion and the Alternating Bit Protocol in CSP; and I have never seen a published concurrent or distributed synchronization algorithm described functionally. As the basis for an easy-to-understand algorithm language, it is hard to justify alternatives to the familiar constructs like assignment, **if/then**, and **while** that have been used for decades and appear in the most popular programming languages.

If simplicity is the goal, why add the **await**, **with**, and **either/or** constructs that were shown in Section 4.2 to be subtle? These constructs are needed to express interprocess synchronization and nondeterminism, and there are no standard ones that can be used instead. The subtlety of these constructs comes from the inherent subtlety of the concepts they express.

Finally, one might want to use a different expression language than TLA$^+$. To achieve expressiveness and familiarity, the language should be based on ordinary mathematics—the kind taught in introductory math classes. A number of languages have been designed for expressing mathematics formally. I obviously prefer TLA$^+$, but others may have different preferences. A replacement for TLA$^+$ should be suitable not just as an expression language, but as a target language for a translator and as a language for expressing liveness properties, including fairness. It should also permit model checking of algorithms.

Upon being shown PlusCal, people often ask if it can be used as a programming language. One can undoubtedly define subsets of the expression language that permit compilation into reasonably efficient code. However, it is not clear if there is any good reason to do so. The features that make programming languages ill-suited to writing algorithms are there for a reason. For example, strong typing is important in a programming language; but one reason PlusCal is good for writing algorithms is the simplicity that comes from its being untyped.

PlusCal is meant to replace pseudo-code. It combines the best features of pseudo-code with the ability to catch errors by model checking. It is suitable for use in books, in articles, and in the classroom. It can also be used by programmers to debug their algorithms before implementing them.

References

1. Wirth, N.: Algorithms + Data Structures = Programs. Prentice-Hall, Englewood Cliffs (1975)
2. Lamport, L.: Specifying Systems. Addison-Wesley, Boston (2003), http://lamport.org

3. Yu, Y., Manolios, P., Lamport, L.: Model checking TLA$^+$ specifications. In: Pierre, L., Kropf, T. (eds.) CHARME 1999. LNCS, vol. 1703, pp. 54–66. Springer, Heidelberg (1999)
4. Lamport, L.: The PlusCal algorithm language,
   `http://research.microsoft.com/users/lamport/tla/pluscal.html`
   The page can also be found by searching the Web for the 25-letter string obtained by removing the "-" from uid-lamportpluscalhomepage
5. Sedgewick, R.: Algorithms. Addison-Wesley, Reading (1988)
6. Hoare, C.A.R.: Algorithm 64: Quicksort. Communications of the ACM 4, 321 (1961)
7. Lamport, L.: A fast mutual exclusion algorithm. ACM Transactions on Computer Systems 5, 1–11 (1987)
8. Lamport, L.: What good is temporal logic? In: Mason, R.E.A. (ed.) Information Processing 83: Proceedings of the IFIP 9th World Congress, Paris, IFIP, pp. 657–668. North-Holland, Amsterdam (1983)
9. Pratt, V.R.: Semantical considerations on Floyd-Hoare logic. In: 17th Symposium on Foundations of Computer Science, pp. 109–121. IEEE, Los Alamitos (1976)
10. Lynch, N.A.: Distributed Algorithms. Morgan Kaufmann, San Mateo (1995)
11. Francez, N.: Fairness. Texts and Monographs in Computer Science. Springer, Heidelberg (1986)
12. Lamport, L.: Checking a multithreaded algorithm with $^+$CAL. In: Dolev, S. (ed.) DISC 2006. LNCS, vol. 4167, pp. 151–163. Springer, Heidelberg (2006)
13. Lamport, L.: The temporal logic of actions. ACM Transactions on Programming Languages and Systems 16, 872–923 (1994)
14. Schwartz, J.T., Dewar, R.B., Schonberg, E., Dubinsky, E.: Programming with sets: An Introduction to SETL. Springer, New York (1986)
15. Jackson, D.: Alloy: a lightweight object modelling notation. ACM Transactions on Software Engineering and Methodology 11, 256–290 (2002)
16. Holzmann, G.J.: The Spin Model Checker. Addison-Wesley, Boston (2004)
17. McMillan, K.L.: Symbolic Model Checking. Kluwer Academic Publishers, Dordrecht (1993)
18. Gurevich, Y.: Can abstract state machines be useful in language theory? Theoretical Computer Science 376, 17–29 (2007)
19. Dijkstra, E.W.: A Discipline of Programming. Prentice-Hall, Englewood Cliffs (1976)
20. Hoare, C.A.R.: Communicating sequential processes. Communications of the ACM 21, 666–677 (1978)

Appendix: The C-Syntax Grammar

Here is a simplified BNF grammar for PlusCal's c-syntax. Terminals like **begin** are distinguished by font and are sometimes quoted like "(" to avoid ambiguity. The grammar omits restrictions on where labels may or must not occur, on what statements may occur in the body of a macro, and on the use of reserved tokens like **if** and **:=** in identifiers and expressions.

Algorithm ::= **--algorithm** *Id*
                { [*VarDecls*] [*Definitions*] *Macro**
                  Procedure* (*CompoundStmt* | *Process*$^+$) }

Definitions ::= **define** { *Defs* } [;]

Macro ::= macro *Id* "(" [*Id* (, *Id*)*] ")" *CompoundStmt* [;]

Procedure ::= procedure *Id* "(" [*PVarDecl* (, *PVarDecl*)*] ")"
          [*PVarDecls*] *CompoundStmt* [;]

Process ::= process "(" *Id* (= | \in) *Expr* ")"
          [*VarDecls*] *CompoundStmt* [;]

PVarDecls ::= variable[s] (*Id* [= *Expr*] (;|,))⁺

VarDecls ::= variable[s] (*Id* [(= | \in) *Expr*] (;|,))⁺

CompoundStmt ::= { *Stmt* [; *Stmt*]* [;] }

Stmt ::= [*Id* :] (*UnlabeledStmt* | *CompoundStmt*)

UnlabeledStmt ::= *Assign* | *If* | *While* | *Either* | *With* | | *Await* | *Print* |
          Assert | skip | return | *Goto* | [call] *Call*

Assign ::= *LHS* := *Expr* ("||" *LHS* := *Expr*)*

LHS ::= *Id* ("[" *Expr* (, *Expr*)* "]" | "." *Id*)*

If ::= if "(" *Expr* ")" *Stmt* [else *Stmt*]

While ::= while "(" *Expr* ")" *Stmt*

Either ::= either *Stmt* (or *Stmt*)⁺

With ::= with "(" *Id* (= | \in) *Expr*
              ((; |,) *Id* (= | \in) *Expr*)* [; |,] ")" *Stmt*

Await ::= (await | when) *Expr*

Print ::= print *Expr*

Assert ::= assert *Expr*

Goto ::= goto *Id*

Call ::= *Id* "(" [*Expr* (, *Expr*)*] ")"

Id ::= A TLA⁺ identifier (string of letters, digits, and "_"s not all digits).

expr ::= A TLA⁺ expression.

Defs ::= A sequence of TLA⁺ definitions.

The Secret Art of Computer Programming

Annabelle K. McIver*

Dept. Computer Science, Macquarie University, NSW 2109 Australia

Abstract. "Classical" program development by refinement [12,2,3] is a technique for ensuring that source-level program code remains faithful to the semantic goals set out in its corresponding specification. Until recently the method has not extended to security-style properties, principally because classical refinement semantics is inadequate in security contexts [7].

The Shadow semantics introduced by Morgan [13] is an abstraction of probabilistic program semantics [11], and is rich enough to distinguish between refinements that do preserve noninterference security properties and those that don't. In this paper we give a formal development of Private Information Retrieval [4]; in doing so we extend the general theory of secure refinement by introducing a new kind of security annotation for programs.

Keywords: Proofs of security, program semantics, compositional security, refinement of ignorance.

1 Introduction

Abstraction and refinement are together one of the core techniques in any formal verifier's toolkit. Yet to date they are rarely applied in security analysis; indeed until recently refinement and security were considered uneasy bedfellows, with any attempt to reconcile the two bound for paradox and confusion [7].

Morgan's *Shadow semantics* [13] for "noninterference security" based originally on an abstraction of probabilistic program semantics [11] succeeded after all in bringing about a détente between nondeterminism (the mathematical encapsulation of abstraction) and hidden state (the mathematical encapsulation of secrets). *Noninterference* security [6] formalises our intuitive notion of "security leaks" — in programming terms it characterises scenarios where data intended to be kept private are exposed by inadvertent correlations with other observable program behaviour. By a careful treatment of nondeterminism and hidden state, the Shadow semantics automatically selects refinements which are "security-aware": a valid "secure refinement" is now not only functionally- but also security-wise compatible with its specification. In some cases this might mean absolute confidentiality; but there are many applications where the required functionality logically forces a disclosure, at least in part. Shadow security proofs guarantee therefore that any implementation leaks *no more* than the specification demands.

* We acknowledge the support of the Australian Research Council Grant DP0879529.

M. Leucker and C. Morgan (Eds.): ICTAC 2009, LNCS 5684, pp. 61–78, 2009.

The Shadow approach is distinguished from other methods for security analysis in its emphasis on compositionality and the development-by-hierarchy that compositionality supports. Specifications are now programs too –though most likely inefficient and tacit as to algorithmic detail– yet as we have learned from many years' experience with the refinement calculus, a focus on what we want pays off "in spades" for understanding systems. Adding detail devolves to the validation of refinement steps, each one small enough for the proofs to be – almost– automatic, and furthermore achieved at the source level. And, as for classical refinement, we often call on specifications of sub-protocols wherever this simplifies the reasoning, leading to the method's ability to accommodate protocols of unbounded state [10].

Our contribution. in this paper is a formal development of a scheme for Private Information Retrieval in public databases [4]. In doing so we extend the theory by the introduction of "visibility annotations" for reasoning about the extent to which a secret is revealed during program execution.

We begin with a summary and commentary on the basics for non-interference security using the Shadow semantics. Throughout we use left-associating dot for function application, so that $f.x.y$ means $(f(x))(y)$ or $f(x, y)$, and we take (un-)Currying for granted where necessary. Comprehensions/quantifications are written uniformly, as $(Qx: T | R \cdot E)$ for quantifier Q, bound variable(s) x of type(s) T, range-predicate R (probably) constraining x and element-constructor E in which x (probably) appears free: for sets the opening "(Q" is "{" and the closing ")" is "}" so that e.g. the comprehension $\{x, y: \mathbb{N} \mid y = 2^x \cdot yz\}$ is the set of numbers $z, 2z, 4z, \cdots$.

2   Semantics for Programming with Secrets

A non-interference -secure program is one where an attacker (discussed below) cannot infer "hidden" variables' initial values from "visible" variables' values (initial or final). With just two variables v, h of class visible, hidden resp. suppose a possibly nondeterministic program r takes initial states (v, h) to sets of final visible states v' and so is of type $\mathcal{V} \to \mathcal{H} \to \mathbb{P}\mathcal{V}$, where $\mathcal{V}, \mathcal{H}$ are the value sets corresponding to the types of v, h. Such a program r is then *non-interference -secure* just when for any initial visible the set of possible final visibles is independent of the initial hidden [8,15], that is for any $v: \mathcal{V}$ we have $(\forall h_0, h_1: \mathcal{H} \cdot r.v.h_0 = r.v.h_1)$.

In our approach [13] we extend this view, in several stages. The first is to concentrate on final- (rather than initial) hidden values and therefore to model programs as $\mathcal{V} \to \mathcal{H} \to \mathbb{P}(\mathcal{V} \times \mathcal{H})$. For two such programs $r_{\{1,2\}}$ we say that $r_1 \sqsubseteq r_2$, that r_1 "is securely refined by" r_2, whenever both the following hold:

(i) For any initial state v, h each possible r_2 outcome v', h' is also a possible r_1 outcome, that is for all $v: \mathcal{V}$ and $h: \mathcal{H}$ we have $r_1.v.h \supseteq r_2.v.h$.

This is the classical "can reduce nondeterminism" form of refinement.

(ii) For all $v\colon \mathcal{V}, h\colon \mathcal{H}$ and $v'\colon \mathcal{V}$ satisfying $\left(\exists h_2'\colon \mathcal{H} \cdot (v', h_2') \in r_2.v.h\right)$, we have that $(v', h') \in r_1.v.h$ implies $(v', h') \in r_2.v.h$ for all $h'\colon \mathcal{H}$.

This second condition says that for any observed visibles v, v' and any initial h the attacker's "deductive powers" w.r.t. final h''s cannot be improved by refinement: there can only be more possibilities, never fewer.

In this simple setting, as an example restrict all our variables' types so that $\mathcal{V}=\mathcal{H}=\{0,1\}$, and let r_1 be the program that can produce from any initial values (v, h) any one of the four possible (v', h') final values in $\mathcal{V} \times \mathcal{H}$ (so that the final values of v and h are uncorrelated). Then the program r_2 that can produce only the two final values $\{(0,0), (0,1)\}$ is a secure refinement of r_1; but the program r_3 that produces only the two final values $\{(0,0), (1,1)\}$ is not a secure refinement (although it is a classical one).

The difference between r_2 and r_3 is that although r_2 reduces r_1's visible nondeterminism, it does not affect the hidden nondeterminism in h'. In r_3, however, variables v' and h' have become correlated.

2.1 The Shadow H of h Records h's Inferred Values

In r_1 above the set of possible final values of h' was $\{0,1\}$ for each v' separately. This set is called "The Shadow," and represents explicitly an attacker's ignorance of h': it is the smallest set of possibilities he can infer. In r_2 that shadow was the same; but in r_3 the shadow was smaller, just $\{v'\}$ for each v', and that is why r_3 was not a secure refinement of r_1.

In the shadow semantics we track this inference, so that our program state becomes a triple (v, h, H) with H a subset of $\mathcal{H}$ — and in each triple the H contains exactly those (other) values that h *might have had*, including the one it actually *does* have. The (extended) output triples of the three example programs are then respectively

$$r_1 \text{ — } \{(0,0,\{0,1\}),\ (0,1,\{0,1\}),\ (1,0,\{0,1\}),\ (1,1,\{0,1\})\}$$
$$r_2 \text{ — } \{(0,0,\{0,1\}),\ (0,1,\{0,1\})\}$$
$$r_3 \text{ — } \{(0,0,\{0\}),\ (1,1,\{1\})\},$$

and we have $r_1 \sqsubseteq r_2$ because r_1's set of outcomes includes all of r_2's. But for r_3 we find that its outcome $(0,0,\{0\})$ does not occur among r_1's outcomes, nor is there even an r_1-outcome $(0,0,H')$ with $H' \subseteq \{0\}$ that would satisfy (ii). That, again, is why $r_1 \not\sqsubseteq r_3$.

For sequential composition of shadow-enhanced programs, not only final- but also initial triples (v, h, H) must be dealt with: the final triples of a first component become initial triples for a second. We now define the shadow semantics exactly, in stages, by showing how those triples are generated for straight-line programs.

2.2 The Shadow Semantics of Atomic Programs

A classical program r is an input-output relation between $\mathcal{V} \times \mathcal{H}$ -pairs. Considered as a single, atomic action its shadow-enhanced semantics addShadow.r is a relation between $\mathcal{V} \times \mathcal{H} \times \mathbb{P}\mathcal{H}$ -triples and is defined as follows:

	Program P	Semantics $[\![P]\!].v.h.H$	
Publish a value	**reveal** $E.v.h$	$\{\,(v, h, \{h'\!:H \mid E.v.h' = E.v.h\})\,\}$	
Assign to visible	$v := E.v.h$	$\{\,(E.v.h, h, \{h'\!:H \mid E.v.h' = E.v.h\})\,\}$	$\star$
Assign to hidden	$h := E.v.h$	$\{\,(v, E.v.h, \{h'\!:H \cdot E.v.h'\})\,\}$	$\star$
Choose visible	$v :\in S.v.h$	$\{v'\!:S.v.h \cdot (v', h, \{h'\!:H \mid v' \in S.v.h'\})\,\}$	$\star$
Choose hidden	$h :\in S.v.h$	$\{h'\!:S.v.h \cdot (v, h', \{h'\!:H; h''\!:S.v.h' \cdot h''\})\,\}$	$\star$
Execute atomically	$\langle\!\langle P \rangle\!\rangle$	addShadow.("classical semantics of P")	
Sequential composition	$P_1; P_2$	$\mathsf{lift}.[\![P_2]\!].([\![P_1]\!].v.h.H)$	
Demonic choice	$P_1 \sqcap P_2$	$[\![P_1]\!].v.h.H \cup [\![P_2]\!].v.h.H$	

$$\text{Conditional} \quad \textbf{if } E.v.h \textbf{ then } P_t \textbf{ else } P_f \textbf{ fi} \qquad [\![P_t]\!].v.h.\{h'\!:H \mid E.v.h' = \textbf{true}\}$$
$$\lhd\, E.v.h\, \rhd$$
$$[\![P_f]\!].v.h.\{h'\!:H \mid E.v.h' = \textbf{false}\}$$

The syntactically atomic commands A marked $\star$ have the property that $A = \langle\!\langle A \rangle\!\rangle$. This is deliberate: syntactic atoms execute atomically. The function $\mathsf{lift}.[\![P_2]\!]$ applies $[\![P_2]\!]$ to all triples in its set-valued argument, un-Currying each time, and then takes the union of all results.

The extension to many variables $v_1, v_2, \cdots$ and $h_1, h_2, \cdots$, including local declarations, is straightforward [13, 14].

Fig. 1. Semantics of non-looping commands

Definition 1. *Atomic shadow semantics.* Given a classical program $r: \mathcal{V} \to \mathcal{H} \to \mathbb{P}(\mathcal{V} \times \mathcal{H})$ we define its *shadow enhancement* addShadow.r of type $\mathcal{V} \to \mathcal{H} \to \mathbb{P}\mathcal{H} \to \mathbb{P}(\mathcal{V} \times \mathcal{H} \times \mathbb{P}\mathcal{H})$ so that addShadow.$r.v.h.H \ni (v', h', H')$ just when

(i) we have both $r.v.h \ni (v', h')$ — *classical*

(ii) and $H' = \{h'\!:\mathcal{H} \mid (\exists h''\!:H \cdot r.v.h'' \ni (v', h'))\}$.   — *shadow*

$\square$

Clause (i) says that the classical projection of addShadow.r's behaviour is the same as the classical behaviour of just r itself. Clause (ii) says that the final shadow H' contains all those values h' compatible with allowing the original hidden value to range as h'' over the initial shadow H.

2.3 Security-Aware Program Refinement

Equality of programs is a special case of refinement, whence compositionality is a special case of monotonicity: two programs with equal semantics in isolation must remain equal in all contexts. With those ideas in place, we define refinement as follows:

Definition 2. *Refinement*   For programs $P_{\{1,2\}}$ we say that P_1 *is securely refined by* P_2 and write $P_1 \sqsubseteq P_2$ just when for all v, h, H we have

$$(\forall\,(v',h',H_2')\colon [\![P_2]\!].v.h.H\,\cdot$$
$$\big(\exists H_1'\colon\mathbb{P}\mathcal{H}\mid H_1'\subseteq H_2'\,\cdot\quad(v',h',H_1')\in [\![P_1]\!].v.h.H\big)\,\big)\,,$$

with $[\![\cdot]\!]$ as defined in Fig. 1.

This means that for each initial triple (v,h,H) every final triple (v',h',H_2') produced by P_2 must be "justified" by the existence of a triple (v',h',H_1'), with equal or smaller shadow, produced by P_1 under the same circumstances.   □

3   Programming with Hidden State

What makes security analysis difficult is the seeming incompatibility of both keeping a secret *and* using it in "public computations." In this section we summarise the characteristics of the Shadow semantics that allow us to analyse the extent to which information is revealed at runtime.

Runtime visibility and *in*-visibility. A *visible* variable is one whose runtime value can be "observed" after each (atomic) execution. For example, the resolution of the nondeterministic choice in the program $v\colon\in\{0,1\}$ can be determined simply by reading the final value of the visible variable v. Assignments to *hidden* variables, in contrast, cannot be observed directly. Thus the program $h\colon\in\{0,1\}$ reveals nothing about h at runtime beyond what can be gleaned statically by examining the source code: we deduce that it is either 0 or 1; but we don't know which.

Interaction and information flow. More interesting is when visible and invisible variables interact, for that is where correlations are formed. Direct publication of the hidden state results in a direct correlation, for example $v\colon=h$ effectively announces h's value. Moreover once the information is in the public domain, no amount of track-covering can erase the knowledge. The program $v\colon=h; v\colon=0$ also leaks h, *even though v is overwritten immediately afterwards —* that is because our *attack model* [10] assumes that an observer can see the the results of visible computations after each "atomic step," which is normally defined by sequential composition (but see atomicity below). In addition an observer may make deductions based on his run-time observations and the structure of the program code. Thus in principle attackers have perfect recall [13,14].

This curious interaction of hidden and visible assignments means sequential composition becomes a somewhat strange operator — for instance it no longer satisfies the rule $(v\colon=h; v\colon=0)=v\colon=0$. Luckily these idiosyncrasies are limited to visible/hidden interactions, with the classical rules continuing to apply as normal in the cases where the reasoning is entirely between visible variables.

Compositionality and refinement. Two programs are judged to be the same if and only if they are both functionally equivalent *and* have identical "security defences." The latter is crucial to our hierarchical development method, for it implies that one program may be replaced by its equivalent *in any context,* without fear of unanticipated security flaws. In our examples below we will use not-necessarily-executable programs as specifications to articulate our overall security goals.

When reasoning about programs we are able to assume the normal structural rules, so for example $P \sqcap Q \sqsubseteq P$, and (**if** $E.v.h$ **then** P_t **else** P_f **fi**); $Q =$ **if** $E.v.h$ **then** $P_t; Q$ **else** $P_f; Q$ **fi**. We also use the fact that decreasing visibility is always a secure refinement, *i.e.* $[\![\textbf{vis } x \cdots]\!] \sqsubseteq [\![\textbf{hid } x \cdots]\!]$, where we have used "visibility declarations" (discussed below) to assign the visibility attribute to the variable x.

Atomicity: controlling granularity. Explicit atomicity is necessary for hiding the results of intermediate computations when secrecy demands it. For example the process of encryption typically is achieved as a result of a number of steps, and it is only safe to publish the final result after obliterating the intermediate computations. We use $\langle\!\langle P \rangle\!\rangle$ to mean that the internals of program P are not revealed at runtime — and within those brackets $\langle\!\langle \cdot \rangle\!\rangle$ we can therefore use classical *equality* reasoning. Proper refinement however is not allowed.

That is, within the safety of atomicity brackets, classical equality reasoning is reinstated so that $\langle\!\langle v := h; v := 0 \rangle\!\rangle = \langle\!\langle v := 0 \rangle\!\rangle$; but we cannot for example reason via refinement that $(h := 0 \sqcap h := 1) \sqsubseteq h := 0$ implies

$$h :\in \{0, 1\} \quad = \quad \langle\!\langle h := 0 \sqcap h := 1 \rangle\!\rangle \quad \sqsubseteq \quad \langle\!\langle h := 0 \rangle\!\rangle \quad = \quad h := 0 \, ,$$

becuase the middle (refinement) step fails.

Removing atomicity brackets is possible only under certain circumstances. The following lemma sets out one such case.

Lemma 1. *atomicity and composition [10].* Given two programs $P_{\{1,2\}}$ over v, h we have $\langle\!\langle P_1; P_2 \rangle\!\rangle = \langle\!\langle P_1 \rangle\!\rangle; \langle\!\langle P_2 \rangle\!\rangle$ just when v's *intermediate* value, i.e. "at the semicolon," can be deduced from its *endpoint* values, i.e. initial and final, possibly in combination. The semicolon is interpreted classically on the left, and as in Fig. 1 on the right. $\qquad\qquad\square$

Lem. 1 prevents us from removing the atomicity brackets for $\langle\!\langle v := h; v := 0 \rangle\!\rangle$, but allows it for $\langle\!\langle v := \{0, 1\}; h := v \oplus E \rangle\!\rangle$, for example. In the former case the intermediate value of v (equal to the hidden h) cannot be deduced from its final value (the constant 0); in the latter case, v's final value is the same as its intermediate value, and atomicity offers no further protection.

Before beginning our real case studies, we elaborate on our treatment of multi-agent systems, and encryption.

4   Agents, Views and Proofs

Our cases studies below are all examples of "multi-agent systems" in that they are composed of a number of independent components, which collaborate to achieve an overall goal. When secrecy is an issue, each agent only has a "partial view" of the system state, and has complementary security goals with respect to the other agents and to the system as a whole. We use the extension of the Shadow semantics introduced elsewhere [10] to express the differing views of the agents in the system. Essentially the simple semantics can reflect a single agent's viewpoint.

Multiple agents, and the attacker's capabilities. Let A be an agent in a multi-agent system; the above simple semantics reflects A's viewpoint, say, by interpreting variables declared to be $\mathbf{vis}_{list}$ as visible ($\mathbf{vis}$) variables if A is in *list* and as hidden ($\mathbf{hid}$) variables otherwise. More precisely,

- **var** means the associated variable's visibility is unknown or irrelevant.
- **vis** means the associated variable is visible to all agents.
- **hid** means the associated variable is hidden from all agents.
- **vis**$_{list}$ means the associated variable is visible to all agents in the (non-empty) list, and is hidden from all others (including third parties).
- **hid**$_{list}$ means the associated variable is hidden from all agents in the list, and is visible to all others (including third parties).

For example $[\![\mathbf{vis}_A\ a; \mathbf{vis}_B\ b; \mathbf{vis}\ c;\ c{:=}a{\oplus}b]\!]$ from A's viewpoint the specification would be interpreted with a and c visible and b hidden; for B the interpretation hides a instead of b. For a third party X, say, both a,b are hidden but c is still visible. We say that a system is *generally secure* provided that it is *specifically secure* (as determined by the Shadow semantics) from all its viewpoints. For us this means that the proof must be checked for all those viewpoints; happily many of these can be carried out schematically.

Visibility declarations can be thought of as placing access restrictions on variables; it does not mean that the value of the variables must always remain unknown to agents not on its visibility list: that depends on the code, since *e.g.* hidden h is known to all once the statement $v{:=}h$ has been executed. They do however have an impact on which refinements will be judged ultimately to be valid.

5   The General Encryption Lemma

Our first case study is a small "toolkit" security idiom which occurs in many protocols: it is the splitting into two pieces of some hidden information, with only "one half" of it then subsequently revealed: the key to the protocols is that this does not introduce a security vulnerability. Perhaps the simplest case is

$$[\![\ \mathbf{vis}\ v;\ \mathbf{hid}\ h;\quad h{:}{\in}\{0,1\}; v{:=}E{\oplus}h\ ]\!]\ , \tag{1}$$

where all types are Boolean (equiv. $\{0,1\}$) and $\oplus$ is exclusive-or. No matter what the visibility characteristics of E might be, the code above reveals nothing (more) about it. In this section, we will discuss a symmetric version of this, and in more general terms than Booleans and exclusive-or.

5.1   The Symmetric Encryption Lemma

With (1) as motivation, we reason about two agents A, B in some context where expression E is meaningful. We take A's point of view, and show as follows that (1) is equivalent to **skip**, and so changes nothing (global) but –more significantly– *reveals* nothing about E:

$$
\begin{array}{llll}
& [\![\; \mathsf{vis}_A \; a; \mathsf{vis}_B \; b; & (a{\oplus}b){:=}\, E \;]\!] & \text{``from (1)''} \\
= & [\![\; \mathsf{vis}_A \; a; \mathsf{vis}_B \; b; & \langle\!\langle (a{\oplus}b){:=}\, E \rangle\!\rangle \;]\!] & \text{``statement is atomic already''} \\
= & [\![\; \mathsf{vis}_A \; a; \mathsf{vis}_B \; b; & \langle\!\langle a{:}{\in}\,\mathcal{E}; b{:=}\, E{\oplus}a \rangle\!\rangle \;]\!] & \text{``}\mathcal{E}\text{ is the type of } a, b, E; \text{ see (i) below'' } \heartsuit \\
= & [\![\; \mathsf{vis}_A \; a; \mathsf{vis}_B \; b; & \langle\!\langle a{:}{\in}\,\mathcal{E} \rangle\!\rangle; \langle\!\langle b{:=}\, E{\oplus}a \rangle\!\rangle \;]\!] & \text{``atomicity lemma''} \\
= & [\![\; \mathsf{vis}_A \; a; \mathsf{vis}_B \; b; & a{:}{\in}\,\mathcal{E}; b{:=}\, E{\oplus}a \;]\!] & \text{``statements are atomic anyway''} \\
= & [\![\; \mathsf{vis}_A \; a; a{:}{\in}\,\mathcal{E}; & [\![\; \mathsf{vis}_B \; b; \; b{:=}\, E{\oplus}a \;]\!] \;]\!] & \text{``}b\text{ is not free in }\mathcal{E}; \text{ see (ii) below'' } \heartsuit \\
= & [\![\; \mathsf{vis}_A \; a; & a{:}{\in}\,\mathcal{E}; \mathsf{skip} \;]\!] & \text{``}b\text{ is hidden from }A\text{'' } \flat \\
= & [\![\; \mathsf{vis}_A \; a; & a{:}{\in}\,\mathcal{E} \;]\!] & \text{``skip''} \\
= & \mathsf{skip} \; . & & \text{``}a\text{ is a local visible''}
\end{array}
$$

The proof for B's point of view is symmetric.[1] The crucial features $\heartsuit$ of the derivation are these:

(i) The correctness of this step has both classical and security aspects. The classical aspect is simply that we must have $(E{\oplus}a) \oplus a = E$.

    The security aspect is that, within atomicity brackets $\langle\!\langle \cdot \rangle\!\rangle$, only *equality* reasoning is allowed; proper refinement is not, and this concerns the introduction of the type-set $\mathcal{E}$. That set must capture *precisely* the possible values of a that could result from the (previous) statement $(a{\oplus}b){:=}\, E$, no more and no less — otherwise it's not an equality. Putting that in words we would say "For all values of E and all $a{\in}\mathcal{E}$ there must be some $b{\in}\mathcal{E}$ so that $a = E{\oplus}b$, and furthermore $\mathcal{E}$ contains all the values that a could have."

(ii) In this step we moved $a{:}{\in}\,\mathcal{E}$ out of the scope of b. This is possible only because in choosing $\mathcal{E}$ from which to pick a we were able to ignore b, i.e. that the choice-range for a is independent of b (and E).

In the next section we illustrate the above Boolean-based encryption with a simple scheme for secure messaging.

6   Secure Messaging in an Untrusted Medium

Sender S is eager to tell R a secret but, as they live far apart, he cannot whisper it in his ear. Instead he sends it with messengers X, Y even though he does not trust either one separately not to read the message he is delivering. First S splits s into two "shares" s_x and s_y in such as way that their exclusive-or is equal to s, *i.e.* so that $s_x \oplus s_y = s$. He gives s_x to X and s_y to Y with the instruction to

---

[1] The $\flat$ is referred to in §8.2.

$\mathbf{vis}_S\ s; \mathbf{vis}_R\ r;$
$\mathbf{vis}_{SX}\ s_x; \mathbf{vis}_{SY}\ s_y;$
$\mathbf{vis}_X\ x; \mathbf{vis}_Y\ y;$
$\mathbf{vis}_{RX}\ r_x; \mathbf{vis}_{RY}\ r_y;$

$(s_x \oplus s_y) := s;$	$\Leftarrow S$ splits the message in two.
$(s_x \oplus s_y) := s;$	$\Leftarrow S$ splits the message in two.
$x, y := s_x, s_y;$	$\Leftarrow$ Messages sent from S to X and to Y separately.
$r_x, r_y := x, y;$	$\Leftarrow$ Messages sent from X and Y to R.
$r := r_x \oplus r_y$.	$\Leftarrow R$ recombines the two halves.

We write $(s_x \oplus s_y) := s$ for the (atomic) choice over all possibilities of splitting the message s, equivalent to the specification statement $s_x, s_y : [s_x \oplus s_y = s]$ and interpreted atomically[12].

Fig. 2. Abstract messaging with non-colluding messengers

deliver their messages to R. Once R receives the two halves he can reassemble them at his leisure to reveal s. The code, including its visibility declarations, is set out at Fig. 2.

Clearly this scheme transfers s to R; as for security, it seems intuitive that if s is split so that neither X nor Y learns its contents, then the message passing reveals no more. Our goal in this section is to check formally that the intuition is sound. We begin with an "obviously correct" specification, namely an atomic transaction between R and S:

$$\mathbf{vis}_S\ s; \quad \mathbf{vis}_R\ r; \quad r := s , \tag{2}$$

which is "as if" the message were indeed whispered; but that is not directly executable because r and s are local only to R and S respectively. Nevertheless it precisely sets out the limited circulation of s — X and Y are excluded from the the visibility lists, and therefore neither X nor Y can know s. The next step is to ensure that the restricted circulation is maintained in spite of introducing untrustworthy agents.

Following the refinement tradition, we gradually introduce the message-passing infrastructure, making sure as we do so that neither by publication nor by careless program structure can X or Y glean anything about s. As we introduce detail it becomes important to identify what is already known, and by whom — we use a new technique of "visibility annotations"[2] to formalise exactly that.

Definition 3. *The statement* **reveal**$_{list} E$ *is just* **reveal** E *if the viewpoint is in agent-list* list, *and is* **skip** *otherwise.*

Definition 4. *We say that an expression E is effectively list-visible at a point in a program just when putting a statement* **reveal**$_{list} E$ *there would not alter the program's meaning.*

---

[2] Thanks to Carroll Morgan for suggesting visibility annotations.

In our case we need to know at what point in the transaction we can assume who knows what; in practice to determine the visibility of an expression we use the visibility declarations as well as other information which has already been revealed. Thus an expression is said to be effectively visible (at a point) just when its value is determined by variables visible (at that same point) and any other expressions that are effectively visible at that point.

Now we begin with the simple specification (2), embellishing it until we reach the message-passing scheme at Fig. 2. At each stage we sill use visibility annotations, visibility declarations or simple program algebra to justify the equality between programs.

Step 1: Visibility annotations. We start by analysing the visibility of s both before and after the assignment in (2); we use the visibility annotations. First, it is clear that r is effectively S-visible after the statement, and that s is effectively R-visible both before and after. Obvious or not, we check this as follows: we use Def. 4 to put **reveal**$_S$ r and **reveal**$_R$ s before and after the assignment.

First, we see that r is effectively S-visible after the assignment:

$$
\begin{aligned}
&r := s;\ \textbf{reveal}_S\ r \\
=\ &r := s;\ \textbf{reveal}_S\ s && \text{``}r = s\text{ at that point''} \\
=\ &r := s\ . && \text{``}s\text{ is }S\text{-visible by declaration''}
\end{aligned}
$$

Similarly s R-visible after the assignment:

$$
\begin{aligned}
&r := s;\ \textbf{reveal}_R\ s \\
=\ &r := s;\ \textbf{reveal}_R\ r && \text{``as above''} \\
=\ &r := s\ .
\end{aligned}
$$

And finally s is r-visible *before* the assignment:

$$
\begin{aligned}
&(\textbf{reveal}_R\ s);\ r := s \\
=\ &r := s;\ \textbf{reveal}_R\ r && \text{`` }s\text{ is unchanged''} \\
=\ &r := s\ . && \text{``as above''}
\end{aligned}
$$

The last one is interesting, since *operationally* one would be inclined to say that s is not R-visible before the statement, since we "can't yet know s" before that assignment has occurred. But here (yet again) is where a logical view helps us to avoid confusions that operational reasoning can cause.

Referring to the "attack model" sketched above, we'd say under an attack from R we'd have that s is visible before the statement $r := s$ just when R really can see it. But he can't see it, can he...? Nevertheless he can reason as if he could: whatever reasoning he wanted to do with s at that point he simply defers, first allowing the program to run one further step. Then s really is visible (by inference, since it's now sitting in r), and then R can go back and continue the reasoning based on s that he had put on hold.

Step 2: Splitting the message. Now we have learned about R and S's viewpoints, we can start adding details of the message-passing. We use encryption to split s, but we need to show that still only R and S learn s. What we need to show is that

$$(2) \quad = \quad [\![\mathbf{vis}_{RXS}\ s_x; \mathbf{vis}_{RYS}\ s_y;\quad (s_x \oplus s_y) := s]\!]; r := s \ ,$$

where we have used the specification statement to make mutually secret shares s_x and s_y.

Here although the encryption guarantees that neither X nor Y learn anything, to ensure equality with the specification, we need to check that the security refinement holds from all points of view, and that includes R and S. The problematic case is R, because on the right since R can see s_x and s_y, he would learn the secret before the assignment to his variable r. Although we don't really "care" about that (after all, he is the intended recipient of s) in our formal proof we are *made to care*, and rightly so — information can be unintentionally leaked and if an agent learns something "early" then he becomes a security risk when he was not intended to be. In this case early knowledge is not a problem, as our visibility analysis above has already checked for us.

1. From S's point of view, everything is visible in the new block (no security problems), and the (generalised) assignment is to new local variables (no classical problems).
2. From X (Y)'s point of view, it's an instance of the encryption lemma.
3. From R's point of view (the only interesting one), we would formerly have been stuck because s_x, s_y are both visible to R but s is hidden from R. But now we can see that although s is hidden from R by declaration, nevertheless it is R-visible (from Step 1 above) and so this case reduces to (1).

Step 3: Delivering the messages. The next step introduces the messengers X and Y, who now carry their halves in variables x and y and give them to R.

$$
\begin{aligned}
&\quad \mathbf{vis}_R\ r;\ \mathbf{vis}_S\ s;\ r := s \\
=&\quad (s_x \oplus s_y) := s; r := s & \text{``}\mathbf{vis}_{RXS}\ s_x; \mathbf{vis}_{RYS}\ s_y\text{''} \\
=&\quad (s_x \oplus s_y) := s; & \text{``}\mathbf{vis}_{RX}\ x; \mathbf{vis}_{RY}\ y\text{''} \\
&\quad x, y := s_x, s_y; \\
&\quad r := s \\
=&\quad (s_x \oplus s_y) := s; & \text{``}\mathbf{vis}_R\ r_x, r_y\text{''} \\
&\quad x, y := s_x, s_y; \\
&\quad r_x, r_y := x, y; \\
&\quad r := s \\
=&\quad (s_x \oplus s_y) := s; & \text{``program algebra''} \\
&\quad x, y := s_x, s_y; \\
&\quad r_x, r_y := x, y; \\
&\quad r := r_x \oplus r_y \ .
\end{aligned}
$$

For the final step from here to Fig. 2, we use the general refinement rule for reducing visibilities, replacing $\mathbf{vis}_{RXS}\ s_x; \mathbf{vis}_{RYS}\ s_y$ by $\mathbf{vis}_X\ s_x; \mathbf{vis}_Y\ s_y$.

7 Secure Remote Computations

We now take another step towards our principal case study. Private Information Retrieval is very similar to secure message-passing as above, but includes structured set-valued messages, and remote computation. We begin by working towards a more general instance of the encryption lemma.

7.1 The Exclusive-or Algebra of Subsets

We take as our type $\mathcal{E}$ the powerset $\mathbb{P}[0..N)$ of the natural numbers below N, which we will abbreviate $\mathbb{P}N$. For our operation $\oplus$ we take the *symmetric set-difference*, which we will write Δ so that for $N_{0,1} \in \mathbb{P}N$ we have $N_0 \Delta N_1 = N_0 - N_1 \cup N_1 - N_0$[3]. As payoff for our generality above, we have immediately for $E \in \mathbb{P}N$ the equality

$$\llbracket\ \mathbf{vis}_A\ a\colon\mathbb{P}N;\ \mathbf{vis}_B\ b\colon\mathbb{P}N;\ (a\Delta b){:=}E\ \rrbracket \quad = \quad \mathbf{skip}\ . \tag{3}$$

It's just the encryption lemma for subsets. Here's how we can use it.

7.2 Secure Use of a Remote Super-Computer

Suppose some user-agent U wants to compute $y{:=}F.x$ with $\mathbf{vis}_A\ x, y$, so that the variables involved are visible only to him. (We do not specify the types of x, y at this stage.) The function F is public; but unfortunately it is so complicated that A does not have the resources to compute it. His first thought is to ship y off to a super-computer -agent A who will compute it for him, thus he hopes for

$$y{:=}F.x \quad \sqsubseteq \quad \llbracket\ \mathbf{vis}_A\ a, a';\quad a{:=}x;\ a'{:=}F.a;\ y{:=}a'\ \rrbracket\ ,$$

in which $a{:=}x$ sends the argument from U to A, and $y{:=}a'$ returns the result. The computation $a'{:=}F.a$ is then carried out entirely by A.

Although this is a classical refinement (obviously), it is not a secure one: the problem is that A learns the values of x, y, and they are supposed to be private to U.

Now let us suppose that the function F distributes $\oplus$ (over the types of x, y), that is that $F.(x_0 \oplus x_1) = F.x_0 \oplus F.x_1$. Moreover we assume that U values his privacy so much that he is prepared to pay for *two* super-computer runs, the second one's being run by Agent B. He now proposes the refinement

$$y{:=}F.x \quad \sqsubseteq \quad \llbracket\ \mathbf{vis}_A\ a;\mathbf{vis}_B\ b;\quad (a\oplus b){:=}x;\ y{:=}F.a\oplus F.b\ \rrbracket$$

in which, to reduce clutter, we have suppressed the assignments (like $a{:=}x$ above) that are simply to do with passing values from one agent to another.

The classical correctness of this second refinement-proposal depends on the $\oplus$-distributivity of F, which we have assumed; but what about its security correctness? That follows from the Encryption Lemma, since we can derive

---

[3] This operator Δ really is just exclusive-or $\oplus$ in different clothes: regard the sets as characteristic functions, and then apply the ordinary Boolean exclusive-or pointwise to those functions.

$y := F.x$

$=$ $[\![\ \mathbf{vis}_A\ a; \mathbf{vis}_B\ b; \quad (a{\oplus}b) := x\ ]\!];$ "Encryption Lemma"
    $y := F.x$

$=$ $[\![\ \mathbf{vis}_A\ a; \mathbf{vis}_B\ b;$ "scope and context"
    $(a{\oplus}b) := x;$
    $y := F.(a{\oplus}b)$
    $]\!]$

$=$ $[\![\ \mathbf{vis}_A\ a; \mathbf{vis}_B\ b;$ "$\oplus$-distributivity of F"
    $(a{\oplus}b) := x;$
    $y := F.a \oplus F.b$
    $]\!]$

This solves U's privacy problems — though he does have to pay for two runs of the function F.

7.3   Explicit Message-Passing

Naturally the two statements $(a{\oplus}b) := x$ and $y := F.a{\oplus}F.b$ above must themselves be implemented via explicit message passing. For the first we argue by analogy with the two-messengers approach of §6, as follows:

    $(a{\oplus}b) := x$

$=$ $[\![\ \mathbf{vis}_{UA}\ x_A; \mathbf{vis}_{UB}\ x_B;$ "Encryption Lemma, scoping and context"
    $(x_A{\oplus}x_B) := x;$
    $a, b := x_a, x_b$
    $]\!]$

$\sqsubseteq$ $[\![\ \mathbf{vis}_U\ x_A, x_B;$ "reduce visibility"
    $(x_A{\oplus}x_B) := x;$
    $a, b := x_a, x_b$
    $]\!]\ .$

For the second, similar reasoning (which we elide) gives

    $y := F.a \oplus F.b$

$\sqsubseteq$ $[\![\ \mathbf{vis}_U\ y_A, y_B;$ "as above"
    $\mathbf{vis}_A\ z_A; \mathbf{vis}_B\ z_B;$
    $z_A, z_B := F.a, F.b;$
    $y_A, y_B := z_A, z_B; \quad y := y_A \oplus y_B$
    $]\!]\ .$

Put together with the refinement of the previous section (and exploiting monotonicity), we have the overall refinement shown in Fig. 3.

$$y := F.x$$

$\sqsubseteq$ $[\![$ $\mathbf{vis}_U$ $x_A, x_B, y_A, y_B;$ "composition of the above"
      $\mathbf{vis}_A$ $z_A;$ $\mathbf{vis}_B$ $z_B;$

$(x_A \oplus x_B) := x;$	$\Leftarrow$ Split x into two shares.
$a, b := x_a, x_b;$	$\Leftarrow$ Send them to Agents A, B separately.
$z_A, z_B := F.a, F.b;$	$\Leftarrow$ Agents A, B compute F on their respective arguments.
$y_A, y_B := z_A, z_B;$	$\Leftarrow$ The results are sent back to U.
$y := y_A \oplus y_B$	$\Leftarrow$ Agent U combines the result shares to get the answer.

$]\!]$

Fig. 3. Using two remote super computers to calculate an expensive function privately

8   Private Information Retrieval

This is our principal case study. In publicly accessible databases security is not about protecting data, but rather about protecting users –this can be an issue if the data concerns medical or share price information– because the user may want his request to be confidential. Hence the objective of *private information retrieval schemes* (*PIR*) is that the *requests* themselves should remain anonymous.

It has been shown that when the data is stored on a single server (a "single-server model") the only way to achieve the anonymity of requests is for the user to download the entire database for local (and therefore private) perusal [4], but the cost of this confidentiality is extremely poor performance. Current research on *PIR* aims to minimise communication complexity, and in this section we study a scheme introduced by Chor et al. [4].

The idea is to uses some number $d \geq 2$ of copies of the database servers. As in the message-passing example above the user splits the request into d shares, sending each share to each server. The trick is to make sure that the shares (a) reveal no information about the actual request (to either server or a third party), and (b) can nevertheless be reconstructed by the user to reveal his actual request.

Chor explains that the performance reduction only emerges when in fact $d > 2$, but that the security aspects are well illustrated (but more easily!) for $d=2$. Following his advice we begin our formalisation for $d=2$, and in any case study only the security aspects in detail. We assume a database D of N (bit-sized) records addressable with an index $1 \leq i \leq N$; we use U for the user, and A, B for the two servers, each of which host (identical) copies D_A and D_B of D. Chor's informal description of the two-server model is as follows:

> Let U's secret request be some $1 \leq c \leq N$, and he wants to know $D.c$ (equivalently $D_A.c$ or $D_B.c$). He chooses randomly a subset $S \in \mathbb{P}N$, and then sends (all of) S to A and $S \odot c$ to B, where
>
> $$S \odot c := \mathbf{if} \ (c \in S) \ \mathbf{then} \ S \backslash c \ \mathbf{else} \ S \cup \{c\} \ \mathbf{fi}.$$

Next A sends to U the result $y_A := (\oplus_{i \in \mathcal{S}} D_A.i)$, and B similarly sends $y_B := (\oplus_{i \in \mathcal{S} \odot z} D_B.i)$; finally U decrypts the two replies by computing $y_A \oplus y_B$.

The functional correctness of this scheme can be seen easily because of the definition of $\odot$. Note that $\mathcal{S} \odot c$ simply includes c if $c \notin \mathcal{S}$, or it removes it if it is already in $\mathcal{S}$. That means that c occurs in exactly one of $\mathcal{S}$ or $\mathcal{S} \odot c$, but all the other items in $\mathcal{S}$ appear in both subsets. Thus in the final computation of the exclusive or, all the terms $D.i$ cancel out except for $D.c$ and hence $y_A \oplus y_B = D.c$ as required.

The security correctness is slightly more involved, but still intuitive. Since the set $\mathcal{S}$ is chosen at random from all possible subsets of $\{1 \ldots N\}$ when a server receives the subset it does not know whether the real query c is contained in the subset or not.[4] Moreover $\mathcal{S} \odot c$ also appears equally likely amongst all subsets, therefore provided A and B do not collude, they are individually none the wiser as to the actual request.

8.1 Solving the *PIR* Problem with Algebra

Using our results from §5, we can legitimise Chor's approach easily.

First, note that Chor's $\mathcal{S} \odot c$ is just $\mathcal{S} \oplus \{c\}$ in our terms. This establishes the connection with exclusive-or. Second, Chor's operation $(\oplus_{i \in \mathcal{S}} D_A.i)$ (and equivalently $(\oplus_{i \in \mathcal{S}} D_B.i)$) is our function F — and it distributes $\oplus$. This means the refinement of Fig. 3 applies immediately, once we notice that $D.c = D_A.c = D_B.c = F.\{c\}$. Thus we obtain by instantiation the refinement of Fig. 4, in which our initial split $(x_A \triangle x_B) := \{c\}$ is equivalent to Chor's $x_A :\in \mathbb{P}N; x_B := x_A \odot c$.

8.2 Collusion and Visibility Declarations

The above derivation explicitly separates the U/A and U/B correspondence by enforced by the visibility declarations $\mathbf{vis}_A$ and $\mathbf{vis}_B$; for Chor that separation is articulated by the "non-collusion" assumption, and theorems there depend upon it. Here there is a similar dependency, and indeed the validity of refinement depends upon it.

To investigate what would happen if A and B do collude, we rename all the A/B variables to belong to a single server C variable, and attempt the same derivation. [5]This means that all $\mathbf{vis}_A; \mathbf{vis}_B$ declarations become $\mathbf{vis}_C$ — then a careful review of the proofs shows that the original encryption §5, on which the whole security is built fails at the step labelled $\flat$. In this case, the relabelling would make both a, b variables $\mathbf{vis}_C$, so that the comment "b *is hidden* ..." is invalid, preventing the replacement of the assignment to b with $\mathbf{skip}$.

---

[4] Of course if the two servers share their partial information by colluding then the value z is revealed. We discuss collusion later.

[5] We do this since we do not assume anything about the nature of the collusion, except that the servers are able to share all correspondence.

$u := D.c$

$\sqsubseteq$ $\lVert$ **vis**$_U$ $x_A, x_B : \mathbb{P}N; y_A, y_B :$ Bool;   "instantiating Fig. 3"
    vis$_A$ $z_A :$ Bool; **vis**$_B$ $z_B :$ Bool;

   $(x_A \Delta x_B) := \{c\};$ $\Leftarrow$ Split c into two "subset" shares.
   $a, b := x_a, x_b;$ $\Leftarrow$ Send to the servers separately.
   $z_A := (\oplus_{i \in a} D_A.i);$ $\Leftarrow$ Each computes the $\oplus$ of its shares.
   $z_B := (\oplus_{i \in b} D_B.i);$ $\Leftarrow$ $\cdots$
   $y_A, y_B := z_A, z_B;$ $\Leftarrow$ Each sends the result back to the requester.
   $u := y_A \oplus y_B$ $\Leftarrow$ The results are $\oplus$-ed together.
$\rVert$

Fig. 4. Using two remote databases to perform a lookup privately

8.3 Efficient Perfect Information Retrieval

The solution presented in §8 actually does not reduce the overhead on the network at all — in fact it is the same as the single-server solution where the whole database must be sent to U.

The full solution, combining privacy and a reduction in average network traffic — from $O(N)$ to $O(\sqrt{N})$ (for example) — needs strictly more than two servers, and a structured addressing scheme. Again each server is sent an apparently random set of requests for which it must compute the $\oplus$ of the results, and return to the user, who can then reassemble to uncover the request. Although the addressing scheme is somewhat detailed, the principles for correctness, and the machinery for proof remain the same, namely generalised encryption §5.1 and the exclusive-or algebra §7.1.

9   Conclusions and Future Work

We have shown how to validate a well known protocol for Perfect Information Retrieval using a novel refinement-style development. Our approach emphasises a hierarchical analysis which refinement supports, allowing us to use specifications of sub-protocols in our proofs. Critically the proofs are carried out ultimately at the level of source code, thus legitimising noninterference security goals at that level of detail.

The relationship to other formal semantics of non-intereference has been summarised in detail elsewhere [13,14]; it is comparable to Leino [8] and Sabelfeld [15], but differs in details; and it shares the goals of the pioneering work of Mantel [9] and Engelhardt [5].

Our work sits between two communities. On the one hand there are those who reason about code at the source level, and in some cases build (semi-)automated tools to help them do so. Reasoning that way about security however is quite rare; and this community generally does not study the advanced theoretical models of semantics for security for their own sake.

On the other hand, there are those who study or create the mathematics upon which cryptography and secrecy depend. But it is rare to find there a serious interest *as well* in the problems of transferring their insights to the source-code level[6].

We try to place our contribution in between the two groups, drawing inspiration from the concerns of both and hoping in return to contribute something towards bridging the gap.

Thus although there are many ingenious protocols involving secret information, there is as yet limited support for their code-level justification: most new algorithmic/theoretical insights are presented as a mixture of pseudo-code and English (or other natural language). Our work can be seen as an early step towards bridging the cryptographic/software gap.

Future work on this topic will be to develop a "probabilistic Shadow" to enable stronger cryptographic guarantees, quantitative rather than only qualitative, to be faithfully transferred to source-level computer code.

References

1. Abadi, M., Rogoway, P.: Reconciling two views of crytography (the computational soundness of formal encrytion) . In: Watanabe, O., Hagiya, M., Ito, T., van Leeuwen, J., Mosses, P.D. (eds.) TCS 2000. LNCS, vol. 1872, pp. 3–22. Springer, Heidelberg (2000)
2. Abrial, J.-R.: The B Book: Assigning Programs to Meanings. Cambridge University Press, Cambridge (1996)
3. Back, R.-J.R.: Correctness preserving program refinements: Proof theory and applications. Tract 131, Mathematisch Centrum, Amsterdam (1980)
4. Chor, B., Goldreich, O., Kushilevitz, E., Sudan, M.: Private information retrieval. J. ACM 45(6), 965–982 (1999)
5. Engelhardt, K., van der Meyden, R., Moses, Y.: A refinement theory that supports reasoning about knowledge and time. In: Nieuwenhuis, R., Voronkov, A. (eds.) LPAR 2001. LNCS, vol. 2250, pp. 125–141. Springer, Heidelberg (2001)
6. Goguen, J.A., Meseguer, J.: Unwinding and inference control. In: Proc IEEE Symp on Security and Privacy, pp. 75–86 (1984)
7. Jacob, J.: Security specifications. In: IEEE Symposium on Security and Privacy, pp. 14–23 (1988)
8. Leino, K.R.M., Joshi, R.: A semantic approach to secure information flow. Science of Computer Programming 37(1–3), 113–138 (2000)
9. Mantel, H.: Preserving information flow properties under refinement. In: Proc IEEE Symp. Security and Privacy, pp. 78–91 (2001)
10. McIver, A.K., Morgan, C.C.: Sums and lovers: Case studies in security, compositionality and refinement. Submitted to Formal Methods 2009 (2009)

---

[6] How many serious programmers do not understand the simple theory of lists underlying *Mergesort*, say? Not many. How many serious implementations of Mergesort contain at least one bug? Probably quite a lot: because of aliasing, source-level reasoning over linked lists is difficult. There really is a gap.

In the area of unifying the cryptological and formal methods communities there is some work, notably Abadi and Rogoway [1].

11. McIver, A.K., Morgan, C.C.: Abstraction, Refinement and Proof for Probabilistic Systems. Tech. Mono Comp. Sci. Springer, New York (2005)
12. Morgan, C.C.: Programming from Specifications, 2nd edn. Prentice-Hall, Englewood Cliffs (1994), `web.comlab.ox.ac.uk/oucl/publications/books/PfS/`
13. Morgan, C.C.: The Shadow Knows: Refinement of ignorance in sequential programs. In: Uustalu, T. (ed.) MPC 2006. LNCS, vol. 4014, pp. 359–378. Springer, Heidelberg (2006); Treats Dining Cryptographers
14. Morgan, C.C.: The Shadow Knows: Refinement of ignorance in sequential programs. Science of Computer Programming 74(8) (2009); Treats Oblivious Transfer
15. Sabelfeld, A., Sands, D.: A PER model of secure information flow. Higher-Order and Symbolic Computation 14(1), 59–91 (2001)

Verification, Testing and Statistics

Sriram K. Rajamani

Microsoft Research India
sriram@microsoft.com

Formal verification is the holy grail of software validation. Practical applications of verification run into two major challenges. The first challenge is in writing detailed specifications, and the second challenge is in scaling verification algorithms to large software. In this talk, we present possible approaches to address these problems:

- We propose using statistical techniques to raise the level of abstraction, and automate the tedium in writing detailed specifications. We present our experience with the MERLIN project [4], where we have used probabilistic inference to infer specifications for secure information flow, and discovered several vulnerabilities in web applications.
- We propose combining testing with verification to help scalability, an reducing false errors. We present our experience with the YOGI project [1,2,3,5], where we have built a verifier that combines static analysis with testing to find bugs and verify properties of low-level systems code.

Acknowledgment. We thank our collaborators Anindya Banerjee, Nels Beckman, Bhargav Gulavani, Patrice Godefroid, Tom Henzinger, Yamini Kannan, Ben Livshits, Aditya Nori, Rob Simmons, Sai Tetali and Aditya Thakur.

References

1. Beckman, N.E., Nori, A.V., Rajamani, S.K., Simmons, R.J.: Proofs from tests. In: ISSTA 2008: International Symposium on Software Testing and Analysis, pp. 3–14. ACM Press, New York (2008)
2. Godefroid, P., Nori, A.V., Rajamani, S.K., Tetali, S.: Compositional May-Must Program Analysis: Unleashing The Power of Alternation. Microsoft Research Technical Report MSR-TR-2009-2, Microsoft Research (2009)
3. Gulavani, B.S., Henzinger, T.A., Kannan, Y., Nori, A.V., Rajamani, S.K.: SYNERGY: A new algorithm for property checking. In: FSE 2006: Foundations of Software Engineering, pp. 117–127. ACM Press, New York (2006)
4. Livshits, B., Nori, A.V., Rajamani, S.K., Banerjee, A.: Merlin: Specification Inference for Explicit Information Flow Problems. To appear in PLDI 2009: Programming Language Design and Implementation. ACM Press, New York (2009)
5. Nori, A.V., Rajamani, S.K., Tetali, S., Thakur, A.V.: The Yogi Project: Software Property Checking via Static Analysis and Testing. In: TACAS 2009: Tools and Algorithms for Constuction and Analysis of Systems. LNCS, vol. 5509, pp. 178–181. Springer, Heidelberg (2009)

M. Leucker and C. Morgan (Eds.): ICTAC 2009, LNCS 5684, p. 79, 2009.
© Springer-Verlag Berlin Heidelberg 2009

ν-Types for Effects and Freshness Analysis

Massimo Bartoletti[1], Pierpaolo Degano[2], Gian Luigi Ferrari[2],
and Roberto Zunino[3]

[1] Dipartimento di Matematica e Informatica, Università degli Studi di Cagliari, Italy
[2] Dipartimento di Informatica, Università di Pisa, Italy
[3] Dipartimento di Ingegneria e Scienza dell'Informazione, Università di Trento, Italy

Abstract. We define a type and effect system for a λ-calculus extended with side effects, in the form of primitives for creating and accessing resources. The analysis correctly over-approximates the sequences of resource accesses performed by a program at run-time. To accurately analyse the binding between the creation of a resource and its accesses, our system exploits a new class of types. Our ν-types have the form $\nu N.\,\tau \triangleright H$, where the names in N are bound both in the type τ and in the effect H, that represents the sequences of resource accesses.

1 Introduction

The paramount goal of static analysis is that of constructing sound, and as precise as possible, approximations to the behaviour of programs. Various kinds of behaviour have been studied, to guarantee that the analysed programs enjoy some properties of interest: for instance, that a program has no type errors, that communication channels are used correctly, that the usage of resources respects some prescribed policy, *etc.* In the classical approach to type systems, one approximates values and expressions as types, and at the same time checks the desired property over the constructed abstraction.

Separating the concerns of constructing the approximation and of verifying it has some advantages, however. First, once the first step is done, one can check the same abstract behaviour against different properties. Second, one can independently improve the accuracy of the first analysis and the efficiency of the verification algorithm. Third, if we devise a complete verification technique (for a given abstraction), then we have a good characterization of the accuracy of the abstraction with respect to the property of interest.

In this paper, we propose a new sort of types (called *ν-types*) for classifying programs according to their abstract behaviour, that we define as follows. Call *resource* any program object (a variable, a channel, a kernel service, *etc.*) relevant for the property of interest, and call *event* any action performed on a resource (a variable assignment, an output along a channel, a system call, *etc.*). Then, the abstract behaviour we are concerned with is the set of all the possible sequences of events (*histories*) that can result from the execution of a program.

Our reference program model is a call-by-value λ-calculus extended with side effects, that model events, and with a primitive for creating new resources. Our

M. Leucker and C. Morgan (Eds.): ICTAC 2009, LNCS 5684, pp. 80–95, 2009.

ν-types have the form $\nu N. \tau \rhd H$, where the names $n \in N$ are bound both in the type τ and in the effect H, that is a *history expression* that represents the possible histories. Essentially, history expressions are Basic Process Algebra [7] processes extended with name restriction *à la* π-calculus [14]. We showed in [5] that history expressions are a suitable model upon which one can develop sound and complete techniques for verifying history-based usage policies of programs.

The possibility of creating new resources poses the non-trivial problem of correctly recording the binding of a fresh name with its possible uses in types and effects. For instance, consider the following function:

$$f = \lambda y. \textbf{new } x \textbf{ in } \alpha(x); x$$

Each application of f creates a new resource r, fires the event $\alpha(r)$, and finally returns r. A suitable ν-type for f would then be $(\mathbf{1} \rightarrow (\nu n.\{n\} \rhd \alpha(n))) \rhd \varepsilon$. The unit type $\mathbf{1}$ for the parameter y is irrelevant here. Since f is a function, the actual effect is empty, denoted by the history expression ε. The return type $\nu n. \{n\} \rhd \alpha(n)$ correctly predicts the behaviour of applying f. The binder νn guarantees the freshness of the name n in the type $\{n\}$ – which indicates that f will return a fresh resource r – and in the history expression $\alpha(n)$. Indeed, $\nu n. \alpha(n)$ abstracts from any sequence $\alpha(r)$, where r is a fresh resource.

Consider now the following term:

$$\textbf{let } f = \lambda y. \textbf{new } x \textbf{ in } \alpha(x); x \textbf{ in } \beta(f*; f*)$$

Here we apply f twice to the value $*$, and we fire β on the resource that results from the second application of f. A suitable ν-type for the above would be:

$$\mathbf{1} \rhd (\nu n. \, \alpha(n)) \cdot (\nu n'. \, \alpha(n') \cdot \beta(n'))$$

The first part $\nu n. \, \alpha(n)$ of the history expression describes the behaviour of the first application of f, while the second part $\nu n'. \, \alpha(n') \cdot \beta(n')$ approximates the second application, and firing β on the returned name n'. The binders ensure that the resources represented by n and n' are kept distinct.

As a more complex example, consider the following recursive function (where z stands for the whole function g within its body):

$$g = \lambda_z x. \textbf{new } y \textbf{ in } (\alpha(y); (b(x)) \, ? \, x : (b'(y)) \, ? \, z \, y : z \, x)$$

The function g creates a new resource upon each loop; if g ever terminates, it either returns the resource passed as parameter, or one of the resources created. If no further information is known about the boolean predicates b and b', we cannot statically predict which resource is returned. A suitable ν-type for g is:

$$(\{?\} \rightarrow (\{?\} \rhd \mu h. \, \nu n. \, \alpha(n) \cdot (h + \varepsilon))) \rhd \varepsilon$$

Being g a function, its actual effect is ε. Its functional type is $\{?\} \rightarrow \{?\}$, meaning that g takes as parameter any resource, and it returns an unknown resource. The latent effect $\mu h. \, \nu n. \, \alpha(n) \cdot (h + \varepsilon)$ represents the possible histories generated when applying g, i.e. any finite sequence $\alpha(r_0) \cdots \alpha(r_k)$ such that $r_i \neq r_j$ for all $i \neq j$.

The examples given above witness some inherent difficulties of handling new names in static analysis. We take as starting point the type and effect system of [18], which handles a λ-calculus with side effects, but without resource creation. We extend the calculus of [18] with the **new** primitive, and we give it a big-step operational semantics. We then define effects (i.e. history expressions) and our ν-types, together with a subtyping/subeffecting relation. We introduce then a type and effect system for our calculus, which associates any well-typed term with a ν-type that correctly approximates the possible run-time histories. We finally present some possible extensions to our work. Further typing examples and the proofs of our statements can be found in [6].

Related work. Our investigation started in [1] to deal with history-based access control in a calculus with side effects, but without creation of resources. In a subsequent paper [3] we featured a preliminary treatment of resource creation, through a conservative extension of simple types. The idea was that of using a special event $new(n)$ as a "weak" binder – a sort of $gensym()$ – instead of using explicit ν-binders. While this allowed for reusing some of the results of [18], e.g. type inference, it also required a further analysis step, called "bindification" to place the ν-binders at the right points in the inferred effect. A first drawback of this approach is that bindification is not always defined, because the introduced scopes of names may interfere dangerously, e.g. in $new(n) \cdot new(n) \cdot \alpha(n)$. A second, more serious, drawback is that our theory of weak binders resulted too complex to be usable in practice [4]. Several definitions (e.g. the bound and free names, the semantics of history expressions, and the subeffecting relation) needed particular care to deal with the corner cases, so leading to extremely intricate proofs. The ν-types presented here are an attempt to solve both these problems. For the first problem, bindification is no longer needed, because ν-binders are already embodied into types. For the second problem, we found the proofs about ν-types, although not immune from delicate steps (e.g. checking capture avoidance in α-conversions) are far easier than those with weak binders. Another technical improvement over [3] is the Subject Reduction Lemma. Actually, in [3] we used a small-step semantics, which "consumes" events as they are fired. As a consequence, the effect of an term cannot be preserved under transitions. To prove type soundness, we had then to deal with a weak version of Subject Reduction, where the effects before and after a transition are in a somewhat convoluted relation. The proof of this statement was extremely complex, because of the weak induction hypothesis. Unlike [3], here we adopt a big-step semantics, which does not consume events. This allows us to establish Subject Reduction in the classical form, where the type is preserved under transitions.

In [2] we combined a type and effect analysis and a model-checking technique in a unified framework, to statically verify history-based policies of programs, in a λ-calculus enriched with primitives to create and use resources, and lexically-scoped usage policies. The present paper extends some results of [2] by presenting further technical achievements about the type and effect system and its relation with the program semantics, in a cleaner setting.

A number of formal techniques have been developed to handle binding and freshness of names. The language FreshML [17] has constructors and destructors for handling bound names. This allows for elegantly manipulating object-level syntactical structures up-to α-conversion, so relieving programmers from the burden of explicitly handling capture-avoidance. The FreshML type system however has a different goal than ours, since it extends the ML type system, while it is not concerned with approximating run-time histories like ours.

Skalka and Smith [18,19] proposed a λ-calculus with local checks that enforce linear μ-calculus properties [8] on the past history. A type and effect system approximates the possible run-time histories, whose validity can be statically verified by model checking μ-calculus formulae over Basic Process Algebras [7,10]. Compared with our type system, [18] also allows for let-polymorphism, subtyping of functional types, and type inference – but it does not handle resource creation. In Sec. 5 we further discuss these issues.

Regions have been used in type and effect systems [20,15] to approximate new names in impure call-by-value λ-calculi. The static semantics of [15], similarly to ours, aims at over-approximating the set of run-time traces, while that of [20] only considers flat sets of events. A main difference from our approach is that, while our ν-types deal with the *freshness* of names, both [20] and [15] use universal polymorphism for typing resource creations. Since a region n stands for a *set* of resources, in an effect $\alpha(n) \cdot \beta(n)$ their static approximation does not ensure that α and β act on the same resource. This property can instead be guaranteed in our system through the effect $\nu n.(\alpha(n) \cdot \beta(n))$. This improvement in the precision of approximations is crucial, since it allows us to model-check in [5] regular properties of traces (e.g. permit $read(file)$ only after an $open(file)$) that would otherwise fail with the approximations of [20,15].

Igarashi and Kobayashi [12] extended the λ-calculus with primitives for creating and accessing resources, and for defining their permitted usage patterns. An execution is resource-safe when the possible patterns are within the permitted ones. A type system guarantees well-typed expressions to be resource-safe. Types abstract the usages permitted at run-time, while typing rules check that resource accesses respect the deduced permitted usages. Since the type system checks resource-safety while constructing the types, type inference is undecidable in the general case. Separating the analysis of effects from their verification, as we did here, led to a simpler model of types. Also, it allowed us to obtain in [5] a sound, complete and PTIME verification algorithm for checking approximations against usage policies. Clearly, also [12] would be amenable to verification, provided that one either restricts the language of permitted usages to a decidable subset, or one uses a sound but incomplete algorithm.

The $\lambda\nu$-calculus of [16] extends the pure λ-calculus with names. In contrast to λ-bound variables, nothing can be substituted for a name, yet names can be tested for equality. Reduction is confluent, and it allows for deterministic evaluation; also, all the observational equivalences of the pure λ-calculus still hold in $\lambda\nu$. Unlike our calculus, names cannot escape their static scope, e.g. $\nu n.n$ is stuck. Consequently, the type system of $\lambda\nu$ is not concerned with name extrusion (and approximation of traces), which is a main feature of ours.

Types and effects are also successfully used in process calculi. Honda, Yoshida and Carbone [11] defined multi-party session types to ensure a correct orchestration of complex systems. Unlike ours, their types do not contain ν binders: the main feature there is not tracking name flow, but reconciling global and local views of multi-party protocols. Igarashi and Kobayashi [13] and Chaki, Rajamani and Rehof [9] defined behavioural types for the π-calculus. In both these proposals, a π-calculus process is abstracted into a CCS-like processes, with no operators for hiding or creating names. Abstractions with ν-binders, however, make it possible to statically verify relevant usage properties about the fresh resources used by a program (see e.g. [5]).

2   A Calculus for Resource Access and Creation

In our model, *resources* are system objects that can either be statically available in the environment (Res_s, a finite set), or be dynamically created (Res_d, a denumerable set). Resources are accessed through a given finite set of *actions*. An *event* $\alpha(r)$ abstracts from accessing the resource r through the action α. When the target resource of an action α is immaterial, we stipulate that α acts on some special (static) resource, and we write just α for the event. A *history* is a finite sequence of events. In Def. 1 we introduce the needed syntactic categories.

Definition 1. Syntactic categories

$r, r', \dots \in \mathsf{Res} = \mathsf{Res}_s \cup \mathsf{Res}_d$	*resources (static/dynamic)*
$\alpha, \alpha', \dots \in \mathsf{Act}$	*actions (a finite set)*
$\alpha(r), \dots \in \mathsf{Ev} = \mathsf{Act} \times \mathsf{Res}$	*events* ($\eta, \eta', \dots \in \mathsf{Ev}^*$ *are histories*)
$x, x', \dots \in \mathsf{Var}$	*variables*
$n, n', \dots \in \mathsf{Nam}$	*names*

We consider an impure call-by-value λ-calculus with primitives for creating and accessing resources. The syntax is in Def. 2. Variables, abstractions, applications and conditionals are as expected. The definition of guards b in conditionals is irrelevant here, and so it is omitted. The variable z in $\lambda_z x . e$ is bound to the whole abstraction, so to allow for an explicit form of recursion. The parameter of an event may be either a resource or a variable. The term **new** represents the creation of a fresh resource. The term *!* models an aborted computation.

Definition 2. Syntax of terms

$e, e' ::= x$	*variable*	
r	*resource*	
$(b) \, ? \, e : e'$	*conditional*	
$\lambda_z x . e$	*abstraction*	$(x, z \in \mathsf{Var})$
$e \, e'$	*application*	
$\alpha(\xi)$	*event*	$(\xi \in \mathsf{Var} \cup \mathsf{Res})$
new	*resource creation*	
!	*aborted computation*	

Values $v, v', \ldots \in$ Val are variables, resources, abstractions, and the term $!$. We write $*$ for a fixed, closed value. We shall use the following abbreviations, the first four of which are quite standard:

$$\lambda_z.\, e = \lambda_z x.\, e \quad \text{if } x \notin fv(e) \qquad \lambda x.\, e = \lambda_z x.\, e \quad \text{if } z \notin fv(e)$$

$$e;\, e' = (\lambda.\, e')\, e \qquad\qquad (\text{let } x = e \text{ in } e') = (\lambda x.\, e')\, e$$

$$\text{new } x \text{ in } e = (\lambda x.\, e)\, (\text{new}) \qquad \alpha(e) = (\text{let } z = e \text{ in } \alpha(z))$$

Some auxiliary notions are needed to define the operational semantics of terms. A *history context* is a finite representation of an infinite set of histories that only differ for the choice of fresh resources. For instance, the set of histories $\{\, \alpha(r) \mid r \in \mathsf{Res} \,\}$ is represented by the context **new** x **in** $\alpha(x);\bullet$. Contexts composition is crucial for obtaining compositionality.

Definition 3. History contexts

A history context C is inductively defined as follows:

$$C \; ::= \; \bullet \; \mid \; \alpha(\xi);\, C \; \mid \; \text{new } x \text{ in } C$$

The free and the bound variables $fv(C)$ and $bv(C)$ of C are defined as expected. We write $C[C']$ for $C[C'[\bullet]]$, also assuming the needed α-conversions of variables so to ensure $bv(C) \cap bv(C') = \emptyset$ (note that $bn(C) \cap fn(C') \neq \emptyset$ is ok).

We specify in Def. 4 our operational semantics of terms, in a big-step style. Transitions have the form $e \stackrel{C}{\Longrightarrow} v$, meaning that the term e evaluates to the value v, while producing a history denoted by C.

Definition 4. Big-step semantics of terms

The big-step semantics of a term e is defined by the relation $e \stackrel{C}{\Longrightarrow} v$, which is the least relation closed under the rules below.

$$\text{E-Val } v \stackrel{\bullet}{\Longrightarrow} v \qquad \text{E-Bang } e \stackrel{\bullet}{\Longrightarrow} ! \qquad \text{E-If } \frac{e_{\mathcal{B}(b)} \stackrel{C}{\Longrightarrow} v}{(b)\,?\,e_{tt} : e_{f\!f} \stackrel{C}{\Longrightarrow} v}$$

$$\text{E-Ev } \alpha(\xi) \stackrel{\alpha(\xi);\bullet}{\Longrightarrow} * \qquad \text{E-New } \textbf{new} \stackrel{\text{new } x \text{ in } \bullet}{\Longrightarrow} x$$

$$\text{E-Beta } \frac{e \stackrel{C}{\Longrightarrow} \lambda_z x.\, e'' \quad e' \stackrel{C'}{\Longrightarrow} v' \neq ! \quad e''\{v'/x, \lambda_z x.\, e''/z\} \stackrel{C''}{\Longrightarrow} v}{e\, e' \stackrel{C[C'[C'']]}{\Longrightarrow} v}$$

$$\text{E-BetaBang1 } \frac{e \stackrel{C}{\Longrightarrow} !}{e\, e' \stackrel{C}{\Longrightarrow} !} \qquad \text{E-BetaBang2 } \frac{e \stackrel{C}{\Longrightarrow} v \neq ! \quad e' \stackrel{C'}{\Longrightarrow} !}{e\, e' \stackrel{C[C']}{\Longrightarrow} !}$$

The rules (E-Val) and (E-Ev) are straightforward. The rule (E-Bang) aborts the evaluation of a term, so allowing us to observe the finite prefixes of its histories. For conditionals, the rule (E-If) assumes as given a total function $\mathcal{B}$ that evaluates the boolean guards. The rule (E-New) evaluates a **new** to a variable x, and records in the context **new** x **in** $\bullet$ that x may stand for any (fresh) resource. The last three rules are for β-reduction of an application $e\,e'$. The rule (E-Beta) is used when both the evaluations of e and e' terminate; (E-BetaBang1) is for when the evaluation of e has been aborted; (E-BetaBang2) is used when the evaluation e terminates while that of e' has been aborted.

Example 1. Let $e = (\lambda y.\,\alpha(y))\,\textbf{new}$. We have that:

$$\frac{\lambda y.\,\alpha(y) \xRightarrow{\bullet} \lambda y.\,\alpha(y) \qquad \textbf{new} \xRightarrow{\textbf{new } x \textbf{ in } \bullet} x \qquad \alpha(x) \xRightarrow{\alpha(x);\bullet} *}{e \xRightarrow{\textbf{new } x \textbf{ in } \alpha(x);\bullet} *}$$

Consider now the following two recursive functions:

$$f = \lambda_z x.\,(\alpha;zx) \qquad g = \lambda_z x.\,\textbf{new } y \textbf{ in } (b(x))\,?\,y : z*$$

The function f fires the event α and recurse. The function g creates a new resource upon each loop; if it ever terminates, it returns the last resource created. For all $k \geq 0$ and for all contexts C, let C^k be inductively defined as $C^0 = \bullet$ and $C^{k+1} = C[C^k]$. Then, for all $k \geq 0$, we have that $f* \xRightarrow{(\alpha;\bullet)^k} \,!$, and, assuming $b(x)$ non-deterministic, $g* \xRightarrow{(\textbf{new } w \textbf{ in } \bullet)^k} \,!$ and $g* \xRightarrow{(\textbf{new } w \textbf{ in } \bullet)^k[\textbf{new } y \textbf{ in } \bullet]} y$. □

We now define the set of histories $\mathcal{H}(e)$ that a term e can produce at run-time. To this purpose, we exploit the auxiliary operator $\mathcal{H}(C, R)$, that constructs the set of histories denoted by the context C under the assumption that R is the set of available resources (Def. 5). Note that all the histories in $\mathcal{H}(e)$ are "truncated" by a !. Only looking at $\mathcal{H}(e)$, gives then no hint about the termination of e. However, this is not an issue, since our goal is not checking termination, but approximating all the possible histories a term can produce.

Definition 5. Run-time histories

For each history context C such that $fv(C) = \emptyset$, for all $R \subseteq$ Res, and for all terms e, we define $\mathcal{H}(C, R)$ and $\mathcal{H}(e)$ inductively as follows:

$$\mathcal{H}(\bullet, R) = \{\,!\,\}$$
$$\mathcal{H}(\alpha(r); C, R) = \{\,!\,\} \cup \{\,\alpha(r)\eta \mid \eta \in \mathcal{H}(C, R)\,\}$$
$$\mathcal{H}(\textbf{new } x \textbf{ in } C, R) = \{\,!\,\} \cup \bigcup_{r \notin R \cup \text{Res}_s} \mathcal{H}(C\{r/x\}, R \cup \{r\})$$
$$\mathcal{H}(e) = \{\,\eta \in \mathcal{H}(C, \emptyset) \mid e \xRightarrow{C} v\,\}$$

Example 2. Recall from Ex. 1 the term $e = (\lambda y.\,\alpha(y))\,\textbf{new}$. All the possible observations (i.e. the histories) of the runs of e are represented by $\mathcal{H}(e) = \mathcal{H}(\textbf{new } x \textbf{ in } \alpha(x); \bullet, \emptyset) = \{\,!\,\} \cup \bigcup_{r \in \text{Res}}\{\alpha(r)\,!\,\}$. Note how the variable x in C was instantiated with all the possible fresh resources r. □

3   Effects and Subeffecting

History expressions are used to approximate the behaviour of terms. They include ε, representing the empty history, variables h, events $\alpha(\rho)$, resource creation $\nu n.H$, sequencing $H \cdot H'$, non-deterministic choice $H + H'$, recursion $\mu h.H$, and !, a nullary event that models an aborted computation. Hereafter, we assume that actions can also be fired on a special, unknown resource denoted by "?", typically due to approximations made by the type and effect system. In $\nu n.H$, the free occurrences of the name n in H are bound by ν; similarly acts μh for the variable h. The free variables $fv(H)$ and the free names $fn(H)$ are defined as expected. A history expression H is *closed* when $fv(H) = \emptyset = fn(H)$.

Definition 6. Syntax of history expressions

$H, H' ::= \varepsilon$	*empty*	
$!$	*truncation*	
h	*variable*	
$\alpha(\rho)$	*event*	$(\rho \in \mathsf{Res} \cup \mathsf{Nam} \cup \{?\})$
$\nu n.H$	*resource creation*	
$H \cdot H'$	*sequence*	
$H + H'$	*choice*	
$\mu h.H$	*recursion*	

We define below a denotational semantics of history expressions. Compared with [18,3], where labelled transition semantics were provided, here we find a denotational semantics more suitable, e.g. for reasoning about the composition of effects. Some auxiliary definitions are needed.

The binary operator $\odot$ (Def. 7) composes sequentially a history η with a set of histories X, while ensuring that all the events after a ! are discarded. For instance, $H = (\mu h.\, h) \cdot \alpha(r)$ will never fire the event $\alpha(r)$, because of the infinite loop that precedes the event. In our semantics, the first component $\mu h.\, h$ will denote the set of histories $\{\,!\,\}$, while $\alpha(r)$ will denote $\{\,!, \alpha(r), \alpha(r)\,!\,\}$. Combining the two semantics results in $\{\,!\,\} \odot \{\,!, \alpha(r), \alpha(r)\,!\,\} = \{\,!\,\}$.

Definition 7. *Let $X \subseteq \mathsf{Ev}^* \cup \mathsf{Ev}^*\,!$, and $x \in \mathsf{Ev} \cup \{\,!\,\}$. We define $x \odot X$ and its homomorphic extension $\eta \odot X$, where $\eta = a_1 \cdots a_n$, as follows:*

$$x \odot X = \begin{cases} \{\, x\,\eta \mid \eta \in X \,\} & \text{if } x \neq \,! \\ \{x\} & \text{if } x = \,! \end{cases} \qquad \eta \odot X = a_1 \odot \cdots \odot a_n \odot X$$

The operator $\boxdot$ (Def. 8) defines sequential composition between semantic functions, i.e. functions from (finite) sets of resources to sets of histories. To do that, it records the resources created, so to avoid that a resource is generated twice. For instance, let $H = (\nu n.\, \alpha(n)) \cdot (\nu n'.\, \alpha(n'))$. The component $\nu n'.\, \alpha(n')$ must not generate the same resources as the component $\nu n.\, \alpha(n)$, e.g. $\alpha(r_0)\alpha(r_0)$ is *not* a possible history of H. The definition of $\boxdot$ exploits the auxiliary function R, that singles out the resources occurring in a history η. Also, $\downarrow \in \mathsf{R}(\eta)$ indicates that η is terminating, i.e. it does not contain any !'s denoting its truncation.

Definition 8. *Let* $Y_0, Y_1 : \mathcal{P}_{fin}(\mathsf{Res}) \to \mathcal{P}(\mathsf{Ev}^* \cup \mathsf{Ev}^*\,!)$. *The composition* $Y_0 \boxdot Y_1$ *is defined as follows:*

$$Y_0 \boxdot Y_1 = \lambda R. \bigcup \{\, \eta_0 \odot Y_1(R \cup \mathsf{R}(\eta_0)) \mid \eta_0 \in Y_0(R) \,\}$$

where, for all histories η, $\mathsf{R}(\eta) \subseteq \mathsf{Res} \cup \{\downarrow\}$ *is defined inductively as follows:*

$$\mathsf{R}(\varepsilon) = \{\downarrow\} \quad \mathsf{R}(\eta\,\alpha(\rho)) = \begin{cases} \mathsf{R}(\eta) \cup \{r\} & \text{if } \rho = r \text{ and } !\notin \eta \\ \mathsf{R}(\eta) & \text{if } \rho = ? \end{cases} \quad \mathsf{R}(\eta\,!) = \mathsf{R}(\eta) \setminus \{\downarrow\}$$

The denotational semantics $\llbracket H \rrbracket_\theta$ of history expressions (Def. 9) is a function from finite sets of resources to the cpo D_0 of sets X of histories such that (i) $!\in X$, and (ii) $\eta\,!\in X$ whenever $\eta \in X$. The finite set of resources collects those already used, so making them unavailable for future creations. As usual, the parameter θ binds the free variables of H (in our case, to values in D_0). Note that the semantics is prefix-closed, i.e. for each H and R, the histories in $\llbracket H \rrbracket(R)$ comprise all the possible truncated prefixes.

Definition 9. Denotational semantics of history expressions

Let D_0 *be the following cpo of sets of histories ordered by set inclusion:* $D_0 = \{ X \subseteq \mathsf{Ev}^* \cup \mathsf{Ev}^*\,! \mid !\in X \,\wedge\, \forall \eta \in X : \eta\,!\in X \}$. *The set* $\{!\}$ *is the bottom element of* D_0. *Let* $D_{den} = \mathcal{P}_{fin}(\mathsf{Res}) \to D_0$ *be the cpo of functions from the finite subsets of* Res *to* D_0. *Note that the bottom element* $\perp$ *of* D_{den} *is* $\lambda R. \{!\}$. *Let* H *be a history expression such that* $fn(H) = \emptyset$, *and let* θ *be a mapping from variables* h *to functions in* D_{den} *such that* $dom(\theta) \supseteq fv(H)$. *The denotational semantics* $\llbracket H \rrbracket_\theta$ *is a function in* D_{den}, *inductively defined as follows.*

$$\llbracket \varepsilon \rrbracket_\theta = \lambda R. \{!, \varepsilon\} \qquad \llbracket ! \rrbracket_\theta = \perp \qquad \llbracket h \rrbracket_\theta = \theta(h) \qquad \llbracket H \cdot H' \rrbracket_\theta = \llbracket H \rrbracket_\theta \boxdot \llbracket H' \rrbracket_\theta$$

$$\llbracket \nu n. H \rrbracket_\theta = \lambda R. \bigcup_{r \notin R \cup \mathsf{Res}_s} \llbracket H\{r/n\} \rrbracket_\theta (R \cup \{r\}) \qquad \llbracket H + H' \rrbracket_\theta = \llbracket H \rrbracket_\theta \sqcup \llbracket H' \rrbracket_\theta$$

$$\llbracket \alpha(\rho) \rrbracket_\theta = \lambda R. \{!, \alpha(\rho), \alpha(\rho)\,!\} \qquad \llbracket \mu h.H \rrbracket_\theta = \bigsqcup_{i \geq 0} f^i(\perp) \quad f(Z) = \llbracket H \rrbracket_{\theta\{Z/h\}}$$

The first three rules are straightforward. The semantics of $H \cdot H'$ combines the semantics of H and H' with the operator $\boxdot$. The semantics of $\nu n. H$ joins the semantics of H, where the parameter R is updated to record the binding of n with r, for *all* the resources r not yet used in R. The semantics of $H + H'$ is the least upper bound of the semantics of H and H'. The semantics of an event comprises the possible truncations. The semantics of a recursion $\mu h. H$ is the least upper bound of the ω-chain $f^i(\lambda R.\{!\})$, where $f(Z) = \llbracket H \rrbracket_{\theta\{Z/h\}}$.

We first check that the above semantics is well-defined. First, the image of the semantic function is indeed in D_0: it is easy to prove that, for all H, θ and R, $!\in \llbracket H \rrbracket_\theta(R)$ and $\eta\,!\in \llbracket H \rrbracket_\theta(R)$ whenever $\eta \in \llbracket H \rrbracket_\theta(R)$. Lemma B3 [6] guarantees that the least upper bound in the last equation exists (since f is monotone). Also, since f is continuous and $\perp$ is the bottom of the cpo D_{den}, by the Fixed Point theorem the semantics of $\mu h. H$ is the least fixed point of f.

Example 3. Consider the following history expressions:

$$H_0 = \mu h.\, \alpha(r) \cdot h \qquad H_1 = \mu h.\, h \cdot \alpha(r) \qquad H_2 = \mu h.\, \nu n.\, (\varepsilon + \alpha(n) \cdot h)$$

Then, $[\![H_0]\!](\emptyset) = \alpha(r)^*!$, i.e. H_0 generates histories with an arbitrary, finite number of $\alpha(r)$. Note that all the histories of H_0 are non-terminating (as indicated by the !) since there is no way to exit from the recursion. Instead, $[\![H_1]\!](\emptyset) = \{!\}$, i.e. H_1 loops forever, without generating any events. The semantics of $[\![H_2]\!](\emptyset)$ consists of all the histories of the form $\alpha(r_1) \cdots \alpha(r_k)$ or $\alpha(r_1) \cdots \alpha(r_k)!$, for all $k \geq 0$ and pairwise distinct resources r_i.   □

We now define a preorder $H \sqsubseteq H'$ betweeen history expressions, that we shall use in subtyping. Roughly, when $H \sqsubseteq H'$ holds, the histories of H are included in those of H'. The preorder $\sqsubseteq$ includes equivalence, and it is closed under contexts. A history expression H can be arbitrarily "weakened" to $H + H'$. An event $\alpha(\rho)$ can be weakened to $\alpha(?)$, as ? stands for an unknown resource.

Definition 10. Subeffecting

The relation $=$ over history expressions is the least congruence including α-conversion such that the operation $+$ is associative, commutative and idempotent; $\cdot$ is associative, has identity ε, and distributes over $+$, and:

$$\mu h.H = H\{\mu h.\, H/h\} \qquad \mu h.\mu h'.H = \mu h'.\mu h.H \qquad \nu n.\nu n'.H = \nu n'.\nu n.H$$

$$\nu n.\varepsilon = \varepsilon \qquad \nu n.(H + H') = (\nu n.H) + H' \;\; if\; n \notin fn(H')$$

$$\nu n.(H \cdot H') = H \cdot (\nu n.H') \;\; if\; n \notin fn(H) \qquad \nu n.(H \cdot H') = (\nu n.H) \cdot H' \;\; if\; n \notin fn(H')$$

The relation $\sqsubseteq$ over history expressions is the least precongruence such that:

$$H \sqsubseteq H' \;\; if\; H = H' \qquad H \sqsubseteq H + H' \qquad \alpha(\rho) \sqsubseteq \alpha(?)$$

We now formally state that the subeffecting relation agrees with the semantics of history expressions, i.e. it implies trace inclusion. Actually, this turns out to be a weaker notion than set inclusion, because the rule $\alpha(\rho) \sqsubseteq \alpha(?)$ allows for abstracting some resource with a ?. We then render trace inclusion with the preorder $\subseteq_?$ defined below. Intuitively, $\eta \subseteq_? \eta'$ means that η concretizes each unknown resource in η' with some $r \in \mathsf{Res}$.

Definition 11. *The preorder $\subseteq_?$ between histories is inductively defined as:*

$$\varepsilon \subseteq_? \varepsilon \qquad \eta\, \alpha(\rho) \subseteq_? \eta'\, \alpha(\rho') \;\; if\; \eta \subseteq_? \eta'\; and\; \rho' \in \{\rho, ?\} \qquad \eta! \subseteq_? \eta'! \;\; if\; \eta \subseteq_? \eta'$$

The preorder $\subseteq_?$ is extended to sets of histories as follows:

$$I \subseteq_? J \qquad if\; \forall \eta \in I : \exists \eta' \in J : \eta \subseteq_? \eta'$$

The correctness of subeffecting is stated in Lemma 1 below. When $H = H'$ (resp. $H \sqsubseteq H'$), the histories of H are equal to (resp. are $\subseteq_?$ of) those of H'.

Lemma 1. *For all closed history expressions H, H' and for all $R \subseteq \mathsf{Res}$:*

- *if $H = H'$ then $[\![H]\!](R) = [\![H']\!](R)$*
- *if $H \sqsubseteq H'$ then $[\![H]\!](R) \subseteq_? [\![H']\!](R)$.*

4 ν-Types and Type and Effect System

In this section we introduce ν-types, and we use them to define a type and effect system for the calculus of Section 2 (Def. 14). Informally, a term with ν-type $\zeta = \nu N.\,\tau \triangleright H$ will have the *pure type* τ, and the *effect* of its evaluation will be a history included in the denotation of the history expression H. The heading νN is used to bind the names $n \in N$ both in τ and H. Pure types comprise:

- the unit type $\mathbf{1}$, inhabited by the value $*$ (and by $!$).
- sets S, to approximate the possible targets of actions. Sets S either contain resources and (possibly) one name, or we have $S = \{?\}$, meaning that the target object is unknown.
- functional types $\tau \to \zeta$. The type ζ is a ν-type, that may comprise the *latent* effect associated with an abstraction.

Example 4. The term $e = (b)\,?\,r : r'$ has type $\{r, r'\} \triangleright \varepsilon$ (we omit the νN when $N = \emptyset$). The pure type $\{r, r'\}$ means that e evaluates to either r or r', while producing an empty history (denoted by the history expression ε).

The term $e' = \mathbf{new}\ x\ \mathbf{in}\ \alpha(x); x$ creates a new resource r, fires on it the action α, and then evaluates to r. A suitable type for e' is then $\nu n.\,\{n\} \triangleright \alpha(n)$.

The function $g = \lambda_z y.\,\mathbf{new}\ x\ \mathbf{in}\ (\alpha(x); (b)\,?\,x : z\,x)$, instead, has type $\mathbf{1} \to (\{?\} \triangleright \mu h.\,\nu n.\,\alpha(n) \cdot (\varepsilon + h)) \triangleright \varepsilon$. The latent effect $\mu h.\,\nu n.\,\alpha(n) \cdot (\varepsilon + h)$ records that g is a recursive function that creates a fresh resource upon each recursion step. The type $\{?\}$ says that g will return a resource with unknown identity, since it cannot be predicted when the guard b will become true. $\qquad\square$

Type environments are finite mappings from variables and resources to pure types. Roughly, a typing judgment $\Delta \vdash e : \nu N.\,\tau \triangleright H$ means that, in a type environment Δ, the term e evaluates to a value of type $\nu N.\,\tau$, and it produces a history represented by $\nu N.\,H$. Note however that the ν-type $\nu N.\,\tau \triangleright H$ is more precise than taking $\nu N.\,\tau$ and $\nu N.\,H$ separately. Indeed, in the ν-type the names N indicate exactly the *same* fresh resources in both τ and H.

Definition 12. Types, type environments, and typing judgements

$$S ::= R \mid R \cup \{n\} \mid \{?\} \qquad R \subseteq \mathsf{Res}, n \in \mathsf{Nam}, S \neq \emptyset \qquad \textit{resource sets}$$

$$\tau ::= \mathbf{1} \mid S \mid \tau \to \zeta \qquad\qquad\qquad\qquad\qquad\qquad\qquad \textit{pure types}$$

$$\zeta ::= \nu n.\,\zeta \mid \tau \triangleright H \qquad\qquad\qquad\qquad\qquad\qquad\qquad \textit{ν-types}$$

$$\Delta ::= \emptyset \mid \Delta; r : \{r\} \mid \Delta; x : \tau \qquad x \notin dom(\Delta) \qquad \textit{type environments}$$

$$\Delta \vdash e : \zeta \qquad\qquad\qquad\qquad\qquad\qquad\qquad\qquad\qquad \textit{typing judgements}$$

We also introduce the following shorthands (we write $N \not\mathrel{\cap} M$ for $N \cap M = \emptyset$):

$$\nu N.\,\zeta = \nu n_1 \cdots \nu n_k.\,\zeta \qquad \textit{if } N = \{n_1, \ldots n_k\}$$

$$H \cdot \zeta = \nu N.\,\tau \triangleright H \cdot H' \qquad \textit{if } \zeta = \nu N.\,\tau \triangleright H' \textit{ and } N \not\mathrel{\cap} fn(H)$$

We say $\nu N.\,\tau \triangleright H$ is in ν-normal form (abbreviated νNF) when $N \subseteq fn(\tau)$.

We now define the subtyping relation $\sqsubseteq$ on ν-types. It builds over the subeffecting relation between history expressions (Def. 10). The first equation in Def. 13 below is a variant of the usual name extrusion. The first two rules for $\sqsubseteq$ allow for weakening a pure type S to a wider one, or to the pure type $\{?\}$. The last rule extends to ν-types the relations $\sqsubseteq$ over pure types and over effects.

Definition 13. Subtypes

The equational theory of types includes that of history expressions (if $H = H'$ then $\tau \triangleright H = \tau \triangleright H'$), α-conversion of names, and the following equation:

$$\nu n.\,(\tau \triangleright H) = \tau \triangleright (\nu n.\,H) \quad \text{if } n \notin \mathit{fn}(\tau)$$

The relation $\sqsubseteq$ over pure types is the least preorder including $=$ such that:

$$S \sqsubseteq S' \ \text{if } S \subseteq S' \text{ and } S \neq \{?\} \qquad S \sqsubseteq \{?\}$$

$$\nu N.\,\tau \triangleright H \sqsubseteq \nu N.\,\tau' \triangleright H' \quad \text{if } \tau \sqsubseteq \tau' \text{ and } H \sqsubseteq H' \text{ and } (\mathit{fn}(\tau') \setminus \mathit{fn}(\tau)) \cap N$$

Note that the side condition in the last rule above prevents from introducing name captures. For instance, let $\zeta = \nu n.\,\{r\} \triangleright \alpha(n)$ and $\zeta' = \nu n.\,\{r,n\} \triangleright \alpha(n)$. Since $n \in \mathit{fn}(\{r,n\}) \setminus \mathit{fn}(\{r\})$, then $\zeta \not\sqsubseteq \zeta'$. Indeed, by the equational theory:

$$\zeta \ = \ \{r\} \triangleright \nu n.\,\alpha(n) \ = \ \{r\} \triangleright \nu n'.\,\alpha(n')$$

After an α-conversion, the subtyping $\zeta \sqsubseteq \zeta'' = \{r,n\} \triangleright \nu n'.\,\alpha(n')$ holds. Indeed, in ζ'' the name n' upon which α acts has nothing to do with name n in the pure type $\{r,n\}$, while in ζ' both α and the pure type refer to the same name.

Remark 1. Note that it is always possible to rewrite any type $\nu N.\,\tau \triangleright H$ in νNF. To do that, let $\hat{N} = N \cap \mathit{fn}(\tau)$, and let $\check{N} = N \setminus \mathit{fn}(\tau)$. Then, the equational theory of types gives: $\nu N.\,\tau \triangleright H = \nu \hat{N}.\,\tau \triangleright (\nu \check{N}.H)$.

We now state in Lemma 2 a fundamental result about subtyping of ν-types. Roughly, whenever $\zeta \sqsubseteq \zeta'$, it is possible to α-convert the names of ζ so to separately obtain subtyping between the pure types of ζ and ζ', and subeffecting between their effects. Note that Remark 1 above enables us to use Lemma 2 on any pair of types, after rewriting them in νNF.

Lemma 2. *Let $\nu N.\,\tau \triangleright H \sqsubseteq \nu N'.\,\tau' \triangleright H'$, where both types are in νNF.*

- *If $\tau' \neq \{?\}$, then there exists a bijective function $\sigma : N \leftrightarrow N'$ such that $\tau\sigma \sqsubseteq \tau'$ and $H\sigma \sqsubseteq H'$.*
- *If $\tau' = \{?\}$, then $\tau \sqsubseteq \tau'$ and $\nu N.H \sqsubseteq H'$.*

Example 5. Let $\zeta = \nu n.\,\{n\} \triangleright \alpha(n)$, let $\zeta' = \nu n'.\,\{n',r\} \triangleright \alpha(n') + \alpha(r)$, and let $\zeta'' = \{?\} \triangleright \nu n''.\,\alpha(n'') + \alpha(?)$. By using Lemma 2 on $\zeta \sqsubseteq \zeta'$, we obtain $\sigma = \{n'/n\}$ such that $\{n\}\sigma \sqsubseteq \{n',r\}$ and $\alpha(n)\sigma \sqsubseteq \alpha(n') + \alpha(r)$. By Lemma 2 on $\zeta' \sqsubseteq \zeta''$, we find $\{n',r\} \sqsubseteq \{?\}$ and $\nu n'.\,\alpha(n') + \alpha(r) \sqsubseteq \nu n''.\,\alpha(n'') + \alpha(?)$. $\qquad\square$

Definition 14. Type and effect system

$$\text{T-Unit } \Delta \vdash * : \mathbf{1} \rhd \varepsilon \qquad \text{T-Bang } \Delta \vdash \, ! : \zeta \qquad \text{T-Var } \Delta; \xi : \tau \vdash \xi : \tau \rhd \varepsilon$$

$$\text{T-New } \Delta \vdash \mathbf{new} : \nu n. \{n\} \rhd \varepsilon \qquad \text{T-Ev } \Delta; \xi : S \vdash \alpha(\xi) : \mathbf{1} \rhd \sum_{\rho \in S} \alpha(\rho)$$

$$\text{T-AddVar} \frac{\Delta \vdash e : \zeta}{\Delta; \xi : \tau \vdash e : \zeta} \qquad \text{T-Abs} \frac{\Delta; x : \tau; z : \tau \to \zeta \vdash e : \zeta}{\Delta \vdash \lambda_z x.e : (\tau \to \zeta) \rhd \varepsilon}$$

$$\text{T-Wk} \frac{\Delta \vdash e : \zeta}{\Delta \vdash e : \zeta'} \; \zeta \sqsubseteq \zeta' \qquad \text{T-If} \frac{\Delta \vdash e : \zeta \quad \Delta \vdash e' : \zeta}{\Delta \vdash (b) ? e : e' : \zeta}$$

$$\text{T-App} \frac{\Delta \vdash e : \nu N.(\tau \to \zeta) \rhd H \quad \Delta \vdash e' : \nu N'.(\tau \rhd H')}{\Delta \vdash e\, e' : \nu(N \cup N'). (H \cdot H' \cdot \zeta)} \quad \begin{array}{l} N \,\not\!\!\!\cap\, N' \\ N \,\not\!\!\!\cap\, fn(\Delta) \,\not\!\!\!\cap\, N' \\ N \,\not\!\!\!\cap\, fn(H') \end{array}$$

Here we briefly comment on the most peculiar typing rules.

- (T-Bang) An aborted computation can be given any type, modelling the fact that nothing is known about the behaviour of the term that was aborted.
- (T-New) The type of a **new** is a set $\{n\}$, where n is bound by an outer νn, and the actual effect is empty. (We could instead record the resource creation in the effect, by handling **new** as we currently do for $(\lambda x. \alpha_{\text{created}}(x); x)\mathbf{new}$.)
- (T-Ev) An event $\alpha(\xi)$ has type $\mathbf{1}$, provided that the type of ξ is a set S. The effect of $\alpha(\xi)$ can be any of the accesses $\alpha(\rho)$ for ρ included in S.
- (T-Abs) The actual effect of an abstraction is the empty history expression, while the latent effect (included in the type ζ) is equal to the actual effect of the function body. Note that ζ occurs twice in the premise: to unify those occurrences, usually one has to resort to recursive history expressions $\mu h. H$.
- (T-Wk) This rule allows for *weakening* of ν-types, according to Def. 13.
- (T-App) The effects in the rule for application are concatenated according to the evaluation order of the call-by-value semantics (function, argument, latent effect). The side conditions ensure that there is no clash of names. In particular, the disjointness condition makes sure that the names created by the function are never used by the argument.

Example 6. We have the following typing judgements, in the (omitted) empty typing environment (detailed typing derivations can be found in [6]):

$$\vdash e_1 = (b) ? \, \lambda_z x. \alpha \; : \; \lambda_z x. \beta : (\mathbf{1} \to (\mathbf{1} \rhd \alpha + \beta)) \rhd \varepsilon$$

$$\vdash e_2 = \lambda_g x. (b') ? * : g(e_1\, x) : (\mathbf{1} \to (\mathbf{1} \rhd \mu h. \varepsilon + (\alpha + \beta) \cdot h)) \rhd \varepsilon$$

$$\vdash e_3 = \alpha(\mathbf{new}\; x\; \mathbf{in}\; (b) ? \, x : r) : \mathbf{1} \rhd \nu n. (\alpha(n) + \alpha(r))$$

$$\vdash e_4 = \mathbf{let}\; f = (\lambda x. \, \mathbf{new}\; y\; \mathbf{in}\; \alpha(y); y)\; \mathbf{in}\; \beta(f*; f*)$$
$$\qquad : \mathbf{1} \rhd (\nu n. \, \alpha(n)) \cdot (\nu n'. \, \alpha(n') \cdot \beta(n'))$$

$$\vdash e_5 = \mathbf{let}\; g = (\mathbf{new}\; y\; \mathbf{in}\; \lambda x. \, \alpha(y); y)\; \mathbf{in}\; \beta(g*; g*) : \mathbf{1} \rhd \nu n. \, \alpha(n) \cdot \alpha(n) \cdot \beta(n)$$

$$\vdash e_6 = (\lambda_z x. \, \mathbf{new}\; y\; \mathbf{in}\; (b) ? \, \alpha(y) : \beta(y); zx) * : \mathbf{1} \rhd \mu h. \, \nu n. (\alpha(n) + \beta(n) \cdot h)$$

$$\vdash e_7 = \alpha((\lambda_z x. \, \mathbf{new}\; y\; \mathbf{in}\; (b) ? \, y : \beta(y); zx) *) : \mathbf{1} \rhd (\mu h. \, \nu n. (\varepsilon + \beta(n) \cdot h)) \cdot \alpha(?)$$

The effects of e_4 and e_5 correctly represent the fact that two distinct resources are generated by e_4, while the evaluation of e_5 creates a single fresh resource. The effect of e_6 is a recursion, at each step of which a fresh resource is generated. The effect of e_7 is more peculiar: it behaves similarly to e_6 until the recursion is left, when the last generated resource is exported. Since its identity is lost, the event α is fired on the unknown resource "?". $\square$

The following lemma relates the histories denoted by a context C with the typing of any term of the form $C[v]$. More precisely, the histories of C are included (modulo concretization of ?) in those denoted by the effect in the ν-type. Since the big-step semantics of terms produces both a value v and a context C, this result will be pivotal in proving the correctness of our type and effect system.

Lemma 3. *For all closed history contexts C, values v, and sets of resources R:*

$$\Delta \vdash C[v] : \nu N.\tau \triangleright H \implies \mathcal{H}(C,R) \subseteq_? [\![\nu N.H]\!](R)$$

We now establish a fundamental result about typing, upon which the proof of the Subject Reduction lemma is based. Roughly, given a history context C and a term e, it allows for constructing a type for $C[e]$ from a type for e, and *viceversa*. The information needed to extend/reduce a type is contained in $\mathcal{T}(C,\Delta)$, that extracts from C a set of binders, a history expression, and a type environment.

Definition 15. *For all C and Δ, we inductively define $\mathcal{T}(C,\Delta)$ as follows:*

$$\mathcal{T}(\bullet,\Delta) = (\varepsilon,\emptyset)$$

$$\mathcal{T}(\alpha(\xi);C',\Delta) = (\textstyle\sum_{\rho\in\Delta(\xi)} \alpha(\rho)\cdot H', \Delta') \text{ if } \mathcal{T}(C',\Delta) = (H',\Delta')$$

$\mathcal{T}(\mathbf{new}\ x\ \mathbf{in}\ C',\Delta) = (\nu n.H',\Delta'; x:\{n\}) \text{ if } \mathcal{T}(C',\Delta;x:\{n\}) = (H',\Delta'), n\notin\Delta$

Hereafter, when writing $\mathcal{T}(C,\Delta) = (\nu N.H,\Delta')$ we always assume $N = \mathit{fn}(\Delta')$. This is always possible by the equational theory of history expressions (Def. 10).

Lemma 4. *Let $\mathcal{T}(C,\Delta) = (\nu N.H,\Delta')$. Then, for all terms e:*

- $\Delta;\Delta' \vdash e : \zeta' \implies \Delta \vdash C[e] : \nu N.H\cdot\zeta'$
- $\Delta \vdash C[e] : \zeta \implies \exists\zeta' : \Delta;\Delta' \vdash e : \zeta'$ *and* $\nu N.H\cdot\zeta' \sqsubseteq \zeta$

We state below the Subject Reduction Lemma, crucial for proving our type and effect system correct. We state it in the traditional form where the type is preserved under computations. This was made possible by the big-step semantics of terms, where all the information about the generated histories is kept in a history context. Note instead this were not the case for a small-step operational semantics, like the one in [3], where histories grow along with computations. This would require Subject Reduction to "consume" the target type, to render the events fired, and the resources created, in execution steps. Not preserving the type would make the inductive statement harder to to write and to prove.

Lemma 5 (Subject Reduction). *If $\Delta \vdash e : \zeta$ and $e \overset{C}{\Longrightarrow} v$, then $\Delta \vdash C[v] : \zeta$.*

Theorem 1 below guarantees that our type and effect system correctly approximates the dynamic semantics, i.e. the effect of a term e represents all the possible run-time histories of e. As usual, precision is lost with conditionals and with recursive functions. Also, you may lose the identity of names exported by recursive functions (see e.g. the type of e_7 in Ex. 6).

Theorem 1 (Correctness of effects). *For all closed terms e:*

$$\Delta \vdash e : \nu N. \tau \rhd H \implies \mathcal{H}(e) \subseteq_? [\![\nu N. H]\!](\emptyset)$$

Proof. By Def. 5, $\mathcal{H}(e) = \bigcup_{e \xRightarrow{C} v} \mathcal{H}(C, \emptyset)$. Let C and v be such that $e \xRightarrow{C} v$. By Lemma 5, $\Delta \vdash C[v] : \nu N. \tau \rhd H$. By Lemma 3, $\mathcal{H}(C, \emptyset) \subseteq_? [\![\nu N. H]\!](\emptyset)$. Therefore, $\mathcal{H}(e) \subseteq_? [\![\nu N. H]\!](\emptyset)$. □

5   Conclusions

We studied how to correctly and precisely record creation and use of resources in a type and effect system for an extended λ-calculus. To do that, we used the ν-quantifier for denoting freshness in types and effects. The main technical result is Theorem 1, which guarantees the type of a program correctly approximates its run-time histories. This enables us to exploit the model-checking technique of [2] to verify history-based usage policies of higher-order programs.

Future Work. To improve the accuracy of types, we plan to relax the constraint that a single name can appear in pure types S. For instance, consider the term:

$$e = \textbf{new } x \textbf{ in new } y \textbf{ in } (\beta(x); \beta(y); (b) ? x : y))$$

Currently, we have the judgements $\vdash e : \{?\} \rhd \nu n. \nu n'. \beta(n) \cdot \beta(n')$, and thus $\vdash \alpha(e) : \mathbf{1} \rhd \nu n. \nu n'. \beta(n) \cdot \beta(n') \cdot \alpha(?)$ whereas by relaxing the single-name assumption on pure types S, we would have the more precise judgements $\vdash e : \nu\{n, n'\}. \{n, n'\} \rhd \beta(n) \cdot \beta(n')$ and $\vdash \alpha(e) : \mathbf{1} \rhd \nu n. \nu n'. \beta(n) \cdot \beta(n') \cdot (\alpha(n) + \alpha(n'))$.

A further improvement would come from allowing subtyping of functional types, e.g. by extending Def. 13 with the rule $\tau \to \zeta \sqsubseteq \tau' \to \zeta'$ if $\tau' \sqsubseteq \tau$ and $\zeta \sqsubseteq \zeta'$ (i.e. contravariant in the argument and covariant in the result). Let e.g. $f = \lambda x. ((b) ? \lambda. \alpha : x); x$. With the current definition, we have $\vdash f (\lambda. \beta) : (\mathbf{1} \to (\mathbf{1} \rhd \alpha + \beta)) \rhd \varepsilon$. Note that the function $\lambda. \alpha$ is discarded, and so we would like to have instead $\vdash f (\lambda. \beta) : (\mathbf{1} \to (\mathbf{1} \rhd \beta)) \rhd \varepsilon$, which is more accurate. Subtyping of functional types would allow for such a judgement, using the weakening $\mathbf{1} \to (\mathbf{1} \rhd \beta) \sqsubseteq \mathbf{1} \to (\mathbf{1} \rhd \alpha + \beta)$ within the typing judgement of f.

The above constraints have been introduced in our model in order to simplify the proofs, only (for instance, the restriction about the number of names in set types helps in the proof of Lemma B20 [6]). Even when exploiting these constraints, the technical burden in our proofs is still quite heavy: yet, we conjecture that these restrictions could be lifted without invalidating our main results.

We plan to develop a type and effect inference algorithm, taking [19] as a starting point. The subtype relation of [19] enjoys some nice properties, e.g. principal types, which we expect to maintain in our setting. The main difference is that, while [19] constructs and resolves separately type constraints and effect constraints, ours demands for dealing with subtyping constraints between whole ν-types. The key issue is unifying α-convertible terms, which we expect to manage by exploiting nominal unification [21].

Acknowledgements. This work has been partially supported by EU-FETPI Global Computing Project IST-2005-16004 SENSORIA (Software Engineering for Service-Oriented Overlay Computers) and by the MIUR-PRIN project SOFT (Tecniche Formali Orientate alla Sicurezza).

References

1. Bartoletti, M., Degano, P., Ferrari, G.L.: History based access control with local policies. In: Sassone, V. (ed.) FOSSACS 2005. LNCS, vol. 3441, pp. 316–332. Springer, Heidelberg (2005)
2. Bartoletti, M., Degano, P., Ferrari, G.L., Zunino, R.: Local policies for resource usage analysis. To appear in ACM Tran. Progr. Lang. and Sys.
3. Bartoletti, M., Degano, P., Ferrari, G.L., Zunino, R.: Types and effects for resource usage analysis. In: Seidl, H. (ed.) FOSSACS 2007. LNCS, vol. 4423, pp. 32–47. Springer, Heidelberg (2007)
4. Bartoletti, M., Degano, P., Ferrari, G.L., Zunino, R.: Hard life with weak binders. In: Proc. EXPRESS (2008)
5. Bartoletti, M., Degano, P., Ferrari, G.L., Zunino, R.: Model checking usage policies. In: Proc. Trustworthy Global Computing (2008)
6. Bartoletti, M., Degano, P., Ferrari, G.L., Zunino, R.: ν-types for effects and freshness analysis. Technical Report DISI-09-033, DISI - Università degli Studi di Trento (2009)
7. Bergstra, J.A., Klop, J.W.: Algebra of communicating processes with abstraction. Theoretical Computer Science 37 (1985)
8. Bradfield, J.: On the expressivity of the modal μ-calculus. In: Puech, C., Reischuk, R. (eds.) STACS 1996. LNCS, vol. 1046. Springer, Heidelberg (1996)
9. Chaki, S., Rajamani, S.K., Rehof, J.: Types as models: model checking message-passing programs. In: Proc. POPL (2002)
10. Esparza, J.: On the decidability of model checking for several μ-calculi and Petri nets. In: Tison, S. (ed.) CAAP 1994. LNCS, vol. 787. Springer, Heidelberg (1994)
11. Honda, K., Yoshida, N., Carbone, M.: Multiparty asynchronous session types. In: Proc. POPL (2008)
12. Igarashi, A., Kobayashi, N.: Resource usage analysis. In: Proc. POPL (2002)
13. Igarashi, A., Kobayashi, N.: A generic type system for the pi-calculus. Theoretical Computer Science 311(1-3) (2004)
14. Milner, R., Parrow, J., Walker, D.: A Calculus of Mobile Processes, I and II. Information and Computation 100(1) (September 1992)
15. Nielson, H.R., Nielson, F.: Higher-order concurrent programs with finite communication topology. In: Proc. POPL (1994)
16. Odersky, M.: A functional theory of local names. In: Proc. POPL (1994)
17. Shinwell, M.R., Pitts, A.M., Gabbay, M.: FreshML: programming with binders made simple. In: Proc. ICFP (2003)
18. Skalka, C., Smith, S.: History effects and verification. In: Chin, W.-N. (ed.) APLAS 2004. LNCS, vol. 3302, pp. 107–128. Springer, Heidelberg (2004)
19. Skalka, C., Smith, S., Horn, D.V.: Types and trace effects of higher order programs. Journal of Functional Programming 18(2) (2008)
20. Talpin, J.-P., Jouvelot, P.: Polymorphic type, region and effect inference. Journal of Functional Programming 2(3) (1992)
21. Urban, C., Pitts, A.M., Gabbay, M.: Nominal unification. Theoretical Compututer Science 323(1-3) (2004)

A First-Order Policy Language for History-Based Transaction Monitoring

Andreas Bauer, Rajeev Goré, and Alwen Tiu

Logic and Computation Group
College of Engineering and Computer Science
The Australian National University

Abstract. Online trading invariably involves dealings between strangers, so it is important for one party to be able to judge objectively the trustworthiness of the other. In such a setting, the decision to trust a user may sensibly be based on that user's past behaviour. We introduce a specification language based on linear temporal logic for expressing a *policy* for categorising the behaviour patterns of a user depending on its transaction history. We also present an algorithm for checking whether the transaction history obeys the stated policy. To be useful in a real setting, such a language should allow one to express realistic policies which may involve parameter quantification and quantitative or statistical patterns. We introduce several extensions of linear temporal logic to cater for such needs: a restricted form of universal and existential quantification; arbitrary computable functions and relations in the term language; and a "counting" quantifier for counting how many times a formula holds in the past. We then show that model checking a transaction history against a policy, which we call the history-based transaction monitoring problem, is PSPACE-complete in the size of the policy formula and the length of the history, assuming that the underlying interpreted functions and relations are polynomially computable. The problem becomes decidable in polynomial time when the policies are fixed. We also consider the problem of transaction monitoring in the case where not all the parameters of actions are observable. We formulate two such "partial observability" monitoring problems, and show their decidability under certain restrictions.

1 Introduction

Internet mediated trading is now a common way of exchanging goods and services between parties who may not have engaged in transactions with each other before. The decision of a seller/buyer to engage in a transaction is usually based on the "reputation" of the other party, which is often provided via the online trading system itself. These so-called *reputation systems* can take the form of numerical ratings, which can be computed based on feedback from users (cf. [11] for a survey of reputation systems). While many reputation systems used in practice seem to serve their purposes, they are not without problems (cf. [11]) and can be too simplistic in some cases. For example, in eBay.com, the rating

M. Leucker and C. Morgan (Eds.): ICTAC 2009, LNCS 5684, pp. 96–111, 2009.
© Springer-Verlag Berlin Heidelberg 2009

of a seller/buyer consists of two components: the number of positive feedbacks she gets, and the number of negative feedbacks. A seller with, say 90 positive feedbacks and 1 negative feedback may be considered trustworthy by some. But one may want to correlate a feedback with the monetary value of the transaction by checking if the one negative feedback was for a very expensive item, or one may want to check other more general relations between different parameters of past transactions.

Here, we consider an alternative (and complementary) method to describe the reputation of a seller/buyer, by specifying explicitly what constitutes a "good" and a "bad" seller/buyer based on the observed patterns of past transactions. More specifically, we introduce a formal language based on linear temporal logic for encoding the desired patterns of behaviours, and a mechanism for checking these patterns against a concrete history of transactions. The latter is often referred to as the *monitoring problem* since the behaviour of users is being monitored, but here, it is just a specific instance of model checking for temporal logic. The patterns of behaviours, described in the logical language, serve as a concise description of the policies for the user on whether to engage with a particular seller/buyer. The approach we follow here is essentially an instance of *history-based access control* (see e.g., [2,4,8,9,10,13]). More precisely, our work is closely related to that of Krukow et al. [13,14].

There are two main ideas underlying the design of our language:

- *Transactions vs. individual actions:* Following Krukow et al., we are mainly interested in expressing properties about transactions seen as a logically connected grouping of actions, for example because they represent a run of a protocol. A history in our setting is a list of such transactions, in contrast to the more traditional notion of history as a list of individual actions (i.e., a trace), e.g., as in [8,10], which is common in monitoring program execution.
- *Closed world assumption:* The main idea underlying the design of our quantified policies is that a policy should only express properties of objects which are observed in the history. For example, in monitoring a typical online transaction, it makes sense to talk about properties that involve "all the payments that have been made". Thus, if we consider a formalisation of events using predicates, where $pay(100)$ denotes the payment of 100 dollars (say), then we can specify a policy like the one below left which states that all payments must obey ψ:

$$\forall x. \ pay(x) \rightarrow \psi(x) \qquad\qquad \forall x. \ \neg pay(x) \rightarrow \psi(x)$$

However, it makes less sense to talk about "for all dollar amounts that a seller did not pay", like the policy above right, since this involves infinitely many possibility (e.g., the seller paid 100, but did not pay 110, did not pay 111, etc.). We therefore restrict our quantification in policies to have a "positive guard", guaranteeing that we always quantify over the finitely many values that have already been observed in the history.

An important consequence of the closed world assumption is that we can only describe relations between known individual objects. Thus we can enrich our logical language with computable functions over these objects and computable relations between these objects without losing decidability of the model checking problem. One such useful extension is arithmetic, which allows one to describe constraints on various quantities and values of transactions.

Our base language for describing policies is the pure past fragment of linear temporal logic [16] since it has been used quite extensively by others [4,10,13,17] for similar purposes. However, the following points distinguish our work from related work in the literature, within the context of history-based access control:

– We believe our work is the first to incorporate both quantified policies and computable functions/relations within the same logic. Combining unrestricted quantifiers with arbitrary computable functions easily leads to undecidability (see Section 7).
– We extend temporal logic with a "counting quantifier", which counts how many times a policy has been satisfied in the past. A similar counting mechanism was proposed in [13,14] as a part of a meta-policy language. But in our work, it is a part of the same logic.
– We consider new monitoring problems based on a notion of *partial observability* which seem to arise quite naturally in online trading platforms where a user (or a system provider) cannot directly observe all parameters of an action. For instance, in eBay, it may not be always possible to observe whether payments have been made, or it may be possible to observe a payment but not the exact amount paid. We model unobservable parameters in an action as variables representing unknown values. Given a policy and a history containing unknown parameters, we ask whether the policy is satisfied under some substitution of the variables (the *potential satisfiability problem*), or under *all* substitutions (the *adherence problem*).

The rest of the paper is organised as follows. Section 2 introduces our policy language $PTLTL^{FO}$, for "past time linear temporal logic with first-order (guarded) quantifiers", and defines its semantics. Section 3 presents some examples using $PTLTL^{FO}$ for specifying access control policies, which include formalisations of known security policies. Section 4 considers the model checking problem for $PTLTL^{FO}$ which we show to be PSPACE-complete. Fixing the policies reduces the complexity to PTIME. Section 5 presents an extension of $PTLTL^{FO}$ with a counting quantifier allowing us to express that a policy depends on the number of times another policy was satisfied in the past. The model checking problem for this extension remains PSPACE-complete. In Section 6, we consider more general (undecidable) monitoring problems where not all the parameters of an action can be observed. By restricting the class of allowed functions and relations, we can obtain decidability of both the potential satisfiability and adherence problems, for example, when the term language of the logic is restricted to linear arithmetic. Section 7 discusses possible decidable extensions to the guarded quantifiers. Section 8 concludes the paper and discusses related work.

Due to space limit, detailed proofs are omitted, but they can be found in a technical report [3].

2 The Policy Language: Definitions and Notation

Since we are interested in the notion of history-based access control, our definition of history is similar of that of [14]. A history is organised as a list of sessions. Each session is a finite set of events, or actions. Each event is represented by a predicate. A session represents a "world" in the sense of a Kripke semantics where the underlying frame is linear and discrete.

The term structures of our policy language are made up of variables and interpreted multi-sorted function symbols. Function symbols of zero arity are called *constants*. Terms are ranged over by s, t, u. Variables of the language, denoted by x, y, z, range over certain domains, such as strings, integers, or other finite domains. We call these domains *base types* or simply *types*. We assume a distinguished type *prop* which denotes the set of propositions of the logic, and which must not be used in the types of the function symbols and variables. That is, we do not allow logical formulae to appear at the term level. Function symbols and variables are typed.

We assume an interpretation where distinct constants of the same type map to distinct elements of the type. We shall use the same symbol, say a, to refer both to an element of some type τ and the constant representing this element. Function symbols of one or more arities admit a fixed interpretation, which can be any total recursive function. We shall assume the usual function symbols for arithmetic, $+, -, \times$, etc., with the standard interpretations. The language we are about to define is open to additional interpreted function symbols, e.g., string related operations, etc. We shall use f, g, h to range over function symbols of arity one or more, and a, b, c, d to range over constants. We also assume a set of interpreted relations, in particular, those for arithmetic, e.g., $<, =, \geq$, etc. These interpreted relations are ranged over by R. All the interpreted functions and relations have first-order types, i.e., their types are of the form $\tau_1 \times \cdots \times \tau_n \rightarrow \tau$, where τ and $\tau_1, \ldots, \tau_n$ are base types. We shall restrict to computable relations R. Of course, there is also the (rigidity) assumption that the function f, constant c and relation R have the same fixed interpretation over all worlds.

Since our term language contains interpreted symbols, we assume that there is a procedure for evaluating terms into values. We also assume that each term can be evaluated to a unique value. Given a term t, we shall denote with $t \downarrow$ the unique value denoted by this term, e.g., if $t = (2+3)$ then $t \downarrow = 5$. Given an atomic formula $p(t_1, \ldots, t_n)$, we shall write $p(t_1, \ldots, t_n) \downarrow$ to denote $p(t_1 \downarrow, \ldots, t_n \downarrow)$. The policy language is given by the following grammar:

$$\psi ::= p(t_1, \ldots, t_m) \mid R(t_1, \ldots, t_n) \mid \psi \wedge \psi \mid \neg \psi$$
$$\mid \mathbf{X}^{-1} \psi \mid \psi \, \mathbf{S} \, \psi \mid \forall (x_1, \ldots, x_n) : p. \; \psi,$$

where $\mathbf{X}^{-1}$ is referred to as the "previously"-operator, and $\mathbf{S}$ as the "since"-operator. In the quantified formula $\forall (x_1, \ldots, x_n) : p. \; \psi$, where $n \geq 1$, the symbol p is an n-ary predicate of type $\tau_1 \times \cdots \times \tau_n \rightarrow prop$, and each x_i is of type τ_i. The intended interpretation of this quantification is that the predicate p defines a subtype of $\tau_1 \times \cdots \times \tau_n$, which is determined by the occurrence of p in the world (session) in which the formula resides. For example,

$(h, i) \models p(t_1, \ldots, t_n)$ iff $p(t_1 \downarrow, \ldots, t_n \downarrow) \in h_i$

$(h, i) \models R(t_1, \ldots, t_n)$ iff $R(t_1 \downarrow, \ldots, t_n \downarrow)$ is true

$(h, i) \models \psi_1 \wedge \psi_2$ iff $(h, i) \models \psi_1$ and $(h, i) \models \psi_2$

$(h, i) \models \neg \psi$ iff $(h, i) \not\models \psi$

$(h, i) \models \mathbf{X}^{-1} \psi$ iff $i > 1$ and $(h, i - 1) \models \psi$

$(h, i) \models \psi_1 \mathbf{S} \psi_2$ iff there exists $j \leq i$ such that $(h, j) \models \psi_2$ and
for all k, if $j < k \leq i$ then $(h, k) \models \psi_1$

$(h, i) \models \forall(x_1, \ldots, x_n) : p. \ \psi$ iff for all $c_1, \ldots, c_n$, if $p(c_1, \ldots, c_n) \in h_i$
then $(h, i) \models \psi[x_1 := c_1, \ldots, x_n := c_n]$.

Fig. 1. Semantics of $PTLTL^{FO}$

in a world consisting of $\{p(1,1), p(1,2), p(1,3), q(4)\}$ the predicate p represents the set $\{(1,1), (1,2), (1,3)\}$, i.e., a subset of $N \times N$. We shall often abbreviate $\forall(x_1, \ldots, x_n) : p. \ \psi$ as simply $\forall \vec{x} : p. \ \psi$ when the exact arity and the information about each x_i is not important or can be inferred from context. The notions of free and bound variables are defined as usual. A formula is *closed* if it has no occurrences of free variables.

Definition 1. *An* event *(or an* action*) is a predicate* $p(c_1, \ldots, c_n)$ *where each* c_i *is a constant and* p *is an uninterpreted predicate symbol. A* session *is a finite set of events. A* history *is a finite list of sessions.*

A standard definition for the semantics of first-order logic uses a mapping of free variables in a formula to elements of the types of the variables. To simplify the semantics, we shall consider only closed formulae. The semantics for quantified statements is then defined by closing these statements under variable mappings. We use the notation σ and θ to range over partial maps from variables to elements of types. We usually enumerate them as, e.g., $[x_1 := a_1, \ldots, x_n := a_n]$. Since we identify a constant with the element represented by that constant, a variable mapping is both a semantic and a syntactic concept. The latter means that we can view a variable mapping as a substitution. Given a formula ψ and variable mapping σ, we write $\psi\sigma$ to denote a formula resulting from replacing each free variable x in ψ with the constant $\sigma(x)$. From now on, we shall use the term variable mapping and substitution interchangeably.

We shall be concerned with judgements of the form $(h, i) \models \psi$, where h is a history, i is an index referring to the i-th session in h, and ψ is a closed formula. The judgement reads "ψ is true at the i-th world in the history h". We denote with $|h|$ the length of h, and with h_i the i-th element of h when $i \leq |h|$.

Definition 2. *The* forcing relation $(h, i) \models \psi$, *where* h *is a history,* i *an integer, and* ψ *a formula, is defined inductively as shown in Figure 1 where* $1 \leq i \leq |h|$. *We denote with* $h \models \psi$ *the relation* $(h, |h|) \models \psi$. *The boolean connectives* $\vee$ *(disjunction) and* $\rightarrow$ *(implication) are defined in the standard way using negation and conjunction. We derive the operators* $\mathbf{F}^{-1} \varphi \equiv \top \mathbf{S} \varphi$ *("sometime in the* *past"), and* $\mathbf{G}^{-1}\varphi \equiv \neg\mathbf{F}^{-1}(\neg\varphi)$ *("always in the past"), where* $\top$ *("true") is short for* $p \vee \neg p$.

Note that allowing unrestricted quantifiers can cause model checking to become undecidable, depending on the interpreted functions and relations. For example, if we allow arbitrary arithmetic expressions in the term language, then we can express solvability of Diophantine equations, which is undecidable [15].

3 Some Example Policies

Let us now examine some example policies known from the literature, and our means of expressing them concisely and accurately. We also examine some policies from applications other than monitoring users in online trading systems to demonstrate that our language can model the requirements of other related domains as well if they can be expressed as trace-based properties.

One-out-of-k policy. The *one-out-of-k policy* as described in [8] concerns the monitoring of web-based applications. More specifically, it concerns monitoring three specific situations: connection to a remote site, opening local files, and creating subprocesses. We model this as follows, with the set of events being

open(file, mode): request to open the file *file* in mode, *mode*, where *file* is a
 string containing the absolute path, and *mode* can be either ro (for read-
 only) or rw (for read-write). There can be other modes but for simplicity we
 assume just these two;
read/write/create(file): request to read/write/create a file;
connect: request to open a socket (to a site which is irrelevant for now);
subproc: request to create a subprocess.

We assume some operators for string manipulation: the function *path(file)* which returns the absolute path to the directory in which the file resides, and the equality predicate = on strings. The history in this setting is one in which every session is a singleton set. Consider one of the policies as described in [8]: allow a program to open local files in user-specified directories for modifications only if it has created them, and it has neither tried to connect to a remote site nor tried to create a sub-process. Suppose that we allow only one user-specified directory called "Document". Then this policy can be expressed as:

$$\forall(x, m) : open.m = \text{rw} \rightarrow [\, path(x) = \text{``Document''} \wedge \mathbf{F}^{-1} create(x) \wedge$$
$$\neg\mathbf{F}^{-1} connect \wedge \neg\mathbf{F}^{-1} subproc].$$

Chinese wall policy. The Chinese wall policy [6] is a common access control policy used in financial markets for managing conflicts of interests. In this setting, each object for which access is requested, is classified as belonging to a *company dataset*, which in turn belongs to a *conflict of interest class*. The idea is that a user (or subject) that accessed an object that belonged to a company A in the past will not be allowed to access another object that belongs to a company B which is in the same conflict of interest class as A.

To model this policy, we assume the following finite sets: U for users, O for objects, D for company datasets, and C for the names of the conflict of interest class. The event we shall be concerned with is access of an object o by a user u. We shall assume that this event carries information about the company dataset to which the object belongs, and the name of the conflict of interest class to which the company dataset belongs. That is, *access* is of type $U \times O \times D \times C \to prop$. A history in this case is a sequence of singletons containing the *access* event. The policy, as given in [6], specifies among others that

> "access is only granted if the object requested: 1.) is in the same company dataset as an object already accessed by that subject, or 2.) belongs to an entirely different conflict of interest class."

Implicit in this description is that first access (i.e., no prior history) is always allowed. We can model the case where no prior history exists simply using the formula $\neg \mathbf{X}^{-1} \top$. This policy can be expressed in our language as follows:

$$\forall(u, o, d, c) : access. \neg \mathbf{X}^{-1} \top \vee$$
$$(\mathbf{X}^{-1} \mathbf{F}^{-1} \exists(u', o', d', c') : access. u = u' \wedge d = d') \vee$$
$$(\mathbf{X}^{-1} \mathbf{G}^{-1} \forall(u', o', d', c') : access. u = u' \to \neg(c = c')).$$

eBay.com. Consider a scenario where a potential buyer wants to engage in a bidding process on an online trading system like eBay.com, but the buyer wants to impose some criteria on what kind of sellers she trusts. A simple policy would be something like "only deal with a seller who was never late in delivery of items". In this model, a session in a history represents a complete exchange between buyer and seller, e.g., the bidding process, winning the bid, payment, confirmation of payment, delivery of items, confirmation of delivery, and the feedbacks. We consider the following events (in the history of a seller):

$win(X, V)$: the bidder won the bid for item X for value V.
$pay(T, X, V)$: payment of item X at date T of the sum V (numerical value of dollars).
$post(X, T)$: the item X is delivered within T days[1].
negative, neutral, positive: represents negative, neutral and positive feedbacks.

There are other actions and parameters that we can formalise, but these are sufficient for an illustration. Now, suppose the buyer sets a criterion such that a posting delay greater than 10 days after payment is unacceptable. This can be expressed as:

$$\mathbf{G}^{-1} [\forall(t, x, v) : pay. \exists(y, t') : post. x = y \wedge t' \leq 10]. \tag{1}$$

Of course, for such a simple purpose, one use eBay's rating system, which computes the number of feedbacks in each category (positive, neutral and negative). However, the seller's rating may sometimes be too coarse a description of a

---

[1] Note that on actual eBay, no concrete number of days is given, but instead buyers can rate the time for posting and handling in the feedback forums in a range of 1–5.

seller's reputation. For instance, one is probably willing to trust a seller with some negative feedbacks, as long as those feedbacks refer to transactions involving only small values. A buyer can specify that she would trust a seller who never received negative feedbacks for transactions above a certain value, say, 200 dollars. This can be specified as follows: $\mathbf{G}^{-1} [\forall(t, x, v) : pay.\ v \geq 200 \rightarrow \neg negative]$.

4   Model Checking $PTLTL^{FO}$

We now consider the model checking problem for $PTLTL^{FO}$, i.e., deciding whether $h \models \varphi$ holds. We show that the problem is PSPACE-complete, even in the case where no interpreted functions or relations occur in the formula.

We prove the complexity of our model checking problem via a terminating recursive algorithm. The algorithm is presented abstractly via a set of rules which successively transform a triple $\langle h, i, \varphi \rangle$ of a history, an index and a formula, and return a truth value of either $\mathbf{t}$ or $\mathbf{f}$ to indicate that $(h, i) \models \varphi$ (resp. $(h, i) \not\models \varphi$). We write $\langle h, i, \varphi \rangle \Downarrow v$ to denote this relation and overload the logical connectives $\wedge$, $\vee$ and $\neg$ to denote operations on boolean values, e.g., $\mathbf{t} \wedge \mathbf{t} = \mathbf{t}$, etc. Since $\psi_1 \mathbf{S} \psi_2 \equiv \psi_2 \vee (\psi_1 \wedge \mathbf{X}^{-1} (\psi_1 \mathbf{S} \psi_2))$, we shall use the following semantic clause for $\psi_1 \mathbf{S} \psi_2$ which is equivalent: $(h, i) \models \psi_1 \mathbf{S} \psi_2$ if and only if

$$(h, i) \models \psi_2 \text{ or } [(h, i) \models \psi_1 \text{ and } i > 1 \text{ and } (h, i - 1) \models \psi_1 \mathbf{S} \psi_2].$$

The rules for the evaluation judgement are given in Figure 2. To evaluate the truth value of $\langle h, i, \varphi \rangle$, we start with the judgement $\langle h, i, \varphi \rangle \Downarrow v$ where v is still unknown. We then successively apply the transformation rules bottom up, according to the main connective of φ and the index i. Each transformation step will create n-child nodes with n unknown values. Only at the base case (i.e., id, R, or $\mathbf{X}^{-1}$) the value of v is explicitly computed and passed back to the parent nodes. A run of this algorithm can be presented as a tree whose nodes are the evaluation judgements which are related by the transformation rules. A straightforward simultaneous induction on the derivation trees yields:

Lemma 1. *The judgement $\langle h, i, \varphi \rangle \Downarrow \mathbf{t}$ is derivable if and only if $(h, i) \models \varphi$ and the judgement $\langle h, i, \varphi \rangle \Downarrow \mathbf{f}$ is derivable if and only if $(h, i) \not\models \varphi$.*

Theorem 1. *Let φ be a $PTLTL^{FO}$ formula and h a history. If the interpreted functions and relations in φ are in PSPACE, then deciding whether $h \models \varphi$ holds is PSPACE-complete.*

Although the model checking problem is PSPACE-complete, in practice, one often has a fixed policy formula which is evaluated against different histories. Then, it makes sense to ask about the complexity of the model checking problem with respect to the size of histories only (while restricting ourselves to interpreted functions and relations computable in polynomial time).

Theorem 2. *The decision problem for $h \models \varphi$, where φ is fixed, is solvable in polynomial time.*

$$(id) \quad \frac{\text{if } p(\vec{t})\downarrow \in h_i \text{ then } v := \mathbf{t} \text{ else } v := \mathbf{f}}{\langle h, i, p(\vec{t})\rangle \Downarrow v} \qquad (R) \quad \frac{\text{if } R(\vec{t})\downarrow \text{ is true then } v := \mathbf{t} \text{ else } v := \mathbf{f}}{\langle h, i, R(\vec{t})\rangle \Downarrow v}$$

$$(\neg) \quad \frac{\langle h, i, \psi\rangle \Downarrow v}{\langle h, i, \neg\psi\rangle \Downarrow \neg v} \qquad\qquad (\wedge) \quad \frac{\langle h, i, \psi_1\rangle \Downarrow v_1 \quad \langle h, i, \psi_2\rangle \Downarrow v_2}{\langle h, i, \psi_1 \wedge \psi_2\rangle \Downarrow v_1 \wedge v_2}$$

$$(\forall) \quad \frac{\langle h, i, \varphi(\vec{t_1})\rangle \Downarrow v_1 \quad \cdots \quad \langle h, i, \varphi(\vec{t_n})\rangle \Downarrow v_n}{\langle h, i, \forall \vec{x} : p.\varphi(\vec{x})\rangle \Downarrow \bigwedge_{i=1}^{n} v_i}$$
$$\text{where } \{\varphi(\vec{t_1}), \cdots, \varphi(\vec{t_n})\} = \{\varphi(\vec{x}) \mid p(\vec{x}) \in h_i\}$$

$$(\mathbf{S}) \quad \frac{\langle h, i, \psi_1\rangle \Downarrow v_1 \quad \langle h, i, \psi_2\rangle \Downarrow v_2 \quad \langle h, i-1, \psi_1 \mathbf{S} \psi_2\rangle \Downarrow v_3}{\langle h, i, \psi_1 \mathbf{S} \psi_2\rangle \Downarrow v_2 \vee (v_1 \wedge v_3)} \quad i > 1$$

$$(\mathbf{S}_1) \quad \frac{\langle h, 1, \psi_2\rangle \Downarrow v}{\langle h, 1, \psi_1 \mathbf{S} \psi_2\rangle \Downarrow v} \qquad (\mathbf{X}^{-1}) \quad \frac{\langle h, i-1, \varphi\rangle \Downarrow v}{\langle h, i, \mathbf{X}^{-1}\varphi\rangle \Downarrow v} \, i > 1 \qquad (\mathbf{X}^{-1}_{1}) \quad \frac{v := \mathbf{f}}{\langle h, 1, \mathbf{X}^{-1}\varphi\rangle \Downarrow v}$$

Fig. 2. Evaluation rules for deciding whether $(h, i) \models \varphi$

An easy explanation for the above hardness result is via a polynomial time encoding of the PSPACE-complete QBF-problem (cf. [18] and Appendix). Given a boolean expression like $E(x_1, x_2, x_3) \equiv (x_1 \vee \neg x_2) \wedge (\neg x_2 \vee x_3)$ and the QBF-formula $F \equiv \forall x_1. \exists x_2. \forall x_3. E(x_1, x_2, x_3)$, we can construct a corresponding $PTLTL^{FO}$-formula, $\varphi \equiv \forall x_1 : p_1. \exists x_2 : p_2. \forall x_3 : p_3. E'(x_1, x_2, x_3)$ where $E'(x_1, x_2, x_3) \equiv (true(x_1) \vee \neg true(x_2)) \wedge (\neg true(x_2) \vee true(x_3))$, and a history, h below, representing all possible interpretations of F's variables in a single session:

$$h = \{p_1(0), p_1(1), p_2(0), p_2(1), p_3(0), p_3(1), true(1)\}.$$

It is then easy to see that F evaluates to $\top$ if and only if $h \models \varphi$ holds.

On the surface it seems that this "blow up" is caused by the multiple occurrences of the same predicate symbol in a single session. It is therefore natural to ask whether the complexity of the problem can be reduced if we consider histories where every predicate symbol can occur at most once in every session. Surprisingly, however, even with this restriction, model checking remains PSPACE-complete. Consider, for example, the following polynomial encoding of the above QBF-instance, using this restriction:

$$\{p_3(0), true(1)\}; \{p_3(1), true(1)\}; \ldots; \{p_1(0), true(1)\}; \{p_1(1), true(1)\} \models$$
$$\mathbf{G}^{-1} \forall x_1 : p_1. \mathbf{F}^{-1} \exists x_2 : p_2. \mathbf{G}^{-1} \forall x_3 : p_3. E'(x_1, x_2, x_3)).$$

Definition 3. *A history h is said to be* trace-like *if for all i such that $1 \leq i \leq |h|$, for all p, $\vec{t}$ and $\vec{s}$, if $p(\vec{t}) \in h_i$ and $p(\vec{s}) \in h_i$, then $\vec{t} = \vec{s}$.*

Theorem 3. *Let φ be a $PTLTL^{FO}$ formula and h a trace-like history. If the interpreted functions and relations in φ are in PSPACE, then deciding whether $h \models \varphi$ holds is PSPACE-complete.*

We have implemented a prototypic model checker for $PTLTL^{FO}$ [2]. The model checker accepts two user inputs: a $PTLTL^{FO}$ policy and a history which is then checked against the policy. We use FOL-RuleML [5] as the input format for the policy since it is due for standardisation as the W3C's first-order logic extension to RuleML [1]. Thus users can even specify policies using graphical XML-editors with a FOL-RuleML DTD extended by our temporal operators. The model checker is currently not optimised for performance, but demonstrates the feasibility and practicality of our approach. to The above web site contains Ocaml source code (as well as a statically linked binary for Linux) and some example policies from Section 3 stored in XML-format.

5   Extending $PTLTL^{FO}$ with a Counting Quantifier

We now consider an extension of our policy language with a counting quantifier. The idea is that we want to count how many times a policy was satisfied in the past, and use this number to write another policy. The language of formulae is extended with the construct $\mathbf{N}x : \psi.\ \phi(x)$ where x binds over the formula $\phi(x)$ and is not free in ψ. The semantics is as follows:

$$(h, i) \models \mathbf{N}x : \psi.\ \phi(x) \text{ iff } (h, i) \models \phi(n),$$

where $n = |\{j \mid 1 \leq j \leq i \text{ and } (h, j) \models \psi\}|$.

Krukow et al. also consider a counting operator, #, which applies to a formula. Intuitively, $\#\psi$ counts the number of sessions in which ψ is true, and can be used inside other arithmetic expressions like $\#\psi \leq 5$. The advantage of our approach is that we can still maintain a total separation of these arithmetic expressions and other underlying computable functions from the logic, thus allowing us to modularly extend these functions. Another difference is that our extension resides in the logic itself, thus allowing one to express policies that combine counting with other logical operators.

Examples: Consider a "meta" policy such as: "engage only with a seller whose past transactions with negative feedbacks constitute at most a quarter of the total transactions". This can be expressed succinctly as

$$\mathbf{N}x : negative.\ \mathbf{N}y : \top.\ \frac{x}{y} \leq \frac{1}{4}$$

since $\mathbf{N}y : \top$ instantiates y to be the length of the transaction history to date. A more elaborate example is the formula in Eq. (1) without the $\mathbf{G}^{-1}$-operator:

$$\psi \equiv \forall(t, x, v) : pay.\ \exists(y, t') : post.\ x = y \wedge t' \leq 10.$$

Then one can specify a policy that demands that "the seller's delivery is *mostly* on-time", where *mostly* can be given as a percentage, such as 90%, via:

$$\mathbf{N}x : \psi.\ \mathbf{N}y : \top.\ \frac{x}{y} \leq 0.9.$$

---

[2] See http://code.google.com/p/ptltl-mc/

Theorem 4. *If the interpreted functions and relations are in* PSPACE, *then the model checking problem for* $PTLTL^{FO}$ *with the counting quantifier is* PSPACE-*complete.*

6   Partial Observability

In some online transaction systems, like eBay, certain events may not be wholly observable all the time, even to the system providers, e.g., payments made through a third-party outside the control of the provider[3]. We consider scenarios where some information is missing from the history of a client (buyer or seller) and the problem of enforcing security policies in this setting.

Examples: Consider the policy $\psi \equiv \mathbf{G}^{-1} [\forall(x, v) : win.\exists(t, y, u) : pay.x = y \wedge v = u]$ which states that every winning bid must be paid with the agreed dollar amount. The history below, where X represents an unknown amount, can *potentially satisfy* ψ when $X = 100$ (say):

$$h = \{win(a, 100), pay(1, a, 100), post(a, 5)\};$$
$$\{win(a, 100), pay(2, a, X), post(a, 4), positive\}$$

Of course it is also possible that the actual amount paid is less than 100, in which case the policy is not satisfied. There are also cases in which the values of the unknowns do not matter. For instance, a system provider may not be able to verify payments, but it may deduce that if a buyer leaves a positive remark, that payment has been made. That is, a policy like the following:

$$\varphi' \equiv \mathbf{G}^{-1} [\forall(x, v) : win.\exists(t, y, u) : pay.x = y \wedge (u = v \vee positive)].$$

In this case, we see that h still satisfies φ' under all substitutions for X.

We consider two problems arising from partial observability. For this, we extend slightly the notion of history and sessions.

Definition 4. *A* partially observable session, *or po-session for short, is a finite set of predicates of the form* $p(u_1, \ldots, u_n)$, *where* p *is an uninterpreted predicate symbol and each* u_i *is either a constant or a variable. A partially observable history (po-history) is a finite list of po-sessions.*

Given a po-history h, we denote with $V(h)$ the set of variables occurring in h. In the following, we consider formulae which may have occurrences of free variables. The notation $V(\psi)$ denotes the set of free variables in the formula ψ.

Definition 5. *Given a po-history* h, *a natural number* i, *and a formula* ψ *such that* $V(\psi) \subseteq V(h)$, *we say that* h potentially satisfies ψ *at* i, *written* $(h, i) \vdash \psi$, *if there exists a substitution* σ *such that* $dom(\sigma) = V(h)$ *and* $(h\sigma, i) \models \psi\sigma$. *We say that* h adheres to ψ *at* i, *written* $(h, i) \Vdash \psi$, *if* $(h\sigma, i) \models \psi\sigma$ *for all* σ *such that* $dom(\sigma) = V(h)$.

---

[3] eBay asks users for confirmation of payment, but does not check whether the payment goes through. This is modelled by an unknown amount in the payment parameters.

Note that the adherence problem is just the dual of the potential satisfiability problem, i.e., $(h, i) \Vdash \psi$ if and only if $(h, i) \not\vdash \neg\psi$. In general the potential satisfiability problem is undecidable, since one can encode solvability of general Diophantine equations: Let $D(x_1, \ldots, x_n)$ be a set of Diophantine equations whose variables are among $x_1, \ldots, x_n$. Assume that we have n uninterpreted unary predicate symbols $p_1, \cdots, p_n$ which take an integer argument. Then solvability of $D(x_1, \ldots, x_n)$ is reducible to the problem

$$\{p_1(x_1), \ldots, p_n(x_n)\} \vdash \exists x_1 : p_1. \cdots \exists x_n : p_n.\psi(x_1, \ldots, x_n)$$

where $\psi(x_1, \ldots, x_n)$ is the conjunction of all the equations in $D(x_1, \ldots, x_n)$.

However, we can obtain decidability results if we restrict the term language. We consider here such a restriction where the term language is the language of linear arithmetic over integers, i.e., terms of the form (modulo associativity and commutativity of $+$): $k_1 x_1 + \cdots + k_n x_n + c$, where c and each k_i are integers. We also assume the standard relations on integers $=$, $\geq$ and $\leq$. It is useful to introduce a class of *constraint formulae* generated from the following grammar:

$$C ::= \top \mid \bot \mid t_1 = t_2 \mid t_1 \leq t_2 \mid t_1 \geq t_2 \mid C_1 \wedge C_2 \mid C_1 \vee C_2 \mid \neg C.$$

A constraint C is *satisfiable* if there exists a substitution σ such that $C\sigma$ is true. Satisfiability of constraint formulae is decidable (see [12] for a list of algorithms). The decidability proof of the potential satisfiability problem involves a transformation of the judgement $(h, i) \vdash \psi$ into an equivalent constraint formula.

Lemma 2. *For every h, i, and ψ, there exists a constraint formula C such that $(h, i) \vdash \psi$ if and only if C is satisfiable.*

Theorem 5. *The potential satisfiability problem and the adherence problem for $PTLTL^{FO}$ with linear arithmetic are decidable.*

We note that the transformation of $(h, i) \vdash \psi$ to C above may result in an exponential blow-up (see [3] for more details).

7   Extended Guarded Quantifiers

An underlying design principle for our quantified policies is the closed-world assumption (CWA). The guarded quantifier in $PTLTL^{FO}$ is the most basic quantifier, and by no means the only one that enforces CWA. It is a natural to ask what other extensions achieve the same effect.

We mentioned earlier that introducing negation in the guard leads to undecidability. Surprisingly, simple extensions with unrestricted disjunction or the **S**-operator also lead to undecidability, as we shall see shortly. Let us first fix the language with extended guarded quantifiers, whose syntax is as follows:

$$\forall \vec{x} : \psi(\vec{x}). \; \varphi(\vec{x}) \qquad \exists \vec{x} : \psi(\vec{x}). \; \varphi(\vec{x}).$$

Here the formula $\psi(\vec{x})$ is a guard, and $\vec{x}$ are its only free variables. The semantics of the quantifiers are a straightforward extension of that of $PTLTL^{FO}$, i.e.,

$$(h, i) \models \forall(x_1, \ldots, x_n) : \psi(x_1, \ldots, x_n). \varphi \text{ iff for all } c_1, \ldots, c_n,$$
$$\text{if } (h, i) \models \psi(c_1, \ldots, c_n) \text{ then } (h, i) \models \varphi[x_1 := c_1, \ldots, x_n := c_n].$$

Now consider a guarded quantifier that allows unrestricted uses of disjunction. Suppose $\varphi(\vec{x})$, where $\vec{x}$ range over integers, is a formula encoding some general Diophantine equation. Let $\psi(\vec{x}, y)$ be a guard formula $p(\vec{x}) \vee q(y)$, for some predicate p and q of appropriate types. Then satisfiability of the entailment $\{q(0)\} \models \exists(\vec{x}, y) : \psi(\vec{x}, y). \varphi(\vec{x})$ is equivalent to the validity of the first-order formula $\exists \vec{x}. \varphi(\vec{x})$, which states the solvability of the Diophantine equations in $\varphi(\vec{x})$. This means that the model checking problem for $PTLTL^{FO}$ with unrestricted disjunctive guards is undecidable. The cause of this undecidability is that satisfiability of the guard, relative to the history, is independent of the variables $\vec{x}$. Similar observations can be made regarding the unrestricted uses of the "since" operator, e.g., if we replace the guard $\psi(\vec{x}, y)$ with $p(\vec{x}) \, \mathbf{S} \, q(y)$.

Unrestricted uses of function symbols in guarded quantifiers can also lead to violation of CWA. For instance, in checking $\{p(0)\} \models \forall(x, y) : p(x + y). \varphi(x, y)$, we have to consider infinitely many combinations of x and y such that $x + y = 0$.

The above considerations led us to the following guarded extension to the quantifiers of $PTLTL^{FO}$. *Simple guards* are formulae generated by the grammar:

$$\gamma ::= p(\vec{u}) \mid \gamma \wedge \gamma \mid \mathbf{G}^{-1} \gamma \mid \mathbf{F}^{-1} \gamma$$

Here the list $\vec{u}$ is a list of variables and constants. We write $\gamma(\vec{x})$ to denote a simple guard whose only free variables are $\vec{x}$. *Positive guards* $G(\vec{x})$ *over variables* $\vec{x}$ are formulae whose only variables are $\vec{x}$, as generated by the grammar:

$$G(\vec{x}) ::= \gamma(\vec{x}) \mid G(\vec{x}) \wedge G(\vec{x}) \mid G(\vec{x}) \vee G(\vec{x}) \mid \mathbf{G}^{-1} G(\vec{x}) \mid \mathbf{F}^{-1} G(\vec{x}) \mid G(\vec{x}) \, \mathbf{S} \, G(\vec{x}).$$

Let $PTLTL^{FO+}$ denote the extension of $PTLTL^{FO}$ with positive guards. We show that the model checking problem for $PTLTL^{FO+}$ is decidable. The key to this is the finiteness of the set of "solutions" for a guard formula.

Definition 6. *Let $G(\vec{x})$ be a positive guard and let h be a history. The guard instantiation problem, written $(h, G(\vec{x}))$, is the problem of finding a list $\vec{u}$ of constants such that $h \models G(\vec{u})$ holds. Such a list is called a solution of the guard instantiation problem.*

Lemma 3. *Let $G(\vec{x})$ be a positive guard over variables $\vec{x}$ and let h be a history. Then the set of solutions for the problem $(h, G(\vec{x}))$ is finite. Moreover, every solution uses only constants that appear in h.*

Theorem 6. *Let φ be a $PTLTL^{FO+}$ formula and h a history. The model checking problem $h \models \varphi$ is decidable.*

8   Conclusions and Related Work

We have presented a formal language for expressing history-based access control policies based on the pure past fragment of linear temporal logic, extended to allow certain guarded quantifiers and arbitrary computable functions and relations. As our examples show, these extensions allow us to write complex policies concisely, while retaining decidability of model checking. Adding a counting quantifier allows us to express some statistical properties in policies. We also consider the monitoring problem in the presence of unobservable or unknown action parameters. We believe this is the first formulation of the problem in the context of monitoring.

There is much previous work in the related area of history-based access control [2,4,8,9,10,13]. Counting the occurrence of specific events was previously described in [7], where a stream-based approach to runtime verification was presented. There, the monitoring algorithm incrementally constructs output streams from input streams, while maintaining a store of partially evaluated expressions for forward references. This way one can count, for example, how often an input stream carried a certain value. Our transaction-based approach to defining policies separates us from the more traditional trace-based approaches in program execution monitoring. Our work is closely related to Krukow, et al. [13,14], but there are a few important differences. Their definition of sessions allows events to be partially ordered using *event structures* [19] whereas our notion of a session as a set with no structure is simpler. The latter is not a real limitation since ordering of events can be explicitly encoded in our setup using first-order quantifiers and a rich term language allowing extra parameters, interpreted functions, timestamps and arithmetic. In the first-order case, they forbid multiple occurrences of the same event in a session, i.e., they correspond to our trace-like histories (see Section 4). Their language does not allow arbitrary computable functions and relations, since allowing these features in the presence of quantifiers can lead to undecidability of model checking. Our policy language is thus more expressive than theirs in describing quantitative properties of histories.

For propositional LTL, there exist efficient means of monitoring, e.g., as in [4,10]. There a so-called *monitor* device is generated for a policy which reads a history as it unfolds and which does not need to re-apply a costly model checking procedure when new sessions are added. Instead in [10], only the truth values of certain subformulae of the policy are kept with respect to the previous session, in order to compute the truth value of the subformulae with respect to the new session; that is, the complexity of the monitor does not depend on the length of a history. Let us refer to policies which can be monitored this way as *monitorable policies*. Obviously, not all policies in $PTLTL^{FO}$ are monitorable. For example, in a policy such as $\forall x : p.\ \mathbf{G}^{-1} \exists y : q.\ y \leq x$, we must, for each new $x : p$, check all the previous sessions in the history whether or not there exists a $y : q$, such that $y \leq x$ holds. A policy such as the one given in the eBay.com example in

Section 3, however, can be monitored efficiently as it does not involve the same nesting of temporal modalities under the scope of quantifiers:

$$\varphi \equiv \mathbf{G}^{-1} \varphi_1 \text{ where } \varphi_1 \equiv \forall(t,x,v) : pay. \ \exists(y,t') : post. \ x = y \wedge t' \leq 10.$$

We can evaluate it w.r.t. the current session only, and keep track of the results from previous evaluations using two arrays of truth values, pre and now like in [10], to store the truth values of subformulae w.r.t. the current (now) and the previous ($pres$) session. In this example, it is sufficient that pre and now each have two entries; the first corresponds to the truth value φ_1 and the second to φ. The values of now are updated for each new session, and subsequently copied to pre. The condition induced by the $\mathbf{G}^{-1}$-operator is that φ_1 has to be true now, and previously, for all sessions, i.e., $now[2] \leftarrow now[1] \wedge pre[2]$.

An obvious class of monitorable policy is one obtained by substituting propositional variables in a propositional LTL formula with closed first-order formulae (without temporal operators). In this case, with straightforward modifications, the procedure in [10] can be applied to construct efficient monitors. It will be interesting to investigate other restrictions to $PTLTL^{FO}$ which are monitorable.

References

1. The RuleML Initiative. Document located, http://www.ruleml.org/
2. Bartoletti, M., Degano, P., Ferrari, G.L.: History-based access control with local policies. In: Sassone, V. (ed.) FOSSACS 2005. LNCS, vol. 3441, pp. 316–332. Springer, Heidelberg (2005)
3. Bauer, A., Goré, R., Tiu, A.: A decidable policy language for history-based transaction monitoring. Technical report, The Australian National University (2009), http://arxiv.org/abs/0903.2904
4. Bauer, A., Leucker, M., Schallhart, C.: Monitoring of real-time properties. In: Arun-Kumar, S., Garg, N. (eds.) FSTTCS 2006. LNCS, vol. 4337, pp. 260–272. Springer, Heidelberg (2006)
5. Boley, H., Dean, M., Grosof, B., Sintek, M., Spencer, B., Tabet, S., Wagner, G.: FOL RuleML: The First-Order Logic Web Language (2005), http://www.ruleml.org/fol
6. Brewer, D.F.C., Nash, M.J.: The chinese wall security policy. In: IEEE Symposium on Security and Privacy. IEEE, Los Alamitos (1989)
7. D'Angelo, B., Sankaranarayanan, S., Sánchez, C., Robinson, W., Finkbeiner, B., Sipma, H.B., Mehrotra, S., Manna, Z.: LOLA: Runtime monitoring of synchronous systems. In: TIME. IEEE, Los Alamitos (2005)
8. Edjlali, G., Acharya, A., Chaudhary, V.: History-based access control for mobile code. In: ACM Conference on Computer and Communications Security, pp. 38–48 (1998)
9. Fong, P.W.L.: Access control by tracking shallow execution history. In: IEEE Symposium on Security and Privacy, pp. 43–55. IEEE Computer Society Press, Los Alamitos (2004)
10. Havelund, K., Rosu, G.: Synthesizing Monitors for Safety Properties. In: Katoen, J.-P., Stevens, P. (eds.) TACAS 2002. LNCS, vol. 2280, p. 342. Springer, Heidelberg (2002)

11. Jøsang, A., Ismail, R., Boyd, C.: A survey of trust and reputation systems for online service provision. Decision Support Systems 43(2), 618–644 (2007)
12. Kroening, D., Strichman, O.: Decision Procedures. Springer, Heidelberg (2008)
13. Krukow, K., Nielsen, M., Sassone, V.: A framework for concrete reputation-systems with applications to history-based access control. In: ACM Conf. Comp. and Commun. Sec. (2005)
14. Krukow, K., Nielsen, M., Sassone, V.: A logical framework for reputation systems and history based access control. Journal of Computer Security (to appear) (2008)
15. Matiyasevich, Y.: Hilbert's 10th Problem. MIT Press, Cambridge (1993)
16. Pnueli, A.: The temporal logic of programs. In: Proc. FOCS 1977, pp. 46–57 (1977)
17. Roger, M., Goubault-Larrecq, J.: Log auditing through model-checking. In: CSFW, pp. 220–234. IEEE, Los Alamitos (2001)
18. Sipser, M.: Introduction to the Theory of Computation. Intl. Thomson Publishing (1996)
19. Winskel, G., Nielsen, M.: Models for concurrency. In: Handbook of logic in computer science. semantic modelling, vol. 4. Oxford University Press, Oxford (1995)

Checking Thorough Refinement on Modal Transition Systems Is EXPTIME-Complete

Nikola Beneš[1],*, Jan Křetínský[1],**, Kim G. Larsen[2],***, and Jiří Srba[2],†

[1] Faculty of Informatics, Masaryk Univ., Botanická 68a, 60200 Brno, Czech Republic
[2] Department of Computer Science, Aalborg Univ., Selma Lagerlöfs Vej 300, 9220 Aalborg East, Denmark

Abstract. Modal transition systems (MTS), a specification formalism introduced more than 20 years ago, has recently received a considerable attention in several different areas. Many of the fundamental questions related to MTSs have already been answered. However, the problem of the exact computational complexity of thorough refinement checking between two finite MTSs remained unsolved.

We settle down this question by showing EXPTIME-completeness of thorough refinement checking on finite MTSs. The upper-bound result relies on a novel algorithm running in single exponential time providing a direct goal-oriented way to decide thorough refinement. If the right-hand side MTS is moreover deterministic, or has a fixed size, the running time of the algorithm becomes polynomial. The lower-bound proof is achieved by reduction from the acceptance problem of alternating linear bounded automata and the problem remains EXPTIME-hard even if the left-hand side MTS is fixed.

1 Introduction

Modal transition systems (MTS) is a specification formalism which extends the standard labelled transition systems with two types of transitions, the *may* transitions that are allowed to be present in an implementation of a given modal transition system and *must* transitions that must be necessarily present in any implementation. Modal transition systems hence allow to specify both safety and liveness properties. The MTS framework was suggested more than 20 years ago by Larsen and Thomsen [14] and has recently brought a considerable attention due to several applications to e.g. component-based software development [16,7], interface theories [20,17], modal abstractions and program analysis [11,12,15] and other areas [10,21], just to mention a few of them. A renewed interest in tool support for modal transition systems is recently also emerging [8,9]. A recent

* Partially supported by the Academy of Sciences of the Czech Republic, project No. 1ET408050503.
** Partially supported by the research centre ITI, project No. 1M0545.
*** Partially supported by the VKR Center of Excellence MT-LAB.
† Partially supported by Ministry of Education of the Czech Republic, project No. MSM 0021622419.

M. Leucker and C. Morgan (Eds.): ICTAC 2009, LNCS 5684, pp. 112–126, 2009.

overview article on the theoretical foundations of MTSs and early tool development is available in [1].

Modal transition systems were designed to support *component-based* system development via a *stepwise refinement* process where abstract specifications are gradually refined into more concrete ones until an *implementation* of the system (where the may and must transitions coincide) is obtained. One of the fundamental questions is the decidability of a *thorough refinement* relation between two specifications S and T. We say that S thoroughly refines T iff every implementation of S is also an implementation of T. While for a number of other problems, like the common implementation problem, a matching complexity lower and upper bounds were given [2,13,3], the question of the exact complexity of thorough refinement checking between two finite MTSs remained unanswered.

In this paper, we prove EXPTIME-completeness of thorough refinement checking between two finite MTSs. The hardness result is achieved by a reduction from the acceptance problem of alternating linear bounded automata, a well known EXPTIME-complete problem, and it improves the previously established PSPACE-hardness [2]. The main reduction idea is based on the fact that the existence of a computation step between two configurations of a Turing machine can be locally verified (one needs to consider the relationships between three tape symbols in the first configuration and the corresponding three tape symbols in the second one, see e.g. [19, Theorem 7.37]), however, a nonstandard encoding of computations of Turing machines (which is crucial for our reduction) and the addition of the alternation required a nontrivial technical treatment. Moreover, we show that the problem remains EXPTIME-hard even if the left-hand side MTS is of a constant size. Some proof ideas for the containment in EXPTIME were mentioned in [2] where the authors suggest a reduction of the refinement problem to validity checking of vectorized modal μ-calculus, which can be solved in EXPTIME—the authors in [2] admit that such a reduction relies on an unpublished popular wisdom, and they only sketch the main ideas hinting at the EXPTIME algorithm. In our paper, we describe a novel technique for deciding thorough refinement in EXPTIME. The result is achieved by a direct goal-oriented algorithm performing a least fixed-point computation, and can be easily turned into a tableau-based algorithm. As a corollary, we also get that if the right-hand side MTS is deterministic (or of a constant size), the algorithm for solving the problem runs in deterministic polynomial time.

A full version of the paper is available in [6].

2   Basic Definitions

A *modal transition system* (MTS) over an action alphabet Σ is a triple $(P, \dashrightarrow, \longrightarrow)$, where P is a set of *processes* and $\longrightarrow \subseteq \dashrightarrow \subseteq P \times \Sigma \times P$ are *must* and *may* transition relations, respectively. The class of all MTSs is denoted by $\mathcal{MTS}$. Because in MTS whenever $S \xrightarrow{a} S'$ then necessarily also $S \dashrightarrow^{a} S'$, we adopt the convention of drawing only the must transitions $S \xrightarrow{a} S'$ in such cases. An MTS is *finite* if P and Σ are finite sets.

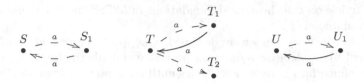

Fig. 1. $S \leq_t T$ but $S \not\leq_m T$, and $S \not\leq_t U$ and $S \not\leq_m U$

An MTS is an *implementation* if $\dashrightarrow = \longrightarrow$. The class of all implementations is denoted $i\mathcal{MTS}$ and as in implementations the must and may relations coincide, we can consider such systems as the standard *labelled transition systems*.

Definition 2.1. *Let* $M_1 = (P_1, \dashrightarrow_1, \longrightarrow_1)$, $M_2 = (P_2, \dashrightarrow_2, \longrightarrow_2)$ *be MTSs over the same action alphabet* Σ *and* $S \in P_1$, $T \in P_2$ *be processes. We say that* S *modally refines* T, *written* $S \leq_m T$, *if there is a relation* $R \subseteq P_1 \times P_2$ *such that* $(S, T) \in R$ *and for every* $(A, B) \in R$ *and every* $a \in \Sigma$:

1. *if* $A \overset{a}{\dashrightarrow}_1 A'$ *then there is a transition* $B \overset{a}{\dashrightarrow}_2 B'$ *s.t.* $(A', B') \in R$, *and*
2. *if* $B \overset{a}{\longrightarrow}_2 B'$ *then there is a transition* $A \overset{a}{\longrightarrow}_1 A'$ *s.t.* $(A', B') \in R$.

We often omit the indices in the transition relations and use symbols $\dashrightarrow$ and $\longrightarrow$ whenever it is clear from the context what transition system we have in mind. Note that on implementations modal refinement coincides with the classical notion of strong bisimilarity, and on modal transition systems without any must transitions it corresponds to the well-studied simulation preorder.

Example 2.2. Consider processes S and T in Fig. 1. We prove that S does not modally refine T. Indeed, there is a may-transition $S \overset{a}{\dashrightarrow} S_1$ on the left-hand side which has to be matched by entering either T_1 or T_2 on the right-hand side. However, in the first case there is a move $T_1 \overset{a}{\longrightarrow} T$ on the right-hand side which cannot be matched from S_1 as it has no must-transition under a. In the second case there is a may-transition $S_1 \overset{a}{\dashrightarrow} S$ on the left-hand side which cannot be matched by any may-transition from T_2. Hence there cannot be any relation of modal refinement containing the pair S and T, which means that $S \not\leq_m T$. Similarly, one can argue that $S \not\leq_m U$. □

We shall now observe that the modal refinement problem, i.e. the question whether a given process modally refines another given process, is tractable for finite MTSs.

Theorem 2.3. *The modal refinement problem for finite MTSs is P-complete.*

Proof. Modal refinement can be computed in polynomial time by the standard greatest fixed-point computation, similarly as in the case of strong bisimulation. P-hardness of modal refinement follows from P-hardness of bisimulation [4] (see also [18]). □

We proceed with the definition of thorough refinement, a relation that holds for two modal specification S and T iff any implementation of S is also an implementation of T.

Definition 2.4. *For a process S let us denote by $[\![S]\!] = \{I \in i\mathcal{MTS} \mid I \leq_m S\}$ the set of all implementations of S. We say that S thoroughly refines T, written $S \leq_t T$, if $[\![S]\!] \subseteq [\![T]\!]$.*

Clearly, if $S \leq_m T$ then also $S \leq_t T$ because the relation $\leq_m$ is transitive. The opposite implication, however, does not hold as demonstrated by the processes S and T in Fig. 1 where one can easily argue that every implementation of S is also an implementation of T. On the other hand, $S \not\leq_t U$ because a process with just a single a-transition is an implementation of S but not of U.

3   Thorough Refinement Is EXPTIME-Hard

In this section we prove that the thorough refinement relation $\leq_t$ on finite modal transition systems is EXPTIME-hard by reduction from the acceptance problem of alternating linear bounded automata.

3.1   Alternating Linear Bounded Automata

Definition 3.1. *An alternating linear bounded automaton (ALBA) is a tuple $\mathcal{M} = (Q, Q_\forall, Q_\exists, \Sigma, \Gamma, q_0, q_{acc}, q_{rej}, \vdash, \dashv, \delta)$ where Q is a finite set of control states partitioned into $Q_\forall$ and $Q_\exists$, universal and existential states, respectively, Σ is a finite input alphabet, $\Gamma \supseteq \Sigma$ is a finite tape alphabet, $q_0 \in Q$ is the initial control state, $q_{acc} \in Q$ is the accepting state, $q_{rej} \in Q$ is the rejecting state, $\vdash, \dashv \in \Gamma$ are the left-end and the right-end markers that cannot be overwritten or moved, and $\delta : (Q \setminus \{q_{acc}, q_{rej}\}) \times \Gamma \rightarrow 2^{Q \times \Gamma \times \{L,R\}}$ is a computation step function such that for all $q, p \in Q$ if $\delta(q, \vdash) \ni (p, a, D)$ then $a = \vdash, D = R$; if $\delta(q, \dashv) \ni (p, a, D)$ then $a = \dashv, D = L$; if $\delta(q, a) \ni (p, \vdash, D)$ then $a = \vdash$; and if $\delta(q, a) \ni (p, \dashv, D)$ then $a = \dashv$.*

Remark 3.2. W.l.o.g. we assume that $\Sigma = \{a, b\}$, $\Gamma = \{a, b, \vdash, \dashv\}$, $Q \cap \Gamma = \emptyset$ and that for each $q \in Q_\forall$ and $a \in \Gamma$ it holds that $\delta(q, a)$ has exactly two elements $(q_1, a_1, D_1), (q_2, a_2, D_2)$ where moreover $a_1 = a_2$ and $D_1 = D_2$. We fix this ordering and the successor states q_1 and q_2 are referred to as the *first* and the *second successor*, respectively. The states q_{acc}, q_{rej} have no successors.

A *configuration* of $\mathcal{M}$ is given by the state, the position of the head and the content of the tape. For technical reasons, we write it as a word over the alphabet $\Xi = Q \cup \Gamma \cup \{\vdash, \dashv, \exists, \forall, 1, 2, *\}$ (where $\exists, \forall, 1, 2, *$ are fresh symbols) in the following way. If the tape contains a word $\vdash w_1 a w_2 \dashv$, where $w_1, w_2 \in \Gamma^*$ and $a \in \Gamma$, and the head is scanning the symbol a in a state q, we write the configuration as $\vdash w_1 \alpha \beta q a w_2 \dashv$ where $\alpha\beta \in \{\exists*, \forall 1, \forall 2\}$.

The two symbols $\alpha\beta$ before the control state in every configuration are non-standard, though important for the encoding of the computations into modal transition systems to be checked for thorough refinement. Intuitively, if a control state q is preceded by $\forall 1$ then it signals that the previous configuration (in a given computation) contained a universal control state and the first successor was chosen; similarly $\forall 2$ reflects that the second successor was chosen. Finally, if the control state is preceded by $\exists *$ then the previous control state was existential and in this case we do not keep track of which successor it was, hence the symbol $*$ is used instead. The *initial configuration* for an input word w is by definition $\vdash \exists * q_0 w \dashv$.

Depending on the present control state, every configuration is called either *universal, existential, accepting* or *rejecting*.

A *step of computation* is a relation $\rightarrow$ between configurations defined as follows (where $w_1, w_2 \in \Gamma^*$, $\alpha\beta \in \{\forall 1, \forall 2, \exists *\}$, $a, b, c \in \Gamma$, $i \in \{1, 2\}$, and $w_1 a w_2$ and $w_1 c a w_2$ both begin with $\vdash$ and end with $\dashv$):

- $w_1 \alpha\beta q a w_2 \rightarrow w_1 b \forall i p w_2$
  if $\delta(q, a) \ni (p, b, R)$, $q \in Q_\forall$ and (p, b, R) is the i'th successor,
- $w_1 \alpha\beta q a w_2 \rightarrow w_1 b \exists * p w_2$
  if $\delta(q, a) \ni (p, b, R)$ and $q \in Q_\exists$,
- $w_1 c \alpha\beta q a w_2 \rightarrow w_1 \forall i p c b w_2$
  if $\delta(q, a) \ni (p, b, L)$, $q \in Q_\forall$ and (p, b, L) is the i'th successor, and
- $w_1 c \alpha\beta q a w_2 \rightarrow w_1 \exists * p c b w_2$
  if $\delta(q, a) \ni (p, b, L)$ and $q \in Q_\exists$.

Note that for an input w of length n all reachable configurations are of length $n + 5$. A standard result is that one can efficiently compute the set $Comp \subseteq \Xi^{10}$ of all compatible 10-tuples such that for each sequence $C = c_1 c_2 \cdots c_k$ of configurations $c_1, c_2, \ldots, c_k$, with the length of the first configuration being $l = |c_1| = n + 5$, we have $c_1 \rightarrow c_2 \rightarrow \cdots \rightarrow c_k$ iff for all i, $0 \leq i \leq (k-1)l - 5$,

$$(C(i+1), C(i+2), C(i+3), C(i+4), C(i+5),$$
$$C(i+1+l), C(i+2+l), C(i+3+l), C(i+4+l), C(i+5+l)) \in Comp.$$

A *computation tree* for $\mathcal{M}$ on an input $w \in \Sigma^*$ is a tree T satisfying the following: the root of T is (labeled by) the initial configuration, and whenever N is a node of T labeled by a configuration c then the following holds:

- if c is accepting or rejecting then N is a leaf;
- if c is existential then N has one child labeled by some d such that $c \rightarrow d$;
- if c is universal then N has two children labelled by the first and the second successor of c, respectively.

Without loss of generality, we shall assume from now on that any computation tree for $\mathcal{M}$ on an input w is finite (see e.g. [19, page 198]) and that every accepting configuration contains at least four other symbols following after the state q_{acc}.

We say that $\mathcal{M}$ accepts w iff there is a (finite) computation tree for $\mathcal{M}$ on w with all leaves labelled with accepting configurations. The following fact is well known (see e.g. [19]).

Proposition 3.3. *Given an ALBA M and a word w, the problem whether M accepts w is EXPTIME-complete.*

3.2   Encoding of Configurations and Computation Trees

In this subsection we shall discuss the particular encoding techniques necessary for showing the lower bound. For technical convenience we will consider only tree encodings and so we first introduce the notion of tree-thorough refinement.

Definition 3.4. *Let Tree denote the class of all MTSs with their graphs being trees. We say that a process S tree-thoroughly refines a process T, denoted by $S \leq_{tt} T$, if $[\![S]\!] \cap$ Tree $\subseteq [\![T]\!] \cap$ Tree.*

Lemma 3.5. *For any two processes S and T, $S \leq_{tt} T$ iff $S \leq_t T$.*

Proof. The if case is trivial. For the only if case, we define an *unfold* $U(S)$ of a process S over an MTS $M = (P, \dashrightarrow, \longrightarrow)$ with an alphabet Σ to be a process S over an MTS $U(M) = (P^*, \dashrightarrow_U, \longrightarrow_U)$ over the same alphabet and where P^* is the set of all finite sequences over the symbols from P. The transition relations are defined as follows: for all $a \in \Sigma$, $T, R \in P$ and $\alpha \in P^*$, whenever $T \overset{a}{\dashrightarrow} R$ then $\alpha T \overset{a}{\dashrightarrow}_U \alpha T R$, and whenever $T \overset{a}{\longrightarrow} R$ then $\alpha T \overset{a}{\longrightarrow}_U \alpha T R$. Since the transitions in $U(S)$ depend only on the last symbol, we can easily see that $U(S) \leq_m S$ and $S \leq_m U(S)$ for every process S.

Let I be now an implementation of S. Its unfold $U(I)$ is also an implementation of S by $U(I) \leq_m I \leq_m S$ and the transitivity of $\leq_m$. By our assumption that $S \leq_{tt} T$ and the fact that $U(I)$ is a tree, we get that $U(I)$ is also an implementation of T. Finally, $I \leq_m U(I) \leq_m T$ and the transitivity of $\leq_m$ allow us to conclude that I is an implementation of T.   □

Let $\mathcal{M} = (Q, Q_\forall, Q_\exists, \Sigma, \Gamma, q_0, q_{acc}, q_{rej}, \vdash, \dashv, \delta)$ be an ALBA and $w \in \Sigma^*$ an input word of length n. We shall construct (in polynomial time) modal transition systems L and R such that $\mathcal{M}$ accepts w iff $L \not\leq_{tt} R$. The system L will encode (almost) all trees beginning with the initial configuration, while the implementations of R encode only the incorrect or rejecting computation trees.

Configurations, i.e. sequences of letters from Ξ, are not encoded straightforwardly as sequences of actions (the reason why this naive encoding does not work is explained later on in Remark 3.12). Instead we have to use two auxiliary actions π a σ. The intended implementations of L and R will alternate between the actions π and σ on a linear path, while the symbols in the encoded configuration are present as side-branches on the path.

Formally, a sequence $a_1 a_2 a_3 \cdots a_n \in \Xi^*$ is encoded as

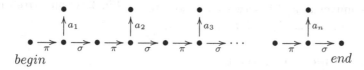

and denoted by $\text{code}(a_1 a_2 \cdots a_n)$.

We now describe how to transform computation trees into their corresponding implementations. We simply concatenate the subsequent codes of configurations in the computation tree such that the end node of the previous configuration is merged with the begin node of the successor configuration. Whenever there is a (universal) branching in the tree, we do not branch in the corresponding implementation at its beginning but we wait until we reach the occurrence of ∀. The branching happens exactly before the symbols 1 or 2 that follow after ∀. This occurs in the same place on the tape in both of the configurations due to the assumption that the first and the second successor move simultaneously either to the left or to the right, and write the same symbol (see Remark 3.2). A formal definition of the encoding of computation trees into implementations follows.

Definition 3.6 (Encoding computation trees into implementations). *Let $\mathcal{T}$ be a (finite) computation tree. We define its tree implementation* $\mathrm{code}(\mathcal{T})$ *inductively as follows:*

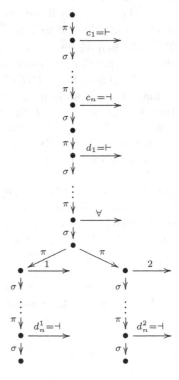

- *if $\mathcal{T}$ is a leaf labelled with a configuration c then $\mathrm{code}(\mathcal{T}) = \mathrm{code}(c)$;*
- *if the root of $\mathcal{T}$ is labelled by an existential configuration c with a tree $\mathcal{T}'$ being its child, then $\mathrm{code}(\mathcal{T})$ is rooted in the begin node of $\mathrm{code}(c)$, followed by $\mathrm{code}(\mathcal{T}')$ where the end node of $\mathrm{code}(c)$ and the begin node of $\mathrm{code}(\mathcal{T}')$ are identified;*
- *if the root of $\mathcal{T}$ is labelled by a universal configuration c with two children $d_1 \ldots \forall 1 \ldots d_n^1$ and $d_1 \ldots \forall 2 \ldots d_n^2$ that are roots of the subtrees $\mathcal{T}_1$ and $\mathcal{T}_2$, respectively, then $\mathrm{code}(\mathcal{T})$ is rooted in the begin node of $\mathrm{code}(c)$, followed by two subtrees $\mathrm{code}(\mathcal{T}_1)$ and $\mathrm{code}(\mathcal{T}_2)$ where the nodes in $\mathrm{code}(d_1 \ldots \forall)$ of the initial part of $\mathrm{code}(\mathcal{T}_1)$ are identified with the corresponding nodes in the initial part of $\mathrm{code}(\mathcal{T}_2)$ (note that by Remark 3.2 this prefix is common in both subtrees), and finally the end node of $\mathrm{code}(c)$ is identified with now the common begin node of both subtrees.*

Fig. 2 illustrates this definition on a part of a computation tree, where the first configuration $c_1 \ldots c_n$ is universal and has two successor configurations $d_1 \ldots \forall 1 \ldots d_n^1$ and $d_1 \ldots \forall 2 \ldots d_n^2$.

Fig. 2. Comp. Tree Encoding

3.3 The Reduction—Part 1

We now proceed with the reduction. As mentioned earlier, our aim is to construct for a given ALBA $\mathcal{M}$ and a string w two modal transition systems L and R such that $L \not\leq_{tt} R$ iff $\mathcal{M}$ accepts w. Implementations of L will include all

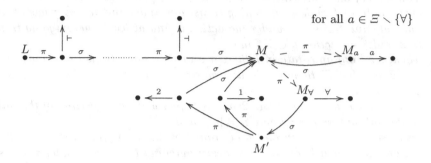

Fig. 3. Full specification of the process L

(also incorrect) possible computation trees. We only require that they start with the encoding of the initial configuration and do not "cheat" in the universal branching (i.e. after the encoding of every symbol $\forall$ there must follow a branching such that at least one of the branches encodes the symbol 1 and at least another one encodes the symbol 2).

As L should capture implementations corresponding to computations starting in the initial configuration, we set L to be the begin of code($\vdash\exists*q_0w\dashv$) and denote its end by M. After the initial configuration has been forced, we allow all possible continuations of the computation. This can be simply done by setting

$$M \overset{\pi}{\dashrightarrow} M_a$$
$$M_a \overset{\sigma}{\longrightarrow} M$$
$$M_a \overset{a}{\longrightarrow} X_a$$

for all letters $a \in \Xi \setminus \{\forall\}$ and there are no outgoing transitions from X_a.

for all $a \in \Xi \setminus \{\forall\}$

$$M \overset{\pi}{\underset{\sigma}{\rightleftarrows}} M_a \overset{a}{\longrightarrow} X_a$$

Finally, we add a fragment of MTS into the constructed process L which will guarantee the universal branching as mentioned above whenever the symbol $\forall$ occurs on a side-branch. The complete modal transition system L is now depicted in Fig. 3.

We shall now state some simple observations regarding tree implementations of the process L.

Proposition 3.7. *Every tree implementation I of the process L satisfies that*

1. *every branch in I is labelled by an alternating sequence of π and σ actions, beginning with the action π, and if the branch is finite then it ends either with the action σ or with an actions $a \in \Xi \setminus \{\forall\}$, and*
2. *every state in I with an incoming transition under the action π has at least one outgoing transition under the action σ and at least one outgoing transition under an action $a \in \Xi$, and*
3. *whenever from any state in I there are two outgoing transitions under some $a \in \Xi$ and $b \in \Xi$ then $a = b$, and moreover no further actions are possible after taking any transition under $a \in \Xi$, and*
4. *every branch in I longer than $2(n+5)$ begins with the encoding of the initial configuration $\vdash\exists*q_0w\dashv$ where $n = |w|$, and*
5. *every state in I with an incoming transition under σ from a state where the action $\forall$ is enabled satisfies that every outgoing transition under π leads to a state where either the action 1 or 2 is enabled (but not both at the same time), and moreover it has at least one such transition that enables the action 1 and at least one that enables the action 2.*

Of course, not every tree implementation of the process L represents a correct computation tree of the given ALBA. Implementations of L can widely (even uncountably) branch at any point and sequences of configurations they encode on some (or all) of their branches may not be correct computations of the given ALBA. Nevertheless, the encoding of any computation tree of the given ALBA is an implementation of the processes L, as stated by the following lemma.

Lemma 3.8. *Let T be a computation tree of an ALBA $\mathcal{M}$ on an input w. Then $\mathrm{code}(T) \leq_m L$.*

Proof (Sketch). To show that the implementation $\mathrm{code}(T)$ modally refines L is rather straightforward. The implementation $\mathrm{code}(T)$ surely starts with the encoding of the initial configuration and all symbols $a \in \Xi \setminus \{\forall\}$ on the side-branches in $\mathrm{code}(T)$ can be matched by entering M_a in the right-hand side process M. In case that the implementation contains a side-branch with the symbol $\forall$, the specification M will enter the state $M_\forall$ and require that two branches with labels 1 and 2 follow, however, from definition of $\mathrm{code}(T)$ this is clearly satisfied. □

3.4   The Reduction—Part 2

We now proceed with the construction of the right-hand side process R. Its implementations should be the codes of all incorrect or rejecting computation trees. To cover the notion of incorrect computation, we define a so-called bad path (see page 116 for definition of the relation $Comp$).

Definition 3.9. *A sequence*

$$c_1c_2c_3c_4c_5 \underbrace{a_1a_2 \ldots a_{n-6}a_{n-5}}_{n-5 \text{ elements from } \Xi} d_1d_2d_3d_4d_5$$

is called a bad path *if $(c_1, c_2, c_3, c_4, c_5, d_1, d_2, d_3, d_4, d_5) \in \Xi^{10} \setminus Comp$.*

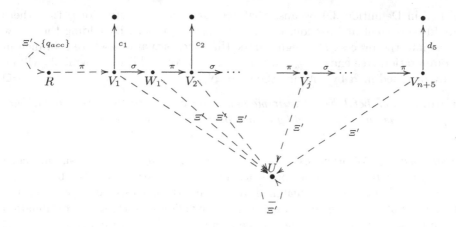

Fig. 4. A fragment of the system R for a bad path $c_1 c_2 c_3 c_4 c_5 \ldots d_1 d_2 d_3 d_4 d_5$

To cover the incorrect or rejecting computations, we loop in the process R under all actions, including the auxiliary ones, except for q_{acc}. For convenience we denote $\Xi' = \Xi \cup \{\pi, \sigma\}$. For any bad path, the process R can at any time nondeterministically guess the beginning of its first quintuple, realize it, then perform $n - 5$ times a sequence of π and σ, and finally realize the second quintuple. Moreover, we have to allow all possible detours of newly created branches to end in the state U where all available actions from Ξ' are always enabled and hence the continuation of any implementation is modally refined by U. Formally, for any $(c_1, c_2, c_3, c_4, c_5, d_1, d_2, d_3, d_4, d_5) \in \Xi^{10} \setminus Comp$ we add (disjointly) the following fragment into the process R (see also Fig. 4).

$$
\begin{aligned}
&R \xdashrightarrow{\pi} V_1 \\
&V_j \xrightarrow{\pi} W_j \xrightarrow{\sigma} V_{j+1} && \text{for } 1 \le j < n + 5 \\
&V_j \xrightarrow{c_j} X_j && \text{for } 1 \le j \le 5 \\
&V_{n+j} \xrightarrow{d_{n+j}} X_{5+j} && \text{for } 1 \le j \le 5 \\
&V_j \xdashrightarrow{x} U, W_j \xdashrightarrow{x} U, V_{n+5} \xdashrightarrow{x} U && \text{for } 1 \le j < n + 5 \text{ and } x \in \Xi' \\
&U \xdashrightarrow{x} U && \text{for all } x \in \Xi' \\
&R \xdashrightarrow{x} R && \text{for all } x \in \Xi' \setminus \{q_{acc}\}
\end{aligned}
$$

We also add ten new states $N_1, \ldots, N_{10}$ and the following transitions: $R \xdashrightarrow{\pi} N_1 \xdashrightarrow{\Xi'} N_2 \xdashrightarrow{\Xi'} N_3 \xdashrightarrow{\Xi'} N_4 \xdashrightarrow{\Xi'} \ldots \xdashrightarrow{\Xi'} N_{10}$ and $N_1 \xrightarrow{q_{acc}} N_{10}$ where any transition labelled by Ξ' is the abbreviation for a number of transitions under all actions from Ξ'.

Remark 3.10. We do not draw these newly added states $N_1, \ldots, N_{10}$ into Fig. 4 in order not to obstruct its readability. The reason why these states are added is purely technical. It is possible that there is an incorrect computation that ends with the last symbol q_{acc} but it cannot be detected by any bad path as defined in Definition 3.9 because that requires (in some situations) that there should be present at least four other subsequent symbols. By adding these new states into the process R, we guarantee that such situations where a branch in a computation tree ends in q_{acc} without at least four additional symbols will be easily matched in R by entering the state N_1.   □

Lemma 3.11. *Let I be a tree implementation of L such that every occurrence of q_{acc} in I is either preceded by a code of a bad path or does not continue with the encoding of at least four other symbols. Then $I \leq_m R$.*

Proof (Sketch). All branches in I that do not contain q_{acc} can be easily matched by looping in R and all branches that contain an error (bad path) before q_{acc} appears on that branch are matched by entering the corresponding state V_1 and at some point ending in the state U which now allows an arbitrary continuation of the implementation I (including the occurrence of the state q_{acc}).   □

Remark 3.12. Lemma 3.11 demonstrates the point where we need our special encoding of configurations using the alternation of π and σ actions together with side-branches to represent the symbols in the configurations. If the configurations were encoded directly as sequences of symbols on a linear path, the construction would not work. Indeed, the must path of alternating σ and π actions in the process R is necessary to ensure that the bad path entered in the left-hand side implementation I is indeed realizable. This path cannot be replaced by a linear path of must transitions containing directly the symbols of the configurations because the sequence of $n - 5$ symbols in the middle of the bad sequence would require exponentially large MTS to capture all such possible sequences explicitly and the reduction would not be polynomial.   □

Let us now finish the definition of the process R. Note that in ALBA even rejecting computation trees can still contain several correct computation paths ending in accepting configurations. We can only assume that during any universal branching in a rejecting tree, *at least one* of the two possible successors forms a rejecting branch. The process R must so have the possibility to discard the possibly correct computation branch in universal branching and it suffices to make sure that the computation will continue with only one of the branches.

So in order to finish the construction of R we add an additional fragment to R as depicted in Fig. 5 (it is the part below R that starts with branching to U_1 and U_2).

The construction of the process R is now finished (recall that the part of the construction going from R to the right is repeated for any bad path of the machine $\mathcal{M}$). Because the newly added part of the construction does not use any must transitions, it does not restrict the set of implementations and hence Lemma 3.11 still holds. The following two lemmas show that the added part of the construction correctly handles the universal branching.

Lemma 3.13. *Let I be a tree implementation of L which is not, even after removing any of its branches, a code of any accepting computation tree of $\mathcal{M}$ on the input w. Then $I \leq_m R$.*

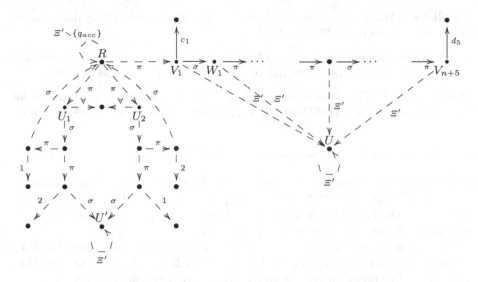

Fig. 5. Full specification of the process R

Proof (Sketch). We should prove that in the universal branching in I, the specification R can choose one of the two possible continuations and discard the checking of the other one. This is achieved by entering either the state U_1 or U_2 whenever the next side-branch in I contains the symbol $\forall$. From U_1 the continuation under the second successor is discarded by entering the state U' and symmetrically from U_2 the continuation under the first successor is discarded. We argued in Lemma 3.11 for the rest. □

Lemma 3.14. *Let T be an accepting computation tree of an ALBA $\mathcal{M}$ on the input w. Then* $\text{code}(T) \not\leq_m R$.

Proof (Sketch). Indeed, in $\text{code}(T)$ any branch ends in a configuration containing q_{acc} and there is no error (bad path), so clearly $\text{code}(T) \not\leq_m R$. □

3.5 Summary

We can now combine the facts about the constructed systems L and R.

Theorem 3.15. *An ALBA $\mathcal{M}$ accepts an input w iff $L \not\leq_t R$.*

Proof. If $\mathcal{M}$ accepts the input w then clearly it has an accepting computation tree T. By Lemma 3.8 $\text{code}(T) \leq_m L$ and by Lemma 3.14 $\text{code}(T) \not\leq_m R$. This implies that $L \not\leq_t R$.

On the other hand, if $\mathcal{M}$ does not accept w then none of the tree implementations of L represents a code of an accepting computation tree of $\mathcal{M}$ on w. By Lemma 3.13 this means that any tree I such that $I \leq_m L$ satisfies that $I \leq_m R$ and hence $L \leq_{tt} R$ which is by Lemma 3.5 equivalent to $L \leq_t R$. □

Corollary 3.16. *The problem of checking thorough refinement on finite modal transition systems is EXPTIME-hard.*

In fact, we can strengthen the result by adapting the above described reduction to the situation where the left-hand side system is of a fixed size (see [6]).

Theorem 3.17. *The problem of checking thorough refinement on finite modal transition systems is EXPTIME-hard even if the left-hand side system is fixed.*

4   Thorough Refinement Is in EXPTIME

In this section we provide a direct algorithm for deciding thorough refinement between MTSs in EXPTIME. Given two processes A and B over some finite-state MTSs, the algorithm will decide if there exists an implementation I that implements A but not B, i.e. $I \leq_m A$ and $I \not\leq_m B$.

For a modal transition systems B, we introduce the syntactical notation $\overline{B}$ to denote the semantical complement of B, i.e. $I \leq_m \overline{B}$ iff $I \not\leq_m B$. Our algorithm now essentially checks for consistency (existence of a common implementation) between A and $\overline{B}$ with the outcome that they are consistent if and only if $A \not\leq_t B$.

In general, we shall check for consistency of sets of the form $\{A, \overline{B}_1, \ldots, \overline{B}_k\}$ in the sense of existence of an implementation I such that $I \leq_m A$ but $I \not\leq_m B_i$ for all $i \in \{1, \ldots, k\}$. Before the full definition is given, let us get some intuition by considering the case of consistency of a simple pair $A, \overline{B}$. During the arguments, we shall use CCS-like constructs (summation and action-prefixing) for defining implementations.

Clearly, if for some B' with $B \xrightarrow{a} B'$ and for all A_i with $A \xrightarrow{a} A_i$ we can find an implementation I_i implementing A_i but not B' (i.e. we demonstrate consistency between all the pairs $A_i, \overline{B'}$), we can claim consistency between A and $\overline{B}$: as a common implementation I simply take $H + \sum_i a.I_i$, where H is some arbitrary implementation of A with all a-derivatives removed.

We may also conclude consistency of A and $\overline{B}$, if for some A' with $A \dashrightarrow^{a} A'$, we can find an implementation I' of A', which is not an implementation of any B' where $B \dashrightarrow^{a} B'$. Here a common implementation would simply be $H + a.I'$ where H is an arbitrary implementation of A. However, in this case we will need to determine consistency of the set $\{A'\} \cup \{\overline{B'} \mid B \dashrightarrow^{a} B'\}$ which is in general not a simple pair.

Definition 4.1. *Let $M = (P, \dashrightarrow, \longrightarrow)$ be an MTS over the action alphabet Σ. The set of* consistent *sets of the form $\{A, \overline{B}_1, \ldots, \overline{B}_k\}$, where $A, B_1, \ldots, B_k \in P$, is the smallest set* Con *such that $\{A, \overline{B}_1, \ldots, \overline{B}_k\} \in$ Con whenever $k = 0$ or for some $a \in \Sigma$ and some $J \subseteq \{1, \ldots, k\}$, where for all $j \in J$ there exists B'_j such that $B_j \xrightarrow{a} B'_j$, we have*

1. *$\{A', \overline{B'_j} \mid j \in J\} \in$ Con for all A' with $A \xrightarrow{a} A'$, and*
2. *$\{A_\ell, \overline{B'_\ell} \mid B_\ell \dashrightarrow^{a} B'_\ell\} \cup \{\overline{B'_j} \mid j \in J\} \in$ Con for all $\ell \notin J$ and some A_ℓ with $A \dashrightarrow^{a} A_\ell$.*

Lemma 4.2. *Given processes* $A, B_1, \ldots, B_k$ *of some finite MTS, there exists an implementation* I *such that* $I \leq_m A$ *and* $I \not\leq_m B_i$ *for all* $i \in \{1, \ldots, k\}$ *if and only if* $\{A, \overline{B}_1, \ldots, \overline{B}_k\} \in \mathsf{Con}$.

Computing the collection of consistent sets $\{A, \overline{B}_1, \ldots, \overline{B}_k\}$ over an MTS $(P, \dashrightarrow, \longrightarrow)$ may be done as a simple (least) fixed-point computation. The running time is polynomial in the number of potential sets of the form $\{A, \overline{B}_1, \ldots, \overline{B}_k\}$ where $A, B_1, \ldots, B_k \in P$, hence it is exponential in the number of states of the underlying MTS. This gives an EXPTIME algorithm to check for thorough refinement.

Theorem 4.3. *The problem of checking thorough refinement on finite modal transition systems is decidable in EXPTIME.*

Example 4.4. Consider S and T from Fig. 1. We have already mentioned in Section 2 that $S \leq_t T$. To see this, we will attempt (and fail) to demonstrate consistency of $\{S, \overline{T}\}$ according to Definition 4.1, which essentially asks for a finite tableau to be constructed. Now, in order for $\{S, \overline{T}\}$ to be concluded consistent, we have to establish consistency of $\{S_1, \overline{T}_1, \overline{T}_2\}$— as T has no must-transitions the only choice for J is $J = \emptyset$. Now, to establish consistency of $\{S_1, \overline{T}_1, \overline{T}_2\}$ both $J = \emptyset$ and $J = \{1\}$ are possibilities. However, in both cases the requirement will be that $\{S, \overline{T}\}$ must be consistent. Given this cyclic dependency together with the minimal fixed-point definition of Con it follows that $\{S, \overline{T}\}$ is *not* consistent, and hence that $S \leq_t T$.   □

Example 4.5. Consider S and U from Fig. 1. Here $S \not\leq_t U$ clearly with $I = a.0$ as a witness implementation. Let us demonstrate consistency of $\{S, \overline{U}\}$. Choosing $J = \emptyset$, this will follow from the consistency of $\{S_1, \overline{U}_1\}$. To conclude this, note that $J = \{1\}$ will leave us with the empty collection of sets—as S_1 has no must-transitions—all of which are obviously consistent.   □

Note that in the case of B being deterministic, we only need to consider pairs of the form $\{A, \overline{B}\}$ for determining consistency. This results in a polynomial time algorithm (see also [5] for an alternative proof of this fact). Similarly, if the process B is of a constant size, our algorithm runs in polynomial time as well.

Corollary 4.6. *The problem of checking thorough refinement between a given finite modal transition system and a finite deterministic or fixed-size modal transition system is in* P.

To conclude, by Theorem 4.3 and Corollary 3.16 we get our main result.

Theorem 4.7. *The problem of checking thorough refinement on finite modal transition systems is EXPTIME-complete.*

References

1. Antonik, A., Huth, M., Larsen, K.G., Nyman, U., Wasowski, A.: 20 years of modal and mixed specifications. Bulletin of the EATCS 1995, 94–129 (2008)
2. Antonik, A., Huth, M., Larsen, K.G., Nyman, U., Wasowski, A.: Complexity of decision problems for mixed and modal specifications. In: Amadio, R.M. (ed.) FOSSACS 2008. LNCS, vol. 4962, pp. 112–126. Springer, Heidelberg (2008)

3. Antonik, A., Huth, M., Larsen, K.G., Nyman, U., Wasowski, A.: EXPTIME-complete decision problems for mixed and modal specifications. In: Proc. of EXPRESS 2008 (July 2008)
4. Balcazar, J.L., Gabarró, J., Santha, M.: Deciding bisimilarity is P-complete. Formal aspects of computing 4(6A), 638–648 (1992)
5. Beneš, N., Křetínský, J., Larsen, K.G., Srba, J.: On determinism in modal transition systems. Theoretical Computer Science (to appear) (2008)
6. Beneš, N., Křetínský, J., Larsen, K.G., Srba, J.: Checking thorough refinement on modal transition systems is EXPTIME-complete. Technical report FIMU-RS-2009-03, Faculty of Informatics, Masaryk University, Brno (2009)
7. Bertrand, N., Pinchinat, S., Raclet, J.-B.: Refinement and consistency of timed modal specifications. In: Dediu, A.H., Ionescu, A.M., Martín-Vide, C. (eds.) LATA 2009. LNCS, vol. 5457, pp. 152–163. Springer, Heidelberg (2009)
8. D'Ippolito, N., Fischbein, D., Chechik, M., Uchitel, S.: MTSA: The modal transition system analyser. In: Proc. of ASE 2008, pp. 475–476. IEEE Computer Society Press, Los Alamitos (2008)
9. D'Ippolito, N., Fischbein, D., Foster, H., Uchitel, S.: MTSA: Eclipse support for modal transition systems construction, analysis and elaboration. In: Proc. of (ETX 2007), pp. 6–10. ACM Press, New York (2007)
10. Fecher, H., Schmidt, H.: Comparing disjunctive modal transition systems with an one-selecting variant. J. of Logic and Alg. Program. 77(1-2), 20–39 (2008)
11. Godefroid, P., Huth, M., Jagadeesan, R.: Abstraction-based model checking using modal transition systems. In: Larsen, K.G., Nielsen, M. (eds.) CONCUR 2001. LNCS, vol. 2154, pp. 426–440. Springer, Heidelberg (2001)
12. Huth, M., Jagadeesan, R., Schmidt, D.A.: Modal transition systems: A foundation for three-valued program analysis. In: Sands, D. (ed.) ESOP 2001. LNCS, vol. 2028, pp. 155–169. Springer, Heidelberg (2001)
13. Larsen, K.G., Nyman, U., Wasowski, A.: On modal refinement and consistency. In: Caires, L., Vasconcelos, V.T. (eds.) CONCUR 2007. LNCS, vol. 4703, pp. 105–119. Springer, Heidelberg (2007)
14. Larsen, K.G., Thomsen, B.: A modal process logic. In: Proc. of LICS 1988, pp. 203–210. IEEE Computer Society Press, Los Alamitos (1988)
15. Nanz, S., Nielson, F., Nielson, H.R.: Modal abstractions of concurrent behaviour. In: Alpuente, M., Vidal, G. (eds.) SAS 2008. LNCS, vol. 5079, pp. 159–173. Springer, Heidelberg (2008)
16. Raclet, J.-B.: Residual for component specifications. In: Proc. of the 4th International Workshop on Formal Aspects of Component Software (2007)
17. Raclet, J.-B., Badouel, E., Benveniste, A., Caillaud, B., Passerone, R.: Why are modalities good for interface theories. In: Proc. of ACSD 2009 (to appear, 2009)
18. Sawa, Z., Jančar, P.: Behavioural equivalences on finite-state systems are PTIME-hard. Computing and informatics 24(5), 513–528 (2005)
19. Sipser, M.: Introduction to the Theory of Computation. Course Technology (2006)
20. Uchitel, S., Chechik, M.: Merging partial behavioural models. In: FSE 2004, pp. 43–52. ACM, New York (2004)
21. Wei, O., Gurfinkel, A., Chechik, M.: Mixed transition systems revisited. In: Jones, N.D., Müller-Olm, M. (eds.) VMCAI 2009. LNCS, vol. 5403, pp. 349–365. Springer, Heidelberg (2009)

Transmission Protocols for Instruction Streams

J.A. Bergstra and C.A. Middelburg

Informatics Institute, Faculty of Science, University of Amsterdam,
Science Park 107, 1098 XG Amsterdam, The Netherlands
J.A.Bergstra@uva.nl, C.A.Middelburg@uva.nl

Abstract. Sequential programs under execution produce behaviours to
be controlled by some execution environment. Threads as considered in
basic thread algebra model such behaviours: upon each action performed
by a thread, a reply from an execution environment – which takes the
action as an instruction to be processed – determines how the thread
proceeds. In this paper, we are concerned with the case where the execution environment is remote: we study some transmission protocols for
passing instructions from a thread to a remote execution environment.

1 Introduction

The behaviours produced by sequential programs under execution are behaviours
to be controlled by some execution environment. The execution environment concerned is increasingly more a remote execution environment. The objective of
the current paper is to clarify the phenomenon of remotely controlled program
behaviours. With the current paper, we carry on the line of research with which
a start was made in [1]. This line of research concerns forms of sequential programs and behaviours produced by sequential programs under execution (see
e.g. [2,3,4]).

Basic thread algebra [1], BTA in short, is a form of process algebra tailored
to the description and analysis of the behaviours produced by sequential programs under execution.[1] Threads as considered in basic thread algebra model
behaviours to be controlled by some execution environment. Threads proceed
by performing steps, called basic actions in what follows, in a sequential fashion.
The execution environment of a thread takes the basic actions performed by the
thread as instructions to be processed. Upon each basic action performed by
the thread, a reply from the execution environment determines how the thread
proceeds. To achieve the objective of the current paper, we study some transmission protocols for passing instructions from a thread to a remote execution
environment.

General process algebras, such as ACP [5,6], CCS [7,8] and CSP [9,10], are
too general for the description and analysis of the behaviours produced by sequential programs under execution. That is, it is quite awkward to describe and

---

[1] In [1], basic thread algebra is introduced under the name basic polarized process
algebra.

M. Leucker and C. Morgan (Eds.): ICTAC 2009, LNCS 5684, pp. 127–139, 2009.
© Springer-Verlag Berlin Heidelberg 2009

analyse behaviours of this kind using such a general process algebra. However, the behaviours considered in basic thread algebra can be viewed as processes that are definable over ACP, see e.g. [11]. This allows for the transmission protocols mentioned above to be described and their correctness to be verified using ACP or rather ACP$^\tau$, an extension of ACP which supports abstraction from internal actions. We consider first a very simple transmission protocol and then a more complex one that is more efficient.

This paper is organized as follows. First, we give brief summaries of BTA (Section 2) and ACP$^\tau$ (Section 3). Next, we make mathematically precise the connection between behaviours as considered in BTA and processes as considered in ACP$^\tau$ (Section 4). After that, we describe and analyse the above-mentioned transmission protocols (Sections 5 and 6). Finally, we make some concluding remarks (Section 7).

2   Thread Algebra

In this section, we review BTA (Basic Thread Algebra). BTA is concerned with behaviours as exhibited by sequential programs under execution. These behaviours are called threads.

In BTA, it is assumed that a fixed but arbitrary set $\mathcal{A}$ of *basic actions* has been given. A thread performs basic actions in a sequential fashion. Upon each basic action performed, a reply from the execution environment of the thread determines how it proceeds. The possible replies are the Boolean values T and F.

To build terms, BTA has the following constants and operators:

- the *deadlock* constant D;
- the *termination* constant S;
- for each $a \in \mathcal{A}$, the binary *postconditional composition* operator $\unlhd\, a \unrhd$.

We assume that there are infinitely many variables, including x, y, z. Terms are built as usual. We use infix notation for the postconditional composition operator.

The thread denoted by a closed term of the form $p \unlhd a \unrhd q$ will first perform a, and then proceed as the thread denoted by p if the reply from the execution environment is T and proceed as the thread denoted by q if the reply from the execution environment is F. The threads denoted by D and S will become inactive and terminate, respectively. This implies that each closed BTA term denotes a thread that will become inactive or terminate after it has performed finitely many basic actions. Infinite threads can be described by guarded recursion.

A *guarded recursive specification* over BTA is a set of recursion equations $E = \{X = t_X \mid X \in V\}$, where V is a set of variables and each t_X is a BTA term of the form D, S or $t \unlhd a \unrhd t'$ with t and t' that contain only variables from V. We write $\mathrm{V}(E)$ for the set of all variables that occur in E. We are only interested in models of BTA in which guarded recursive specifications have unique solutions, such as the projective limit model of BTA presented in [12].

For each guarded recursive specification E and each $X \in \mathrm{V}(E)$, we introduce a constant $\langle X | E \rangle$ standing for the unique solution of E for X. The axioms for these

Table 1. Axioms for guarded recursion

$$\langle X|E\rangle = \langle t_X|E\rangle \quad \text{if } X = t_X \in E \quad \text{RDP}$$
$$E \Rightarrow X = \langle X|E\rangle \quad \text{if } X \in \text{V}(E) \quad \text{RSP}$$

constants are given in Table 1. In this table, we write $\langle t_X|E\rangle$ for t_X with, for all $Y \in \text{V}(E)$, all occurrences of Y in t_X replaced by $\langle Y|E\rangle$. X, t_X and E stand for an arbitrary variable, an arbitrary BTA term and an arbitrary guarded recursive specification over BTA, respectively. Side conditions are added to restrict what X, t_X and E stand for.

In the sequel, we will make use of a version of BTA in which the following additional assumptions relating to $\mathcal{A}$ are made: (i) a fixed but arbitrary set $\mathcal{F}$ of *foci* has been given; (ii) a fixed but arbitrary set $\mathcal{M}$ of *methods* has been given; (iii) $\mathcal{A} = \{f.m \mid f \in \mathcal{F}, m \in \mathcal{M}\}$. These assumptions are based on the view that the execution environment provides a number of services. Performing a basic action $f.m$ is taken as making a request to the service named f to process command m. As usual, we will write $\mathbb{B}$ for the set $\{\mathsf{T}, \mathsf{F}\}$.

3   Process Algebra

In this section, we review ACP$^\tau$ (Algebra of Communicating Processes with abstraction). This is the process algebra that will be used in Section 4 to make precise what processes are produced by the threads denoted by closed terms of BTA with guarded recursion. For a comprehensive overview of ACP$^\tau$, the reader is referred to [6,13].

In ACP$^\tau$, it is assumed that a fixed but arbitrary set A of *atomic actions*, with $\tau, \delta \notin$ A, and a fixed but arbitrary commutative and associative function $| : \text{A} \times \text{A} \to \text{A} \cup \{\delta\}$ have been given. The function $|$ is regarded to give the result of synchronously performing any two atomic actions for which this is possible, and to give δ otherwise. In ACP$^\tau$, τ is a special atomic action, called the silent step. The act of performing the silent step is considered unobservable. Because it would otherwise be observable, the silent step is considered an atomic action that cannot be performed synchronously with other atomic actions.

ACP$^\tau$ has the following constants and operators:

- for each $e \in$ A, the *atomic action* constant e;
- the *silent step* constant τ;
- the *deadlock* constant δ;
- the binary *alternative composition* operator $+$;
- the binary *sequential composition* operator $\cdot$;
- the binary *parallel composition* operator $\parallel$;
- the binary *left merge* operator $\lfloor\!\lfloor$;
- the binary *communication merge* operator $|$;

Table 2. Axioms of ACP^τ

$x + y = y + x$	A1	$x \cdot \tau = x$	B1
$(x + y) + z = x + (y + z)$	A2	$x \cdot (\tau \cdot (y + z) + y) = x \cdot (y + z)$	B2
$x + x = x$	A3		
$(x + y) \cdot z = x \cdot z + y \cdot z$	A4	$\partial_H(a) = a$ if $a \notin H$	D1
$(x \cdot y) \cdot z = x \cdot (y \cdot z)$	A5	$\partial_H(a) = \delta$ if $a \in H$	D2
$x + \delta = x$	A6	$\partial_H(x + y) = \partial_H(x) + \partial_H(y)$	D3
$\delta \cdot x = \delta$	A7	$\partial_H(x \cdot y) = \partial_H(x) \cdot \partial_H(y)$	D4

$x \parallel y = x \lfloor\!\lfloor y + y \lfloor\!\lfloor x + x \mid y$	CM1	$\tau_I(a) = a$ if $a \notin I$	TI1
$a \lfloor\!\lfloor x = a \cdot x$	CM2	$\tau_I(a) = \tau$ if $a \in I$	TI2
$a \cdot x \lfloor\!\lfloor y = a \cdot (x \parallel y)$	CM3	$\tau_I(x + y) = \tau_I(x) + \tau_I(y)$	TI3
$(x + y) \lfloor\!\lfloor z = x \lfloor\!\lfloor z + y \lfloor\!\lfloor z$	CM4	$\tau_I(x \cdot y) = \tau_I(x) \cdot \tau_I(y)$	TI4
$a \cdot x \mid b = (a \mid b) \cdot x$	CM5		
$a \mid b \cdot x = (a \mid b) \cdot x$	CM6	$a \mid b = b \mid a$	C1
$a \cdot x \mid b \cdot y = (a \mid b) \cdot (x \parallel y)$	CM7	$(a \mid b) \mid c = a \mid (b \mid c)$	C2
$(x + y) \mid z = x \mid z + y \mid z$	CM8	$\delta \mid a = \delta$	C3
$x \mid (y + z) = x \mid y + x \mid z$	CM9	$\tau \mid a = \delta$	C4

- for each $H \subseteq A$, the unary *encapsulation* operator ∂_H ;
- for each $I \subseteq A$, the unary *abstraction* operator τ_I .

We assume that there are infinitely many variables, including x, y, z. Terms are built as usual. We use infix notation for the binary operators.

Let p and q be closed ACP^τ terms, $e \in A$, and $H, I \subseteq A$. Intuitively, the constants and operators to build ACP^τ terms can be explained as follows:

- e first performs atomic action e and next terminates successfully;
- τ performs an unobservable atomic action and next terminates successfully;
- δ can neither perform an atomic action nor terminate successfully;
- $p + q$ behaves either as p or as q, but not both;
- $p \cdot q$ first behaves as p and on successful termination of p it next behaves as q;
- $p \parallel q$ behaves as the process that proceeds with p and q in parallel;
- $p \lfloor\!\lfloor q$ behaves the same as $p \parallel q$, except that it starts with performing an atomic action of p;
- $p \mid q$ behaves the same as $p \parallel q$, except that it starts with performing an atomic action of p and an atomic action of q synchronously;
- $\partial_H(p)$ behaves the same as p, except that atomic actions from H are blocked;
- $\tau_I(p)$ behaves the same as p, except that atomic actions from I are turned into unobservable atomic actions.

Table 3. RDP, RSP and AIP

$\langle X|E\rangle = \langle t_X|E\rangle$ if $X = t_X \in E$ RDP	$\pi_0(a) = \delta$	PR1
$E \Rightarrow X = \langle X|E\rangle$ if $X \in V(E)$ RSP	$\pi_{n+1}(a) = a$	PR2
	$\pi_0(a \cdot x) = \delta$	PR3
$\bigwedge_{n \geq 0} \pi_n(x) = \pi_n(y) \Rightarrow x = y$ AIP	$\pi_{n+1}(a \cdot x) = a \cdot \pi_n(x)$	PR4
	$\pi_n(x + y) = \pi_n(x) + \pi_n(y)$	PR5
	$\pi_n(\tau) = \tau$	PR6
	$\pi_n(\tau \cdot x) = \tau \cdot \pi_n(x)$	PR7

The axioms of ACP^τ are given in Table 2. CM2–CM3, CM5–CM7, C1–C4, D1–D4 and TI1–TI4 are actually axiom schemas in which a, b and c stand for arbitrary constants of ACP^τ, and H and I stand for arbitrary subsets of A.

A *recursive specification* over ACP^τ is a set of recursion equations $E = \{X = t_X \mid X \in V\}$, where V is a set of variables and each t_X is an ACP^τ term containing only variables from V. Let t be an ACP^τ term without occurrences of abstraction operators containing a variable X. Then an occurrence of X in t is *guarded* if t has a subterm of the form $e \cdot t'$ where $e \in$ A and t' is a term containing this occurrence of X. Let E be a recursive specification over ACP^τ. Then E is a *guarded recursive specification* if, in each equation $X = t_X \in E$: (i) abstraction operators do not occur in t_X and (ii) all occurrences of variables in t_X are guarded or t_X can be rewritten to such a term using the axioms of ACP^τ in either direction and/or the equations in E except the equation $X = t_X$ from left to right. We only consider models of ACP^τ in which guarded recursive specifications have unique solutions, such as the models of ACP^τ presented in [6].

For each guarded recursive specification E and each variable X that occurs in E, we introduce a constant $\langle X|E\rangle$ standing for the unique solution of E for X. The axioms for these constants are RDP and RSP given in Table 3. In RDP, we write $\langle t_X|E\rangle$ for t_X with, for all $Y \in V(E)$, all occurrences of Y in t_X replaced by $\langle Y|E\rangle$. RDP and RSP are actually axiom schemas in which X stands for an arbitrary variable, t_X stands for an arbitrary ACP^τ term, and E stands for an arbitrary guarded recursive specification over ACP^τ.

Closed terms of ACP with guarded recursion that denote the same process cannot always be proved equal by means of the axioms of ACP together with RDP and RSP. To remedy this, we introduce AIP (Approximation Induction Principle). AIP is based on the view that two processes are identical if their approximations up to any finite depth are identical. The approximation up to depth n of a process behaves the same as that process, except that it cannot perform any further atomic action after n atomic actions have been performed. AIP is given in Table 3. Here, approximation up to depth n is phrased in terms of a unary *projection* operator π_n. The axioms for these operators are axioms PR1–PR7 in Table 3. PR1–PR7 are actually axiom schemas in which a stands for arbitrary constants of ACP^τ different from τ and n stands for an arbitrary natural number.

Table 4. Defining equations for process extraction operation

$$|X|^c = X$$
$$|S|^c = \text{stop}$$
$$|D|^c = i \cdot \delta$$
$$|t_1 \trianglelefteq f.m \trianglerighteq t_2|^c = s_f(m) \cdot (r_f(T) \cdot |t_1|^c + r_f(F) \cdot |t_2|^c)$$
$$|\langle X|E \rangle|^c = \langle X | \{ Y = |t_Y|^c \mid Y = t_Y \in E \} \rangle$$

We will write $\sum_{i \in S} p_i$, where $S = \{i_1, \ldots, i_n\}$ and $p_{i_1}, \ldots, p_{i_n}$ are ACP^τ terms, for $p_{i_1} + \ldots + p_{i_n}$. The convention is that $\sum_{i \in S} p_i$ stands for δ if $S = \emptyset$. We will often write X for $\langle X|E \rangle$ if E is clear from the context. It should be borne in mind that, in such cases, we use X as a constant.

4   Process Extraction

In this section, we use ACP^τ with guarded recursion to make mathematically precise what processes are produced by the threads denoted by closed terms of BTA with guarded recursion.

For that purpose, A and $|$ are taken such that the following conditions are satisfied:

$$\mathsf{A} \supseteq \{ s_f(d) \mid f \in \mathcal{F}, d \in \mathcal{M} \cup \mathbb{B} \} \cup \{ r_f(d) \mid f \in \mathcal{F}, d \in \mathcal{M} \cup \mathbb{B} \} \cup \{ \text{stop}, i \}$$

and for all $f \in \mathcal{F}$, $d \in \mathcal{M} \cup \mathbb{B}$, and $e \in \mathsf{A}$:

$$s_f(d) \mid r_f(d) = i \,,$$
$$s_f(d) \mid e = \delta \qquad \text{if } e \neq r_f(d) \,, \qquad \text{stop} \mid e = \delta \,,$$
$$e \mid r_f(d) = \delta \qquad \text{if } e \neq s_f(d) \,, \qquad i \mid e = \delta \,.$$

Actions of the forms $s_f(d)$ and $r_f(d)$ are send and receive actions, respectively, stop is an explicit termination action, and i is a concrete internal action.

The *process extraction* operation $|_-|$ determines, for each closed term p of BTA with guarded recursion, a closed term of ACP^τ with guarded recursion that denotes the process produced by the thread denoted by p. The process extraction operation $|_-|$ is defined by $|p| = \tau_{\{\text{stop}\}}(|p|^c)$, where $|_-|^c$ is defined by the equations given in Table 4 (for $f \in \mathcal{F}$ and $m \in \mathcal{M}$).

Two atomic actions are involved in performing a basic action of the form $f.m$: one for sending a request to process command m to the service named f and another for receiving a reply from that service upon completion of the processing. For each closed term p of BTA with guarded recursion, $|p|^c$ denotes a process that in the event of termination performs a special termination action just before termination. Abstracting from this termination action yields the process denoted by $|p|$. Some atomic actions introduced above are not used in the definition of the process extraction operation for BTA. Those atomic actions are commonly used in the definition of the process extraction operation for extensions of BTA in which operators for thread-service interaction occur, see e.g. [11].

Let p be a closed term of BTA with guarded recursion. Then we say that $|p|$ is the *process produced by* p.

The process extraction operation preserves the axioms of BTA with guarded recursion. Roughly speaking, this means that the translations of these axioms are derivable from the axioms of ACP^τ with guarded recursion. Before we make this fully precise, we have a closer look at the axioms of BTA with guarded recursion.

A proper axiom is an equation or a conditional equation. In Table 1, we do not find proper axioms. Instead of proper axioms, we find axiom schemas without side conditions and axiom schemas with side conditions. The axioms of BTA with guarded recursion are obtained by replacing each axiom schema by all its instances.

We define a function $|_-|$ from the set of all equations and conditional equations of BTA with guarded recursion to the set of all equations of ACP^τ with guarded recursion as follows:

$$|t_1 = t_2| \;=\; |t_1| = |t_2|\,,$$
$$|E \Rightarrow t_1 = t_2| \;=\; \{|t_1'| = |t_2'| \mid t_1' = t_2' \in E\} \Rightarrow |t_1| = |t_2|\,.$$

Proposition 1. *Let ϕ be an axiom of* BTA *with guarded recursion. Then $|\phi|$ is derivable from the axioms of* ACP^τ *with guarded recursion.*

Proof. The proof is trivial.   □

Proposition 1 would go through if no abstraction of the above-mentioned special termination action was made. Notice further that ACP^τ without the silent step constant and the abstraction operator, better known as ACP, would suffice if no abstraction of the special termination action was made.

5   A Simple Protocol

In this section, we consider a very simple transmission protocol for passing instructions from a thread to a remote execution environment.

At the location of the thread concerned, two atomic actions are involved in performing a basic action: one for sending a message containing the basic action via a transmission channel to a receiver at the location of the execution environment and another for receiving a reply via a transmission channel from the receiver upon completion of the processing at the location of the execution environment. The receiver waits until a message containing a basic action can be received. Upon reception of a message containing a basic action $f.m$, the receiver sends a request to process command m to the service named f at the location of the execution environment. Next, the receiver waits until a reply from that service can be received. Upon reception of a reply, the receiver forwards the reply to the thread. Deadlocking and terminating are treated like performing basic actions.

We write $\mathcal{A}'$ for the set $\mathcal{A} \cup \{\mathsf{stop}, \mathsf{dead}\}$.

Table 5. Process extraction for remotely controlled threads

$$|X|_{\text{rct}} = X$$
$$|\mathsf{S}|_{\text{rct}} = \mathsf{s}_1(\mathsf{stop})$$
$$|\mathsf{D}|_{\text{rct}} = \mathsf{s}_1(\mathsf{dead})$$
$$|t_1 \trianglelefteq a \trianglerighteq t_2|_{\text{rct}} = \mathsf{s}_1(a) \cdot (\mathsf{r}_4(\mathsf{T}) \cdot |t_1|_{\text{rct}} + \mathsf{r}_4(\mathsf{F}) \cdot |t_2|_{\text{rct}})$$
$$|\langle X|E\rangle|_{\text{rct}} = \langle X| \{Y = |t_Y|_{\text{rct}} \mid Y = t_Y \in E\}\rangle$$

For the purpose of describing the very simple transmission protocol outlined above in ACP^τ, A and $|$ are taken such that, in addition to the conditions mentioned at the beginning of Section 4, the following conditions are satisfied:

$$\mathsf{A} \supseteq \{\mathsf{s}_i(d) \mid i \in \{1,2\}, d \in \mathcal{A}'\} \cup \{\mathsf{r}_i(d) \mid i \in \{1,2\}, d \in \mathcal{A}'\}$$
$$\cup \{\mathsf{s}_i(r) \mid i \in \{3,4\}, r \in \mathbb{B}\} \cup \{\mathsf{r}_i(r) \mid i \in \{3,4\}, r \in \mathbb{B}\} \cup \{\mathsf{j}\}$$

and for all $i \in \{1,2\}$, $j \in \{3,4\}$, $d \in \mathcal{A}'$, $r \in \mathbb{B}$, and $e \in \mathsf{A}$:

$$\mathsf{s}_i(d) \mid \mathsf{r}_i(d) = \mathsf{j}\,, \qquad\qquad \mathsf{s}_j(r) \mid \mathsf{r}_j(r) = \mathsf{j}\,,$$
$$\mathsf{s}_i(d) \mid e = \delta \quad \text{if } e \neq \mathsf{r}_i(d)\,, \qquad \mathsf{s}_j(r) \mid e = \delta \quad \text{if } e \neq \mathsf{r}_j(r)\,,$$
$$e \mid \mathsf{r}_i(d) = \delta \quad \text{if } e \neq \mathsf{s}_i(d)\,, \qquad e \mid \mathsf{r}_j(r) = \delta \quad \text{if } e \neq \mathsf{s}_j(r)\,,$$

$$\mathsf{j} \mid e = \delta\,.$$

We introduce a process extraction operation $|_-|_{\text{rct}}$ which determines, for each closed term p of BTA with guarded recursion, a closed term of ACP^τ with guarded recursion that denotes the process produced by the thread denoted by p in the case where the thread is remotely controlled. This operation is defined by the equations given in Table 5 (for $a \in \mathcal{A}$).

Let p be a closed term of BTA with guarded recursion. Then the process representing the remotely controlled thread p is described by

$$\partial_H(|p|_{\text{rct}} \parallel CHA \parallel CHR \parallel RCV)\,,$$

where

$$CHA = \sum_{d \in \mathcal{A}'} \mathsf{r}_1(d) \cdot \mathsf{s}_2(d) \cdot CHA\,,$$

$$CHR = \sum_{r \in \mathbb{B}} \mathsf{r}_3(r) \cdot \mathsf{s}_4(r) \cdot CHR\,,$$

$$RCV = \sum_{f.m \in \mathcal{A}'} \mathsf{r}_2(f.m) \cdot \mathsf{s}_f(m) \cdot (\mathsf{r}_f(\mathsf{T}) \cdot \mathsf{s}_3(\mathsf{T}) + \mathsf{r}_f(\mathsf{F}) \cdot \mathsf{s}_3(\mathsf{F})) \cdot RCV$$
$$+ \mathsf{r}_2(\mathsf{stop}) + \mathsf{r}_2(\mathsf{dead}) \cdot \mathsf{i} \cdot \delta$$

and

$$H = \{\mathsf{s}_i(d) \mid i \in \{1,2\}, d \in \mathcal{A}'\} \cup \{\mathsf{r}_i(d) \mid i \in \{1,2\}, d \in \mathcal{A}'\}$$
$$\cup \{\mathsf{s}_i(r) \mid i \in \{3,4\}, r \in \mathbb{B}\} \cup \{\mathsf{r}_i(r) \mid i \in \{3,4\}, r \in \mathbb{B}\}\,.$$

CHA is the transmission channel for messages containing basic actions, *CHR* is the transmission channel for replies, and *RCV* is the receiver.

If we abstract from all atomic actions for sending and receiving via the transmission channels *CHA* and *CHR*, then the processes denoted by $|p|$ and $\partial_H(|p|_{\text{rct}} \| CHA \| CHR \| RCV)$ are equal modulo an initial silent step.

Theorem 1. *For each closed term p of BTA with guarded recursion:*

$$\tau \cdot |p| = \tau \cdot \tau_{\{j\}}(\partial_H(|p|_{\text{rct}} \| CHA \| CHR \| RCV)) .$$

Proof. By AIP, it is sufficient to prove that for all $n \geq 0$:

$$\pi_n(\tau \cdot |p|) = \pi_n(\tau \cdot \tau_{\{j\}}(\partial_H(|p|_{\text{rct}} \| CHA \| CHR \| RCV))) .$$

This is easily proved by induction on n and in the inductive step by case distinction on the structure of p, using the axioms of ACP^τ and RDP.   □

6   A More Complex Protocol

In this section, we consider a more complex transmission protocol for passing instructions from a thread to a remote execution environment.

The general idea of this protocol is that:

- while the last basic action performed by the thread in question is processed at the location of the receiver, the first basic actions of the two ways in which the thread may proceed are transmitted together to the receiver;
- while the choice between those two basic actions is made by the receiver on the basis of the reply produced at the completion of the processing, the reply is transferred to the thread.

To simplify the description of the protocol, the following extensions of ACP from [14] will be used:

- We will use conditionals. The expression $p \triangleleft b \triangleright q$, is to be read as if b then p else q. The defining equations are

$$x \triangleleft \mathsf{T} \triangleright y = x \quad \text{and} \quad x \triangleleft \mathsf{F} \triangleright y = y .$$

- We will use the generalization of restricted early input action prefixing to process prefixing. Restricted early input action prefixing is defined by the equation $\text{er}_i^D(u) \,;\, t = \sum_{d \in D} \text{r}_i(d) \cdot t[d/u]$. We use the extension to processes to express binary parallel input: $(\text{er}_i^{D_1}(u_1) \| \text{er}_j^{D_2}(u_2)) \,;\, P$. For this particular case, we have the following equation:

$$(\text{er}_i^{D_1}(u_1) \| \text{er}_j^{D_2}(u_2)) \,;\, t = \sum_{d_1 \in D_1} \text{r}_i(d_1) \cdot (\text{er}_j^{D_2}(u_2) \,;\, t[d_1/u_1])$$
$$+ \sum_{d_2 \in D_2} \text{r}_j(d_2) \cdot (\text{er}_i^{D_1}(u_1) \,;\, t[d_2/u_2]) .$$

Table 6. Alternative process extraction for remotely controlled threads

$|X|_{\mathrm{rct2}} = X$

$|S|_{\mathrm{rct2}} = \mathsf{s}_1(\mathsf{stop})$

$|D|_{\mathrm{rct2}} = \mathsf{s}_1(\mathsf{dead})$

$|t_1 \unlhd a \unrhd t_2|_{\mathrm{rct2}} = \mathsf{s}_1(a, init(t_1), init(t_2)) \cdot (\mathsf{r}_4(\mathsf{T}) \cdot |t_1|'_{\mathrm{rct2}} + \mathsf{r}_4(\mathsf{F}) \cdot |t_2|'_{\mathrm{rct2}})$

$|\langle X|E\rangle|_{\mathrm{rct2}} = \langle X| \{Y = |t_Y|_{\mathrm{rct2}} \mid Y = t_Y \in E\}\rangle$

$|X|'_{\mathrm{rct2}} = X$

$|S|'_{\mathrm{rct2}} = \mathsf{s}_1(\mathsf{void})$

$|D|'_{\mathrm{rct2}} = \mathsf{s}_1(\mathsf{void})$

$|t_1 \unlhd a \unrhd t_2|'_{\mathrm{rct2}} = \mathsf{s}_1(init(t_1), init(t_2)) \cdot (\mathsf{r}_4(\mathsf{T}) \cdot |t_1|'_{\mathrm{rct2}} + \mathsf{r}_4(\mathsf{F}) \cdot |t_2|'_{\mathrm{rct2}})$

$|\langle X|E\rangle|'_{\mathrm{rct2}} = \langle X| \{Y = |t_Y|'_{\mathrm{rct2}} \mid Y = t_Y \in E\}\rangle$

$init(S) = \mathsf{stop}$

$init(D) = \mathsf{dead}$

$init(t_1 \unlhd a \unrhd t_2) = a$

$init(\langle X|E\rangle) = init(\langle t_X|E\rangle)$ if $X = t_X \in E$

We write $\mathcal{A}''_2$ for the set $\mathcal{A}' \times \mathcal{A}'$, $\mathcal{A}''_3$ for the set $\mathcal{A} \times \mathcal{A}' \times \mathcal{A}'$, and $\mathcal{A}''$ for the set $\mathcal{A}''_2 \cup \mathcal{A}''_3 \cup \{\mathsf{stop}, \mathsf{dead}, \mathsf{void}\}$.

For the purpose of describing the more complex transmission protocol outlined above in ACP^τ, A and | are taken such that, in addition to the conditions mentioned at the beginning of Section 4, the following conditions are satisfied:

$$\mathsf{A} \supseteq \{\mathsf{s}_i(d) \mid i \in \{1,2\}, d \in \mathcal{A}''\} \cup \{\mathsf{r}_i(d) \mid i \in \{1,2\}, d \in \mathcal{A}''\}$$
$$\cup \ \{\mathsf{s}_i(r) \mid i \in \{3,4\}, r \in \mathbb{B}\} \cup \{\mathsf{r}_i(r) \mid i \in \{3,4\}, r \in \mathbb{B}\} \cup \{\mathsf{j}\}$$

and for all $i \in \{1,2\}$, $j \in \{3,4\}$, $d \in \mathcal{A}''$, $r \in \mathbb{B}$, and $e \in \mathsf{A}$:

$$\mathsf{s}_i(d) \mid \mathsf{r}_i(d) = \mathsf{j}\,, \qquad\qquad \mathsf{s}_j(r) \mid \mathsf{r}_j(r) = \mathsf{j}\,,$$
$$\mathsf{s}_i(d) \mid e = \delta \quad \text{if } e \neq \mathsf{r}_i(d)\,, \qquad \mathsf{s}_j(r) \mid e = \delta \quad \text{if } e \neq \mathsf{r}_j(r)\,,$$
$$e \mid \mathsf{r}_i(d) = \delta \quad \text{if } e \neq \mathsf{s}_i(d)\,, \qquad e \mid \mathsf{r}_j(r) = \delta \quad \text{if } e \neq \mathsf{s}_j(r)\,,$$
$$\mathsf{j} \mid e = \delta\,.$$

We introduce a process extraction operation $|_-|_{\mathrm{rct2}}$ which determines, for each closed term p of BTA with guarded recursion, a closed term of ACP^τ with guarded recursion that denotes the process produced by the thread denoted by p in the case where the thread is remotely controlled by means of the alternative transmission protocol. This operation is defined by the equations given in Table 6 (for $a \in \mathcal{A}$).

Let p be a closed term of BTA with guarded recursion. Then the process representing the remotely controlled thread p is described by

$$\partial_H(|p|_{\mathrm{rct2}} \parallel CHA_2 \parallel CHR \parallel RCV_2) ,$$

where

$$CHA_2 \quad = \quad \sum_{d \in \mathcal{A}''} \mathrm{r}_1(d) \cdot \mathrm{s}_2(d) \cdot CHA_2 ,$$

$$CHR \quad = \quad \sum_{r \in \mathbb{B}} \mathrm{r}_3(r) \cdot \mathrm{s}_4(r) \cdot CHR ,$$

$$RCV_2 \quad = \quad \sum_{(f.m,a,a') \in \mathcal{A}_3''} \mathrm{r}_2(f.m, a, a') \cdot \mathrm{s}_f(m)$$
$$\cdot (\mathrm{r}_f(\mathsf{T}) \cdot RCV_2'(\mathsf{T}, a) + \mathrm{r}_f(\mathsf{F}) \cdot RCV_2'(\mathsf{F}, a'))$$
$$+ \mathrm{r}_2(\mathsf{stop}) + \mathrm{r}_2(\mathsf{dead}) \cdot \mathrm{i} \cdot \delta ,$$

$$RCV_2'(r, f.m) = (\mathrm{s}_3(r) \parallel \mathrm{s}_f(m)) \cdot RCV_2'' ,$$
$$RCV_2'(r, \mathsf{stop}) = \mathrm{r}_2(\mathsf{void}) ,$$
$$RCV_2'(r, \mathsf{dead}) = \mathrm{r}_2(\mathsf{void}) \cdot \mathrm{i} \cdot \delta ,$$

$$RCV_2'' \quad = (\mathrm{er}_2^{\mathcal{A}''}(u, v) \parallel \mathrm{er}_f^{\mathbb{B}}(\beta)) ; (RCV_2'(\beta, u) \triangleleft \beta \triangleright RCV_2'(\beta, v))$$

and

$$H = \{\mathrm{s}_i(d) \mid i \in \{1,2\}, d \in \mathcal{A}''\} \cup \{\mathrm{r}_i(d) \mid i \in \{1,2\}, d \in \mathcal{A}''\}$$
$$\cup \{\mathrm{s}_i(r) \mid i \in \{3,4\}, r \in \mathbb{B}\} \cup \{\mathrm{r}_i(r) \mid i \in \{3,4\}, r \in \mathbb{B}\} .$$

Notice that the first cycle of the alternative transmission protocol differs fairly from all subsequent ones. This difference gives rise to a slight complication in the proof of Theorem 2 below.

If we abstract from all atomic actions for sending and receiving via the transmission channels CHA_2 and CHR, then the processes denoted by $|p|$ and $\partial_H(|p|_{\mathrm{rct2}} \parallel CHA_2 \parallel CHR \parallel RCV_2)$ are equal modulo an initial silent step.

Theorem 2. *For each closed term p of BTA with guarded recursion:*

$$\tau \cdot |p| = \tau \cdot \tau_{\{j\}}(\partial_H(|p|_{\mathrm{rct2}} \parallel CHA_2 \parallel CHR \parallel RCV_2)) .$$

Proof. By AIP, it is sufficient to prove that for all $n \geq 0$:

$$\pi_n(\tau \cdot |p|) = \pi_n(\tau \cdot \tau_{\{j\}}(\partial_H(|p|_{\mathrm{rct2}} \parallel CHA_2 \parallel CHR \parallel RCV_2))) .$$

For $n = 0, 1, 2$, this is easily proved. For $n \geq 3$, it is easily proved in the cases $p \equiv \mathsf{S}$ and $p \equiv \mathsf{D}$, but in the case $p \equiv p_1 \trianglelefteq f.m \trianglerighteq p_2$ we get:

$$\tau \cdot \mathrm{s}_f(m) \cdot (\mathrm{r}_f(\mathsf{T}) \cdot \pi_{n-2}(|p_1|) + \mathrm{r}_f(\mathsf{F}) \cdot \pi_{n-2}(|p_2|))$$
$$= \tau \cdot \mathrm{s}_f(m)$$
$$\cdot (\mathrm{r}_f(\mathsf{T}) \cdot \pi_{n-2}(\tau_{\{j\}}(\partial_H(|p_1|_{\mathrm{rct2}}' \parallel CHA_2 \parallel CHR \parallel RCV_2'(\mathsf{T}, init(p_1)))))$$
$$+ \mathrm{r}_f(\mathsf{F}) \cdot \pi_{n-2}(\tau_{\{j\}}(\partial_H(|p_2|_{\mathrm{rct2}}' \parallel CHA_2 \parallel CHR \parallel RCV_2'(\mathsf{F}, init(p_2))))))) .$$

We have that

$$\pi_{n-2}(\tau_{\{j\}}(\partial_H(|p'|'_{\text{rct2}} \parallel CHA_2 \parallel CHR \parallel RCV'_2(\mathsf{T}, init(p')))))$$
$$= \pi_{n-2}(\tau_{\{j\}}(\partial_H(|p'|'_{\text{rct2}} \parallel CHA_2 \parallel CHR \parallel RCV'_2(\mathsf{F}, init(p')))))$$

in the cases $p' \equiv \mathsf{S}$ and $p' \equiv \mathsf{D}$, but not in the case $p' \equiv p'_1 \trianglelefteq f'.m' \trianglerighteq p'_2$. Therefore, we cannot prove

$$\pi_n(\tau \cdot |p|) = \pi_n(\tau \cdot \tau_{\{j\}}(\partial_H(|p|_{\text{rct2}} \parallel CHA_2 \parallel CHR \parallel RCV_2)))$$

by induction on n. However, in the case $p' \equiv p'_1 \trianglelefteq f'.m' \trianglerighteq p'_2$ we have that

$$\mathsf{r}_f(r) \cdot \pi_{n-2}(|p'|)$$
$$= \mathsf{r}_f(r) \cdot \mathsf{s}_{f'}(m') \cdot \pi_{n-3}(\mathsf{r}_{f'}(\mathsf{T}) \cdot |p'_1| + \mathsf{r}_{f'}(\mathsf{F}) \cdot |p'_2|)$$

and

$$\mathsf{r}_f(r) \cdot \pi_{n-2}(\tau_{\{j\}}(\partial_H(|p'|'_{\text{rct2}} \parallel CHA_2 \parallel CHR \parallel RCV'_2(r, f'.m'))))$$
$$= \mathsf{r}_f(r) \cdot \mathsf{s}_{f'}(m') \cdot \pi_{n-3}(\tau_{\{j\}}(\partial_H(|p'|'_{\text{rct2}} \parallel CHA_2 \parallel CHR \parallel RCV''_2))) .$$

Therefore, it is sufficient to prove that for all closed terms p_1 and p_2 of BTA with guarded recursion, $f \in \mathcal{F}$ and $m \in \mathcal{M}$, for all $n \geq 0$:

$$\pi_n(\tau \cdot (\mathsf{r}_f(\mathsf{T}) \cdot |p_1| + \mathsf{r}_f(\mathsf{F}) \cdot |p_2|))$$
$$= \pi_n(\tau \cdot \tau_{\{j\}}(\partial_H(|p_1 \trianglelefteq f.m \trianglerighteq p_2|'_{\text{rct2}} \parallel CHA_2 \parallel CHR \parallel RCV''_2))) .$$

This is easily proved by induction on n and in the inductive step by case distinction on the structure of p_1 and p_2, using the axioms of ACP$^\tau$, RDP and the axioms concerning process prefixing and conditionals given in [14].   □

7   Conclusions

Using ACP$^\tau$, we have described a very simple transmission protocol for passing instructions from a thread to a remote execution environment and a more complex one that is more efficient, and we have verified the correctness of these protocols. In this way, we have clarified the phenomenon of remotely controlled program behaviours to a certain extent.

One option for future work is to describe the protocols concerned in a version of ACP with discrete relative timing (see e.g. [15,16]) and then to show that the more complex one leads to a speed-up indeed. Another option for future work is to devise, describe and analyse more efficient protocols, such as protocols that allow for two or more instructions to be processed in parallel.

By means of the protocols, we have presented a way to deal with the instruction streams that turn up with remotely controlled program behaviours. By that we have ascribed a sense to the term instruction stream which makes clear that an instruction stream is dynamic by nature, in contradistinction with an instruction sequence. We have not yet been able to devise a basic definition of instruction streams.

References

1. Bergstra, J.A., Loots, M.E.: Program algebra for sequential code. Journal of Logic and Algebraic Programming 51(2), 125–156 (2002)
2. Bergstra, J.A., Bethke, I., Ponse, A.: Decision problems for pushdown threads. Acta Informatica 44(2), 75–90 (2007)
3. Bergstra, J.A., Middelburg, C.A.: Program algebra with a jump-shift instruction. Journal of Applied Logic 6(4), 553–563 (2008)
4. Ponse, A., van der Zwaag, M.B.: An introduction to program and thread algebra. In: Beckmann, A., Berger, U., Löwe, B., Tucker, J.V. (eds.) CiE 2006. LNCS, vol. 3988, pp. 445–458. Springer, Heidelberg (2006)
5. Bergstra, J.A., Klop, J.W.: Process algebra for synchronous communication. Information and Control 60(1–3), 109–137 (1984)
6. Baeten, J.C.M., Weijland, W.P.: Process Algebra. Cambridge Tracts in Theoretical Computer Science, vol. 18. Cambridge University Press, Cambridge (1990)
7. Hennessy, M., Milner, R.: Algebraic laws for non-determinism and concurrency. Journal of the ACM 32(1), 137–161 (1985)
8. Milner, R.: Communication and Concurrency. Prentice-Hall, Englewood Cliffs (1989)
9. Brookes, S.D., Hoare, C.A.R., Roscoe, A.W.: A theory of communicating sequential processes. Journal of the ACM 31(3), 560–599 (1984)
10. Hoare, C.A.R.: Communicating Sequential Processes. Prentice-Hall, Englewood Cliffs (1985)
11. Bergstra, J.A., Middelburg, C.A.: Thread algebra with multi-level strategies. Fundamenta Informaticae 71(2–3), 153–182 (2006)
12. Bergstra, J.A., Bethke, I.: Polarized process algebra and program equivalence. In: Baeten, J.C.M., Lenstra, J.K., Parrow, J., Woeginger, G.J. (eds.) ICALP 2003. LNCS, vol. 2719, pp. 1–21. Springer, Heidelberg (2003)
13. Fokkink, W.J.: Introduction to Process Algebra. Texts in Theoretical Computer Science, An EATCS Series. Springer, Berlin (2000)
14. Baeten, J.C.M., Bergstra, J.A.: On sequential composition, action prefixes and process prefix. Formal Aspects of Computing 6(3), 250–268 (1994)
15. Baeten, J.C.M., Bergstra, J.A.: Discrete time process algebra. Formal Aspects of Computing 8(2), 188–208 (1996)
16. Baeten, J.C.M., Middelburg, C.A.: Process Algebra with Timing. Monographs in Theoretical Computer Science, An EATCS Series. Springer, Berlin (2002)

A Deadlock-Free Semantics for Shared Memory Concurrency*

Gérard Boudol

INRIA, 06902 Sophia Antipolis, France

Abstract. We design a deadlock-free semantics for a concurrent, functional and imperative programming language where locks are implicitly and univocally associated with pointers. The semantics avoids unsafe states by relying on a static analysis of programs, by means of a type and effect system. The system uses singleton reference types, which allow us to have a precise information about the pointers that are anticipated to be locked by an expression.

1 Introduction

In this paper we revisit, from a programming language perspective, one of the most annoying problems with concurrent systems, namely the risk of entering into a deadlocked situation. Deadlocks arise in particular from synchronization mechanisms like locking, when several threads of computation are circularly blocked, each waiting for a resource that is locked by another thread. As is well-known, locking is sometimes necessary. To illustrate this, as well as some other points, we shall use an example which is often considered as regards synchronization problems. This is the example of manipulating bank accounts. In our setting, a bank account will simply be a memory location containing an integer value.[1] Now suppose that we want to define a function to deposit some amount x on the account y. Using ML's notation $(!\,y)$ to get the contents of the memory location y (i.e. to dereference it, in ML's jargon where memory locations are called references – we shall also use the word "pointer"), this function can be defined as $\lambda x \lambda y (y := \,!\,y + x)$. There is a problem however with this definition, which is that two concurrent deposits may have the effect of only one of them, if both read the current amount before it has been updated by the other thread.

To solve this problem, it is enough to make the deposit function taking, for the update operation $y := \,!\,y + x$, an exclusive access to the bank account to update, that is y. In this paper we shall assume that there is in the programming language a construct, say (lock y in e), to lock the reference y for the purpose of performing the operation e with an exclusive access to y. Indeed, we think that the programmer should be offered constructs to control access to memory locations (as they appear in the language), rather than having to explicitly

---

* Work partially supported by the ANR-SETI-06-010 grant.
[1] The operations we shall consider dealing with accounts should actually be packaged into a module.

M. Leucker and C. Morgan (Eds.): ICTAC 2009, LNCS 5684, pp. 140–154, 2009.

manipulate locks. In other words, we are assuming here that the locks are, transparently for the programmer, associated with the resources, as in JAVA. Then we can conveniently define the deposit function as follows:

$$\text{deposit} \;=\; \lambda x \lambda y (\text{lock } y \text{ in } y := \,! \, y + x)$$

Similarly, we can define a function to withdraw some amount from an account:

$$\text{withdraw} \;=\; \lambda x \lambda y (\text{lock } y \text{ in } (\text{if } ! \, y \geq x \text{ then } (y := \,! \, y - x) \text{ else error}))$$

From this we can define another function, to transfer some amount x from an account y to another one z, as $\lambda x \lambda y \lambda z ((\text{withdraw } xy) \, ; \, (\text{deposit } xz))$. It has been argued (see [9]) that this function should ensure the property that another thread cannot see the intermediate state where y has decreased, but z has not yet been credited. This can be achieved by defining

$$\text{transfer} \;=\; \lambda x \lambda y \lambda z (\text{lock } y \text{ in } (\text{withdraw } xy) \, ; \, (\text{deposit } xz))$$

We are assuming here that the locks are reentrant: a thread that temporarily "possesses" a reference, like y in this example, is not blocked in locking it twice. Now suppose that two transfers are performed concurrently, from account a to account b, and in the converse direction. That is, we have to execute something like

$$(\text{transfer } 100 \, a \, b) \; \| \; (\text{transfer } 10 \, b \, a) \tag{1}$$

Clearly there is a danger of deadlock here: if both operations first perform the withdrawals, locking respectively a and b, they are then blocked in trying to lock the other account in order to perform the deposits.

There are three ways out of deadlocks, that have been identified long ago in the area of operating systems development (see [2]):

(i) deadlock *prevention* aims at only accepting for execution concurrent systems that are determined to be deadlock-free, in the sense that none of their interleaved executions runs into a deadlock;

(ii) deadlock *avoidance* aims at ensuring, by monitoring the execution at run-time, that unsafe states that could lead to a deadlocked situation are avoided;

(iii) deadlock *detection* and *recovery* uses run-time monitoring and rollback mechanisms to analyse the current state, and undo some computations[2] in case there is a deadlock.

Despite the existence of the well-known Dijkstra's Banker's algorithm, solutions (i) and (iii) are, by far, the most popular. Deadlock detection and recovery is similar to optimistic concurrency control in database transactions implementation. By contrast, deadlock avoidance may be qualified as pessimistic concurrency. (See [7] for a recent use of this technique).

Solution (i), deadlock prevention, lends itself to using static analysis techniques. Indeed, a lot of work has been done in this direction – see [1,3,5,10,11], to mention just a few recent works on this topic. One has to notice that, with

---

[2] Provided these are not irrevocable, such as I/O operations.

no exception, all these works (also including [7]) use the standard approach to precluding deadlocks, which is to assume an ordering on locking to prevent circularities. This is an assumption we would like to avoid: in our bank account example, where one can do concurrent transfers from an account to another in any direction, like in Example (1), such an assumption would entail that there should be a unique lock associated with all the accounts, which obviously limits the concurrency in a drastic, and sometimes unjustified way. In this paper we shall explore a different direction, namely (ii), deadlock avoidance.

To implement solution (ii), one has to know in advance what are the resources that are needed, in an exclusive way, by a thread. Then this also seems amenable to static analysis techniques. This is what this paper is proposing: we define, for a standard multithreaded programming style, a *type and effect system* that allows us to design a *prudent* semantics, that is then proved to be deadlock-free. The idea is quite simple: one should not lock a pointer whenever one anticipates, by typing, to take some other pointer that is currently held by another thread. As one can see, this is much lighter than implementing optimistic concurrency, and the proof of correctness is not very complicated. Surprisingly enough, I could not find in the literature any reference to a similar work – except [12], which however uses a Petri net model, and Discrete Control Theory –, so ours appears to be the first one to define a deadlock-free semantics, following the deadlock avoidance approach, based on a type and effect system for standard multithreading.

To conclude this introduction, let us discuss some more technical points of our contribution. In analysing an expression such as (lock e_0 in e_1), we need a way to get, statically, an approximative idea of what will be the value of e_0, the pointer to be locked, in order to assign it as an effect to the locking expression, and then use it in the types. An idea could be to use dependent types, but dependent types for imperative, call-by-value languages is a topic which largely remains unexplored, and the existing proposals (see [8] for instance) seem to be over-elaborate for our purpose. A standard approach to statically get information about pointer accesses is to use *regions* in a type and effect system [6]: in an ML-like language, one assigns (distinct) region names to the subexpressions (ref e) creating a reference, and one can then record as an effect the region where a reference that has to be locked resides. In this way, locks are actually associated with regions, rather than with references. However, this is too coarse grained for our purpose: again using the bank account example, we could define a (very simplified) function for creating accounts with an initial value as $\lambda x(\text{ref } x)$, but then, this would mean that all accounts would be assigned the same lock, and we already rejected such a scenario.

To solve this problem, we shall introduce in the programming language a new construct (cref e) which is a function that, when applied to some (dummy) argument, then creates a reference with initial value the one of e. Typically, (cref e)() has the same meaning as (ref e). We shall then restrict, by typing, the use of such a function f to a particular form, namely (let $x = (f())$ in e) where e does not export x. In this way, we shall be able to know exactly the name of the pointer denoted by e_0 in (lock e_0 in e_1)[3], using *singleton types* [4], which are both dependent types of a very simple kind, as well as types with (singleton) regions. This provides us with a fine grained locking policy, where locks are univocally associated with references.

Note. For lack of space, the proofs are omitted, or only sketched.

2   Source and Target Languages

Our source language is an extension of CoreML, that is a functional (embedding the call-by-value λ-calculus) and imperative language, enriched with concurrent programming primitives, namely a thread spawning construct (thread e) and a locking construct (lock e_0 in e_1). The main feature of ML we are interested in here is not the polymorphic let, but rather the explicit distinction between values and references to values. Typically, in ML – as opposed to SCHEME or JAVA for instance –, one cannot write $x := x+1$, because x cannot be both an integer, as in $x+1$, and a reference to an integer, as in $x := 1$. As explained in the Introduction, we refine the reference creation construct (ref e) of ML into (cref e), which is a function that needs to be applied (to a dummy argument) to actually create a mutable reference, with the value of e as initial value. Then (ref e) is here an abbreviation for ((cref e)()). For simplicity, we omit from the language the constructs relying on basic types such as the booleans or integers. Considering these constructs (and recursion) does not cause any technical difficulty, and we shall use them in the examples. The syntax of our source language is as follows:

$v,\ w\ldots ::= x \mid \lambda x e$		*values*
$e ::= v \mid (e_1 e_0)$		*expressions (functional)*
$\mid$ (cref e) $\mid$ (! e) $\mid$ ($e_0 := e_1$)		*(imperative)*
$\mid$ (thread e) $\mid$ (lock e_0 in e_1)		*(concurrent)*

The abstraction $\lambda x e$ is the only binder in this language. We denote by $\{x \mapsto v\}e$ the capture-avoiding substitution of the variable x by the value v in its free occurrences in e, and we shall always consider expressions up to α-conversion, that is up to the renaming of bound variables. We shall use the standard abbreviation (let $x = e_0$ in e_1) for $(\lambda x e_1 e_0)$, also denoted $e_0\ ;\ e_1$ whenever x is not free in e_1. The use of expressions e reducing to values of the form (cref v) will be restricted, by typing, to a particular form, namely (let $x = (e())$ in e'). A particular case of this is (let $x = $ (ref e) in e').

In order to be evaluated (or executed), the expressions of the source language will be first translated into a slightly different language. This run-time language, or more appropriately *target language* differs from the source one on the following points:

(i) the construct (cref e) is removed, as well as the values (cref v);

---

[3] This does not mean that one can statically predict which pointers will be created at run-time, since an expression such as (let $x = $ ((cref e)()) in e') can be passed as an argument, and duplicated.

(ii) *references* (or pointers), ranged over by p, $q \ldots$ are introduced. These are run-time values;

(iii) the locking construct ($\text{lock } e_0 \text{ in } e_1$) is replaced by the family of constructs ($\text{lock}_\varphi \, e_0 \text{ in } e_1$) where φ is any *effect*, that is any finite set of pointer names (either constant or variable);

(iv) a family of constructs $(e \backslash p)_{\psi, P}$ is introduced, to represent the fact that the pointer p is currently held, and will be released upon termination of e. In this construct ψ and P are finite sets of pointers (they are there for technical convenience only);

(v) a construct ($\text{new } x \text{ in } e$), also written simply $\nu x e$, is introduced for creating new pointers. This is a binder for x.

An expression ($\text{cref } e$) of the source language will be represented as

$$(\text{let } x = e \text{ in } \lambda y((y := x) \, ; y))$$

in the target language, where it will take (and return) a pointer as argument (see the next Section). The (pointer) variables occurring in the effect φ in ($\text{lock}_\varphi \, e_0 \text{ in } e_1$) are free in this expression. An expression of the target language is called *pure* if it does not contain any pointer (which does not mean that its evaluation does not produce side effects). In particular, a pure expression does not contain any subexpression of the form $(e \backslash p)_{\psi, P}$.

3   Translation

In this section we define a translation, guided by a type and effect system, from the source language into the target language. The purpose of this translation is twofold:

(i) we compute the effect φ of an expression e, which is the set of pointers that this expression may have to lock during its execution. This effect is then used to annotate, by translating them, the expressions ($\text{lock } e' \text{ in } e$) (which are also the ones which produce an effect, namely of locking the pointer denoted by e'), in order to guide the evaluation, avoiding deadlocks. This is the main purpose of the type and effect system.

(ii) we restrict the use of expressions of the form ($\text{cref } e$) in a way that allows us to have, in the types, a precise information about the pointer names.

The types for the source language are as follows:

$$\tau, \sigma, \theta \ldots \; ::= \; \text{unit} \; | \; \theta \, \text{ref}_x \; | \; \theta \, \text{cref} \; | \; (\tau \xrightarrow{\varphi} \sigma)$$

Here $\theta \, \text{ref}_x$ is a *singleton* type [4], meaning that the only value of this type is the pointer name x. (This is a very primitive form of dependent type.) We abbreviate $(\tau \xrightarrow{\emptyset} \sigma)$ into $(\tau \to \sigma)$. In $(\theta \, \text{ref}_x \xrightarrow{\varphi} \sigma)$ the (pointer) variable x is *universally quantified*, with scope φ and σ, and will be instantiated when applying a function of this type. The capture-avoiding substitution $\{x \mapsto y\}\tau$ is defined in the standard way, and we always consider types up to α-conversion,

$$\frac{\Gamma, x : \tau \vdash_s e : \varphi, \sigma \;\Rightarrow\; \bar{e}}{}$$

$$\frac{}{\Gamma, x : \tau \vdash_s x : \emptyset, \tau \;\Rightarrow\; x} \qquad \frac{}{\Gamma \vdash_s \lambda x e : \emptyset, (\tau \xrightarrow{\varphi} \sigma) \;\Rightarrow\; \lambda x \bar{e}} \qquad \frac{}{\Gamma \vdash_s () : \emptyset, \mathsf{unit} \;\Rightarrow\; ()}$$

$$\frac{\Gamma \vdash_s e_0 : \varphi_0, (\tau \xrightarrow{\varphi_2} \sigma) \;\Rightarrow\; \bar{e_0} \qquad \Gamma \vdash_s e_1 : \varphi_1, \tau \;\Rightarrow\; \bar{e_1}}{\Gamma \vdash_s (e_0 e_1) : \varphi_0 \cup \varphi_1 \cup \varphi_2, \sigma \;\Rightarrow\; (\bar{e_0}\bar{e_1})} \; \tau \neq \theta \, \mathsf{ref}_x$$

$$\frac{\Gamma \vdash_s e_0 : \varphi_0, (\theta \, \mathsf{ref}_x \xrightarrow{\varphi_2} \sigma) \;\Rightarrow\; \bar{e_0} \qquad \Gamma \vdash_s e_1 : \varphi_1, \theta \, \mathsf{ref}_y \;\Rightarrow\; \bar{e_1}}{\Gamma \vdash_s (e_0 e_1) : \varphi_0 \cup \varphi_1 \cup \{x \mapsto y\}\varphi_2, \{x \mapsto y\}\sigma \;\Rightarrow\; (\bar{e_0}\bar{e_1})}$$

$$\frac{\Gamma \vdash_s e_0 : \varphi_0, \theta \, \mathsf{cref} \;\Rightarrow\; \bar{e_0} \qquad \Gamma, x : \theta \, \mathsf{ref}_x \vdash_s e_1 : \varphi_1, \tau \;\Rightarrow\; \bar{e_1}}{\Gamma \vdash_s (\lambda x e_1(e_0())) : \varphi_0 \cup (\varphi_1 - \{x\}), \tau \;\Rightarrow\; \nu y (\lambda x \bar{e_1}(\bar{e_0}y))} \; y \text{ fresh}, \; x \notin \Gamma, \varphi_0, \tau$$

$$\frac{\Gamma \vdash_s e : \varphi, \theta \;\Rightarrow\; \bar{e}}{\Gamma \vdash_s (\mathsf{cref}\, e) : \varphi, \theta \, \mathsf{cref} \;\Rightarrow\; (\lambda x \lambda y ((y := x) \,;\, y)\bar{e})}$$

$$\frac{\Gamma \vdash_s e : \varphi, \theta \, \mathsf{ref}_x \;\Rightarrow\; \bar{e}}{\Gamma \vdash_s (!e) : \varphi, \theta \;\Rightarrow\; (!\bar{e})} \qquad \frac{\Gamma \vdash_s e_0 : \varphi_0, \theta \, \mathsf{ref}_x \;\Rightarrow\; \bar{e_0} \qquad \Gamma \vdash_s e_1 : \varphi_1, \theta \;\Rightarrow\; \bar{e_1}}{\Gamma \vdash_s (e_0 := e_1) : \varphi_0 \cup \varphi_1, \mathsf{unit} \;\Rightarrow\; (\bar{e_0} := \bar{e_1})}$$

$$\frac{\Gamma \vdash_s e : \varphi, \mathsf{unit} \;\Rightarrow\; \bar{e}}{\Gamma \vdash_s (\mathsf{thread}\, e) : \emptyset, \mathsf{unit} \;\Rightarrow\; (\mathsf{thread}\, \bar{e})}$$

$$\frac{\Gamma \vdash_s e_0 : \varphi_0, \theta \, \mathsf{ref}_x \;\Rightarrow\; \bar{e_0} \qquad \Gamma \vdash_s e_1 : \varphi_1, \tau \;\Rightarrow\; \bar{e_1}}{\Gamma \vdash_s (\mathsf{lock}\, e_0 \, \mathsf{in}\, e_1) : \{x\} \cup \varphi_0 \cup \varphi_1, \tau \;\Rightarrow\; (\mathsf{lock}_{\varphi_1} \bar{e_0} \, \mathsf{in}\, \bar{e_1})}$$

——————— **Figure 1: Type and Effect System (Source Language)** ———————

that is, up to the renaming of bound variables. The typing judgements for the source language are as follows:

$$\Gamma \vdash_s e : \varphi, \tau$$

where Γ is a typing context, that is a mapping from a finite set $\mathrm{dom}(\Gamma)$ of variables to types. In this judgement the effect φ is the set of pointer names that the expression e may have to lock during its evaluation. In the following we shall only consider *well-formed* judgements, meaning that if a type $\theta \, \mathsf{ref}_x$ occurs in the judgement then x does not occur in θ, and if $\Gamma(y) = \theta \, \mathsf{ref}_x$ then $y = x$. This assumption is left implicit in the following.

We shall give a simultaneous definition for both the type and effect system and the translation from the source to the target languages. That is, we define inductively the predicate

$$\Gamma \vdash_s e : \varphi, \tau \;\Rightarrow\; \bar{e}$$

meaning that the source expression e is well-typed in the typing context Γ, with effect φ and type τ, and translates into the target expression $\bar{e}$. The rules are given in Figure 1, where, when we write $x \notin \Gamma, \varphi, \tau$, we mean that x does not occur in Γ (neither in the domain, nor in the types assigned by this typing context), nor in φ, nor in τ. By forgetting the "$\Rightarrow \bar{e}$" parts one obtains the rules of the type system for the source language. One should notice that if $\Gamma \vdash_s e : \varphi, \tau \Rightarrow \bar{e}$ then $\bar{e}$ is pure. One should also notice that the type and effect system only *builds* effects, but does not (other than by implicit type unification, as usual) use them to constrain the typing.

The most interesting rule is the one for the $(\mathsf{lock}\ e_0\ \mathsf{in}\ e_1)$ constructs. This expression is the only one introducing an effect, which is the name of the pointer that is intended to be locked, that is the reference resulting from the evaluation of e_0. In the translation of this expression, that is $(\mathsf{lock}_{\varphi_1}\ \bar{e}_0\ \mathsf{in}\ \bar{e}_1)$, one records the anticipated effect φ_1 of e_1. Indeed, the operational semantics will rely on the idea that, in order to avoid deadlocks, one should not lock the pointer which is denoted by $\bar{e}_0$ if a pointer from φ_1 is already held by another thread. Notice that the use of a singleton type for e_0, namely $\theta\ \mathsf{ref}_x$, allows us to build the effect as a set of names (i.e. variables, in the source language), and not expressions (or regions).

As announced, reference creation is restricted to the form $(\mathsf{let}\ x = (e_0()) \mathsf{\ in\ } e_1)$, where the name (that is, x) of the reference in known in e_1. In the translation of this expression, namely $\nu y (\mathsf{let}\ x = (\bar{e}_0 y) \mathsf{\ in\ } \bar{e}_1)$, one first creates, by means of νy, a fresh pointer name (see the following Section), which is passed as an argument, and then bound to the value v "handled" by $\bar{e}_0$ (as one can see, $\bar{e}_0$ is constrained, by typing, to reduce to an expression of the form $\lambda z((z := v)\ ; z))$. By reduction the name y will be substituted for x in $\bar{e}_1$, and in particular in the effects involving the name x, in subexpressions of the form $(\mathsf{lock}_\varphi\ \_\mathsf{\ in\ }\_)$.

One can see that, assuming that we have the obvious typing rules for boolean and integer constructs, the deposit and transfer functions considered in the Introduction can be typed as follows, using polymorphic types, where y and z are universally quantified:

$$\Gamma \vdash_s \mathsf{deposit} : \emptyset, \mathsf{int} \to (\mathsf{int\ ref}_y \xrightarrow{\{y\}} \mathsf{unit})$$

$$\Gamma \vdash_s \mathsf{transfer} : \emptyset, \mathsf{int} \to (\mathsf{int\ ref}_y \to (\mathsf{int\ ref}_z \xrightarrow{\{y,z\}} \mathsf{unit}))$$

and their definitions are translated as follows:

$$\lambda x \lambda y (\mathsf{lock}_\emptyset\ y \mathsf{\ in\ } y := \ !\,y + x)$$

$$\lambda x \lambda y \lambda z (\mathsf{lock}_{\{y,z\}}\ y \mathsf{\ in\ } (\mathsf{withdraw}\ xy)\ ; (\mathsf{deposit}\ xz))$$

Then (assuming that error has any type) one can check that the following is typable, in a context where the functions deposit, withdraw and transfer have been defined, as above:

$$
\begin{aligned}
&\mathsf{let\ create\_account} = \lambda x (\mathsf{cref}\ x) \mathsf{\ in}\\
&\quad \mathsf{let}\ a = (\mathsf{create\_account}\ 100)() \mathsf{\ in}\\
&\quad \mathsf{let}\ b = (\mathsf{create\_account}\ 10)() \mathsf{\ in}\\
&\qquad ((\mathsf{thread}\ (\mathsf{transfer}\ 50\ ab)))\ ; (\mathsf{deposit}\ 10\ b)
\end{aligned}
\tag{2}
$$

and the translation is, with some optimization in the translation of create_account:

$$\text{let create\_account } = \lambda x \lambda y((y := x) \, ; y) \text{ in}$$
$$\text{new } y \text{ in let } a = (\text{create\_account } 100)y \text{ in}$$
$$\text{new } z \text{ in let } b = (\text{create\_account } 10)z \text{ in}$$
$$((\text{thread } (\text{transfer } 50 \, ab))) \, ; (\text{deposit } 10 \, b)$$

4 Prudent Operational Semantics

As usual, evaluation consists in reducing a *redex* (reducible expression) in an *evaluation context*, possibly performing a side effect. In our (run-time) language, redexes and evaluation contexts are defined as follows:

$$
\begin{aligned}
r ::= &\ (\lambda x e v) \mid (!\, p) \mid (p := v) & \text{redexes}\\
      &\mid (\text{thread } e) \mid (\text{lock}_\psi \, p \text{ in } e) \mid (v\backslash p)_{\psi,P} \mid \nu x \, e\\[4pt]
\mathbf{E} ::= &\ [] \mid \mathbf{E}[\mathbf{F}] & \text{evaluation contexts}\\[4pt]
\mathbf{F} := &\ ([]\, e) \mid (v\, []) & \text{frames}\\
      &\mid (\text{cref}\, []) \mid (!\, []) \mid ([] := e) \mid (v := [])\\
      &\mid (\text{lock}_\psi \, [] \text{ in } e) \mid ([]\backslash p)_{\psi,P}
\end{aligned}
$$

To define the semantics of reentrant locks, we shall use the set $\lceil \mathbf{E} \rceil$ of pointers held in the context $\mathbf{E}$, computed by a kind of "stack inspection" mechanism, as follows:

$$
\begin{aligned}
\lceil [] \rceil &= \emptyset\\
\lceil \mathbf{E}[\mathbf{F}] \rceil &= \lceil \mathbf{E} \rceil \cup \lceil \mathbf{F} \rceil
\end{aligned}
\qquad \text{where} \qquad
\lceil \mathbf{F} \rceil =
\begin{cases}
\{p\} & \text{if } \mathbf{F} = ([]\backslash p)_{\psi,P}\\
\emptyset & \text{otherwise}
\end{cases}
$$

We now describe our operational semantics for expressions of the target language, defined as a small-step transition system between *configurations* (S, L, T) where S is the *store*, that is a partial mapping from a finite set $\text{dom}(S)$ of pointers to values, L is a finite set of *locked pointers*, and T is a multiset of *threads*, which are simply expressions. The store is only partial because in some state, some pointers may have been created but not yet initialized. As regards the store, we shall use the following notations: $S + p$, where $p \notin \text{dom}(S)$, is the store obtained by adding p to $\text{dom}(S)$, but not providing a value for p; $S[p := v]$, where p is supposed to be in $\text{dom}(S)$, is the store obtained by initializing or updating the value of p to be v. The set L is the set of pointers that are currently held by some thread. As regards multisets, our notations are as follows. Given a set X, a *multiset* over X is a mapping E from X to the set $\mathbb{N}$ of non-negative integers, indicating the multiplicity $E(x)$ of an element. We denote by x the singleton multiset such that $x(y) = (\text{if } y = x \text{ then } 1 \text{ else } 0)$. Multiset union $E \parallel E'$ is given by $(E \parallel E')(x) = E(x) + E'(x)$. In the following we only consider multisets of expressions, ranged over by T.

The semantics is given in Figure 2, that we now comment. The general form of the rules is

$$(S, L, \mathbf{E}[r] \parallel T) \to (S', L', \mathbf{E}[e] \parallel T')$$

$$(S, L, \mathbf{E}[(\lambda x e v)] \parallel T) \rightarrow (S, L, \mathbf{E}[\{x \mapsto v\} e] \parallel T)$$

$$(S, L, \mathbf{E}[(!\, p)] \parallel T) \rightarrow (S, L, \mathbf{E}[v] \parallel T) \qquad\qquad S(p) = v$$

$$(S, L, \mathbf{E}[(p := v)] \parallel T) \rightarrow (S[p := v], L, \mathbf{E}[()] \parallel T)$$

$$(S, L, \mathbf{E}[(\mathsf{thread}\ e)] \parallel T) \rightarrow (S, L, \mathbf{E}[()] \parallel T \parallel e)$$

$$(S, L, \mathbf{E}[(\mathsf{lock}_\psi\ p\ \mathsf{in}\ e)] \parallel T) \rightarrow (S, L, \mathbf{E}[e] \parallel T) \qquad\qquad p \in \lceil \mathbf{E} \rceil$$

$$(S, L, \mathbf{E}[(\mathsf{lock}_\psi\ p\ \mathsf{in}\ e)] \parallel T) \rightarrow (S, L', \mathbf{E}[(e \backslash p)_{\psi,P}] \parallel T) \qquad\begin{array}{l} p \notin \lceil \mathbf{E} \rceil\ \&\ (\spadesuit)\ \& \\ P = \mathsf{dom}(S) \end{array}$$

$$(S, L, \mathbf{E}[(v \backslash p)_{\psi,P}] \parallel T) \rightarrow (S, L - \{p\}, \mathbf{E}[v] \parallel T)$$

$$(S, L, \mathbf{E}[\nu x e] \parallel T) \rightarrow (S + p, L, \mathbf{E}[\{x \mapsto p\} e] \parallel T) \qquad p \notin \mathsf{dom}(S)$$

$(\spadesuit)$ $L \cap (\{p\} \cup (\psi - \lceil \mathbf{E} \rceil)) = \emptyset,\ L' = L \cup \{p\}$

———————————— **Figure 2: Prudent Operational Semantics** ————————————

meaning that any thread ready to be reduced can be non-deterministically chosen for evaluation. Again, the most interesting case is the one of expressions $(\mathsf{lock}_\psi\ e_0\ \mathsf{in}\ e_1)$. To evaluate such an expression, one first has to evaluate e_0, since $(\mathsf{lock}_\psi\ []\ \mathsf{in}\ e_1)$ is [part of] an evaluation context. The expected result is a pointer p. Then, to reduce $(\mathsf{lock}_\psi\ p\ \mathsf{in}\ e_1)$, one first looks in the evaluation context $\mathbf{E}$ to see if the thread has already locked p, that is $p \in \lceil \mathbf{E} \rceil$. If this is the case, the locking instruction is ignored, that is $(\mathsf{lock}_\psi\ p\ \mathsf{in}\ e_1)$ is reduced to e_1, with no effect. Otherwise, one consults the set L to see if p, *or any pointer in* ψ, is locked by another thread. If this is the case, the expression $(\mathsf{lock}_\psi\ p\ \mathsf{in}\ e_1)$ is blocked, waiting for this condition to become false. Otherwise, the pointer p is locked,[4] and one proceeds executing e_1 in a context where the fact that p is currently held is recorded, namely $([] \backslash p)_{\psi,P}$. On termination of e_1, the pointer p is released. One should compare the precondition in $(\spadesuit)$ for taking a lock with the usual one, which is $L \cap \{p\} = \emptyset$. It is then obvious that our prudent semantics avoids some paths explored in the standard interleaving semantics.

Notice that the sets ψ and P in the context $([] \backslash p)_{\psi,P}$ are actually not used in the operational semantics, and could therefore be removed from the syntax. We include them for the sole purpose of proving our safety result. Here ψ is the set of pointers that are anticipated, by the $(\mathsf{lock}_\psi\ p\ \mathsf{in}\ e_1)$ instruction, as possibly locked in the future, before p is released. The set P is the one of known pointers at the time where p is locked.

In the following we shall only consider *well-formed* configurations, which are triples (S, L, T) such that if a pointer p occurs in the configuration, either in some thread or in some value in the store, or in L, then $p \in \mathsf{dom}(S)$. It is easy to check that well-formedness is preserved by reduction, since references are allocated in the store when they are created.

---

[4] The computations expressed by $(\spadesuit)$ must be performed in an atomic way. This means that in an implementation one would use a global lock on the set L.

In the rest of this section we establish some results about the operational semantics, and discuss it on an example. Let us say that a configuration (S, L, T) is *regular* if it satisfies

(i) $T = \mathbf{E}[(e\backslash p)_{\psi,P}] \parallel T' \Rightarrow p \notin \lceil \mathbf{E} \rceil$ & $(T' = \mathbf{E}'[e'] \parallel T'' \Rightarrow p \notin \lceil \mathbf{E}' \rceil)$

(ii) $p \in L \Leftrightarrow \exists \mathbf{E}, e, \psi, P, T'. \, T = \mathbf{E}[(e\backslash p)_{\psi,P}] \parallel T'$

Clearly, if e is a pure expression, the initial configuration $(\emptyset, \emptyset, e)$ is regular. Moreover, this property is preserved by reduction:

LEMMA 4.1.   *If (S, L, T) is regular and $(S, L, T) \rightarrow (S', L', T')$ then (S', L', T') is regular.*

The following notion of a *safe* expression is central to our safety result:

DEFINITION (SAFE EXPRESSION) 4.2.   *A closed pure expression e of the target language is safe if $(\emptyset, \emptyset, e) \xrightarrow{*} (S, L, T)$ implies*

$$T = \mathbf{E}[(\mathbf{E}'[(\mathsf{lock}_{\psi_1} \, p_1 \, \mathsf{in} \, e)]\backslash p_0)_{\psi_0,P_0}] \parallel T' \, \& \, p_1 \in P_0 \Rightarrow p_1 \in \psi_0$$

That is, when a reference p_1 is about to be locked while some other pointer p_0 was previously locked by the same thread, with p_1 known to exist at that point, then the possibility of locking p_1 was anticipated when locking p_0. (this is where we need ψ and P in $(e\backslash p)_{\psi,P}$).

DEFINITION (DEADLOCK) 4.3.   *A configuration (S, L, T) is deadlocked if*

$$T = \mathbf{E}_0[(\mathsf{lock}_{\psi_0} \, p_0 \, \mathsf{in} \, e_1)] \parallel \cdots \parallel \mathbf{E}_n[(\mathsf{lock}_{\psi_n} \, p_n \, \mathsf{in} \, e_n)] \parallel T'$$

with $n > 0$ and $p_{i+1} \in \lceil \mathbf{E}_i \rceil$ (mod $n + 1$). A pure expression e is deadlock-free if no configuration reachable from $(\emptyset, \emptyset, e)$ is deadlocked.

The main property of our operational semantics is the following:

PROPOSITION 4.4.   *Any safe expression is deadlock-free.*

PROOF SKETCH: let us assume the contrary, that is $(\emptyset, \emptyset, e) \xrightarrow{*} (S, L, T)$ where (S, L, T) is deadlocked. For simplicity, let us assume that there are two threads in T that block each other, that is

$$T = \mathbf{E}_0^0[(\mathbf{E}_1^0[(\mathsf{lock}_{\varphi_0} \, p_1 \, \mathsf{in} \, e_0)]\backslash p_0)_{\psi_0,P_0}] \parallel \mathbf{E}_0^1[(\mathbf{E}_1^1[(\mathsf{lock}_{\varphi_1} \, p_0 \, \mathsf{in} \, e_1)]\backslash p_1)_{\psi_1,P_1}] \parallel T'$$

(the general case where there is a cycle of blocked threads of length greater than 2 is just notationally more cumbersome). Since e is safe, we have $p_1 \in \psi_0$ if $p_1 \in P_0$, and $p_0 \in \psi_1$ if $p_0 \in P_1$. Assume for instance that p_0 is the pointer that is locked the first (and then not released), that is:

$$(\emptyset, \emptyset, e) \xrightarrow{*} (S_0, L_0, \mathbf{E}_0^0[(\mathsf{lock}_{\psi_0} \, p_0 \, \mathsf{in} \, e_0')] \parallel T_0)$$
$$\rightarrow (S_0, L_0', \mathbf{E}_0^0[(e_0'\backslash p_0)_{\psi_0,P_0}] \parallel T_0) \qquad\qquad P_0 = \mathsf{dom}(S_0)$$
$$\xrightarrow{*} (S_1, L_1, \mathbf{E}_0^0[(e_0''\backslash p_0)_{\psi_0,P_0}] \parallel \mathbf{E}_0^1[(\mathsf{lock}_{\psi_1} \, p_1 \, \mathsf{in} \, e_1')] \parallel T_1)$$
$$\rightarrow (S_1, L_1', \mathbf{E}_0^0[(e_0''\backslash p_0)_{\psi_0,P_0}] \parallel \mathbf{E}_0^1[(e_1'\backslash p_1)_{\psi_1,P_1}] \parallel T_1) \qquad P_1 = \mathsf{dom}(S_1)$$
$$\xrightarrow{*} (S, L, T)$$

Since e is pure, the configurations reachable from $(\emptyset, \emptyset, e)$ are regular (Lemma 4.1), and therefore $p_0 \in L_1 \subseteq P_1$, but then reducing $(\mathsf{lock}_{\psi_1} \, p_1 \, \text{in} \, e_1')$ in the context of L_1 is not possible – a contradiction. $\square$

To conclude this section, let us revisit and discuss Example (2), where the multiset of threads is

$$(\mathsf{transfer} \, 50 \, a \, b) \, \| \, (\mathsf{deposit} \, 10 \, b)$$

Assuming that the pointers a and b contain some integers in the store, with $S(a) \geq 50$, and both of them are free (i.e. not locked), one can see that a reachable state is $(S, \{a\}, ((a := \, ! \, a - 50) \backslash a) \, \| \, (\mathsf{deposit} \, 10 \, b))$, where we omit the ψ and P components annotating the context $(\_\backslash a)$. Then, from this state one can reach for instance the state

$$(S, \{a, b\}, ((a := \, ! \, a - 50) \backslash a) \, \| \, ((b := \, ! \, b + 10) \backslash b))$$

This means that there is some real concurrency in executing a transfer from a to b and a deposit to b in parallel, even though both these operations need to lock b at some point. However, if $(\mathsf{deposit} \, 10 \, b)$ starts executing, this blocks $(\mathsf{transfer} \, 50 \, a \, b)$, because the latter cannot lock a, while anticipating to lock b, since b is already locked. Then the condition ($\spadesuit$) is sometimes too strong in preventing deadlocks, precluding some harmless interleavings, and one may wonder how we could relax it, adopting for instance a more informative structure than L for locked pointers. However, one must be careful with pointer creation, as the following example shows:

$$\mathsf{new} \, x \, \text{in} \, \mathsf{lock}_\emptyset \, x \, \text{in} \, \mathsf{new} \, y \, \text{in} \, (\mathsf{thread} \, (\mathsf{lock}_{\{x\}} \, y \, \text{in} \, (\mathsf{lock}_\emptyset \, x \, \text{in} \, ())));$$
$$(\mathsf{lock}_\emptyset \, y \, \text{in} \, ())$$

Starting with $S = \emptyset = L$, this expression reduces to

$$(\{p \mapsto, q \mapsto\}, \{p\}, ((\mathsf{lock}_\emptyset \, q \, \text{in} \, ()) \backslash p)_{\emptyset, \{p\}} \, \| \, (\mathsf{lock}_{\{p\}} \, q \, \text{in} \, (\mathsf{lock}_\emptyset \, p \, \text{in} \, ())))$$

where the second thread is (as it should be) not allowed to lock q. Notice that to detect a potential cycle out of the static information contained in this expression one has to look into the evaluation context.

5 Safety

In this section we establish our main result (Type Safety, Theorem 5.8 below), stating that typable expressions are safe. The types for the target language are as follows:

$$\rho ::= x \mid p \qquad\qquad \text{pointer names}$$
$$\tau, \, \sigma, \, \theta \ldots ::= \mathsf{unit} \mid \theta \, \mathsf{ref}_\rho \mid (\tau \xrightarrow{\varphi} \sigma) \quad \text{types}$$

We define a translation $\tau \Rightarrow \bar{\tau}$ from the types of the source language to the types of the target language by

$$\theta \, \mathsf{cref} \;\Rightarrow\; (\theta \, \mathsf{ref}_x \to \theta \, \mathsf{ref}_x)$$

$$\frac{}{\Gamma, x : \tau \vdash_t x : \emptyset, \tau} \qquad \frac{}{\Gamma, p : \theta \operatorname{ref}_p \vdash_t p : \emptyset, \theta \operatorname{ref}_p} \qquad \frac{\Gamma, x : \tau \vdash_t e : \varphi, \sigma}{\Gamma \vdash_t \lambda x e : \emptyset, (\tau \xrightarrow{\varphi} \sigma)} \ x \notin \Gamma$$

$$\frac{}{\Gamma \vdash_t () : \emptyset, \operatorname{unit}} \qquad \frac{\Gamma \vdash_t e_0 : \varphi_0, (\tau \xrightarrow{\varphi_2} \sigma) \quad \Gamma \vdash_t e_1 : \varphi_1, \tau}{\Gamma \vdash_t (e_0 e_1) : \varphi_0 \cup \varphi_1 \cup \varphi_2, \sigma} \ \tau \neq \theta \operatorname{ref}_x$$

$$\frac{\Gamma \vdash_t e_0 : \varphi_0, (\theta \operatorname{ref}_x \xrightarrow{\varphi_2} \sigma) \quad \Gamma \vdash_t e_1 : \varphi_1, \theta \operatorname{ref}_\rho}{\Gamma \vdash_t (e_0 e_1) : \varphi_0 \cup \varphi_1 \cup \{x \mapsto \rho\}\varphi_2, \{x \mapsto \rho\}\sigma}$$

$$\frac{\Gamma \vdash_t e : \varphi, \theta \operatorname{ref}_\rho}{\Gamma \vdash_t (!\, e) : \varphi, \theta} \qquad \frac{\Gamma \vdash_t e_0 : \varphi_0, \theta \operatorname{ref}_\rho \quad \Gamma \vdash_t e_1 : \varphi_1, \theta}{\Gamma \vdash_t (e_0 := e_1) : \varphi_0 \cup \varphi_1, \operatorname{unit}}$$

$$\frac{\Gamma \vdash_t e : \varphi, \operatorname{unit}}{\Gamma \vdash_t (\operatorname{thread} e) : \emptyset, \operatorname{unit}} \qquad \frac{\Gamma \vdash_t e_0 : \varphi_0, \theta \operatorname{ref}_\rho \quad \Gamma \vdash_t e_1 : \varphi_1, \tau}{\Gamma \vdash_t (\operatorname{lock}_{\varphi_1} e_0 \operatorname{in} e_1) : \{\rho\} \cup \varphi_0 \cup \varphi_1, \tau}$$

$$\frac{\Gamma \vdash_t e : \varphi, \tau}{\Gamma \vdash_t (e \backslash p)_{\psi, P} : \varphi, \tau} \ \varphi \cap P \subseteq \psi, \ P \subseteq \operatorname{dom}(\Gamma) \qquad \frac{\Gamma, x : \theta \operatorname{ref}_x \vdash_t e : \varphi, \tau}{\Gamma \vdash_t \nu x e : \varphi - \{x\}, \tau} \ x \notin \Gamma, \tau$$

—————— **Figure 3: Type and Effect System (Target Language)** ——————

(where x is not in θ). The judgements of the type system for the target language are $\Gamma \vdash_t e : \varphi, \tau$ where Γ, the typing context, is a mapping from a finite set $\operatorname{dom}(\Gamma)$ of variables and pointers to types.

As in the case of the source language, we only consider *well-formed* judgements, meaning that if a type $\theta \operatorname{ref}_\rho$ occurs in the judgement then ρ does not occur in θ, and if $\Gamma(\rho') = \theta \operatorname{ref}_\rho$ then $\rho' = \rho$. The typing rules are given in Figure 3. These are essentially the same as for the source language, with some new rules. One should in particular notice the constraints on the typing of $(e \backslash p)_{\psi, P}$: the anticipated effect of e must be recorded, as far as the known pointers are concerned, in the ψ component. This is the condition that will ensure the safety of typable expressions. First, we wish to show that the translation from the source to the target language preserves typability. To this end, we need a standard weakening property:

LEMMA (WEAKENING) 5.1. *If $\Gamma \vdash_t e : \varphi, \tau$ and x and p do not occur in this judgement then $\Gamma, x : \sigma \vdash_t e : \varphi, \tau$ and $\Gamma, p : \theta \vdash_t e : \varphi, \tau$.*

Then we have, denoting by $\overline{\Gamma}$ the typing context obtained from Γ by translating the types assigned to the variables:

LEMMA 5.2. *If $\Gamma \vdash_s e : \varphi, \tau \Rightarrow \bar{e}$ then $\overline{\Gamma} \vdash_t \bar{e} : \varphi, \bar{\tau}$.*

PROOF SKETCH: by induction on the definition of $\Gamma \vdash_s e : \varphi, \tau \Rightarrow \bar{e}$. The only cases to consider are the rule for $(\lambda x e_1(e_0()))$ with e_0 of type $\theta \operatorname{cref}$, using the Lemma 5.1, and the rules for $(\operatorname{cref} e)$ and $e = (\operatorname{lock} e_0 \operatorname{in} e_1)$. $\qquad\square$

Some obvious properties are:

REMARK 5.3.

(i) If $\Gamma \vdash_t v : \varphi, \tau$ then $\varphi = \emptyset$, and if $\tau = \theta \operatorname{ref}_\rho$ then $v = \rho$.

(ii) If $\Gamma \vdash_t e : \varphi, \tau$ and x is free in e then $x \in \operatorname{dom}(\Gamma)$.

(iii) If $\Gamma \vdash_t e : \varphi, \tau$ and p occurs in e then $p \in \operatorname{dom}(\Gamma)$.

LEMMA (STRENGTHENING) 5.4.

(i) If $\Gamma, x : \tau \vdash_t e : \varphi, \tau$ and x is not free in e then $\Gamma \vdash_t e : \varphi, \sigma$.

(ii) If $\Gamma, p : \sigma \vdash_t e : \varphi, \tau$ and p does not occur in e then $\Gamma \vdash_t e : \varphi, \tau$.

Our type safety result is established following the standard steps (see [13]), that is, the main property to show is that typability is preserved by reduction (the so-called "Subject Reduction" property). To this end, we need a lemma regarding typing and substitution, and another one regarding the typing of expressions of the form $\mathbf{E}[e]$ (the "Replacement Lemma"). We denote by $\{x \mapsto \rho\}(\Gamma \vdash_t e : \varphi, \tau)$ the substitution of x by ρ in all its free occurrences in this judgement. This is only defined if $x \in \operatorname{dom}(\Gamma)$ & $\rho \in \operatorname{dom}(\Gamma) \Rightarrow \Gamma(x) = \Gamma(\rho)$.

LEMMA (SUBSTITUTION) 5.5.

(i) If $\Gamma \vdash_t e : \varphi, \tau$ and $\rho' \in \operatorname{dom}(\Gamma) \Rightarrow \Gamma(\rho') = \theta \operatorname{ref}_{\rho'}$ for $\rho' \in \{x, \rho\}$ then $\{x \mapsto \rho\}(\Gamma \vdash_t e : \varphi, \tau)$.

(ii) If $x \notin \Gamma$ then $\Gamma, x : \sigma \vdash_t e : \varphi, \tau$ & $\Gamma \vdash_t v : \emptyset, \sigma \Rightarrow \Gamma \vdash_t \{x \mapsto v\}(e : \varphi, \tau)$.

PROOF SKETCH:

(i) The proof, by induction on the inference of $\Gamma \vdash_t e : \varphi, \tau$, is straightforward.

(ii) This is a standard property, established by induction on the inference of $\Gamma, x : \sigma \vdash_t e : \varphi, \tau$ (using the Weakening Lemma 5.1, and the previous point). In the case where $e = (\operatorname{lock}_{\varphi_1} e_0 \text{ in } e_1)$ with $\Gamma, x : \sigma \vdash_t e_0 : \varphi_0, \theta \operatorname{ref}_x$ and $\Gamma, x : \sigma \vdash_t e_1 : \varphi_1, \tau$, we have $\sigma = \theta \operatorname{ref}_x$ by the well-formedness assumption, and we use Remark 5.3(i), that is $v = x$.   □

LEMMA (REPLACEMENT) 5.6. If $\Gamma \vdash_t \mathbf{E}[e] : \varphi, \tau$ then there exist ψ and σ such that $\Gamma \vdash_t e : \psi, \sigma$ and if $\Gamma' \vdash_t e' : \psi', \sigma$ with $\Gamma \subseteq \Gamma'$ and $\psi' \cap \operatorname{dom}(\Gamma) \subseteq \psi$ then there exists φ' such that $\Gamma' \vdash_t \mathbf{E}[e'] : \varphi', \tau$ with $\varphi' \cap \operatorname{dom}(\Gamma) \subseteq \varphi$.

PROOF SKETCH: by induction on the evaluation context, and then by case on the frame $\mathbf{F}$ such that $\mathbf{E} = \mathbf{E}'[\mathbf{F}]$. We only examine some cases.

• $\mathbf{F} = (\operatorname{lock}_{\varphi''} [] \text{ in } e'')$. We have $\varphi = \{\rho\} \cup \psi \cup \varphi''$ with $\Gamma \vdash_t e : \psi, \theta \operatorname{ref}_\rho$ for some θ and $\Gamma \vdash_t e'' : \varphi'', \tau$. If $\Gamma' \vdash_t e' : \psi', \theta \operatorname{ref}_\rho$ with $\Gamma \subseteq \Gamma'$ and $\psi' \cap \operatorname{dom}(\Gamma) \subseteq \psi$ then $\Gamma' \vdash_t (\operatorname{lock}_{\varphi''} e' \text{ in } e'') : \{\rho\} \cup \psi' \cup \varphi'', \tau$, and we conclude using the induction hypothesis on $\mathbf{E}'$.

• $\mathbf{F} = ([] \backslash p)_{\varphi'', P}$. We have $\Gamma \vdash_t e : \varphi, \tau$ with $\varphi \cap P \subseteq \varphi''$ and $P \subseteq \operatorname{dom}(\Gamma)$. If $\Gamma' \vdash_t e' : \varphi', \tau$ with $\Gamma \subseteq \Gamma'$ and $\varphi' \cap \operatorname{dom}(\Gamma) \subseteq \varphi$ then $\varphi' \cap P \subseteq \varphi''$, and therefore $\Gamma' \vdash_t (e' \backslash p)_{\varphi'', P} : \varphi', \tau$, and we conclude using the induction hypothesis on $\mathbf{E}'$.   □

In order to show the type safety result, we have to extend the typing to configurations. The extension of typing to multisets of threads, that is $\Gamma \vdash T$, is given by

$$\frac{\Gamma \vdash_t e : \varphi, \tau}{\Gamma \vdash e} \qquad \frac{\Gamma \vdash T \qquad \Gamma \vdash T'}{\Gamma \vdash T \,\|\, T'}$$

Typing the store is defined as follows:

$$\Gamma \vdash S \quad \Leftrightarrow_{\mathrm{def}} \quad \begin{cases} \mathrm{dom}(S) \subseteq \mathrm{dom}(\Gamma) \,\&\, \\ \forall p.\ \Gamma(p) = \theta\, \mathrm{ref}_p \,\&\, S(p) = v \,\Rightarrow\, \Gamma \vdash_t v : \emptyset, \theta \end{cases}$$

Finally one defines

$$\Gamma \vdash (S, L, T) \quad \Leftrightarrow_{\mathrm{def}} \quad \Gamma \vdash S \,\&\, \Gamma \vdash T$$

PROPOSITION (SUBJECT REDUCTION) 5.7. *If* $\Gamma \vdash (S, L, T)$ *and* $(S, L, T) \to (S', L', T')$ *then* $\Gamma' \vdash (S', L', T')$ *for some* Γ' *such that* $\Gamma \subseteq \Gamma'$.

PROOF SKETCH: by case on the transition $(S, L, T) \to (S', L', T')$, where $T = \mathbf{E}[r] \,\|\, T''$ and r is the redex that is reduced. We only examine some cases.

• $r = (\lambda x e v)$. We have $S' = S$, $L' = L$ and $T' = \mathbf{E}[\{x \mapsto v\}e] \,\|\, T''$. There are two cases.

(i) $\Gamma, x : \zeta \vdash_t e : \varphi, \sigma$ and $\Gamma \vdash_t v : \emptyset, \zeta$ with $\zeta \neq \theta\, \mathrm{ref}_y$ and $\Gamma \vdash_t r : \varphi, \sigma$. We use the Substitution Lemma 5.5(ii) and the Replacement Lemma 5.6.

(ii) $\Gamma, x : \theta\, \mathrm{ref}_y \vdash_t e : \varphi, \sigma$ and $\Gamma \vdash_t v : \emptyset, \theta\, \mathrm{ref}_\rho$ with $\Gamma \vdash_t r : \{y \mapsto \rho\}(\varphi, \sigma)$ then by the well-formedness assumption we have $y = x$, and $v = \rho$ by Remark 5.3(i), and therefore by the Substitution Lemma 5.5(i) we have $\Gamma \vdash_t \{x \mapsto v\}e : \{y \mapsto \rho\}(\varphi, \sigma)$, and we conclude using the Replacement Lemma 5.6.

• $r = (\mathrm{lock}_\psi\ p\ \mathrm{in}\ e)$. We have $S = S'$ and $\Gamma \vdash_t r : \{p\} \cup \psi, \tau$ with $\Gamma = \Gamma', p : \theta\, \mathrm{ref}_p$ and $\Gamma \vdash_t e : \psi, \tau$. There two cases.

(i) $p \in \lceil \mathbf{E} \rceil$ and $L' = L$ and $T' = \mathbf{E}[e]$. We use the Replacement Lemma 5.6 to conclude.

(ii) $p \notin \lceil \mathbf{E} \rceil$, $L' = L \cup \{p\}$ and $T' = \mathbf{E}[(e \backslash p)_{\psi, P}]$ where $P = \mathrm{dom}(S)$. Then $P \subseteq \mathrm{dom}(\Gamma)$, and therefore $\Gamma \vdash_t (e \backslash p)_{\psi, P} : \psi, \tau$, and we conclude using the Replacement Lemma 5.6.

• $r = \nu x e$. We have $S' = S + p$ where $p \notin \mathrm{dom}(S)$ and $L' = L$ and $T = \mathbf{E}[\{x \mapsto p\}e] \,\|\, T''$. Then $\Gamma \vdash_t \nu x e : \varphi - \{x\}, \tau$ with $x \notin \Gamma, \tau$ and $\Gamma, x : \theta\, \mathrm{ref}_x \vdash_t e : \varphi, \tau$. By the Strengthening Lemma 5.4 (and well-formedness of configurations) we may assume that $p \notin \mathrm{dom}(\Gamma)$, and therefore $\Gamma, p : \theta\, \mathrm{ref}_p \vdash_t \{x \mapsto p\}e : \{x \mapsto p\}\varphi, \tau$ by the Substitution Lemma 5.5(i), and we use the Replacement Lemma 5.6 to conclude. $\square$

THEOREM (TYPE SAFETY) 5.8. *For any closed expression e of the source language, if* $\Gamma \vdash_s e : \varphi, \tau \Rightarrow \bar{e}$ *then* $\bar{e}$ *is safe.*

PROOF: this is a consequence of Lemma 5.2 and the Subject Reduction property, since if

$$\mathbf{E}[(\mathbf{E}'[(\mathrm{lock}_{\psi_1}\ p_1\ \mathrm{in}\ e)] \backslash p_0)_{\psi_0, P_0}]$$

is typable, we have $p_1 \in P_0 \Rightarrow p_1 \in \psi_0$, for

$$\Gamma \vdash_t \mathbf{E}'[(\mathrm{lock}_{\psi_1}\ p_1\ \mathrm{in}\ e)] : \varphi, \tau \Rightarrow p_1 \in \varphi \cap \mathrm{dom}(\Gamma)$$

$\square$

An obvious consequence of this result and Proposition 4.4 is that, if the closed expression e of the source language is typable, and translates into $\bar{e}$, then executing the latter (in the initial configuration where $S = \emptyset = L$) is free from deadlocks.

6 Conclusion

Designing a semantics for shared variable concurrency that is provably free of deadlocks is a step towards a *modular* concurrent programming style, where one can compose a system from several (typable) threads and modules without running the risk of entering into a deadlock. We have proposed such a deadlock-free semantics, that relies on a static analysis of programs which is not much more constraining than usual typing. Moreover, thanks to the use of singleton reference types, we obtain a fine grained locking policy, where each pointer has its own lock. That is, the programmer does not have to think about locks, but only about pointers.

References

1. Boyapati, C., Lee, R., Rinard, M.: Ownership types for safe programming: preventing data-races and deadlocks. In: OOPSLA 2002, pp. 211–230 (2002)
2. Coffman Jr, E.G., Elphick, M.J., Shoshani, A.: System Deadlocks. ACM Comput. Surveys 3(2), 67–78 (1971)
3. Flanagan, C., Abadi, M.: Types for safe locking. In: Swierstra, S.D. (ed.) ESOP 1999. LNCS, vol. 1576, pp. 91–108. Springer, Heidelberg (1999)
4. Hayashi, S.: Singleton, union and intersection types for program extraction. In: Ito, T., Meyer, A.R. (eds.) TACS 1991. LNCS, vol. 526, pp. 701–730. Springer, Heidelberg (1991)
5. Kobayashi, N.: A new type system for deadlock-free processes. In: Baier, C., Hermanns, H. (eds.) CONCUR 2006. LNCS, vol. 4137, pp. 233–247. Springer, Heidelberg (2006)
6. Lucassen, J.M., Gifford, D.K.: Polymorphic effect systems. In: POPL 1988, pp. 47–57 (1988)
7. McCloskey, B., Zhou, F., Gray, D., Brewer, E.: Autolocker: synchronization inference for atomic sections. In: POPL 2006, pp. 346–358 (2006)
8. Nanevski, A., Morrisett, G., Shinnar, A., Birkedal, L.: Ynot: dependent types for imperative programs. In: ICFP 2008, pp. 229–240 (2008)
9. Peyton Jones, S.L.: Beautiful concurrency. In: Oram, A., Wilson, G. (eds.) Beautiful Code. O'Reilly, Sebastopol (2007)
10. Suenaga, K.: Type-based deadlock-freedom verification for non-block-structured lock primitives and mutable references. In: Ramalingam, G. (ed.) APLAS 2008. LNCS, vol. 5356, pp. 155–170. Springer, Heidelberg (2008)
11. Vasconcelos, V., Martins, F., Cogumbreiro, T.: Type inference for deadlock detection in a multithreaded polymorphic typed assembly language. In: Proceedings of PLACES 2009 (2009)
12. Wang, Y., Lafortune, S., Kelly, T., Kudlur, M., Mahlke, S.: The theory of deadlock avoidance via discrete control. In: POPL 2009, pp. 252–263 (2009)
13. Wright, A., Felleisen, M.: A syntactic approach to type soundness. Information and Computation 115(1), 38–94 (1994)

On the Expressiveness of Forwarding in Higher-Order Communication*

Cinzia Di Giusto, Jorge A. Pérez, and Gianluigi Zavattaro

Dipartimento di Scienze dell'Informazione, Università di Bologna, Italy

Abstract. In higher-order process calculi the values exchanged in communications may contain processes. There are only two capabilities for received processes: execution and forwarding. Here we propose a limited form of forwarding: output actions can only communicate the parallel composition of statically known closed processes and processes received through previously executed input actions. We study the expressiveness of a higher-order process calculus featuring this style of communication. Our main result shows that in this calculus termination is decidable while convergence is undecidable.

1 Introduction

Higher-order process calculi are calculi in which processes can be communicated. They have been put forward in the early 1990s, with CHOCS [1], Plain CHOCS [2], the Higher-Order π-calculus [3], and others. Higher-order (or process-passing) concurrency is often presented as an alternative paradigm to the first order (or name-passing) concurrency of the π-calculus for the description of mobile systems. These calculi are inspired by, and formally close to, the λ-calculus, whose basic computational step — β-reduction — involves term instantiation. As in the λ-calculus, a computational step in higher-order calculi results in the instantiation of a variable with a term, which is then copied as many times as there are occurrences of the variable.

HOCORE is a core calculus for higher-order concurrency, recently introduced in [4]. It is *minimal*, in that only the operators strictly necessary to obtain higher-order communications are retained. This way, continuations following output messages have been left out, so communication in HOCORE is asynchronous. More importantly, HOCORE has no restriction operator. Thus all channels are global, and dynamic creation of new channels is impossible. This makes the absence of recursion also relevant, as known encodings of fixed-point combinators in higher-order process calculi require the restriction operator. The grammar of HOCORE processes is:

$$P ::= a(x).\, P \mid \overline{a}\langle P \rangle \mid P \parallel P \mid x \mid \mathbf{0} \qquad (*)$$

An input prefixed process $a(x).\, P$ can receive on name (or channel) a a process to be substituted in the place of x in the body P; an output message $\overline{a}\langle P \rangle$ can send P (the output object) on a; parallel composition allows processes to interact. Despite this

* Research partially funded by EU Integrated Projects HATS (contract number 231620) and SENSORIA (contract number 016004).

M. Leucker and C. Morgan (Eds.): ICTAC 2009, LNCS 5684, pp. 155–169, 2009.

minimality, via a termination preserving encoding of Minsky machines [5], HOCORE was shown to be Turing complete. Therefore, in HOCORE, properties such as *termination* (i.e. non existence of divergent computations) and *convergence* (i.e. existence of a terminating computation) are both undecidable. In contrast, somewhat surprisingly, strong bisimilarity is decidable, and several sensible bisimilarities coincide with it.

In this paper, we shall aim at identifying the intrinsic source of expressive power in HOCORE. A substantial part of the expressive power of a concurrent language comes from the ability of accounting for infinite behavior. In higher-order process calculi there is no explicit operator for such a behavior, as both recursion and replication can be encoded. We then find that infinite behavior resides in the interplay of higher-order communication, in particular, in the ability of *forwarding* a received process within an *arbitrary context*. For instance, consider the process $R = a(x).\overline{b}\langle P_x \rangle$ (here P_x stands for a process P with free occurrences of a variable x). Intuitively, R receives a process on name a and forwards it on name b. It is easy to see that since objects in output actions are built following the syntax given by $(*)$, the actual structure of P_x can be fairly complex. One could even "wrap" the process to be received in x using an arbitrary number of k "output layers", i.e., by letting $P_x \equiv \overline{b_1}\langle \overline{b_2}\langle \ldots \overline{b_k}\langle x \rangle \rangle \ldots \rangle$. This *nesting capability* embodies a great deal of the expressiveness of HOCORE: as a matter of fact, the encoding of Minsky machines in [4] depends critically on nesting-based counters. Therefore, investigating suitable limitations to the kind of processes that can be communicated in an output action appears as a legitimate approach to assess the expressive power of higher-order concurrency.

With the above consideration in mind, in this paper we propose HO^{-f}, a sublanguage of HOCORE in which output actions are limited so as to rule out the nesting capability (Section 2). In HO^{-f}, output actions can communicate the parallel composition of two kinds of objects: (i) statically known closed processes (i.e. that do not contain free variables), and (ii) processes received through previously executed input actions. Hence, the context in which the output action resides can only contribute to communication by "appending" pieces of code that admit no inspection, available in the form of a black-box. More formally, the grammar of HO^{-f} processes is that in $(*)$, except for the production for output actions, which is replaced by the following one:
$$\overline{a}\langle x_1 \parallel \cdots \parallel x_k \parallel P \rangle$$
where $k \geq 0$ and P is a closed process. This modification directly restricts forwarding capabilities for output processes, which in turn, leads to a more limited structure of processes along reductions.

The limited style of higher-order communication enforced in HO^{-f} is relevant from a pragmatic perspective. In fact, communication in HO^{-f} is inspired by those cases in which a process P is communicated in a translated format $[\![P]\!]$, and the translation is not compositional. That is, the cases in which, for any process context C, the translation of $C[P]$ cannot be seen as a function of the translation of P, i.e. there exists no context D such that $[\![C[P]]\!] = D[P]$. This setting can be related to several existing programming scenarios. The simplest example is perhaps mobility of already compiled code, on which it is not possible to apply inverse translations (such as reverse engineering). Other examples include *proof-carrying code* [6] and communication of *obfuscated code* [7]. The former features communication of executable code that comes with a certificate: a recipient can only check the certificate and decide whether to execute the code or not. The latter consists of the communication of source code that is made difficult to understand for, e.g., security/copyright reasons, while preserving its functionality.

The main contribution of the paper is the study of the expressiveness of HO^{-f} in terms of decidability of termination and convergence. Our main results are:

1. Similarly as HOCORE, HO^{-f} is Turing complete (Section 3). The calculus thus retains a significant expressive power despite of the limited forwarding capability. This result is obtained by exhibiting an encoding of Minsky machines.
2. In sharp contrast with HOCORE, termination in HO^{-f} is *decidable* (Section 4). This result is obtained by appealing to the theory of well-structured transition systems [8], following the approach used in [9].

As for (1), it is worth commenting that the encoding is not *faithful* in the sense that, unlike the encoding of Minsky machines in HOCORE, it may introduce computations which do not correspond to the expected behavior of the modeled machine. Such computations are forced to be infinite and thus regarded as non-halting computations which are therefore ignored. Only the finite computations correspond to those of the encoded Minsky machine. This way, we prove that a Minsky machine terminates if and only if its encoding in HO^{-f} converges. Consequently, convergence in HO^{-f} is *undecidable*.

As for (2), the use of the theory of well-structured transition systems is certainly not a new approach to obtain expressiveness results. However, to the best of our knowledge, this is the first time it is applied in the higher-order setting. This is significant because the adaptation to the HO^{-f} case is far from trivial. Indeed, as we shall discuss, this approach relies on approximating an upper bound on the depth of the (set of) derivatives of a process. By *depth* of a process we mean its maximal nesting of input/output actions. Notice that, even with the limitation on forwarding enforced by HO^{-f}, because of the "term copying" feature of higher-order calculi, variable instantiation might lead to a potentially larger process. Hence, finding suitable ways of bounding the set of derivatives of a process is rather challenging and needs care.

We comment further on the consequences of our results in Section 5. In this presentation we omit most proofs; these can be found in the extended version [10].

2 The Calculus

We now introduce the syntax and semantics of HO^{-f}. We use a, b, c to range over names, and x, y, z to range over variables; the sets of names and variables are disjoint.

$$P, Q ::= \overline{a}\langle x_1 \parallel \cdots \parallel x_k \parallel P \rangle \quad \text{(with } k \geq 0, \, \text{fv}(P) = \emptyset\text{)} \quad \text{output}$$
$$\mid \quad a(x).\,P \qquad\qquad\qquad\qquad\qquad\qquad \text{input prefix}$$
$$\mid \quad P \parallel Q \qquad\qquad\qquad\qquad\qquad\qquad\; \text{parallel composition}$$
$$\mid \quad x \qquad\qquad\qquad\qquad\qquad\qquad\qquad \text{process variable}$$
$$\mid \quad \mathbf{0} \qquad\qquad\qquad\qquad\qquad\qquad\qquad \text{nil}$$

An input $a(x).\,P$ binds the free occurrences of x in P. We write $\text{fv}(P)$ and $\text{bv}(P)$ for the set of free and bound variables in P, respectively. A process is *closed* if it does not have free variables. We abbreviate $a(x).\,P$, with $x \notin \text{fv}(P)$, as $a.\,P$, $\overline{a}\langle \mathbf{0} \rangle$ as $\overline{a}$, and

$P_1 \| \ldots \| P_k$ as $\prod_{i=1}^{k} P_i$. Hence, an output action can be written as $\overline{a}\langle \prod_{k \in K} x_k \| P \rangle$. We write $\prod_1^n P$ as an abbreviation for the parallel composition of n copies of P. Further, $P\{Q/x\}$ denotes the substitution of the free occurrences of x with process Q in P.

The Labeled Transition System (LTS) of HO^{-f} is defined on closed processes. There are three forms of transitions: τ transitions $P \xrightarrow{\tau} P'$; input transitions $P \xrightarrow{a(x)} P'$, meaning that P can receive at a a process that will replace x in the continuation P'; and output transitions $P \xrightarrow{\overline{a}\langle P' \rangle} P''$ meaning that P emits P' at a, and in doing so it evolves to P''. We use α to indicate a generic label of a transition.

$$\text{INP} \quad a(x).\, P \xrightarrow{a(x)} P \qquad\qquad \text{OUT} \quad \overline{a}\langle P \rangle \xrightarrow{\overline{a}\langle P \rangle} 0$$

$$\text{ACT1} \quad \frac{P_1 \xrightarrow{\alpha} P_1'}{P_1 \| P_2 \xrightarrow{\alpha} P_1' \| P_2} \qquad \text{TAU1} \quad \frac{P_1 \xrightarrow{\overline{a}\langle P \rangle} P_1' \quad P_2 \xrightarrow{a(x)} P_2'}{P_1 \| P_2 \xrightarrow{\tau} P_1' \| P_2'\{P/x\}}$$

(We have omitted ACT2 and TAU2, the symmetric counterparts of the last two rules.)

Remark 1. Since we consider closed processes, in rule ACT1, P_2 has no free variables and no side conditions are necessary. As a consequence, alpha-conversion is not needed.

Definition 1. *The* structural congruence *relation is the smallest congruence generated by the following laws:*

$$P \| 0 \equiv P, \; P_1 \| P_2 \equiv P_2 \| P_1, \; P_1 \| (P_2 \| P_3) \equiv (P_1 \| P_2) \| P_3.$$

The *alphabet* of an HO^{-f} process is defined as follows:

Definition 2 (Alphabet of a process). *Let P be a HO^{-f} process. The alphabet of P, denoted $\mathcal{A}(P)$, is inductively defined as:*

$$\mathcal{A}(0) = \emptyset \qquad \mathcal{A}(P \| Q) = \mathcal{A}(P) \cup \mathcal{A}(Q) \qquad \mathcal{A}(x) = \{x\}$$

$$\mathcal{A}(a(x).\,P) = \{a, x\} \cup \mathcal{A}(P) \qquad \mathcal{A}(\overline{a}\langle P \rangle) = \{a\} \cup \mathcal{A}(P)$$

Proposition 1. *Let P be a HO^{-f} process. The set $\mathcal{A}(P)$ is finite. Also, if $P \xrightarrow{\alpha} P'$ then $\mathcal{A}(P') \subseteq \mathcal{A}(P)$.*

The internal runs of a process are given by sequences of *reductions*. Given a process P, its reductions $P \longrightarrow P'$ are defined as $P \xrightarrow{\tau} P'$. We denote with $\longrightarrow^*$ the reflexive and transitive closure of $\longrightarrow$; notation $\longrightarrow^j$ is to stand for a sequence of j reductions. We use $P \nrightarrow$ to denote that there is no P' such that $P \longrightarrow P'$. Following [9] we now define process convergence and process termination. Observe that termination implies convergence while the opposite does not hold.

Definition 3. *Let P be a HO^{-f} process. We say that P converges iff there exists P' such that $P \longrightarrow^* P'$ and $P' \nrightarrow$. We say that P terminates iff there exist no $\{P_i\}_{i \in \mathbb{N}}$ such that $P_0 = P$ and $P_j \longrightarrow P_{j+1}$ for any j.*

Termination and convergence are sometimes also referred to as *universal* and *existential* termination, respectively.

Table 1. Reduction of Minsky machines

$$\text{M-INC} \quad \frac{i : \text{INC}(r_j) \quad m'_j = m_j + 1 \quad m'_{1-j} = m_{1-j}}{(i, m_0, m_1) \longrightarrow_M (i+1, m'_0, m'_1)} \qquad \text{M-JMP} \quad \frac{i : \text{DECJ}(r_j, s) \quad m_j = 0}{(i, m_0, m_1) \longrightarrow_M (s, m_0, m_1)}$$

$$\text{M-DEC} \quad \frac{i : \text{DECJ}(r_j, s) \quad m_j \neq 0 \quad m'_j = m_j - 1 \quad m'_{1-j} = m_{1-j}}{(i, m_0, m_1) \longrightarrow_M (i+1, m'_0, m'_1)}$$

3   Convergence Is Undecidable

In this section we show that HO^{-f} is powerful enough to model Minsky machines [5], a Turing complete model. We present an encoding that is not *faithful*: unlike the encoding of Minsky machines in HOCORE, it may introduce computations which do not correspond to the expected behavior of the modeled machine. Such computations are forced to be infinite and thus regarded as non-halting computations which are therefore ignored. Only finite computations correspond to those of the encoded Minsky machine. More precisely, given a Minsky machine N, its encoding $[\![N]\!]$ has a terminating computation if and only if N terminates. This allows to prove that convergence is undecidable.

We begin by briefly recalling the definition of Minsky machines; we then present the encoding into HO^{-f} and discuss its correctness.

Minsky machines. A Minsky machine is a Turing complete model composed of a set of sequential, labeled instructions, and two registers. Registers r_j $(j \in \{0, 1\})$ can hold arbitrarily large natural numbers. Instructions $(1 : I_1), \ldots, (n : I_n)$ can be of two kinds: $\text{INC}(r_j)$ adds 1 to register r_j and proceeds to the next instruction; $\text{DECJ}(r_j, s)$ jumps to instruction s if r_j is zero, otherwise it decreases register r_j by 1 and proceeds to the next instruction. A Minsky machine includes a program counter p indicating the label of the instruction being executed. In its initial state, the machine has both registers set to 0 and the program counter p set to the first instruction. The Minsky machine stops whenever the program counter is set to a non-existent instruction, i.e. $p > n$. A *configuration* of a Minsky machine is a tuple (i, m_0, m_1); it consists of the current program counter and the values of the registers. Formally, the reduction relation over configurations of a Minsky machine, denoted $\longrightarrow_M$, is defined in Table 1.

In the encoding of a Minsky machine into HO^{-f} we will find it convenient to have a simple form of guarded replication. This construct can be encoded in HO^{-f} as follows.

Input-guarded replication. We follow the standard encoding of replication in higher-order process calculi, adapting it to input-guarded replication so as to make sure that diverging behaviors are not introduced. As there is no restriction in HO^{-f}, the encoding is not compositional and replications cannot be nested. In [4] the following encoding is shown to preserve termination.

Definition 4. *Assume a fresh name c. The encoding of* input-guarded replication *is as follows:*

$$[\![!a(z).P]\!]_{i!} = a(z).(Q_c \parallel P) \parallel \overline{c}\langle a(z).(Q_c \parallel P)\rangle$$

Table 2. Encoding of Minsky machines

REGISTER r_j $[\![r_j = m]\!]_M = \prod_1^m \overline{u_j}$

INSTRUCTIONS $(i : I_i)$
$[\![(i : \text{INC}(r_j))]\!]_M = {!}p_i.\,(\overline{u_j} \parallel set_j(x).\,\overline{set_j}\langle x \parallel \text{INC}_j\rangle \parallel \overline{p_{i+1}})$
$[\![(i : \text{DECJ}(r_j, s))]\!]_M = {!}p_i.\,\overline{m_i}$
$\qquad\qquad\qquad \parallel {!}m_i.\,(\overline{loop} \parallel u_j.\,loop.\,set_j(x).\,\overline{set_j}\langle x \parallel \text{DEC}_j\rangle \parallel \overline{p_{i+1}})$
$\qquad\qquad\qquad \parallel {!}m_i.\,set_j(x).\,(x \parallel \overline{set_j}\langle 0\rangle \parallel \overline{p_s}))$

where

$\qquad \text{INC}_j = \overline{loop} \parallel check_j.\,loop \qquad\qquad \text{DEC}_j = \overline{check_j}$

where $Q_c = c(x).\,(x \parallel \overline{c}\langle x\rangle)$, P contains no replications (nested replications are forbidden), and $[\![\cdot]\!]_{i!}$ is an homomorphism on the other process constructs in HO^{-f}.

Encoding Minsky machines into HO^{-f}. The encoding of Minsky machines into HO^{-f} is denoted by $[\![\cdot]\!]_M$ and presented in Table 2. We begin by defining the encoding of the configurations of a Minsky machine; we then discuss the encodings of registers and instructions.

Definition 5 (Encoding of Configurations). *Let N be a Minsky machine with registers r_0, r_1 and instructions $(1 : I_1), \ldots, (n : I_n)$. For $j \in \{0, 1\}$, suppose fresh, pairwise different names r_j, $p_1, \ldots, p_n$, set_j, $loop$, $check_j$. Also, let DIV be a divergent process (e.g. $\overline{w} \parallel {!}w.\,\overline{w}$). Given the encodings in Table 2, we have:*

1. *The initial configuration $(1, 0, 0)$ of N is encoded as:*

$$[\![(1, 0, 0)]\!]_M ::= \overline{p_1} \parallel \prod_{i=1}^{n} [\![(i : I_i)]\!]_M \parallel loop.\,\text{DIV} \parallel \overline{set_0}\langle 0\rangle \parallel \overline{set_1}\langle 0\rangle\,.$$

2. *A configuration (i, m_0, m_1) of N, after k_j increments and l_j decrements of register r_j, is encoded as:*

$$[\![(i, m_0, m_1)]\!]_M = \overline{p_i} \parallel [\![r_0 = m_0]\!]_M \parallel [\![r_1 = m_1]\!]_M \parallel \prod_{i=1}^{n} [\![(i : I_i)]\!]_M \parallel$$
$$loop.\,\text{DIV} \parallel \overline{set_0}\langle \text{LOG}_0[k_0, l_0]\rangle \parallel \overline{set_1}\langle \text{LOG}_1[k_1, l_1]\rangle\,.$$

A register r_j that stores the number m is encoded as the parallel composition of m copies of the unit process $\overline{u_j}$. To implement the test for zero it is necessary to record how many increments and decrements have been performed on the register r_j. This is done by using a special process LOG_j, which is communicated back and forth on name set_j. More precisely, every time an increment instruction occurs, a new copy of the process $\overline{u_j}$ is created, and the process LOG_j is updated by adding the process INC_j in parallel. Similarly for decrements: a copy of $\overline{u_j}$ is consumed and the process DEC_j is added to LOG_j. As a result, after k increments and l decrements on register r_j, we have that $\text{LOG}_j = \prod_k \text{INC}_j \parallel \prod_l \text{DEC}_j$, which we abbreviate as $\text{LOG}_j[k, l]$.

Each instruction $(i : I_i)$ is a replicated process guarded by p_i, which represents the program counter when $p = i$. Once p_i is consumed, the instruction is active and an interaction with a register occurs. We already described the behavior of increments. Let us now focus on decrements, the instructions that can introduce divergent —unfaithful— computations. In this case, the process can internally choose either to actually perform a decrement and proceed with the next instruction, or to jump. This can be seen as a guess the process makes on the actual number stored by the register r_j. Therefore, two situations can occur:

1. *The process chooses to decrement r_j.* In this case instruction p_{i+1} is immediately enabled, and the process launches process $\overline{loop}$ and then tries to consume a copy of $\overline{u_j}$. If this operation succeeds (i.e. the content of r_j is greater than 0) then a synchronization with the input on $loop$ that guards the updating of LOG_j (represented as an output on name set_j) takes place. Otherwise, the unit process $\overline{u_j}$ could not be consumed (i.e. the content of r_j is zero and the process made a wrong guess). Process $\overline{loop}$ then synchronizes with the external process $loop$. DIV, thus spawning a divergent computation.

2. *The process chooses to jump to instruction p_s.* In this case instruction p_s is immediately enabled, and it is necessary to check if the actual value stored by r_j is zero. To do so, the process receives the process LOG_j and launches it. If the number of increments is equal to the number of decrements then complementary signals on the name $check_j$ will match each other. In turn, this allows each signal $\overline{loop}$ executed by an INC_j process to be matched by a complementary one. Otherwise, then it is the case that at least one of those $\overline{loop}$ signals remains active (i.e. the content of the register is not zero); a synchronization with the process $loop$. DIV then takes place, and a divergent computation is spawned.

Before executing the instructions, we require both registers in the Minsky machine to be set to zero. This is to guarantee correctness: starting with values different from zero in the registers (without proper initialization of the logs) can lead to inconsistencies. For instance, the test for zero would succeed (i.e. without spawning a divergent computation) even for a register whose value is different from zero.

We now state that the encoding is correct.

Theorem 1. *Let N be a Minsky machine with registers $r_0 = m_0$, $r_1 = m_1$, instructions $(1 : I_1), \ldots, (n : I_n)$, and configuration (i, m_0, m_1). Then (i, m_0, m_1) terminates if and only if process $[\![(i, m_0, m_1)]\!]_M$ converges.*

As a consequence of this theorem we have that convergence is undecidable.

Corollary 1. *Convergence is undecidable in HO^{-f}.*

4   Termination Is Decidable

In this section we prove that termination is decidable for HO^{-f} processes. As hinted at in the introduction, this is in sharp contrast with the analogous result for HOCORE. The proof appeals to the theory of well-structured transition systems, whose main definitions and results we summarize next.

Well-Structured Transition Systems. The following results and definitions are from [8], unless differently specified. Recall that a *quasi-order* (or, equivalently, preorder) is a reflexive and transitive relation.

Definition 6 (Well-quasi-order). *A well-quasi-order (wqo) is a quasi-order $\leq$ over a set X such that, for any infinite sequence $x_0, x_1, x_2 \ldots \in X$, there exist indexes $i < j$ such that $x_i \leq x_j$.*

Note that if $\leq$ is a wqo then any infinite sequence $x_0, x_1, x_2, \ldots$ contains an infinite increasing subsequence $x_{i_0}, x_{i_1}, x_{i_2}, \ldots$ (with $i_0 < i_1 < i_2 < \ldots$). Thus well-quasi-orders exclude the possibility of having infinite strictly decreasing sequences.

We also need a definition for (finitely branching) transition systems. This can be given as follows. Here and in the following $\rightarrow^*$ denotes the reflexive and transitive closure of the relation $\rightarrow$.

Definition 7 (Transition system). *A transition system is a structure $TS = (S, \rightarrow)$, where S is a set of states and $\rightarrow \subseteq S \times S$ is a set of transitions. We define $Succ(s)$ as the set $\{s' \in S \mid s \rightarrow s'\}$ of immediate successors of S. We say that TS is finitely branching if, for each $s \in S$, $Succ(s)$ is finite.*

Fact 1. *The LTS for* HO^{-f} *given in Section 2 is finitely branching.*

The function $Succ$ will also be used on sets by assuming the point-wise extension of the above definitions. The key tool to decide several properties of computations is the notion of *well-structured transition system*. This is a transition system equipped with a well-quasi-order on states which is (upward) compatible with the transition relation. Here we will use a strong version of compatibility; hence the following definition.

Definition 8 (Well-structured transition system). *A well-structured transition system with strong compatibility is a transition system $TS = (S, \rightarrow)$, equipped with a quasi-order $\leq$ on S, such that the two following conditions hold:*

1. *$\leq$ is a well-quasi-order;*
2. *$\leq$ is strongly (upward) compatible with $\rightarrow$, that is, for all $s_1 \leq t_1$ and all transitions $s_1 \rightarrow s_2$, there exists a state t_2 such that $t_1 \rightarrow t_2$ and $s_2 \leq t_2$ holds.*

The following theorem is a special case of Theorem 4.6 in [8] and will be used to obtain our decidability result.

Theorem 2. *Let $TS = (S, \rightarrow, \leq)$ be a finitely branching, well-structured transition system with strong compatibility, decidable $\leq$, and computable $Succ$. Then the existence of an infinite computation starting from a state $s \in S$ is decidable.*

We will also need a result due to Higman [11] which allows to extend a well-quasi-order from a set S to the set of the finite sequences on S. More precisely, given a set S let us denote by S^* the set of finite sequences built by using elements in S. We can define a quasi-order on S^* as follows.

Definition 9. *Let S be a set and $\leq$ a quasi-order over S. The relation $\leq_*$ over S^* is defined as follows. Let $t, u \in S^*$, with $t = t_1 t_2 \ldots t_m$ and $u = u_1 u_2 \ldots u_n$. We have* *that* $t \leq_* u$ *if and only if there exists an injection* f *from* $\{1, 2, \ldots m\}$ *to* $\{1, 2, \ldots n\}$ *such that* $t_i \leq u_{f(i)}$ *and* $i \leq f(i)$ *for* $i = 1, \ldots, m$.

The relation $\leq_*$ is clearly a quasi-order over S^*. It is also a wqo, since we have the following result.

Lemma 1 ([11]). *Let* S *be a set and* $\leq$ *a wqo over* S. *Then* $\leq_*$ *is a wqo over* S^*.

Finally we will use also the following proposition, whose proof is immediate.

Proposition 2. *Let* S *be a finite set. Then the equality is a wqo over* S.

Termination is Decidable in HO^{-f}. Here we prove that termination is decidable in HO^{-f}. The crux of the proof consists in finding an upper bound for a process and its derivatives. This is possible in HO^{-f} because of the limited structure allowed in output actions. We proceed as follows. First we define a notion of normal form for HO^{-f} processes. We then characterize an upper bound for the derivatives of a given process, and define an ordering over them. This ordering is then shown to be a wqo that is strongly compatible with respect to the LTS of HO^{-f} given in Section 2. The decidability result is then obtained by resorting to the results from [8] reported before.

Definition 10 (Normal Form). *Let* $P \in \text{HO}^{-f}$. P *is in* normal form *iff*

$$P = \prod_{k=1}^{l} x_k \parallel \prod_{i=1}^{m} a_i(y_i).\, P_i \parallel \prod_{j=1}^{n} \overline{b_j}\langle P_j' \rangle$$

where each P_i *and* P_j' *are in normal form.*

Lemma 2. *Every process* $P \in \text{HO}^{-f}$ *is structurally congruent to a normal form.*

We now define an ordering over normal forms. Intuitively, a process is larger than another if it has more parallel components.

Definition 11 (Relation $\preceq$). *Let* $P, Q \in \text{HO}^{-f}$. *We write* $P \preceq Q$ *iff there exist* $x_1 \ldots x_l$, $P_1 \ldots P_m$, $P_1' \ldots P_n'$, $Q_1 \ldots Q_m$, $Q_1' \ldots Q_n'$, *and* R *such that*

$$P \equiv \prod_{k=1}^{l} x_k \parallel \prod_{i=1}^{m} a_i(y_i).\, P_i \parallel \prod_{j=1}^{n} \overline{b_j}\langle P_j' \rangle$$
$$Q \equiv \prod_{k=1}^{l} x_k \parallel \prod_{i=1}^{m} a_i(y_i).\, Q_i \parallel \prod_{j=1}^{n} \overline{b_j}\langle Q_j' \rangle \parallel R$$

with $P_i \preceq Q_i$ *and* $P_j' \preceq Q_j'$, *for* $i \in [1 .. m]$ *and* $j \in [1 .. n]$.

The normal form of a process can be intuitively represented in a tree-like manner. More precisely, given the process in normal form

$$P = \prod_{k=1}^{l} x_k \parallel \prod_{i=1}^{m} a_i(y_i).\, P_i \parallel \prod_{j=1}^{n} \overline{b_j}\langle P_j' \rangle$$

we shall decree its associated tree to have a root node labeled $x_1, \ldots, x_k$. This root node has $m + n$ children, corresponding to the the trees associated to processes $P_1, \ldots, P_m$ and $P_1', \ldots, P_m'$; the outgoing edges connecting the root node and the children are labeled $a_1(y_1), \ldots, a_m(y_m)$ and $\overline{b_1}, \ldots, \overline{b_n}$.

This intuitive representation of processes in normal form as trees will be useful to reason about the structure of HO^{-f} terms. We begin by defining the *depth* of a process. Notice that such a depth corresponds to the maximum depth of its tree representation.

Definition 12 (Depth). *Let* $P = \prod_{k=1}^{l} x_k \parallel \prod_{i=1}^{m} a_i(y_i).P_i \parallel \prod_{j=1}^{n} \overline{b_j}\langle P_j' \rangle$ *be a* HO^{-f} *process in normal form. The* depth *of* P *is given by*

$$\mathsf{depth}(P) = \max\{1 + \mathsf{depth}(P_i), 1 + \mathsf{depth}(P_j') \mid i \in [1..m] \wedge j \in [1..n]\}.$$

Given a natural number n and a process P, the set $\mathcal{P}_{P,n}$ contains all those processes in normal form that can be built using the alphabet of P and whose depth is at most n.

Definition 13. *Let* n *be a natural number and* $P \in \text{HO}^{-f}$. *We define the set* $\mathcal{P}_{P,n}$ *as follows:*

$$\mathcal{P}_{P,n} = \{Q \mid Q \equiv \prod_{k \in K} x_k \parallel \prod_{i \in I} a_i(y_i).Q_i \parallel \prod_{j \in J} \overline{b_j}\langle Q_j' \rangle$$
$$\wedge \ \mathcal{A}(Q) \subseteq \mathcal{A}(P)$$
$$\wedge \ Q_i, Q_j' \in \mathcal{P}_{P,n-1} \ \forall i \in I, j \in J\}$$

where $\mathcal{P}_{P,0}$ *contains processes that are built out only of variables in* $\mathcal{A}(P)$.

As it will be shown later, the set of all derivatives of P is a subset of $\mathcal{P}_{P,2\cdot\mathsf{depth}(P)}$.

When compared to processes in languages such as Milner's CCS, higher-order processes have a more complex structure. This is because, by virtue of reductions, an arbitrary process can take the place of possibly several occurrences of a single variable. As a consequence, the depth of (the syntax tree of) a process cannot be determined (or even approximated) before its execution: it can vary arbitrarily along reductions. Crucially, in HO^{-f} it is possible to bound such a depth. Our approach is the following: rather than solely depending on the depth of a process, we define measures on the relative position of variables within a process. Informally speaking, such a position will be determined by the number of prefixes guarding a variable. Since variables are allowed only at the top level of the output objects, their relative distance will remain invariant during reductions. This allows to obtain a bound on the structure of HO^{-f} processes. Finally, it is worth stressing that even if the same notions of normal form, depth, and distance can be defined for HOCORE, a finite upper bound for such a language does not exist. We first define the maximum distance between a variable and its binder.

Definition 14. *Let* $P = \prod_{k \in K} x_k \parallel \prod_{i \in I} a_i(y_i).P_i \parallel \prod_{j \in J} \overline{b_j}\langle P_j' \rangle$ *be a* HO^{-f} *process in normal form. We define the* maximum distance *of* P *as:*

$$\mathsf{maxDistance}(P) = \max\{\mathsf{maxDist}_{y_i}(P_i),$$
$$\mathsf{maxDistance}(P_i), \mathsf{maxDistance}(P_j') \mid i \in I, j \in J\}$$

where

$$\mathsf{maxDist}_x(P) = \begin{cases} 1 & \text{if } P = x, \\ 1 + \mathsf{maxDist}_x(P_z) & \text{if } P = a(z).P_z \wedge x \neq z, \\ 1 + \mathsf{maxDist}_x(P') & \text{if } P = \overline{a}\langle P' \rangle, \\ \max\{\mathsf{maxDist}_x(R), \mathsf{maxDist}_x(Q)\} & \text{if } P = R \parallel Q, \\ 0 & \text{otherwise.} \end{cases}$$

Lemma 3 (Properties of maxDistance). *Let* P *be a* HO^{-f} *process. It holds that:*

1. $\mathsf{maxDistance}(P) \leq \mathsf{depth}(P)$
2. *For every* Q *such that* $P \xrightarrow{\alpha} Q$, $\mathsf{maxDistance}(Q) \leq \mathsf{maxDistance}(P)$.

We now define the maximum depth of processes that can be communicated. Notice that the continuations of inputs are considered as they could become communication objects themselves along reductions:

Definition 15. *Let* $P = \prod_{k \in K} x_k \parallel \prod_{i \in I} a_i(y_i). P_i \parallel \prod_{j \in J} \overline{b_j}\langle P'_j \rangle$ *be a* HO^{-f} *process in normal form. We define the* maximum depth *of a process that can be communicated* (maxDepCom(P)) *in* P *as:*

$$\text{maxDepCom}(P) = \max\{\text{maxDepCom}(P_i), \text{depth}(P'_j) \mid i \in I, j \in J\}.$$

Lemma 4 (Properties of maxDepCom). *Let* P *be a* HO^{-f} *process. It holds that:*

1. $\text{maxDepCom}(P) \leq \text{depth}(P)$
2. *For every* Q *such that* $P \xrightarrow{\alpha} Q$, $\text{maxDepCom}(Q) \leq \text{maxDepCom}(P)$.

Notation 1. *We use* $P \xrightarrow{\tilde{\alpha}} P'$ *if, for some* $n \geq 0$, *there exist* $\alpha_1, \dots, \alpha_n$ *such that* $P \xrightarrow{\alpha_1} \cdots \xrightarrow{\alpha_n} P'$.

Generalizing Lemmata 3 and 4 we obtain:

Corollary 2. *Let* P *be a* HO^{-f} *process. For every* Q *such that* $P \xrightarrow{\tilde{\alpha}} Q$, *it holds that:*

1. $\text{maxDistance}(Q) \leq \text{depth}(P)$
2. $\text{maxDepCom}(Q) \leq \text{depth}(P)$.

We are interested in characterizing the derivatives of a given process P. We shall show that they are over-approximated by means of the set $\mathcal{P}_{P,2 \cdot \text{depth}(P)}$. We will investigate the properties of the relation $\preceq$ on such an approximation; such properties will also hold for the set of derivatives.

Definition 16. *Let* $P \in \text{HO}^{-f}$. *Then we define* $\text{Deriv}(P) = \{Q \mid P \longrightarrow^* Q\}$

The following results hold because of the limitations we have imposed on the output actions for HO^{-f} processes. Any process that can be communicated in P is in $\mathcal{P}_{P,n-1}$ and its maximum depth is also bounded by $\text{depth}(P)$. The deepest position for a variable is when it is a leaf in the tree associated to the normal form of P. That is, when its depth is exactly $\text{depth}(P)$. Hence the following:

Proposition 3. *Let* P *be a* HO^{-f} *process. Suppose, for some* n, *that* $P \in \mathcal{P}_{P,n}$. *For every* Q *such that* $P \xrightarrow{\alpha} Q$, *it holds that* $Q \in \mathcal{P}_{P,2 \cdot n}$.

The lemma below generalizes Proposition 3 to a sequence of transitions.

Lemma 5. *Let* P *be a* HO^{-f} *process. Suppose, for some* n, *that* $P \in \mathcal{P}_{P,n}$. *For every* Q *such that* $P \xrightarrow{\tilde{\alpha}} Q$, *it holds that* $Q \in \mathcal{P}_{P,2 \cdot n}$.

Corollary 3. *Let* $P \in \text{HO}^{-f}$. *Then* $\text{Deriv}(P) \subseteq \mathcal{P}_{P,2 \cdot \text{depth}(P)}$.

To prove that $\preceq$ is a wqo, we first show that it is a quasi order.

Proposition 4. *The relation* $\preceq$ *is a quasi-order.*

We are now in place to state that $\preceq$ is a wqo.

Theorem 3 (Well-quasi-order). *Let* $P \in \mathrm{HO}^{-\mathrm{f}}$ *and* $n \geq 0$. *The relation* $\preceq$ *is a well-quasi-order over* $\mathcal{P}_{P,n}$.

Proof. The proof is by induction on n.

(–) Let $n = 0$. Then $\mathcal{P}_{P,0}$ contains processes containing only variables taken from $\mathcal{A}(P)$. The equality on finite sets is a well-quasi-ordering; by Lemma 1 (Higman's Lemma) also $=_*$ is a well quasi-ordering: it corresponds to the ordering $\preceq$ on processes containing only variables.

(–) Let $n > 0$. Take an infinite sequence of processes $s = P_1, P_2, \ldots, P_l, \ldots$ with $P_l \in \mathcal{P}_{P,n}$. We shall show that the thesis holds by means of successive filterings of the normal forms of the processes in s. By Lemma 2 there exist K_l, I_l and J_l such that

$$P_l \equiv \prod_{k \in K_l} x_k \parallel \prod_{i \in I_l} a_i(y_i) . P_i^l \parallel \prod_{j \in J_l} \overline{b_j}\langle P_j''^l \rangle$$

with P_i^l and $P_j''^l \in \mathcal{P}_{P,n-1}$. Hence each P_l can be seen as composed of 3 finite sequences: (i) $x_1 \ldots x_k$, (ii) $a_1(y_1) . P_1^l \ldots a_i(y_i) . P_i^l$, and (iii) $\overline{b_1}\langle P_1''^l \rangle \ldots \overline{b_j}\langle P_j''^l \rangle$. We note that the first sequence is composed of variables from the finite set $\mathcal{A}(P)$ whereas the other two sequences are composed by elements in $\mathcal{A}(P)$ and $\mathcal{P}_{P,n-1}$. Since we have an infinite sequence of $\mathcal{A}(P)^*$, as $\mathcal{A}(P)$ is finite, by Proposition 2 and Lemma 1 we have that $=_*$ is a wqo over $\mathcal{A}(P)^*$. By inductive hypothesis, we have that $\preceq$ is a wqo on $\mathcal{P}_{P,n-1}$, hence by Lemma 1 relation $\preceq_*$ is a wqo on $\mathcal{P}_{P,n-1}^*$. We start filtering out s by making the finite sequences $x_1 \ldots x_k$ increasing with respect to $=_*$; let us call this subsequence t. Then we filter out t, by making the finite sequence $a_1(y_1) . P_1^l \ldots a_i(y_i) . P_i^l$ increasing with respect to both $\preceq_*$ and $=_*$. This is done in two steps: first, by considering the relation $=_*$ on the subject of the actions (recalling that $a_i, y_i \in \mathcal{A}(P)$), and then by applying another filtering to the continuation using the inductive hypothesis. For the first step, it is worth remarking that we do not consider symbols of the alphabet but pairs of symbols. Since the set of pairs on a finite set is still finite, we know by Higman's Lemma that $=_*$ is a wqo on the set of sequences of pairs (a_i, y_i). For the sequence of outputs $\overline{b_1}\langle P_1''^l \rangle \ldots \overline{b_j}\langle P_j''^l \rangle$ this is also done in two steps: the subject of the outputs are ordered with respect to $=_*$ and the objects of the output action are ordered with respect to $\preceq_*$ using the inductive hypothesis. At the end of the process we obtain an infinite subsequence of s that is ordered with respect to $\preceq$. $\qquad \square$

The last thing to show is that the well-quasi-ordering $\preceq$ is strongly compatible with respect to the LTS associated to $\mathrm{HO}^{-\mathrm{f}}$. We need the following auxiliary lemma:

Lemma 6. *Let* P, P', Q, *and* Q' *be* $\mathrm{HO}^{-\mathrm{f}}$ *processes in normal form such that* $P \preceq P'$ *and* $Q \preceq Q'$. *Then it holds that* $P\{Q/x\} \preceq P'\{Q'/x\}$.

Theorem 4 (Strong Compatibility). *Let* $P, Q, P' \in \mathrm{HO}^{-\mathrm{f}}$. *If* $P \preceq Q$ *and* $P \xrightarrow{\alpha} P'$ *then there exists* Q' *such that* $Q \xrightarrow{\alpha} Q'$ *and* $P' \preceq Q'$.

Theorem 5. *Let* $P \in \mathrm{HO}^{-\mathrm{f}}$. *The transition system* $(\mathrm{Deriv}(P), \longrightarrow, \preceq)$ *is a finitely branching well-structured transition system with strong compatibility, decidable* $\preceq$, *and computable* $Succ$.

Proof. The transition system of HO^{-f} is finitely branching (Fact 1). The fact that $\preceq$ is a well-quasi-order on $Deriv(P)$ follows from Corollary 3 and Theorem 3. Strong compatibility follows from Theorem 4.   □

We can now state the main result of the section. It follows from Theorems 2 and 5.

Corollary 4. *Let* $P \in HO^{-f}$. *Termination of* P *is decidable.*

5 Concluding Remarks

We have studied HO^{-f}, a higher-order process calculus featuring a limited form of higher-order communication. In HO^{-f}, output actions can only include previously received processes in composition with closed ones. This is reminiscent of programming scenarios with forms of code mobility in which the recipient is not authorized or capable of accessing/modifying the structure of the received code. We have shown that such a weakening of the forward capabilities of higher-order processes has consequences both on the expressiveness of the language and on the decidability of termination.

As for the expressiveness issues, by exhibiting an encoding of Minsky machines into HO^{-f}, we have shown that convergence is undecidable. Hence, from an *absolute expressiveness* standpoint, HO^{-f} is Turing complete. Now, given the analogous result for HOCORE [4], a *relative expressiveness* issue also arises. Indeed, our encoding of Minsky machines into HO^{-f} is not faithful, which reveals a difference on the criteria each encoding satisfies. This reminds us of the situation in [12], where faithful and unfaithful encodings of Turing complete formalisms into calculi with interruption and compensation are compared. Using the terminology in [12], we can say that the presented encoding satisfies a *weakly Turing completeness* criterion, as opposed to the (stronger) *Turing completeness* criterion that is satisfied by the encoding of Minsky machines into HOCORE in [4]. The discrepancy on the criteria satisfied by each encoding might be interpreted as an expressiveness gap between HO^{-f} and HOCORE; nevertheless, it seems clear that the loss of expressiveness resulting from limiting the forwarding capabilities in HOCORE is much less dramatic than what one would have expected.

We have shown that the communication style of HO^{-f} causes a separation result with respect to HOCORE. In fact, because of the limitation on output actions, it was possible to prove that termination in HO^{-f} is decidable. This is in sharp contrast with the situation in HOCORE, for which termination is undecidable. In HO^{-f}, it is possible to provide an upper bound on the depth (i.e. the level of nesting of actions) of the (set of) derivatives of a process. In HOCORE such an upper bound does not exist. This was essential for obtaining the decidability result; for this, we appealed to the approach developed in [9], which relies on the theory of well-structured transition systems [8]. As far as we are aware, this approach to studying expressiveness issues has not previously been used in the higher-order setting. The decidability of termination might shed light on the development of verification techniques for higher-order processes.

The HO^{-f} calculus is a sublanguage of HOCORE. As such, HO^{-f} inherits the many results and properties of HOCORE [4]; most notably, a notion of (strong) bisimilarity which is decidable and coincides with a number of sensible equivalences in the higher-order context. Our results thus complement those in [4] and deepen our understanding of the expressiveness of core higher-order calculi as a whole. Furthermore, by recalling that CCS without restriction is not Turing complete and has decidable convergence, the present results shape an interesting expressiveness hierarchy, namely one in which HOCORE is strictly more expressive than HO^{-f} (because of the discussion above), and in which HO^{-f} is strictly more expressive than CCS without restriction.

Remarkably, our undecidability result can be used to prove that (weak) barbed bisimilarity is undecidable in the calculus obtained by extending HO^{-f} with restriction. Consider the encoding of Minsky machines used in Section 3 to prove the undecidability of convergence in HO^{-f}. Consider now the restriction operator $(\nu \widetilde{x})$ used as a binder for the names in the tuple $\widetilde{x}$. Take a Minsky machine N (it is not restrictive to assume that it executes at least one increment instruction) and its encoding P, as defined in Definition 5. Let $\widetilde{x}$ be the tuple of the names used by P, excluding the name w. We have that N terminates if and only if $(\nu \widetilde{x})P$ is (weakly) barbed equivalent to the process $(\nu d)(\overline{d} \mid d \mid d . (\overline{w} \mid !w . \overline{w}))$.

Related Work. The most closely related work is [4], which was already discussed along the paper. We do not know of other works that study the expressiveness of higher-order calculi by restricting higher-order outputs. The recent work [13] studies finite-control fragments of Homer [14], a higher-order process calculus with locations. While we have focused on decidability of termination and convergence, in [13] the interest is in decidability of barbed bisimilarity. One of the approaches explored in [13] is based on a type system that bounds the size of processes in terms of their syntactic components (e.g. number of parallel components, location nesting). Although the restrictions such a type system imposes might be considered as similar in spirit to the limitation on outputs in HO^{-f} (in particular, location nesting resembles the output nesting HO^{-f} forbids), the fact that the synchronization discipline in Homer depends heavily on the structure of locations makes it difficult to establish a more detailed comparison with HO^{-f}.

Also similar in spirit to our work, but in a slightly different context, are some studies on the expressiveness (of fragments) of the Ambient calculus [15]. Ambient and higher-order calculi are related in that both allow the communication of objects with complex structure. Some works on the expressiveness of fragments of Ambient calculi are similar to ours. In particular, [16] shows that termination is decidable for the fragment without both restriction (as HO^{-f} and HOCORE) and movement capabilities, and featuring replication; in contrast, the same property turns out to be undecidable for the fragment with recursion. Hence, the separation between fragments comes from the source of infinite behavior, and not from the structures allowed in output action, as in our case. However, we find that the connections between Ambient-like and higher-order calculi are rather loose, so a proper comparison is difficult also in this case.

Future Work. As already mentioned, a great deal of the expressive power in higher-order calculi resides in the interplay of input and output actions. Here we have studied an alternative for limiting output capabilities; it would be interesting to investigate if suitable limitations on input actions are possible, and whether they have influence on expressiveness. Another interesting direction would be to compare higher-order and Ambient calculi from the expressiveness point of view.

Acknowledgments. We are grateful to Julian Gutierrez for his helpful comments on an earlier version of this paper.

References

1. Thomsen, B.: A calculus of higher order communicating systems. In: Proc. of POPL 1989, pp. 143–154. ACM Press, New York (1989)
2. Thomsen, B.: Plain CHOCS: A second generation calculus for higher order processes. Acta Inf. 30(1), 1–59 (1993)
3. Sangiorgi, D.: Expressing Mobility in Process Algebras: First-Order and Higher-Order Paradigms. PhD thesis CST–99–93, University of Edinburgh, Dept. of Comp. Sci. (1992)
4. Lanese, I., Pérez, J.A., Sangiorgi, D., Schmitt, A.: On the expressiveness and decidability of higher-order process calculi. In: Proc. of LICS 1908, pp. 145–155. IEEE Computer Society Press, Los Alamitos (2008)
5. Minsky, M.: Computation: Finite and Infinite Machines. Prentice-Hall, Englewood Cliffs (1967)
6. Necula, G.C., Lee, P.: Safe, untrusted agents using proof-carrying code. In: Vigna, G. (ed.) Mobile Agents and Security. LNCS, vol. 1419, pp. 61–91. Springer, Heidelberg (1998)
7. Collberg, C.S., Thomborson, C.D., Low, D.: Manufacturing cheap, resilient, and stealthy opaque constructs. In: Proc. of POPL 1998, pp. 184–196. ACM Press, New York (1998)
8. Finkel, A., Schnoebelen, P.: Well-structured transition systems everywhere! Theor. Comput. Sci. 256(1-2), 63–92 (2001)
9. Busi, N., Gabbrielli, M., Zavattaro, G.: On the expressive power of recursion, replication, and iteration in process calculi. Math. Struct. Comp. Sci. (to appear, 2009)
10. Di Giusto, C., Pérez, J.A., Zavattaro, G.: On the Expressiveness of Forwarding in Higher-Order Communication (Extended Version) (2009),
    http://www.cs.unibo.it/~perez/hocore
11. Higman, G.: Ordering by divisibility in abstract algebras. Proceedings of the London Mathematical Society (3) 2(7), 326–336 (1952)
12. Bravetti, M., Zavattaro, G.: On the expressive power of process interruption and compensation. Math. Struct. Comp. Sci. (to appear, 2009)
13. Bundgaard, M., Godskesen, J.C., Haagensen, B., Huttel, H.: Decidable fragments of a higher order calculus with locations. In: Proc. of EXPRESS 2008. Electronic Notes in Theoretical Computer Science. Elsevier, Amsterdam (2008) (to appear)
14. Bundgaard, M., Godskesen, J.C., Hildebrandt, T.: Bisimulation congruences for homer — a calculus of higher order mobile embedded resources. Technical Report TR-2004-52, IT University of Copenhagen (2004)
15. Cardelli, L., Gordon, A.D.: Mobile ambients. Theor. Comput. Sci. 240(1), 177–213 (2000)
16. Busi, N., Zavattaro, G.: On the expressive power of movement and restriction in pure mobile ambients. Theor. Comput. Sci. 322(3), 477–515 (2004)

On the Hairpin Completion of Regular Languages

Volker Diekert[1], Steffen Kopecki[1], and Victor Mitrana[2]

[1] Universität Stuttgart, FMI, Germany
[2] Faculty of Mathematics, University of Bucharest, Romania
and
Department of Information Systems and Computation
Technical University of Valencia, Spain
diekert@fmi.uni-stuttgart.de, steffen.kopecki@web.de,
mitrana@fmi.unibuc.ro

Abstract. The hairpin completion is a natural operation of formal languages which has been inspired by molecular phenomena in biology and by DNA-computing. The hairpin completion of a regular language is linear context-free and we consider the problem to decide whether the hairpin completion remains regular. This problem has been open since the first formal definition of the operation.

In this paper we present a positive solution to this problem. Our solution yields more than decidability because we present a polynomial time procedure. The degree of the polynomial is however unexpectedly high, since in our approach it is more than n^{14}. Nevertheless, the polynomial time result is surprising, because even if the hairpin completion $\mathcal{H}$ of a regular language L is regular, there can be an exponential gap between the size of a minimal DFA for L and the size of a smallest NFA for $\mathcal{H}$.

1 Introduction

The origin of this paper is motivated by biological and DNA-computing. But although our motivation is based on biological phenomena, the present paper is more about an interesting decidability result on regular languages. Let us explain the background first and the connection to Formal Language Theory later.

Single-stranded DNA (ssDNA) are composed by nucleotides which differ from each other by their bases: A (adenine), G (guanine), C (cytosine), and T (thymine). Therefore each ssDNA may be viewed as a finite string over the four-letter alphabet $\{A, C, G, T\}$. Two single strands can bind to each other forming the secondary structure of DNA if they are pairwise Watson-Crick complementary: A is complementary to T, and C to G. The binding of two strands is also called *annealing*.

An intramolecular base pairing, known as *hairpin*, is a pattern that can occur in single-stranded DNA and, more commonly, in RNA. Hairpin or hairpin-free structures have numerous applications to DNA computing and molecular genetics. In many DNA-based algorithms, these DNA molecules cannot be used

M. Leucker and C. Morgan (Eds.): ICTAC 2009, LNCS 5684, pp. 170–184, 2009.

in the subsequent computations. Therefore, it is important to design methods for constructing sets of DNA sequences which are unlikely to lead to "bad" hybridizations. This problem was considered in a series of papers, see e.g. [2,3,4,7,8].

In [1,12] a new formal operation on words is introduced, namely the *hairpin completion*. It consists of three biological principles. Besides the Watson-Crick complementarity and annealing the third biological phenomenon is that of *lengthening DNA by polymerases*. In our case the phenomenon produces a complete molecule as follows: one starts with hairpins which are here single strands such that for each of them one end is annealed to a part of itself by Watson-Crick complementarity; and a *polymerization buffer* with many copies of the four nucleotides. Then polymerases will concatenate to the hairpin by complementing the template.

What happens in this situation is, informally, best explained in Fig. 1. In that picture as in the rest of the paper we mean by putting a *bar* on a word (like $\overline{\alpha}$) to read it from right-to-left in addition to replacing a by $\overline{a}$ for letters.

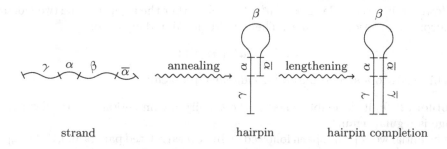

Fig. 1. Hairpin completion of a strand

This is a good starting point to translate the biologically inspired motivation to a purely abstract formalism. On that level, we have just a finite alphabet Σ together with an *involution*. This is a bijection $^- : \Sigma \to \Sigma$ such that $\overline{\overline{a}} = a$ for all $a \in \Sigma$. In the concrete situation above $\Sigma = \{A, C, G, T\}$ and $\overline{A} = T$ and $\overline{C} = G$. We extend the involution to words $a_1 \cdots a_n$ by $\overline{a_1 \cdots a_n} = \overline{a_n} \cdots \overline{a_1}$. (Just like taking inverses in groups.)

We start with a (formal) language $L \subseteq \Sigma^*$ (the set of strands). Then hairpin completion can arise in one-sided way. The *right-sided hairpin completion* of L is formally defined by the set of words $\gamma \alpha \beta \overline{\alpha} \overline{\gamma}$ with $\gamma \alpha \beta \overline{\alpha} \in L$ being the strand and $\gamma \alpha \beta \overline{\alpha} \overline{\gamma}$ being the completion, see again Fig. 1. Still inspired by biological facts, a binding in a hairpin can be *stable*, only if α is long enough, say $|\alpha| \geq 10$. Formally we fix a (small) constant k and ask $|\alpha| \geq k$. The *left-sided hairpin completion* can be defined analogously.

Clearly, the hairpin completion of a finite language is finite. If L is regular then, sometimes the right/left-sided k-hairpin completion is regular again, sometimes it is not. But then it is a linear context-free language as the reader will immediately recognize. For example, if $L = ab^*b^k c\overline{b}\,^k$, then the right-sided k-hairpin completion is not regular, but linear context-free, because it is:

$$\left\{ab^m b^k c\overline{b}\,^k \overline{b}\,^n \overline{a} \mid m \geq n\right\}.$$

This leads to a first natural decidability problem:

Problem 1. Is it decidable whether the right-sided k-hairpin completion of a regular language is regular again?

We can see directly from the hairpin picture that it is not always natural to distinguish between left and right. Therefore we consider the two-sided case, too. The *(two-sided) hairpin completion* of L is therefore defined by the set of words $\gamma\alpha\beta\overline{\alpha}\,\overline{\gamma}$ with either $\gamma\alpha\beta\overline{\alpha} \in L$ or $\alpha\beta\overline{\alpha}\,\overline{\gamma} \in L$ or both. If we simply speak about the *hairpin completion* we always mean the two-sided case. As above we see two possibilities, and, moreover, we see that the behaviors are different. Let us consider $L = ab^*b^k c\overline{b}\,^k \cup b^k c\overline{b}\,^k \overline{b}\,^*\overline{a}$. The right- and left-sided k-hairpin completion is still not regular, but the two-sided is.

However, if we consider $L = a^+ b^k c\overline{b}\,^k$, then neither the right- nor the two-sided k-hairpin completion is regular. They are identical and equal to:

$$\left\{a^n b^k c\overline{b}\,^k \overline{a}\,^n \mid n \geq 1\right\}.$$

This leads to a second natural decidability problem:

Problem 2. Is it decidable whether the k-hairpin completion of a regular language is regular again?

The initial work [1] has been followed up by several related papers [6,9,10,11,12], where both the hairpin completion as well as its inverse operation, namely the hairpin reduction, considered as formal operations on strings and languages were further investigated. But the decidability status of Problems 1 and 2 remained open. Actually, the difficulty in solving Problems 1 and 2 is perhaps not that surprising since we are immediately confronted with decidability questions on linear context-free languages. Every linear context-free language is a weak code image of an hairpin completion of some regular language. (A *weak code* is a homomorphism which is the identity on a subset of letters and maps the other letters to the empty word.) To see this let us quote a theorem from [1]:

Theorem 1. *A language is linear context-free if and only if it is the weak-code image of the hairpin completion of a regular language.*

Natural problems well-known to be undecidable for context-free languages are already undecidable for linear context-free languages, see e.g. [5] for a classical reference. In particular it is undecidable whether linear context-free languages are universal or equal to a given regular language or whether a linear context-free language is regular.

Thus, Problems 1 and 2 are problems about a subclass of linear context-free languages where no general results were known to solve them. In this paper we give positive answers to both problems. Actually, they are decidable in polynomial time (if the input size is given as the size of a DFA for L plus the size of a

DFA accepting the reversal language of L. Clearly, there might be an exponential gap between these sizes.)

The history of the solution shows several steps. First we solved Problem 1 and we realized that, retrospective, it was not difficult to find the solution, but we had no good estimation for the complexity. The solution to Problem 2 was much more difficult, and it became rather technical. The complexity was again unclear. A very rough estimation led us to something like triple exponential, but we worked in syntactic monoids and raised, whenever possible, elements to idempotent powers. So it was clear that there was room for improvement, and the intermediate results were never published.

The present solution is more ambitious. We prove a polynomial time result, which is more than expected when we started our work. What we find also quite amazing is the following: We treat natural problems about regular languages which we now know to be decidable in polynomial time. But the degree for the polynomial as we present the algorithm here might be about 20. So it is very high. With more efforts we were able to bring the degree down to 14, but this is not shown here. Such a huge time complexity is however no indication that for real life examples the problem is difficult. For most regular languages L it is probably very easy to decide whether the k-hairpin completion is regular again. Being regular is the exception and puts many constraints on L as we will see below. The formal statement of our result is in Section 3.

2   Notation

We assume the reader to be familiar with the fundamental concepts of formal language theory, context-free grammars and automata theory, see [5]. We also use *syntactic monoids*, but very little of this rich theory. What we use is the following elementary fact. If L is a regular language then there is a constant $s \in \mathbb{N}$ such that for all words x, y, z we have $xy^s z \in L$ if and only if $xy^{2s} z \in L$. Note that this implies $xy^s z \in L$ if and only if $x(y^s)^+ z \subseteq L$.

We use non-deterministic finite automata (NFA) and deterministic finite automata (DFA). Whenever convenient we use that all states are reachable and co-reachable. Thus, if g is a state then there is a path from the initial state to g and a path from g to some final state.

An *alphabet* is a finite set of *letters*. Here the alphabet is Σ. The set of words over Σ is denoted Σ^*, as usual, and the *empty word* is denoted by 1. Given a word w, we denote by $|w|$ its length. If $w = xyz$ for some $x, y, z \in \Sigma^*$, then x, y, z are called *prefix, factor, suffix*, respectively. For the prefix relation we also use the notation $x \leq w$. By a proper factor y of w we mean a factor such that $x \neq w$, but in our paper we allow $x = 1$.

As said above, Σ is equipped with an involution such that $\overline{\overline{a}} = a$ for all letters $a \in \Sigma$. The involution is extended to words by $\overline{1} = 1$ and $\overline{uv} = \overline{v}\,\overline{u}$, thus the involution reverses the order as well. Due to this law some authors call it an anti-involution, but we prefer our convention (which is also the more standard one).

If L is a language, then its *reversal language* is given by reading words right-to-left, i.e. by the set of words $a_n \cdots a_1$ where $a_1 \cdots a_n \in L$ and $a_i \in \Sigma$. Note that a DFA of minimal size for the reversal language yields also a DFA for $\overline{L} = \{\overline{w} \in \Sigma^* \mid w \in L\}$ of exactly the same size, and vice versa.

We intend to solve Problem 1 and 2 simultaneously, therefore we introduce a more general notion of hairpin completion.

Throughout the paper L and R denote two regular languages and $k > 0$ is a positive integer. We define the *hairpin completion* $\mathcal{H}(L, R, k)$ by

$$\mathcal{H}(L, R, k) = \{\gamma \alpha \beta \overline{\alpha} \, \overline{\gamma} \mid (\gamma \alpha \beta \overline{\alpha} \in L \lor \alpha \beta \overline{\alpha} \, \overline{\gamma} \in R) \land |\alpha| = k \}$$

Note that the definition does not change if we replace $|\alpha| = k$ by $|\alpha| \geq k$. For simplicity of the presentation we treat k as a (small) constant.

3   Main Result

Note that the right-sided k-hairpin completion is nothing but $\mathcal{H}(L, \emptyset, k)$, whereas the two-sided version appears as $\mathcal{H}(L, L, k)$. Thus, the notion $\mathcal{H}(L, R, k)$ is adopted to treat both cases simultaneously.

Problem 3. *Input:* A DFA accepting L of at most n states and a DFA accepting the reversal language of L (or for $\overline{L}$) of at most n states.

Question: Is the hairpin completion $\mathcal{H}(L, R, k)$ regular?

The purpose of this paper is to prove the following theorem.

Theorem 2. *Let Σ be a fixed alphabet and $k > 0$ be a constant. Let L and R be regular languages. Then it is decidable whether the hairpin completion $\mathcal{H}(L, R, k)$ is regular.*

As we have explained above, Problem 3 is more general than Problem 1 and 2. Obviously, for Problem 1 we do not need a DFA for the reversal language.

An NFA of minimal size accepting the hairpin completion may have exponentially more states than a DFA for L and $\overline{L}$. Thus, although we have a polynomial time decision algorithm there is no time to construct the NFA (in plain form). Indeed let

$$L_n = \{bv\overline{a}^k ba^k \mid v \in \{a, b\}^n\}.$$

Then we have $\mathcal{H}(L_n, \emptyset, k) = \mathcal{H}(L_n, L_n, k) = \{bv\overline{a}^k ba^k \overline{v} \overline{b} \mid v \in \{a, b\}^n\}.$

Thus, the sizes of a minimal DFA accepting L_n and $\overline{L_n}$ are in $\mathcal{O}(n)$. But every NFA accepting $\mathcal{H}(L_n, \emptyset, k)$ must keep track of v and thus its size is in $\Omega(2^n)$.

The proof of Theorem 2 is quite technical and relies on some non-standard constructions for finite automata and context-free grammars.

The key idea is to use a linear grammar which produces exactly those $\gamma \alpha \beta \overline{\alpha} \, \overline{\gamma}$ where $|\gamma|$ is minimal. We show that, due to the minimality of $|\gamma|$, the context-free grammar has either a very special structure or the hairpin completion is not regular. This leads to a series of decidable conditions for the regularity of the hairpin completion which are either sufficient or necessary. The last test in this series yields the result.

3.1   An NFA for L and R

Regular languages can be specified by deterministic finite automata (DFA). A DFA is essentially a finite set Q together with a monoid action of Σ^* on the right. The action is written as a product $q \cdot u$ with the usual laws $q \cdot uv = (q \cdot u) \cdot v$ and $q \cdot 1 = q$, where $q \in Q$ and $u, v \in \Sigma^*$. By 1 we denote the empty word and the neutral element in other monoids. The action is defined by a function $Q \times \Sigma^* \to Q$. In the following we assume that the regular language L is specified by a DFA with state set Q_L, $q_{0,L} \in Q_L$ as initial state, and $\mathcal{F}_L \subseteq Q_L$ as final states. We fix $n_L = |Q_L|$ to be the number of states. For R we need however a DFA reading R from right-to-left. Such an automaton is essentially equivalent to a DFA accepting the *reversal language* of R.

We start with a finite set Q_R and a *left-action* of Σ^*. For simplicity we use a product sign again, but we write it on the left: $u \cdot q$ satisfying $uv \cdot q = u \cdot (v \cdot q)$ and $1 \cdot q = q$. We choose Q_R, $q_{0,R} \in Q_R$ and $\mathcal{F}_R \subseteq Q_R$ such that

$$R = \{u \in \Sigma^* \mid u \cdot q_{0,R} \in \mathcal{F}_R\}.$$

Let $n_R = |Q_R|$. For the rest of the paper we fix $n = n_L + n_R$. We view n as input size for our decidability problem (stated in Theorem 2) to test whether the hairpin completion $\mathcal{H}(L, R, k)$ is regular.

What we are really interested in is the product automaton with state space

$$Q = Q_L \times Q_R.$$

Although we started with deterministic automata, we content to read Q as the state space of a non-deterministic automaton which accepts L reading words from left-to-right and accepts R reading words from right-to-left. Since this construction is crucial, we make it precise: Let $P = (p_1, p_2)$, $Q = (q_1, q_2)$ be states of Q and $a \in \Sigma$ be a letter. We define an *arc* (P, a, Q), if $p_1 \cdot a = q_1$ and $p_2 = a \cdot q_2$. Note that P may have several outgoing arcs labeled by a because for each p_2 and each a there might be several q_2 with $p_2 = a \cdot q_2$.

Let $u \in \Sigma^*$ be a word. Then for each pair (p, q) there is a unique pair $(r, s) \in Q_R \times Q_L$ such that there is u-labeled path in the NFA from (p, r) to (s, q). Moreover the path is uniquely defined. This is easily seen by induction on the length of u.

In particular, u is in L if and only if there is such a path from $(q_{0,L}, r)$ to $(s, q_{0,R})$ with $s \in \mathcal{F}_L$. By symmetry, u is in R if and only if $r \in \mathcal{F}_R$ for that path.

Now for each pair $(P, Q) \in Q \times Q$ we define a regular language $\mathcal{R}[P, Q]$ by

$$\mathcal{R}[P, Q] = \{u \in \Sigma^* \mid \text{There is a } u\text{-labeled path from } P \text{ to } Q\}.$$

There are at most n^4 such regular languages and for each of them we can test emptiness in polynomial time. For $P = (p, r)$ and $Q = (s, q)$ we obtain

$$\mathcal{R}[P, Q] = \{u \in \Sigma^* \mid p \cdot u = s \wedge r = u \cdot q\}.$$

3.2   A First Linear Context-Free Grammar

We continue with the same notations. In addition we view each symbol $[P, Q]$ with $(P, Q) \in \mathcal{Q} \times \mathcal{Q}$ as a variable of a context-free grammar. First we define productions of the form

$$[P, Q] \longrightarrow a[R, S]\bar{a}$$

with $a \in \Sigma$. We do so for all $[P, Q], [R, S]$ and a, where (P, a, R) and $(S, \bar{a}, Q)$ are arcs in the NFA above. For example, let $P = (p_1, p_2)$ and $R = (r_1, r_2)$, then we must have $p_1 \cdot a = r_1$ and $p_2 = a \cdot r_2$.

Moreover, we introduce chain rules

$$[P, Q] \longrightarrow \mathcal{R}_0[P, Q],$$

where $\mathcal{R}_i[P, Q]$ denotes a variable for $0 \leq i < k$; and $\mathcal{R}_k[P, Q]$ denotes a new terminal symbol. Of course, the idea is that we are free to substitute $\mathcal{R}_k[P, Q]$ by the regular language $\mathcal{R}[P, Q]$.

The index i can be viewed as a level where we produce the words α and $\bar{\alpha}$ used in the hairpin. This idea leads us to the third type of productions. These productions are of the form

$$\mathcal{R}_{i-1}[P, Q] \longrightarrow a\mathcal{R}_i[R, S]\bar{a}$$

where $1 \leq i \leq k$ and again $a \in \Sigma$. In order to have rules of the third type we impose again that (P, a, R) and $(S, \bar{a}, Q)$ are arcs in the NFA above.

We obtain a linear grammar with variables $[P, Q]$, $\mathcal{R}_i[P, Q]$, $0 \leq i < k$, and terminal symbols a, $\bar{a}$, and $\mathcal{R}_k[P, Q]$ with $a \in \Sigma$, and $\mathcal{R}_i[P, Q]$ as above. Note that the symbols $\mathcal{R}_0[P, Q]$ produce finite languages of the form $\alpha \mathcal{R}_k[R, S]\bar{\alpha}$ with $|\alpha| = k$. In particular, replacing the symbol $\mathcal{R}_k[R, S]$ by the language $\mathcal{R}[R, S]$, the symbol $\mathcal{R}_0[P, Q]$ produces a regular language, too.

Consider next a derivation

$$[P, Q] \overset{*}{\Longrightarrow} \gamma \mathcal{R}_i[R, S]\bar{\gamma}.$$

Let $P = (p_1, p_2)$, $Q = (q_1, q_2)$, $R = (r_1, r_2)$, $S = (s_1, s_2)$ be states in the NFA and $w \in \mathcal{R}_i[R, S]$ be a word.

This implies:

$$
\begin{array}{ll}
p_1 \cdot \gamma = r_1, & p_2 = \gamma \cdot r_2, \\
r_1 \cdot w = s_1, & r_2 = w \cdot s_2, \\
s_1 \cdot \bar{\gamma} = q_1, & s_2 = \bar{\gamma} \cdot q_2.
\end{array}
$$

In particular, we have

$$p_1 \cdot \gamma w \bar{\gamma} = q_1, \qquad p_2 = \gamma w \bar{\gamma} \cdot q_2.$$

For the other direction, assume we have $p_1 \cdot \gamma w \bar{\gamma} = q_1$ and $p_2 = \gamma w \bar{\gamma} \cdot q_2$ with $|\gamma| \geq k$. Then, for each $1 \leq i \leq k$, there are uniquely defined symbols

$[P, Q], \mathcal{R}_i[R, S]$ with $P = (p_1, p_2)$, $Q = (q_1, q_2)$, $R = (r_1, r_2)$, $S = (s_1, s_2)$ and a word $w \in \mathcal{R}_i[R, S]$ such that we find a derivation:

$$[P, Q] \stackrel{*}{\Longrightarrow} \gamma \mathcal{R}_i[R, S]\overline{\gamma}.$$

In the next step we fix six states $P_0 = (p_1, p_2)$, $Q_0 = (q_1, q_2)$, $R_0 = (r_1, r_2)$, $S_0 = (s_1, s_2)$, $I_0 = (i_1, i_2)$, and $J_0 = (j_1, j_2)$, with the following properties:

1.) $p_1 = q_{0,L}$ is the initial state in the DFA above accepting L.
2.) $q_2 = q_{0,R}$ is the initial state in the right-to-left DFA above accepting R.
3.) Either $s_1 \in \mathcal{F}_L$ or $r_2 \in \mathcal{F}_R$ or both.
4.) There is a k-step derivation $\mathcal{R}_0[R_0, S_0] \stackrel{k}{\Longrightarrow} \alpha \mathcal{R}_k[I_0, J_0]\overline{\alpha}$.

The number of possible ways to choose these six states is bounded by $n_L^5 \cdot n_R^5$, hence at most n^{10}. By symmetry we assume in addition that we have $s_1 \in \mathcal{F}_L$, thus whenever $[P_0, Q_0] \stackrel{*}{\Longrightarrow} \gamma \mathcal{R}_0[R_0, S_0]\overline{\gamma}$ and $w \in \mathcal{R}[R_0, S_0]$, then we know $\gamma w \in L$.

We continue as follows: We choose the variable $[P_0, Q_0]$ to be the single axiom of the linear grammar G_0 we are going to define. We restrict the terminal alphabet to be the set $\Sigma \cup \{\mathcal{R}_k[I_0, J_0]\}$.

Next, we remove more productions and variables. On level 0 we only keep one single variable, namely $\mathcal{R}_0[R_0, S_0]$. Thus, all terminal derivations admit the form:

$$[P_0, Q_0] \stackrel{*}{\Longrightarrow} \gamma \mathcal{R}_0[R_0, S_0]\overline{\gamma} \stackrel{k}{\Longrightarrow} \gamma \alpha \mathcal{R}_k[I_0, J_0]\overline{\alpha}\,\overline{\gamma}.$$

So far, the productions can be assumed to be of three types:

$$[P, Q] \longrightarrow a[R, S]\overline{a},$$
$$[R_0, S_0] \longrightarrow \mathcal{R}_0[R_0, S_0],$$
$$\mathcal{R}_{i-1}[P, Q] \longrightarrow a\mathcal{R}_i[R, S]\overline{a}$$

Now we remove all productions $[P, Q] \longrightarrow a[R, S]\overline{a}$ where $P = (p_1, p_2)$ and $Q = (q_1, q_2)$ with either $q_1 \in \mathcal{F}_L$ or $p_2 \in \mathcal{F}_R$ or both. Let us call this new linear grammar G_0. Derivation in the grammar G_0 look as follows.:

$$[P_0, Q_0] \stackrel{*}{\Longrightarrow} \gamma_1[P, Q]\overline{\gamma_1} \stackrel{*}{\Longrightarrow} \gamma \mathcal{R}_0[R_0, S_0]\overline{\gamma} \stackrel{k}{\Longrightarrow} \gamma \alpha \mathcal{R}_k[I_0, J_0]\overline{\alpha}\,\overline{\gamma}.$$

Now let $\beta \in \mathcal{R}[I_0, J_0]$ and $w = \alpha\beta\overline{\alpha}$, then we know that either $\gamma w = \gamma\alpha\beta\overline{\alpha} \in L$ or $w\overline{\gamma} = \alpha\beta\overline{\alpha}\,\overline{\gamma} \in R$ or both, but every prefix of $\gamma w\overline{\gamma}$ belonging to L is a prefix of γw and every suffix belonging to R is a suffix of $w\gamma$.

As usual, the generated language is called $L(G_0)$. By $\mathcal{H}(G_0)$ we mean the language where we substitute the terminal symbol $\mathcal{R}_k[I_0, J_0]$ by the (non-empty) regular language $\mathcal{R}[I_0, J_0]$. Thus,

$$\mathcal{H}(G_0) = \left\{ \gamma\alpha\beta\overline{\alpha}\,\overline{\gamma} \;\middle|\; [P_0, Q_0] \stackrel{*}{\underset{G_0}{\Longrightarrow}} \gamma\alpha\mathcal{R}_k[I_0, J_0]\overline{\alpha}\,\overline{\gamma} \wedge \beta \in \mathcal{R}[I_0, J_0] \right\}.$$

By the very construction $\mathcal{H}(G_0) \subseteq \mathcal{H}(L,R,k)$. Moreover, every word in the hairpin completion $\mathcal{H}(L,R,k)$ belongs to one of these $\mathcal{H}(G_0)$. Thus, $\mathcal{H}(L,R,k)$ is regular if and only if for all these $\mathcal{H}(G_0)$ we find regular languages $\mathcal{R}(G_0)$ such that $\mathcal{H}(G_0) \subseteq \mathcal{R}(G_0) \subseteq \mathcal{H}(L,R,k)$.

Thus, it is enough to show that we can decide in polynomial time whether there is such a regular language $\mathcal{R}(G_0)$ for a given grammar G_0 as above.

Note that we can test in polynomial time whether $L(G_0) \subseteq \Sigma^* \mathcal{R}_k[I_0, J_0]\Sigma^*$ is finite. In the case that $L(G_0)$ is finite, we are done, because $\mathcal{H}(G_0)$ is obtained by substituting $\mathcal{R}_k[I_0, J_0]$ by a regular language. So we can choose $\mathcal{R}(G_0) = \mathcal{H}(G_0)$.

In the spirit of an algorithm we could also say:

Test 1. Check whether $L(G_0)$ is finite. If yes, we construct the next grammar of this type.

We continue with the linear grammar G_0 under the assumption that $L(G_0)$ is infinite and that the grammar is reduced. This means all symbols are reachable and productive. Since $L(G_0)$ is infinite there must be variables of the form $[P,Q]$ and non-trivial derivations:

$$[P,Q] \xRightarrow[G_0]{+} [P,Q].$$

There are at most n^4 such symbols. They are called *self-reproducing* symbols in the following. Let us fix one self-reproducing symbol and denote it by $[P',Q']$. We define a linear context-free grammar G_1 and a language $L(G_1)$ given as the following set:

$$\left\{ \pi\gamma\alpha\mathcal{R}_k[I_0, J_0]\overline{\alpha}\ \overline{\gamma}\overline{\pi} \ \middle| \ [P_0,Q_0] \xRightarrow[G_0]{\leq n^4} \pi[P',Q']\overline{\pi} \xRightarrow[G_0]{*} \pi\gamma\alpha\mathcal{R}_k[I_0, J_0]\overline{\alpha}\ \overline{\gamma}\overline{\pi} \right\}.$$

This gives us at most n^4 grammars G_1 of polynomial size such that $L(G_0)$ is, up to finitely many elements, the union of languages $L(G_1)$. Note also that each language $L(G_1)$ is infinite by construction.

As above, we also have a linear context-free language $\mathcal{H}(G_1)$ by defining:

$$\mathcal{H}(G_1) = \left\{ \pi\gamma\alpha\beta\overline{\alpha}\ \overline{\gamma}\ \overline{\pi} \ \middle| \ \pi\gamma\alpha\mathcal{R}_k[I_0, J_0]\overline{\alpha}\ \overline{\gamma}\overline{\pi} \in L(G_1) \wedge \beta \in \mathcal{R}[I_0, J_0] \right\}.$$

This reduces the proof of Theorem 2 to the following statement: We can decide in polynomial time whether there is a regular language $\mathcal{R}$ such that $\mathcal{H}(G_1) \subseteq \mathcal{R} \subseteq \mathcal{H}(L,R,k)$.

For $[P',Q']$ we compute two words π and p with length $0 < |\pi|, |p| \leq n^4$ such that we have:

$$[P_0,Q_0] \xRightarrow[G_1]{+} \pi[P',Q']\overline{\pi} \xRightarrow[G_1]{+} \pi p[P',Q']\overline{p}\ \overline{\pi}.$$

N.B., there are perhaps many choices for π and p, but we content to fix one pair (π, p) for each $[P',Q']$. As we will see below, the solution to Problems 1 and 2 can be based on these fixed pairs!

The main idea is from now to investigate the effect of pumping the word p under the assumption that the hairpin completion is regular. This means we consider derivations $[P_0, Q_0] \xLongrightarrow[G_1]{+} \pi p^s [P', Q'] \overline{p}^s \overline{\pi}$, where s is huge and $\mathcal{H}(L, R, k)$ is regular.

Consider some $\beta \in \mathcal{R}[I_0, J_0]$ and $\pi v \alpha \mathcal{R}_k[I_0, J_0] \overline{\alpha} \ \overline{v} \ \overline{\pi} \in L(G_1)$. The choice of the word p implies $[P', Q'] \xLongrightarrow[G_1]{+} p[P', Q'] \overline{p}$ and hence, for all $s \in \mathbb{N}$ we have

$$z_s = \pi p^s v \alpha \beta \overline{\alpha} \ \overline{v} \overline{p}^s \overline{\pi} \in \mathcal{H}(G_1)$$

and the word $\pi p^s v \alpha \beta \overline{\alpha}$ is the longest prefix of z_s in L; and moreover, if a suffix of z_s belongs to R, then it is a suffix of $\alpha \beta \overline{\alpha} \ \overline{v} \overline{p}^s \overline{\pi}$.

Assume for a moment that $\mathcal{H}(L, R, k)$ is regular, then we find $s > 0$ such that p^s is idempotent in the syntactic monoid of $\mathcal{H}(L, R, k)$. However, this means that $\pi p^{sy} v \alpha \beta \overline{\alpha} \ \overline{v} \overline{p}^s \overline{\pi} \in \mathcal{H}(L, R, k)$ where s is perhaps large, but y can be taken as huge as we need. Now, for the hairpin we do not have the option to build it on the right, because $\alpha \beta \overline{\alpha} \ \overline{v} \overline{p}^s \overline{\pi}$ is too short compared to length of the whole word (it must cover more than half of the length). Thus, we must use the longest prefix $\pi p^{sy} v \alpha \beta \overline{\alpha}$ in L for the hairpin. But this implies that $v \alpha$ is a prefix of some power of p.

This leads to the following lemma:

Lemma 1. Let $\mathcal{H}(L, R, k)$ be regular. Then $v \alpha$ is a prefix of some power of the word p for all derivations $[P', Q'] \xLongrightarrow[G_1]{*} v \alpha \mathcal{R}_k[I_0, J_0] \overline{\alpha} \ \overline{v}$.

Proof. This is clear, choose some $\beta \in \mathcal{R}[I_0, J_0]$ and derivation $[P_0, Q_0] \xLongrightarrow[G_1]{*} \pi v \alpha \beta \overline{\alpha} \ \overline{v} \overline{\pi}$; and argue as above.

We have also the following complexity result:

Lemma 2. There is a polynomial time algorithm which checks whether for all derivations $[P', Q'] \xLongrightarrow[G_1]{*} v \alpha \mathcal{R}_k[I_0, J_0] \overline{\alpha} \ \overline{v}$ if we have that $v \alpha$ is a prefix of some power of p.

Proof. This follows from a standard construction. For the language

$$X = \left\{ w \mathcal{R}_k[I_0, J_0] w' \in \Sigma^* \mathcal{R}_k[I_0, J_0] \Sigma^* \mid w \text{ is no prefix of a word in } p^+ \right\}$$

we find a DFA with $|p| + 3$ states. Therefore we can check in polynomial time whether the following intersection is empty:

$$X \cap \left\{ v \alpha \mathcal{R}_k[I_0, J_0] \overline{\alpha} \ \overline{v} \in \Sigma^* \mathcal{R}_k[I_0, J_0] \Sigma^* \mid [P', Q'] \xLongrightarrow[G_1]{*} v \alpha \mathcal{R}_k[I_0, J_0] \overline{\alpha} \ \overline{v} \right\}$$

The intersection is empty if and only if for all derivations

$$[P', Q'] \xLongrightarrow[G_1]{*} v \alpha \mathcal{R}_k[I_0, J_0] \overline{\alpha} \ \overline{v}$$

we have that $v \alpha$ is a prefix of some power of p.

This gives a non-trivial necessary condition.

Test 2. We check for all self-reproducing symbols $[P', Q']$ the condition in Lemma 2.

If one of the test fails, we know that the hairpin completion $\mathcal{H}(L, R, k)$ is not regular. Thus, in the following we assume that all self-reproducing symbols $[P', Q']$ passed this test.

3.3   Candidates

Thus by Test 2, for the rest of the proof we assume that all self-reproducing symbols $[P', Q']$ produce only terminal words of the form $p^s p' \alpha \mathcal{R}_k[I_0, J_0] \overline{\alpha} \, \overline{p'} \, \overline{p}^{\, s}$ where $s \geq 0$ and $p' \leq p$ and $p' \alpha$ is a prefix of some power of p. This condition remains valid if we replace p by some fixed power, say p^k. In particular, we may assume henceforth that $|p| \geq k$ and therefore α becomes a prefix of some conjugated word $q = p'' p'$ with $p = p' p''$.

We use all these (at most n^4) symbols $[P', Q']$ and we collect all words p and all their conjugates $q = p'' p'$ in a list of *candidates* $\mathcal{C}$. This list contains at most n^8 words, and $q \in \mathcal{C}$ defines a word α of length k such that $\alpha \leq q$.

We now need the reference to specific states in the DFAs. We have $P_0 = (q_{0,L}, p_2)$ and $P' = (p'_1, p'_2)$ and hence $q_{0,L} \cdot \pi = p'_1$ and $p'_1 \cdot p = p'_1$. Let $q = p'' p'$ with $p = p' p''$ and $c \in \mathcal{Q}_L$ such that $c = p'_1 \cdot p'$. Then we have $c \cdot q = c$, too.

Moreover, let $J_0 = (j_1, j_2)$ and $f = j_1 \cdot \overline{\alpha}$, then we know that $f \in \mathcal{F}_L$ and (starting in f) reading any non-empty prefix of a word in $\overline{q}^+ \overline{p'} \, \overline{\pi}$ cannot take us back to a final state. For the symmetric consideration we content that if $d = \overline{p'} \, \overline{\pi} \cdot q_{0,R} \in \mathcal{Q}_R$, then $d = \overline{q} \cdot d$.

The next step is to create a list $\mathcal{L}$ of tuples

$$(c, d, e, f, g, h, q) \in \mathcal{Q}_L \times \mathcal{Q}_R \times \mathcal{Q}_L \times \mathcal{Q}_L \times \mathcal{Q}_R \times \mathcal{Q}_R \times \mathcal{C},$$

which satisfy the following additional conditions:

1.) $f \in \mathcal{F}_L$ and reading any non-empty prefix of a word in $\overline{q}^+$ cannot take us back from f to a final state.
2.) $c = c \cdot q$ and $d = \overline{q} \cdot d$.
3.) $e \cdot \overline{q} = e$ and $f \cdot \overline{q}^n = e$.
4.) $g = q \cdot g$ and $g = q^n \cdot h$.

There are at most n^{14} elements in $\mathcal{L}$. We consider (c, d, e, f, g, h, q) one after another. For each tuple we define $\alpha \leq q$ by $|\alpha| = k$. We define a finite (!) language Π by all words $\pi \in \Sigma^*$ satisfying the following conditions:

1.) $|\pi| \leq 2n^4 + k$.
2.) $q_{0,L} \cdot \pi = c$, and $d = \overline{\pi} \cdot q_{0,R}$,
3.) For all $\eta \leq \overline{\pi}$ we have $e \cdot \eta \notin \mathcal{F}_L$.
4.) For all suffixes σ of π we have $\sigma \cdot g \notin \mathcal{F}_R$.

Note that an NFA of polynomial size for Π can be constructed in polynomial time, but the size of Π can be exponential, $|\Pi| \leq |\Sigma|^{2n^4 + k}$. We also define a (possibly infinite) regular language B by all words $\beta \in \Sigma^*$ satisfying $c \cdot \alpha\beta\overline{\alpha} = f$, $h = \alpha\beta\overline{\alpha} \cdot d$, and $q\alpha$ is not a prefix of $\alpha\beta$. Again, an NFA of polynomial size for B can be constructed in polynomial time.

The idea behind this definition is as follows. Assume $\pi q^t q^n \alpha\beta\overline{\alpha} \, \overline{q}^{\,n} \overline{q}^{\,s} \overline{\pi}$ is in the hairpin closure, then we see these states as follows:

$$q_{0,L} \xrightarrow{\pi} c \xrightarrow{q^t q^n} c \xrightarrow{\alpha\beta\overline{\alpha}} f \xrightarrow{\overline{q}^{\,n}} e \xrightarrow{\overline{q}^{\,s}} e \xrightarrow{\overline{\pi}}$$

$$\xleftarrow{\pi} g \xleftarrow{q^t} g \xleftarrow{q^n} h \xleftarrow{\alpha\beta\overline{\alpha}} d \xleftarrow{\overline{q}^{\,n}\overline{q}^{\,s}} d \xleftarrow{\overline{\pi}} q_{0,R}$$

Let

$$\mathcal{H}(c,d,e,f,g,h,q) = \left\{ \pi q^t \alpha\beta\overline{\alpha} \, \overline{q}^{\,s} \overline{\pi} \mid \pi \in \Pi \wedge \beta \in B \wedge 0 \leq s \leq t \right\}.$$

Then obviously, $\mathcal{H}(c,d,e,f,g,h,q) \subseteq \mathcal{H}(L,R,k)$ because $\pi q^t \alpha\beta\overline{\alpha} \in L$. We claim that for the grammar G_1 as above and all words $w \in \mathcal{H}(G_1)$ there exists at least one tuple $(c,d,e,f,g,h,q) \in \mathcal{L}$ such that $w \in \mathcal{H}(c,d,e,f,g,h,q)$.

The crucial observation here is that we have introduced the states h and g just for the following purpose: We can write a word $w = \alpha\beta'\overline{\alpha}$ as $w = q^j \alpha\beta\overline{\alpha}$ such that $q\alpha$ is not a prefix of $\alpha\beta$. Then let $h = \alpha\beta\overline{\alpha} \cdot d$. The words w which play a role for $\mathcal{H}(G_1)$ are of the type that if we are during the right-to-left run in state h after reading $\alpha\beta\overline{\alpha}$, then for some perhaps huge t we reach the state $g = q^t \cdot h$ with $g = q \cdot g$. Indeed, we can use $g = p'' \cdot p_2'$ where $P' = (p_1', p_2')$. But this means $g = q^n \cdot h$, too. We obtain a symmetric statement for e and f.

Thus, $\mathcal{H}(L,R,k)$ is regular if and only if for all $(c,d,e,f,g,h,q) \in \mathcal{L}$ we find regular languages $\mathcal{R}$ such that $\mathcal{H}(c,d,e,f,g,h,q) \subseteq \mathcal{R} \subseteq \mathcal{H}(L,R,k)$.

Note that for $\pi q^t \alpha\beta\overline{\alpha} \, \overline{q}^{\,s} \overline{\pi}$ in $\mathcal{H}(c,d,e,f,g,h,q)$ the longest prefix in L is the word $\pi q^t \alpha\beta\overline{\alpha}$, but we lost the control over the suffixes which are in R.

Clearly,

$$\left\{ \pi q^t \alpha\beta\overline{\alpha} \, \overline{q}^{\,s} \overline{\pi} \mid \pi \in \Pi \wedge \beta \in B \wedge 0 \leq s < n \wedge s \leq t \right\} \subseteq \mathcal{H}(L,R,k)$$

is a regular language because Π is finite and B is regular. Thus all we will have to show is the following.

Proposition 1. *Let*

$$\mathcal{H} = \mathcal{H}(c,d,e,f,g,h,q,n) = \left\{ \pi q^t \alpha\beta\overline{\alpha} \, \overline{q}^{\,s} \overline{\pi} \mid \pi \in \Pi \wedge \beta \in B \wedge n \leq s \leq t \right\}.$$

Then we can decide in polynomial time whether there is a regular language $\mathcal{R}$ such that $\mathcal{H} \subseteq \mathcal{R} \subseteq \mathcal{H}(L,R,k)$.

For the proof of Proposition 1 we start with the following test.

Test 3. Check in polynomial time whether there exists a suffix σ of q^n such that $\sigma \cdot h \in \mathcal{F}_R$ is a final state for R.

If Test 3 yields *yes*, then we can put

$$\mathcal{R} = \left\{ \pi q^t \alpha\beta\overline{\alpha} \, \overline{q}^{\,s} \overline{\pi} \mid \pi \in \Pi \wedge \beta \in B \wedge n \leq s \wedge n \leq t \right\}.$$

The set $\mathcal{R}$ is regular and satisfies $\mathcal{H} \subseteq \mathcal{R} \subseteq \mathcal{H}(L, R, k)$.

Thus, for the rest we assume that Test 3 is negative. Then the language $\mathcal{H}$ has some additional special features.

For $z_{t,s} = \pi q^t \alpha \beta \overline{\alpha} \, \overline{q}^s \overline{\pi} \in \mathcal{H}$ with $\pi \in \Pi$ and $\beta \in B$ and $n \leq s \leq t$ we know that the prefix $\pi' q^t \alpha \beta \overline{\alpha}$ belongs to L and it is the longest prefix with this property. If a suffix of $z_{t,s}$ belongs to R, then it is a suffix of $\alpha \beta \overline{\alpha} \, \overline{q}^s \overline{\pi}$, due to Test 3. Moreover, $q\alpha$ is not a prefix of $\alpha\beta$ which was the main purpose of defining B in such a way.

Let us assume that $\mathcal{H}(L, R, k)$ is regular, then there exists some $x > n$ such that $\overline{q}^x$ is idempotent in the syntactic monoid of $\mathcal{H}(L, R, k)$. Consider $t + 1 = s = 2x$.

Consider $z_t = \pi q^t \alpha \beta \overline{\alpha} \, \overline{q}^{t+1} \overline{\pi}$ with $\pi \in \Pi$ and $\beta \in B$. As $\overline{q}^x$ is idempotent and $\pi' q^t \alpha \beta \overline{\alpha} \, \overline{q}^{t+1-x} \overline{\pi'} \in \mathcal{H}(L, R, k)$ we see that $z_t \in \mathcal{H}(L, R, k)$, too. Since $q\alpha$ is not a prefix of $\alpha\beta$ the longest prefix in L becomes too short to create a hairpin completion for $\pi q^t \alpha \beta \overline{\alpha} \, \overline{q}^{t+1} \overline{\pi}$; we must use a suffix in R for that purpose. The longest suffix in R has the form $\delta u \in R$ with $|\delta| = k$, and it is a suffix of $\alpha \beta \overline{\alpha} \, \overline{q}^{t+1} \overline{\pi}$. Moreover as $|\alpha| = |\delta|$ we see that $\pi q^t \alpha$ must be a prefix of $\overline{u}$.

Thus, we must be able to write

$$\alpha \beta \overline{\alpha} \, \overline{q} = v \delta w \overline{\delta} \, \overline{v}$$

such that $\delta w \overline{\delta} \, \overline{v} \overline{q}^t \overline{\pi} \in R$. Now consider some huge y, say $y > |z_t|$. Then $\pi q^t \alpha \beta \overline{\alpha} \, \overline{q}^{t+1+xy} \overline{\pi} \in \mathcal{H}(L, R, k)$, too. Similar to an earlier observation this says that we can write $v\delta = q^m q' \delta$ with $m \geq 0$ and $q'\delta$ is a proper prefix of $q\alpha$. But we cannot have $m > 0$, since, again, $q\alpha$ is not a prefix of $\alpha\beta$.

Thus, if $\mathcal{H}(L, R, k)$ is regular, then $v\delta < q\alpha$ and $\alpha \beta \overline{\alpha} \, \overline{q} = v \delta u \overline{\delta} \, \overline{v}$ such that $\delta u \overline{\delta} \, \overline{v} \cdot d \in \mathcal{F}_R$.

This leads finally to another necessary condition. If $\mathcal{H}(L, R, k)$ is regular, then it must pass the following test:

Test 4. Check in polynomial time whether for all $\beta \in B$ there exist v, δ with $|\delta| = k$, $v\delta \leq q\alpha$ and $\alpha \beta \overline{\alpha} \, \overline{q} = v \delta w$ with $|w| \geq |v\delta|$ and $\delta w \cdot d \in \mathcal{F}_R$.

In order to perform a test in polynomial time we start with any NFA accepting the language

$$\{\alpha \beta \overline{\alpha} \, \overline{q} \mid \beta \in B\}.$$

Then we may take e.g. the cross product with the NFA constructed in Section 3.1, which, in particular, *knows* the state in $\mathcal{Q}_R$. This means if, in the new automaton, state Q *knows* $r \in \mathcal{Q}_R$ and if we can reach via a word z a final state, then we may infer $r = z \cdot d$. (This is because we may assume that in the right-to-left DFA d is an initial state for the right quotient $R(\overline{q}^n \overline{\pi})^{-1}$.) Recall that whenever we investigate properties of NFA, we first do a clean-up. Thus, we assume that all states are reachable and co-reachable.

We continue to modify the new NFA as follows. We duplicate each state Q several times so that each state becomes the form $[i, Q, j]$ with $i \in \{0, \ldots, |q|, *\}$ and $j \in \{0, \ldots, |q| + 2k, *\}$, where $*$ is a special symbol standing for integers greater than $|q|$, respectively greater than $|q| + 2k$.

After a transformation we may assume that if the NFA accepts a word uz with $|u| = i$ and $|z| = j$, then we are sure that reading u we reach some state $[i, Q, j]$. Vice versa if we reach after reading u a state $[i, Q, j]$, then $|u| = i$ and $|z| = j$ for every word z which takes $[i, Q, j]$ to some final state.

We duplicate the states again, and we introduce upper and lower states. We start in the upper part, but as soon as we deviate from reading a prefix $q\alpha$ we switch to the lower part. We switch also to the lower part if $j < k$. Once we are in the lower part we remain there. Note that the last k states on an accepting path are lower.

On every accepting path there is exactly one upper state U where the next state is a lower state.

Remember that our NFA of Section 3.1 transfers the following property: If we accept now a word uz with $|u| = i$ and if after reading u we reach $[i, Q, j]$, then we know the state $z \cdot d$ of the right-to-left DFA for R. Let us mark all upper states $[i, Q, j]$ as *good*, if both $z \cdot d \in \mathcal{F}_R$ and $i + 2k \leq j$.

It is clear that every accepting path must go through some good upper state, otherwise Test 4 fails. This can be decided via a reachability algorithm. Finally consider all accepting paths and compute the set of good upper states $[i, Q, j]$ which are seen first on such paths. For each such states all outgoing paths of length k must stay in the upper part, otherwise Test 4 fails. If no such $[i, Q, j]$ leads to a failure, Test 4 is positive.

Now, all tests have been performed; and we get our result due to the following conclusion: Assume Test 4 is positive. Then we have for all $s, t \geq n$ the following fact:

$$z_{t,s} = \pi q^t \alpha \beta \overline{\alpha}\, \overline{q}\, \overline{q}^{\,s} \overline{\pi} \in \mathcal{H}(L, R, k)$$

Indeed for $t > s$ this holds because $\pi q^t \alpha \beta \overline{\alpha} \in L$. For $n \leq t \leq s$ we use that there exist v, δ with $|\delta| = k$, $v\delta \leq p\alpha$, and $\alpha\beta\overline{\alpha}\,\overline{q} = v\delta w$ with $|w| \geq |v\delta|$, and $\delta w \overline{\pi} \cdot q_{0,R} \in \mathcal{F}_R$. Thus $z_{t,s} = \pi q^t v\delta u\overline{\delta}\,\overline{v}\,\overline{q}^{\,s} \overline{\pi}$ and $z_{t,s} \in \mathcal{H}(L, R, k)$ because $\delta u\overline{\delta}\,\overline{v}\,\overline{q}^{\,s}\overline{\pi} \in R$.

Open problems

We conclude with four questions which might be interesting for future research.

Question 1. What is the complexity of our decision algorithm in terms of n, if we start with a finite monoid of size n recognizing both L and R?

Question 2. What is the *practical performance* of our decision algorithm?

Let us define the *partial hairpin completion* of L by the set of words $\gamma\alpha\beta\overline{\alpha}\,\overline{\gamma}'$ where γ' is a prefix γ and $\gamma\alpha\beta\overline{\alpha} \in L$ or γ is a prefix γ' and $\alpha\beta\overline{\alpha}\,\overline{\gamma}' \in L$. (In particular, L becomes a subset of its partial hairpin completion.)

Question 3. Is it decidable whether the partial hairpin completion applied to a regular language is regular again?

Given a language L we can iterate the (partial) hairpin completion and can define the *iterated (partial) hairpin completion* as the union over all iterations.

Question 4. Is it decidable whether the iterated (partial) hairpin completion applied to a regular language (finite language resp.) is regular again?

Acknowledgement

We thank the anonymous referees for many useful remarks and hints.

References

1. Cheptea, D., Martin-Vide, C., Mitrana, V.: A new operation on words suggested by DNA biochemistry: Hairpin completion. Transgressive Computing, 216–228 (2006)
2. Deaton, R., Murphy, R., Garzon, M., Franceschetti, D., Stevens, S.: Good encodings for DNA-based solutions to combinatorial problems. Proc. of DNA-based computers DIMACS Series 44, 247–258 (1998)
3. Garzon, M., Deaton, R., Neathery, P., Murphy, R., Franceschetti, D., Stevens, E.: On the encoding problem for DNA computing. In: The Third DIMACS Workshop on DNA-Based Computing, pp. 230–237 (1997)
4. Garzon, M., Deaton, R., Nino, L., Stevens Jr., S., Wittner, M.: Genome encoding for DNA computing. In: Proc. Third Genetic Programming Conference, pp. 684–690 (1998)
5. Hopcroft, J.E., Ulman, J.D.: Introduction to Automata Theory, Languages and Computation. Addison-Wesley, Reading (1979)
6. Ito, M., Leupold, P., Mitrana, V.: Bounded hairpin completion. In: LATA. LNCS, vol. 5457, pp. 434–445. Springer, Heidelberg (2009)
7. Kari, L., Konstantinidis, S., Losseva, E., Sosík, P., Thierrin, G.: Hairpin structures in DNA words. In: Carbone, A., Pierce, N.A. (eds.) DNA 2005. LNCS, vol. 3892, pp. 158–170. Springer, Heidelberg (2006)
8. Kari, L., Mahalingam, K., Thierrin, G.: The syntactic monoid of hairpin-free languages. Acta Inf. 44(3-4), 153–166 (2007)
9. Manea, F., Martín-Vide, C., Mitrana, V.: On some algorithmic problems regarding the hairpin completion. Discrete Applied Mathematics 27, 71–72 (2006)
10. Manea, F., Mitrana, V.: Hairpin completion versus hairpin reduction. In: Cooper, S.B., Löwe, B., Sorbi, A. (eds.) CiE 2007. LNCS, vol. 4497, pp. 532–541. Springer, Heidelberg (2007)
11. Manea, F., Mitrana, V., Yokomori, T.: Some remarks on the hairpin completion. In: 12th International Conference on Automata and Formal Languages, pp. 302–313 (2008)
12. Manea, F., Mitrana, V., Yokomori, T.: Two complementary operations inspired by the DNA hairpin formation: Completion and reduction. Theor. Comput. Sci. 410(4-5), 417–425 (2009)

Context-Free Languages of Countable Words*

Zoltán Ésik and Szabolcs Iván

Dept. of Computer Science, University of Szeged, Hungary

Abstract. We define context-free grammars with Büchi acceptance condition generating languages of countable words. We establish several closure properties and decidability results for the class of Büchi context-free languages generated by these grammars. We also define context-free grammars with Müller acceptance condition and show that there is a language generated by a grammar with Müller acceptance condition which is not a Büchi context-free language.

1 Introduction

A word over an alphabet Σ is an isomorphism type of a labeled linear order. In this paper, in addition to finite words and ω-words, we also consider words whose underlying linear order is any countable linear order, including scattered and dense linear orders, cf. [21].

Finite automata on ω-words were introduced by Büchi [9]. He used automata to prove the decidability of the monadic second-order theory of the ordinal ω. Automata on ω-words have since been extended to automata on ordinal words beyond ω, cf. [10,11,1,25,26], to words whose underlying linear order is not necessarily well-ordered, cf. [3,8], and to automata on finite and infinite trees, cf. [14,22,20]. Many decidability results have been obtained using the automata theoretic approach, both for ordinals and other linear orders, and for first-order and monadic second-order theories in general.

Countable words were first investigated in [13], where they were called "arrangements". It was shown that any arrangement can be represented as the frontier word (i.e., the sequence of leaf labels) of a possibly infinite labeled binary tree. Moreover, it was shown that words definable by finite recursion schemes are exactly those words represented by the frontiers of regular trees. These words were called regular in [6]. Courcelle [13] raised several problems that were later solved in the papers [17,23,5]. In [23], it was shown that it is decidable for two regular trees whether they represent the same regular word. In [17], an infinite collection of regular operations has been introduced and it has been shown that each regular word can be represented by a regular expression. Complete axiomatizations have been obtained in [4] and [5] for the subcollections of the regular operations that allow for the representation of the regular ordinal words and the regular scattered words, respectively. Complete axiomatization of the full

* Research supported by grant no. K 75249 from the National Foundation of Hungary for Scientific Research.

M. Leucker and C. Morgan (Eds.): ICTAC 2009, LNCS 5684, pp. 185–199, 2009.

collection of the regular operations has been obtained in [6], where it is also proved that there is a polynomial time algorithm to decide whether two regular expressions represent the same regular word. In [8,3], the authors proposed regular expressions to represent languages (i.e., sets) of scattered countable words and languages of possibly dense words with no upper bound on the size of the words. They have established Kleene theorems stating that a language of infinite words is recognizable by a finite automaton iff it can be represented by a regular expression.

In addition to automata and expressions (or terms), a third common way of representing languages of finite words is by generative grammars. Context-free grammars have been used to generate languages of ω-words in [12] and in [18]. However, we are not aware of any work on context-free grammars as a device generating languages of countable words possibly longer than ω, except for the recent [15] that deals only with linear grammars. In this paper we consider languages of countable words generated by context-free grammars equipped with a Büchi-type acceptance condition, called BCFG's. A BCFG is a system $G = (N, \Sigma, P, S, F)$, where (N, Σ, P, S) is an ordinary context-free grammar and $F \subseteq N$ is the set of repeated (or final) nonterminals. A derivation tree t of a grammar G is a possibly infinite tree whose vertices are labeled in the set $N \cup \Sigma \cup \{\epsilon\}$, so that each vertex is labeled by a nonterminal in N, a letter in the terminal alphabet Σ, or by the empty word ϵ. The labeling is locally consistent with the rules contained in P in the usual way. Moreover, it is required that each derivation tree satisfies the "Büchi condition F", i.e., on each infinite path of t at least one repeated nonterminal has to occur infinitely many times. The frontier of a derivation tree t determines a countable word w over the alphabet $N \cup \Sigma$. When w is a word over the terminal alphabet Σ and the root of t is labeled by the start symbol S, we say that w is contained in the Büchi context-free language generated by G. The language class BCFL consists of all such Büchi context-free languages.

It is well-known (see e.g., [16]) that ordinary context-free languages of finite words are precisely the frontier languages of sets of finite trees recognizable by finite tree automata. Tree automata over infinite trees have been introduced in [20]. Just as automata over ω-words, a tree automaton may be equipped with different acceptance conditions such as the Büchi and Müller acceptance conditions, or the Rabin, Streett and parity conditions, cf. [19,24]. In the setting of ω-words, these conditions are equally powerful (at least for nondeterministic automata). Nevertheless, some yield more succinct representation than others, or have different algorithmic properties. On the other hand, in the setting of infinite trees, the Büchi acceptance condition is strictly less powerful than the Müller acceptance condition which is equivalent to the Rabin, Streett, and parity conditions, cf. [19,24]. While in the present paper we are mainly concerned with the Büchi condition for generating context-free languages of countable words, we still show that the Müller condition is strictly more powerful also in the setting of countable words. This result is not immediate from the tree case.

2 Linear Orders and Words

In this section we recall some concepts for linear orders and words. A good reference on linear orders is [21].

A partial order, or partial ordering is a set P equipped with a (partial) order relation usually denoted $\leq$. We sometimes write $x < y$ if $x \leq y$ and $x \neq y$. A linear order is a partial order $(P, \leq)$ whose order relation is total, so that $x \leq y$ or $y \leq x$ for all $x, y \in P$. A countable (finite or infinite, respectively) linear order is a linear order which is a countable (finite or infinite, respectively) set. When $(P, \leq)$ and $(Q, \leq)$ are linear orders, an isomorphism (embedding, respectively) $(P, \leq) \to (Q, \leq)$ is a bijection (injection, respectively) $h : P \to Q$ such that $x \leq y$ implies $h(x) \leq h(y)$ for all $x, y \in P$. When two linear orders are isomorphic, we also say that they have the same order type (or isomorphism type).

Below when there is no danger of confusion, we will denote a linear order just by $P, Q, \ldots$. Suppose that P is a linear order. Then any subset X of P determines a sub-order of P whose order relation is the restriction of the order relation of P to X. Note that the inclusion function $X \hookrightarrow P$ is an embedding of X into P. When in addition X is such that for all $x, y \in X$ and $z \in P$, $x < z < y$ implies that $z \in X$, then we call X an interval. In particular, for any $x, y \in P$, the set $[x, y] = \{z : x \leq z \leq y\}$ is an interval.

We recall that a linear order $(P, \leq)$ is a *well-order* if each nonempty subset of P has a least element, and is *dense* if it has at least two elements and for any $x < y$ in P there is some z with $x < z < y$.[1] A *quasi-dense* linear order is a linear order $(P, \leq)$ containing a dense linear sub-order, so that P has a subset P' such that $(P', \leq)$ is a dense order. Finally, a *scattered* linear order is a linear order which is not quasi-dense.

It is clear that every finite linear order is a well-order, every well-order is a scattered order, and every dense order is quasi-dense. It is well-known that up to isomorphism there are 4 countable dense linear orders, the rationals $\mathbb{Q}$ with the usual order, $\mathbb{Q}$ endowed with a least or a greatest element, and $\mathbb{Q}$ endowed with both a least and a greatest element.

An ordinal is an order type of a well-order. The finite ordinals n are the isomorphism types of the finite linear orders. As usual, we denote by ω the least infinite ordinal, which is the order type of the finite ordinals, and of the positive integers $\mathbb{N}$ equipped with the usual order. The order type of $\mathbb{Q}$ is denoted η.

When τ and τ' are order types, we say that $\tau \leq \tau'$ if there is an embedding of a linear order of type τ into a linear order of type τ'. The relation $\leq$ defined above is a linear order of the ordinals.

We define several operations on linear orders. First, the reverse $(P, \leq')$ of a linear order $(P, \leq)$ is defined by $x \leq' y$ iff $y \leq x$, for all $x, y \in P$. We will sometimes denote the reverse order $(P, \leq')$ by P^r. It is clear that the reverse of a scattered (dense, respectively) linear order is scattered (dense, respectively).

Suppose that P and Q are linear orders. Then the sum $P + Q$ is the linear order on the disjoint union of P and Q such that P and Q are intervals of $P + Q$

---

[1] In [21], a singleton linear order is also called dense.

and $x \leq y$ holds for all $x \in P$ and $y \in Q$. There is a more general notion. Suppose that I is a linear order and for each $i \in I$, P_i is a linear order. Then the generalized sum $P = \sum_{i \in I} P_i$ is obtained by replacing each point i of I with the linear order P_i. Formally, the generalized sum P is the linear order on the disjoint union $\bigcup_{i \in I} P_i$ equipped with the order relation such that each P_i is an interval and for all $i, j \in I$ with $i < j$, if $x \in P_i$ and $y \in P_j$ then $x < y$. The generalized sum gives rise to a product operation. Let P and Q be linear orders, and for each $y \in Q$, let P_y be an isomorphic copy of P. Then $P \times Q$ is defined as the linear order $\sum_{y \in Q} P_y$. Note that this linear order is isomorphic to the linear order on the cartesian product of P and Q equipped with the order relation $(x, y) \leq (x', y')$ iff $y < y'$ or $(y = y'$ and $x \leq x')$.

Lemma 1. *[21] Any scattered generalized sum of scattered linear orders is scattered. Similarly, any well-ordered generalized sum of well-orders is a well-order. Every quasi-dense linear order is a dense generalized sum of (nonempty) scattered linear orders.*

Thus, when I is a scattered linear order and for each $i \in I$, P_i is a scattered linear order, then so is $\sum_{i \in I} P_i$, and similarly for well-orders. And if P is a quasi-dense linear order, then there is a dense linear order D and (nonempty) scattered linear orders P_x, $x \in D$ such that P is isomorphic to $\sum_{x \in D} P_x$.

The above operations preserve isomorphism, so that they give rise to corresponding operations $\tau + \tau'$ and $\tau \times \tau'$ on order types. In particular, the sum and product of two ordinals is well-defined (and is an ordinal). The reverse of an order type τ will be denoted $-\tau$. The ordinals are also equipped with the exponentiation operation, cf. [21].

An alphabet Σ is a finite nonempty set. A word over an alphabet Σ is a labeled linear order, i.e., a system $u = (P, \leq, \lambda)$, where $(P, \leq)$ is a linear order, sometimes denoted $\mathrm{dom}(u)$, and λ is a labeling function $P \to \Sigma$. The underlying linear order $\mathrm{dom}(\epsilon)$ of the empty word ϵ is the empty linear order. We say that a word is finite (infinite or countable, respectively), if its underlying linear order is finite (infinite or countable, respectively). An isomorphism of words is an isomorphism of the underlying linear orders that preserves the labeling. Embeddings of words are defined in the same way. We usually identify isomorphic words. We will say that a word u is a subword of a word v if there is an embedding $u \hookrightarrow v$. When in addition the image of the underlying linear order of u is an interval of the underlying linear order of v we call u a factor of v.

The order type of a word is the order type of its underlying linear order. Thus, the order type of a finite word is a finite linear order. A word whose order type is ω is called an ω-word.

Let $\Sigma = \{a, b\}$. Some examples of words over Σ are the finite word aab which is the (isomorphism class of the) 3-element labeled linear order $0 < 1 < 2$ whose points are labeled a, a and b, in this order, and the infinite words a^ω and $a^{-\omega}$, whose order types are ω and $-\omega$, respectively, with each point labeled a. For another example, consider the linear order $\mathbb{Q}$ of the rationals and label each point a. The resulting word of order type η is denoted a^η. More generally, let Σ be the alphabet $\{a_1, \ldots, a_n\}$ of size n. Then up to isomorphism there is a unique labeling of the rationals such that between any two points there are n points labeled $a_1, \ldots, a_n$, respectively. This word is denoted $(a_1, \ldots, a_n)^\eta$, cf. [17].

The reverse of a word $u = (P, \leq, \lambda)$ is $u^r = (P, \leq', \lambda)$, where $(P, \leq')$ is the reverse of $(P, \leq)$. Suppose that $u = (P, \leq, \lambda)$ and $v = (Q, \leq, \lambda')$ are words over Σ. Then their concatenation (or product) uv is the word over Σ whose underlying linear order is $P + Q$ and whose labeling function agrees with λ on points in P, and with λ' on points in Q. More generally, when I is a linear order and u_i is a word over Σ with underlying linear order $P_i = \mathrm{dom}(u_i)$, for each $i \in I$, then the generalized concatenation $\prod_{i \in I} u_i$ is the word whose underlying linear order is $\sum_{i \in I} P_i$ and whose labeling function agrees with the labeling function of P_i on the elements of each P_i. In particular, when $u_0, u_1, \ldots, u_n, \ldots$ are words over Σ, and I is the linear order ω or its reverse, then $\prod_{i \in I} u_i$ is the word $u_0 u_1 \ldots u_n \ldots$ or $\ldots u_n \ldots u_1 u_0$, respectively. When $u_i = u$ for each i, these words are denoted u^ω and $u^{-\omega}$, respectively.

In the sequel, we will make use of the substitution operation on words. Suppose that u is a word over Σ and for each letter $a \in \Sigma$, u_a is a word over Δ. Then the word $u[a \leftarrow u_a]_{a \in \Sigma}$ obtained by substituting u_a for each occurrence of a letter a in u (or replacing each occurrence of a letter a with u_a) is formally defined as follows. Let $u = (P, \leq, \lambda)$ and $u_a = (P_a, \leq_a, \lambda_a)$ for each $a \in \Sigma$. Then for each $i \in P$ let $u_i = (P_i, \leq_i, \lambda_i)$ be an isomorphic copy of $P_{\lambda(i)}$. We define

$$u[a \leftarrow u_a]_{a \in \Sigma} = \prod_{i \in P} u_i.$$

Note that when $u = a^\omega$, then $u[a \leftarrow v]$ is v^ω, and similarly for $v^{-\omega}$. For any words $u_1, \ldots, u_n$ over an alphabet Σ, we define

$$(u_1, \ldots, u_n)^\eta = (a_1, \ldots, a_n)^\eta[a_1 \leftarrow u_1, \ldots, a_n \leftarrow u_n].$$

We call a word over an alphabet Σ well-ordered, scattered, dense, or quasi-dense if its underlying linear order has the appropriate property. For example, the words a^ω, $a^\omega b^\omega a$, $(a^\omega)^\omega$ over the alphabet $\{a, b\}$ are well-ordered, the words $a^\omega a^{-\omega}$, $a^{-\omega} a^\omega$ are scattered, the words a^η, $a^\eta b a^\eta$, $(a, b)^\eta$ are dense, and the words $(ab)^\eta$, $(a^\omega)^\eta$, $(a^\eta b)^\omega$ are quasi-dense. From Lemma 1 we immediately have:

Lemma 2. *Any scattered generalized product of scattered words is scattered. Any well-ordered generalized product of well-ordered words is well-ordered. Moreover, every quasi-dense word is a dense product of (nonempty) scattered words.*

As already mentioned, we will usually identify isomorphic words, so that a word is an isomorphism type (or isomorphism class) of a labeled linear order. When Σ is an alphabet, we let Σ^*, Σ^ω and Σ^∞ respectively denote the set of all finite words, ω-words, and countable words over Σ. Σ^+ is the set of all finite nonempty words. The length of a finite word w will be denoted $|w|$.

A language over Σ is any subset L of Σ^∞. When $L \subseteq \Sigma^*$ or $L \subseteq \Sigma^\omega$, we sometimes call L a language of finite words or ω-words, or an ω-language.

Languages are equipped with several operations, including the usual set theoretic operations. We now define the generic operation of language substitution.

Suppose that $u \in \Sigma^\infty$ and for each $a \in \Sigma$, $L_a \subseteq \Delta^\infty$. Then the words in the language $u[a \leftarrow L_a]_{a\in\Sigma} \subseteq \Delta^\infty$ are obtained from u by substituting in all possible ways a word in L_a for each occurrence of each letter $a \in \Sigma$. Different occurrences of the same letter a may be replaced by different words in L_a.

Formally, suppose that $u = (P, \leq, \lambda)$. For each $x \in P$ with $\lambda(x) = a$, let us choose a word $u_x = (P_x, \leq_x, \lambda_x)$ which is isomorphic to some word in L_a. Then the language $u[a \leftarrow L_a]_{a\in\Sigma}$ consists of all words $\prod_{x\in P} u_x$.

Suppose now that $L \subseteq \Sigma^\infty$ and for each $a \in \Sigma$, $L_a \subseteq \Delta^\infty$. Then

$$L[a \leftarrow L_a]_{a\in\Sigma} = \bigcup_{u\in L} u[a \leftarrow L_a]_{a\in\Sigma}.$$

We call $L[a \leftarrow L_a]_{a\in\Sigma}$ the language obtained from L by substituting the language L_a for each $a \in \Sigma$.

As mentioned above, set theoretic operations on languages in Σ^∞ have their standard meaning. Below we define some other operations.

Let $L, L_1, L_2, \ldots, L_m \subseteq \Sigma^\infty$. Then we define:

1. $L_1 L_2 = ab[a \leftarrow L_1, b \leftarrow L_2] = \{uv : u \in L_1, v \in L_2\}$.
2. $L^* = \{a\}^*[a \leftarrow L] = \{u_1 \ldots u_n : n < \omega,\ u_i \in L\}$.
3. $L^\omega = \{a^\omega\}[a \leftarrow L] = \{u_0 u_1 \ldots u_n \ldots : u_i \in L\}$.
4. $L^{-\omega} = \{a^{-\omega}\}[a \leftarrow L] = \{\ldots u_n \ldots u_1 u_0 : u_i \in L\}$.
5. $(L_1, \ldots, L_m)^\eta = \eta(a_1, \ldots, a_m)[a_1 \leftarrow L_1, \ldots, a_m \leftarrow L_m]$.
6. $L^\infty = \{a\}^\infty[a \leftarrow L]$.

The above operations are respectively called concatenation, star, $^\omega$-power, $^{-\omega}$-power, $^\eta$-power, and $^\infty$-power.

Some more operations. The reverse L^r of a language $L \subseteq \Sigma^\infty$ is defined as $L^r = \{u^r : u \in L\}$. The prefix language $\mathrm{Pre}(L)$ is given by $\mathrm{Pre}(L) = \{u : \exists v\ uv \in L\}$ and the suffix language $\mathrm{Suf}(L)$ is defined symmetrically. The infix (or factor) language $\mathrm{In}(L)$ is $\{u : \exists v, w\ vuw \in L\}$, and the language $\mathrm{Sub}(L)$ of subwords of L is the collection of all words u such that there is an embedding $u \hookrightarrow v$ for some $v \in L$.

3   Büchi Context-Free Languages

Recall that an ordinary context-free grammar (CFG) is a system $G = (N, \Sigma, P, S)$ where N and Σ are the disjoint alphabets of nonterminals and terminal symbols (or letters), P is a finite set of productions of the form $A \to p$ where $A \in N$ and $p \in (N \cup \Sigma)^*$, and $S \in N$ is the start symbol. Each context-free grammar $G = (N, \Sigma, P, S)$ generates a context-free language $L(G) \subseteq \Sigma^*$ which can be defined either by using the derivation relation $\Rightarrow^*$ or by using the concept of derivation trees.

We recall that for finite words $p, q \in (N \cup \Sigma)^*$ it holds that $p \Rightarrow q$ if p and q can be written as $p = p_1 A p_2$, $q = p_1 r p_2$ such that $A \to r$ is in P. The relations $\Rightarrow^+$ and $\Rightarrow^*$ are respectively the transitive closure and the reflexive-transitive closure of the direct derivation relation $\Rightarrow$. The context-free language generated by G is $L(G) = \{u \in \Sigma^* : S \Rightarrow^* u\}$. Two context-free grammars G and G' having the same terminal alphabet are called equivalent if $L(G) = L(G')$. We let CFL denote the class of all context-free languages.

A derivation tree is a partial mapping $t : \mathbb{N}^* \to N \cup \Sigma \cup \{\epsilon\}$ whose domain $\mathrm{dom}(t)$ is finite, nonempty and prefix closed (i.e., $uv \in \mathrm{dom}(t) \Rightarrow u \in \mathrm{dom}(t)$). The elements of $\mathrm{dom}(t)$ are the vertices of t, and for any vertex v, $t(v)$ is the label of v. The empty word ϵ is the root of t, and $t(\epsilon)$ is the root symbol. The vertices in $\mathrm{dom}(t)$ are equipped with both the lexicographic order and the prefix order. Let $x, y \in \mathrm{dom}(t)$. We say that $x \leq y$ in the prefix order if $y = xz$ for some $z \in \mathbb{N}^*$. Moreover, we say that $x < y$ in the lexicographic order if $x = uiz$ and $y = ujz'$ for some $u, z, z' \in \mathbb{N}^*$ and $i, j \in \mathbb{N}$ with $i < j$. The leaves of t are the maximal elements of $\mathrm{dom}(t)$ with respect to the prefix order. When $x, y \in \mathrm{dom}(t)$ and $y = xi$ for some $i \in \mathbb{N}$, then we say that y is the ith successor of x and x is the predecessor of y. The function t is required to satisfy the local consistency condition that whenever $t(u) = A$ with $A \in N$ and u is not a leaf, then either $A \to \epsilon \in P$ and $t(u1) = \epsilon$ and $t(ui)$ is not defined for any $i \in \mathbb{N}$ with $i > 1$, or there is a production $A \to p$ such that $|p| = n$ with $n > 0$ and $t(ui)$ is defined for some $i \in \mathbb{N}$ iff $i \leq n$, moreover, $t(ui)$ is the ith letter of p for each $i \leq n$. The frontier of t is the linearly ordered set of leaves whose order is the lexicographic order. The frontier determines a word in $(N \cup \Sigma)^*$ whose underlying linear order is obtained from the frontier of t by removing all those vertices whose label is ϵ. The labeling function is the restriction of the function t to the remaining vertices. This word is sometimes called the frontier word of t. It is well-known that a word u in Σ^* belongs to $L(G)$ iff there is a derivation tree whose root is labeled S and whose frontier word is u.

We now define context-free grammars generating countable words.

Definition 1. *A context-free grammar with Büchi acceptance condition, or BCFG is a system* $G = (N, \Sigma, P, S, F)$ *where* N, Σ, P, S *are the same as above, and* $F \subseteq N$ *is the set of* repeated nonterminals.

Note that each BCFG has an underlying CFG. Suppose $G = (N, \Sigma, P, S, F)$ is a BCFG. A derivation tree t is defined as above except that $\mathrm{dom}(t)$ may now be infinite. However, we require that at least one repeated nonterminal occurs infinitely often along each infinite path. When the root symbol of t is A and the frontier word of t is p, we also write $A \Rightarrow^\infty p$. (Here, it is allowed that A is a terminal in which case $A = p$.) The language (of countable words) generated by G is $L^\infty(G) = \{u \in \Sigma^\infty : S \Rightarrow^\infty u\}$. When G and G' are BCFG's with the same terminal alphabet Σ generating the same language, then we say that G and G' are equivalent.

Definition 2. *We call a set* $L \subseteq \Sigma^\infty$ *a Büchi context-free language, or a BCFL, if it can be generated by some BCFG, i.e., when* $L = L^\infty(G)$ *for some BCFG* $G = (N, \Sigma, P, S, F)$.

Suppose that $G = (N, \Sigma, P, S, F)$ is a BCFG with underlying CFG $G' = (N, \Sigma, P, S)$. Then we define $L^*(G)$ as the CFL $L(G')$. Note that in general it does not hold that $L^*(G) = L^\infty(G) \cap \Sigma^*$. Later we will see that for every BCFG $G = (N, \Sigma, P, S, F)$ it holds that $L^\infty(G) \cap \Sigma^*$ is a CFL. It is clear that CFL $\subseteq$ BCFL, for if $G = (N, \Sigma, P, S, F)$ is a BCFG with $F = \emptyset$, then $L^\infty(G) = L^*(G)$.

Example 1. Consider the sequence $(w_n)_{n<\omega}$ of words over $\{a\}$ defined inductively by $w_0 = a$, and for each $n < \omega$, $w_{n+1} = w_n^\omega$. Note that the order type of w_n is ω^n. For each n, the BCFG $G_n = (N, \{a\}, P, S_n, N)$ with

$$N = \{S_0, \ldots, S_n\} \quad \text{and} \quad P = \{S_0 \to a\} \cup \{S_i \to S_{i-1}S_i : 1 \leq i \leq n\}$$

generates the singleton language $\{w_n\}$, cf. [7]. Using this, it follows that the BCFG $G'_n = (N \cup \{S\}, \{a\}, P \cup \{S \to S_i : 0 \leq i \leq n\}, S, N)$ generates the set $\{w_i : 0 \leq i \leq n\}$.

Example 2. Let Σ be an alphabet and let $a_1, \ldots, a_n \in \Sigma$ be letters in Σ. The singleton language containing the word $(a_1, \ldots, a_n)^\eta$ is a BCFL generated by $G = (\{S\}, \Sigma, \{S \to Sa_1Sa_2 \ldots Sa_nS\}, S, \{S\})$.

Example 3. Consider the language L over the 1-letter alphabet $\{a\}$ consisting of all words in $\{a\}^\infty$ whose domain is well-ordered of order type $< \omega^n$. Then L is generated by the BCFG $G = (N, \{a\}, P, S_n, N - \{S_n\})$ with $N = \{S_n, \ldots, S_0\}$ and $P = \{S_i \to \epsilon : 0 \leq i \leq n\} \cup \{S_0 \to a\} \cup \{S_i \to S_{i-1}S_i : 1 \leq i \leq n\}$.

Let L' be the subset of L consisting of those words whose domain is a limit ordinal. Then L' is the set of all finite concatenations of the words w_i, $1 \leq i < n$ of Example 1. L' is generated by the BCFG $G = (N, \{a\}, P, S, N - \{S\})$ with $N = \{S, S_0, \ldots, S_{n-1}\}$ and

$$P = \{S \to S_iS : 1 \leq i < n\} \cup \{S \to \epsilon\} \cup \{S_0 \to a\} \cup \{S_i \to S_{i-1}S_i : 1 \leq i < n\}.$$

Example 4. The language $\{a^\omega b^{-\omega}\}^* \cup \{a^\omega b^{-\omega}\}^\omega$ is a BCFL generated by $G = (N, \{a, b\}, P, S, N)$ with $N = \{S, X\}$ and $P = \{S \to XS, S \to \epsilon, X \to aXb\}$.

Example 5. Using the fact (see e.g., Theorem 2.5 in [21]) that any countable linear order can be embedded into $\mathbb{Q}$, we get that Σ^∞ is a BCFL for any alphabet Σ, generated by the BCFG $G = (\{S\}, \Sigma, \{S \to \epsilon, S \to SS\} \cup \{S \to SaS : a \in \Sigma\}, S, \{S\})$.

4   Normal Forms

The results of this section show that each BCFG can be transformed in polynomial time into an equivalent BCFG which is "weakly ϵ-free" and does not contain useless nonterminals nor any chain productions. Moreover, each BCFG can be transformed into an equivalent "ϵ-free" BCFG having no useless nonterminals.

Definition 3. *Let $G = (N, \Sigma, P, S, F)$ be a BCFG. We say that a nonterminal A is useful if there exist words $p, q \in (N \cup \Sigma)^*$ and $u \in \Sigma^\infty$ such that $S \Rightarrow^* pAq$ and $A \Rightarrow^\infty u$. We say that G contains no useless nonterminals if either $N = \{S\}$, $P = \emptyset$ and $F = \emptyset$, or each nonterminal is useful.*

Note that when $G = (N, \Sigma, P, S, F)$ contains no useless nonterminals, then $L^\infty(G)$ is empty iff $N = \{S\}$, $P = \emptyset$ and $F = \emptyset$. Moreover, if $L^\infty(G)$ is not empty, then for each $A \in N$ there are words $u, v \in \Sigma^\infty$ with $S \Rightarrow^\infty uAv$.

Definition 4. *Let $G = (N, \Sigma, P, S, F)$ be a BCFG. We call G weakly ϵ-free if either $L^\infty(G) = \emptyset$, or for each nonterminal A there is a nonempty word $u \in \Sigma^\infty$ with $A \Rightarrow^\infty u$, or $S \to \epsilon$ is the only production.*

As usual, a chain production is of the form $A \to B$, where A, B are nonterminals.

Proposition 1. *For each BCFG G one can construct in polynomial time an equivalent weakly ϵ-free BCFG G' without any chain productions which contains no useless nonterminals.*

Definition 5. *We say that the BCFG $G = (N, \Sigma, P, S, F)$ is ϵ-free if the following conditions hold: 1. G is weakly ϵ-free. 2. Except possibly for the production $S \to \epsilon$, the right side of any other production is a nonempty word. Moreover, if $S \to \epsilon$ is a production, then S does not occur on the right side of any other production. 3. For each derivation tree t whose frontier determines a nonempty word in Σ^∞ there is a derivation tree t' with the same root symbol and frontier word which is well-founded in the following strict sense: For each vertex $x \in \mathrm{dom}(t')$, the subtree $t'|_x$ of t' rooted at x has at least one leaf labeled in Σ.*

Proposition 2. *For each BCFG G one can construct in polynomial time an equivalent ϵ-free grammar without useless nonterminals.*

Proposition 3. *Suppose that $G = (N, \Sigma, P, S, F)$ is an ϵ-free BCFG. Then $L^\infty(G) \cap \Sigma^* = L^*(G)$.*

Corollary 1. *A language $L \subseteq \Sigma^*$ is in BCFL iff L is in CFL.*

Remark 1. Suppose that $G = (N, \Sigma, P, S, F)$ is a BCFG with $F = N$. By an argument similar to the proof of the well-known pumping lemma for ordinary context-free languages we show that if $L^\infty(G) \cap \Sigma^*$ is infinite, then $L^\infty(G)$ contains an infinite word. Indeed, without loss of generality we may assume that G is ϵ-free without chain productions and useless nonterminals. Since $L^\infty(G) \cap \Sigma^*$ is infinite, there is a word $w \in L^\infty(G) \cap \Sigma^+$ with a finite strictly well-founded derivation tree rooted S such that at least one nonterminal is repeated along some path. This implies that w can be written as $xyuvz$ such that $yv \neq \epsilon$ and for some nonterminal A we have $S \Rightarrow^* xAz$, $A \Rightarrow^* yAv$ and $A \Rightarrow^* u$. Since $F = N$ we have $A \in F$. Thus, $S \Rightarrow^\infty xy^\omega v^{-\omega} z$, showing that $L^\infty(G)$ contains the infinite word $xy^\omega v^{-\omega} z$.

5 Closure Properties

In this section we establish the fact that BCFL's are effectively closed under substitution and use this result to derive the closure of BCFL's under the operations of union, concatenation, $^\omega$-power, $^{-\omega}$-power, $^\eta$-power and $^\infty$-power. Recall the definition of language substitution from Section 2.

Theorem 1. *If the languages L, L_a, $a \in \Sigma$ are BCFL's then so is $L' = L[a \leftarrow L_a]_{a \in \Sigma}$. Moreover, given BCFG's generating the languages L, L_a, $a \in \Sigma$, one can effectively construct a BCFG generating L'.*

Corollary 2. *The class BCFL is effectively closed under binary set union, concatenation, ω-power, $-\omega$-power, η-power and ∞-power.*

Thus, for example, given a BCFG generating L, one can effectively construct a BCFG generating L^η. Moreover, for any ordinary context-free language $L \subseteq \Sigma^*$, L^ω, $L^{-\omega}$, L^η, L^∞ are BCFL's. We mention the following results.

Proposition 4. *If L is a Büchi context-free language, then L^r, $\mathrm{Pre}(L)$, $\mathrm{Suf}(L)$, $\mathrm{In}(L)$ and $\mathrm{Sub}(L)$ are all effectively Büchi context-free languages.*

Proposition 5. *For every alphabet Σ, the set of all dense words in Σ^∞ and the set of all quasi-dense words in Σ^∞ are BCFL's.*

Remark 2. Since a language of finite words $L \subseteq \Sigma^*$ is a BCFL iff it is a CFL, and since CFL's are not closed under intersection, it follows that BCFL's are not closed under complementation and intersection either.

6   Some Decidable Properties

In this section we show that it is decidable in polynomial time for a Büchi context free language given by a BCFG whether it is empty, consists of finite words, consists of infinite words, consists of ω-words, consists of well-ordered words, consists of scattered words, or it consists of dense words. We also establish a limitedness property of BCFL's.

Let $G = (N, \Sigma, P, S, F)$ be a BCFG. We define a directed graph Γ_G whose set of vertices is N. There is an edge $A \to B$ exactly when B occurs on the right side of a production whose left side is A. We partition N into strongly connected components. As usual, the strongly connected components can be partially ordered by $S \leq S'$ iff there is a sequence of nonterminals $A_0, \ldots, A_m$ such that $A_0 \in S'$, $A_m \in S$ and for each $i < m$ there is an edge from A_i to A_{i+1}.

The first fact is clear, since for every BCFG one can construct in polynomial time an equivalent BCFG without useless nonterminals.

Theorem 2. *It is decidable in polynomial time whether a BCFG generates an empty language.*

Theorem 3. *Let $G = (N, \Sigma, P, S, F)$ be a weakly ϵ-free BCFG having no useless nonterminal. Then $L^\infty(G)$ contains an infinite word iff there is a strongly connected component S of Γ_G which contains a nonterminal in F, and there is a production $A \to p$ with $A \in S$ such that $|p| \geq 2$ and at least one nonterminal in S occurs in p.*

Corollary 3. *It is decidable in polynomial time whether the language $L^\infty(G)$ generated by a given BCFG G consists of finite words.*

Theorem 4. *It is decidable in polynomial time whether the language $L^\infty(G)$ generated by a given BCFG $G = (N, \Sigma, P, S, F)$ contains only infinite words.*

Below, we will make use of the notion of the *rank* of a scattered countable word. Let Σ be an alphabet. We define the sequence $(V_\alpha^\Sigma)_\alpha$ of subsets of Σ^∞, where α ranges over all countable ordinals. Let $V_0^\Sigma = \Sigma^*$. Then for any countable ordinal $\alpha > 0$, let V_α^Σ be the least set of words closed under finite concatenation which contains $\bigcup_{\beta < \alpha} V_\beta^\Sigma$ together with all words of the form $u_0 u_1 \ldots u_i \ldots$ and $\ldots u_i \ldots u_1 u_0$, where each u_i, $i < \omega$ is in $V_{\beta_i}^\Sigma$ for some β_i with $\beta_i < \alpha$. The following fact is immediate from Hausdorff's theorem [21].

Proposition 6. *A word in Σ^∞ is scattered iff it belongs to V_α^Σ for some countable ordinal α.*

Definition 6. *The* rank *of a scattered word w in Σ^∞ is the least ordinal α such that w is in V_α^Σ. If this ordinal is finite we say that w is of finite rank.*

Example 6. Consider the following languages over the singleton alphabet. Let $L_0 = \{a\}$ and $L_{n+1} = \{w^\omega, w^{-\omega} : w \in L_n\}$, for all $n < \omega$. Then for each n and for each word $w \in L_n$, we have that w is scattered of rank n. In particular, let $w_0 = a$ and $w_{n+1} = w_n^\omega$, for all $n < \omega$. Then each w_n is scattered of rank n.

Example 7. For any alphabet Σ and $n < \omega$, the set L_n of all scattered words in Σ^∞ of rank at most n is a BCFL: $L_0 = \Sigma^*$ and $L_{n+1} = (L_n^\omega \cup L_n^{-\omega})^*$.

Theorem 5. *Let $G = (N, \Sigma, P, S, F)$ be a weakly ϵ-free BCFG with no useless nonterminals. Then $L^\infty(G)$ consists of scattered words iff for each strongly connected component S of Γ_G with $S \cap F \neq \emptyset$ and for each production $A \to p$ with $A \in S$, the word p contains at most one occurrence of a nonterminal in S.*

Corollary 4. *It is decidable in polynomial time whether the language $L^\infty(G)$ generated by a given BCFG G contains only scattered words.*

Corollary 5. *Suppose that $G = (N, \Sigma, P, S, F)$ is a BCFG such that $L^\infty(G)$ contains only scattered words. Then the rank of each word in $L^\infty(G)$ is at most the number of nonterminals in N.*

Corollary 6. *Let $w_0 = a$ and $w_{n+1} = (w_n)^\omega$ for all $n < \omega$. There exists no BCFL consisting only of scattered words containing all words w_n, for all $n < \omega$. In particular, for any alphabet Σ, the set of all scattered words in Σ^∞ is not a BCFL. Similarly, the set of all well-ordered words in Σ^∞ is not a BCFL.*

The language of all quasi-dense words in Σ^∞ is a BCFL, while its complement, the language of all scattered words in Σ^∞ is not. Thus we have:

Corollary 7. *For every alphabet Σ, including the singleton alphabet, the set of all BCFL's in Σ^∞ is not closed under complementation.*

Definition 7. *Suppose that $L \subseteq \Sigma^\infty$ is a language consisting of scattered words of finite rank bounded by some $n < \omega$. Then we define the rank of L as the maximum rank of a word in L.*

Theorem 6. *There is a polynomial time algorithm to compute the rank of a BCFL of scattered words generated by a BCFG.*

Theorem 7. *Let $G = (N, \Sigma, P, S, F)$ be a weakly ϵ-free BCFG with no useless nonterminals. Then $L^\infty(G)$ contains only well-ordered words iff for each strongly connected component S of Γ_G containing a nonterminal in F and for each production $A \to p$ with $A \in S$, if p contains a nonterminal in S then it contains a single occurrence of such a nonterminal, and moreover, this nonterminal is the rightmost letter of p.*

Corollary 8. *It is decidable in polynomial time whether the language $L^\infty(G)$ generated by a given BCFG G contains only well-ordered words.*

Theorem 8. *Suppose that $G = (N, \Sigma, P, S.F)$ is a weakly ϵ-free BCFG without useless nonterminals and chain productions. Then $L^\infty(G)$ consists of finite and ω-words iff the following holds: Whenever S is a strongly connected component of Γ_G containing a nonterminal in F such that for at least one production whose left side is in S, the right side of the production contains a nonterminal in S, and whenever $A \in S$, then there is no finite derivation $S \Rightarrow^* pAp'$ for any words $p, p' \in (N \cup \Sigma)^*$ such that $p' \neq \epsilon$.*

Corollary 9. *It can be decided in polynomial time whether the language generated by a BCFG contains only finite or ω-words, or only ω-words.*

Theorem 9. *It is decidable in polynomial time for a BCFG $G = (N, \Sigma, P, S, F)$ whether each word in $L^\infty(G)$ is dense.*

7   A Comparison

In this section, we compare the class of regular ω-languages [19] and the class of context-free ω-languages as defined by Cohen and Gold [12] with the class of those ω-languages that are BCFL's.

Recall that a Büchi automaton is a system $\mathbf{A} = (Q, \Sigma, \delta, q_0, F)$ which consists of an alphabet Q of states, an alphabet Σ of letters, a transition relation $\delta \subseteq Q \times \Sigma \times Q$, an initial state $q_0 \in Q$ and a set F of repeated states. A run of the automaton $\mathbf{A}$ on a word $w = a_0 a_1 \ldots \in \Sigma^\omega$ is a sequence of states $q_0, q_1, \ldots$ where q_0 is the initial state and $(q_i, a_i, q_{i+1}) \in \delta$ holds for all i. Moreover, it is required that at least one state in F occurs infinitely often in the run. The automaton $\mathbf{A}$ accepts the language $L(\mathbf{A}) \subseteq \Sigma^\omega$ consisting of those words having at least one run. An ω-language is regular if some Büchi automaton accepts it.

Proposition 7. *Every regular language $L \subseteq \Sigma^\omega$ is a BCFL.*

Theorem 10. *An ω-language is a BCFL if and only if it is context-free in the sense of Cohen and Gold [12].*

Remark 3. The papers [8,3] define finite automata acting on infinite words and using this automaton model, provide a definition of recognizable languages of both countable words and all words with no upper bound on the cardinality of the word. Here we briefly compare BCFL's with the class REC of recognizable languages of countable words. On one hand, for any alphabet Σ, the set of all well-ordered words in Σ^{∞} is in REC but not in BCFL. On the other hand, any nonregular context-free language in Σ^* is a BCFL which is not in REC. Thus, the two classes REC and BCFL are incomparable.

8 An Undecidable Property

The main result of this section is that for any fixed alphabet Σ, it is undecidable whether a BCFL given by a BCFG is the universal language Σ^{∞}.

First we note that the language $\Sigma^{+\infty} = \Sigma^{\infty}\Sigma\Sigma^{\infty}$ of all nonempty words in Σ^{∞} is a BCFL. Next, the set of all words in Σ^{∞} with no first letter is also a BCFL since it can be given as $(\Sigma^{+\infty})^{-\omega} \cup \{\epsilon\}$. Consider now the set of all words in Σ^{∞} having a first letter. This set can be subdivided into two sets: 1. All words starting with an ω-word which is a BCFL given by $\Sigma^{\omega}\Sigma^{\infty}$. 2. All words starting with a nonempty finite word followed by a word that does not have a first letter. This is again a BCFL given by the expression $\Sigma^+((\Sigma^{+\infty})^{-\omega} \cup \{\epsilon\})$.

Suppose now that $G = (N, \Sigma, P, S)$ is an ordinary CFG with no ϵ-productions generating the language of finite words $L = L(G) \subseteq \Sigma^+$. Then consider the following language $L' \subseteq \Sigma^{\infty}$. L' consists of all words in Σ^{∞} not having a first letter together with all words that start with an ω-word as well as those words starting with a finite word in L followed by a word not having a first letter. An expression for this language is $((\Sigma^{+\infty})^{-\omega} \cup \{\epsilon\}) \cup \Sigma^{\omega}\Sigma^{\infty} \cup L((\Sigma^{+\infty})^{-\omega} \cup \{\epsilon\})$, showing that L' is a BCFL.

Lemma 3. $L' = \Sigma^{\infty}$ *iff* $L = \Sigma^+$.

Since it is undecidable for an ordinary context-free grammar without ϵ-productions over a fixed alphabet of size at least two whether it generates the language of all finite nonempty words, and since BCFL's are effectively closed under the operations that appear in the above expressions, we immediately have that the universality problem is undecidable for BCFL's.

Proposition 8. *Let Σ be an alphabet of size at least two. Then it is undecidable for a BCFG $G = (N, \Sigma, P, S, F)$ whether $L^{\infty}(G) = \Sigma^{\infty}$.*

Theorem 11. *It is undecidable for a BCFG G over the unary alphabet $\{a\}$ whether $L^{\infty}(G) = \{a\}^{\infty}$.*

9   Müller Context-Free Languages

In this section we define context-free grammars with Müller acceptance condition and show that their generative power strictly exceeds the generating power of context-free grammars with Büchi acceptance condition.

Definition 8. *A context-free grammar with Müller acceptance condition, or MCFG is a system $G = (N, \Sigma, P, S, \mathcal{F})$ where (N, Σ, P, S) is an (ordinary) CFG and $\mathcal{F}$ is a set of subsets of N.*

When G is such an MCFG, a derivation tree t over G is defined as for BCFG's except that we require that for every infinite path π of t, the set of nonterminals occurring infinitely often as a vertex label along π belongs to $\mathcal{F}$. We write $X \Rightarrow^\infty p$ when there is a derivation tree with root symbol X and frontier word p.

Definition 9. *Let $G = (N, \Sigma, P, S, \mathcal{F})$ be an MCFG. The language $L^\infty(G)$ generated by G is the collection of all words $u \in \Sigma^\infty$ that are frontier words of some derivation tree whose root symbol is S. A language $L \subseteq \Sigma^\infty$ is called a Müller context-free language, or an MCFL, if L is generated by some MCFG.*

Theorem 12. *BCFL is strictly included in MCFL.*

In fact, an MCFL that is not a BCFL is provided by Corollary 6.

10   Conclusion and Further Research Topics

We have defined two types of context-free grammars generating languages of countable words, BCFG's and MCFG's, corresponding to the Büchi- and Müller-type acceptance conditions of automata on ω-words and automata on infinite trees. We showed that BCFG's can be transformed into equivalent BCFG's that are (weakly) ϵ-free and do not have chain productions or useless nonterminals. We established several closure properties of the class BCFL of languages that can be generated by BCFG's. We proved that many properties, including several order theoretic properties of BCFL's are decidable in polynomial time, whereas the universality problem is undecidable even for the single letter alphabet. We showed that the BCFL's of finite words are exactly the usual CFL's, and that the ω-languages that are BCFL's are exactly the context-free ω-languages of Cohen and Gold [12]. We showed that every BCFL of scattered words consists of words of finite bounded rank. Finally we showed that there is a language that can be generated by an MCFG which is not a BCFL.

It follows from our proof of Theorem 4 that it is decidable in polynomial time whether a finite word belongs to the language generated by a BCFG. The same question for regular words seems very interesting, where a regular word may be defined as a word generated by a BCFG which contains exactly one production for each nonterminal.

The present paper focuses on BCFG's and BCFL's. It would be interesting to see how much differently MCFG's behave. We have seen that they have a strictly larger generative power, and they also have different algorithmic properties. It would also be interesting to develop a suitable pushdown automaton model.

References

1. Bedon, N.: Finite automata and ordinals. Theor. Comp. Sci. 156, 119–144 (1996)
2. Bedon, N., Bès, A., Carton, O., Rispal, C.: Logic and rational languages of words indexed by linear orderings. In: Hirsch, E.A., Razborov, A.A., Semenov, A., Slissenko, A. (eds.) CSR 2008. LNCS, vol. 5010, pp. 76–85. Springer, Heidelberg (2008)
3. Bès, A., Carton, O.: A Kleene theorem for languages of words indexed by linear orderings. In: De Felice, C., Restivo, A. (eds.) DLT 2005. LNCS, vol. 3572, pp. 158–167. Springer, Heidelberg (2005)
4. Bloom, S.L., Choffrut, Ch.: Long words: the theory of concatenation and ω-power. Theor. Comp. Sci. 259, 533–548 (2001)
5. Bloom, S.L., Ésik, Z.: Axiomating omega and omega-op powers of words. Theor. Inform. Appl. 38, 3–17 (2004)
6. Bloom, S.L., Ésik, Z.: The equational theory of regular words. Inform. and Comput. 197, 55–89 (2005)
7. Bloom, S.L., Ésik, Z.: Regular and algebraic words and ordinals. In: Mossakowski, T., Montanari, U., Haveraaen, M. (eds.) CALCO 2007. LNCS, vol. 4624, pp. 1–15. Springer, Heidelberg (2007)
8. Bruyère, V., Carton, O.: Automata on linear orderings. J. Comput. System Sci. 73, 1–24 (2007)
9. Büchi, J.R.: Weak second-order arithmetic and finite automata. Z. Math. Logik und Grundlagen Math. 6, 66–92 (1960)
10. Büchi, J.R.: The monadic second order theory of ω_1. In: Decidable theories, II. Lecture Notes in Math., vol. 328, pp. 1–127. Springer, Heidelberg (1973)
11. Choueka, Y.: Finite automata, definable sets, and regular expressions over ω^n-tapes. J. Comput. System Sci. 17(1), 81–97 (1978)
12. Cohen, R.S., Gold, A.Y.: Theory of ω-languages, parts one and two. Journal of Computer and System Science 15, 169–208 (1977)
13. Courcelle, B.: Frontiers of infinite trees. RAIRO Theor. Inf. 12, 319–337 (1978)
14. Doner, J.: Tree acceptors and some of their applications. J. Comput. System Sci. 4, 406–451 (1970)
15. Ésik, Z., Ito, M., Kuich, W.: Linear languages of finite and infinite words (to appear)
16. Gécseg, F., Steinby, M.: Tree automata. Akadémiai Kiadó, Budapest (1984)
17. Heilbrunner, S.: An algorithm for the solution of fixed-point equations for infinite words. RAIRO Theor. Inf. 14, 131–141 (1980)
18. Nivat, M.: Sur les ensembles de mots infinis engendrés par une grammaire algébrique (French). RAIRO Inform. Théor. 12(3), 259–278 (1978)
19. Perrin, D., Pin, J.-E.: Infinite Words. Elsevier, Amsterdam (2004)
20. Rabin, M.O.: Decidability of second-order theories and automata on infinite trees. Trans. Amer. Math. Soc. 141, 1–35 (1969)
21. Rosenstein, J.G.: Linear Orderings. Academic Press, London (1982)
22. Thatcher, J.W., Wright, J.B.: Generalized finite automata theory with an application to a decision problem of second-order logic. Math. Systems Theory 2, 57–81 (1968)
23. Thomas, W.: On frontiers of regular sets. RAIRO Theor. Inf. 20, 371–381 (1986)
24. Thomas, W.: Automata on infinite objects. In: Handbook of Theoretical Computer Science, vol. B, pp. 135–191. Elsevier, Amsterdam (1990)
25. Wojciechowski, J.: Classes of transfinite sequences accepted by finite automata. Fundamenta Informaticæ 7, 191–223 (1984)
26. Wojciechowski, J.: Finite automata on transfinite sequences and regular expressions. Fundamenta Informaticæ 8, 379–396 (1985)

Automatic Conflict Detection on Contracts*

Stephen Fenech[1], Gordon J. Pace[1], and Gerardo Schneider[2]

[1] Dept. of Computer Science, University of Malta, Malta
[2] Dept. of Informatics, University of Oslo, Norway
{sfen002,gordon.pace}@um.edu.mt, gerardo@ifi.uio.no

Abstract. Many software applications are based on collaborating, yet compet-
ing, agents or virtual organisations exchanging services. Contracts, expressing
obligations, permissions and prohibitions of the different actors, can be used to
protect the interests of the organisations engaged in such service exchange. However, the potentially dynamic composition of services with different contracts, and
the combination of service contracts with local contracts can give rise to unex-
pected conflicts, exposing the need for automatic techniques for contract analysis.
In this paper we look at automatic analysis techniques for contracts written in the
contract language $\mathcal{CL}$. We present a trace semantics of $\mathcal{CL}$ suitable for conflict
analysis, and a decision procedure for detecting conflicts (together with its proof
of soundness, completeness and termination). We also discuss its implementation
and look into the applications of the contract analysis approach we present. These
techniques are applied to a small case study of an airline check-in desk.

1 Introduction

Today's trend towards Service-Oriented Architectures (SOA), in which different decou-
pled services distributed not only on different machines within a single organisation but
also outside of it, provides new challenges to reliability and trust. Since an organisation
may need to execute code provided by third parties, it requires mechanisms to protect
itself — one such mechanism is the use of *contracts* giving restrictions on the service
behaviours. Clearly, it is important that such contracts are conflict-free — meaning that
the contracts will never lead to conflicting or contradictory directives.

Services are frequently composed of different sub-services, each of which comes
with its own contract. The top-level service, not only needs to ensure that each single
contract is conflict-free, but also that the composition of all the contracts is itself also
conflict-free. This is true not only for SOA but for any application domain with a need
to specify and monitor prescriptive behaviour.

The concept of contracts has been widely interpreted in the literature, from simple pre/post-conditions, to QoS properties. In this paper, we take the deontic view of
contracts — a contract specifies the normative behaviour of a system, specifying obligations, permissions and prohibitions of actions, as well as the reparations in case of
not respecting an obligation or prohibition. We build upon the contract language $\mathcal{CL}$
[10], which enables formal specification of deontic electronic contracts, and we extend

---

* Partially supported by the Nordunet3 project COSoDIS: "Contract-Oriented Software Development for Internet Services".

the trace semantics given in [6] in order to define and discover potential conflicts in contracts.

Although useful for runtime monitoring of $\mathcal{CL}$ contracts, the semantics given in [6] is not concerned with permissions, and it loses the deontic information (obligations, etc.) of the parties involved in the contract, making it unsuitable for conflict analysis. In this paper, we present an extension of this trace semantics to support conflict analysis, which is proved correct with respect to the original trace semantics. Based on the extended semantics we define the concept of conflicting contracts, and develop and prove the correctness of a decision procedure to detect conflicts in $\mathcal{CL}$ contracts. The algorithm has also been implemented into the tool CLAN for $\mathcal{CL}$ contract analysis.

The paper is organised as follows. We start by presenting $\mathcal{CL}$ in section 2, whose deontic trace semantics is introduced in section 3. The definition and algorithm for conflict analysis is then presented in section 4, where we also present theoretical results concerning correctness of the algorithm. Section 5 presents a small case study to illustrate the use of the analysis, which is compared to related work in section 6. We finally conclude in section 7.

2   The Contract Language $\mathcal{CL}$

Deontic logic [13] enables reasoning about non-normative and normative behaviour (e.g., obligations, permissions and prohibitions), including not only the ideal behaviours but also the exceptional and actual behaviours. One of the main problems of the logic is the difficulty theoreticians have to define a consistent yet expressive formal system, free from paradoxes [8].

Instead of trying to solve the problem of having a complete paradox-free deontic logic, $\mathcal{CL}$ has been designed with the aim to be used on a restricted application domain: electronic contracts. In this way the expressivity of the logic is reduced, resulting in a language free from most classical paradoxes, but still of practical use. $\mathcal{CL}$ is based on a combination of deontic, dynamic and temporal logics, allowing the representation of obligations, permissions and prohibitions, as well as temporal aspects. Moreover, it also gives a means to specify *exceptional* behaviours arising from the violation of obligations (what is to be demanded in case an obligation is not fulfilled) and of prohibitions (what is the penalty in case a prohibition is violated). These are usually known in the deontic community as *Contrary-to-Duties* (CTDs) and *Contrary-to-Prohibitions* (CTPs) respectively. $\mathcal{CL}$ contracts are written using the following syntax:

$$C := C_O \mid C_P \mid C_F \mid C \wedge C \mid [\beta]C \mid \top \mid \bot$$
$$C_O := O_C(\alpha) \mid C_O \oplus C_O$$
$$C_P := P(\alpha) \mid C_P \oplus C_P$$
$$C_F := F_C(\alpha)$$
$$\alpha := 0 \mid 1 \mid \bar{a} \mid a \mid \alpha \,\&\, \alpha \mid \alpha; \alpha \mid \alpha + \alpha$$
$$\beta := \epsilon \mid 0 \mid 1 \mid \bar{a} \mid a \mid \beta \,\&\, \beta \mid \beta; \beta \mid \beta + \beta \mid \beta^*$$

Being $\mathcal{CL}$ an action-based language, we assume a non-empty set of actions $\Sigma = \{a, b, \ldots\}$, together with the three special actions 0, 1 and ϵ explained below. A contract clause C can be either an obligation (C_O), a permission (C_P) or a prohibition (C_F) clause, a conjunction of two clauses, the trivially satisfied contract ($\top$), the impossible contract ($\bot$) or a clause preceded by the dynamic logic square brackets. $O_C(\alpha)$ is interpreted as the obligation to perform α in which case, if violated, then the reparation contract C must be executed (a CTD). An obligation clause may be an exclusive disjunction of two other obligation clauses. This is interpreted as being obliged to satisfy one of the obligations but not both. $F_C(\alpha)$ is interpreted as forbidden to perform α and if α is performed then the reparation C must be executed (a CTP). In what follows we will write $F(\alpha)$ (respectively $O(\alpha)$) instead of $F_\bot(\alpha)$ (respectively $O_\bot(\alpha)$) to denote that there is no CTP (respectively CTD) associated. $[\beta]C$ is interpreted as if action β^1 is performed then the contract C must be executed — if β is not performed, the contract is trivially satisfied. The conjunction of two clauses is interpreted as both clauses have to be satisfied. The trivially satisfied contract $\top$ is satisfied by any sequence of actions whereas the impossible contract $\bot$ cannot be satisfied with any sequence of actions. ϵ is an empty action, 1 is the action that matches any action, while 0 is the impossible action.

Action expressions can be constructed from basic ones using the operators $\&$, ;, $+$ and $*$ where $\&$ stands for the actions occurring concurrently, ; stands for the actions to occur in sequence, $+$ stands for a choice between actions and $*$ is the Kleene star. $\overline{\cdot}$ is the complement, so $\overline{a}$ means "any action except a". In the rest of the paper $\alpha_\&$ will denote basic actions or complex actions constructed from basic actions only using the concurrent operator $\&$ (for example $a, a\&b$). It can be shown that every action expression can be transformed into an equivalent representation where $\&$ appears only at the innermost level. This representation is referred to as the *canonical form*. In the rest of this paper we assume that action expressions have been reduced to this form. We also allow the negation of compound actions in the formal syntax (and semantics). However, one can push negations on action expressions down to the constituent actions. Throughout the rest of the paper, whenever the negation of action expressions is used, it is assumed that the expression will be reduced appropriately. Following [10], we assume there is an action dictionary containing all possible actions, including which actions are contradictory: we write $a\#b$ to denote that a and b are contradictory (for instance "send a message shorter than 5 characters" and "send a message longer than 10 characters").

In order to avoid paradoxes the operators combining obligations, permissions and prohibitions are restricted syntactically. See [10,6] for more details on $\mathcal{CL}$.

As a simple example, let us consider the following clause from an airline company contract: 'When checking in, the traveller is obliged to have a luggage within the weight limit — if exceeded, the traveller is obliged to pay extra.' This would be represented in $\mathcal{CL}$ as $[checkIn]O_{O(pay)}(withinWeightLimit)$.

---

[1] Note that the only differences between the syntactic categories representing actions (α and β) is $\cdot^*$. α is restricted to be used only under obligations, permissions and prohibitions, while β only in "conditions".

3   Deontic Trace Semantics

In this section, we will introduce a new finite trace semantics of $\mathcal{CL}$ that includes deontic information — which obligations, permissions and prohibitions are enacted at each step of the trace. This will enable us to detect conflicts in a contract, by looking at finite traces allowed by the semantics leading to incompatible normative behaviour — for example both obliging and forbidding the same action at the same time.

Let us consider a simple example to better understand the need of a finite trace semantics with deontic information. Let $C = [a]O(b) \wedge [b]F(b)$ be a contract on the action alphabet $\{a, b\}$ we want to check for conflicts. According to the $\mathcal{CL}$ (infinite) trace semantics given in [6], the set of traces "accepted" by the contract C is $\{\langle a, b, any\rangle \mid any = (a + b)^\omega\} \cup \{\langle b, a, any\rangle \mid any = (a + b)^\omega\}$. According to the semantics, no trace starting with action $\{a, b\}$ (i.e., with a and b occurring concurrently) will be accepted by the contract, since this would imply a contract violation due to the enacted conflicting obligation and prohibition. Moreover, there is no deontic information in the trace, making it difficult to capture the notion of conflict. Since our aim is to obtain a witness of such a conflict, and in particular a systematic way to obtain an automaton that recognises such prefixes containing conflicts, it is necessary to extend the trace semantics. This extension includes: (1) The addition of deontic information (which obligations, permissions and prohibitions are satisfied at any moment), (2) The addition of a trace semantics for permission (this was not present in the original trace semantics), (3) The addition of the possibility to "accept" certain finite prefixes (in order to get the witness for conflicts). With this new semantics we will be able to automatically obtain an automaton accepting exactly the (finite prefix) traces "accepted" by the contract, including those witnesses for conflict detection.

For a contract with action alphabet Σ, we will introduce its deontic alphabet Σ_d which consists of O_a, P_a and F_a for each action $a \in \Sigma$, that will be used to represent which normative behaviour is enacted at a particular moment. Given a set of concurrent actions α, we will write O_α to represent $\{O_a \mid a \in \alpha\}$.

Given a $\mathcal{CL}$ contract C with action alphabet Σ, the semantics will be expressed in the form $\sigma, \sigma_d \vDash C$, where σ is a finite trace of sets of concurrent actions in Σ and σ_d is a finite trace consisting on sets of sets[2] of deontic information in Σ_d. The statement $\sigma, \sigma_d \vDash C$ is said to be well-formed if $length(\sigma) = length(\sigma_d)$. In the rest of the paper we will consider only well-formed semantic statements.

A well-formed statement $\sigma, \sigma_d \vDash C$ will correspond to the statement that action sequence σ is possible under (will not break) contract C, with σ_d being the deontic statements enforced from the contract.

Let us consider again the contract $C = [a]O(b) \wedge [b]F(b)$, and the trace $\sigma = \langle\{a\}, \{b\}\rangle$, then $\sigma_d = \langle\{\emptyset\}, \{\{O_b\}\}\rangle$, and we have that $\sigma, \sigma_d \vDash C$. The contract $C' = F(c) \wedge [1](O(a) \wedge F(b))$, for example, stipulates that it is forbidden to perform action c and that after the execution of any action, there is an obligation to perform an a (while prohibiting the execution of b), so we can write $\sigma_d = \langle\{\{F_c\}\}, \{\{O_a\}, \{F_b\}\}\rangle$. The contract allows the execution of actions a and b concurrently, and then a concurrently with c ($\sigma = \langle\{a, b\}, \{a, c\}\rangle$), and we have that $\sigma, \sigma_d \vDash C'$. As a final example, let

---

[2] This is needed to distinguish choices from conjunction.

$$\sigma, \sigma_d \vDash C \quad \text{if} \quad length(\sigma) = length(\sigma_d) = 0 \tag{1}$$

$$\sigma, \sigma_d \vDash \top \quad \text{if} \quad \sigma_d(0) = \emptyset \text{ and } \sigma(1..), \sigma_d(1..) \vDash \top \tag{2}$$

$$\sigma, \sigma_d \vDash C_1 \wedge C_2 \quad \text{if} \quad \sigma, \sigma_d' \vDash C_1 \text{ and } \sigma, \sigma_d'' \vDash C_2 \text{ and } \sigma_d = \sigma_d' \cup \sigma_d'' \tag{3}$$

$$\sigma, \sigma_d \vDash C_1 \oplus C_2 \quad \text{if} \quad (\sigma, \sigma_d \vDash C_1 \text{ and } \sigma, \sigma_d \nvDash C_2) \text{ or } (\sigma, \sigma_d \vDash C_2 \text{ and } \sigma, \sigma_d \nvDash C_1) \tag{4}$$

$$\sigma, \sigma_d \vDash [\epsilon]C \quad \text{if} \quad \sigma, \sigma_d \vDash C \tag{5}$$

$$\sigma, \sigma_d \vDash [\alpha_\&]C \quad \text{if} \quad (\alpha_\& \nsubseteq \sigma(0) \Rightarrow \sigma, \sigma_d \vDash \top) \text{ and} \tag{6}$$

$$(\alpha_\& \subseteq \sigma(0) \Rightarrow (\sigma_d(0) = \emptyset \text{ and } \sigma(1..), \sigma_d(1..) \vDash C)) \tag{7}$$

$$\sigma, \sigma_d \vDash [\overline{\alpha_\&}]C \quad \text{if} \quad (\alpha_\& \subseteq \sigma(0) \Rightarrow \sigma, \sigma_d \vDash \top) \text{ and} \tag{8}$$

$$(\alpha_\& \nsubseteq \sigma(0) \Rightarrow (\sigma_d(0) = \emptyset \text{ and } \sigma(1..), \sigma_d(1..) \vDash C)) \tag{9}$$

$$\sigma, \sigma_d \vDash [\beta; \beta']C \quad \text{if} \quad \sigma, \sigma_d \vDash [\beta][\beta']C \tag{10}$$

$$\sigma, \sigma_d \vDash [\beta + \beta']C \quad \text{if} \quad \sigma, \sigma_d \vDash [\beta]C \wedge [\beta']C \tag{11}$$

$$\sigma, \sigma_d \vDash [\beta^*]C \quad \text{if} \quad \sigma, \sigma_d \vDash C \wedge [\beta][\beta^*]C \tag{12}$$

$$\sigma, \sigma_d \vDash O_C(\alpha_\&) \quad \text{if} \quad \sigma_d(0) = O_{\alpha_\&} \text{ and} \tag{13}$$

$$(\alpha_\& \subseteq \sigma(0) \Rightarrow \sigma(1..), \sigma_d(1..) \vDash \top) \text{ and} \tag{14}$$

$$(\alpha_\& \nsubseteq \sigma(0) \Rightarrow \sigma(1..), \sigma_d(1..) \vDash C) \tag{15}$$

$$\sigma, \sigma_d \vDash O_C(\alpha; \alpha') \quad \text{if} \quad \sigma, \sigma_d \vDash O_C(\alpha) \wedge [\alpha]O_C(\alpha') \tag{16}$$

$$\sigma, \sigma_d \vDash O_C(\alpha + \alpha') \quad \text{if} \quad \sigma, \sigma_d \vDash O_\top(\alpha) \wedge O_\top(\alpha') \wedge [\overline{\alpha + \alpha'}]C \tag{17}$$

$$\sigma, \sigma_d \vDash F_C(\alpha_\&) \quad \text{if} \quad \sigma_d(0) = F_{\alpha_\&} \text{ and} \tag{18}$$

$$(\alpha_\& \subseteq \sigma(0) \Rightarrow \sigma(1..), \sigma_d(1..) \vDash C) \text{ and} \tag{19}$$

$$(\alpha_\& \nsubseteq \sigma(0) \Rightarrow \sigma(1..), \sigma_d(1..) \vDash \top) \tag{20}$$

$$\sigma, \sigma_d \vDash F_C(\alpha; \alpha') \quad \text{if} \quad \sigma, \sigma_d \vDash F_\perp(\alpha) \text{ or } \sigma, \sigma_d \vDash [\alpha]F_C(\alpha') \tag{21}$$

$$\sigma, \sigma_d \vDash F_C(\alpha + \alpha') \quad \text{if} \quad \sigma, \sigma_d \vDash F_C(\alpha) \wedge F_C(\alpha') \tag{22}$$

$$\sigma, \sigma_d \vDash P(\alpha_\&) \quad \text{if} \quad \sigma_d(0) = P_{\alpha_\&} \text{ and } \sigma(1..), \sigma_d(1..) \vDash \top \tag{23}$$

$$\sigma, \sigma_d \vDash P(\alpha; \alpha') \quad \text{if} \quad \sigma, \sigma_d \vDash P(\alpha) \wedge [\alpha]P(\alpha') \tag{24}$$

$$\sigma, \sigma_d \vDash P(\alpha + \alpha') \quad \text{if} \quad \sigma, \sigma_d \vDash P(\alpha) \wedge P(\alpha') \tag{25}$$

Fig. 1. The deontic trace semantics of $\mathcal{CL}$

us consider the contract $C'' = [a]O(b+c) \wedge [b]F(b)$. In this case, due to the choice inside the obligation, we get that given the trace $\sigma = \langle \{a\}, \{b\} \rangle$ then $\sigma_d = \langle \{\emptyset\}, \{\{O_b, O_c\}\} \rangle$, and we have that $\sigma, \sigma_d \vDash C''$.

Given two traces σ_1 and σ_2, we will use $\sigma_1; \sigma_2$ to denote their concatenation, and $\sigma_1 \cup \sigma_2$ (provided the length of σ_1 is equal to that of σ_2) to denote the point-wise union of the traces: $\langle \sigma_1(0) \cup \sigma_2(0), \sigma_1(1) \cup \sigma_2(1), \ldots \sigma_1(n) \cup \sigma_2(n) \rangle$. In what follows we explain our new trace semantics, shown in Fig. 1.[3]

Basic conditions: Empty traces satisfy any contract, as shown in Fig. 1-(1).

---

[3] Due to lack of space, we do not present the trivial cases of actions 0 and 1, and they are omitted in the rest of the paper.

Done, Break: The simplest definitions are those of the trivially satisfiable contract $\top$, and the unsatisfiable contract $\bot$. In the case of $\bot$, only an empty sequence will not have yet broken the contract, while in the case of $\top$, any sequence of actions satisfies the contract (whenever no obligation, prohibition, or permission is present on the trace). See Fig. 1 line (2).

Conjunctions: For the conjunction of two contracts, the action trace must satisfy both contracts, and the deontic traces are combined point-wise. See Fig. 1 line (3).

Exclusive disjunction: Similar to conjunctions. See Fig. 1 line (4). (Note that the rule is valid only for C_1 and C_2 being both of the form C_O, or C_P. In the rest of the paper we will continue to write $C_1 \oplus C_2$ with the understanding that the above restriction applies.)

Conditions: Conditions are handled structurally. Note that using the normal form defined in [6], one can push concurrent actions to the bottom level. See Fig. 1 lines (5)–(12).

Obligations: Obligations, like conditions, are defined structurally on action expressions. The base case of the action simply consisting of a conjunction of actions that can be dealt with by ensuring that if the actions are present in the action trace, then the contract is satisfied, otherwise the reparation is enacted. The case for the sequential composition of two action sequences is handled simply by rewriting into a pair of obligations. The case of choice (+) is the most complex case, in which we have to consider the possibility of having either obligation satisfied or neither satisfied, hence triggering the reparation. Recall that the star operator cannot appear within obligations. See Fig. 1 lines (13)–(17).

Prohibitions: Dealing with prohibitions is similar to obligations, with the main difference being that prohibition of choice is more straightforward to express. See Fig. 1 lines (18)–(22).

Permissions: The aim of the original trace semantics of $\mathcal{CL}$ [6] was to provide a linear time semantics to the language, appropriate for applications such as runtime verification. Since a single linear trace does not give any information whether a permission clause has been found to be in conflict with other clauses or not, the original semantics simply discarded permission clauses. However, to reason about conflicts, the fact that a permission operator has been enacted is important. See Fig. 1 lines (23)–(25) for the semantics.

4   Conflict Analysis

Conflicts in contracts arise from four different reasons. The first two reasons are being obliged and forbidden to perform the same action (e.g., $O(a) \wedge F(a)$), and being permitted and forbidden to perform the same action (e.g., $P(a) \wedge F(a)$). In the first conflict we would end up in a situation where whatever is performed will violate the contract. The second conflict would not result in having a trace that violates the contract since in the trace semantics permissions cannot be broken, however, we can still identify these situations due to the deontic trace. The remaining two kinds of conflicts correspond to obligations of contradictory actions (e.g., $O(a) \wedge O(b)$ with $a \# b$), and permissions and obligations of contradictory actions (e.g., $P(a) \wedge O(b)$ with $a \# b$).

Before defining formally what a conflict-free contract is, we recall our motivating example, the contract $[a]O(b) \wedge [b]F(b)$ with allowed actions a and b. It is clear that both traces $\sigma_1 = \langle \{a\}, \{b\} \rangle$ and $\sigma_2 = \langle \{b\}, \{a\} \rangle$ satisfy the contract. However, any trace starting with concurrent actions $\{a, b\}$ (e.g., $\langle \{a, b\}, \{b\} \rangle$) will not be accepted by the contract since any action following it will violate either the obligation to perform b or the prohibition from performing b. In this case, since unspecified, the reparation is the $\perp$ clause which cannot be satisfied regardless of what action is performed.

In what follows we define the notion of conflict-free contract at the semantic level, formalising the four cases. We show how to obtain an automaton from a contract and discuss an automata-based model checking algorithm for detecting conflicts.

Definition 1. *For a given trace σ_d of a contract C, let $D, D' \subseteq \sigma_d(i)$ (with $i \geq 0$). We say that D is in conflict with D' if and only if there exists at least one element $e \in D$ such that:*

$$e = O_a \wedge (F_a \in D' \vee (P_b \in D' \wedge a\#b) \vee (O_b \in D' \wedge a\#b))$$
$$\text{or } e = P_a \wedge (F_a \in D' \vee (P_b \in D' \wedge a\#b) \vee (O_b \in D' \wedge a\#b))$$
$$\text{or } e = F_a \wedge (P_a \in D' \vee O_a \in D').$$

A contract C is said to be conflict-free *if for all traces σ and σ_d such that $\sigma, \sigma_d \vDash C$, then for any $D, D' \subseteq \sigma_d(i)$ $(0 \leq i \leq len(\sigma_d))$, D and D' are not in conflict.*

Let us consider the contract $C = [a]O(b + c) \wedge [b]F(b)$, then we have that C is not conflict-free since $\langle \{a, b\}, \{b\} \rangle, \langle \{\emptyset\}, \{\{O_b, O_c\}, \{F_b\}\} \rangle \vDash C$, and there are $D, D' \subseteq \sigma_d(1)$ such that D and D' are in conflict. To see this, let us take $D = \{O_b, O_c\}$ and $e = O_b$. We have then that for $D' = \{F_b\}$, $F_b \in D'$ (satisfying the first line of definition 1).

We have then characterised the notion of conflict in contracts by analysing the set of traces accepted by the contract. We now show how to generate a finite-state automaton from a $\mathcal{CL}$ contract C, with the property that the language accepted by the automaton corresponds to the traces given by the semantics of the contract. We also define the notion of conflict in the generated automaton.

Generation of an automaton from a $\mathcal{CL}$ contract. Given a contract C, over an action alphabet Σ and corresponding deontic alphabet Σ_d, we can construct an automaton $A(C) = \langle S, A_\&, s_0, T, V, l, \delta \rangle$ where S is the set of states, $A_\&$ is the set of concurrent actions from Σ, s_0 is the initial state, $T \subseteq S \times A_\& \times S$ is the set of labelled transitions, V is a special violation state, l is a function labelling states with the $\mathcal{CL}$ clause that holds in that state $(l : S \rightarrow \mathcal{CL})$ and $\delta : S \rightarrow 2^{\Sigma_d}$ is a function labelling states with the set of deontic notions that hold in that state. We say that a *run* (sequence of states) is accepted by the automaton if none of the states of the run is V. Similarly, we say that the automaton *accepts a word* w, consisting of a sequence of actions, if none of the actions of w is the label of a transition containing the state V, in which case we write $\text{Accept}(A(C), w)$. Note that the automaton is deterministic.

The construction of the automaton uses the residual contract function f which, given a $\mathcal{CL}$ formula C and an action α, will return the clause that needs to hold in the following step, similarly to the CTL sub-formula construction [2]. f is defined in Fig. 2. The

$$f \;:\; \mathcal{CL} \times A_\& \to \mathcal{CL}$$

$$f(\top, \varphi) = \top$$

$$f(\bot, \varphi) = \bot$$

$$f(C_1 \wedge C_2, \varphi) = f(C_1, \varphi) \wedge f(C_2, \varphi)$$

$$f(C_1 \oplus C_2, \varphi) = \begin{cases} \top & \text{if } (f(C_1,\varphi) = \top \wedge f(C_2,\varphi) = \bot) \vee \\ & \quad (f(C_1,\varphi) = \bot \wedge f(C_2,\varphi) = \top) \\ \bot & \text{if } (f(C_1,\varphi) = f(C_2,\varphi) = \top) \vee \\ & \quad (f(C_1,\varphi) = f(C_2,\varphi) = \bot) \\ f(C_1,\varphi) \oplus f(C_2,\varphi) & \text{otherwise} \end{cases}$$

$$f([\alpha_\&]C, \varphi) = \begin{cases} C & \text{if } \alpha_\& \subseteq \varphi \\ \top & \text{otherwise} \end{cases}$$

$$f([\overline{\alpha_\&}]C, \varphi) = \begin{cases} C & \text{if } \alpha_\& \not\subseteq \varphi \\ \top & \text{otherwise} \end{cases}$$

$$f([\overline{\alpha;\alpha'}]C, \varphi) = \begin{cases} C & \text{if } (\alpha;\alpha')/\varphi = 0 \\ [\overline{(\alpha;\alpha')/\varphi}]C & \text{otherwise} \end{cases}$$

$$f([\overline{\alpha + \alpha'}]C, \varphi) = f([\overline{\alpha}]C, \varphi) \wedge f([\overline{\alpha'}]C, \varphi)$$

$$f([\beta;\beta']C, \varphi) = f([\beta][\beta']C, \varphi)$$

$$f([\beta + \beta']C, \varphi) = f([\beta]C \wedge [\beta']C, \varphi)$$

$$f([\beta^*]C, \varphi) = f(C \wedge [\beta][\beta^*]C, \varphi)$$

$$f(O_C(\alpha_\&), \varphi) = \begin{cases} \top & \text{if } \alpha_\& \subseteq \varphi \\ C & \text{otherwise} \end{cases}$$

$$f(O_C(\alpha;\alpha'), \varphi) = f(O_C(\alpha) \wedge [\alpha]O_C(\alpha'), \varphi)$$

$$f(O_C(\alpha + \alpha'), \varphi) = \begin{cases} \top & \text{if } f(O_\bot(\alpha), \varphi) = \top \text{ or } f(O_\bot(\alpha'), \varphi) = \top \\ C & \text{if } f(O_\bot(\alpha), \varphi) = \bot \text{ and } f(O_\bot(\alpha'), \varphi) = \bot \\ O_C(\alpha + \alpha'/\varphi) & \text{otherwise} \end{cases}$$

$$f(F_C(\alpha_\&), \varphi) = \begin{cases} C & \text{if } \alpha_\& \subseteq \varphi \\ \top & \text{otherwise} \end{cases}$$

$$f(F_C(\alpha;\alpha'), \varphi) = f([\alpha]F_C(\alpha'), \varphi)$$

$$f(F_C(\alpha + \alpha'), \varphi) = f(F_C(\alpha) \wedge F_C(\alpha'))$$

$$f(P(\alpha_\&), \varphi) = \top$$

$$f(P(\alpha \cdot \alpha'), \varphi) = f(P(\alpha) \wedge [\alpha]P(\alpha'), \varphi)$$

$$f(P(\alpha + \alpha'), \varphi) = f(P(\alpha) \wedge P(\alpha'), \varphi)$$

Fig. 2. The residual function f

binary operator $/$ used in f, that gives the tail of the left-hand side sequence of actions if its head matches the right-hand side action, is defined inductively as follows:

$$\alpha'_\&/\alpha_\& = \epsilon \text{ if } \alpha'_\& \subseteq \alpha_\&, \text{ otherwise } 0$$
$$(0;\alpha)/\alpha_\& = 0$$
$$(1;\alpha)/\alpha_\& = \alpha$$
$$(\alpha;\alpha')/\alpha_\& = (\alpha/\alpha_\&);\alpha'$$
$$(\alpha + \alpha')/\alpha_\& = \alpha/\alpha_\& + \alpha'/\alpha_\&$$

For example, $(a;b)/a$ will give b whereas $((a;b) + (a;c))/a$ will result in $b + c$.

The automaton is built using the construction function f_c shown in Fig. 3, that takes as argument an initial state s_0 where $l(s_0) = C$. Besides the residual function f, f_c

$f_c(s) =$ if $l(s) = 1$ then
$\qquad T := T \cup (s, 1, s)$
$\qquad$ if $l(s) = 0$ then
$\qquad\quad V := s$
$\qquad\quad T := T \cup (V, 1, V)$
$\qquad$ otherwise $\quad \forall a \in A_\&$
$\qquad\quad$ if $\exists\, s' \in S$ s.t. $l(s') = f(l(s), a)$
$\qquad\quad$ then $T := T \cup (s, a, s')$
$\qquad\quad$ otherwise
$\qquad\qquad$ new s'
$\qquad\qquad l(s') := f(l(s), a)$
$\qquad\qquad S := S \cup s'$
$\qquad\qquad T := T \cup (s, a, s')$
$\qquad\qquad d(s') := f_d(l(s'))$
$\qquad\qquad f_c(s')$

$$
\begin{aligned}
f_d(C_1 \wedge C_2) &= f_d(C_1) \cup f_d(C_2) \\
f_d(O(\alpha_\&)) &= \{\{O_{a_1}\}, \dots, \{O_{a_n}\}\} \\
f_d(F(\alpha_\&)) &= \{\{F_{a_1}\}, \dots, \{F_{a_n}\}\} \\
f_d(P(\alpha_\&)) &= \{\{P_{a_1}\}, \dots, \{P_{a_n}\}\} \\
f_d(O(\alpha + \alpha')) &= \{x \cup y \mid x \in f_d(O(\alpha)) \\
&\qquad \text{and } y \in f_d(O(\alpha'))\} \\
f_d(\text{otherwise}) &= \emptyset
\end{aligned}
$$

Fig. 3. The construction function f_c **Fig. 4.** The deontic labelling function f_d

uses function f_d (shown in Fig. 4) that adds all the relevant deontic information to each state (we take $\alpha_\&$ to be equal to $a_1 \& \dots \& a_n$).[4]

As an example, let us consider the contract $[a]O(b) \wedge [b]F(b)$. The automaton is constructed by applying f_c to the state s_0 where $l(s_0) = [a]O(b) \wedge [b]F(b)$. Every possible transition is created (in this case, transitions labelled with a, b and $a\&b$) from this state to a new state labelled with the result of applying function f to the original formula and the label of the transition as parameters. Thus, the state that is reached with the transition labelled with action a is $f([a]O(b) \wedge [b]F(b), a) = O(b)$. If there is another state with the same label, the transition will connect to the existing state and the new one will be discarded (this ensures termination). If there is no such a state, f_c is then recursively called on this new state. Eventually we either reach a satisfying state, a violating state, or a state already labeled with the formula. The corresponding automaton is shown in Fig. 5.[5]

Since our objective is to find conflicts analysing the constructed automaton, we need to define what a conflict is at the automaton level. The definition is straightforward and it is very similar to the definition given for $\mathcal{CL}$ traces.

---

[4] We have omitted the case for $\oplus$ in the deontic labelling function description. In practice, two different automata are created for each one of the choices, and the analysis proceeds as usual. Also note that there is no explicit labelling function for $F(\alpha + \alpha')$ and $P(\alpha + \alpha')$ since these cases are reduced to conjunction.

[5] Note that what is written in each state is the *sub-formula* remaining to be satisfied. Formally speaking, each state will be "marked" with the deontic information as defined by the function f_d. So, $O(a)$ is a syntactic expression in $\mathcal{CL}$, while O_a is the corresponding "marking" at the state saying there is an obligation of doing a.

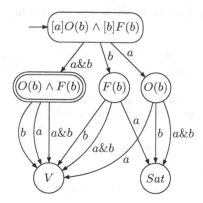

Fig. 5. Automaton for $[a]O(b) \wedge [b]F(b)$

Definition 2. *Given a state s of an automaton $A(C)$, let $D, D' \subseteq f_d(s)$. We say that D is in* conflict *with D' if and only if there exists at least one element e of D such that:*

$$e = O_a \wedge (F_a \in D' \vee (P_b \in D' \wedge a \# b) \vee (O_b \in D' \wedge a \# b))$$
$$or \; e = P_a \wedge (F_a \in D' \vee (P_b \in D' \wedge a \# b) \vee (O_b \in D' \wedge a \# b))$$
$$or \; e = F_a \wedge (P_a \in D' \vee O_a \in D').$$

An automaton $A(C)$ is said to be conflict-free *if for every state $s \in S$, then for any $D, D' \subseteq f_d(s)$, D and D' are not in conflict.*

The automaton shown in Fig. 5 is not conflict-free since there exists a state which is not conflict-free. Consider that s is the double-lined state labelled with $O(b) \wedge F(b)$ then $f_d(s) = \{\{O_b\}, \{F_b\}\}$. Using definition 2, let $e = O_b$. For this state to be conflict-free, any subset $D \in f_s(s)$ should not contain F_b, which is not the case.

Conflict detection algorithm. The main algorithm takes a contract written in $\mathcal{CL}$ and decides whether or not the given contract may reach a state of conflict. Once the automaton was generated from the contract as explained above, the conflict detection algorithm simply consists of a standard forward or backward reachability analysis based on a fix-point computation, looking for states containing conflicts.

For example, performing reachability analysis on the simple contract whose automaton is shown in Fig. 5 would identify that the conflict state labelled $O(b) \wedge F(b)$ is reachable from the initial state upon receiving action $a \& b$, since the state contains the deontic information $\{\{O_b\}, \{F_b\}\}$.

Correctness of the algorithm. We now prove the correctness and completeness of the algorithm, which includes proving the following auxiliary results: (1) The traces accepted by the automaton coincide with those "accepted" by the contract in $\mathcal{CL}$ (according to the trace semantics); (2) A contract C in $\mathcal{CL}$ is conflict-free iff the generated automaton $A(C)$ is conflict-free.

We first prove that the automaton will accept all and only those traces which satisfy the contract.

Lemma 1. *Given a* $\mathcal{CL}$ *contract* C, *the automaton* $A(C)$ *accepts all and only those traces* σ *that satisfy the contract:* $\sigma, \sigma_d \vDash C$ *if and only if* $\mathrm{Accept}(A(C), \sigma)$.

The proof is based on a long and tedious induction on the structure of the formula, proving that f_c (and the auxiliary functions f and f_d) are complete and correct.

Note that our algorithm checks that no state contains a conflict rather than checking all possible satisfying runs. In order to prove that this is correct we need to prove that we generate only and all the reachable states.

Proposition 1. *The function* f_c *generates all and only reachable states.*

Based on the above proposition and the definition of conflict at the trace and the automaton level, we can prove that the automata construction function preserves conflict-freedom, and that no spurious conflicts are generated.

Lemma 2. *A contract* C *written in* $\mathcal{CL}$ *is conflict-free if and only if the automaton* $A(C)$ *is conflict-free.*

Based on the above results, and the correctness and completeness proofs of standard forward reachability analysis, we can finally prove our main result. Termination is trivially guaranteed since the generated automaton is finite and the reachability analysis is based on a standard fix-point computation.

Theorem 1. *The* $\mathcal{CL}$ *conflict detection algorithm is correct and complete.*

5   Case Study

In this section, the use of conflict analysis will be illustrated through a small case study, starting from a draft contract written in English, translated in $\mathcal{CL}$ and analysed using the techniques developed in this paper.

Consider a contract between an airline company and a company taking care of the ground crew (mainly the check-in process), where the normative specification is given as the following *contract*:

1. *The ground crew is obliged to open the check-in desk and request the passenger manifest two hours before the flight leaves.*
2. *The airline is obliged to reply to the passenger manifest request made by the ground crew when opening the desk with the passenger manifest.*
3. *After the check-in desk is opened the check-in crew is obliged to initiate the check-in process with any customer present by checking that the passport details match what is written on the ticket and that the luggage is within the weight limits. Then they are obliged to issue the boarding pass.*
4. *If the luggage weighs more than the limit, the crew is obliged to collect payment for the extra weight and issue the boarding pass.*
5. *The ground crew is prohibited from issuing any boarding cards without inspecting that the details are correct beforehand.*

6. *The ground crew is prohibited from issuing any boarding cards before opening the check-in desk.*
7. *The ground crew is obliged to close the check-in desk 20 minutes before the flight is due to leave and not before.*
8. *After closing check-in, the crew must send the luggage information to the airline.*
9. *Once the check-in desk is closed, the ground crew is prohibited from issuing any boarding pass or from reopening the check-in desk.*
10. *If any of the above obligations and prohibitions are violated a fine is to be paid.*

The contract can be represented in $\mathcal{CL}$ as shown below. Note that the last clause is introduced as a reparation for breaking the previous clauses.[6] Also, all the natural language clauses include an implicit universal quantification — statements of the form 'After the check-in desk is open...' should be interpreted as 'At any time, after the check-in desk is open...'. Hence, $[1^*]$ precedes such clauses.

Note that the last clause corresponds to the penalty (reparation) of all the obligations and prohibitions appearing in the contract, and thus they are represented as CTDs and CTPs with the secondary obligation $O(fine)$.

1. $[1^*][2hBefore]O_{O(fine)}(openCheckIn \ \& \ requestInfo)$
2. $[1^*][openCheckIn\&requestInfo]O_{O(fine)}(replyInfo)$
3. $[1^*][openCheckIn][1^*](O(correctDetails \ \& \ luggageInLimit) \ \wedge$
$\qquad\qquad [correctDetails \ \& \ luggageInLimit]O_{O(fine)}(boardingCard))$
4. $[1^*][openCheckIn][1^*][correctDetails \ \& \ luggageOverLimit]$
$\qquad\qquad\qquad O_{O(fine)}(collectPayment\&boardingCard)$
5. $[1^*][\overline{correctDetails}]F_{O(fine)}(boardingCard)$
6. $[\overline{openCheckIn}^*]F_{O(fine)}(boardingCard)$
7. $([1^*][20mBefore]O_{O(fine)}(closeCheckIn)) \wedge ([\overline{20mBefore}^*]F_{O(fine)}(closeCheckIn))$
8. $[1^*][closeCheckIn]O_{O(fine)}(sendLuggageInfo)$
9. $[1^*][closeCheckIn][1^*](F_{O(fine)}(openCheckIn) \wedge F_{O(fine)}(boardingCard))$

Running the contract through the conflict discovery algorithm, we discover a number of problems. The first conflict we encounter is being obliged and forbidden to issue a boarding pass.

The tool will identify a state in conflict labelled with the obligation to perform action *boardingCard* and the prohibition of performing action *boardingCard* together with a trace leading to this state. Looking at clause 3, once the crew opens the check-in desk, they are always obliged to issue a boarding pass if the client has the correct details. However, according to clause 9 it is prohibited to issue of boarding pass once the check-in desk is closed. These two clauses are in conflict once the check-in desk is closed and a client arrives to the desk with the correct details. To fix this problem we require to change clause 3 so that after the check-in desk is opened, the ground crew is obliged to issue the boarding pass as long as the desk has not been closed. This issue can also be found in clause 4 and the solution is similar.

The trace returned identifies the situation in which the check-in desk is closed at the same time the client provides his correct details:

---

[6] Note that the payment is supposed to be immediate.

⟨*openCheckIn*, *closeCheckIn* & *correctDetails*, $O(boardingCard)$ & $F(boardingCard)$⟩.

In reality, a check-in desk cannot close and accept the passport details at the same time, and thus these two are mutually exclusive actions. Adding these two actions as mutually exclusive will solve this conflict.

To ensure that *2hBefore* and *20mBefore* occur in the correct order, we make use of path constraints. Similar constraints are used for *openCheckIn* and *closeCheckIn*. Thus, clauses number 3 and 4 have to be modified as follows:

3′. $[1^*][openCheckIn][\overline{closeCheckIn}^*][correctDetails$ & $luggageInLimit]O_{O(fine)}(boardingCard)$

4′. $[1^*][openCheckIn][\overline{closeCheckIn}^*][correctDetails$ & $luggageOverLimit]$
$$O_{O(fine)}(collectPayment\&boardingCard)$$

This could be represented in textual form as:

3′. *After the check-in desk is opened the check-in crew is obliged to initiate the check-in process with any customer present until the check-in desk is closed[7]. This is done by checking that passport details match the ticket and that luggage is within the weight limits. Then the crew is obliged to issue the boarding pass.*

4′. *If the luggage weighs more than the limit, the crew is obliged to collect payment for the extra weight and issue the boarding pass.*

Note that 4′ is stated in the same way as in the original contract since what have changed are the common conditions stated in 3′. From this small case study, it should be evident that the resolution of conflicts in a contract require human intervention, to ensure that the amendments to the contract correspond the what one had in mind in the first place. Although one could define automated ways of changing, removing or adding clauses to resolve conflicts, the sheer number of possibilities one has (making certain actions mutually exclusive, removing parts of a contract, delaying the triggering of a contract, etc) and the fact that most of the options would not make sense in the real-world interpretation of the contract makes automated conflict resolution impractical.

6 Related Work

The use of model checking techniques for logics other than temporal logic is quite new, and it focuses mainly in multi-agent systems (see for instance [12]). There is not much work on the verification of logics containing the deontic notions of obligation, permission and prohibition, and including CTDs and CTPs. An extended temporal logic with conditional obligations and permissions is presented in [4] for checking whether an organisation conforms to a body of regulation. In the context of SOA, model checkers have recently been used to verify compliance of web-service composition [7], where the specifications are given in the so-called temporal deontic interpreted systems. However, we are not aware of any work that automatically detects conflicts in deontic contracts as presented here.

---

[7] Recall that we made *closeCheckIn* and *correctDetails* mutually exclusive, and cannot thus happen at the same instance of time. This ensures the submission of the correct details before the desk is closed.

The trace semantics used in our paper extends the one introduced for monitoring purposes in [6]. The automaton they generate is different and cannot be used for conflict analysis since it does not consider permissions, and does not keep deontic information in the states, determining only if a trace has been satisfied, violated or neither. Moreover, we can create a monitor directly from the automaton generated thus enabling both monitoring and conflict analysis.

In [9], a labelled transition system is generated in an *ad hoc* manner from a $\mathcal{CL}$ contract in order to be model checked using nuSMV, against properties expressed in LTL. The process is subject to error since many of the steps are manual, and the encoding of the deontic information into nuSMV is complicated. Our method is completely automatic, and though it is specific for conflict analysis it could be extended for other uses as we explain in the next section.

7 Conclusions

We have presented a finite trace semantics for $\mathcal{CL}$ augmented with deontic information, and showed its use for automatic contract analysis for conflict discovery. Remarkably, we do not use $\mathcal{CL}$ branching semantics [11] for conflict detection, which has the advantage of allowing a simpler automaton and algorithm for conflict detection. The automata we create can also be used as a basis for other kinds of analysis, including the possibility of performing queries, the detection of unreachable clauses, and the identification of superfluous clauses. In particular, the detection of unreachable clauses can be very useful in identifying parts of a contract which may be useless. This would generate more lightweight monitors, for runtime verification.

Based on the constructions presented, we have implemented a model checker for detecting conflicts in $\mathcal{CL}$ (the tool CLAN [1]). In other ongoing work using the semantics presented in this paper, we are using the automata created from $\mathcal{CL}$ contracts for runtime verification using LARVA [3]. This enables the writing of contracts about Java programs and automatically obtaining monitors ensuring conformance at runtime.

We believe that contract analysis is essential in dynamic contract composition. Even in the case of a single contract, conflict analysis can be a useful aid, as shown in the case study we present. Moreover, when dynamically generated contracts are to be used, the analysis becomes even more valuable. The main advantage of using a deontic approach is that the obligations, permissions and prohibitions are explicitly identified, and differentiated from conditionals. This enables an analysis focusing only on conflicts at the deontic level.

Please refer to [5] for more details and full proofs.

References

1. CLAN. CL ANalyser – A tool for Contract Analysis,
   www.cs.um.edu.mt/~svrg/Tools/CLTool/
2. Clarke, E.M., Grumberg, O., Peled, D.A.: Model checking. The MIT Press, Cambridge (1999)
3. Colombo, C., Pace, G.J., Schneider, G.: Dynamic event-based runtime monitoring of real-time and contextual properties. In: FMICS. LNCS. Springer, Heidelberg (2008) (to appear)

4. Dinesh, N., Joshi, A., Lee, I., Sokolsky, O.: Reasoning about conditions and exceptions to laws in regulatory conformance checking. In: van der Meyden, R., van der Torre, L. (eds.) DEON 2008. LNCS, vol. 5076, pp. 110–124. Springer, Heidelberg (2008)
5. Fenech, S.: Conflict analysis of deontic contracts. Master's thesis, Dept. of Computer Science, Univ. of Malta (2008)
6. Kyas, M., Prisacariu, C., Schneider, G.: Run-time monitoring of electronic contracts. In: Cha, S(S.), Choi, J.-Y., Kim, M., Lee, I., Viswanathan, M. (eds.) ATVA 2008. LNCS, vol. 5311, pp. 397–407. Springer, Heidelberg (2008)
7. Lomuscio, A., Qu, H., Solanki, M.: Towards verifying compliance in agent-based web service compositions. In: AAMAS, pp. 265–272 (2008)
8. McNamara, P.: Deontic logic. In: Handbook of the History of Logic, vol. 7, pp. 197–289. North-Holland Publishing, Amsterdam (2006)
9. Pace, G., Prisacariu, C., Schneider, G.: Model Checking Contracts –a case study. In: Namjoshi, K.S., Yoneda, T., Higashino, T., Okamura, Y. (eds.) ATVA 2007. LNCS, vol. 4762, pp. 82–97. Springer, Heidelberg (2007)
10. Prisacariu, C., Schneider, G.: A Formal Language for Electronic Contracts. In: Bonsangue, M.M., Johnsen, E.B. (eds.) FMOODS 2007. LNCS, vol. 4468, pp. 174–189. Springer, Heidelberg (2007)
11. Prisacariu, C., Schneider, G.: CL: A Logic for Reasoning about Legal Contracts – Semantics. Technical Report 371, Univ. Oslo (2008)
12. Wozna, B., Lomuscio, A., Penczek, W.: Bounded model checking for knowledge and real time. In: AAMAS, pp. 165–172. ACM Press, New York (2005)
13. Wright, G.H.V.: Deontic logic. Mind (60), 1–15 (1951)

A Sound Observational Semantics for Modal Transition Systems

Dario Fischbein[1], Victor Braberman[2], and Sebastian Uchitel[1,2]

[1] Imperial College London, 180 Queen's Gate, London, SW7 2RH, UK
[2] University of Buenos Aires, C1428EGA, Argentina
d.fischbein@doc.ic.ac.uk, {suchitel,vbraber}@dc.uba.ar

Abstract. Modal Transition Systems (MTS) are an extension of Labelled Transition Systems (LTS) that distinguish between required, proscribed and unknown behaviour and come equipped with a notion of refinement that supports incremental modelling where unknown behaviour is iteratively elaborated into required or proscribed behaviour. The original formulation of MTS introduces two alternative semantics for MTS, strong and weak, which require MTS models to have the same communicating alphabet, the latter allowing the use of a distinguished unobservable action. In this paper we show that the requirement of fixing the alphabet for MTS semantics and the treatment of observable actions are limiting if MTS are to support incremental elaboration of partial behaviour models. We present a novel semantics, branching alphabet semantics, for MTS inspired by branching LTS equivalence, we show that some unintuitive refinements allowed by weak semantics are avoided, and prove a number of theorems that relate branching refinement with alphabet refinement and consistency. These theorems, which do not hold for other semantics, support the argument for considering branching implementation of MTS as the basis for a sound semantics to support behaviour model elaboration.

1 Introduction

Labelled Transition Systems [13] (LTS) have been used successfully to reason about system behaviour. Modal Transition Systems [16] (MTS) are an extension of LTS that distinguish between required, proscribed and unknown behaviour. MTS have been studied for some time as a means for formally describing partial knowledge of the intended behaviour of software systems.

An MTS can be naturally interpreted as the set of implementations, in the form of LTS, that conform to the MTS. Hence, with a view to support elaboration of partial behaviour models operations over MTS and the implementations they describe have been studied. These include refinement [1,11,19] (does an MTS describe a subset of the implementations of another MTS?), consistency [19,7] (is the intersection of implementations described by two MTS non-empty?) and merge [15,7,19] (which are the implementations that conform to two MTS?).

M. Leucker and C. Morgan (Eds.): ICTAC 2009, LNCS 5684, pp. 215–230, 2009.

The original formulation of MTS by Larsen [16] defined two semantics by presenting two refinement relations between MTS. The first, strong refinement, requires MTS to have the same alphabet, i.e. the same set of transition labels, the second, weak refinement, allows the use of a distinguished unobservable action as in, for instance, process algebraic approaches to behaviour modelling.

Although strong semantics for MTS has a number of convenient qualities [7,16], the requirement of a fixed set of action labels and the inability to distinguish observable from non-observable actions results in a serious limitation for using MTS as the basis for behaviour model elaboration: Incremental elaboration typically involves gradually extending the scope of a description (i.e. augmenting the alphabet of MTS) and also merging models with different scopes.

Weak semantics for MTS supports the distinction between observable and non-observable actions, hence when combined with hiding operations, MTS under weak semantics supports a variety of elaboration tasks including merge [19,3]. However, as we show in this paper, this semantics allows some counter-intuitive LTS implementations and lacks some expected theoretical properties. In particular, it does not behave as expected with respect to alphabet hiding.

In this paper we discuss the limitations of existing semantics for MTS and propose a novel semantics, inspired by the notion of branching equivalence and branching simulation [21,9] for LTS, that addresses these limitations. More specifically, we present branching semantics for MTS and define notions of branching implementation and branching alphabet implementation. We show that unintuitive implementations allowed by weak semantics are avoided by branching semantics and prove a number of theorems that relate branching refinement with alphabet extension that do not hold for weak semantics. In addition,we study the notion of consistency, a key notion in the context of partial behaviour model elaboration, and show results for branching semantics that do not hold for weak semantics, thus, further supporting the argument for considering branching implementation of MTS as the basis for a sound semantics to support behaviour model elaboration.

2   Background

In this section, we recall definitions and fix notation for Labelled Transition Systems, related equivalences, and Modal Transition Systems.

Labelled transition systems (LTSs) [13] are widely used for modelling and analysing the behaviour of software systems. An LTS is a state transition system where transitions are labelled with actions. The set of actions of an LTS is called its *communicating alphabet* and constitutes the interactions that the modelled system can have with its environment. In addition, LTSs can have transitions labelled with τ, representing actions that are not observable by the environment. Figure 2 shows an example of an LTS.

Definition 1. (Labelled Transition Systems) *Let States be a universal set of states, $Act_\tau = Act \cup \{\tau\}$ where Act is the universal set of observable action labels and τ an unobservable action label. A labelled transition system (LTS) is* *a tuple* $P = (S, L, \Delta, s_0)$, *where* $S \subseteq States$ *is a finite set of states,* $L \subseteq Act_\tau$ *a set of labels,* $\Delta \subseteq (S \times L \times S)$ *a transition relation between states, and* $s_0 \in S$ *the initial state. We use* $\alpha P = L \setminus \{\tau\}$ *to denote the communicating alphabet of* P.

Given an LTS $P = (S, L, \Delta, s_0)$ we say P transitions on ℓ to P', denoted $P \xrightarrow{\ell} P'$, if $P' = (S, L, \Delta, s_0')$ and $(s_0, \ell, s_0') \in \Delta$. Similarly, we write $P \xrightarrow{\hat{\ell}} P'$ to denote that either $P \xrightarrow{\ell} P'$ or $\ell = \tau$ and $P = P'$ are true. We use $P \overset{\ell}{\Longrightarrow} P'$ to denote $P(\xrightarrow{\tau})^* \xrightarrow{\ell} (\xrightarrow{\tau})^* P'$, and $P \overset{\hat{\ell}}{\Longrightarrow} P'$ to denote $P(\xrightarrow{\tau})^* \xrightarrow{\hat{\ell}} (\xrightarrow{\tau})^* P'$.

A number of equivalence relations have been proposed that provide a criteria for deciding if syntactically different LTS models describe the same behaviour.

Definition 2. (Strong Bisimulation Equivalence) *Let* $\wp$ *be the universe of all LTS, and* $P, Q \in \wp$. *P and Q are strong equivalent, written* $P \sim Q$, *if* $\alpha P = \alpha Q$ *and* (P, Q) *is contained in some bisimulation relation* $R \subseteq \wp \times \wp$ *for which the following holds for all* $\ell \in Act_\tau$:

1. $(P \xrightarrow{\ell} P') \implies (\exists Q' \cdot Q \xrightarrow{\ell} Q' \wedge (P', Q') \in R)$
2. $(Q \xrightarrow{\ell} Q') \implies (\exists P' \cdot P \xrightarrow{\ell} P' \wedge (P', Q') \in R)$

This equivalence does not distinguish τ as special or unobservable actions. A property of this equivalence is that it preserves the branching structure of processes [9]. In contrast Weak Bisimulation equivalence compares the observable behaviour of models and ignores internal computations (τ-transitions). Some authors call this equivalence *observational equivalence*, but we use this expression to refer to any equivalence that considers τ-transitions as unobservable actions.

Definition 3. (Weak Bisimulation Equivalence) *Let* $\wp$ *be the universe of all LTS, and* $P, Q \in \wp$. *P and Q are weak bisimulation equivalent, written* $P \approx_w Q$, *if* $\alpha P = \alpha Q$ *and* (P, Q) *is contained in some weak bisimulation relation* $R \subseteq \wp \times \wp$ *for which the following holds for all* $\ell \in Act_\tau$:

1. $(P \xrightarrow{\ell} P') \implies (\exists Q' \cdot Q \overset{\hat{\ell}}{\Longrightarrow} Q' \wedge (P', Q') \in R)$
2. $(Q \xrightarrow{\ell} Q') \implies (\exists P' \cdot P \overset{\hat{\ell}}{\Longrightarrow} P' \wedge (P', Q') \in R)$

Finally, branching equivalence is the coarsest observational equivalence that preserves the branching structure of processes [9], it is coarser than strong equivalence yet finer than weak bisimulation equivalence.

Definition 4. (Branching Bisimulation Equivalence)
Let $\wp$ *be the universe of all LTS, and* $P, Q \in \wp$. *P and Q are branching bisimulation equivalent, written* $P \approx_b Q$, *if* $\alpha P = \alpha Q$ *and* (P, Q) *is contained in some observational bisimulation relation* $R \subseteq \wp \times \wp$ *for which the following holds for all* $\ell \in Act_\tau$:

1. $(P \xrightarrow{\ell} P') \implies (\exists Q', Q'' \cdot Q \overset{\hat{\tau}}{\Longrightarrow} Q' \xrightarrow{\hat{\ell}} Q'' \wedge (P, Q') \in R \wedge (P', Q'') \in R)$
2. $(Q \xrightarrow{\ell} Q') \implies (\exists P', P'' \cdot P \overset{\hat{\tau}}{\Longrightarrow} P' \xrightarrow{\hat{\ell}} P'' \wedge (P', Q) \in R \wedge (P'', Q') \in R)$

MTSs [16] extend LTSs by defining two sets of transitions. The first, similarly to LTS, describe the actions provided by the system in different states. The second set of transitions describes actions that may be provided by the system. If there is no transition from that a state on a particular action in either set of transitions, then the system will never provide the action on that state.

Definition 5. (Modal Transition Systems) *A modal transition system (MTS) M is a structure $(S, L, \Delta^r, \Delta^p, s_0)$, where $\Delta^r \subseteq \Delta^p$, (S, L, Δ^r, s_0) is an LTS representing required transitions of the system and (S, L, Δ^p, s_0) is an LTS representing possible (but not necessarily required) transitions of the system.*

Given an MTS $M = (S, L, \Delta^r, \Delta^p, s_0)$ we say M transitions on ℓ through a required (resp. possible) transition to M', denoted $M \xrightarrow{\ell}_r M'$ (resp. $M \xrightarrow{\ell}_p M'$), if $M' = (S, L, \Delta^r, \Delta^p, s'_0)$ and $(s_0, \ell, s'_0) \in \Delta^r$ (resp. $(s_0, \ell, s'_0) \in \Delta^p$).

We refer to transitions in $\Delta^p \setminus \Delta^r$ as *maybe* transitions. Maybe transitions are denoted with a question mark following the label. Note that LTS are a special case of MTS where there are no maybe transitions.

3   Motivation

In this section we analyse the adequacy of existing MTS semantics for incremental modelling of system behaviour using a simple motivating example.

3.1   Motivating Example

Consider a behaviour model of the control software for an electronic device at an early stage of the modelling process. The device offers different functions grouped into several menus. The general behaviour of the system is basically as follows: the user selects a desired menu and the system offers the functions associated with the menu. If the user does not choose any function after an elapsed time, the system beeps and returns to the initial state. The MTS that models the controller's behaviour is shown in Figure 1. Note that the model abstracts away using τ transitions how the functionality selected by a user works. From the initial state there are n transitions labelled $menu_1$ to $menu_n$ each one representing the selection of a menu by the user. These transitions are either required or maybe, the former corresponding to the menu items that must be in the final product and the latter corresponding to those whose inclusion is still in doubt. States labelled M_i model that the user has selected the menu i and that a functions $func_1$ to $func_{xi}$ are available. The user can select one of these functions and the system will do the associated task and and then return to the initial state, or an internal timeout occurs, making the system leave the M_i state and return to the initial state with a *beep*. This timeout is an internal event and therefore not visible to the user, so it has been modelled with a τ transition.

The explanation given above for Figure 1, although intuitive, is informal. We now discuss its precise meaning by recalling existing semantics for MTS.

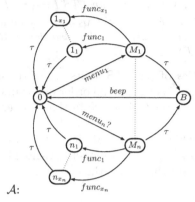

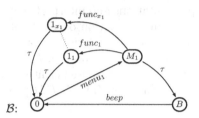

Fig. 1. MTS for Controller

Fig. 2. A strong refinement of Figure 1 where only $menu_1$ is available

3.2   Strong Semantics

Strong refinement [16] of MTS captures the notion of elaboration of a partial description into a more comprehensive one, in which some knowledge over the maybe behaviour has been gained. It can be seen as being a "more defined than" relation between two partial models. Intuitively, refinement in MTS is about converting maybe transitions into required transitions or removing them altogether: an MTS N refines M if N preserves all of the required and all of the proscribed behaviours of M. Alternatively, an MTS N refines M if N can simulate the required behaviour of M, and M can simulate the possible behaviour of N.

Definition 6 (Strong Refinement). *[16] Let δ be the universe of all MTS. N is a refinement of M, written $M \preceq N$, if $\alpha M = \alpha N$ and (M, N) is contained in some refinement relation $R \subseteq \delta \times \delta$ for which the following holds for all $\ell \in Act_\tau$:*

$$1.\ (M \xrightarrow{\ell}_r M') \implies (\exists N' \cdot N \xrightarrow{\ell}_r N' \land (M', N') \in R)$$
$$2.\ (N \xrightarrow{\ell}_p N') \implies (\exists M' \cdot M \xrightarrow{\ell}_p M' \land (M', N') \in R)$$

Note that *strong refinement* for MTS does not distinguish τ as an unobservable action and is equivalent to strong bisimulation when restricted to LTS models.

Consider the MTS shown in Figure 1. If modellers decide to exclude $menu_n$ then the model that would represent that decision is the one shown in Figure 2. According to strong semantics this latter model is a valid possible evolution of the initial one since the MTS $\mathcal{A}$ is refined by the MTS $\mathcal{B}$ ($\mathcal{A} \preceq \mathcal{B}$), incorporating as new knowledge that the $menu_n$ has been removed from the functionalities of the system. The refinement relation between these models is $R = \{(0,0), (B,B), (M_1, M_1), (1_1, 1_1), \ldots, (1_{x_1}, 1_{x_1})\}$.

Note the MTS $\mathcal{B}$ in Figure 2 has no maybe transitions, thus it can be considered an LTS. We say that it is an implementation of the model in Figure 1.

Definition 7 ((Strong) Implementation). *We say that an LTS* $I = (S_I, L_I,$ $\Delta_I, i_0)$ *is a* (strong) implementation *of an MTS* $M = (S_M, L_M, \Delta_M^r, \Delta_M^p, m_0)$, *written* $M \preceq I$, *if* $M \preceq M_I$ *with* $M_I = (S_I, L_I, \Delta_I, \Delta_I, i_0)$. *We also define the set of implementations of* M *as* $\mathcal{I}[M] = \{I \; LTS \mid M \preceq I\}$.

In fact, we shall consider the *strong semantics* of an MTS as its set of strong implementations and interpret strong refinement as the partial order determined by the subset relation over sets of strong implementations. Note that Larsen's strong refinement relation is transitive [16] and therefore it is straightforward to proof that $M \preceq M'$ implies $\mathcal{I}[M] \supseteq \mathcal{I}[M']$, which means that the $\preceq$ relation is of great use to reason efficiently about elaborating partial models. Although it was thought that $\mathcal{I}[M] \supseteq \mathcal{I}[M'] \Leftrightarrow M \preceq M'$ [10] this is not the case [6].

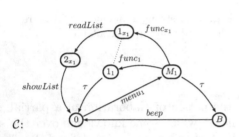 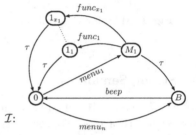

Fig. 3. A model where the behaviour of functionality associated to $func_{x_1}$ has been detailed

Fig. 4. A valid implementation of the initial model according to weak refinement

Strong semantics does not adequately support iterative model elaboration because in practice such an activity often requires progressively extending the alphabet of the system to describe behaviour aspects that previously had not been taken into account. For instance, we may want to produce a model for the electronic device's controller which describes in more detail how a particular function works (see Figure 3, states 1_{x_1} and 2_{x_1}), and then check if this model conforms to the initial, more abstract model of the controller. Such check cannot be done with strong semantics as the models have different alphabets. A standard workaround for checking if Figure 3 conforms to Figure 1 is to hide actions *readList* and *showList* (i.e. replace them with τ) to obtain models with the same alphabet and then comparing them. Strong refinement is not appropriate in this case as it does not consider τ transitions as unobservable. Indeed, the model obtained by hiding *readList* and *showList* in Figure 3 is not a strong refinement of Figure 1. However, these models can be compared using an observational semantics. We discuss this below.

3.3   Weak Semantics

Weak MTS refinement also defined by Larsen [11] allows comparing the observable behaviour of models while ignoring the possible differences that they may have in terms of internal computation. In other words, this notion of refinement considers τ-labelled transitions differently from other transitions.

Definition 8 (Weak Refinement). *[11] N is a weak refinement of M, written* $M \preceq_w N$, *if* $\alpha M = \alpha N$ *and* (M, N) *is contained in some refinement relation* $R \subseteq \delta \times \delta$ *for which the following holds for all* $\ell \in Act_\tau$:

$$1.\ (M \xrightarrow{\ell}_r M') \implies (\exists N' \cdot N \xRightarrow{\hat{\ell}}_r N' \wedge (M', N') \in R)$$
$$2.\ (N \xrightarrow{\ell}_p N') \implies (\exists M' \cdot M \xRightarrow{\hat{\ell}}_p M' \wedge (M', N') \in R)$$

It is worth noting that weak refinement results in weak LTS bisimulation when restricted to MTS with no maybe transitions, and that strong MTS refinement implies weak refinement. Finally, as with strong refinement, a notion of implementation can be defined between MTSs and LTSs, the *weak semantics* of MTS can be defined in terms of sets of weak implementations, and it can be shown that $\preceq_w$ implies inclusion of weak implementations.

Returning to our running example, recall model C described in Figure 3. If we hide actions *readList* and *showList* and then use weak refinement to compare it with the initial model A, we can conclude that C is a refinement of A based upon the weak refinement relation $R = \{(0,0), (B,B), (M_1, M_1), (1_1, 1_1),$ $\ldots, (1_{x_1}, 1_{x_1})\ , (0, 2_{x_1})\}$. Thus, as expected, under weak semantics the more detailed model C is an adequate elaboration of the initial model A.

One of the problems of weak MTS semantics is that it allows implementations that can be considered unintuitive: Consider the MTS $\mathcal{I}$ in Figure 4 which is an implementation of the original controller MTS A based on the weak implementation relation $R = \{(0,0), (B,B), (M_1, M_1), (1_1, 1_1), \ldots, (1_{x_1}, 1_{x_1})\}$.

Note that in A (Figure 1) the availability of $menu_n$ is yet to be defined, but if the system were to have this menu included we would expect all the functionalities associated with this menu to be reachable by the user. However in the implementation proposed above the user never has the possibility of selecting functionalities $func_1 \ldots func_{xn}$ after selecting $menu_n$. This breaks the intuition behind the notion of implementation. The implementation shown above is not satisfactory since it does not reflect the expected behaviour: if a menu is included, all its associated functionality will be available to users. This example shows that weak semantics does not seem to be adequate to support evolving software modelling since it accepts as valid refinements counter intuitive implementations. In subsequent sections we shall also show that weak semantics lacks some properties that relate refinement with action hiding, these properties are linked to some degree with the existence of such unintuitive implementations that weak semantics allows.

In summary, we have seen that although an observational semantics is required to support incremental elaboration of partial behaviour models, the observational semantics based on weak refinement not adequately fit with the intended meaning of MTS. In the next sections we show a semantics that not only resolves the case discussed above but that also provides a number of theoretical results that support the argument for a novel observational semantics for MTS.

4   Branching Semantics

In the previous section we analysed the shortcomings of strong and weak semantics as a foundation for characterising conformance and supporting model elaboration. Succinctly, strong semantics does not distinguish unobservable actions and hence does not support comparing models whose behaviour has been described to varying levels of detail. The latter allows implementations of partial models that contradict the intuition modellers may have of conformance. We now define a novel semantics for MTS that draws from desirable characteristics of both weak and strong semantics, in other words it is an observational semantics that captures the intuition that modellers might have of refinement. This novel semantics is based on LTS branching bisimulation.

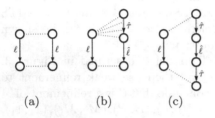
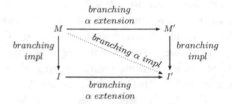

Fig. 5. Depiction of how a transition is simulated in bisimulation: (a) strong; (b) branching; (c) weak

Fig. 6. Informally, alphabet extension and branching implementations commute

Unlike strong bisimulation, branching bisimulation allows one LTS to simulate the occurrence of an ℓ transition in the other LTS by taking a number of τ transitions beforehand. Unlike weak bisimulation, branching bisimulation requires the intermediate states reached through τ transitions to fall within the equivalence relation. Figure 5 shows a graphical representation of how an ℓ transition is simulated in each of these three bisimulations. A branching implementation relation for MTS can be derived from LTS branching bisimulation in a similar manner as weak and strong implementation can be derived from weak and strong bisimulation.

Definition 9 (Branching Implementation Relation). *A branching implementation relation is a binary relation R from MTS to LTS such that whether $(M, I) \in R$ and $\ell \in Act_\tau$ the following holds:*

1. $(M \xrightarrow{\ell}_r M') \implies (\exists I_0, \ldots, I_n, I') \cdot (I_0 = I \wedge I_i \xrightarrow{\tau} I_{i+1} \forall 0 \leq i < n \wedge$
$$I_n \xrightarrow{\hat{\ell}} I' \wedge (M', I') \in R \wedge (M, I_i) \in R \,\forall 0 \leq i \leq n)$$

2. $(I \xrightarrow{\ell} I') \implies (\exists M_0, \ldots, M_n, M') \cdot (M_0 = M \wedge M_i \xrightarrow{\tau}_p M_{i+1} \forall 0 \leq i < n \wedge$
$$M_n \xrightarrow{\hat{\ell}}_p M' \wedge (M', I') \in R \wedge (M_i, I) \in R \,\forall 0 \leq i \leq n)$$

Definition 10 (Branching Implementation). *Let M be an MTS and I be an LTS, we say that I is a branching implementation of M, $M \preceq_b I$, if there* *exists a branching implementation relation R such as $(M, I) \in R$. We also define the set of implementations of M as $\mathcal{I}_b[M] = \{I\ LTS \mid M \preceq_b I\}$.*

As expected if this relation is restricted to LTS it coincides with branching equivalence. It can also be easily proved that if $M \preceq_b I$ and $I \approx_b I'$ then $M \preceq_b I'$, and so this novel implementation relation is a sound extension of branching equivalence. It is worth mentioning that this new implementation relation does not accept as a valid implementation of model $\mathcal{A}$ depicted on Figure 1 the counter intuitive implementation shown on Figure 4.

Recalling that an MTS semantics is completely defined by stating which are valid implementations for a model, we define branching semantics based on the novel implementation relation instead of a refinement relation. An associated notion of refinement comes naturally as N is a refinement of M if all the implementations of N are implementations of M, as stated on definition 11.

Definition 11 (Branching Refinement). *Let M and N be MTSs, we say that N is a refinement of M, written $M \preceq_b N$, iff $\mathcal{I}_b[M] \supseteq \mathcal{I}_b[N]$.*

Unlike refinement notions given by a simulation relation between MTSs this refinement notion is by definition complete. A co-inductive relation between MTS that implies branching implementation relation, mimicking Larsen's strong and weak refinement can easily be defined too. In the following section we will see how it is possible to demonstrate properties of this complete notion of refinement and to compare it against weak and strong refinement.

Definition 12 (Hiding). *Let $M = (S, L, \Delta^r, \Delta^p, s_0)$ be an MTS and $X \subseteq Act$. M with actions X hidden, denoted $M \backslash X$, is an MTS $(S, L \backslash X, \Delta^{r'}, \Delta^{p'}, s_0)$, where $\Delta^{r'} = \{(s, \ell, s') \mid \ell \notin X \wedge (s, \ell, s') \in \Delta^r\} \cup \{(s, \tau, s') \mid \ell \in X \wedge (s, \ell, s') \in \Delta^r\}$ and analogously for $\Delta^{p'}$. We use $M@X$ to denote $M \backslash (Act \backslash X)$.*

Branching refinement, similarly to weak refinement, does not allow for the comparison of models with different alphabets. However, we can do so by using the hiding operator, i.e. hiding the new labels of the extended alphabet. For example, given a model M and a model N, the latter with an alphabet that extends the alphabet of M, i.e. $\alpha M \subseteq \alpha N$, in order to assess whether N is a refinement of M we compute $M \preceq N@\alpha M$.

This operation gives a new refinement, therefore defining a new semantics for MTSs for which is possible to extend the alphabet of the models. In previous work [19,2] a similar extension has been applied to weak semantics, although this has been done implicitly without distinguishing between weak semantics and the extended alphabet semantics. However, since the set of implementations defined by branching implementation and the set obtained by applying this new refinement operator are different, they refer to two different semantics and we will make that distinction clear by formally defining this new semantics.

Definition 13 (Branching Alphabet Refinement). *An MTS N is a branching alphabet refinement of an MTS M, written $M \preceq_{ab} N$, if $\alpha M \subseteq \alpha N$ and $M \preceq_b N@\alpha M$.*

Note that this new semantics is an extension of branching semantics, as they behave in the same way when comparing models with identical alphabets. Similarly, we can define *Weak Alphabet Refinement* as an extension of weak refinement.

We now show that a sound relationship between branching implementation semantics and alphabet extension exists, but previously we define formally *equivalence* and *alphabet extension* for MTS.

Definition 14 (Equivalence). *Given a refinement for MTS, $\preceq$, we say that M and N are equivalent, written $M \approx N$, iff $M \preceq N$ and $N \preceq M$. We shall sometimes subindex $\approx$ to explicit the underlying refinement relation, e.g. $\approx_b$ for branching refinement $\preceq_b$.*

Definition 15 (Alphabet Extension). *Given an observational refinement for MTS, $\preceq$, we say that M' is an* alphabet extension *of M iff $M'@\alpha M \approx_w M$.*

Theorem 1 (Branching semantics is sound w.r.t Alphabet Extension).
Let M be an MTS and I be an LTS such that I is a branching implementation of M, i.e. $M \preceq_b I$. Given M' an MTS such that is a branching alphabet extension of M then there exists I' a branching alphabet extension of I such that $M' \preceq_b I'$.

Intuitively, if a model M is extended into a model M' then all implementations of M can be extended to be an implementation of M'. Figure 6 provides an intuition of Theorem 1. We say, informally, that the diagram commutes, meaning that it is possible to obtain the same result by taking an implementation of M and then extending the alphabet of that implementation; or by extending the alphabet of M and then taking an implementation of that model.

From an engineering perspective this result implies that whatever implementation we have in mind for a given partial model, refining the alphabet of the partial model will not rule out that implementation: extending the original implementation to make it an implementation of the new model is possible.

It is important to note that it is not possible to formulate a similar soundness result as the one above under weak semantics:

Remark 1 (Weak semantics is not sound w.r.t Alphabet Extension). Let M and M' be MTSs such that M' is a weak alphabet extension of M. It is not the case that for all LTS I such that $M \preceq_w I$ then there exists I' such that $M' \preceq_w I'$ and I' is weak alphabet extension of I.

Proof. Consider the example described in the previous section. Assume we extend model $\mathcal{A}$ given in Figure 4 to produce $\mathcal{A}'$ by extending its alphabet with the label *timeout*, and replacing τ transitions from M_i to state B with a *timeout* transition. It would be reasonable to expect that model I could be extended with *timeout* into a I' to obtain an implementation of $\mathcal{A}'$. However, this is not possible. If we analyse this in further detail, we can see that we would need I' to be able to perform a *timeout* after $menu_n$ and before reaching state B. Hence, I' would have a new state in between $menu_n$ and *timeout*. This leads to one of two options, either the new state does not simulate the require behaviour of M_n because it does not have transitions $func_1...func_{x_n}$, and therefore I' could not be an implementation of A'; or it does have those transitions and refines state M_n, but in this case $I'@\alpha I$ would not be equivalent to I since I does not have any of the functionalities available after $menu_n$ and therefore I' could not be an alphabet extension of I.

Summarising, in this section we have defined a new observational semantics for MTS that preserves the branching structure and resolves the unintuitive example provided in the motivation section. Furthermore, we have formally defined an extension of this semantics that supports not only the elaboration of model behaviour but also the extension of their alphabets, laying the foundations for a sound elaboration process where the level of the detail of the models can be increased over time. We have also shown that extending the alphabet of a partial behaviour model is a sound operation with respect branching semantics, while it is not for weak semantics.

5 Consistency

In this section we discuss the notion of consistency which is central to MTS semantics. We provide a complete characterization of consistency under branching semantics (result unavailable for weak semantics) and show that, unlike in weak semantics, consistency is preserved by hiding non-shared actions.

In order to support elaboration of partial behaviour models, a number of operations over MTS have been studied. Most notably, Larsen defined two co-inductive relations [16,11] which allow checking efficiently if there is a subset relation between the implementations of two MTS. This allows elaborating an MTS and checking if the new MTS effectively only "adds information", i.e. reduces acceptable implementations, to the first MTS. Another useful operation is that of merge [7,19], which attempts to produce an MTS that characterises the common implementations of two given MTS. This operation which is a form of conjunction [15] supports composing partial descriptions provided by different modellers possibly with different scopes or viewpoints of the same system. Finally, checking if two partial descriptions are consient, in other words that there is at least one implementation that conforms to both descriptions is a precondition for merging and a usefull operation in its own right for understanding the relation between different partial descriptions.

In this section, we analyse the notion of consistency under branching semantics and also compare with weak semantics. The study of a co-inductive refinement relation, which can be easily formulated, and merge under branching semantics is left out of this paper due to space restrictions and the fact that within consistency lie some key results that distinguish branching from weak semantics. We start with a formal definition of consistency.

Definition 16 (Consistency). *Two MTSs M and N are consistent if there exists an MTS P such that P is a common refinement of M and N.*

The problem of characterising consistency has been solved for strong semantics in [7] where a sufficient and necessary condition for determining if there exist a common strong refinement for two models is presented. We now define a new relation, *branching alphabet consistency relation*, and show that it characterises branching alphabet consistency.

Definition 17 (Branching Alphabet Consistency Relation). *A* branching alphabet consistency relation *is a binary relation* $C \subseteq \delta \times \delta$, *such that the following conditions hold for all* $(M, N) \in C$:

1. $(M \xrightarrow{\ell}_r M') \implies (\exists N_0, \ldots, N_n, N') \cdot ((N_i \xrightarrow{v}_p N_{i+1} \wedge v \notin \alpha M) \; \forall 0 \leq i < n \; \wedge$
$$N_0 = N \wedge N_n \xrightarrow{\ell}_p N' \wedge (M, N_i) \in C \; \forall 0 \leq i \leq n \; \wedge \; (M', N') \in C$$
2. $(N \xrightarrow{\ell}_r N') \implies (\exists M_0, \ldots, M_n, M') \cdot ((M_i \xrightarrow{v}_p M_{i+1} \wedge v \notin \alpha N) \; \forall 0 \leq i < n \; \wedge$
$$M_0 = M \wedge M_n \xrightarrow{\ell}_p M' \wedge (M_i, N) \in C \; \forall 0 \leq i \leq n \; \wedge \; (M', N') \in C$$

Intuitively, this relation requires that one model provides as possible behaviour at least all the required behaviour of the other, and vice versa.

The branching consistency relation defined above characterises branching alphabet consistency in the sense that there is a branching alphabet consistency relation between two MTS if and only if there exists an LTS that is a branching alphabet implementation of the two MTS.

Theorem 2 (Characterisation of Branching Alphabet Consistency). *MTSs M and N are branching alphabet consistent if and only if there exists a branching alphabet consistency relation C_{MN} such that (M, N) is in C_{MN}.*

Note that the Branching Alphabet Consistency Relation is equivalent to branching bisimulation when restricted to LTSs with the same alphabet This result is as expected, since an LTS is an MTS that characterises only one implementation, itself. Hence, it can only be consistent with any LTS that is equivalent to it; equivalence which in this case is that of LTS branching bisimulation.

Similar results do not exist for weak semantics. In [2] a first attempt to characterise weak consistency was published, however the definition has some problems. An improvement of the weak consistency relation in [2] is:

Definition 18. (Weak Alphabet Consistency Relation) *A* weak alphabet consistency relation *is a binary relation $C \subseteq \wp \times \wp$, such that the following conditions hold for all* $(M, N) \in C$:

1. $(M \xrightarrow{\ell}_r M') \implies (\exists N') \cdot (N \xRightarrow{v \hat{\ell} w}_p N' \wedge v, w \in (\alpha N \setminus \alpha M)^* \wedge (M', N') \in C))$
2. $(N \xrightarrow{\ell}_r N') \implies (\exists M') \cdot (M \xRightarrow{v \hat{\ell} w}_p M' \wedge v, w \in (\alpha M \setminus \alpha N)^* \wedge (M', N') \in C))$

Theorem 3 (Characterisation of Weak Consistency). *Two MTSs M and N, such that $\alpha M = \alpha N$, are weak consistent if and only if there exists a weak alphabet consistency relation C_{MN} such that (M, N) is contained in C_{MN}.*

The weak alphabet consistency relation restricted to models with the same alphabet characterises weak consistency, this can be easily proved using the Theorem 1 presented in [7]. However, it does not characterise weak alphabet consistency. Figure 7 shows a counter example, models M and N with alphabets

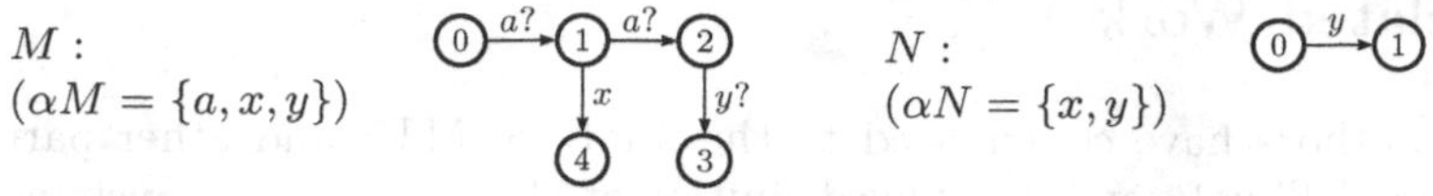

M :
$(\alpha M = \{a, x, y\})$

N :
$(\alpha N = \{x, y\})$

Fig. 7. Counter example for weak alphabet consistency characterisation

$\alpha M = \{a, x, y\}$ and $\alpha M = \{x, y\}$ are not consistent but $C_{MN} = \{(0, 0), (3, 1)\}$ is a valid relation. Definition 18 can be made more restrictive giving it a branching feel in line with [2] obtaining a relation that is a sufficient but not a necessary condition for weak alphabet consistency. This relation is out of the scope of this paper and for space limitation is not included.

In the same way Theorem 1 relates refinement with alphabet extension, it is interesting and relevant to analyse the relation between consistency and alphabet extension. Here we also find that the expected results hold for branching semantics but do not for weak semantics.

The following theorem establishes that models are branching alphabet consistent if and only if they are branching consistent over their common alphabet.

Theorem 4. *Let M and N be MTSs, and $A = \alpha M \cap \alpha N$ be the common alphabet of M and N. $M@A$ and $N@A$ are branching consistent iff M and N are branching alphabet consistent.*

From an engineering point of view this theorem expresses the fact that in order to assess whether two models are consistent it is sufficient to evaluate whether they are consistent in their common alphabet. On the other hand, it tells us that given two consistent models with the same alphabet it is possible to elaborate those models independently, extending their alphabets over different labels, knowing that the models will always remain consistent. This is a useful feature, especially when comparing two models taken from different viewpoints of the system, and for which there is a requirement to increase the level of detail with regards to different aspects. Interestingly, the natural candidate for weak alphabet consistency relation does not satisfy the left-to-right implication of the above theorem. In other words that if two models are weak consistent, extending them over new labels does not guarantee that they will remain consistent.

A related result, that in a way is more general than Theorem 4 is shown below. Note that the converse Theorem 5 is not generally true, but in the particular case of Theorem 4 the converse is also true and it can be trivially proved.

Theorem 5. *Let M' and N' be MTSs, and $A = \alpha M' \cap \alpha N'$ be the common alphabet of M' and N'. If there exist M and N MTSs such as $M'@A \preceq_{ab} M$, $N'@A \preceq_{ab} N$ and M and N are branching alphabet consistent then M' and N' are branching alphabet consistent.*

In summary, have provided a complete characterization for consistency under branching semantics and shown that it has the expected properties when considered in the context of alphabet extension. These results do not exist for weak refinement of MTS.

6   Related Work

Various authors have contributed to the study of MTS and other partial behaviour modelling formalisms. Our definition of Modal Transition Systems differs
from the original [16] in that MTS can have different communication alphabets.
Expliciting the communication alphabet allows scoping models and capturing
the fact that components control and monitor a subset of all events [12].

Related work regarding MTS refinement and simulation has been discussed
extensively throughout the paper. Our notions of branching refinement and
branching implementation are heavily inspired on that of branching bisimulation, although as shown, the extension of branching bisimulation from LTS to
MTS cannot be done straightforwardly. Numerous other refinement notions exist, both for LTS (such as trace, failures [18], and testing [4] refinement) and
for other state-based modelling formalisms such as kripke structures. We have
also compared extensively the notion of refinement we propose with respect to
strong [16] and weak refinement [16] over MTS. Regarding consistency, as mentioned previously, a characterization of consistency under strong semantics has
been developed previously [7], while up to now no characterization of consistency
for weak nor weak alphabet semantics had been provided (the definition in [2]
fails to do so completely). In [8] we sketch the idea of a branching semantics
however the theoretical results presented in this paper are novel.

Numerous extensions and variants of MTS exist such as Mixed Transition
Systems [5] and disjunctive modal transition systems [14]. The semantics we
propose could be studied for these formalisms too. We believe that existing
weak and strong refinement notions in these settings will suffer from the same
shortcomings as in MTSs. A slightly different approach to modelling unknown
behaviour is taken in [20,17]. In [20] Partial Labelled Transition Systems, each
state is associated with a set of actions that are explicitly proscribed from hap-
pening. Extended Transition Systems [17] also associate a set of actions with
each state, but in this case it models the actions for which the state has been
fully described. The relation between these models and MTS, and in particular,
our notion of refinement has yet to be studied.

In [1] a study of the complexity of different decision problems for MTS and
Mixed transition systems is presented. In particular it is shown that thorough
refinement for strong and weak semantics is PSPACE-hard, considering that
branching alphabet refinement is between these two is expected to have the
same complexity but further study is necessary.

7   Conclusions and Future Work

In this paper we have analysed the limitations of existing semantics for MTS and
presented a new observational semantics, called branching semantics, based on
the notion of branching equivalence. Furthermore, we have shown how this new
semantics does not allow for the counter-intuitive implementations permitted

by weak semantics. Moreover, in order to allow for the elaboration of models' alphabets, we have distinguished branching semantics from branching alphabet semantics. Lastly, we have shown how branching alphabet semantics presents a series of desirable properties that are not valid for weak semantics, making it a more adequate option for model elaboration.

In future work we aim to study the problem of merging under alphabet branching semantics.

References

1. Antonik, A., Huth, M., Larsen, K.G., Nyman, U., Wasowski, A.: Complexity of decision problems for mixed and modal specifications. In: Amadio, R.M. (ed.) FOSSACS 2008. LNCS, vol. 4962, pp. 112–126. Springer, Heidelberg (2008)
2. Brunet, G.: A Characterization of Merging Partial Behavioural Models. Master's thesis, Univ. of Toronto (January 2006)
3. Brunet, G., Chechik, M., Uchitel, S.: Properties of behavioural model merging. In: Misra, J., Nipkow, T., Sekerinski, E. (eds.) FM 2006. LNCS, vol. 4085, pp. 98–114. Springer, Heidelberg (2006)
4. Cleaveland, R., Hennessy, M.: Testing equivalence as a bisimulation equivalence. Formal Asp. Comput. 5(1), 1–20 (1993)
5. Dams, D.: Abstract Interpretation and Partition Refinement for Model Checking. PhD thesis, Eindhoven University of Technology, The Netherlands (July 1996)
6. Fischbein, D., Uchitel, S.: Behavioural model elaboration using mts. In: "Copenhagen" Meeting on Modal Transition Systems (2007)
7. Fischbein, D., Uchitel, S.: On correct and complete strong merging of partial behaviour models. In: SIGSOFT 2008/FSE-16, pp. 297–307. ACM Press, New York (2008)
8. Fischbein, D., Uchitel, S., Braberman, V.: A foundation for behavioural conformance in software product line architectures. In: ROSATEA (2006)
9. van Glabbeek, R.: What is branching time semantics and why to use it? In: Nielsen, M. (ed.) The Concurrency Column, pp. 190–198 (1994); Bulletin of the EATCS 53
10. Huth, M.: Refinement is complete for implementations. Formal Asp. Comput. 17(2), 113–137 (2005)
11. Hüttel, H., Larsen, K.G.: The use of static constructs in a modal process logic. In: Logic at Botik, pp. 163–180 (1989)
12. Jackson, M.: Software requirements & specifications: a lexicon of practice, principles and prejudices. ACM Press/Addison-Wesley Publishing Co. (1995)
13. Keller, R.M.: Formal verification of parallel programs. Commun. ACM (1976)
14. Larsen, K., Xinxin, L.: Equation Solving Using Modal Transition Systems. In: 5th Annual IEEE Symposium on Logic in Computer Science, pp. 108–117 (1990)
15. Larsen, K.G., Steffen, B., Weise, C.: A constraint oriented proof methodology based on modal transition systems. In: Brinksma, E., Steffen, B., Cleaveland, W.R., Larsen, K.G., Margaria, T. (eds.) TACAS 1995. LNCS, vol. 1019. Springer, Heidelberg (1995)
16. Larsen, K.G., Thomsen, B.: A modal process logic. In: LICS (1988)

17. Milner, R.: A modal characterisation of observable machine-behaviour. In: Astesiano, E., Böhm, C. (eds.) CAAP 1981. LNCS, vol. 112, pp. 25–34. Springer, Heidelberg (1981)
18. Schneider, S., Schneider, S.A.: Concurrent and Real Time Systems: The CSP Approach. John Wiley & Sons, Inc., New York (1999)
19. Uchitel, S., Chechik, M.: Merging partial behavioural models. In: Taylor, R.N., Dwyer, M.B. (eds.) SIGSOFT FSE, pp. 43–52. ACM Press, New York (2004)
20. Uchitel, S., Kramer, J., Magee, J.: Behaviour Model Elaboration using Partial Labelled Transition Systems. In: ESEC/FSE 2003, pp. 19–27 (2003)
21. van Gabbeek, R.J., Weijland, W.P.: Branching time and abstraction in bisimulation semantics. J. ACM 43(3), 555–600 (1996)

Regular Expressions with Numerical Constraints and Automata with Counters

Dag Hovland

Department of Informatics, University of Bergen, Norway
dag.hovland@uib.no

Abstract. Regular expressions with numerical constraints are an extension of regular expressions, allowing to bound numerically the number of times that a subexpression should be matched. Expressions in this extension describe the same languages as the usual regular expressions, but are exponentially more succinct.

We define a class of *finite automata with counters* and a *deterministic* subclass of these. Deterministic finite automata with counters can recognize words in linear time. Furthermore, we describe a subclass of the regular expressions with numerical constraints, a polynomial-time test for this subclass, and a polynomial-time construction of deterministic finite automata with counters from expressions in the subclass.

1 Introduction

Regular expressions with numerical constraints add the possibility to express that a subexpression must be matched a number of times specified by a lower and a upper limit. The Single UNIX Specification [1] requires this as a standard part of regular expressions. In the GNU version of the UNIX program grep [2] and in the programming language Perl they are included as standard and in XML Schemas [3] the 1-unambiguous subclass is allowed. In GNU grep you can, for example, write ([0-9]{1,3}\.){3}[0-9]{1,3} to match any IPv4 address in dotted-decimal notation.

Common uses of regular expressions with numerical constraints are matching and searching. With matching we mean the problem of deciding whether a given word is in the language defined by the regular expression. Searching means to decide whether one or more of the sub-strings of a given text match the regular expression. Kilpeläinen and Tuhkanen [4] showed that for the regular expressions with numerical constraints, matching can be done with a dynamic programming algorithm in quadratic space and time, relative to the size of the word being matched. Using this algorithm, one can also search in polynomial time.

However, many programs that search using regular expressions with numerical constraints use algorithms with super-polynomial behaviour in the size of the regular expression. These programs typically have as input one short regular expression and many, long, texts to be searched. It is therefore common to construct a deterministic finite automaton (DFA) for matching or searching, as a DFA can be used to search in time linear in the length of the text, although

M. Leucker and C. Morgan (Eds.): ICTAC 2009, LNCS 5684, pp. 231–245, 2009.

a quadratic algorithm is usually preferred, as it is faster in most practical cases. The known algorithms for constructing a DFA from a given regular expression with numerical constraints use super-polynomial space.

As an example, consider an experiment lasting 100 hours, where we need to record the moments at which some (unspecified) events take place. We will use one string to describe each 100-hour experiment. For each hour when there is an event, the hour is given, followed by "h", followed by a string describing the events occurring that hour. This string is formatted in the following way: for each minute when there is an event, the minute is given, followed by "m", followed by the second and "s" for each second at which there was an event during that minute. If there were, e.g., a total of three events during one experiment, at 3:12:22, 3:12:43 and 20:45:01, then the string describing the experiment is 3h12m22s43s20h45m1s. For testing the strings we decide to use the regular expression $((0 + \cdots + 9)^{1..2}h((1 + \cdots + 5)^{0..1}(0 + \cdots + 9)m((1 + \cdots + 5)^{0..1}(0 + \cdots + 9)s)^{1..60})^{1..60})^{0..100}$ by executing the command in Fig. 1 (See next section for syntax and semantics of the regular expressions). However, this command turns out to use over 2 gigabytes of memory[1], independent of the length of the text.

```
grep -E "([0-9]{1,2}h([1-5]?[0-9]m([1-5]?[0-9]s){1,60}){1,60}){0,100}"
```

Fig. 1. Example execution of grep

An algorithm for the matching problem will be called a *fast-matcher*, if there is a constant c such that the algorithm runs in time $O(|r|^c \cdot |w|)$ (where r is the regular expression and w is the word to be matched). There exists a fast-matcher for the usual regular expressions without numerical constraints. The algorithm constructs a non-deterministic finite automaton (NFA) recognizing the regular expression, and runs the NFA on the word by maintaining the set of reachable states. The latter set is limited by the size of the NFA, and the number of steps is exactly the length of the word. Construction of an NFA recognizing a regular expression is possible in polynomial time. Brüggemann-Klein [5] describes a different fast-matcher for a subset of the regular expressions, called 1-unambiguous regular expressions. Their algorithm constructs in polynomial time a deterministic finite automaton from a 1-unambiguous regular expression. However, no polynomial-time construction is known for 1-unambiguous regular expressions with numerical constraints.

In this article we describe *finite automata with counters*, and a fast-matcher for a subset of the regular expressions with numerical constraints, called *counter-1-unambiguous regular expressions*. The algorithm works by constructing deterministic finite automata with counters from these expressions. The construction can also be used to test in polynomial time whether a regular expression with

---

[1] Measurements done with procps version 3.2.7 running GNU grep version 2.5.3 compiled with GNU cc version 4.1.2 on a machine with four 2,0 GHz 32-bit CPU running CentOS-5.2 with Linux 2.6.18 and GNU C library version 2.5.

numerical constraints is counter-1-unambiguous. The algorithm has been implemented[2] in C in a manner inspired by grep. The command in Fig. 1 executed with our implementation on the same machine uses less memory by three orders of magnitude.

The next section describes the regular expressions with numerical constraints, the languages they denote, and the 1-unambiguous regular expressions. Section 3 describes the finite automata with counters and shows an example of such an automaton. Section 4 shows how to construct a finite automaton with counters from a regular expression, and defines the counter-1-unambiguous regular expressions. The article ends with a section on related work and a conclusion.

2   Regular Expressions with Numerical Constraints

Fix an alphabet Σ and let $\mathbb{N} = \{1, 2, \ldots\}$ be the positive integers and $\mathbb{N}_{/1} = \{2, 3, 4, \ldots\} \cup \{\infty\}$.

Definition 1. *[6,7] Given an alphabet Σ, $\mathcal{R}_\Sigma$ is the set of (non-empty) regular expressions with numerical constraints over Σ, defined in the following manner:*

$$\mathcal{R}_\Sigma ::= \mathcal{R}_\Sigma + \mathcal{R}_\Sigma \mid \mathcal{R}_\Sigma \cdot \mathcal{R}_\Sigma \mid \mathcal{R}_\Sigma^{\mathbb{N}..\mathbb{N}_{/1}} \mid \Sigma \mid \epsilon$$

We disallow expressions of the form $r^{n..m}$ where $n > m$. We will use the abbreviations r^n for $r^{n..n}$, $r^{0..u}$ for $\epsilon + r^{1..u}$, $r^{n..}$ for $r^{n..\infty}$, r^+ for $r^{1..}$, and r^* for $r^{0..}$. Intuitively, $r^{n..}$ means that subexpression r must be matched n or more times, while $r^{n..m}$ means that r must be matched at least n and at most m times. In this paper, "regular expression" will mean regular expressions with numerical constraints.

The set of symbols from the alphabet occurring in a regular expression r, is denoted $\mathsf{sym}(r)$. We lift concatenation of words to sets of words, such that if $L_1, L_2 \subseteq \Sigma^*$, then $L_1 \cdot L_2 = \{w_1 \cdot w_2 \mid w_1 \in L_1 \wedge w_2 \in L_2\}$. Moreover, ϵ denotes the *empty word* of zero length, such that for all $w \in \Sigma^*$, $\epsilon \cdot w = w \cdot \epsilon = w$. Further, we allow non-negative integers as exponents meaning repeated concatenation, such that for any $L \subseteq \Sigma^*$, we have $L^n = L^{n-1} \cdot L$ for $n > 0$ and $L^0 = \{\epsilon\}$. For convenience, we recall in Definition 2 the language denoted by a regular expression, and extend it to numerical constraints. Since we will compare arbitrary members of $\mathbb{N}$ and $\mathbb{N}_{/1}$ below, we define that $i < \infty$ for all $i \in \mathbb{N}$.

Definition 2 (Language). *The language $L(r)$ denoted by a regular expression $r \in \mathcal{R}_\Sigma$, is defined in the following inductive way:*

$$L(r_1 + r_2) = L(r_1) \cup L(r_2)$$
$$L(r_1 \cdot r_2) = L(r_1) \cdot L(r_2)$$
$$L(r^{n..m}) = \bigcup_{n \le i \le m} L(r)^i$$
$$\textit{for } a \in \Sigma \cup \{\epsilon\}, L(a) = \{a\}$$

Some examples of regular expressions and their languages are: $L((a + b)^{0..2}) = \{\epsilon, a, b, aa, ab, ba, bb\}$ and $L((a^2b)^2) = \{aabaab\}$.

---

[2] Available from http://www.ii.uib.no/~dagh/fac

2.1   Term Trees and Positions

Given a regular expression r, we follow Terese [8] and define the term tree of r as the tree where the root is labelled with the main operator (choice, concatenation or numerical constraint) and the subtrees are the term trees of the subexpression(s) combined by the operator. If $a \in \Sigma \cup \{\epsilon\}$ the term tree is a single root-node with a as label.

We use $\langle n_1, \ldots, n_k \rangle$, a possibly empty sequence of natural numbers, to denote a position in a term tree. We let p, q, including subscripted variants, be variables for such possibly empty sequences of natural numbers. The position of the root is $\langle \rangle$. If $r = r_1 \cdot r_2$ or $r = r_1 + r_2$, and $n_1 \in \{1, 2\}$, the position $\langle n_1, \ldots, n_k \rangle$ in r is the position $\langle n_2, \ldots, n_k \rangle$ in the subtree of child n_1, that is, in the term tree of r_{n_1}. If $r = r_1{}^{l..u}$, the position $\langle 1, n_2, \ldots, n_k \rangle$ in r is the position $\langle n_2, \ldots, n_k \rangle$ in r_1, and $\langle 2 \rangle$ and $\langle 3 \rangle$ are the positions of the nodes containing the lower and upper limits l and u, respectively. For two positions $p = \langle m_1, \ldots, m_k \rangle$ and $q = \langle n_1, \ldots, n_l \rangle$, the notation $p \odot q$ will be used for the concatenated position $\langle m_1, \ldots, m_k, n_1, \ldots, n_l \rangle$. For a position p in r we will denote the subexpression rooted at this position by $r|_p$. Note that $r|_{\langle \rangle} = r$. Let $\mathsf{pos}(r)$ be the set of positions in r.

Note that for $r \in \mathcal{R}_\Sigma$, $p \in \mathsf{pos}(r)$, and $q \in \mathsf{pos}(r|_p)$, we have $r|_{p \odot q} = r|_p|_q$. This can be shown by induction on $r|_p$ (see, e.g., Terese [8]).

The concept of *marked expressions* will be important in this article. It has been used by Kilpeläinen & Tuhkanen [7] and by Brüggemann-Klein & Wood [9], but the definition given here is somewhat different.

Definition 3 (Marked Expressions). *If* $r \in \mathcal{R}_\Sigma$ *is a regular expression,* $\mu(r) \in \mathcal{R}_{\mathsf{pos}(r)}$ *is the marked expression, that is, the expression where every instance of any symbol from Σ is substituted with its position in the expression.*

It follows that if $p \in \mathsf{sym}(\mu(r))$, then $r|_p \in \mathsf{sym}(r)$. Note that, e.g., $\mu(b) = \mu(a) = \langle \rangle$, which shows that marking is not injective.

Example 1. As an example, consider $\Sigma = \{a, b, c\}$ and $r = (a^2 + bc)^{3..5}$. Then $\mu(r) = (\langle 1, 1, 1 \rangle^2 + \langle 1, 2, 1 \rangle \cdot \langle 1, 2, 2 \rangle)^{3..5}$. The term trees of r and $\mu(r)$ are shown in Fig. 2.

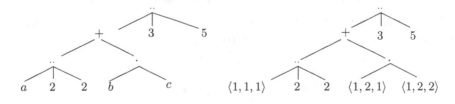

Fig. 2. Term trees for $(a^2 + bc)^{3..5}$ and $\mu((a^2 + bc)^{3..5})$

2.2   1-Unambiguous Regular Expressions

Definition 4. *[5,9] A regular expression r is 1-unambiguous if for any two* $upv, uqw \in L(\mu(r))$, *where* $p, q \in \mathsf{sym}(\mu(r))$ *and* $u, v, w \in \mathsf{sym}(\mu(r))^*$ *such that* $r|_p = r|_q$, *we have* $p = q$.

Examples of 1-unambiguous regular expressions are $(a^{1..2})^{1..2}$ and $b^*a(b^*a)^*$, while $(\epsilon + a)a$ and $(a + b)^*a$ are not 1-unambiguous. The languages denoted by 1-unambiguous regular expressions without numerical constraints will be called *1-unambiguous regular languages*. Brüggemann-Klein & Wood [9] showed that there exist regular languages that are not 1-unambiguous regular languages, e.g. $L((a + b)^*(ac + bd))$. However, it is easy to modify a searching algorithm to search backwards, and the reverse of $(a+b)^*(ac+bd)$, namely $(ca+db)(a+b)^*$ is 1-unambiguous. There are of course also expressions like $(a+b)^*(ac+bd)(c+d)^*$, which denotes a 1-ambiguous language, read both backwards and forwards.

3   Finite Automata with Counters

3.1   Counter States and Update Instructions

We define *counter states*, which will be used to keep track of the number of times subexpressions with numerical constraints have been matched. Let $\mathcal{C}$ be the set of positions of subexpressions we need to keep track of. Let the mapping $\gamma : \mathcal{C} \mapsto \mathbb{N}$ denote a counter state. Let γ_1 be the counter state that maps all members of the domain to 1. We define an *update instruction* ψ as a partial mapping from $\mathcal{C}$ to $\{\mathsf{inc}, \mathsf{res}\}$ (inc for *increment*, res for *reset*). Update instructions ψ define mappings f_ψ between counter states in the following way: If $\psi(p) = \mathsf{inc}$, then $f_\psi(\gamma)(p) = \gamma(p) + 1$, if $\psi(p) = \mathsf{res}$ then $f_\psi(\gamma)(p) = 1$, and otherwise $f_\psi(\gamma)(p) = \gamma(p)$. Furthermore, we define the *counter-conditions* min and max, which map each member of $\mathcal{C}$ to lower and upper limits, respectively, such that $\min(p) \le \max(p)$ for all $p \in \mathcal{C}$.

Definition 5 (Satisfaction of Update Instructions). *We define a satisfaction relation between update instructions, counter states and the two counterconditions. Given* $\min : \mathcal{C} \mapsto \mathbb{N}$, $\max : \mathcal{C} \mapsto \mathbb{N}_{/1}$, $\gamma : \mathcal{C} \mapsto \mathbb{N}$ *and* $\psi : \mathcal{C} \mapsto \{\mathsf{inc}, \mathsf{res}\}$, *then* $(\gamma, \min, \max) \models \psi$ *holds if and only if the following holds for all* p *in the domain of* ψ: *whenever* $\psi(p) = \mathsf{inc}$, *then* $\gamma(p) < \max(p)$, *and whenever* $\psi(p) = \mathsf{res}$, *then* $\gamma(p) \ge \min(p)$.

The intuition of Definition 5 is that the value of a counter state can only be increased if the value is smaller than the maximum allowed value, while a value can only be reset if it is at least as large as the minimum value.

Example 2. Assume $\mathcal{C} = \{p_1, p_2\}$, $\min(p_1) = \max(p_1) = 2$, $\min(p_2) = 1$, $\max(p_2) = \infty$ and $\gamma = \{p_1 \mapsto 2, p_2 \mapsto 1\}$, and let $\psi_1 = \{p_1 \mapsto \mathsf{inc}\}$, $\psi_2 = \{p_1 \mapsto \mathsf{res}, p_2 \mapsto \mathsf{inc}\}$ and $\psi_3 = \{p_1 \mapsto \mathsf{res}, p_2 \mapsto \mathsf{res}\}$. Then $f_{\psi_1}(\gamma) = \{p_1 \mapsto 3, p_2 \mapsto 1\}$, $f_{\psi_2}(\gamma) = \{p_1 \mapsto 1, p_2 \mapsto 2\}$ and $f_{\psi_3}(\gamma) = \{p_1 \mapsto 1, p_2 \mapsto 1\}$. Furthermore, $(\gamma, \min, \max) \models \psi_2$ and $(\gamma, \min, \max) \models \psi_3$ hold, while it does not hold that $(\gamma, \min, \max) \models \psi_1$.

3.2   Overlapping Update Instructions

Given mappings max and min, two update instructions are called *overlapping*, if there is a counter state that satisfies both of the update instructions.

Definition 6 (Overlapping Update Instructions). *Given mappings* max *and* min, *update instructions* ψ_1 *and* ψ_2 *are overlapping, if and only if there is a counter state* γ, *such that both* $(\gamma, \mathsf{min}, \mathsf{max}) \models \psi_1$ *and* $(\gamma, \mathsf{min}, \mathsf{max}) \models \psi_2$ *hold.*

Whether two update instructions are overlapping can be decided in linear time, relative to the size of $\mathcal{C}$, by the algorithm presented in the following proposition.

Proposition 1. *Given mappings* max *and* min, *two update instructions are overlapping if and only if: for every p that is mapped to different values by the two update instructions, it must hold that* $\mathsf{min}(p) < \mathsf{max}(p)$.

Proof. The proof is by treating the two parts of "if and only if" separately. First assume that for every p which is mapped to different values by the two update instructions, it holds that $\mathsf{min}(p) < \mathsf{max}(p)$. We must show that the update instructions are overlapping. A counter state γ satisfying both update instructions can be constructed as follows: For each member p of $\mathcal{C}$, if p is mapped to res by at least one of the update instructions, then let $\gamma(p) = \mathsf{min}(p)$, otherwise let $\gamma(p) = 1$. For the second part, that is, the "only if"-part of the proposition, assume the update instructions are overlapping. Thus there is at least one counter state γ which satisfies both update instructions ψ_1 and ψ_2. Now, for every p such that $\psi_1(p) = \mathsf{inc}$ and $\psi_2(p) = \mathsf{res}$, we get that $\mathsf{min}(p) \leq \gamma(p) < \mathsf{max}(p)$ from Definition 5, such that $\mathsf{min}(p) < \mathsf{max}(p)$. The opposite case where $\psi_1(p) = \mathsf{res}$ and $\psi_2(p) = \mathsf{inc}$ follows by symmetry. $\square$

Recall Example 2. ψ_1 and ψ_2 are not overlapping, while ψ_3 is overlapping with ψ_2. The counter state satisfying both ψ_2 and ψ_3 constructed as in the argument above is γ. ψ_1 and ψ_3 are not overlapping.

3.3   Finite Automata with Counters

Definition 7 (Finite Automata with Counters). *A* Finite Automaton with Counters *(FAC) is a tuple* $(\Sigma, Q, \mathcal{C}, \mathcal{A}, \Phi, \mathsf{min}, \mathsf{max}, q^I, \mathcal{F})$. *The members of the tuple are summarized in Table 1 and described below:*

- Σ *is a finite, non-empty set (the alphabet).*
- Q *and* $\mathcal{C}$ *are finite sets of* states *and* counters, *respectively.*
- $q^I \in Q$ *is the initial state.*
- $\mathcal{A} : Q \mapsto \Sigma$ *maps each non-initial state to the letter which is matched when entering the state.*
- Φ *maps each state to a set of pairs. The latter pairs consist of a state and an update instruction.*

$$\Phi : Q \mapsto \wp(Q \times (\mathcal{C} \mapsto \{\mathsf{res}, \mathsf{inc}\})) \,.$$

Table 1. The members of the tuple describing an FAC

Symbol	Short description	Formally
Σ	Alphabet	Finite set
Q	States	Finite set
$\mathcal{C}$	Counters	Finite set
$\mathcal{A}$	Matching letter	$Q \mapsto \Sigma$
Φ	Transitions	$Q \mapsto \wp(Q \times (\mathcal{C} \mapsto \{\mathsf{res}, \mathsf{inc}\}))$
min	Counter minimum	$\mathcal{C} \mapsto \mathbb{N}$
max	Counter maximum	$\mathcal{C} \mapsto \mathbb{N}_{/1}$
q^I	Initial state	$q^I \in Q$
$\mathcal{F}$	Final configurations	$Q \mapsto \wp(\mathcal{C}) \cup \{\bot\}$

- min $: \mathcal{C} \mapsto \mathbb{N}$ *and* max $: \mathcal{C} \mapsto \mathbb{N}_{/1}$ *are the counter-conditions.*
- $\mathcal{F} : Q \mapsto \wp(\mathcal{C}) \cup \{\bot\}$ *describes the* final configurations *(See Definition 8). The symbol $\bot$ is used to indicate that a configuration is not final.*

Running or executing an FAC is defined in terms of *transitions* between *configurations*. The configurations of an FAC are pairs, where the first element is a member of Q, and the second element is a counter state.

Definition 8 (Configuration of an FAC). *A* configuration *of an FAC is a pair (q, γ), where $q \in Q$ is the current state and $\gamma : \mathcal{C} \mapsto \mathbb{N}$ is the counter state. A configuration (q, γ) is final, if $\mathcal{F}(q) \neq \bot$, and for all $c \in \mathcal{F}(q)$, $(\gamma, \mathsf{min}, \mathsf{max}) \models \{c \mapsto \mathsf{res}\}$. Thus, $\mathcal{F}(q)$ specifies which counters should be "resettable".*

Intuitively, the first member of each of the pairs mapped to by Φ, is the state that can be entered, and the second member describes the changes to the current counter state of the automaton in this step. Thus, Φ and $\mathcal{A}$ together describe the possible transitions of the automaton. This is formalized as the transition function δ.

Definition 9 (Transition Function of an FAC). *For an FAC $(\Sigma, Q, \mathcal{C}, \mathcal{A}, \Phi, \mathsf{min}, \mathsf{max}, q^I, \mathcal{F})$, the transition function δ is defined for any configuration (q, γ) and letter l by*

$$\delta((q, \gamma), l) = \{(p, f_\psi(\gamma)) \mid \mathcal{A}(p) = l \wedge (p, \psi) \in \Phi(q) \wedge (\gamma, \mathsf{min}, \mathsf{max}) \models \psi\}.$$

Definition 10 (Deterministic FAC). *An FAC $(\Sigma, Q, \mathcal{C}, \mathcal{A}, \Phi, \mathsf{min}, \mathsf{max}, q^I, \mathcal{F})$ is deterministic if and only if $|\delta((q, \gamma), l)| \leq 1$ for all $q \in Q, l \in \Sigma$ and $\gamma : \mathcal{C} \mapsto \mathbb{N}$.*

Deciding whether an FAC is deterministic can be done in polynomial time as follows: For each state p, for each two different $(p_1, \psi_1), (p_2, \psi_2)$ both in $\Phi(p)$, assure that either $\mathcal{A}(p_1) \neq \mathcal{A}(p_2)$ or, otherwise, that ψ_1 and ψ_2 are not overlapping. That this test is sound and complete follows by the definition of δ and the properties of overlapping update instructions.

3.4 Word Recognition

Given a word as input, an FAC can either *accept* or *reject* this. A deterministic FAC recognizes a word by treating letters in the word one by one. It starts in the *initial configuration* (q^I, γ_1). An FAC in configuration (q, γ), with letter $l \in \Sigma$ next in the word, will reject the word if $\delta((q, \gamma), l)$ is empty. Otherwise it enters the unique configuration $(q', \gamma') \in \delta((q, \gamma), l)$. If the whole word has been read, a deterministic FAC accepts the word if and only if it is in a final configuration. The subset of Σ^* consisting of words being accepted by an FAC A is denoted $L(A)$.

Example 3. Let $\Sigma = \{a, b, c\}$, $Q = \{q^I, \langle 1,1,1 \rangle, \langle 1,2,1 \rangle, \langle 1,2,2 \rangle\}$ and $C = \{\langle \rangle, \langle 1,1 \rangle\}$. Figure 3 illustrates a deterministic FAC $(\Sigma, Q, C, A, \Phi, \min, \max, q^I, \mathcal{F})$ which recognizes $L((a^2 + bc)^{3..5})$. The sequence of configurations of this FAC while recognizing *aabcaa* is :

$$
\begin{aligned}
&(q^I, \gamma_1) \\
&(\langle 1,1,1 \rangle, \{\langle \rangle \mapsto 1, \langle 1,1 \rangle \mapsto 1\}) \\
&(\langle 1,1,1 \rangle, \{\langle \rangle \mapsto 1, \langle 1,1 \rangle \mapsto 2\}) \\
&(\langle 1,2,1 \rangle, \{\langle \rangle \mapsto 2, \langle 1,1 \rangle \mapsto 1\}) \\
&(\langle 1,2,2 \rangle, \{\langle \rangle \mapsto 2, \langle 1,1 \rangle \mapsto 1\}) \\
&(\langle 1,1,1 \rangle, \{\langle \rangle \mapsto 3, \langle 1,1 \rangle \mapsto 1\}) \\
&(\langle 1,1,1 \rangle, \{\langle \rangle \mapsto 3, \langle 1,1 \rangle \mapsto 2\})
\end{aligned}
$$

The last configuration is final, since $\min(\langle \rangle) \leq 3$ and $\min(\langle 1,1 \rangle) \leq 2$.

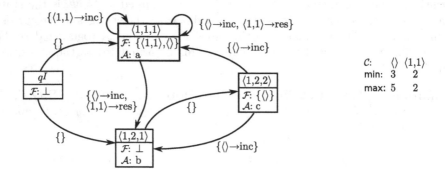

Fig. 3. Illustration of FAC recognizing $L((a^2 + bc)^{3..5})$. Every state is depicted as a rectangle separated in two by a line. The name of the state is in the upper part of the rectangle, and the values of $\mathcal{F}$ and A are in the lower part. Every member of ϕ is shown as an arrow, annotated with the corresponding update instruction. C, min and max are shown on the right hand side.

Proposition 2 (Linear-Time Recognition). *For any textual representation of FACs, and for any deterministic FAC $A = (\Sigma, Q, \mathcal{C}, \mathcal{A}, \Phi, \mathsf{min}, \mathsf{max}, q^I, \mathcal{F})$, if $\sigma(A)$ is the size of the textual representation of A, then for any word $w \in \Sigma^*$, the FAC A can in time $O(|w|\sigma(A)^2)$ decide whether w is rejected or accepted.*

Proof. The FAC makes no more than $|w|$ steps in the recognition, and at each step, there can be no more than $\max\{|\Phi(q)| \,|\, q \in Q\}$ outgoing edges, and for each of these we might have to check the counter state γ against no more than $|\mathcal{C}|$ constraints. Testing whether the last configuration is accepting, takes time $O(|\mathcal{C}| \cdot \max\{|\mathcal{F}(q)| \,|\, q \in Q\})$. Thus we get the result, as $|\mathcal{C}|$, $\max\{|\mathcal{F}(q)| \,|\, q \in Q\}$ and $\max\{|\Phi(q)| \,|\, q \in Q\}$ are all $O(\sigma(A))$.

3.5   Searching with FACs

We formalize the problems called matching and searching as the binary predicates $\mathsf{m}, \mathsf{s} \subseteq \mathcal{R}_\Sigma \times \Sigma^*$, defined as follows: $\mathsf{m}(r, w) \Leftrightarrow w \in L(r)$ and $\mathsf{s}(r, w) \Leftrightarrow \exists u, v, v' : (w = u \cdot v \cdot v' \wedge v \in L(r))$. A deterministic FAC recognizing $L(r)$ can decide $\mathsf{m}(r, w)$ in time linear in $|w|$. If the alphabet (Σ) is fixed, we can solve $\mathsf{s}(r, w)$ in time linear in the length of w by solving $\mathsf{m}(\Sigma^* \cdot r \cdot \Sigma^*)$, where Σ here denotes the disjunction of all the letters. In practical cases, though, the size of Σ can be prohibitively large. Another option is therefore to decide $\mathsf{s}(r, w)$ by using $O(|w|^2)$ executions of an algorithm for m. A deterministic FAC can also decide in linear time the *prefix problem*. The latter is also formalized as a binary predicate, namely $\mathsf{p} \subseteq \mathcal{R}_\Sigma \times \Sigma^*$, where $\mathsf{p}(r, w) \Leftrightarrow \exists u, v : (w = u \cdot v \wedge u \in L(r))$. $O(|w|)$ executions of an algorithm for p is sufficient to decide s. Thus, deterministic FACs can be used to search in time quadratic in the length of the text. The last approach is similar to that used in GNU grep.

4   Constructing Finite Automata with Counters

Following Brüggemann-Klein & Wood [9] and Glushkov [10], we define three mappings, first, last, and follow. They will be used below in an alternative definition of the language denoted by a regular expression, and will be central in the construction of FACs from regular expressions. first takes a regular expression as parameter and returns the set of positions that could be matching the first letter in a word in the language of the regular expression. Similarly, the mapping last takes a regular expression as parameter and returns the set of positions that could be matching the last letter in a word in the language of the regular expression.

follow takes a regular expression and a position in the expression as parameters, and returns a set of pairs (p, ψ). Assume the position given as argument to follow is used to match a letter in a word in the language of the regular expression. If follow returns a set containing (p, ψ), then p is a position in the regular expression which could match the next letter in the word, and ψ is the update instructions, describing what changes must be done to the counters in the step to p from the position given as the second argument.

Before we can define first, last and follow, we need some auxiliary definitions.

Definition 11 (Concatenating Positions with Update Instructions and Sets of Positions)

- *For $p \in \mathbb{N}^*$ and $S \subseteq \mathbb{N}^*$, let $p \odot S = \{p \odot q \mid q \in S\}$*
- *For $p \in \mathbb{N}^*$ and $\psi : (\mathbb{N}^* \mapsto \{\text{res}, \text{inc}\})$, let $p \odot \psi = \{p \odot q \mapsto \psi(q) \mid q \in \text{dom}(\psi)\}$.*
- *For $S \subseteq \mathbb{N}^* \times (\mathbb{N}^* \mapsto \{\text{inc}, \text{res}\})$ let $p \odot S = \{(p \odot q, p \odot \psi) \mid (q, \psi) \in S\}$.*

Definition 12 (Subposition). *We use the notation $p \leq q$ for p a prefix or subposition of q, that is, $p \leq q \Leftrightarrow \exists p_1 : q = p \odot p_1$.*

Definition 13. *Let $r \in \mathcal{R}_\Sigma$ and $q \in \text{pos}(r)$.*

1. *Let $\mathsf{C}(r) \subseteq \text{pos}(r)$ be the positions of all subexpressions of r that are of the form $r_1^{n..m}$, and that are not of the form r_1^+. Expressed formally,*

$$\mathsf{C}(r) = \{q \in \text{pos}(r) \mid \exists n \in \mathbb{N}, m \in \mathbb{N}_{/1}, r_1 \in \mathcal{R}_\Sigma : r|_q = r_1^{n..m} \neq r_1^+\}.$$

2. *Let $\mathsf{C}(r, q) \subseteq \mathsf{C}(r)$ be the set of positions in $\mathsf{C}(r)$ above q, that is, $\mathsf{C}(r, q) = \{p \in \mathsf{C}(r) \mid p \leq q\}$.*

In the sequel we need to express the set of regular expressions whose language contains the empty word. The set of nullable expressions, $\mathfrak{N}_\Sigma$, is therefore defined as follows:

Definition 14 (Nullable Expressions). *Given an alphabet Σ, the set of nullable expressions, $\mathfrak{N}_\Sigma$, is defined in the following inductive manner*

$$\mathfrak{N}_\Sigma ::= \mathfrak{N}_\Sigma \cdot \mathfrak{N}_\Sigma \mid \mathfrak{N}_\Sigma + \mathcal{R}_\Sigma \mid \mathcal{R}_\Sigma + \mathfrak{N}_\Sigma \mid \mathfrak{N}_\Sigma^{\mathbb{N}..\mathbb{N}_{/1}} \mid \epsilon$$

We can prove that $\mathfrak{N}_\Sigma = \{r \in \mathcal{R}_\Sigma \mid \epsilon \in L(r)\}$ by induction on r.

We will define inductively first : $\mathcal{R}_\Sigma \mapsto \wp(\mathbb{N}^*)$ (Table 2), last : $\mathcal{R}_\Sigma \mapsto \wp(\mathbb{N}^*)$ (Table 2) and follow : $(\mathcal{R}_\Sigma \times \mathbb{N}^*) \mapsto \wp(\mathbb{N}^* \times (\mathbb{N}^* \mapsto \{\text{res}, \text{inc}\}))$ (Table 3). first and last map from an expression r to a subset of $\text{sym}(\mu(r))$, such that first$(r) = \{p \in \text{sym}(\mu(r)) \mid \exists w \in \text{sym}(\mu(r))^* : pw \in L(\mu(r))\}$ and last$(r) = \{p \in \text{sym}(\mu(r)) \mid \exists w \in \text{sym}(\mu(r))^* : wp \in L(\mu(r))\}$. follow maps an expression r and a position $q \in \text{pos}(r)$ to a set of pairs of the form (p, ψ), where $p \in \text{sym}(\mu(r))$ and $\psi : \mathsf{C}(r) \mapsto \{\text{inc}, \text{res}\}$.

Recall the example expression $r = (a^2 + bc)^{3..5}$ from Example 1. We get first$(r) = \{\langle 1, 1, 1 \rangle, \langle 1, 2, 1 \rangle\}$, last$(r) = \{\langle 1, 1, 1 \rangle, \langle 1, 2, 2 \rangle\}$, and follow is shown in Table 4.

4.1   Basic Properties

The following lemma basically summarizes that first, last and follow have the intended properties.

Lemma 1. *For all regular expressions $r \in \mathcal{R}_\Sigma$ and all positions $q \in \text{sym}(\mu(r))$:*

Table 2. first : $\mathcal{R}_\Sigma \mapsto \wp(\mathbb{N}^*)$ and last : $\mathcal{R}_\Sigma \mapsto \wp(\mathbb{N}^*)$

first$(\epsilon) = $ last$(\epsilon) = \varnothing,$ $\qquad\qquad$ $r \in \Sigma \Rightarrow$ first$(r) = $ last$(r) = \{\langle\rangle\}$
$r = r_1 + r_2 \Rightarrow$ first$(r) = (\langle 1\rangle \odot $ first$(r_1)) \cup (\langle 2\rangle \odot $ first$(r_2))$ $\wedge$ last$(r) = (\langle 1\rangle \odot $ last$(r_1)) \cup (\langle 2\rangle \odot $ last$(r_2))$
$r = r_1 \cdot r_2 \wedge r_1 \in \mathfrak{N}_\Sigma \;\Rightarrow\;$ first$(r) = (\langle 1\rangle \odot $ first$(r_1)) \cup (\langle 2\rangle \odot $ first$(r_2))$ $r = r_1 \cdot r_2 \wedge r_2 \in \mathfrak{N}_\Sigma \;\Rightarrow\;$ last$(r) = (\langle 1\rangle \odot $ last$(r_1)) \cup (\langle 2\rangle \odot $ last$(r_2))$
$r = r_1 \cdot r_2 \wedge r_1 \notin \mathfrak{N}_\Sigma \;\Rightarrow\;$ first$(r) = \langle 1\rangle \odot $ first(r_1) $r = r_1 \cdot r_2 \wedge r_2 \notin \mathfrak{N}_\Sigma \;\Rightarrow\;$ last$(r) = \langle 2\rangle \odot $ last(r_2)
$r = r_1^{n..m} \Rightarrow$ first$(r) = \langle 1\rangle \odot $ first$(r_1) \;\wedge\;$ last$(r) = \langle 1\rangle \odot $ last(r_1)

Table 3. follow : $(\mathcal{R}_\Sigma \times \mathbb{N}^*) \mapsto \wp(\mathbb{N}^* \times (\mathbb{N}^* \mapsto \{\mathsf{res}, \mathsf{inc}\}))$

$r \in \Sigma \Rightarrow$ follow$(r, \langle\rangle) = \varnothing$
$r = r_1 + r_2 \Rightarrow \big($ follow$(r, \langle 1\rangle \odot q) = \langle 1\rangle \odot $ follow$(r_1, q) \big)$ $\wedge \big($ follow$(r, \langle 2\rangle \odot q) = \langle 2\rangle \odot $ follow$(r_2, q) \big)$
$r = r_1 \cdot r_2 \Rightarrow$ follow$(r, \langle 2\rangle \odot q) = \langle 2\rangle \odot $ follow(r_2, q)
$r = r_1 \cdot r_2 \wedge q \in $ last$(r_1) \Rightarrow$ follow$(r, \langle 1\rangle \odot q) = \langle 1\rangle \odot $ follow$(r_1, q) \cup$ $\{(q_1, \{\langle 1\rangle \odot p_1 \mapsto \mathsf{res} \mid p_1 \in \mathsf{C}(r_1, q)\}) \mid q_1 \in \langle 2\rangle \odot $ first$(r_2)\}$
$r = r_1 \cdot r_2 \wedge q \notin $ last$(r_1) \Rightarrow$ follow$(r, \langle 1\rangle \odot q) = \langle 1\rangle \odot $ follow(r_1, q)
$r = r_1^+ \wedge q \in $ last$(r_1) \Rightarrow$ follow$(r, \langle 1\rangle \odot q) =$ $\langle 1\rangle \odot $ follow$(r_1, q) \cup \big\{ \big(q_1, \{\langle 1\rangle \odot p_1 \mapsto \mathsf{res} \mid p_1 \in \mathsf{C}(r_1, q)\}\big) \mid q_1 \in \langle 1\rangle \odot $ first$(r_1) \big\}$
$r = r_1^{n..m} \wedge q \in $ last$(r_1) \wedge (n, m) \neq (1, \infty) \Rightarrow$ follow$(r, \langle 1\rangle \odot q) = \langle 1\rangle \odot $ follow$(r_1, q) \cup$ $\big\{ \big(q_1, \{\langle\rangle \mapsto \mathsf{inc}\} \cup \{\langle 1\rangle \odot p_1 \mapsto \mathsf{res} \mid p_1 \in \mathsf{C}(r_1, q)\}\big) \mid q_1 \in \langle 1\rangle \odot $ first$(r_1) \big\}$
$r = r_1^{n..m} \wedge q \notin $ last$(r_1) \Rightarrow$ follow$(r, \langle 1\rangle \odot q) = \langle 1\rangle \odot $ follow(r_1, q)

Table 4. The mapping follow for $r = (a^2 + bc)^{3..5}$

$$\text{follow}(r, \langle 1, 1, 1\rangle) = \left\{ \begin{array}{l} (\langle 1, 1, 1\rangle, \{\langle 1, 1\rangle \mapsto \mathsf{inc}\}), \\ (\langle 1, 1, 1\rangle, \{\langle 1, 1\rangle \mapsto \mathsf{res}, \langle\rangle \mapsto \mathsf{inc}\}), \\ (\langle 1, 2, 1\rangle, \{\langle 1, 1\rangle \mapsto \mathsf{res}, \langle\rangle \mapsto \mathsf{inc}\}) \end{array} \right\}$$

follow$(r, \langle 1, 2, 1\rangle) = \{(\langle 1, 2, 2\rangle, \{\})\}$

follow$(r, \langle 1, 2, 2\rangle) = \{(\langle 1, 1, 1\rangle, \{\langle\rangle \mapsto \mathsf{inc}\}), (\langle 1, 2, 1\rangle, \{\langle\rangle \mapsto \mathsf{inc}\})\}$

1. first$(r) = \{p \in \text{sym}(\mu(r)) \mid \exists w \in \text{sym}(\mu(r))^* : pw \in L(\mu(r))\}$
2. last$(r) = \{p \in \text{sym}(\mu(r)) \mid \exists w \in \text{sym}(\mu(r))^* : wp \in L(\mu(r))\}$
3. follow(r, q) is well-defined.
4. $\forall (p, \psi) \in $ follow$(r, q) : \exists u, v \in \text{sym}(\mu(r))^* : uqpv \in L(\mu(r))$
5. $\forall (p, \psi) \in $ follow$(r, q) : \forall q' \in \mathsf{C}(r) :$

$\quad q' \notin \text{dom}(\psi) \Rightarrow (q' \notin \mathsf{C}(r, q) \vee (\exists u, v \in \text{sym}(\mu(r)|_{q'})^* : uqpv \in L(\mu(r)|_{q'})))$
$\quad \wedge \;\; \psi(q') = \mathsf{inc} \Rightarrow (q \in q' \odot $ last$(r|_{q'}) \wedge p \in q' \odot $ first$(r|_{q'}))$
$\quad \wedge \;\; \psi(q') = \mathsf{res} \Leftrightarrow (q \in q' \odot $ last$(r|_{q'}) \wedge q' \notin \mathsf{C}(r, p))$

All items can be proved by induction on r, using the preceding items. The proofs are omitted for space considerations.

Theorem 1 (Polynomial Runtime). *For all regular expressions $r \in \mathcal{R}_\Sigma$ and all positions $q \in \mathsf{sym}(\mu(r))$:*

1. *Computing $\mathsf{first}(r)$ and $\mathsf{last}(r)$ takes time $O(|r|)$.*
2. *Computing $\mathsf{follow}(r, q)$ for all q, takes time $O(|r|^3)$.*

Proof. 1. For part 1 note first that $|\mathsf{first}(r)| = O(|r|)$ and $|\mathsf{last}(r)| = O(|r|)$ follows from parts 1 and 2 of Lemma 1. We will assume that union of sets can be done in linear time, and that prefixing a number to a position (as in $\langle 1 \rangle \odot p$) can be done in constant time. We can then show that the run-time is $O(|r|)$ by induction on r.
2. For part 2, start with computing first and last for all subexpressions of r. This takes time $O(|r|^3)$. Computing $\mathsf{follow}(r, q)$ will then mean a linear number of *calls* to follow, each of which takes maximally $O(|r|^2)$ time in addition to the recursive call to follow.   □

4.2   Counter-1-Unambiguity

We can now define the right unambiguity we need for constructing deterministic automata. *Counter-1-unambiguous* regular expressions are introduced in this section. Section 4.3 describes how a deterministic FAC can be constructed in polynomial time from such expressions. However, the construction of FACs can be applied to regular expressions in a larger class, namely, the regular expressions in *constraint normal form*. The construction of an FAC from an expression in this class can also be done in polynomial time, but the FAC might not be deterministic. An expression is in constraint normal form if, for every subexpression of the form $r^{n..m}$, r is not nullable.

Definition 15. *A regular expression r is in constraint normal form if and only if there is no subexpression of r of the form $r_1^{n..m}$ where $r_1 \in \mathfrak{N}_\Sigma$.*

For example, $(a^*a)^{2..3}$ is in constraint normal form, while $(a^*)^{2..3}$ is not.

Given a regular expression r, let mappings $\min : \mathsf{C}(r) \mapsto \mathbb{N}$ and $\max : \mathsf{C}(r) \mapsto \mathbb{N}_{/1}$ be such that $\min(q) = r|_{q \odot \langle 2 \rangle}$ and $\max(q) = r|_{q \odot \langle 3 \rangle}$, and define a binary relation $\simeq$ between the pairs $\mathsf{sym}(\mu(r)) \times (\mathcal{C} \mapsto \{\mathsf{inc}, \mathsf{res}\})$, where $(q_2, \psi_2) \simeq (q_1, \psi_1)$ if and only if $r|_{q_2} = r|_{q_1}$ and ψ_1 and ψ_2 are overlapping update instructions (as according to Definition 6).

Definition 16 (Counter-1-Unambiguity). *A regular expression r in constraint normal form is* counter-1-unambiguous, *if $\forall p, q \in \mathsf{first}(r) : r|_p = r|_q \Rightarrow p = q$ and $\forall q \in \mathsf{sym}(\mu(r)) : \forall (q_2, \psi_2), (q_1, \psi_1) \in \mathsf{follow}(r, q) : (q_2, \psi_2) \simeq (q_1, \psi_1) \Rightarrow (q_2, \psi_2) = (q_1, \psi_1)$.*

The regular expressions used as examples in Sect. 1 are counter-1-unambiguous. Examples of expressions that are not counter-1-unambiguous are $(a^{1..2})^{1..2}$,

$(a^*a)^{2..3}$ and $(a^{1..2} + b)^{1..2}$, while $(a + b)^{1..4}$ is counter-1-unambiguous. For some of the expressions that are not counter-1-unambiguous, we can multiply the numerical constraints to possibly get counter-1-unambiguous expressions. In general, for regular expressions of the form $(r^{l_1..u_1})^{l_2..u_2}$, if $l_2 \geq \frac{l_1 - 1}{u_1 - l_1}$, then $L(r^{l_1 \cdot l_2..u_1 \cdot u_2}) = L((r^{l_1..u_1})^{l_2..u_2})$. For example, $L((a^{1..2})^{1..2}) = L(a^{1..4})$.

4.3   Constructing FACs

Given a regular expression r and the mappings first, last and follow as defined above, we construct the FAC(r), an FAC $(\Sigma, Q, C(r), \mathcal{A}, \Phi, \min, \max, q^I, \mathcal{F})$, where $Q = \text{sym}(\mu(r)) \cup \{q^I\}$ and where min and max are as above. $\forall q \in \text{sym}(\mu(r))$, let $\mathcal{A}(q) = r|_q$ and $\Phi(q) = \text{follow}(r, q)$. Let $\Phi(q^I) = \{(q, \varnothing) \mid q \in \text{first}(r)\}$.

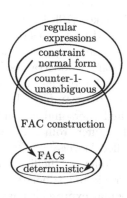

The initial configuration is final if and only if r is nullable. For the other configurations, two conditions must be met: the position the current state represents must be in last(r), and the numerical constraints containing this position must be satisfied. Thus, the mapping $\mathcal{F}$ is defined as follows. Let first $\mathcal{F}' = \{p \mapsto C(r, p) \mid p \in \text{last}(r)\} \cup \{q \mapsto \bot \mid q \in \text{sym}(\mu(r)) - \text{last}(r)\}$. If $r \in \mathfrak{N}_\Sigma$, then let $\mathcal{F} = \mathcal{F}' \cup \{q^I \mapsto \varnothing\}$, and otherwise let $\mathcal{F} = \mathcal{F}' \cup \{q^I \mapsto \bot\}$.

Figure 4 illustrates some properties of this algorithm. The result of applying this algorithm to $r = (a^2 + bc)^{3..5}$ from Example 1 is the FAC in Example 3.

Fig. 4. Some properties of the construction of FACs

4.4   Equivalence of $L(r)$ and $L'(r)$

We will now define $L'(r)$, which is the language recognized by the FAC constructed from r as described above.

Definition 17 ($L'(r)$). *For $r \in \mathcal{R}_\Sigma$, $L'(r)$ is the subset of Σ^*, such that $\epsilon \in L'(r)$ iff $r \in \mathfrak{N}_\Sigma$ and for all $w \in L'(r)$ where $n = |w| > 0$, there exist $p_1, \ldots, p_n \in \text{sym}(\mu(r))$, and if $n > 1$ there are also $\psi_2, \ldots, \psi_n \in (C(r) \mapsto \{\text{inc}, \text{res}\})$, such that all of the following five items hold:*

1. $r|_{p_1} \cdots r|_{p_n} = w$.
2. $p_1 \in \text{first}(r)$.
3. $p_n \in \text{last}(r)$.
4. *If $n > 1$, then $\forall i \in \{1, \ldots, n - 1\} : (p_{i+1}, \psi_{i+1}) \in \text{follow}(r, p_i)$.*
5. $\forall i \in \{1, \ldots, n\} : (f_{\psi_i}(\cdots f_{\psi_1}(\gamma_1) \cdots), \min, \max) \models \psi_{i+1}$, *where $\psi_1 = \varnothing$, $\psi_{n+1} = \{p \mapsto \text{res} \mid p \in C(r, p_n)\}$.*

Theorem 2. *If $r \in \mathcal{R}_\Sigma$ is in constraint normal form, then $L(r) = L'(r)$.*

The proof is by induction on r and uses the definitions of $L'(r)$ and $L(r)$ and the facts in Lemma 1. The proof is omitted for space considerations.

5 Related Work and Conclusion

5.1 Related Work

The inspiration for Finite Automata with Counters comes, of course, from finite automata as defined, e.g., by Hopcroft & Ullman [11], by Kleene [12] or by Glushkov [10]. Kilpeläinen & Tuhkanen [4,7,13], and Gelade et al. [6] also investigated properties of the regular expressions with counters, and give algorithms for membership, and definitions of automata classes for regular expressions with numerical constraints. Tuhkanen & Kilpeläinen's counter automata seem to handle a larger class of expressions than FACs, but they are not defined formally, only by examples. The technical report referred to in the paper was never finished (personal communication). Tuhkanen & Kilpeläinen's counter automata also differ from FACs in the way iterations are kept track of, with extra states, called "levels".

Colazzo, Ghelli & Sartiani describe in [14] an algorithm for linear-time membership in a subclass of regular expressions called collision-free. The collision-free regular expressions have at most one occurrence of each symbol from Σ, and the counters (and the Kleene star) can only be applied directly to letters or disjunctions of letters. The latter class is smaller than, and included in, the class of counter-1-unambiguous regular expressions. The main focus of Colazzo, Ghelli & Sartiani is on the extension of regular expressions used in *XML Schemas*. This extension includes *interleaving*, which is not covered by the algorithm presented here.

A class of tree automata with counting are described by Zilio & Lugiez [15]. Our approach also has similarities to the tagged automata found in Laurikari [16]. The results by Brüggemann-Klein & Wood in [5,9,17] concerning 1-unambiguous regular expressions, are in some ways what the current article attempts to extend to the regular expressions with counters.

5.2 Conclusion

We have defined *Finite Automata with Counters* (FAC), and a translation from the regular expressions with numerical constraints to these automata. We defined *constraint normal form*, a subset of the regular expressions with numerical constraints, for which the translation to FACs can be done in polynomial time. Further we defined *counter-1-unambiguous regular expressions*, a subset of the regular expressions of constraint normal form, and for which the FAC resulting from the translation is deterministic. The deterministic FAC can recognize the language of the given regular expression in time linear in the size of word to be tested. Testing whether an FAC is deterministic can be done in polynomial time.

References

1. The Open Group: The Open Group Base Specifications Issue 6, IEEE Std 1003.1.
   2 edn. (1997)
2. GNU: GNU grep manual
3. Fallside, D.C.: XML Schema part 0: Primer, W3C recommendation. Technical
   report, World Wide Web Consortium (W3C) (2001)
4. Kilpeläinen, P., Tuhkanen, R.: Regular expressions with numerical occurrence indicators - preliminary results. In: Kilpeläinen, P., Päivinen, N. (eds.) SPLST,
   pp. 163–173. University of Kuopio, Department of Computer Science (2003)
5. Brüggemann-Klein, A.: Regular expressions into finite automata. Theoretical Computer Science 120(2), 197–213 (1993)
6. Gelade, W., Martens, W., Neven, F.: Optimizing schema languages for XML: Numerical constraints and interleaving. In: Schwentick, T., Suciu, D. (eds.) ICDT
   2007. LNCS, vol. 4353, pp. 269–283. Springer, Heidelberg (2006)
7. Kilpeläinen, P., Tuhkanen, R.: One-unambiguity of regular expressions with nu-
   meric occurrence indicators. Information and Computation 205(6), 890–916 (2007)
8. Bezem, M., Klop, J.W., de Vrijer, R. (eds.): Term Rewriting Systems. Cambridge
   University Press, Cambridge (2003)
9. Brüggemann-Klein, A., Wood, D.: One-unambiguous regular languages. Information and Computation 140(2), 229–253 (1998)
10. Glushkov, V.M.: The abstract theory of automata. Russian Mathematical Sur-
    veys 16(5), 1–53 (1961)
11. Hopcroft, J.E., Ullman, J.D.: Introduction to Automata Theory, Languages and
    Computation. Addison-Wesley, Reading (1979)
12. Kleene, S.C.: Representation of events in nerve sets and finite automata. Automata
    Studies, 3–41 (1956)
13. Kilpeläinen, P., Tuhkanen, R.: Towards efficient implementation of XML schema
    content models. In: Munson, E.V., Vion-Dury, J.Y. (eds.) ACM Symposium on
    Document Engineering, pp. 239–241. ACM, New York (2004)
14. Ghelli, G., Colazzo, D., Sartiani, C.: Linear time membership in a class of regular
    expressions with interleaving and counting. In: Shanahan, J.G., Amer-Yahia, S.,
    Manolescu, I., Zhang, Y., Evans, D.A., Kolcz, A., Choi, K.S., Chowdhury, A. (eds.)
    CIKM, pp. 389–398. ACM, New York (2008)
15. Dal-Zilio, S., Lugiez, D.: Xml schema, tree logic and sheaves automata. In:
    Nieuwenhuis, R. (ed.) RTA 2003. LNCS, vol. 2706, pp. 246–263. Springer,
    Heidelberg (2003)
16. Laurikari, V.: NFAs with tagged transitions, their conversion to deterministic au-
    tomata and application to regular expressions. In: SPIRE, pp. 181–187 (2000)
17. Brüggemann-Klein, A.: Regular expressions into finite automata. In: Simon, I. (ed.)
    LATIN 1992. LNCS, vol. 583, pp. 87–98. Springer, Heidelberg (1992)

On the Relative Expressive Power of Contextual Grammars with Maximal and Depth-First Derivations

Lakshmanan Kuppusamy[1,*] and Kamala Krithivasan[2]

[1] ALPAGE, INRIA-Rocquencourt
Le Chesnay - 78153, France
klakshma@vit.ac.in
[2] Department of Computer Science and Engineering
Indian Institute of Technology Madras
Chennai - 600 036, India
kamala@iitm.ac.in

Abstract. In the recent years, several new classes of contextual grammars have been introduced to give an appropriate model description to natural languages. With this aim, some new families of contextual languages have been introduced based on maximal and depth-first conditions and analyzed in the framework of so-called mildly context sensitive languages. However, the relationship among these families of languages have not yet been analyzed in detail. In this paper, we investigate the relationship between the families of languages whose grammars are based on maximal and depth-first conditions. We prove an interesting result that all these families of languages are incomparable to each other, but they are not disjoint.

Keywords: internal contextual grammars, maximal, depth-first, incomparable.

1 Introduction

Contextual grammars produce languages starting from a finite set of *axioms* and adjoining *contexts*, iteratively, according to the *selector* present in the current sentential form. As introduced in [15], if the contexts are adjoined at the ends of the strings, the grammar is called *external. Internal* contextual grammars were introduced by Păun and Nguyen in 1980 [20], where the contexts are adjoined to the selector strings which appear as substrings of the derived string. The main motivation for introducing contextual grammars was to obtain languages that are more appropriate from natural languages point of view. In fact, the class of languages should (i) contain basic non-context-free languages, (ii) be parsable in polynomial time (iii) contain *semilinear* languages only, and these three properties together define the so-called *mildly context sensitive* (MCS) formalisms and languages, as introduced by A.K. Joshi in 1985 [5].

---

* Currently on leave from parent Institution VIT University, Vellore - 632 014, India.

M. Leucker and C. Morgan (Eds.): ICTAC 2009, LNCS 5684, pp. 246–260, 2009.

When contextual grammars are analyzed from the perspective of MCS formalisms, the basic classes, external and internal contextual languages fail to contain some desirable non-context-free languages. Further, they contain non-semilinear languages too [4],[6]. Also, at present only exponential time algorithms are known for the membership problem of internal contextual grammars [2] and whether it can be solved in polynomial time algorithm remains open [8]. Therefore, some attempts have been made in the last decade or so to introduce variants of contextual grammars by restricting the selector chosen in the derivation, to obtain certain specific classes of contextual languages which satisfy the above said MCS properties. The first such main variant was *depth-first* contextual grammars [18] where the main catch is to track the previously adjoined contexts in the selector. Though this idea might be useful while parsing (especially for backtracking), these grammars fail to generate one of the basic non-context-free languages, like *multiple agreement:* $\{a^n b^n c^n \mid n \geq 1\}$. So, other new classes of grammars have been introduced, for instance, *maximal* contextual grammars [17]. Though they generate the basic non-context-free languages, they also generate non-semilinear languages [16]. Besides, in [2], it was proved that these maximal and internal contextual grammars can be transformed into equivalent *dynamic range concatenation grammars*, an extended formalism of *range concatenation grammars* [1]). However, parsing dynamic range concatenation grammar allows exponential time complexity and thus this strategy is not useful.

Further, in [11], a variant namely *maximal depth-first* grammars have been introduced, by combining the maximal and depth-first conditions. Like maximal grammars, the family of languages generated by these grammars contain non-context-free languages, but their membership and semilinear problems have been left open. Later in [12], two variants, namely *end-marked maximal depth-first* and *inner end-marked maximal depth-first* grammars have been introduced with the aim to solve the membership problem and semilinearity issue for maximal depth-first derivation. In [7], Ilie considered a new variant called *maximal local*. Ilie showed that the languages generated by maximal local grammars with regular selectors contain basic non-context-free languages and the membership problem for these languages is solvable in polynomial time. But the question of semilinearity was left open for these languages and in [11], a restricted variant of maximal local contextual grammars, called *absorbing right context grammar* has been introduced in order to solve the semilinear problem of maximal local.

Many of these variants were obtained by refining the previous variants (i.e., imposing further restrictions in the existing variants) with the hope that they could clear the failed properties of MCS and at the same time the properties which are shown to satisfy are also preserved. Out of all these variants discussed above, the classes of languages generated by maximal local, absorbing right context, inner end-marked depth-first grammars with regular selectors were shown to satisfy the properties of MCS languages [9],[11],[12]. Since all the above variants have been introduced with a single aim to satisfy the properties of MCS languages (and thus to give a model description for natural languages from the domain of contextual grammars), the relative expressive power of these variants have not been discussed so far. Our motivation in this paper is to analyze the expressive power of these grammars.

When several classes of grammars originate from one grammar, it would be interesting to analyze their power of generating languages and to form the hierarchical structures with the results we obtain. When such hierarchical order is not possible between the families of languages, they become incomparable. In this paper, we analyze the generative power of the above mentioned variants of the internal contextual grammars with regular selectors. We prove that all these families of the above said variants are incomparable to one another. Also, we prove that they are not disjoint as there are common languages that are shared by these families of languages.

As a word of caution we would like to mention that so far no unanimous definition of MCS has been agreed to. For example, the semilinear property is considered to be too strong and is replaced by a weaker property, *constant growth property*. Also non-compliance of these mentioned properties does not rule out a formalism being useful, for example, "back-end" general formalisms like range concatenation grammars [1] or abstract categorial grammars [19]. Also, several other variants of contextual grammars have been introduced and analyzed from the perspective of formal languages. However, we do not discuss them here as it is out of scope of this paper and we refer to the monograph [21] for more variants.

2 Preliminaries

We assume the readers are familiar with the basic formal language theory notions. We refer to [22] for more details on formal language theory. We now present the definition of a few classes of contextual grammars considered in this paper.

An *internal contextual grammar* is $G = (V, A, (S_1, C_1), \ldots, (S_m, C_m)), m \geq 1$, where V is an alphabet, $A \subseteq V^*$ is a finite set called *axioms*, $S_j \subseteq V^*$, $1 \leq j \leq m$, are the sets of *selectors* or *choice*, and $C_j \subseteq V^* \times V^*$, C_j finite, $1 \leq j \leq m$, are the sets of *contexts* associated with the selector S_j. The usual *derivation* in the *internal mode* is defined as $x \Longrightarrow_{in} y$ iff $x = x_1 x_2 x_3$, $y = x_1 u x_2 v x_3$, for $x_1, x_2, x_3 \in V^*$, $x_2 \in S_j, (u, v) \in C_j$, $1 \leq j \leq m$.

Given an internal contextual grammar G as above, the maximal and depth-first derivations are given as below. In maximal mode (denoted by max), at each derivation, the chosen selector $x_2 \in S_i$, for the next derivation should be of maximal length than the other possible selectors $x_2' \in S_i$ (for the formal representation of maximal condition, refer the below condition (iii) alone). In depth-first mode (denoted by df), for every derivation, the selector for the next derivation must contain one of the contexts u or v which was adjoined in the previous derivation (for the formal representation of depth-first condition, refer below condition (ii) alone). Next, we define maximal depth-first grammar, obtained by combining maximality and depth-first conditions. More formally, given a contextual grammar G as above, a *maximal depth-first derivation* (denoted by mdf) in G is a derivation $w_1 \Longrightarrow_{mdf} w_2 \Longrightarrow_{mdf} \cdots \Longrightarrow_{mdf} w_n$, $n \geq 1$, where

(i) $w_1 \in A$, $w_1 \Longrightarrow_{in} w_2$ (i.e., in the usual internal mode),

(ii) For each $i = 2, 3, \ldots, n - 1$, if $w_{i-1} = z_1 z_2 z_3$, $w_i = z_1 u z_2 v z_3$ ((u, v) is the context adjoined to w_{i-1} in order to get w_i), then $w_i = x_1 x_2 x_3$, $w_{i+1} = x_1 s x_2 t x_3$, such that $x_2 \in S_j$, $(s, t) \in C_j$, for some j, $1 \le j \le m$, and x_2 contains one of the contexts u or v as a substring (thus, satisfying the depth-first condition). Note that here the chosen next selector contains not any s or t occurred in the string, but the same s or t adjoined in the previous derivation step.

(iii) For each $i = 2, 3, \ldots, n - 1$, if $w_i \Longrightarrow_{df} w_{i+1}$, then there will be no other derivation in G with $w_i \Longrightarrow_{df} w'_{i+1}$ such that $w_i = x'_1 x'_2 x'_3$, $x'_2 \in S_j$ and $|x'_2| > |x_2|$ where $x_2 \in S_j$ (note that the selector x_2 is of maximal length with respect to S_j only, and not with respect to all selectors).

Given a contextual grammar G, we next define the *local* mode in the following way. For $z \in A$, $z \Longrightarrow_{in} x$ such that $z = z_1 z_2 z_3$, $x = z_1 u z_2 v z_3$, $z_2 \in S_k$, $(u, v) \in C_k$, for $z_1, z_2, z_3 \in V^*$, $1 \le k \le m$, then $x \Longrightarrow_{loc} y$ is called local with respect to $z \Longrightarrow x$, iff we have $u = u'u''$, $v = v'v''$, $u', u'', v', v'' \in V^*$, $y = z_1 u' s u'' z_2 v' t v'' z_3$, for $u'' z_2 v' \in S_j$, $(s, t) \in C_j$, $1 \le j \le m$. That is, at each derivation, the contexts are introduced adjacent to the contexts (or to the side of the previous selector itself, when $u'' = \lambda = v'$) which were introduced in the previous derivation. Note that, at every derivation, the selector may expand on its left side or right side or both sides, but expands not more than the contexts introduced in the previous derivation step. Therefore, once a selector is chosen, that selector should be a subword for the selectors used in the further derivations (this point is often used in the proofs). When the maximality condition is included with this local variant, the grammar is said to be *maximal local* (denoted by *mloc*).

Now, we define a variant obtained by imposing further restriction to the above *mloc* grammar and we call it as *absorbing right contextual grammar* (denoted by *arc*) [11]. In this variant, the selector (say y_{i+1}) for the next derivation (step) is obtained by adjoining the first half v'_i of the current right context to the current selector y_i where $v_i = v'_i v''_i$, $|v'_i| = \lceil \frac{|v_i|}{2} \rceil$, $|v''| = \lfloor \frac{|v_i|}{2} \rfloor$. That is, $y_{i+1} = y_i v'_i$, $y_i \in S_j$, $y_i \in V^*, v'_i \in V^+$.

An *end-marked maximal depth-first* (denoted by *emdf*) contextual grammar [12] is a construct $G = (V, A, \{(S_1, C_1), \ldots, (S_m, C_m)\}), m \ge 1$, where $V, A, S_1, \ldots S_m$, are as mentioned in the definition of internal contextual grammar and $C_j \subseteq (V^+_{\{L,R\}} \times V^*) \cup (V^* \times V^+_{\{L,R\}})$, C_j finite, $1 \le j \le m$, are the set of contexts. The elements of C_j's are of the form $(u_L, v), (u_R, v), (u, v_L)$, and (u, v_R). The suffix L and R represents end marker (left and right) for the selector of the next derivation. u_L (or v_L) indicates the selector for the next derivation should start with u (or v), thus u (or v) is the left end of the next selector. Similarly, u_R (or v_R) indicates the selector for the next derivation should end with the context u (or v). Given such a grammar G, an *emdf* derivation in G is a derivation $w_1 \Longrightarrow_{emdf} w_2 \Longrightarrow_{emdf} \cdots \Longrightarrow_{emdf} w_n$, $n \ge 1$, where

- $w_1 \in A$, $w_1 \Longrightarrow w_2$ in the usual way,

- For each $i = 2, 3, \ldots, n - 1$, if $w_{i-1} = z_1 z_2 z_3$, $w_i = z_1 u z_2 v z_3$, such that $z_2 \in S_k$, $1 \leq k \leq m$, then $w_i = x_1 x_2 x_3$, $w_{i+1} = x_1 s x_2 t x_3$, such that $x_2 \in S_j$, $1 \leq j \leq m$, and x_2 will be one of the following four cases:
  - (i) $x_2 = u z_2'$, $u \neq \lambda$, if $(u_L, v) \in C_k$, with $z_2' \in V^*$ is of maximal (i.e., there exists no $z_2'' \in V^*$, such that $u z_2'' \in S_j$, with $|z_2''| > |z_2'|$).
  - (ii) $x_2 = z_1' u$, $u \neq \lambda$, if $(u_R, v) \in C_k$, with $z_1' \in V^*$ is of maximal (i.e., there exists no $z_1'' \in V^*$, such that $z_1'' u \in S_j$, with $|z_1''| > |z_1'|$).
  - (iii) $x_2 = z_2' v$, $v \neq \lambda$, if $(u, v_R) \in C_k$, with $z_2' \in V^*$ is of maximal (i.e., there exists no $z_2'' \in V^*$, such that $z_2'' v \in S_j$, with $|z_2''| > |z_2'|$).
  - (iv) $x_2 = v z_3'$, $v \neq \lambda$, if $(u, v_L) \in C_k$, with $z_3' \in V^*$ is of maximal (i.e., there exists no $z_3'' \in V^*$, such that $v z_3'' \in S_j$, with $|z_3''| > |z_3'|$).

Now, we introduce the next variant. Given a *emdf* grammar G, we can define the *inner end-marked maximal depth-first grammar* (denoted by *iemdf*) by imposing the following changes in the grammar and in derivation.

- $C_j \subseteq (V_L^+ \times V^*) \cup (V^* \times V_R^+)$.
- As the elements of C_j's are of the form (u_L, v) and (u, v_R), the cases (ii) and (iv) discussed above are void and only the cases (i) and (iii) are valid.
- The selector for the next derivation should lie inside the contexts u and v which were adjoined in the previous derivation. More precisely, the next chosen selector cannot have both the adjoined contexts u and v, but it may contain the proper prefixes of v (if u is end-marked, i.e., u_L) or proper suffixes of u (if v is end-marked, i.e., v_R). Obviously the end-marked context is included in the next chosen selector in order to satisfy the depth-first and end-marked conditions. More formally, if u and v are the contexts adjoined to the selector, say z_2, then the next selector, say x_2, will be a strict subword of $u z_2 v$ and x_2 should either begin with u or end with v.

From the above definitions, we can see that the definition of each of the grammars is interlinked with the other and all the grammars share the maximality condition in common (except *arc*) and many grammars share the depth-first condition also (some grammars share this condition partially, like *mloc* and *arc*).

The language generated by a grammar G in the mode β, $\beta \in \{max, mdf, mloc, arc, emdf, iemdf\}$ is given by $L_\beta(G) = \{w \in V^* \mid x \Longrightarrow_\beta^* w, \ x \in A\}$, where $\Longrightarrow_\beta^*$ is the reflexive transitive closure of the relation $\Longrightarrow_\beta$. If all the sets of selectors $S_1, \ldots, S_m$ are in a family F of languages, then we say that the grammar G is with F choice. As usual, the family of languages for G working in $\beta \in \{max, mdf, mloc, arc, emdf, iemdf\}$ mode with F choice is given as $ICC_{max}(F), ICC_{mdf}(F), ICC_{mloc}(F), ICC_{arc}(F), ICC_{emdf}(F)$, and $ICC_{iemdf}(F)$, respectively. In this paper, we consider $F \in \{FIN, REG\}$.

The following assumption is made throughout this paper. We do not consider the empty contexts (λ, λ) here, but one-sided contexts of the form $(\lambda, v), (u, \lambda)$ are considered (but the λ context cannot be an end-marker). Also, the underlined symbols denote the newly inserted contexts and the word in between the two down arrows indicates the selector used for the next derivation. We call maximal length as maximal in many places for the sake of brevity. Also, we refer the selector for the next derivation as simply next selector in many occurrences.

3 Results

In this section, we discuss the generative power of the internal contextual grammars when we put different types of restrictions on the derivations such as $max, mloc, arc, mdf, emdf, iemdf$. Here, the generative power of a class of grammars deals with the limitation of the grammars in generating the languages (like what languages can or cannot be produced by these grammars). We aim to show that there are some languages which can be generated when putting one type of restriction on the derivation but they cannot be generated when some other types of restriction is imposed on the derivation. Also we aim to show that there are lanaguges which can be generated by all types of restricted derivations mentioned in the previous section.

Lemma 1. $ICC_\alpha(FIN) \subset ICC_\alpha(REG)$, $\alpha \in \{max, mdf, mloc, arc, emdf, iemdf\}$.

Proof. The relation $ICC_\alpha(FIN) \subseteq ICC_\alpha(REG)$ is obvious. The strict inclusion follows from the following result. Consider the crossed dependency language $L_1 = \{a^n b^m c^n d^m \mid n, m \geq 1\}$. This language cannot be generated by any of the above α grammars with finite choice since in order to increase the occurrences of a, c equally and b, d equally, the grammar needs regular selectors of the form $a^{k_1} b^+ c^{k_2}$ and $b^{k_3} c^+ d^{k_4}, k_1, k_2, k_3, k_4 \geq 0$, respectively. However, in previous papers ([7],[9],[11],[12],[17]), all these grammars were shown to generate L_1 with regular selectors. □

Lemma 2. $L_2 = \{a, b\}^+ \in ICC_\alpha(REG)$, $\alpha \in \{max, mdf, mloc, arc, emdf, iemdf\}$.

Proof. The language $L_2 = \{a, b\}^+$ can be generated by $G_\alpha = (\{a, b\}, \{a, b\}, (\{a, b\}, \{(a_L, \lambda), (b_L, \lambda)\}))$ for $\alpha \in \{max, mdf, emdf, iemdf\}$ (for max, mdf modes, there is no suffix L in the contexts). Any string $w = w_1 \ldots w_n \in L_2$ can be produced by starting from w_n, adding the context on the left, iteratively. For $\beta = \{mloc, arc\}$ modes, $G_\beta = (\{a, b\}, \{a, b\}, (\{a, b\}^+, \{(\lambda, a), (\lambda, b)\}))$. It is easy to see that $L(G_\beta) = L_2$. □

The above result shows that the language $\{a, b\}^+$ is included in all families of languages $ICC_\alpha(REG)$, $\alpha \in \{max, mdf, mloc, arc, emdf, iemdf\}$.

Lemma 3. $ICC_\alpha(REG) - ICC_{max}(REG) \neq \emptyset$, $\alpha \in \{mdf, mloc, arc, emdf, iemdf\}$.

Proof. The language $L_3 = \{a^n \mid n \geq 1\} \cup \{a^n b^n c^n \mid n \geq 1\}$ can be generated by the grammars

$$G_{mdf} = (\{a, b, c\}, \{a, aa, abc\}, (aa, (a, \lambda)), (b^+ c^+, (ab, c))).$$
$$G_{mloc} = (\{a, b, c\}, \{a, aa, abc\}, (aa, (a, \lambda)), (b^+ c, (ab, c))).$$
$$G_{arc} = (\{a, b, c\}, \{a, aa, abc\}, (aa^+, (\lambda, a)), (b^+, (a, bc))).$$
$$G_{\{emdf, iemdf\}} = (\{a, b, c\}, \{a, aa, abc\}, (aa, (a_L, \lambda)), (b^+ c^+, (ab, c_R))).$$

In order to get a better understanding on how the strings are generated using these grammars, we provide some details about the selectors used in the derivations.

To generate the strings of the form a^n, aa (or aa^+ for arc mode) is chosen as selector for all derivations and a is adjoined to the side of the selector. For strings of the other part of the language $(a^n b^n c^n)$, the selector $b^+ c^+$ covers the adjoined right context c in mdf mode. In $mloc$ mode, we have $u_2' = a, u_2'' = b$ and $v_2' = \lambda, v_2'' = c$, at every derivation. In arc mode, every time the selector b^+ absorbs half of the right context b in bc. In $emdf$ mode, whenever (a_L, λ) is introduced, the next selector starts with a (a is the left end of the selector aa) and whenever (ab, c_R) is introduced, the next selector ends with the adjoined right context c (c is the right end of the selector $b^+ c^+$). In $iemdf$ mode, the condition (u_L, v) or (u, v_R) is satisfied and the selector is inside the previously introduced contexts. In all modes, the selectors are chosen of maximal length.

However, the language L_3 is not in $ICC_{max}(REG)$. Assume that the language $L_3 \in ICC_{max}(REG)$ for a maximal grammar G_{max}. In order to generate the strings $a^n, n \geq 1$, we need a selector $a^k, k \geq 0$, with the context $(a^{i_1}, a^{i_2}), i_1 + i_2 \geq 1$. Now, consider a string $a^p b^p c^p$ for a large $p \geq k$. As the context (a^{i_1}, a^{i_2}) can be applied to $a^p b^p c^p$ by choosing a subword a^k in a^p, we can produce strings of the form $a^{p+i_1+i_2} b^p c^p \notin L_3$. A contradiction.   □

The following result is the counterpart for the above lemma.

Lemma 4. $ICC_{max}(REG) - ICC_\beta(REG) \neq \emptyset$, $\beta \in \{mdf, mloc, arc, emdf, iemdf\}$.

Proof. Consider the language $L_4 = \{a^n cb^n a^m cb^m \mid n, m \geq 0\}$. It is in $ICC_{max}(FIN)$, because this language can be generated by the grammar $G_{max} = (\{a, b, c\}, cc, (c, (a, b)))$. By Lemma 1, $L_4 \in ICC_{max}(REG)$.

However, $L_4 \notin ICC_\beta(REG)$ for the above β. Assume that $L_4 \in ICC_\beta(REG)$ for any grammar $G_\beta = (\{a, b, c\}, A, (S_1, C_1), \ldots, (S_r, C_r))$. First, we give the proof for the case $\beta = mdf$. As axiom is also present in the language, the axiom A must have a word of the form $a^i cb^i a^j cb^j, i, j \geq 0$, and a context of the form $(a^k, b^k), k \geq 1$, is adjoined to such a word, then either the number of occurrences of a and b around the first c, or the number of occurrences of a and b around the second c is increased. Assume that the occurrences of a and b around the first c is increased equally (the case of a and b increased equally around the second c is symmetric). Therefore, we have $a^i cb^i a^j cb^j \implies a^{i_1} \underline{a^k} a^{i_2} cb^{i_3} \underline{b^k} b^{i_4} a^j cb^j$ for $i_1 + i_2 = i_3 + i_4 = i$. The derivation must continue using a selector which covers at least one of the contexts a^k or b^k. Continuing the derivation in this fashion, at some point of time, we have to increase the number of occurrences of a and b around the second c. In such a case, we have to use a context of the form $(a^p, b^p), p \geq 1$, and the selector should contain the subword b^k which was introduced in the previous derivation. As a^p is a left context, it cannot be added to the right side of b^k and so a^p should be adjoined to the left of b^k (but not necessarily immediate left). Then, we will have unequal number of a and b around the second c, which results in a word not in L_4. Other possibilities of derivations also lead to generation of strings not in the language. Therefore, $L(G_{mdf}) = L_4$ is impossible. For $\beta = emdf$ mode, as the definition is based on depth-first concept, the above argument about the context and selector are applicable. Continuing in that line, we have the context (a^k, b^k) is end-marked. Therefore, we have either $a_{L,R}^k$ or $b_{L,R}^k$. Obviously, a_R^k and b_L^k are failed to increase the occurrences of a and b around the second c. If a_L^k is the case, the occurrences of a around the second c cannot be increased and if b_R^k is the case, the occurrences of b around the second c cannot be increased, thus unequal occurrences a and b is generated. It is not hard to come-up with a similar argument to prove that the language cannot be generated by *iemdf* grammars. Now, let us take $\beta = mloc$. By definition of the grammar, every time the contexts are introduced adjacent to the previously introduced contexts or to the previously used selector, pumping equal number of a and b is possible only on one part of the language. Otherwise, we can derive a word which is not in the language using a similar technique as above.

Finally, let us consider the case for $\beta = arc$. From the language, it is obvious that no selector can have both c as a subword. Otherwise, b and a cannot be increased in between the two c. Since the selector accumulates only on its right side in this mode, if we use a selector contains the second c as a subword in the axiom, then we cannot pump equal occurrences of a and b around the first c. On the other hand, if we choose a selector which contains the first c as a subword, then a^*cb^+ will be a selector for further derivations. However, from this selector, we can increase the occurrences of a only in the second part, thus unequal number of a and b around the second c is generated. A contradiction.

$\square$

From Lemma 2, 3 and 4, we have the following theorem.

Theorem 1. $ICC_{max}(REG)$ *is incomparable with the families* $ICC_\alpha(REG)$, *for* $\alpha \in \{mdf, mloc, arc, emdf, iemdf\}$, *but not disjoint.*

Lemma 5. $ICC_\alpha(REG) - ICC_{mdf}(REG) \neq \emptyset$, $\alpha \in \{mloc, arc, emdf, iemdf\}$.

Proof. Consider the language $L_5 = \{a^n cb^n \mid n \geq 1\} \cup \{a^n \mid n \geq 1\}$. This language is in the family $ICC_\alpha(REG)$ for the above α. Because this language can be generated by the grammar $G_{arc} = (\{a, b, c\}, \{acb, a, aa\}, (aa^+, (\lambda, a)), (cb^+, (a, b)))$, in *arc* mode. For maximal local mode, the grammar $G_{mloc} = (\{a, b, c\}, \{acb, a, aa\}, (aa, (\lambda, a)), (acb, (a, b)))$ generates L_5. Note that, the selector aa cannot be used in the subword a^+cb^+ since once a selector is chosen in this mode, it will always be a subword to the further subwords. For *emdf* and *iemdf*, the grammar $G_5 = (\{a, b, c\}, \{acb, a, aa\}, (aa^+, (\lambda, a_R)), (acb^+, (a, b_R)))$ generates L_5.

However, $L_5 \notin ICC_{mdf}(REG)$. On contrary, let us assume that $L_5 \in ICC_{mdf}(REG)$ for a *mdf* grammar G_{mdf}. In order to generate the strings of the first part, we need a context of the form $(a^m, b^m), m \geq 1$. In order to obtain words of the form a^n for a large n, we need a context $(a^i, a^j), i+j \geq 1$, associated with the selector $a^k, k \geq 1$. Assume a word $a^{m+r}cb^{m+r}$ in the language where $m+r \geq k$. Also, assume that this word is derived from $a^r cb^r, r \geq 1$ by adjoining the context (a^m, b^m). The selector for the next derivation should contain one of the contexts a^m or b^m. Now we can use the selector a^k and obtain a word $a^{i+j+m+r}cb^{m+r} \notin L_5$. A contradiction.

$\square$

Lemma 6. $ICC_\alpha(REG) - ICC_\beta(REG) \neq \emptyset$, $\alpha \in \{mloc, mdf, emdf\}$, $\beta \in \{arc, iemdf\}$.

Proof. Consider the marked mirror image language $L_6 = \{wcw^r \mid w \in \{a,b\}^*\}$. This language can be generated by the grammars

$$G_{mloc} = (\{a,b,c\}, c, (c, \{(a,a),(b,b)\})).$$
$$G_{mdf} = (\{a,b,c\}, c, (\{w'cw'' \mid w',w'' \in \{a,b\}^*\}, \{(a,a),(b,b)\})).$$
$$G_{emdf} = (\{a,b,c\}, c, (\{w'cw'' \mid w',w'' \in \{a,b\}^*\}, \{(a_L,a),(b_L,b)\})).$$

However, this language does not belong to $ICC_{arc}(REG), ICC_{iemdf}(REG)$. Because, for any type of grammar, generating the strings of the form wcw^r is possible only when the context of the form $(a^i, a^i), i \geq 1$ or $(b^j, b^j), j \geq 1$, is adjoined to the selector c in each derivation, or when the above contexts are adjoined to the selector $w'cw''$, $w',w'' \in \{a,b\}^*$ and the selector $w'cw''$ is of maximal length. So, starting from c, either the selector c should absorb both right and left context or should not absorb any context. In arc grammars, as the selector absorbs the right context only, we cannot generate the language L_6 or otherwise, we can generate words which are not in L_6. In $iemdf$ mode, though the selector can absorb right and left contexts, it is not permitted to absorb both contexts at a time since the chosen selector for the next derivation should be inside the adjoined contexts. Therefore, choosing a selector $w'cw''$ of maximal length is not possible. □

From Lemma 2, 5 and 6, we have the following theorem.

Theorem 2. $ICC_{mdf}(REG)$ *is incomparable with* $ICC_{iemdf}(REG)$, *but not disjoint.*

Lemma 7. $ICC_\alpha(REG) - ICC_\beta(REG) \neq \emptyset$, $\alpha \in \{arc, iemdf\}$, $\beta \in \{mloc, mdf, emdf\}$.

Proof. Consider the non-marked duplication language $L_7 = \{ww \mid w \in \{a,b\}^*\}$. This language can be generated by the grammars

$$G_{arc} = (\{a,b\}, \lambda, (\{w' \mid w' \in \{a,b\}^*\}, \{(a,a),(b,b)\})),$$
$$G_{iemdf} = (\{a,b\}, \lambda, (\{w' \mid w' \in \{a,b\}^*\}, \{(a,a_R),(b,b_R)\})).$$

In arc mode, starting with the initial selector λ, it accumulates the right context a or b every time. In $iemdf$ mode, every time, the selector for the next derivation is chosen inside the adjoined contexts (but right context is included for meeting the depth-first condition) and of maximal length. A sample derivation in α mode $\alpha \in \{arc, iemdf\}$ is given as

$$\lambda \Longrightarrow_\alpha \underline{w_1}^\downarrow \underline{w_1}^\downarrow \Longrightarrow_\alpha w_1\underline{w_2}^\downarrow w_1\underline{w_2}^\downarrow \Longrightarrow_\alpha w_1w_2\underline{w_3}^\downarrow w_1w_2\underline{w_3}^\downarrow \Longrightarrow_\alpha^* ww.$$

However L_7 does not belong to $ICC_\beta(REG)$ for the above β. In order to generate the strings of the form ww, at each derivation, from the derived string

$w'' \in L_7$, the context (x, x), $x \in \{a, b\}^+$ is adjoined at the beginning of w''(left context x) and at the center of w''(right context x) or at the center of w''(left context x) and at the end of w''(right context x). This implies, the chosen selector should expand only at one side from the center. Assume that $w' \in L_7$ is derived from w'' in such a way. Then, $w' = z\underline{x}z\underline{x}$ or $w' = \underline{x}z\underline{x}z$, for $z \in \{a, b\}^*$, $x \in \{a, b\}^+$ is the context adjoined and $w'' = zz$. For $\beta = mloc$ mode, at each derivation, the contexts are adjoined to the side of previously adjoined contexts and the selector (which is over $\{a, b\}$) is chosen of maximal length, from w' we can derive $zy\underline{x}zx\underline{y} \notin L_7$ or $\underline{y}x\underline{z}xz\underline{y} \notin L_7$, where y is the context adjoined (which should be near the last adjoined context x). Next, we assume $\beta = emdf$. In $emdf$ mode, we have the contexts are end-marked, thus $(x_{\{L,R\}}, x)$ or $(x, x_{\{L,R\}})$ is the case. If (x_R, x) is the case, we have $w' = zx_R z\underline{x}$ or $\underline{x}_R z\underline{x}z$ and from w' we obtain, $w' \implies \underline{y}_R zx\underline{y}zx$ or $w' \implies \underline{y}_R x\underline{y}zxz \notin L_7$ for the adjoined context y. Though $\underline{y}_R zx\underline{y}zx \in L_7$, in the next derivation while adjoining another context (y'_R, y'), we would have $\underline{y}'_R y\underline{y}'zxyzx \notin L_7$. If (x_L, x) is the case, we have $w' = zx_L z\underline{x}$ or $\underline{x}_L z\underline{x}z$ and from w', we obtain $w' \implies zy\underline{L}xz\underline{x}\underline{y} \notin L_7$ or $w' \implies \underline{y}_L x\underline{y}zxz \notin L_7$, where is the adjoined context. For the other case $(x, x_{\{L,R\}})$, a similar proof can be given. Note that it is look like L_7 can be generated in $emdf$ mode (from $w' = zx_R z\underline{x}$), if the contexts of the form (x_R, x) and (y, y_L) are applied alternatively, however, since their corresponding selectors are same, the contexts need not be applied alternatively and one context can be applied two times to arrive to a contradiction. For $\beta = mdf$ mode, assume that $w' = z\underline{x}z\underline{x}$ or $\underline{x}z\underline{x}z \in L_7$ is derived from $w'' = zz$. Since $w' \in \{a, b\}^*$, and the selector is over $\{a, b\}$ with maximal length, from w' we can derive $\underline{y}zxzx\underline{y} \notin L_7$ or $\underline{y}x\underline{z}xzy \notin L_7$.

$\square$

The above result is the converse relation for the Lemma 6. Therefore from the above two lemmas and Lemma 2, we have the following theorem.

Theorem 3. *The families $ICC_{arc}(REG)$ and $ICC_{iemdf}(REG)$ are incomparable with the families $ICC_\beta(REG)$, $\beta \in \{mloc, mdf, emdf\}$, but not disjoint.*

Lemma 8. $ICC_{arc}(REG) - ICC_{iemdf}(REG) \neq \emptyset$.

Proof. Consider the language $L_8 = \{b^n a^m c b^n a^m b^n \mid n, m \geq 0\}$. This language can be generated by $G_{arc} = (\{a, b, c\}, c, (cb^*, \{(b, bb), (a, a)\}), (cb^*a^*, (a, a)))$. Initially, starting with the axiom c, the arc grammar generates strings of the form $b^n cb^{2n}, n \geq 1$, using the context (b, bb). As half of the right context is absorbed every time to the selector, the next selector (for the word $b^n cb^2 n$) will be cb^n and now the context (a, a) is applied several times to generate the language L_8. A sample derivation in arc mode is given by

$$c \implies_{arc} \underline{b}^{\downarrow} cb^{\downarrow}\underline{b} \implies_{arc} b\underline{b}^{\downarrow} cbb\underline{b}^{\downarrow} bb \implies_{arc} bb\underline{b}^{\downarrow} cbbb\underline{b}^{\downarrow} bbb \implies_{arc}^* b^{n-1}\underline{b}^{\downarrow} cb^{n-1}\underline{b}^{\downarrow} bb^{n-1}$$
$$\implies_{arc} b^n \underline{a}^{\downarrow} cb^n \underline{a}^{\downarrow} b^n \implies_{arc} b^n a\underline{a}^{\downarrow} cb^n a\underline{a}^{\downarrow} b^n \implies_{arc}^* b^n a^m cb^n a^m b^n.$$

However, this language does not belong to $ICC_{iemdf}(REG)$. On contrary, let us assume an $iemdf$ grammar generates L_8. Notice that the occurrences of b are pumped equally at three places in the language. In general, no internal contextual grammar can pump more than two occurrences since at every derivation, we ad-join only two contexts. Therefore, the necessary occurrences of b must be pumped before a is pumped, using a context of the form $(b^i, b^{2i}), i \geq 1$, with the associated selector is of the form $b^* c b^*$. Since the contexts are end-marked, we have either b_L^i or bb_R^{2i}. If bb_R^{2i} is the case, then the occurrences of a cannot be inserted in be-tween bs. When b_L^i is the case, we can only generate $b^n c b^n b^n$ and the occurrences of a cannot be inserted at the correct place on the left of c (a sample derivation is $c \Longrightarrow_{iemdf} {}^{\downarrow}\underline{b_L}cb^{\downarrow}\underline{b} \Longrightarrow_{iemdf} {}^{\downarrow}\underline{b_L}bcbb^{\downarrow}\underline{bb} \Longrightarrow_{iemdf} {}^{\downarrow}\underline{b_L}bbcbbb^{\downarrow}\underline{bbb} \Longrightarrow^* b^n c b^n b^n$). Note that, in $iemdf$ mode, the selector should not cover both the adjoined contexts.   □

Lemma 9. $ICC_\alpha(REG) - ICC_{arc}(REG) \neq \emptyset$, $\alpha \in \{iemdf, mdf\}$.

Proof. Consider the language $L_9 = \{a^n b^n c b^n \mid n \geq 1\}$. This language can be generated by the grammar $G_\alpha = (\{a, b, c\}, abcb, (b^+ c b^+, (ab, b_R)))$, $\alpha \in \{mdf, iemdf\}$ (for mdf grammar, there is no subscript R in the context).

However, $L_9 \notin ICC_{arc}(REG)$. On contrary, let us assume that $L_9 \in ICC_{arc}(REG)$ for an arc grammar G_{arc}. As c is a marker in the language, it is easy to see that any context which uses to generate the language will be of the form $(a^i b^i, b^i)$, $i \geq 1$, and the associated selector will be of the form $b^{j_1} c b^{j_2}, j_1, j_2 \geq 1$. In this mode, the selector never absorbs the left context. So, there is no change in the left end of the selector in every derivation. In order to generate the strings of the language, at each derivation, the selector should absorb the substring b^i from the left adjoined context $a^i b^i$. Otherwise, the symbols a and b do not occur in order. This results misplaced occurrences of a and b in the generated string. A contradiction.   □

From the above two lemmas and Lemma 2, we have the following result.

Theorem 4. $ICC_{arc}(REG)$ *is incomparable with* $ICC_{iemdf}(REG)$, *but not disjoint.*

Lemma 10. $ICC_{mdf}(REG) - ICC_{mloc}(REG) \neq \emptyset$.

Proof. Consider the language $L_{10} = \{a^n c b^{n+m} d a^m \mid n, m \geq 1\}$. This can be generated by $G_{mdf} = (\{a, b, c, d\}, acbbda, (cb^+, (a, b)), (b^+ d, (b, a)))$. However this language is not in $ICC_{mloc}(REG)$. Assume that $L_{10} \in ICC_{mloc}(REG)$ for a $mloc$ grammar. To generate the language, the grammar will have the contexts of the form (a^i, b^i) and (b^j, a^j), $i, j \geq 1$, and their associated selectors will be of the form $a^{k_1} c b^{k_2}$, $b^{k_3} d a^{k_4}$, respectively for $k_1, k_2, k_3, k_4 \geq 0$. Consider the word $a^{n'} c b^{n'} b d a \in L_{10}$ for a large n' (thus the word is not in the axiom). To reach this word from the axiom, we might have used the context (a^i, b^i) (may be sev-eral times) and the selector $a^{k_1} c b^{k_2}$. As we work in $mloc$ mode, any further se-lector must have this selector as a subword. However, from this word, we cannot reach a word $a^{n'} c b^{n'+m'} d a^{m'} \in L_{10}$ for a large m'. To reach this word, the selector $b^{k_3} d a^{k_4}$ must be used, but it does not have the previously used selector $a^{k_1} c b^{k_2}$ as a substring. A similar argument can be given to the word $a^{n'} c b^{n'+m'} d a^{m'}$, if we drive from $acb^{m'} d a^{m'}$, for a large m'.   □

From Lemma 2, 5 and 10, we have the following result.

Theorem 5. $ICC_{mdf}(REG)$ *is incomparable with* $ICC_{mloc}(REG)$, *but not disjoint.*

Lemma 11. $ICC_{mdf}(REG) - ICC_{emdf}(REG) \neq \emptyset$.

Proof. Consider the language $L_{11} = \{a^n cb^m cb^m ca^n \mid n, m \geq 1\}$. This can be generated by $G_{mdf} = (\{a, b, c\}, acbcbca, (b^+ cb^+, (b, b)), (a^* cb^+ cb^+ ca^*, (a, a)))$. However this language is not in $ICC_{emdf}(REG)$. On contrary, let $L_{11} \in ICC_{emdf}(REG)$ for a *emdf* grammar Assume that first we pump the occurrences of b and then the occurrences of a. As b is equally pumped around the second c, there will be a context of the form $(b^i, b^i), i \geq 1$. As at least one of the context is end-marked, we have either b_L^i or b_R^i. Let the left context be end-marked. Then, if b_L^i is the case, then the next selector should begin with b^i and therefore the left context used in the next derivation should be adjoined to the left of b_L^i. Hence, we cannot pump the occurrences of a on the left of first c, using a context of the form $(a^j, a^j), j \geq 1$. Similarly, if b_R^i is the case, then the next selector should end with b^i and therefore the right context used in the next derivation should be adjoined to the right of b^i. Hence, we cannot pump the occurrences of a on the right of third c, using a context of the form $(a^p, a^p), p \geq 1$. Otherwise, we can produce a word which is not in the language. We can give a similar proof if the right context b^i is end-marked. If we assume that first we pump the occurrences of a and then b, then there should be a context of the form $(a^k, a^k), k \geq 1$, in order to pump the occurrences of a equally at the ends. As one of the contexts is end-marked, we have either a_L^k or a_R^k. We assume that the left context a^k is end-marked (i.e., a_L^k or a_R^k). Then, it is easy to see that we cannot pump the occurrences of b equally around the second c. If the right context a^k is end-marked, we can give a similar reasoning for not pumping the occurrences b equally.   □

From Lemma 2, 5 and 11, we have the following result.

Theorem 6. $ICC_{mdf}(REG)$ *is incomparable with* $ICC_{emdf}(REG)$, *but not disjoint.*

Lemma 12. $ICC_{emdf}(REG) - ICC_\beta(REG) \neq \emptyset$, $\beta \in \{max, mloc, mdf, arc, iemdf\}$.

Proof. Consider the language $L_{12} = \{a^{2m} ca^{m+n-1} ca^{2n} \mid n, m \geq 1\}$. This can be generated by the grammar $G_{emdf} = (\{a, c\}, \{aacacaa\}, (aa^+ ca^+, \{(aa_L, a), (aa, a_L)\}), (acaa^+, (a, aa_R)))$. Intuitively, the first selector $aa^+ caa^+$ is used to increase the necessary occurrences of m and $2m$ of a around the first c and the second selector $acaa^+$ is used to increase the necessary occurrences of n and $2n$ of a around the second c. Whenever, the first selector $aa^+ ca^+$ and the context (aa_L, a) is applied, we can continue further derivations with the same selector $aa^+ ca^+$ itself. If the context (aa, a_L) is applied, in the next derivation the second selector $acaa^+$ must be chosen. Once this selector is chosen, the same selector $acaa^+$ can only be used in the further derivations and choosing the first selector is not possible thereafter. However, this does not affect generating the language L_{12} as the first selector can be used for the required $2m$ and m occurrences of as and then the second selector can be used to generate the required number of n and $2n$ occurrences of as. Note that, due to the maximal condition of the selector, whenever the context (aa_L, a) or (aa, a_L) is applied, the right context a is always adjoined just before the second c and this feature helps to switch over to use the second selector. It is easy to see that $L(G_{emdf}) = L_{12}$.

However, the language L_{12} is not in $ICC_\beta(REG)$ for the above β. Assume that the language $L_{12} \in ICC_\beta(REG)$ for any grammar $G_\beta = (\{a, b, c\}, A, (S_1, C_1), \ldots, (S_r, C_r))$. In order to pump the as around the first c we need a context of the form $(a^{2i}, a^i), i \geq 1$, and the associated selector will be of the form $a^{k_1} c a^{k_2}, k_1, k_2 \geq 0$. Similarly, in order to pump the as around the second c we need a context of the form $(a^j, a^{2j}), j \geq 1$, and the associated selector will be of the form $a^{k_3} c a^{k_4}, k_3, k_4 \geq 0$. Let $\beta = max, mdf$. Assume that $a^{2m'} c a^{m'} a^{n'} c a^{2n'} \in L_{12}$ is obtained by adjoining the context (a^{2i}, a^i) and the selector is used around the second c (i.e., $a^{k_1} c a^{k_2}$); the other case of adjoining the context (a^j, a^{2j}) is similar. Since the right context a^i can be covered by the as in between the two cs (i.e., by the selector $a^{k_3} c a^{k_4}$) and the chosen selector can be locally maximal, we can adjoin the context (a^j, a^{2j}) and derive a word $a^{2m'} \underline{a^j} c a^{m'} \underline{a^{2j}} a^{n'} c a^{2n'} \notin L_{12}$. For $\beta = mloc, arc$ mode, we can generate only one part of the language as we have seen that these variants do not pump symbols across the two markers. The case $\beta = iemdf$ mode is similar to $arc, mloc, mldf$, because the next selector should be inside the adjoined contexts, thus the selector cannot go across the two markers. $\square$

From Lemma 2, 6 and 12, we have the following result.

Theorem 7. $ICC_{emdf}(REG)$ *is incomparable with* $ICC_{iemdf}(REG)$, *but not disjoint.*

Lemma 13. $ICC_{mloc}(REG) - ICC_{emdf}(REG) \neq \emptyset$.

Proof. Consider the language $L_{13} = \{a^n \mid n \geq 1\} \cup \{b^n \mid n \geq 1\} \cup \{a^n c b^n \mid n \geq 1\}$. This can be generated by the $mloc$ grammar $G_{mloc} = (\{a, b, c\}, \{a, aa, b, bb, acb\}, (aa, (\lambda, a)), (bb, (\lambda, b)), (acb, (a, b)))$. However, this language cannot be generated by an $emdf$ grammar. Assume that $L_{13} \in ICC_{emdf}(REG)$ for any grammar $G_{emdf} = (\{a, b, c\}, A, (S_1, C_1), \ldots, (S_r, C_r))$. In order to generate the strings a^n and b^n, we need contexts of the form $(a_E^{i_1}, a_E^{i_2}), i_1 + i_2 \geq 1$, and $(b_E^{j_1}, b_E^{j_2}), j_1 + j_2 \geq 1$, with their associated selectors of the form $a^i, i \geq 1$, and $b^j, j \geq 1$. Also, in order to generate the strings $a^n c b^n$, we need a context of the form $(a_E^k, b_E^k), k \geq 1$, with the associated selector of the form $a^{k_1} c b^{k_2}, k_1, k_2 \geq 1$. The suffix E denotes the (right or the left) end-marker. Consider a word $a^{n'} c b^{n'} \in L_{12}$ for a large n'. Then, to reach this word, we should have used the context (a_E^k, b_E^k). In $emdf$ mode, at each derivation, the selector should cover and start/end with one of the adjoined contexts. Therefore, the next selector should start or end with the context a^k (the other case for the context b^k is similar). Such a context can be covered by a selector $a^{m'}$, thus we can apply the context (a^{i_1}, a^{i_2}) to $a^{n'} c b^{n'}$, resulting a word $a^{n'+i_1+i_2} c b^{n'} \notin L_{13}$. A contradiction. $\square$

From the above two lemmas and Lemma 2, we have the following theorem.

Theorem 8. $ICC_{mloc}(REG)$ *is incomparable with* $ICC_{emdf}(REG)$, *but not disjoint.*

4 Conclusion

In this paper, we have considered the generative power of various classes of internal contextual grammars where the restrictions are considered in the derivations, namely, $max, mloc, mdf, arc, emdf, iemdf$. We conjecture that Lemma 2 can be strengthened as the class of regular languages is in the family of languages $ICC_\alpha(REG)$ for the variants discussed in this paper.

In the Chomsky hierarchy of languages, when the restrictions are increased in the form of production rules (from unrestricted to context sensitive (i.e. context dependent), from context dependent to context-free, from context-free to regular), the generative power of the class of grammars is decreased. On the other hand, in regulated rewriting, when the rules are context-free (for instance, matrix grammars, programmed grammars, periodically time varying grammars and grammars with regular control), putting restrictions in the manner of applying the rules, the generative power of the grammars is increased (but for type-3 rules of regulated rewriting, the generative power is unaltered) [3],[22]. Therefore, it will be a nice result in the field of formal languages to show that there are families of languages whose grammars are obtained by imposing more restrictions on the manner of applying the rules, but the generative power of the grammars is neither increased nor decreased; they are incomparable. In this paper, we have identified the families of languages in the domain of contextual grammars which possess this interesting property. Also, we showed that there are languages which are common to all these families of languages. Hence these families are not disjoint.

Thus, we have found that there is a class of languages obtained by putting restrictions in the derivation of the same basic class of grammars (internal contextual grammars) whose behaviour is different from the existing class of grammars in formal languages theory. How these restrictions play a role in natural language processing is an interesting problem which could be explored in future. A study of descriptional complexity measures of the internal contextual grammars under these restrictions can also be explored. We refer to [10], [13], [14] for recent works where descriptional complexity measures of internal contextual grammars and ambiguity of contextual languages were considered.

Acknowledgments. The authors thank the three anonymous referees for their insightful remarks and comments which helped to improve the presentation of the paper. The first author's work was partially carried out during the tenure of an ERCIM "Alain Bensoussan" Fellowship Programme. Also, he mentions his special thanks to Dr. Eric Villemonte de la Clergerie, INRIA, for his support and encouragement.

References

1. Boullier, P.: Range concatenation grammars. In: Proceedings of Sixth International Workshop on Parsing Technologies (IWPT 2000), pp. 53–64 (2000)

2. Boullier, P.: From contextual grammars to range concatenation grammars. Electronic Notes in Theoretical Computer Science 53, 41–52 (2001)
3. Dassow, J., Păun, G.: Regulated Rewriting in Formal Language Theory. EATCS monographs on TCS. Springer, Heidelberg (1989)
4. Ehrenfeucht, A., Ilie, L., Păun, G., Rozenberg, G., Salomaa, A.: On the generative capacity of certain classes of contextual grammars. In: Mathematical Ling. and Related Topics, pp. 105–118. The Publ. House of the Romanian Academy, Bucharest (1995)
5. Joshi, A.K.: How much context-sensitivity is required to provide structural descriptions: Tree adjoining grammars. In: David, D., Lauri, K., Arnold, Z. (eds.) Natural Language Processing: Psycholinguistic, Computational, and Theoretical Perspectives, pp. 206–250. Cambridge University Press, New York (1985)
6. Ilie, L.: A non-seminlinear language generated by an internal contextual grammar with finite selection. Ann. Univ. Bucharest Math. Inform. Series 45, 63–70 (1996)
7. Ilie, L.: On computational complexity of contextual languages. Theo. Comp. Science 183(1), 33–44 (1997)
8. Ilie, L.: Some recent results in contextual grammars. Bull. EATCS 62, 172–194 (1997)
9. Lakshmanan, K.: New Classes of Contextual Grammars for Mildly Context Sensitive Formalisms. In: Terikhovsky, O.N., Burton, W.N. (eds.) New Topics in Theoretical Computer Science, pp. 1–25. Nova Publishers, USA (2008)
10. Lakshmanan, K., Anand, M., Krithivasan, K.: On the trade-off between ambiguity and measures in internal contextual grammars. In: Proceedings of 10th International Workshop on Descriptional Complexity of Formal Systems, pp. 216–223 (2008)
11. Lakshmanan, K., Krishna, S.N., Rama, R., Martin-Vide, C.: Internal contextual grammars for mildly context sensitive languages. Research on Language and Computation 5(2), 181–197 (2007)
12. Lakshmanan, K.: End-marked maximal depth-first contextual grammars. In: Ibarra, O.H., Dang, Z. (eds.) DLT 2006. LNCS, vol. 4036, pp. 339–350. Springer, Heidelberg (2006)
13. Lakshmanan, K.: A note on Ambiguity of Internal Contextual Grammars. Theo. Comp. Science 369, 436–441 (2006)
14. Lakshmanan, K.: Incompatible measures of internal contextual grammars. In: Proceedings of DCFS 2005, pp. 253–260 (2005)
15. Marcus, S.: Contextual grammars. Rev. Roum. Pures. Appl. 14, 1525–1534 (1969)
16. Marcus, S., Martin-Vide, C., Păun, Gh.: Contextual grammars as generative models of natural languages. Computational Linguistics 24(2), 245–274 (1998)
17. Marcus, S., Martin-Vide, C., Păun, Gh.: On internal contextual grammars with maximal use of selectors. In: Proc. 8th Conf. Automata & Formal Lang., vol. 54, pp. 933–947. Salgotarjan. Publ. Math., Debrecen (1999)
18. Martin-Vide, C., Miquel-Verges, J., Păun, Gh.: Contextual grammars with depth-first derivation. In: Tenth Twente Workshop on Language Tech.; Algebraic Methods in Language Processing, Twente, pp. 225–233 (1995)
19. de Groote, P.: Towards abstract categorial grammars. In: ACL 2009. ACL Press (2001), http://www.aclweb.org/anthology/P01-1-33
20. Păun, Gh., Nguyen, X.M.: On the inner contextual grammars. Rev. Roum. Pures. Appl. 25, 641–651 (1980)
21. Păun, Gh.: Marcus Contextual Grammars. Kluwer Academic Publishers, Dordrecht (1997)
22. Salomaa, A.: Formal Languages. Academic Press, London (1973)

Integration Testing from Structured First-Order Specifications via Deduction Modulo

Delphine Longuet[1] and Marc Aiguier[2]

[1] Laboratoire Spécification et Vérification, ENS Cachan,
61 avenue du Président Wilson, F-94235 Cachan Cedex
delphine.longuet@lsv.ens-cachan.fr
[2] Laboratory of Mathematics Applied to Systems (MAS), École Centrale Paris,
Grande voie des vignes, F-92295 Châtenay-Malabry
marc.aiguier@ecp.fr

Abstract. Testing from first-order specifications has mainly been studied for flat specifications, that are specifications of a single software module. However, the specifications of large software systems are generally built out of small specifications of individual modules, by enriching their union. The aim of integration testing is to test the composition of modules assuming that they have previously been verified, i.e. assuming their correctness. One of the main method for the selection of test cases from first-order specifications, called axiom unfolding, is based on a proof search for the different instances of the property to be tested, thus allowing the coverage of this property. The idea here is to use deduction modulo as a proof system for structured first-order specifications in the context of integration testing, so as to take advantage of the knowledge of the correctness of the individual modules.

Testing is a very common practice in the software validation process. The principle of testing is to execute the software system on a subset of its possible inputs in order to detect failures. A failure is detected if the system behaves in a non-conformant way with respect to its specification.

The testing process is usually decomposed into three phases: the *selection* of a relevant subset of the set of all the possible inputs of the system, called a test set; the *submission* of this test set to the system; the *decision* of the success or the failure of the test set submission, called the *oracle problem*. We focus here on the selection phase, which is the crucial point for the relevance and the efficiency of the testing process. In the approach called black-box testing, tests are selected from a (formal or informal) specification of the system, without any knowledge about the implementation.

Our work follows the framework defined by Gaudel, Bernot and Marre [1], for testing from specifications expressed in a logical formalism. One approach to selection consists first in dividing an exhaustive test set into subsets, and then in choosing one test case in each of these subsets, thus building a finite test set which covers the initial exhaustive test set. One of the most studied selection method for testing from equational (and then first-order) specifications is known as *axiom unfolding* [1–4]. Its principle is to divide the initial exhaustive test set according to criteria derived from the axioms of the

M. Leucker and C. Morgan (Eds.): ICTAC 2009, LNCS 5684, pp. 261–276, 2009.
© Springer-Verlag Berlin Heidelberg 2009

specification, using the well-known and efficient proof techniques associated to first-order logic.

Contribution. Test case selection from first-order specifications have mainly been studied for flat specifications (and then flat programs), that are specifications of a single software module. However, for the description of large systems, it is convenient to compose specifications in a modular way [5]. The specification of a large system is generally built from small specifications of individual modules, that are composed by making their union and enriching it with new features in order to get new (larger) specifications, that are themselves composed and so on. The aim of integration testing is to test the composition of modules, assuming that these modules have previously been tested and then are correct. The assumption here is that the system under test is structured according to the structuration of its specification.

Here, we propose to use the knowledge of the correctness of individual modules to make the test selection method based on axiom unfolding more efficient. Since the modules are correct (i.e. they have already been sufficiently tested or completely proved), it is reasonable to assume to have an executable and complete specification of these modules, either from which their implementations has been build or which would have been generated from their implementations. Our selection method being defined for first-order specifications, it is important for this executable specification to be written in first-order logic. Of course, in the case where the specification has to be generated from the implementation, the generation may be more or less easy according to the programming language used (imperative or functional), but this is the price to pay to make the selection method efficient by taking advantage of the specification structure. However, we can observe that the obtained specification is most often composed of (conditional) equations that can be oriented from left to right into confluent and terminating (conditional) rewrite rules, and of predicate definition formulas of the form $p(t_1, \ldots, t_n) \Leftrightarrow \varphi$, where φ is a quantifier-free formula, that can be oriented into confluent and terminating rewrite rules on propositions (see Section 2). We will then suppose to have, for each individual module, a confluent and terminating rewrite system that completely specifies its behaviour. To preserve the black-box aspect of the approach (the tester has no knowledge about the implementation of the system and its modules), we suppose that these executable and complete specifications of modules have been written beforehand by the programmer.

In order to make our selection method more efficient, we propose to use the deduction modulo proposed by Dowek, Hardin and Kirchner [6] as a proof system for structured specifications. Deduction modulo is a formalism introduced to separate computations from deductions in proofs by reasoning modulo a congruence on propositions, which is defined by a rewrite relation over first-order terms and propositions. The idea behind deduction modulo is to hide the computational part of the proof in the congruence, in order to focus on its deductive part. In the context of integration testing, the same idea can be used to focus the proof on the new features coming from the composition of modules, relying on the correct behaviour of these modules which is embedded in the congruence. It leads to shorter proofs which take advantage of the structuration of specifications, thus making the selection procedure more efficient.

Related Work. Testing from structured first-order specifications has already been studied in the framework of institutions. Machado's works deal with the oracle problem [7], that is, whether a finite and executable procedure can be defined for interpreting the results of tests. When dealing with structured specifications, problems arise in particular with the union of specifications. Since the same sort and operations may be introduced and specified in different modules, the union will be consistent only if the different specifications of the same operations are. Doche and Wiels define an extension of the notion of institution to take test cases into account [8]. They incrementally generate tests from structured specifications, generating tests from small specifications and composing them according to a push-out of specifications.

Both of these works aim at building a general test set for the whole structured specification, composing individual test sets obtained for each of its part. The structuration of the specification helps to incrementally build the test set but not to actually test the program in an incremental way. We are here interested in incrementally testing from a structured specification, basing the construction of a test set on the success of the previous ones. Moreover, from the selection point of view, none of the mentioned works propose any particular strategy, but the substitution of axiom variables for some arbitrarily chosen data.

Organisation of the Paper. We first recall standard definitions about structuration of specifications (Section 1) and deduction modulo (Section 2). Section 3 introduces the general framework for testing from logical specifications and gives the result of the existence of an exhaustive test set for quantifier-free first-order specifications. We also prove the existence of an exhaustive test set for structured first-order specifications, relying on the correctness of the smaller modules. We restrict to quantifier-free formulas since we showed in [9] that existential formulas are not testable. Testing a formula of the form $\exists x \varphi(x)$ actually comes down to exhibiting a witness value a such that $\varphi(a)$ is interpreted as true by the system. Of course, there is no general way to exhibit such a relevant value, but notice that surprisingly, exhibiting such a value would amount to simply prove the system with respect to the initial property. In Section 4, the selection method by means of selection criteria is presented. We develop in Section 5 our test selection method from structured first-order specifications, by unfolding axioms using deduction modulo. We give the algorithm of the procedure and prove the soundness and completeness of the method, i.e. the preservation of exhaustiveness through unfolding.

1 Structured First-Order Specifications

A multi-sorted first-order signature $\Sigma = (S, F, P, V)$ is composed of a set of sorts S, a set of operations F, a set of predicates P and a set of variables V over these sorts. $T_\Sigma(V)$ and T_Σ are both S-indexed sets of terms with variables in V and ground terms, respectively, freely generated from variables and operations in Σ and preserving arity of operations. A substitution is any mapping $\sigma : V \rightarrow T_\Sigma(V)$ that preserves sorts. Substitutions are naturally extended to terms with variables. *Formulas* (or *propositions*) are built as usual in first-order logic from atomic formulas $p(t_1, \ldots, t_n)$, where p is a predicate and $t_1, \ldots, t_n$ are first-order terms, and Boolean connectives. Here, we only consider quantifier-free formulas. As usual, variables of quantifier-free formulas are implicitly universally quantified. A formula over Σ is said *ground* if it does not contain variables. Let us denote $For(\Sigma)$ the set of all formulas over the signature Σ.

A model of a signature Σ is a first-order structure giving an interpretation to sorts, operations and predicates of Σ. $Mod(\Sigma)$ is the set of models of Σ. The satisfaction of a quantifier-free formula φ by a given model $\mathcal{M}$ of Σ is inductively defined on the structure of φ as usual and denoted by $\mathcal{M} \models \varphi$. Given a set of formulas Ψ over Σ and two models $\mathcal{M}$ and $\mathcal{M}'$ of Σ, we say that $\mathcal{M}$ is Ψ-equivalent to $\mathcal{M}'$, denoted by $\mathcal{M} \equiv_\Psi \mathcal{M}'$, if and only if for every formula φ in Ψ, $\mathcal{M} \models \varphi$ if and only if $\mathcal{M}' \models \varphi$.

Given a specification $Sp = (\Sigma, Ax)$, a model $\mathcal{M}$ of Σ is a *model of Sp* if $\mathcal{M}$ satisfies all the formulas in Ax. $Mod(Sp)$ is the subset of $Mod(\Sigma)$ whose elements are the models of Sp. A formula φ over Σ is a *semantic consequence* of Sp, denoted by $Sp \models \varphi$, if and only if every model $\mathcal{M}$ of Sp satisfies φ. $Sp^\bullet$ is the set of all the semantic consequences of Sp.

The semantics of a specification $Sp = (\Sigma, Ax)$ is given by its signature $Sig(Sp) = \Sigma$ and its class of models $[\![Sp]\!] = Mod(Sp)$. The specification building operators allow to write *basic* (flat) specifications, to make the *union* of two specifications and to *enrich* specifications with additional sorts, operation and/or predicate and axioms [5]. In general, small specifications are written, for instance specifying basic operations and predicates for a given sort (Booleans, naturals, lists...), then they are composed by the union operator, and finally enriched by new sorts, operations, predicates and axioms involving several of the initial specifications (empty list, list length, list of the divisors of a natural...). The union and enrichment operators are defined as follows.

Basic $Sp = (\Sigma, Ax)$ **Union** $Sp = Sp_1 \text{ union } Sp_2$

$$Sig(Sp) = \Sigma \qquad\qquad\qquad Sig(Sp) = Sig(Sp_1) \cup Sig(Sp_2)$$
$$[\![Sp]\!] = Mod(Sp) \qquad\qquad\qquad [\![Sp]\!] = [\![Sp_1]\!] \cap [\![Sp_2]\!]$$

Enrich[1] $Sp = \text{enrich } Sp_1$
                 by sorts S_2, ops F_2, preds P_2, axioms Ax_2

$$Sig(Sp) = Sig(Sp_1) \cup (S_2, F_2, P_2)$$
$$[\![Sp]\!] = \{\mathcal{M} \in Mod(Sig(Sp)) \mid \mathcal{M}_{|Sig(Sp_1)} \in [\![Sp_1]\!] \wedge \mathcal{M} \models Ax_2\}$$

2   Deduction Modulo

A term rewrite rule $l \to r$ is a pair of terms l, r such that all free variables of r appear in l. A term rewrite system is a set of term rewrite rules. A proposition rewrite rule $A \to P$ is a pair composed of an atomic proposition A and a proposition P, such that all free variables of P appear in A. A rewrite system $\mathcal{R}$ is a pair consisting of a term rewrite system and a proposition rewrite system. We denote by $P \to_\mathcal{R} Q$ the fact that P can be rewritten to Q in the rewrite system $\mathcal{R}$ in one step. $\mathcal{R}$ may be omitted if it is clear from the context. $\xrightarrow{+}_\mathcal{R}$ (resp. $\xrightarrow{*}_\mathcal{R}$) is the transitive (resp. reflexive transitive) closure of this rewrite relation. We denote by $\equiv_\mathcal{R}$ the congruence generated by $\mathcal{R}$.

In the context of integration testing, we consider a system built from modules composed by union and enrichment and we assume the correctness of these modules. As we already explained in the introduction, since each module is correct, we suppose to have the most concrete specification of each individual module. When expressed in

---

[1] $\mathcal{M}_{|\Sigma}$ stands for the reduct of $\mathcal{M}$ over the signature Σ.

first-order logic, this concrete specification (most often) leads to a terminating and confluent rewrite system. We will assume that the behaviour of the module is modelled by this terminating and confluent rewrite system, where the behaviour of functions and predicates is defined by rewrite rules over first-order terms and quantifier-free formulas respectively. For instance, if we take the simple example of the greatest common divisor (gcd) whose possible implementation written in Caml is:

```
let rec gcd(x,y) = if y > x then gcd(y,x)
                   else if x mod y = 0 then y
                   else gcd(y,x mod y);;
```

we obtain the following specification:

$$y > x \Rightarrow \gcd(x, y) = \gcd(y, x)$$
$$\neg(y > x) \land x \bmod y = 0 \Rightarrow \gcd(x, y) = y$$
$$\neg(y > x) \land \neg(x \bmod y = 0) \Rightarrow \gcd(x, y) = \gcd(y, x \bmod y)$$
$$x > y \Leftrightarrow (\neg(x = 0) \land y = 0) \lor (\mathrm{pred}(x) > \mathrm{pred}(y))$$

This specification can obviously be transformed into a set of confluent and terminating (conditional) rewrite rules on terms and propositions. On the contrary, the specification from which this implementation of gcd has been tested would rather be:

$$x \bmod \gcd(x, y) = 0 \qquad x \bmod z = 0 \land y \bmod z = 0 \Rightarrow \gcd(x, y) \geq z$$
$$y \bmod \gcd(x, y) = 0$$

A congruence relation $\equiv$ over formulas is naturally induced by these rewrite rules. For instance, we have the following equivalences:

$$\neg\big(\gcd(2x + 1, 2) = \gcd(2x, 2)\big) \equiv \big(\neg \gcd(2, 2x + 1 \mod 2) = 2\big) \equiv \neg(1 = 2)$$

Using deduction modulo to guide the selection of test cases thus allows to internalise in the congruence the knowledge of the individual modules correctness, in order to focus the testing procedure on the new features of the system coming from the composition of modules.

In order to deal with structured specifications, we must ensure that termination and confluence of the rewrite systems underlying the individual modules are preserved through the union of these modules. It has been proved that these properties of (simple) termination and confluence are preserved for finite rewrite systems that are composable [10] (the rewrite rules in different systems defining the same operation are the same). This property of composability is reasonable in a testing framework, since it is natural to suppose that an operation or a predicate appearing in different modules comes from the same underlying module (used by these modules) and then is implemented in the same way in every module. From now on, we will assume that the rewrite systems underlying the modules are composable pairwise, so their union is also terminating and confluent.

The sequent calculus modulo extends the usual sequent calculus by allowing to work modulo the rewrite system $\mathcal{R}$. When the congruence $\equiv_\mathcal{R}$ is the identity, this sequent calculus collapses to the usual one. The sequent calculus modulo is as powerful as the usual sequent calculus: it is shown in [6] that a formula is provable in the sequent calculus modulo if and only if it is provable in the usual sequent calculus using an appropriate set of axioms which are called compatible.

Here, the sequent calculus modulo is dedicated to the inference of quantifier-free formulas, so the rules for the introduction of quantifiers are omitted. Moreover, the rules associated to Boolean connectives are reversible. Since we assume that the rewrite system $\mathcal{R}$ is terminating and confluent, the rules for Booleans connectives can be used to transform any sequent $\vdash \varphi$, where φ is a quantifier-free formula, into a set of sequents $\Gamma_i \vdash \Delta_i$ where every formula in Γ_i and Δ_i is atomic. Such sequents will be called *normalised sequents*. This transformation is obtained from basic transformations defined as rewriting rules between elementary proof trees. We showed in [11] that for the sequent calculus associated to quantifier-free formulas, every proof tree can be transformed into a proof tree of same conclusion and such that Cut and Subs rules never occur under rule instances associated to Boolean connectives. This result states that every sequent is equivalent to a set of normalised sequents, which allows to deal with normalised sequents only. Therefore, in the following, we will suppose that the specification axioms are given under the form of normalised sequents. We present the sequent calculus modulo for normalised sequents, which is defined by the following rules where $\Gamma \vdash_{\mathcal{R}} \Delta$ is a sequent such that Γ and Δ are two multisets of first-order formulas.

$$\frac{}{\Gamma, P \vdash_{\mathcal{R}} \Delta, Q}\text{Taut if } P \equiv_{\mathcal{R}} Q \qquad\qquad \frac{}{\vdash_{\mathcal{R}} P}\text{Axiom if } \exists ax \in Ax \text{ such that } P \equiv_{\mathcal{R}} ax$$

$$\frac{\Gamma \vdash_{\mathcal{R}} \Delta}{\Gamma' \vdash_{\mathcal{R}} \Delta'}\text{Subs if } \Gamma' \equiv_{\mathcal{R}} \sigma(\Gamma) \text{ and } \Delta' \equiv_{\mathcal{R}} \sigma(\Delta) \qquad \frac{\Gamma, P \vdash_{\mathcal{R}} \Delta \qquad \Gamma' \vdash_{\mathcal{R}} Q, \Delta'}{\Gamma, \Gamma' \vdash_{\mathcal{R}} \Delta, \Delta'}\text{Cut if } P \equiv_{\mathcal{R}} Q$$

where for a multiset Γ, $\sigma(\Gamma)$ is the multiset $\{\sigma(\varphi) \mid \varphi \in \Gamma\}$.

It is possible to show that, when normalised sequents are transformed into formulas in clausal form, the cut and substitution rules can be combined to obtain the classical resolution rule (see [12] for more details). Actually, as we will see afterwards, this is the rule of resolution which is implemented in our unfolding algorithm. However, we use the sequent calculus since it makes the correctness proof of this algorithm easier (see Theorem 3). It is well-known that resolution is complete for quantifier-free formulas. Then it follows from the results of [6] that the resolution modulo as defined above is also complete. Since the resolution modulo is equivalent to the sequent calculus modulo restricted to normalised sequents, this calculus is complete. From now on, we will then speak about theorems and semantic consequences without making any difference.

Example 1. We give here a specification of rationals, built as an enrichment of a specification of naturals NAT. Rationals are defined as pairs of naturals and the comparison predicate *strictly less than* is defined as usual from the same predicate over naturals.

>   **spec** RAT =
>   **enrich** NAT **by**
>   **type** $Rat ::= \_/\_ (Nat, Nat)$
>   **pred** $\ll: Rat \times Rat$
>   **vars** $x, y, u, v: Nat$
>   • $x/s(y) \ll u/s(v) \Leftrightarrow x \times s(v) < u \times s(y)$
>   **end**

This axiom gives the two following normalised sequents:

(1) $x/s(y) \ll u/s(v) \vdash x \times s(v) < u \times s(y)$
(2) $x \times s(v) < u \times s(y) \vdash x/s(y) \ll u/s(v)$

The module implementing NAT can be defined by the following rewrite system:

$$x + 0 \to x \qquad\qquad x \times 0 \to 0 \qquad\qquad x < 0 \to \bot$$
$$x + s(y) \to s(x + y) \qquad x \times s(y) \to x + x \times y \qquad 0 < s(x) \to \top$$
$$s(x) < s(y) \to x < y$$

3 Testing from Logical Specifications

From now on, we assume that the specification of the system to be tested is given as a (structured) first-order specification $Sp = (\Sigma, Ax)$. Following previous works [1, 2, 13], we make the two following assumptions. First, the behaviour of the system under test can be described as a first-order structure, sharing the same signature as its specification. The system under test is thus considered to be a Σ-model. Secondly, test cases can be expressed as quantifier-free first-order formulas over the signature Σ. Some observability constraints must be imposed so that the system is able to evaluate the formulas chosen to be test cases as true or false. Such formulas are called *observable*. Test cases being quantifier-free first-order formulas, they must not contain non-instantiated variables to be evaluated by the system. Therefore here, observable formulas are all ground formulas. We will denote by Obs the set of observable formulas.

The success of the submission of test cases to the system is defined in terms of formula satisfaction. Since the system is considered to be a formal model $S \in Mod(\Sigma)$ and a test case is a ground formula $\varphi \in For(\Sigma)$, φ is said to be *successful* for S if and only if $S \models \varphi$. A test set T being a set of test cases, that is $T \subseteq For(\Sigma)$, T will be said successful for S if and only if every test case in T is successful: $S \models T$ if and only if for all $\varphi \in T, S \models \varphi$.

Following an observational approach [14], a system will be considered as a correct implementation of its specification if, as a model, it cannot be distinguished from a model of the specification. Since the system can only be observed through the observable formulas it satisfies, it is required to be equivalent to a model of the specification up to this notion of observability.

Definition 1 (Correctness). S *is correct for Sp via Obs, denoted by $Correct_{Obs}(S, Sp)$, if and only if there exists a model $\mathcal{M}$ in $Mod(Sp)$ such that $\mathcal{M}$ validates exactly the same observable formulas as S: $\mathcal{M} \equiv_{Obs} S$.*

The correctness of the system could then be proved if we were able to submit to the system the test set composed of all the observable formulas satisfied by the specification. Such a set is then said to be *exhaustive*.

Definition 2 (Exhaustiveness). *Let $\mathcal{K} \subseteq Mod(\Sigma)$ be a class of models. A test set T is exhaustive for $\mathcal{K}$ with respect to Sp and Obs if and only if for all $S \in \mathcal{K}, S \models T \Leftrightarrow Correct_{Obs}(S, Sp)$.*

The existence of an exhaustive test set ensures that for any incorrect system, there exists a test case making this system fail. To put it in a dual way, it ensures that it is relevant to test this system with respect to its specification since its correctness can be asymptotically approached by submitting a potentially infinite test set. As a correctness reference, the exhaustive test set is then appropriate to start the selection of a finite test set of reasonable size. Note that, as we proved in [9], depending on the nature of the specification, on the observability restrictions and on the class of systems $\mathcal{K}$, an exhaustive test set does not necessarily exist.

Theorem 1 ([11]). *Let $Sp = (\Sigma, Ax)$ be a quantifier-free first-order specification and Obs be the set of ground first-order formulas. Then $Sp^\bullet \cap Obs$ is exhaustive for $Mod(\Sigma)$.*

In the context of integration testing, we consider a system built from the composition of individual modules which have already been proved to be correct. The specification Sp of this system is structured by the union and the enrichment of its modules specifications. Since these modules are correct, what remains to be tested are the new behaviours coming from their composition. These new behaviours are properties involving several modules in the case of a union or involving new sorts, operations or predicates in the case of an enrichment. They are properties that do not involve a module alone, i.e. formulas over the new signature that are not formulas of a module's signature alone: formulas in $For(\Sigma) \setminus (For(\Sigma_1) \cup For(\Sigma_2))$ if Σ is the union of Σ_1 and Σ_2; formulas in $For(\Sigma) \setminus For(\Sigma_1)$ if Σ is the enrichment of Σ_1. Let us denote $NewFor$ these sets of new formulas. Then, the new properties of the system coming from the composition are the formulas of $NewFor$ which are semantic consequences of the whole specification Sp. Let us denote $NewPr$ the set $NewFor \cap Sp^\bullet$. We have the following important result.

Theorem 2. *Let $Sp = $ enrich Sp_1 by S_2, F_2, P_2, Ax_2 (resp. $Sp = Sp_1$ union Sp_2). Let $\mathcal{K} = Mod(Sig(Sp))$. For every $S \in \mathcal{K}$, if $Correct_{Obs}(S_{|\Sigma_1}, Sp_1)$ (resp. and $Correct_{Obs}(S_{|\Sigma_2}, Sp_2)$), then $NewPr \cap Obs$ is exhaustive for S.[1]*

The proof may be found in the long version of this paper [15]. The key argument is that the behaviour of the modules is completely known, so their specifications are complete and $S_{|\Sigma_i}$ is fully characterised by the set of ground consequences of its specification Sp_i (it satisfies exactly all formulas of $Sp_i^\bullet \cap Obs$ and not any other). Therefore there are no new properties about the modules in $NewPr$, since the observability is the same.

4   Selection Criteria

When it exists, the exhaustive test set is the starting point for the selection of a practical test set. In practice, experts apply selection criteria on a reference test set in order to extract a test set of reasonable size to submit to the system. The aim is to divide the initial set according to a given criterion, in order to obtain subsets corresponding to particular behaviours representing this criterion. This selection method is called partition testing.

---

[1] $S_{|\Sigma}$ stands for the reduct of S over the signature Σ.

Definition 3 (Selection criterion). *Let Exh be an exhaustive test set. A selection criterion C is a mapping*[2] $\mathcal{P}(Exh) \rightarrow \mathcal{P}(\mathcal{P}(Exh))$.

For $C(T)$ a set of test sets T_i, we denote by $|C(T)|$ the set $\bigcup_i T_i$.

Different selection criteria may be applied one after the other to get a finer and finer partition of the initial test set. When the subdivision of the initial test set is fine enough according to the tester, the construction of a finite test set covering this partition remains to be done. This is the *generation* phase. Here, an important assumption is needed, which is called the *uniformity hypothesis*. It states that in each of the obtained subsets, test cases all are equivalent to make the system fail [1]. In other words, every test case in a subset is representative of the whole subset, with respect to the selection criterion that has been applied. It is then sufficient to choose one test case in each subset to cover the whole initial test set. The construction of a test set relevant to a selection criterion must benefit from the division obtained by the application of this criterion. Test cases must be chosen so as not to loose any of the cases captured by the criterion.

Definition 4 (Satisfaction of a selection criterion). *Let $T \subseteq Exh$ be a test set and C be a selection criterion. A test set T' satisfies the criterion C applied to T if and only if:*

$$T' \subseteq |C(T)| \wedge \forall T_i \in C(T), T_i \neq \emptyset \Rightarrow T' \cap T_i \neq \emptyset$$

A test set satisfying a selection criterion contains at least one test case of each subset T_i of the initial test set, when T_i is not empty. A selection criterion may then be considered as a coverage criterion, according to the way it divides the initial test set. It can be used to cover a particular aspect of the specification. In this paper, the definition of selection criteria will be based on the coverage of the specification axioms.

The relevance of a selection criterion is determined by the link between the initial test set and the family of test sets obtained by the application of this criterion.

Definition 5 (Properties). *Let C be a selection criterion and T be a test set. C is sound for T if and only if $|C(T)| \subseteq T$. C is complete for T if and only if $|C(T)| \supseteq T$.*

These properties are essential for the definition of an appropriate selection criterion. The soundness of a criterion ensures that test cases are really selected among the initial test set, the application of the criterion does not add any new test case. Additional test cases may actually make a correct system fail. Reciprocally, if the selection criterion is complete, no test case of the initial test set is lost. If some test cases are missing, an incorrect system may pass the test set, while it should have failed on the missing test cases. A sound and complete selection criterion then has the property to preserve exactly all the test cases of the test set it divides, and then to preserve the exhaustiveness of the initial test set.

5   Axiom Unfolding for Structured Specifications

We present here our method for defining relevant selection criteria in order to guide the final choice of the test cases. The method we follow is called axiom unfolding [1–4]

---

[2] For a given set X, $\mathcal{P}(X)$ denotes the set of all subsets of X.

and is adapted here to structured specifications in the context of integration testing. It basically consists of a case analysis of a property to test with respect to the specification axioms. The application of the selection criterion defined by this case analysis allows to refine the initial test set associated to the property by characterising test subsets which respect given constraints on the input data.

5.1   Test Sets for Quantifier-Free First-Order Formulas

Since the exhaustive test set is the set

$$NewPr \cap Obs = \{\rho(\varphi) \mid \varphi \in NewFor, \rho : V \to T_\Sigma, \rho(\varphi) \in Sp^\bullet\}$$

one way to divide it is to divide the test set $\{\rho(\varphi) \mid \rho : V \to T_\Sigma, \rho(\varphi) \in Sp^\bullet\}$ associated to each formula φ in $NewFor$, i.e. the set of all the ground instances of φ that are semantic consequences of Sp. The selection criteria we are going to define allow to divide a test set associated to a formula, we will explain at the end of this section how to actually cover the whole exhaustive test set $NewPr \cap Obs$.

Definition 6 (Test set for a formula). *Let $\varphi \in NewFor$ be a formula, called* test purpose. *The* test set for *φ, denoted by T_φ, is the following set:*

$$T_\varphi = \{\rho(\varphi) \mid \rho : V \to T_\Sigma, \rho(\varphi) \in Sp^\bullet\}$$

Note that the formula taken as a test purpose may be any formula, not necessarily a semantic consequence of the specification. However, only ground substitutions ρ such that $\rho(\varphi)$ is a semantic consequence of Sp will be built at the generation step.

As we will see in the next subsection, the division of a test set associated to a formula will result in a set of test subsets, representing sets of particular instances of the initial formula. These instances, called constrained test purposes, are characterised by a substitution of the variables and a set of constraints.

Definition 7 (Constrained test set). *Let $\varphi \in NewFor$ be a formula. Let $C \subseteq For(\Sigma)$ be a set of formulas called* constraints *and $\sigma : V \to T_\Sigma(V)$ be a substitution. A test set for φ constrained by C and σ, denoted by $T_{(C,\sigma),\varphi}$, is the following set:*

$$T_{(C,\sigma),\varphi} = \{\rho(\sigma(\varphi)) \mid \rho : V \to T_\Sigma, \rho(\sigma(\varphi)) \in Sp^\bullet, \forall \psi \in C, \rho(\psi) \in Sp^\bullet\}$$

The pair $((C,\sigma), \varphi)$ is called a constrained test purpose.

5.2   Unfolding Procedure

The aim of the procedure is to compute a selection criterion dividing the test set associated to an initial test purpose, using the specification axioms. Each step of the procedure returns a partition of the initial test set, where each subset is characterised by a constrained test purpose. These subsets can themselves be divided again and so on, until the tester is satisfied with the obtained partition.

The initial test purpose φ can be seen as the constrained test purpose $((\{\varphi\}, \mathrm{Id}), \varphi)$, or even $((C_0, \mathrm{Id}), \varphi)$ where C_0 is the set of normalised sequents obtained from φ. Let

Ψ_0 be the set containing the initial constraints of test purpose φ, the pair $(\mathcal{C}_0, \mathrm{Id})$. Constrained test sets for formulas are naturally extended to sets of pairs Ψ as follows: $T_{\Psi,\varphi} = \bigcup_{(\mathcal{C},\sigma)\in\Psi} T_{(\mathcal{C},\sigma),\varphi}$. The initial test set T_φ then is the set $T_{\Psi_0,\varphi}$.

The aim of the procedure is to divide this set according to the different cases in which formula φ holds. These cases correspond to the different instances of φ that can be proved as theorems. In the context of integration testing, the idea is to use the sequent calculus modulo presented in Section 2 to search for proofs of instances of φ relying on the correctness of the smaller modules of the implementation. So basically, the procedure searches for those proof trees that allow to deduce (instances of) the initial test purpose from the specification axioms modulo $\mathcal{R}$, where $\mathcal{R}$ is the rewrite system defined from the correct modules. However, the aim is not to build the complete proofs of these instances of φ, but only to make a partition of $T_{\Psi_0,\varphi}$ increasingly fine. A first step in the construction of the proof tree of each instance will give us pending lemmas, constraints remaining to prove that, together with the right substitution, characterise this instance of φ. We will thus be able to replace Ψ_0 with a set of constraints Ψ_1 characterising each instance of φ that can be proved from the axioms. The set Ψ_1 can itself be replaced by a bigger set Ψ_2 obtained from a second step in the construction of the previous proof trees, and so on. The procedure can be stopped at any moment, as soon as the tester is satisfied with the obtained partition.

Note that the procedure only intends to divide the test set associated to a given formula, by returning a set of constraints which characterise each set of the partition. The generation phase, not handled in this paper, consists in choosing one test case in each set of the partition, assuming the uniformity hypothesis, by solving the constraints associated to each set (which might be an issue in itself, due to the nature of these constraints).

To find a proof of an instance of φ, the procedure tries to unify φ with an axiom modulo $\mathcal{R}$. Only new axioms coming from an enrichment of a previous specification are considered here, since the behaviour of this previous specification is embedded in the congruence induced by $\mathcal{R}$. We denote this set of axioms $NewAx$ to avoid ambiguity. More precisely, it tries to unify a subset of the test purpose's subformulas with a subset of an axiom's subformulas, modulo $\mathcal{R}$. Hence, if the test purpose is a normalised sequent of the form

$$P_1, \ldots, P_p, \ldots, P_m \vdash Q_1, \ldots, Q_q, \ldots, Q_n$$

the procedure tries to unify a subset of $\{P_1, \ldots, P_m, Q_1, \ldots, Q_n\}$ with a subset of the formulas of an axiom. Then it looks for a specification axiom of the form

$$A_1, \ldots, A_p, A_{p+1}, \ldots, A_k \vdash B_1, \ldots, B_q, B_{q+1}, \ldots, B_l$$

such that it is possible to unify A_i and P_i modulo $\mathcal{R}$ for all i, $1 \le i \le p$, and to unify B_i and Q_i modulo $\mathcal{R}$ for all i, $1 \le i \le q$.

If the unification modulo with an axiom in $NewAx$ is possible, then the corresponding instance of the test purpose is provable from this axiom. Since A_i and P_i $(1 \le i \le p)$ on one hand and B_i and Q_i $(1 \le i \le q)$ on the other hand are unifiable modulo $\mathcal{R}$, there exists a substitution σ such that $\sigma(A_i) \equiv_\mathcal{R} \sigma(P_i)$ for all i, $1 \le i \le p$, and such that $\sigma(B_i) \equiv_{\mathcal{R}} \sigma(Q_i)$ for all i, $1 \le i \le q$. Let us take the following notations: $\Lambda = \{A_1, \ldots, A_p\}$, $\Omega = \{B_1, \ldots, B_q\}$, $\Gamma = \{P_1, \ldots, P_p\}$, $\Gamma' = \{P_{p+1}, \ldots, P_m\}$, $\Delta = \{Q_1, \ldots, Q_q\}$, $\Delta' = \{Q_{q+1}, \ldots, Q_n\}$. We then get a proof tree of the following form:

$$
\cfrac{
\text{Subs} \cfrac{
\cfrac{
\cfrac{
\cfrac{
\cfrac{
\Lambda, C_1, \ldots, C_k \vdash \Omega, D_1, \ldots, D_l
}{\sigma(\Gamma), \sigma(C_1), \ldots, \sigma(C_k) \vdash \sigma(\Delta), \sigma(D_1), \ldots, \sigma(D_l)} \text{Ax} \quad \vdots \ \vdash R_1
}{\sigma(\Gamma), \sigma(C_2), \ldots, \sigma(C_k) \vdash \sigma(\Delta), \sigma(D_1), \ldots, \sigma(D_l)} \text{Cut} \quad \vdots \ \text{Cut}
}{\vdots}
}{
\cfrac{
\cfrac{\sigma(\Gamma), \sigma(C_k) \vdash \sigma(\Delta), \sigma(D_1), \ldots, \sigma(D_l) \quad \vdots \ \vdash R_k}{\sigma(\Gamma) \vdash \sigma(\Delta), \sigma(D_1), \ldots, \sigma(D_l)} \text{Cut} \text{Cut}
}{\vdots}
}
}{\sigma(\Gamma'), S_l \vdash \sigma(\Delta') \qquad S_1 \vdash \qquad \sigma(\Gamma) \vdash \sigma(\Delta), \sigma(D_l)}
}{\sigma(\Gamma), \sigma(\Gamma') \vdash \sigma(\Delta), \sigma(\Delta')} \text{Cut}
$$

where $R_i \equiv_{\mathcal{R}} \sigma(C_i)$ for all i, $1 \le i \le k$ and where $S_i \equiv_{\mathcal{R}} \sigma(D_i)$ for all i, $1 \le i \le l$. The substitution σ together with the set of lemmas

$$c = \{\vdash R_1, \ldots, \vdash R_k, \ S_1 \vdash, \ldots, \sigma(\Gamma'), S_l \vdash \sigma(\Delta')\}$$

characterise the instance of the test purpose φ derived from this proof tree, which corresponds to the constrained test purpose $((c, \sigma), \varphi)$.

Note that a priori, the lemmas R_i and S_i can be any formulas equivalent up to the congruence $\equiv_{\mathcal{R}}$. To avoid this non-determinism, we choose R_i and S_i in normal form: for all i, $1 \le i \le k$, R_i is the normal form of $\sigma(C_i)$ and for all i, $1 \le i \le l$, S_i is the normal form of $\sigma(D_i)$.

The Algorithm. The unfolding procedure is formally described by the following algorithm. What it unfolds is a constraint ψ from a set of constraints $\mathcal{C}$ associated to some substitution σ in a pair of constraints $(\mathcal{C}, \sigma)$. The first set of constraints $\mathcal{C}_0$ only contains the set of normalised sequents obtained from the initial test purpose, so the procedure starts with unfolding one of these sequents. It builds a set $Unf(\psi)$ corresponding to the unfolding of ψ and containing all the pairs of constraints and substitution obtained by unfolding. Then it will unfold the obtained constraints, which will be considered themselves as test purposes, and so on. Given a constraint $\psi = \gamma_1, \ldots, \gamma_m \vdash \delta_1, \ldots, \delta_n$, the algorithm can be synthesised in the following way.

(Reduce) The first verification to make is whether some instances of the constraint are tautologies. If it is possible to unify some γ_i with some δ_j modulo $\mathcal{R}$ thanks to a substitution σ, then $\sigma(\psi)$ always holds and is useless. The formula $\sigma(\psi)$ is then removed from the set of constraints associated to the corresponding instance of the test purpose.

(Unfold) As explained before, if a part of the constraint can be unified with a part of an axiom in $NewAx$ modulo $\mathcal{R}$, then we know that the constraint can be proved from this axiom with a certain number of applications of the Cut rule where each $\vdash R_i$ ($1 \le i \le k$) and each $S_i \vdash$ ($1 \le i \le l$) is a lemma remaining to prove. One of those lemmas must bring the formulas of ψ not occurring in the axiom, so S_l is in the context $\sigma'(P_{p+1}), \ldots, \sigma'(P_m) \vdash S_l, \sigma'(Q_{q+1}), \ldots, \sigma'(Q_n)$.

Then the procedure replaces the initial constraint ψ with the sets of constraints in $Unf(\psi)$. Each unification with an axiom leads to a pair (c, σ'), so the initial constraint ψ is replaced with as many sets of formulas as there are axioms with which it can be unified. The definition of $Unf(\psi)$ being based on unification, this set is computable if the specification has finitely many axioms.

Given a formula ψ, the unfolding procedure defines the selection criterion C_ψ which maps $T_{(C,\sigma),\varphi}$ to the family of test sets $T_{(\sigma'(C \smallsetminus \{\psi\}) \cup c, \sigma' \circ \sigma), \varphi}$ for each (c, σ') in $Unf(\psi)$ if ψ belongs to C, and to itself otherwise. To ensure the relevance of this selection criterion, it must be shown that its application does not add new test cases to $T_{(C,\sigma),\varphi}$ (soundness) or remove test cases from it (completeness). These results are proved in the next subsection.

Coverage of the Exhaustive Test Set. Here, our unfolding procedure has been defined in order to cover behaviours of one test purpose, represented by the formula φ. When we are interested in covering more widely the exhaustive set $NewPr^\bullet \cap Obs$, a strategy consists in ordering quantifier-free first-order formulas with respect to their length:

$$\Phi_0 = \left\{ \begin{array}{l} \vdash p(x_1, \ldots, x_n), \\ \vdash f(x_1, \ldots, x_n) = y \end{array} \left| \begin{array}{l} p : s_1 \times \ldots \times s_n \in P, \\ f : s_1 \times \ldots \times s_n \to s \in F, \\ \forall i, 1 \le i \le n, x_i \in V_{s_i}, y \in V_s \end{array} \right. \right\}$$

$$\Phi_{n+1} = \left\{ \begin{array}{l} p(x_1, \ldots, x_n), \Gamma \vdash \Delta, \\ f(x_1, \ldots, x_n) = y, \Gamma \vdash \Delta, \\ \Gamma \vdash \Delta, p(x_1, \ldots, x_n), \\ \Gamma \vdash \Delta, f(x_1, \ldots, x_n) = y \end{array} \left| \begin{array}{l} \Gamma \vdash \Delta \in \Phi_n, \\ p : s_1 \times \ldots \times s_n \in P, \\ f : s_1 \times \ldots \times s_n \to s \in F, \\ \forall i, 1 \le i \le n, x_i \in V_{s_i}, y \in V_s \end{array} \right. \right\}$$

Then, to manage the (often infinite) size of $NewPr^\bullet \cap Obs$, we start by choosing $k \in \mathbb{N}$, and then we apply for every $i, 1 \le i \le k$, the above unfolding procedure to each formula belonging to Φ_i. Of course, this requires that signatures are finite so that each set Φ_i is finite too.

Example 2. We choose as a test purpose the formula $x < y \Rightarrow z/y \ll z/x$. The associated constrained test purpose for this formula is:

$$((\{ x < y \vdash z/y \ll z/x \}, \ \mathrm{Id} \ ), \ x < y \Rightarrow z/y \ll z/x \ )$$

We denote by Ψ_0 the set containing this first pair of constraints. After a loop of the algorithm, we obtain a set Ψ_1 of constrained test purposes. To give a better intuition, we give the associated test subsets. The first set is obtained thanks to a unification of the test purpose with the left-hand side of axiom (2), and the second with the right-hand side of the same axiom.

$$\{ x \times s(v) < u \times s(y) \Rightarrow z/(u \times s(y)) \ll z/(x \times s(v))$$
$$| \ x/s(y) \ll u/s(v) \Rightarrow z/(u \times s(y)) \ll z/(x \times s(v)) \}$$
$$\{ s(x) < s(y) \Rightarrow z/s(y) \ll z/s(x) \ | \ x < y \Rightarrow z \times s(x) < z \times s(y) \}$$

Algorithm 1. Axiom unfolding

Inputs : structured quantifier-free first-order specification $Sp = (\Sigma, Ax)$,
            rewrite system $\mathcal{R}$, test purpose $\varphi \in NewFor$
Output : set of constraints Ψ

$\Psi \leftarrow \{(C_0, \mathrm{Id})\}$ where C_0 is the set of normalised sequents obtained from φ
loop
   Take (C, σ) from Ψ and remove it
   Take $\psi = P_1, \ldots, P_m \vdash Q_1, \ldots, Q_n$ from C s.t. $\psi \in NewFor$ and remove it
   $Unf(\psi) \leftarrow \emptyset$

(Reduce)
   if there exists $\sigma' \in T_\Sigma(V)^V$ mgu, $1 \le i \le m$ and $1 \le j \le n$
   such that $\sigma'(P_i) \equiv_\mathcal{R} \sigma'(Q_j)$ **then**
       Add $(\emptyset, \sigma')$ to $Unf(\psi)$

   else
       for all axioms $ax \in NewAx$ **do**

(Unfold)
           if ax is of the form $A_1, \ldots, A_p, C_1, \ldots, C_k \vdash B_1, \ldots, B_q, D_1, \ldots, D_l$
           with $1 \le p \le m, 1 \le q \le n$, and
           there exists $\sigma' \in T_\Sigma(V)^V$ mgu such that
           for all $1 \le i \le p, \sigma'(A_i) \equiv_\mathcal{R} \sigma'(P_i)$ and
           for all $1 \le i \le q, \sigma'(B_i) \equiv_\mathcal{R} \sigma'(Q_i)$ **then**
               $c \leftarrow \{\vdash R_i\}_{1 \le i \le k} \cup \{S_i \vdash\}_{1 \le i \le l-1}$
                       $\cup \{\sigma'(P_{p+1}), \ldots, \sigma'(P_m), S_l \vdash \sigma'(Q_{q+1}), \ldots, \sigma'(Q_n)\}$
               such that $R_i = \sigma(C_i)\!\downarrow$ and $S_i = \sigma(D_i)\!\downarrow$
               Add (c, σ') to $Unf(\psi)$

   Add $\displaystyle\bigcup_{(c,\sigma') \in Unf(\psi)} \{(\sigma'(\mathcal{C}) \cup c, \sigma' \circ \sigma)\}$ to Ψ

The premises of the constraint in the second subset is actually the normal form of the corresponding formula obtained after unification, which was $s(x) < s(y)$. Deduction modulo allows here to have a more concise proof, and then a more efficient selection procedure, thanks to the simplification allowed by the congruence.

5.3   Properties of the Selection Criterion

Here, we prove the two properties that make the unfolding procedure relevant for the selection of appropriate test cases, i.e. that the selection criterion defined by the procedure is sound and complete for the initial test set we defined. The entire proof may be found in [15].

Theorem 3 (Soundness and completeness). *Let φ be a quantifier-free first-order formula, $\mathcal{C}$ a set of constraints and $\sigma : V \rightarrow T_\Sigma(V)$ a substitution. Let $\psi \in \mathcal{C}$. The* selection criterion for ψ is sound and complete *for the test set for φ constrained by C and σ:* $|C_\psi(T_{(C,\sigma),\varphi})| = T_{(C,\sigma),\varphi}$.

To prove the soundness of the procedure comes down to proving that the instance $\sigma'(\varphi)$ of the initial formula φ can be derived from the set of constraints c and the axiom with which it has been unified. Thus we prove that the test set obtained by the application of the procedure does not contain new test cases, since it is only composed of instances of the initial test purpose.

To prove the completeness, we prove that all the possible instances of the test purpose can be proved with a proof tree of the form we showed earlier, and that the procedure generates all possible constraints for proving this instance. We thus prove that no test case is lost. Actually, we can observe that our unfolding procedure defines a proof search strategy that enables to limit the search space to the class of proof trees having the following structure: no instance of cut occurs over instances of substitution; there is no instance of cut whose premises both are instances of cut. We then have to prove that the derivability defined by our unfolding strategy coincides with the full derivability. To achieve this purpose, we define basic transformations to rewrite proof trees into ones having the above structure, and show that the induced global proof tree transformation is weakly normalising.

6 Conclusion

In this paper, we investigated the problem of test case selection from structured specifications in the context of integration testing. The problem was to use the structuration of the specification as well as the unit testing result on the smaller modules of the system to select test cases allowing to test the new features of the system only, relying on the correctness of the modules. We used deduction modulo to guide the test case selection because it allows to easily integrate the knowledge of the correctness of the smaller modules in the rewrite system used as a congruence.

The definition of test selection criteria is the first step towards the construction of a practical test set to submit to the system. The next step is the generation of a test set satisfying these criteria. In our framework, the generation consists in applying the uniformity hypothesis to the constrained test sets obtained by unfolding an initial test purpose. It actually comes down to solve the constraints associated to each constrained test purpose, in order to build one test case corresponding to this purpose. Therefore, we plan to study the definition of an efficient algorithm of test case generation for (structured) quantifier-free first-order specifications.

References

1. Bernot, G., Gaudel, M.C., Marre, B.: Software testing based on formal specifications: a theory and a tool. Software Engineering Journal 6(6), 387–405 (1991)
2. Bernot, G.: Testing against formal specifications: a theoretical view. In: Abramsky, S. (ed.) TAPSOFT 1991, CCPSD 1991, and ADC-Talks 1991. LNCS, vol. 494, pp. 99–119. Springer, Heidelberg (1991)

3. Marre, B.: LOFT: a tool for assisting selection of test data sets from algebraic specifications. In: Mosses, P.D., Schwartzbach, M.I., Nielsen, M. (eds.) CAAP 1995, FASE 1995, and TAPSOFT 1995. LNCS, vol. 915, pp. 799–800. Springer, Heidelberg (1995)
4. Aiguier, M., Arnould, A., Boin, C., Le Gall, P., Marre, B.: Testing from algebraic specifications: test data set selection by unfolding axioms. In: Grieskamp, W., Weise, C. (eds.) FATES 2005. LNCS, vol. 3997, pp. 203–217. Springer, Heidelberg (2006)
5. Wirsing, M.: Algebraic specification. In: Handbook of Theoretical Computer Science. Formal Models and Semantics, vol. B, ch. 13, pp. 675–788. Elsevier, Amsterdam (1990)
6. Dowek, G., Hardin, T., Kirchner, C.: Theorem proving modulo. Journal of Automated Reasoning 31(1), 33–72 (2003)
7. Machado, P.: Testing from structured algebraic specifications. In: Rus, T. (ed.) AMAST 2000. LNCS, vol. 1816, pp. 529–544. Springer, Heidelberg (2000)
8. Doche, M., Wiels, V.: Extended institutions for testing. In: Rus, T. (ed.) AMAST 2000. LNCS, vol. 1816, pp. 514–528. Springer, Heidelberg (2000)
9. Aiguier, M., Arnould, A., Le Gall, P., Longuet, D.: Exhaustive test sets for algebraic specification correctness. Technical report, IBISC, Université d'Évry (2008)
10. Ohlebush, E.: Modular properties of composable term rewriting systems. Journal of Symbolic Computation 20, 1–41 (1995)
11. Aiguier, M., Arnould, A., Le Gall, P., Longuet, D.: Test selection criteria from quantifier-free first-order specifications. In: Arbab, F., Sirjani, M. (eds.) FSEN 2007. LNCS, vol. 4767, pp. 144–159. Springer, Heidelberg (2007)
12. Longuet, D., Aiguier, M., Le Gall, P.: Proof-guided test selection from first-order specifications with equality. Journal of Automated Reasoning (to appear, 2009)
13. Le Gall, P., Arnould, A.: Formal specification and test: correctness and oracle. In: Haveraaen, M., Dahl, O.-J., Owe, O. (eds.) Abstract Data Types 1995 and COMPASS 1995. LNCS, vol. 1130, pp. 342–358. Springer, Heidelberg (1996)
14. Orejas, F., Navarro, M., Sánchez, A.: Implementation and behavioural equivalence: a survey. In: Bidoit, M., Choppy, C. (eds.) Abstract Data Types 1991 and COMPASS 1991. LNCS, vol. 655, pp. 144–163. Springer, Heidelberg (1993)
15. Longuet, D., Aiguier, M.: Integration testing from structured first-order specifications via deduction modulo. Technical report, LSV, ENS Cachan (2009)

A Minimized Assumption Generation Method for Component-Based Software Verification

Pham Ngoc Hung, Toshiaki Aoki, and Takuya Katayama

School of Information Science
Japan Advanced Institute of Science and Technology
{hungpn,toshiaki,katayama}@jaist.ac.jp

Abstract. An assume-guarantee verification method has been recognized as a promising approach to verify component-based software with model checking. The method is not only fitted to component-based software but also has a potential to solve the state space explosion problem in model checking. This method allows us to decompose a verification target into components so that we can model check each of them separately. In this method, assumptions which are environments of the components are generated. The number of states of the assumptions should be minimized because the computational cost of model checking is influenced by that number. Thus, we propose a method for generating minimal assumptions for the assume-guarantee verification of component-based software. The key idea of this method is finding the minimal assumptions in the search spaces of the candidate assumptions. These assumptions are seen as the environments needed for the components to satisfy a property and for the rest of the system to be satisfied. The minimal assumptions generated by the proposed method can be used to recheck the whole system at much lower computational cost. We have implemented a tool for generating the minimal assumptions. Experimental results are also presented and discussed.

Keywords: model checking, assume-guarantee reasoning, modular verification, learning algorithm, minimal assumption.

1 Introduction

Component-based development is one of the most important technical initiatives in software engineering as it is considered to be an open, effective and efficient approach to reduce development cost and time while increasing software quality. Component-based software (CBS) technology also supports rapid development of complex evolving software applications by enhancing reuse and adaptability. CBS can be evolved by evolving one or more software components.

To realize such an ideal CBS paradigm, one of the key issues is to ensure that those separately specified and implemented components do not conflict with each other when composed - the *component consistency* issue. The current well-known technologies such as CORBA (OMG), COM/DCOM or .NET (Microsoft), Java and JavaBeans (Sun), etc. only support component *plugging*.

M. Leucker and C. Morgan (Eds.): ICTAC 2009, LNCS 5684, pp. 277–291, 2009.

However, components often fail to co-operate, i.e., the *plug-and-play* mechanism fails. Currently, the popular solution to deal with this issue is the verification of CBS via model checking [5]. Model checking is a practical approach for improving software reliability. It provides exhaustive state space coverage for systems being checked and is particularly effective in detecting difficult coordination errors which frequently result from component composition. Nonetheless, a major problem of model checking is the *state space explosion*. In order to deal with this problem, a powerful method called assume-guarantee verification was proposed in [6,10,14,15] by decomposing a verification target about a component-based system into parts about the individual components. The key idea of this method is to generate assumptions as environments needed for components to satisfy a property. These assumptions are then discharged by the rest of the system. For example, consider a simple case where a CBS is made up of two components M_1 and M_2. The method proposed in [6] verifies whether this system satisfies a property p *without composing* M_1 with M_2. For this goal, an assumption $A(p)$ is generated by applying a learning algorithm called L* [1,17] such that $A(p)$ is strong enough for M_1 to satisfy p but weak enough to be discharged by M_2 (i.e., $\langle A(p) \rangle M_1 \langle p \rangle$ and $\langle true \rangle M_2 \langle A(p) \rangle$ which are called compositional rules, both hold). From these rules, this system satisfies p. In order to check these compositional rules, the number of states of the assumption $A(p)$ should be minimized because the computational cost of model checking of these rules is influenced by that number. This means that the cost of verification of CBS is reduced with a smaller assumption. Moreover, when a component is evolved after adapting some refinements in the context of the software evolution, the whole evolved CBS of many existing components and the evolved component is required to be rechecked [8,9]. In this case, we also can reduce the cost of rechecking the evolved CBS by reusing the smaller assumption. These observations imply that the size of the generated assumptions is of primary importance. However, the method proposed in [6,7] focuses only on generating the assumptions which satisfies the compositional rules. The number of states of the generated assumptions is not mentioned in this work. Thus, the assumptions generated by the method are not minimal. A more detailed discussion of this issue can be found in Section 4.

This paper proposes a method for generating the minimal assumptions for assume-guarantee verification of component-based software to deal with the above issue. The key idea of this method is finding the minimal assumption that satisfies the compositional rules thus is considered as a search problem in a search space of the candidate assumptions. These assumptions are seen as the environments needed for components to satisfy a property and for the rest of the CBS to be satisfied. With regard to the effectiveness, the proposed method can generate the minimal assumptions which have the minimal sizes and a smaller number of transitions than the assumptions generated by the method proposed in [6]. These minimal assumptions generated by the proposed method can be used to recheck the whole CBS by checking the compositional rules at much lower computational costs.

The paper is organized as follows. We first review some background in Section 2. Section 3 describes the current method for assumption generation by using the L* learning algorithm. Section 4 is about a minimized L*-based assumption generation method to find the minimal assumptions for component-based software verification. Section 5 shows an implementation, experimental results, and discussion. Section 6 presents related works. Finally, we conclude the paper in Section 7.

2   Background

This section presents some basic concepts which are used in our work as follows.

LTSs. This paper uses *Labeled Transition Systems* (LTSs) to model behaviors of communicating components. Let $\mathcal{A}ct$ be the universal set of observable actions and let τ denote a local action unobservable to a component's environment. We use π to denote a special error state. An LTS M is a quadruple $\langle Q, \alpha M, \delta, q_0 \rangle$ where: Q is a non-empty set of states, $\alpha M \subseteq \mathcal{A}ct$ is a finite set of observable actions called the alphabet of M, $\delta \subseteq Q \times \alpha M \cup \{\tau\} \times Q$ is a transition relation, and $q_0 \in Q$ is the initial state. The size of an LTS $M = \langle Q, \alpha M, \delta, q_0 \rangle$ is the number of states of M, denoted $|M|$. We use $\prod$ to denote the LTS $\langle \{\pi\}, \mathcal{A}ct, \phi, \pi \rangle$. An LTS $M = \langle Q, \alpha M, \delta, q_0 \rangle$ is *non-deterministic* if it contains τ-transition or if $\exists (q, a, q'), (q, a, q'') \in \delta$ such that $q' \neq q''$. Otherwise, M is *deterministic*.

Traces. A trace t of an LTS M is a sequence of observable actions that M can perform starting at its initial state. For $\Sigma \subseteq \mathcal{A}ct$, we use $t{\uparrow}\Sigma$ to denote the trace obtained by removing from t all occurrences of actions $a \notin \Sigma$. The set of all traces of M is called the language of M, denoted $L(M)$. Let $\sigma = a_1 a_2 ... a_n$ be a finite trace of an LTS M. We use $[\sigma]$ to denote the LTS $M_\sigma = \langle Q, \alpha M, \delta, q_0 \rangle$ with $Q = \langle q_0, q_1, ..., q_n \rangle$, and $\delta = \{(q_{i-1}, a_i, q_i)\}$, where $1 \leq i \leq n$.

Parallel Composition. The parallel composition operator $\|$ is a commutative and associative operator that combines behaviors of two components by synchronizing the actions common to their alphabets and interleaving the remaining actions. For example, when composing two components, *Input* and *Output* illustrated in Fig. 2, actions *send* and *ack* will each be synchronized and the others are interleaved. Details of this concept are in [6,7].

Safety LTS, Safety Property and Satisfiability. We call a deterministic LTS that contains no π states a *safety LTS*. A *safety property* is specified as a safety LTS p, whose language $L(p)$ defines the set of acceptable behaviors over αp. An LTS M satisfies p, denoted as $M \models p$, if and only if $\forall \sigma \in L(M): (\sigma{\uparrow}\alpha p) \in L(p)$. When checking whether the LTS M satisfies a property p, an *error LTS*, denoted p_{err}, is created which traps possible violations with the π state. Details of error LTS can be found in [6,7].

Deterministic Finite State Automata (DFAs). We use the L* learning algorithm [1,17] to update the inaccurate model of the evolved component. The L* learning algorithm produces DFAs, which our work then uses as LTSs. A DFA M is a five tuple $\langle Q, \alpha M, \delta, q_0, F \rangle$ where: Q, αM, δ, q_0 are defined as for deterministic LTSs, and $F \subseteq Q$ is a set of accepting states.

For a DFA M and a string σ, we use $\delta(q, \sigma)$ to denote the state that M will be in after reading σ starting at state q. A string σ is said to be *accepted* by a DFA $M = \langle Q, \alpha M, \delta, q_0, F \rangle$ if $\delta(q_0, \sigma) \in F$. The language of a DFA M is defined as $L(M) = \{\sigma \mid \delta(q_0, \sigma) \in F\}$.

A DFA M is *prefix-closed* if $L(M)$ is prefix-closed. The DFAs returned by the L* learning algorithm in the proposed method are *unique, complete, minimal, and prefix-closed* [17]. These DFAs therefore contain a single non-accepting state. To get a safety LTS A from a DFA M, we remove the non-accepting state denoted nas and all its ingoing transitions. Formally, for a DFA $M = \langle Q \cup \{nas\}, \alpha M, \delta, q_0, F \rangle$, the safety LTS is chosen to be $A = \langle Q, \alpha M, \delta \cap (Q \times \alpha M \times Q), q_0 \rangle$.

Assume-Guarantee Reasoning. In the assume-guarantee paradigm, a formula is a triple $\langle A(p) \rangle \, M \, \langle p \rangle$, where M is a component, p is a property, and $A(p)$ is an assumption about M's environment. The formula is *true* if whenever M is part of a system satisfying $A(p)$, then the system must also guarantee p. In our work, to check an assume-guarantee formula $\langle A(p) \rangle \, M \, \langle p \rangle$, where both $A(p)$ and p are safety LTSs, we use a tool called LTSA [11] to compute $A(p) \| M \| p_{err}$ and check if the error state π is reachable in the composition. If it is, then the formula is violated, otherwise it is satisfied.

Given two component models M_1, M_2 and a property p, assume-guarantee reasoning finds an assumption $A(p)$ by applying the L* learning algorithm such that $A(p)$ is strong enough for M_1 to satisfy p but weak enough to be discharged by M_2 (i.e., $\langle A(p) \rangle \, M_1 \, \langle p \rangle$ and $\langle true \rangle \, M_2 \, \langle A(p) \rangle$ both hold). From these compositional rules, this system satisfies p. Formally, assume-guarantee reasoning finds an assumption $A(p)$ such that $L(A(p) \| M_1) {\uparrow} \alpha p \subseteq L(p)$ and $L(M_2) {\uparrow} \alpha A(p) \subseteq L(A(p))$. The iterative fashion for generating $A(p)$ is illustrated in Fig. 1. Details of this fashion can be found in [6].

An assumption with which the compositional rules is guaranteed to work is the weakest assumption A_W defined in [7], which restricts the environment of M_1 no more and no less than necessary for p to be satisfied. Assumption A_W describes exactly those traces over the alphabet $\Sigma = (\alpha M_1 \cup \alpha p) \cap \alpha M_2$ so that the error state π is not reachable in the compositional system $M_1 \| p_{err}$. Weakest assumption A_W means that for any environment component E, $M_1 \| E \models p$ iff $E \models A_W$.

Minimal Assumption. Given two component models M_1, M_2 and a property p, $A(p)$ is an assumption if and only if $A(p)$ satisfies the compositional rules. *An assumption $A(p)$ represented by a LTS is minimal if and only if the number of states of $A(p)$ is less than or equal to the number of states of any other assumptions.*

3 Assume-Guarantee Verification

3.1 The L* Learning Algorithm

The L* learning algorithms was developed by Angluin [1] and later was improved by Rivest and Schapire [17]. L* learns an unknown regular language and produces a DFA that accepts it. The main idea of the L* learning algorithms is based on the *"Myhill-Nerode Theorem"* [12] in the theory of formal languages. It said that for every regular set $U \subseteq \Sigma^*$, there exists *a unique minimal deterministic automata* whose states are isomorphic to the set of equivalence classes of the following relation: $w \approx w'$ iff $\forall u \in \Sigma^*$: $wu \in U \iff w'u \in U$. Therefore, the main idea of L* is to learn the equivalence classes, i.e., two prefix are not in the same class if and only if there is a distinguishing suffix u.

Let U be an unknown regular language over some alphabet Σ. L* will produce a DFA M such that M is a minimal deterministic automata corresponding to U and $L(M) = U$. In order to learn U, L* needs to interact with a *Minimally Adequate Teacher*, called Teacher. The Teacher must be able to correctly answer two types of questions from L*. The first type is a membership query, consisting of a string $\sigma \in \Sigma^*$; the answer is *true* if $\sigma \in U$, and *false* otherwise. The second type of these questions is a conjecture, i.e., a candidate DFA M whose language the algorithm believes to be identical to U. The answer is *true* if $L(M) = U$. Otherwise the Teacher returns a counterexample, which is a string σ in the symmetric difference of $L(M)$ and U.

At a higher level, L* maintains a table T that records whether string s in Σ^* belong to U. It does this by making membership queries to the Teacher to update the table. At various stages L* decides to make a conjecture. It uses the table T to build a candidate DFA M_i and asks the Teacher whether the conjecture is correct. If the Teacher replies *true*, the algorithm terminates. Otherwise, L* uses the counterexample returned by the Teacher to maintain the table with string s that witness differences between $L(M_i)$ and U.

3.2 L*-Based Assumption Generation Method

The assume-guarantee paradigm is a powerful *"divide-and-conquer"* mechanism for decomposing a verification process of a CBS into subtasks about the individual components. Consider a simple case where a system is made up of two components including a framework M_1 and an extension M_2. The goal is to verify whether this system satisfies a property p *without composing M_1 with M_2*. For this purpose, an assumption $A(p)$ is generated [6] by applying the L* learning algorithm such that $A(p)$ is strong enough for M_1 to satisfy p but weak enough to be discharged by M_2 (i.e., $\langle A(p) \rangle M_1 \langle p \rangle$ and $\langle true \rangle M_2 \langle A(p) \rangle$ both hold). From these compositional rules, this system satisfies p.

In order to obtain appropriate assumptions, this method applies the compositional rules in an iterative fashion illustrated in Fig. 1. At each iteration i, a candidate assumption A_i is produced based on some knowledge about the system and the results of the previous iteration. The two steps of the compositional rules are then applied. Step 1 checks whether M_1 satisfies p in an environment that guarantees A_i by computing formula $\langle A_i \rangle$ M_1 $\langle p \rangle$. If the result is *false*, it means that this candidate assumption is *too weak*. The candidate assumption A_i therefore must be strengthened with the help of the counterexample *cex* produced by this step. Otherwise, the result is *true*, it means that A_i is strong enough for the property to be satisfied. The step 2 is then applied to check that if component M_2 satisfies A_i by computing formula $\langle true \rangle$ M_2 $\langle A_i \rangle$. If this step returns *true*, the property p holds in the compositional system $M_1 \| M_2$ and the algorithm terminates. Otherwise, this step returns *false*; further analysis is required to identify whether p is indeed violated in $M_1 \| M_2$ or the candidate A_i is too strong to be satisfied by M_2. Such analysis is based on the counterexample *cex* returned by this step. The L* algorithm must check that the counterexample *cex* belong to the unknown language $U = L(A_W)$. If it does not, the property p does not hold in the system $M_1 \| M_2$. Otherwise, A_i is too strong. The candidate assumption A_i must be weakened (i.e., behaviors must be added with the help of *cex*) in iteration $i + 1$. A new candidate assumption may of course be too weak, and therefore the entire process must be repeated.

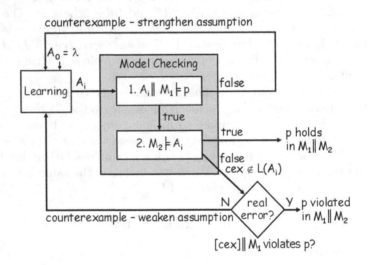

Fig. 1. A framework for L*-based assumption generation

4   Minimized Assumption Generation Method

The assume-generation verification proposed in [6] is a powerful method for checking component-based software by decomposing a verification target about a component-based software into parts about the individual components. In this method, assumptions which are seen as environments of the components are generated. The number of states of the assumptions should be minimized because this number influences on the computational cost of model checking. However, the assumptions generated by this method are not minimal. Fig. 2 is a counterexample to prove this fact. In this counterexample, given two component models M_1 (*Input*), M_2 (*Output*), and a required property p, the method proposed in [6] generates the assumption $A(p)$. However, there is a smaller assumption with a smaller size and a smaller number of transitions. The reason why this method does not generate a minimal assumption is presented as follows. The L* used in this method learns the language of the weakest assumption A_W over the alphabet $\Sigma = (\alpha M_1 \cup \alpha p) \cap \alpha M_2$ and produces a DFA that accepts it. In order to learn this language, L* builds an observation table (S, E, T) where S and E are a set of prefixes and suffixes respectively, both over Σ^*. T is a function which maps $(S \cup S.\Sigma).E$ to $\{true, false\}$, where the operator "." is defined as follows. Given two sets of event sequences P and Q, $P.Q = \{pq \mid p \in P, q \in Q\}$, where pq presents the concatenation of the event sequences p and q. The technique for answering membership queries used in this method means that for any string $s \in (S \cup S.\Sigma).E$, $T(s) = true$ if $s \in L(A_W)$, and $false$ otherwise. In the counterexample showed in Fig. 2, if $s \in L(A_W)$ but $s \notin L(A(p))$, then $T(s)$ is set to $true$ (in this case, $T(s)$ should be $false$). For this reason, the assumption $A(p)$ generated by this method contains some strings/traces which do not belong to the language of the assumption being learned.

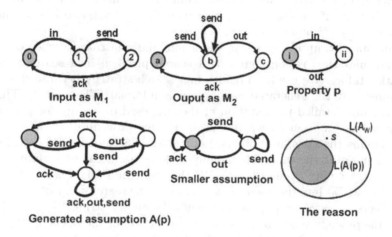

Fig. 2. A counterexample and the reason to show that the assumptions generated in [6] are not minimal

This section proposes a method for generating minimal assumptions for assume-guarantee verification of component-based software. We also define a new technique for answering membership queries to deal with the above issue. The minimal assumption is generated by combining the L* learning algorithm and the breadth-first search strategy. We ensure that the assumptions generated by this method are minimal (Theorem 2).

4.1   Minimal Assumption Generation

An Improved Technique for Answering Membership Queries. As mentioned above, in order to learn the language of the assumption, the L* learning algorithm used in [6] builds an observation table (S, E, T) where T is a function which maps $(S \cup S.\Sigma).E$ to $\{true, false\}$. For any string $s \in (S \cup S.\Sigma).E$, $T(s) = true$ if $s \in L(A_W)$, and $false$ otherwise. In the case where $s \in L(A_W)$, we cannot ensure that whether s belongs to the language being learned or not (i.e., whether $s \in L(A(p))$?). If $s \notin L(A(p))$ then $T(s)$ should be $false$. However, the work in [6] set $T(s)$ to $true$ in this case. For this reason, the generated assumptions are not minimal in this work. In order to solve this issue, we use a new value called "?" to represent the value of $T(s)$ in such cases. We define an improved technique for answering membership queries as follows. To generate a minimal assumption, the L* learning algorithm used in our work builds an observation table (S, E, T), where S and E are a set of prefixes and suffixes respectively, both over Σ^*. T is a function which maps $(S \cup S.\Sigma).E$ to $\{true, false, "?"\}$, where "?" can be seen as "don't know" value. The "don't know" value means that for each string $s \in (S \cup S.\Sigma).E$, even if $s \in L(A_W)$, we do not know whether s belongs to the language of the assumption being learned or not. The technique for answering membership queries used in our method means that for any string $s \in (S \cup S.\Sigma).E$, if s is the empty string then $T(s) = true$, else $T(s) = false$ if $s \notin L(A_W)$, and "?" otherwise.

Finding an assumption where it has a minimal size that satisfies the compositional rules thus is considered as a search problem in a search space of observation tables. We use the breadth-first search strategy because this strategy ensures that the generated assumption is minimal (Theorem 2). The following is more detailed presentation of the proposed procedure for generating the minimal assumption shown in Fig. 3. In this procedure, we use a queue which contains the generated observation tables. These observation tables are used for generating the candidate assumptions. Initially, the procedure sets the queue q to the empty queue (line 1). We then put the initial observation table $OT_0 = (S_0, E_0, T_0)$ into the queue q as the root of the search space of observation tables, where $S_0 = E_0 = \{\lambda\}$ (λ represents the empty string) (line 2). Subsequently, the procedure gets a table OT_i from the top of the queue q (line 3). If OT_i contains the "don't know" value "?" (line 4), we obtain all instances of OT_i by replacing all "?" entries in OT_i with both $true$ and $false$ (line 5). For example, the initial observation table of the illustrative system presented in Fig. 2 and one of its instance obtained by replacing all "?" entries with $true$ value are showed in Fig. 4. The obtained instances then are put into the queue q (line 6). Otherwise, the table OT_i does not contain the "?" value. In this case, if OT_i is not closed (line 7), an updated table OT is obtained by calling the procedure $make\_closed(OT_i)$ (line 8). OT then is put into q (line 9). In the case where the table OT_i is closed, a candidate assumption A_i is generated from OT_i (line 10). If A_i is an actual assumption then the procedure returns A_i as the minimal assumption and terminates (line 11), otherwise a counterexample cex is given. The counterexample cex is analyzed to find a suffix e of cex that witnesses a

1. Initially, q:= empty; //q is empty
    //putting the initial table as root into q
2. q.put(OT_0) ; // $OT_0 = (S_0, E_0, T_0)$, $S_0 = E_0 = \{\lambda\}$
    While q <> empty {
3. OT_i := q.get(); //getting a table form the top of q
4.   If OT_i contains "?" value
5.   For every instance OT of OT_i
6. q.put(OT);
        Else
7.   If OT_i is not closed {
8. OT := make_closed(OT_i);
9. q.put(OT);
                } Else { //OT_i is closed
10.   Construct a candidate assumption A_i from OT_i ;
11.   If A_i is an actual assumption, then return A_i ;
                    Else {
12.   Add the counterexample e to E_i ;
13. OT := Update(OT_i);
14. q.put(OT);
                    }
                }
    }

Fig. 3. The procedure for finding the minimal assumption

difference between $L(A_i)$ and the language of the assumption being learned. e then is added to E_i of the table OT_i (line 12). After that, an updated table OT is obtained by calling the procedure $Update(OT_i)$ (line 13). OT then is put into q (line 14). The procedure iterates the entire process by looping from line 3 to line 14 until the queue q is empty or a minimal assumption is generated.

Characteristics of the Search Space. The search space of observation tables used in the proposed method exactly contains the generated observation tables which are used to generate the candidate assumptions. This search space is seen as a search tree where its root is the initial observation table OT_0. We can conveniently define the size of an observation table $OT = (S, E, T)$ as $|S|$, denoted $|OT|$. We use A_{ij} to denote the jth candidate assumption generated from the jth observation table (denoted OT_{ij}) at the depth i of the search tree. From the way to build the search tree presented in Fig. 3 we have a theorem as follows.

Theorem 1. *Let A_{ij} and A_{kl} be two candidate assumptions generated at the depth i and k respectively. $|A_{ij}| < |A_{kl}|$ implies that $i < k$.*

Proof. The observation tables at the depth $i+1$ are generated from the observation tables at the depth i exactly in one of the following cases:

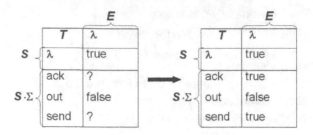

Fig. 4. The initial observation table and one of its instances

- There is at least a table OT_{ij} of the tables at the depth i which contains the "?" value. In this case, the instances of this table are the tables at the depth $i+1$. These tables have the same size with the table OT_{ij}.
- There is at least a table OT_{ij} of the tables at the depth i which is not closed. An updated table $OT_{(i+1)k}$ at the depth $i+1$ is obtained from this table by adding a new element to S_{ij}. This mean that $|OT_{ij}| < |OT_{(i+1)k}|$.
- Finally, there is at least a table OT_{ij} of the tables at the depth i which is not an actual assumption. In this case, an updated table $OT_{(i+1)k}$ at the depth $i+1$ is obtained from this table by adding a suffix e of the given counterexample cex to E_{ij}. This mean that $|OT_{ij}| = |OT_{(i+1)k}|$.

These observations imply that if the size of the candidate generated from a table at the depth i less than the size of the candidate generated from a table at the depth k, then $i < k$. □

4.2 Termination and Correctness

The termination and correctness of the proposed procedure for the minimized assumption generation showed in Fig. 3 are proved by the following theorem.

Theorem 2. *Given two component models M_1 and M_2, and a property p, the proposed procedure for the minimized assumption generation presented in Fig. 3 terminates and returns true and an assumption $A_m(p)$ with a minimal size such that it is strong enough for M_1 to satisfy p but weak enough to be discharged by M_2, if the compositional system $M_1 \| M_2$ satisfies p, and false otherwise.*

Proof. At any iteration, the proposed method returns *true* or *false* (i.e., the compositional system $M_1 \| M_2$ violates p) and terminates or continues by providing a counterexample or continues to update the current observation table (if this table contains "?" or it is not closed). Because the proposed method is based on the L* learning algorithm, by the correctness of L* [1,17], we ensure that if the L* learning algorithm keeps receiving counterexamples, in the worst case, the algorithm will eventually produce the weakest assumption A_W and terminates, by the definition of A_W [7]. This means that the search space exactly contains the observation table OT_W which is used to generate A_W. In the worst case, the proposed method reaches to OT_W and terminates.

With regard to correctness, the proposed method uses two steps of the compositional rules (i.e., $\langle A_i \rangle$ M_1 $\langle p \rangle$ and $\langle true \rangle$ M_2 $\langle A_i \rangle$) to answer the question of whether the candidate assumption A_i produced by the method is an actual assumption or not. It only returns $true$ and a minimal assumption $A_m(p) = A_i$ when both steps return $true$, and therefore its correctness is guaranteed by the compositional rules. The proposed method returns a real error when it detects a trace σ of M_2 which violates the property p when simulated on M_1. In this case, it implies that $M_1 \| M_2'$ violates p. The remaining problem is to prove that the assumption $A_m(p)$ generated by the proposed method is minimal. Suppose that there exists an assumption A such that $|A| < |A_m(p)|$. By using Theorem 1 for this fact, we can imply that the depth of the table used to generate A less than the depth of the table used to generate $A_m(p)$. This means that the table used to generate A has been visited by our procedure. In this case, the procedure has generated A as a candidate assumption and A was not an actual assumption. These facts imply that such assumption A does not exist. $\square$

5   Experiment and Discussion

This section presents our implemented tools for L*-based assumption generation and experimental results by applying these tools for some illustrative systems. We also discuss the advantages and disadvantages of the proposed method.

5.1   Experiment

In order to evaluate the effectiveness of the proposed method, we have implemented the assumption generation method proposed in [6] and the proposed minimized assumption generation method in the Objective Caml (OCaml) functional progamming language [13]. We tested our method by using several illustrative systems and compared the method with that proposed in [6]. The size, the number of transitions, and the generating time of the generated assumptions are evaluated in this experiment. We also evaluate the rechecking time for each system by reusing the generated assumptions for checking the compositional rules. Table 1 shows experimental results for this purpose. In the results, the system size is the product of the sizes of the software components and the size of the required property for each CBS. Our obtained experimental results imply that the generated minimal assumptions have smaller sizes and number of transitions than the generated ones by the method proposed in [6]. These minimal assumptions are effective for rechecking the systems with a lower cost. However, our method has a higher cost for generating the assumption.

We also use the tool for verifying concurrent systems called LTSA [11] to check correctness of the minimal assumption $A_m(p)$ which is generated by our proposed method. For this purpose, we check that whether $A_m(p)$ satisfies the compositional rules (i.e., $\langle A_m(p) \rangle$ M_1 $\langle p \rangle$ and $\langle true \rangle$ M_2 $\langle A_m(p) \rangle$ both hold) by checking the compositional systems $A_m(p) \| M_1 \| p_{err}$ and $M_2 \| A_m(p)_{err}$ in the LTSA tool. For each compositional system, the LTSA tool returns the same result as our verification result for each system.

Table 1. Experimental results

System	Sys. size	The current AG Method				Minimized AG Method			
		$|A|$	Trans. of A	Generating Time (ms)	Rechecking Time (ms)	$|A|$	Trans. of A	Generating Time (ms)	Rechecking Time (ms)
Simple Channel	18	2	4	93	7.8	2	3	94	7.6
Modified Channel	18	4	9	97	9.5	2	4	102	6.3
Two Channels	75	3	12	94	37.5	3	6	107	23.5

The implemented tool and the illustrative systems which are used in our experimental results is available at the site [16].

5.2   Discussion

With regard to the importance of the minimal assumptions, obtaining smaller assumptions is interesting for several advantages as follows:

- Modular verification of CBS is done by model checking the parallel compositional rules which has the assumption as one of its components. The computational cost of this checking is influenced by the size of the assumption. This means that the cost of verification of CBS is reduced with a smaller assumption which has a smaller size and smaller number of transitions.
- When a component is evolved after adapting some refinements in the context of the software evolution, the whole evolved CBS of many existing components and the evolved component is required to be rechecked [8]. In this case, we can reduce the cost of rechecking the evolved CBS by reusing the smaller assumption.
- Finally, a smaller assumption means less complex behavior so this assumption is easier for a human to understand. This is interesting for checking the large-scale systems.

The experimental results show that the difference between the generating time in our method and the current method is not so much because the systems used in our experiment are small. In fact, the method proposed in [6] always generates the assumptions at a lower generating time. If we are not interesting in the above advantages, the method proposed in [6] is better than our method for generating assumptions. Otherwise, the generated assumptions are used for rechecking the CBS or are reused for regenerating the new assumptions for rechecking the evolved CBS [8]. In this case, the minimal assumptions generated by our method are useful. However, the breadth-first-search which is used in our work, may be not practical because it consumed too much memory. For larger systems, the computational cost for generating the minimal assumption is very expensive.

An idea to solve this issue is using the iterative-deepening depth first search. The search strategy combines the space efficiency of the depth-first search with the optimality of breadth-first search. It proceeds by running a depth-limited depth-first search repeatedly, each time increasing the depth limit by one. The assumptions generated by using this search strategy are smaller than the assumption generated in [6] but they may be not minimal. Another problem in the proposed method is that the queue has to hold an exponentially growing of the number of the observation tables. This makes our method unpractical for large-scale systems. In order to reduce the search space of the observation tables, we improve the technique for answering membership queries to reduce the number of instances of each table which contains the "?" entries. At any step i of the learning process, if the current candidate assumption A_i is too strong for M_2 to be satisfied, then $L(A_i)$ is exactly a subset of the language of the assumption being learned. For every $s \in (S \cup S.\Sigma).E$, if $s \in L(A_W)$ and $s \in L(A_i)$, instead of setting $T(s)$ to "?", we should set $T(s)$ to $true$. We can reduce several number of the "?" entries by reusing such candidate assumptions.

6   Related Work

There are many works that have been recently proposed in assume-guarantee verification of component-based systems, by several authors. Focusing only on the most recent and closest ones we can refer to [2,6,7], to [4], and [3,8,9].

D. Giannakopoulou et al. proposes an algorithm for automatically generating the weakest possible assumption for a component to satisfy a required property [7]. Although the motivation of this work is different, the ability to generate the weakest assumption can be used for assume-guarantee verification of component-based software. Based on this work, the work proposed in [6] presents a framework to generate a stronger assumption incrementally and may terminate before the weakest assumption is computed. The key idea of the framework is to generate assumptions as environment for components to satisfy the property. The assumptions are then discharged by the rest of the CBS. However, this framework focuses only on generating the assumptions. The number of states of the generated assumptions is not mentioned in this work. Thus, the assumptions generated by this work are not minimal. This work has been extended in [2] for modular verification of component-based systems at the source code level. Our work improves these works to generate the minimal assumptions in order to reduce the computational cost for rechecking the CBS.

An approach about optimized L*-based assume-guarantee reasoning was proposed by Chaki et al. [4]. The work suggests three optimizations to the L*-based automated assume-guarantee reasoning algorithm for the compositional verification of concurrent systems. The purposes of this work is to reduce the number of the membership queries and the number of the candidate assumptions which are used for generating the assumption, and to minimize the alphabet used by the assumption. However, the core of this approach is the framework proposed in [6]. Thus, the assumptions generated by this work are not minimal. Our work and this work share the motivation for optimizing the framework presented in [6] but we focus on generating the minimal assumptions.

Finally, several works for assume-guarantee verification of evolving software were suggested in [3,8]. The work in [3] focuses on component substitutability directly from the verification point of view. The purpose of this work is to provide an effective verification procedure that decides whether a component can be replaced with a new one without violation. The work improves the L* algorithm to an improved version called the dynamic L* algorithm by reusing the previous assumptions. However, this work assumes the availability and correctness of models that describe the behaviors of the software components. The works proposed in [8] were suggested to deal with this issue by providing a method for updating the inaccurate models of the evolved component. These updated models then are used to verify the evolved CBS by applying the improved L* algorithm. Even these works improve the L* algorithm to optimize it, the core of these works is the framework proposed in [6]. As a result, the assumptions generated by these works are not minimal. On the contrary, we focus on generating the minimal assumptions. The minimal assumptions generated by our work may be useful for these works to recheck the evolved at much lower computational costs.

7   Conclusion

We have presented a method for generating minimal assumptions for assume-guarantee verification of component-based software. The key idea of this method is finding the minimal assumptions in the search space of the candidate assumptions. These assumptions are strong enough for the components to satisfy a property and weak enough to be satisfied by the rest of the component-based software. In this method, we have improved the technique for answering membership queries of the Teacher which helps the L* to correctly answer the membership query questions by using the "don't know" value. By using this technique, the proposed method ensures that every trace which belongs to the language of the generated assumption exactly belongs to the language being learned. The search space of observation tables used in the proposed method exactly contains the generated observation tables which are used to generate the candidate assumptions. This search space is seen as a search tree where its root is the initial observation table. Finding an assumption with a minimal size such that it satisfies the compositional rules thus is considered a search problem in this search tree. We apply the breadth-first search strategy because this strategy ensures that the generated assumptions are minimal (see Theorem 2). The minimal assumptions generated by the proposed method can be used to recheck the whole component-based software at a lower computational cost. We also have implemented a tool for the assumption generation method proposed in [6] and our minimized assumption generation method. This implementation is used to verify some illustrative component-based software to show the effectiveness of the proposed method.

We are investigating to generalize the proposed method for the larger CBS, i.e., CBS containing more than two components. We are also improving our method and applying some CBS with their sizes are larger than the sizes of the CBS which are used in our experiment, to show the practical usefulness of our proposed method.

References

1. Angluin, D.: Learning Regular Sets from Queries and Counterexamples. Information and Computation 75(2), 87–106 (1987)
2. Blundell, C., Giannakopoulou, D., Pasareanu, C.: Assume-Guarantee Testing. In: 4th Microsoft Research – Specification and Verification of Component-Based Systems Workshop (SAVCBS), pp. 7–14 (2005)
3. Chaki, S., Clarke, E., Sharygina, N., Sinha, N.: Verification of Evolving Software. In: 3rd Microsoft Research – Specification and Verification of Component-Based Systems Workshop (SAVCBS), pp. 55–61 (2004)
4. Chaki, S., Strichman, O.: Three Optimizations for Assume-Guarantee Reasoning with L*. Formal Methods in System Design 32(3), 267–284 (2008)
5. Clarke, E.M., Grumberg, O., Peled, D.: Model Checking. MIT Press, Cambridge (1999)
6. Cobleigh, J.M., Giannakopoulou, D., Pasareanu, C.: Learning Assumptions for Compositional Verification. In: Garavel, H., Hatcliff, J. (eds.) TACAS 2003. LNCS, vol. 2619, pp. 331–346. Springer, Heidelberg (2003)
7. Giannakopoulou, D., Pasareanu, C., Barringer, H.: Assumption Generation for Software Component Verification. In: 17th IEEE International Conference on Automated Software Engineering (ASE), pp. 3–12 (2002)
8. Hung, P.N., Katayama, T.: Modular Conformance Testing and Assume-Guarantee Verification for Evolving Component-Based Software. In: 15th Asia-Pacific Softw. Eng. Conf. (APSEC), pp. 479–486. IEEE Computer Society Press, Los Alamitos (2008)
9. Hung, P.N., Thang, N.T., Katayama, T.: An Assume-Guarantee Method for Modular Verification of Evolving Component-Based Software. In: 6th WADS in conjunction with the 37th Annual IEEE/IFIP Intenational Conference on Dependable Systems and Networks (DSN), pp. 160–165 (2007)
10. Jones, C.B.: Tentative Steps Toward a Development Method for Interfering Programs. ACM Transactions on Programming Languages and Systems (TOPLAS) 5(4), 596–619 (1983)
11. Magee, J., Kramer, J.: Concurrency: State Models & Java Programs. John Wiley & Sons, Chichester (1999)
12. Nerode, A.: Linear automaton transformations. American Mathematical Society 9, 541–544 (1958)
13. French National Institute for Research in Computer Science and Control (INRIA), Objective caml (2004), http://caml.inria.fr/ocaml/index.en.html
14. Pnueli, A.: In Transition from Global to Modular Temporal Reasoning about Programs. In: Apt, K.R. (ed.) Logics and Models of Concurrent Systems. Nato Asi Series F: Computer And Systems Sciences, vol. 13, pp. 123–144. Springer, Heidelberg (1985)
15. Stark, E.W.: A Proof Technique for Rely/Guarantee Properties. In: The 5th Conf. on Found. of Soft. Tech. and Theoretical Computer Science, pp. 369–391 (1985)
16. A Minimized Assumption Generation Tool for Modular Verification of Component-Based Software (2009), http://www.jaist.ac.jp/~s0620204/MAGTool/
17. Rivest, R.L., Schapire, R.E.: Inference of finite automata using homing sequences. Information and Computation 103(2), 299–347 (1993)

A Formal Approach to Heuristically Test Restorable Systems*

Pablo Rabanal, Ismael Rodríguez, and Fernando Rubio

Dept. Sistemas Informáticos y Computación
Universidad Complutense de Madrid, 28040 Madrid, Spain
prabanal@fdi.ucm.es, {isrodrig,fernando}@sip.ucm.es

Abstract. In order to test a Finite State Machine (FSM), first we typically have to identify some short interaction sequences allowing to reach
those states or transitions considered as *critical*. If these sequences are
applied to an *implementation under test* (IUT), then equivalent states
or transitions would be reached and observed in the implementation –
provided that the implementation were actually defined as the specification. In this paper we study how to obtain such sequences in a scenario
where previous configurations can be restored at any time. In general,
this feature enables sequences to reach the required parts of the machine
in less time, because some repetitions can be avoided. However, finding
optimal sequences is NP-hard when configurations can be restored. We
use an evolutionary method, River Formation Dynamics, to heuristically
solve this problem.

1 Introduction

The field of formal testing methods [1,4,5,11] has considered several graph theory
techniques to find short test sequences allowing to reach, at least once, all/some
states or transitions in an FSM specification. In this paper we formally generalize testing methods allowing to reach some/all FSM states or transitions to the
case where the tester can *restore* any previous configuration of the system. Let
us assume that the IUT is a software system and the tester can *save* the complete current configuration of the system at any time. Then, at any subsequent
time, the tester could *restore* such configuration and execute the system from
that configuration on. In particular, after restoring the configuration she could
follow a different path to the one she followed the previous time. Notice that,
if configurations can be saved/restored, then the tester can use this feature to
avoid *repeating* some execution sequences. Thus, some time assigned to testing
activities could be saved. Let us also note that saving/restoring the complete
configuration of a system could be time-expensive. These costs are similar to
the costs of executing *process suspending* and *process restoring* operations in any
operating system, which in turn are due to copying the program state from/to

---

* Work supported by projects TIN2006-15578-C02-01, CCG08-UCM/TIC-4124, and
the UCM-BSCH programme (GR58/08 - group number 910606).

M. Leucker and C. Morgan (Eds.): ICTAC 2009, LNCS 5684, pp. 292–306, 2009.

RAM to/from hard disk, respectively. Thus, a testing technique using these features should take these costs into account.

The idea of considering specific methods to test these systems was informally introduced in [10]. In this paper, the proposed problem is formally presented and studied, and an heuristic method based on a series of formal properties is developed. Given a FSM specification (including the costs of the transitions), the cost of saving/restoring a configuration, and a set of *critical* system configurations that are required to be observed, we provide an heuristic method to find a plan to sequentially interact with the system (possibly including saving/restoring operations) that allows to reach all critical configurations in a low overall time. We prove that obtaining the *optimal* interaction sequence is an NP-hard problem.

An interaction plan where saving/restoring operations are allowed is, in fact, a plan where each save/restore point represents a *bifurcation*: Initially, we will take a path, and then we will return to a previous point and follow another path. Thus, our goal will be finding a tree where the sum of the costs of all the transitions of the tree (including the sum of the costs of saving/restoring operations) is minimal. We will prove that considering interaction *trees*, instead of interaction sequences, does not restrict the possibility to find good paths. In particular, we will show that, for all path σ, there exists an equivalent path that can be represented by a tree, which implies that all steps of σ can be sorted in such a way that each load refers *only* to states appearing in the *same* branch of some tree. Consequently, interaction plans constructed by our method will not be represented by a sequential path, but by a tree covering all critical points.

The rest of the paper is structured as follows. Next, we formally describe the problem to be solved. In Section 3 we introduce our general heuristic method, while in Section 4 we show how to apply it to our particular problem. Afterwards, in Section 5 we report the results obtained in some experiments. Finally, in Section 6 we present our conclusions.

2   Problem Definition

In this section we formally introduce the problem to be solved as well as some related notions. Next we introduce some preliminary notation:

- Given a pair $x = (a, b)$, we assume $\mathtt{fst}(x) = a$ and $\mathtt{snd}(x) = b$.
- Given a list $l = [x_1, \ldots, x_n]$, we represent by $l[i]$ the i-th element of l, i.e. $l[i] = x_i$. Besides, $\mathtt{length}(l)$ returns the number of elements of l, i.e. $\mathtt{length}(l) = n$.

We introduce the formalism used to define specifications, called *Weighted Finite State Machine* (WFSM). This is an FSM where the cost of restoring a previous configuration, as well as the cost of taking each transition, are explicitly denoted.

Definition 1. A *Weighted Finite State Machine* (from now on WFSM) is a tuple $(S, s_{in}, I, O, C, \Delta)$ where

- S is a finite set of states and $s_{in} \in S$ is the initial state.

- I and O are the finite sets of *input* and *output* actions, respectively.
- $C \in \mathbb{N}$ is the *cost of restoring* a previously traversed state.
- $\Delta \subseteq S \times S \times I \times O \times \mathbb{N}$ is the set of transitions. A transition $\delta \in \Delta$ is a tuple (s_1, s_2, i, o, c) where s_1 is the origin state, s_2 is the destination state, i is the input that triggers the transition, o is the output produced by the transition, and c is a positive natural value that represents the cost of the transition. We write $s_1 \xrightarrow{i/o/c} s_2$ as a shorthand of $(s_1, s_2, i, o, c) \in \Delta$.

A WFSM is *deterministic* if for all $s \in S$ and $i \in I$ we have

$$\| \{s \xrightarrow{i/o/c} s' \mid \exists\, o, c, s' : s \xrightarrow{i/o/c} s' \in \Delta \} \| \leq 1 \qquad \square$$

We will assume that specifications are defined by deterministic WFSMs. From now on, in all definitions we will assume that a WFSM $W = (S, s_0, I, O, C, \Delta)$ is implicitly given.

Executions of WFSMs will be denoted by *load sequences*. Each step in a load sequence consists in either taking some WFSM transition or restoring a previously traversed configuration. The latter action will be denoted by a symbol $\psi(s_k)$ in the sequence meaning that, at the current step of the sequence, we move from the current state to a previously traversed state s_k by *loading* it (instead of by traversing actual transitions of the WFSM). The goal of our method will be finding the cheapest load sequence belonging to the set of all load sequences that cover some given states and/or transitions. Constraining the notion of load sequence in such a way that some *useless* sequences are discarded from scratch will allow us to reduce the searching space. In particular, a condition will be imposed to *ban* some sequences that are equivalent, in terms of cost, to other available sequences that do fulfill the condition. Load sequences (regardless of whether they fulfill the additional condition or not) and load sequences that *actually* fulfill it will be called *load sequences* and *α-load sequences*, respectively. Later we will show that constraining our search to sequences fulfilling the additional condition does not limit the possibility to find cheap sequences.

Definition 2. A *load sequence* is a sequence $\sigma = s_1 \xrightarrow{\delta_1} s_2 \ldots s_{n-1} \xrightarrow{\delta_{n-1}} s_n$ where, for each $1 \leq k \leq n-1$, δ_k is either $i_k/o_k/c_k$ (if $s_k \xrightarrow{i_k/o_k/c_k} s_{k+1} \in \Delta$) or $\psi(s_j)$ (if $s_j \in \{s_1, ..., s_k\}$ and $s_{k+1} = s_j$). In addition, σ is also an *α-load sequence* if for all $s, s' \in S$ such that the first appearance of s in σ is before the first appearance of s' (i.e. such that we have $s = s_i$ and $s' = s_j$ for some $i < j$ such that $s_k \neq s$ for all $k < i$ and $s_l \neq s'$ for all $l < j$) there do not exist δ_p and δ_q with $p < q$ such that $\delta_p = \psi(s)$ and $\delta_q = \psi(s')$.

The set of all load sequences of a WFSM W is denoted by $\text{Sequences}(W)$. The set of all α-load sequences of W is denoted by $\alpha\text{-Sequences}(W)$.

Given $\sigma = s_1 \xrightarrow{\delta_1} \ldots \xrightarrow{\delta_{n-2}} s_{n-1} \xrightarrow{\delta_{n-1}} s_n \in \text{Sequences}(W)$, we consider $\sigma^- = s_1 \xrightarrow{\delta_1} \ldots \xrightarrow{\delta_{n-2}} s_{n-1}$.

Let $\sigma_1, \ldots, \sigma_n \in \text{Sequences}(W)$ be such that for all $1 \leq i \leq n$ we have $\sigma_i = s_{i,1} \xrightarrow{\delta_{i,1}} \ldots \xrightarrow{\delta_{i,k_i-1}} s_{i,k_i}$ and for all $1 \leq i \leq n-1$ we have

$s_{i,k_i} = s_{i+1,1}$. The *concatenation* of $\sigma_1, \ldots, \sigma_n$, denoted by $\sigma_1 \cdots \sigma_n$, is defined as

$$s_{1,1} \xrightarrow{\delta_{1,1}} \cdots \xrightarrow{\delta_{1,k_1-1}} s_{1,k_1} \xrightarrow{\delta_{2,1}} s_{2,2} \xrightarrow{\delta_{2,2}} \cdots \xrightarrow{\delta_{2,k_2-1}} s_{2,k_2} \cdots \xrightarrow{\delta_{n,k_n-1}} s_{n,k_n}.$$

□

Clearly, α-Sequences$(W) \subseteq$ Sequences(W). For instance, let us consider

$$\sigma_1 = s_1 \xrightarrow{i_1/o_1/c_1} s_2 \xrightarrow{i_2/o_2/c_2} s_3 \xrightarrow{\psi(s_1)} s_1 \xrightarrow{i_3/o_3/c_3} s_4 \xrightarrow{\psi(s_2)} s_2 \xrightarrow{i_4/o_4/c_4} s_5.$$

We have $\sigma_1 \in$ Sequences(W) for some WFSM W, but $\sigma_1 \notin \alpha$-Sequences(W) (see states s_1 and s_2 and the positions of $\psi(s_1)$ and $\psi(s_2)$ in σ_1). Let us consider

$$\sigma_2 = s_1 \xrightarrow{i_5/o_5/c_5} s_6 \xrightarrow{i_7/o_7/c_7} s_7 \xrightarrow{i_8/o_8/c_8} s_8 \xrightarrow{\psi(s_7)} s_7 \xrightarrow{i_9/o_9/c_9} s_{10} \xrightarrow{\psi(s_6)} s_6.$$

We have $\sigma_2 \in \alpha$-Sequences(W) (provided that these transitions also exist in W).

The *cost* of a load sequence is given by the addition of transition costs and load costs. Note that a state (or transition) can appear several times in a given load sequence. There are two possible reasons for this: Either a previous state is *loaded*, or an already traversed state/transition is reached again by traversing some transitions. The latter possibility is useful if we want to come back to some state and we realize that doing it *manually* (i.e. by taking transitions) is cheaper than making a *load*.

Definition 3. Let $\sigma = s_1 \xrightarrow{\delta_1} \cdots \xrightarrow{\delta_{n-1}} s_n \in$ Sequences(W). If $1 \leq k \leq n-1$ then the *cost* of δ_k, denoted by CostTran(δ_k), is defined as

$$\text{CostTran}(\delta_k) = \begin{cases} c_k & \text{if } \delta_k = i_k/o_k/c_k \\ C & \text{if } \delta_k = \psi(s_j) \end{cases}$$

The *cost* of σ, denoted by CostSeq(σ), is defined as $\sum_{k=1}^{n-1}$ CostTran(δ_k).   □

Given the load sequence σ_1 considered before, we have CostSeq$(\sigma_1) = c_1 + c_2 + C + c_3 + C + c_4$. Next we define the target problem of this paper.

Definition 4. Given a WFSM $W = (S, s_0, I, O, C, \Delta)$, some sets $S' \subseteq S$ and $\Delta' \subseteq \Delta$, and a natural number $K \in \mathbb{N}$, the *Minimum Load Sequence* problem, denoted by MLS, is stated as follows: Is there a load sequence $\sigma \in$ Sequences(W) such that CostSeq$(\sigma) \leq K$ and, for all $s \in S'$ and $\delta \in \Delta'$, s and δ appear in σ?   □

To the best of our knowledge, MLS has not been defined or studied before in the literature. Thus, before describing our method to solve it, we prove that it is an NP-complete problem. The proofs of all results presented in this paper can be found in [9].

Theorem 1. MLS $\in$ NP-complete.   □

Next we show that, by constraining our search for good testing sequences to α-load sequences (instead of considering all load sequences) we do not lose the possibility to find sequences whose cost is under some given upper bound.

Proposition 1. For all $\sigma \in$ Sequences(W) there exists $\sigma' \in \alpha$-Sequences(W) such that CostSeq$(\sigma) =$ CostSeq(σ').   □

Let us revisit σ_1. Since $\sigma_1 \in \mathsf{Sequences}(W)$, we have $\sigma_3 \in \alpha\text{-}\mathsf{Sequences}(W)$ for

$$\sigma_3 = s_1 \xrightarrow{\ i_1/o_1/c_1\ } s_2 \xrightarrow{\ i_2/o_2/c_2\ } s_3 \xrightarrow{\ \psi(s_2)\ } s_2 \xrightarrow{\ i_4/o_4/c_4\ } s_5 \xrightarrow{\ \psi(s_1)\ } s_1 \xrightarrow{\ i_3/o_3/c_3\ } s_4.$$

The property $\mathsf{CostSeq}(\sigma_1) = \mathsf{CostSeq}(\sigma_3)$ trivially holds because we traverse the same transitions and we make the same number of loads.

The condition imposed to load sequences to be considered as α-load sequences implies that, in particular, α-load sequences can be equivalently represented as *trees*. A *load tree* is a tree-like version of an α-load sequence, where loads are represented by *bifurcations* in the tree. In particular, a bifurcation represents that, after we complete one of the choices appearing at the bifurcation (i.e. after we complete the *subtree* representing this choice), we will restore the bifurcation state and we will go on through another choice (another subtree). As in the case of sequences, states and transitions can appear several times in the tree. Since loads are represented *only* by bifurcations, a repeated appearance of a state represents that this state is reached again by taking some transitions, rather than by loading.

Definition 5. A *load tree* is a term t belonging to the language induced by the term Lt in the following E-BNF:

$$
\begin{aligned}
Lt &::= \ empty \,|\, (St, Ch) \\
Ch &::= \ [(Tr, Lt), ..., (Tr, Lt)] \\
St &::= \ s_1 \,|\, ... \,|\, s_n \qquad\qquad \text{where } S = \{s_1, \ldots, s_n\} \\
Tr &:= \ (i, o, n) \qquad\qquad\quad\ \text{where } (i, o, n) \in I \times O \times \mathbf{N}
\end{aligned}
$$

such that, if t follows the form $t = (st, [(tr_1, child_1), \ldots, (tr_n, child_n)])$, then for all $1 \leq k \leq n$ the conditions $child_k \neq empty$ and $st \xrightarrow{\ tr_k\ } \mathtt{fst}(child_k) \in \Delta$ must hold.

The set of all load trees for a WFSM W is denoted by $\mathtt{Trees}(W)$. □

Next we formally define the *cost* of a load tree $t = (root, children)$. In the next definition, the term $C \cdot (n - 1)$ represents the cost spent in restoring the state $root$ in t: Assuming t has n children, $n - 1$ loads are necessary to come back from the last state visited by each child to $root$. In the next recursive definition, the anchor case is reached when the list of children is empty i.e. when we have $t = (root, [\,])$ (note that, in this case, no recursive calls are made).

Definition 6. The cost of a tree $t = (root, children)$, denoted by $\mathtt{CostTree}(t)$, is defined as

$$\mathtt{CostTree}(t) = \sum_{k=1}^{n} \left(\begin{array}{l} \mathtt{CostTran}(\mathtt{fst}(children[k])) + \\ \mathtt{CostTree}(\mathtt{snd}(children[k])) \end{array} \right) + C \cdot (n - 1)$$

where $n = \mathtt{length}(children)$. □

We define a boolean predicate $\sigma \triangleright t$ returning *true* if the sequence σ *corresponds* to the tree t, that is, if σ could be a sequential realization of the plan described by t. Intuitively, the sequence must be one of the possible *preorder* traversals of the tree. More technically, in order to compare the sequence σ and the tree t, we transform σ into a tree and next we compare the resulting tree with t. In order to create a tree from a sequence σ, we set the first state s_1 of the sequence as the root of the tree. Then, we split the rest of the sequence into *subsequences*, dividing them at the places where we load s_1. Next we recursively construct the tree of each of these subsequences, and returned trees are taken as children of t. In functions `createTree` and `createSeq` given in the next definition, anchor cases are again reached when the target tree has no children. In addition note that, in function `createSeq`, the term σ^- denotes that the last step of the sequence is removed. This step is the last load to *root*, so this load in unnecessary.

Definition 7. Let $t_1 = (root_1, children_1)$ and $t_2 = (root_2, children_2)$ with $t_1, t_2 \in \text{Trees}(W)$. Let $n_1 = \text{length}(children_1)$ and $n_2 = \text{length}(children_2)$. We say that t_1 and t_2 are *equivalent*, denoted by $t_1 \equiv_T t_2$, if

(1) $root_1 = root_2$,
(2) $n_1 = n_2$,
(3) There exists a bijection $f : [1..n_1] \longrightarrow [1..n_2]$ such that, for all $1 \le i \le n_1$, we have $\text{fst}(children_1[i]) = \text{fst}(children_2[f(i)])$ (i.e. transitions leading to each children coincide) and $\text{snd}(children_1[i]) \equiv_T \text{snd}(children_2[f(i)])$ (i.e. subtrees are equivalent).

Let $\sigma = \sigma_1 \cdot \ldots \cdot \sigma_n \in \alpha\text{-Sequences}(W)$ be such that for all $1 \le i \le n$ we have $\sigma_i = s_1 \xrightarrow{\delta_{1,i}} \ldots \xrightarrow{\delta_{k_i,i}} s_1$, where $\delta_{k_i,i} = \psi(s_1)$ and for all $1 \le j < k_i$ we have $\delta_{j,i} \ne \psi(s_1)$. The *tree of* σ, denoted by $\text{createTree}(\sigma)$, is defined as

$$\text{createTree}(\sigma) = (s_1, [(\delta_{1,1}, \text{createTree}(\sigma_1)), \ldots, (\delta_{1,n}, \text{createTree}(\sigma_n))])$$

Let $\sigma \in \alpha\text{-Sequences}(W)$ and $t \in \text{Trees}(W)$. We say that σ *corresponds to* t, denoted by $\sigma \triangleright t$, if $\text{createTree}(\sigma) \equiv_T t$.

Given a tree $t = (root, children)$, the *set of α-load sequences* of t, denoted by $\text{createSeq}(t)$, is defined as $\{root\}$ if $children = [\,]$; otherwise

$$\text{createSeq}(t) = \left\{ \sigma^- \left|
\begin{array}{l}
\sigma = \sigma_{f(1)} \cdot \ldots \cdot \sigma_{f(n)} \wedge n = \text{length}(children) \wedge \\
f : [1..n] \longrightarrow [1..n] \text{ is a bijective function} \wedge \\
\forall\, 1 \le i \le n : \\
\left(\sigma_i = root \xrightarrow{\text{fst}(children[i])} \sigma_i' \xrightarrow{\psi(root)} root \wedge \right. \\
\left. \sigma_i' \in \text{createSeq}(\text{snd}(children[i])) \right)
\end{array}
\right. \right\}$$

$\square$

Proposition 2. We have the following properties:

(a) $\text{createSeq}(t) = \{\sigma | \sigma \triangleright t\}$
(b) for all $\sigma, \sigma' \in \text{createSeq}(t)$ we have $\text{CostSeq}(\sigma) = \text{CostSeq}(\sigma') = \text{CostTree}(t)$.

$\square$

The previous result guarantees that, if we want to find the cheapest α-load sequence for a given WFSM, then we can concentrate on searching for the equivalent cheapest load tree. Given such cheapest tree t, the α-load sequence to be used can be any sequence σ such that $\sigma \in$ createSeq(t). Recall that Proposition 1 showed that, if we want to search for a good load sequence, we can concentrate on considering α-load sequences. We conclude by transitivity that, if we want to search for a good load sequence, we can focus on searching a good *load tree*. This idea will be exploited later in Section 4, where we will apply an evolutionary computation approach [2] to find trees rather than sequences.

3   Brief Introduction to River Formation Dynamics

In this section we briefly introduce the basic structure of River Formation Dynamics (RFD) (for further details, see [6,7,8]). Given a working graph, we associate *altitude* values to nodes. *Drops* erode the ground (they reduce the altitude of nodes) or deposit the sediment (increase it) as they move. The probability of the drop to take a given edge instead of others is proportional to the gradient of the down slope in the edge, which in turn depends on the difference of altitudes between both nodes and the distance (i.e. the *cost* of the edge). At the beginning, a flat environment is provided, that is, all nodes have the same altitude. The exception is the destination node, which is a hole (the *sea*). Drops are unleashed (i.e. it *rains*) at the origin node/s, and they spread around the flat environment until some of them fall in the destination node. This erodes adjacent nodes, which creates new down slopes, and in this way the erosion process is propagated. New drops are inserted in the origin node/s to transform paths and reinforce the erosion of promising paths. After some steps, good paths from the origin/s to the destination are found. These paths are given in the form of sequences of decreasing edges from the origin to the destination. Several improvements are applied to this basic general scheme (see [6,8]).

Compared to a related well-known evolutionary computation method, *Ant Colony Optimization* ACO [3], RFD provides some advantages that were briefly outlined in the introduction. On the one hand, local cycles are not created and reinforced because they would imply an *ever decreasing cycle*, which is contradictory. Though ants usually take into account their past path to avoid repeating nodes, they cannot avoid to be led by pheromone trails through some edges in such a way that a node must be repeated in the next step[1]. However, *altitudes* cannot lead drops to these situations. Moreover, since drops do not have to worry about following cycles, in general drops do not need to be endowed with *memory* of previous movements, which releases some computational memory and reduces some execution time. On the other hand, when a shorter path is found in RFD, the subsequent reinforcement of the path is fast: Since the same origin and destination are concerned in both the old and the new path, the difference of altitude is the same but the distance is different. Hence, the edges of the shorter path

---

[1] Usually, this implies either to repeat a node or to *kill* the ant. In both cases, the last movements of the ant were useless.

necessarily have higher down slopes and are immediately preferred (in average) by subsequent drops. Finally, the erosion process provides a method to avoid inefficient solutions because sediments tend to be cumulated in blind alleys (in our case, in *valleys*). These nodes are filled until eventually their altitude matches adjacent nodes, i.e., the valley disappears. This differs from typical methods to reduce pheromone trails in ACO: Usually, the trails of *all* edges are periodically reduced at the same rate. On the contrary, RFD intrinsically provides a *focused* punishment of bad paths where, in particular, those nodes blocking alternative paths are modified.

When there are several departing points (i.e. it rains at several points), RFD does not tend in general to provide the shortest path (i.e. river) from each point to the sea. Instead, as it happens in nature, it tends to provide a tradeoff between quickly gathering individual paths into a small number of main flows (which minimizes the total size of the formed *tree* of tributaries) and actually forming short paths from each point to the sea. For instance, meanders are caused by the former goal: We deviate from the shortest path just to collect drops from a different area, thus reducing the number of flows. On the other hand, new tributaries are caused by the latter one: By *not* joining the main flows, we can form tailored short paths.[2] These characteristics make RFD a good heuristic method to solve problems consisting in forming a kind of covering tree [7], which motivates using RFD to solve MLS.

4   Applying RFD to Solve MLS

In this section we show how the general RFD scheme, described in the previous section, is adapted to solve MLS. First, let us note that our goal will be constructing load trees where the root is the *initial state* of the given WFSM. In terms of RFD, we will make this node be the final goal of all drops, i.e. the *sea*. In order to make drops go in this direction, each transition of the WFSM will be represented in the working graph of RFD by an edge leading to the *opposite* direction. Thus, final trees constructed by RFD will have to be inverted in order to constitute valid MLS solutions. Besides, since solutions consist in paths covering some configurations, a modification must be introduced to avoid drops *skip* some required steps. Let us suppose that we have to cover nodes A, B, and C and the optimal path is $A \rightarrow B \rightarrow C$. If this path were formed by RFD then the altitudes x_A, x_B, x_C of these nodes would be such that $x_A > x_B > x_C$. Let us suppose there also exists an edge $A \rightarrow C$. Then, drops will tend to prefer going directly from A to C, which is not optimal because then B is not covered. To avoid this problem, a node will be inserted at each *edge*. In particular, going from A to C will actually imply going from A to a new node ac and next going from ac to C. Since this choice provides an *uncomplete* covering, drops following this path will not be successful and the erosion in this path will be low. Thus, the altitude of ac will remain high and hence taking $A \rightarrow B \rightarrow C$

---

[2] We can make RFD tend towards either of these choices by changing a single parameter (see [7]).

(in fact, $A \rightarrow ab \rightarrow B \rightarrow bc \rightarrow C$) will be preferable for drops. These additional nodes will be called *barrier nodes*. In terms of MLS, barrier nodes will represent WFSM *transitions*, while standard nodes will represent WFSM *states*. During the execution of RFD, new drops will be introduced in nodes representing critical states and transitions (i.e. it *rains* in these nodes). After executing RFD for some time, a solution tree will be constructed by taking, for each critical node, the path leading to the sea through the highest available decreasing gradient. This policy guarantees that the subgraph depicted by these paths is a tree indeed; if it were not a tree then, for some node N, two outgoing edges would be included in the subgraph. This is not possible because only the edge having the highest gradient is taken.

Let us note that load trees may include repeated states. In particular, a repeated state denotes that we return to a previously traversed state by taking transitions instead of by loading (a load is simply represented by a bifurcation). Thus, solutions constructed by RFD must be able to include repetitions as well. If repetitions are represented by actually making drops pass more than once through the same node in the working graph (and, perhaps, leaving it through a different edge each time), then formed solutions will not be *stable*: In the long term, only one of the edges leaving each node would be *reinforced* by drops, and thus only this edge would prevail. This argument applies to similar methods, such as ACO: In the long term, only one choice would be reinforced by ants. In RFD, there is an additional reason for needing an alternative way to denote repetitions: The formation of gradients implicitly makes RFD avoid following a path from a node to itself. Thus, the general RFD scheme must be adapted. In particular, the working graph of RFD will be modified. One possibility consists in introducing several instances of each state in the graph, so that each instance can have its own altitude. In this case, paths formed by RFD could go from an instance of a node to another instance of the *same* node, and these paths would explicitly denote not only state repetitions, but also *when* states must be repeated. Let us note that nodes may be repeated more than twice in a load tree, so this solution would force us to strongly increase the number of nodes of the working graph. Instead, an alternative solution will be applied. Let us note that the purpose of repeating some nodes through transitions (i.e. not by using loads) is reaching some state or transition that has not been traversed before. In particular, we will never load *right after* traversing some repeated states and transitions: Directly loading, instead of traversing some repeated states and transitions and next loading, would have the same effect in terms of covering target entities, but at a lower cost (recall that the load cost C does not depend on the current state or the state to be loaded). Thus, our target tree does not need to *repeat* states or transitions; it just needs to be able to reach the destinations we could reach if states or transitions could be repeated.

In order to allow this, *additional edges* connecting each state with the rest of states through the *shortest available path* will be added to the graph. Let us suppose that we wish to go from A to an (unvisited) critical node B, and the cheapest way to do it is traversing some (repeated and/or non critical) nodes and transitions $N_1 \rightarrow \ldots \rightarrow N_m$ and next taking a transition from node N_m to B. Rather than doing this, we will take a single *direct* transition from A to B whose cost will be the addition of costs of transitions $A \rightarrow N_1 \rightarrow \ldots \rightarrow N_m \rightarrow B$. Technically, no state or transition will be repeated in the working graph of RFD by taking this direct edge. Let us note that, if some states or transitions in the sequence $N_1 \rightarrow \ldots \rightarrow N_m$ were critical and unvisited, then we could take either this direct edge (and count traversed critical configurations) or some standard transitions to traverse the required configurations (combined with other direct edges to skip repeated parts). Let us note that there is no reason to take a direct edge more than once: Since the goal of repeating nodes is reaching a *new* configuration, we can take the direct edge leading to that new configuration (which, obviously, has not been taken yet).

The previous idea must be refined to deal with some particular situations. In fact, a direct edge will *not* connect an origin state A with a destination state B. Instead, a different direct edge will be added to connect A with each (standard) *edge* leading to B. Thus, in our previous example, some direct edge will connect A with a node representing the *transition* connecting N_m and B (rather than directly connecting A with B). As we said before, edges are represented by barrier nodes. Thus, the direct edge will connect the origin edge with the *barrier node* representing such transition. The reason for this is the following: Let us suppose that the edge connecting N_m with B is unvisited and critical, but N_m was visited before. This implies that the edge we used to leave N_m before was not the one leading to B. How can we reach and take the transition from N_m to B? On the one hand, since N_m has already been visited, taking the direct transition connecting A with N_m would imply following a *loop*, which is implicitly avoided by RFD. On the other hand, taking a direct transition from A to B would allow to implicitly cover the transition from N_m and B *only* if this transition were included in the shortest path from A to B. In order to cover the transition from N_m to B without actually repeating N_m in our graph, we will use a direct edge from A to the *edge* between N_m and B. Let us note that having only this alternative notion of direct edge (that is, not having direct edges leading to *states*) does not disable our first example in the previous paragraph: If the goal is not covering the edge between N_m and B but covering B itself, then we can take the direct edge leading to the transition connecting N_m and B, and next move to B (the edge between N_m and B is necessarily unvisited; otherwise, B would have already been visited before).

In order to compute the cost of these additional edges, before launching RFD we will execute the *Floyd* algorithm for the graph representing our WFSM. Given a graph, the Floyd algorithm finds the shortest paths connecting each pair of nodes. After obtaining these shortest paths, for each pair of nodes A an B we will do as follows. Let us suppose that the (standard) transitions reaching B are $N_1 \xrightarrow{i_1/o_1/c_1} B, \ldots, N_m \xrightarrow{i_m/o_m/c_m} B$. Let us suppose that, according to Floyd algorithm, the shortest path from A to N_i has c_i' cost. Then, for all $1 \le j \le m$, the direct edge from A to the barrier node representing the transition $N_j \xrightarrow{i_j/o_j/c_j} B$ is given a cost $c_j' + c_j/2$. In addition, the transition connecting this barrier node with B will be given cost $c_j/2$. Thus, the total cost of moving from A to B through N_j will be $c_j' + c_j$, as expected.

Next we formally present the proposed graph transformation, and we prove the correctness of the approach.

Definition 8. Let $W = (S, s_{in}, I, O, C, \Delta)$ be a WFSM. The shortcut machine of W, denoted by $\mathrm{shortcut}(W)$, is a WFSM $W' = (S', s_{in}, I', O', C, \Delta')$ where

- $S' = S \cup \Delta$, $I' = I \cup \{-\}$, and $O' = O \cup \{-\}$
- $\Delta' = \{(s, \delta, i, o, c/2) \mid \delta = (s, s', i, o, c) \in \Delta\} \cup$
$\qquad \{(\delta, s', -, -, c/2) \mid \delta = (s, s', i, o, c) \in \Delta\} \cup$
$\qquad \left\{ (s, \delta, -, -, c + c_1/2) \,\middle|\, \begin{array}{l} s \in S, \delta = (s', s'', i, o, c_1) \in \Delta, \\ \text{the shortest path from } s \text{ to } s' \text{ has cost } c \end{array} \right\}$

Let $W = (S, s_{in}, I, O, C, \Delta)$, $S' \subseteq S$, and $\Delta' \subseteq \Delta$. Let $W' = \mathrm{shortcut}(W)$ and $t' \in \mathrm{Trees}(W')$. We say that t' *covers* S' (respectively, t' *covers* Δ') if for all $q \in S'$ (resp. $q \in \Delta'$) either q appears in t' or t' has a transition δ representing a shortest path α of W such that q is traversed by α. The maximal sets $S' \subseteq S$ and $\Delta' \subseteq \Delta$ such that t' covers S' and Δ' are denoted by $\mathrm{stCover}(t')$ and $\mathrm{trCover}(t')$, respectively.   □

Next we show that, given a machine W, searching for good trees where states and transitions are allowed to be repeated is equivalent to searching, in the machine $\mathrm{shortcut}(W)$, good trees where no state or transition is repeated. In particular, for all tree in W we can find an equivalent tree in $\mathrm{shortcut}(W)$ that is free of repetitions and whose cost is equal or lower, that is, no relevant tree is lost by considering repetition-free trees in $\mathrm{shortcut}(W)$. Besides, for all tree in $\mathrm{shortcut}(S)$ that is free of repetitions we can find an equivalent tree in W with the same cost, that is, all trees in $\mathrm{shortcut}(W)$ are possible in W. Thus, $\mathrm{shortcut}(W)$ provides an appropriate working graph for applying RFD to solve our target problem. In the next result, let us note that numbers of *occurrences* refer to states and transitions of the *shortcut* machine. Thus, these numbers do not count the number of times we implicitly traverse states and transitions of the original machine by means of shortest paths represented by added direct transitions.

Proposition 3. Let $W = (S, s_{in}, I, O, C, \Delta)$ and $W' = \mathrm{shortcut}(W)$, where $W' = (S', s_{in}', I', O', C', \Delta')$.

(a) If $t \in \mathrm{Trees}(W)$ then there exists $t' \in \mathrm{Trees}(W')$ such that $\mathrm{CostTree}(t) \geq \mathrm{CostTree}(t')$, $\mathrm{stCover}(t) = \mathrm{stCover}(t')$, $\mathrm{trCover}(t) = \mathrm{trCover}(t')$, and for all $s' \in S'$ (respectively, for all $\delta' \in \Delta'$) the number of occurrences of s' (resp. δ') in t' is less than or equal to 1.

(b) If $t' \in \mathrm{Trees}(W')$ and for all $s' \in S'$ (respectively, for all $\delta' \in \Delta'$) the number of occurrences of s' (resp. δ') in t' is less than or equal to 1 then there exists $t \in \mathrm{Trees}(W)$ such that $\mathrm{CostTree}(t) = \mathrm{CostTree}(t')$, $\mathrm{stCover}(t) = \mathrm{stCover}(t')$, $\mathrm{trCover}(t) = \mathrm{trCover}(t')$.   □

Let us note that, in order to (implicitly) allow repetitions, adding new transitions directly connecting pairs of points through the shortest path is, in general, a better choice than adding several instances of each state in the graph. Let us note that if we want to reach X by traversing some repeated states then there is no reason for not taking the shortest path to X. Making an evolutionary computation method, such as RFD, find these shortest paths in a graph with several instances of each node is inefficient because the Floyd algorithm *optimally* solves this problem in polynomial time. In fact, adding direct transitions is a good choice unless repeating nodes is *rarely* preferable to loading, which happens only if the load cost C is very low. In this case, running the Floyd algorithm before executing RFD could be almost a waste of time because direct transitions would be rarely taken. Alternatively, we can bound the execution of the Floyd algorithm in such a way that we do not consider any direct edge whose cost is already known to be higher than C (in this case loading is better, so all direct transitions costing more than C can be ignored).

The second main modification of the general RFD scheme concerns load costs. The general RFD scheme does not include any negative incentive to form bifurcation points, i.e. points where two or more flows join together. However, a negative incentive should be included because these points will represent *loads* in our solutions, which imply some additional cost. Negative incentives should be proportional to the load cost, in such a way that loads are preferred only if repeating nodes is more expensive than loading. We consider the following incentive approach. Let us suppose that a drop can take an edge connecting its current node to a node N where some drop has already moved this turn. Note that moving to N would imply that the hypothetical solution formed by both drops would include a load at N. We will bias the *perception* of drops in such a way that, when the drop makes the (probabilistic) decision of where to move next, it will perceive as if the edge leading to N were C units longer than it actually is, where C is the load cost. Since the chances to take a path depend on the gradient, which in turn depends on the edge cost, this will reduce the probability to go to N. In fact, the drop will choose to go to N only if it is a good choice despite of the additional cost. Moreover, the erosion introduced after the drop moves to N, which in turn also depends on the edge gradient, will be calculated as if the edge cost were C units longer.

5   Experimental Results

In this section we apply our method to empirically find good load trees for some WFSMs. Our experiments have two goals: (a) showing that being able to load previously traversed states may allow to reduce the time needed to cover some states and transitions; and (b) showing that solutions provided by our heuristic method are good enough though not being optimal. Regarding (a), we compare the time required to cover some critical configurations in the cases where load operations are allowed and not allowed. This comparison is made for three load cost assumptions: (i) the load cost is similar to the cost of taking a few edges (so loading is usually preferable); (ii) the load cost is a bit less than the cost of the shortest path between two distant nodes (so loading is seldom preferable); and (iii) an intermediate point. In the alternative case where we cannot restore configurations, we assume that a *reliable reset button* is available, which is a typical assumption in testing methods. Thus, we actually assume we can only restore the initial state of the WFSM. An adapted version of RFD is also used to find solutions in this alternative case. Regarding (b), we compare the performance and optimality of results given by our method with those given by an optimal branch and bound (B&B) strategy.

All experiments were performed in an Intel T2400 processor with 1.83 Ghz. RFD was executed fifty times for each of the graphs during five minutes, while the B&B method was executed (only once) during one hour (note that B&B is deterministic, so running it more times is pointless). For each method, Table 1 summarizes the best solution found (best), the arithmetic mean (average), the variance, and the best solution found for the alternative case where we cannot load any state different to the initial state (reset).

In Table 1, symbol '–' denotes a non-applicable case. The input of both algorithms are randomly generated graphs with 50, 100 and 200 nodes where the cost of edges is between 0 and 100. In the case that the graphs are sparse (✓), each node is connected with 2-5 nodes. However, when the graphs are dense (x), each node is connected with the 80% of the nodes. We present the results when the load cost is relatively cheap (20), when the load cost is medium (100) and when the load cost is high (1000) with respect to the cost of an edge of the WFSM. Furthermore, the cost associated to a reset of the system is set to 100, that is, the average cost of traversing two edges in the WFSM.

As we can see in Table 1, being able to load previously traversed states reduces the time needed to cover all the critical points in sparse graphs (see columns *Best* and *Reset*). Let us notice that in the case of dense graphs it is relatively easy to find paths covering all the critical points without requiring any load or reset. Thus, columns *Best* and *Reset* are nearly equal. However, in the case of sparse graphs (in fact, the most typical case of FSM specification) the advantages are obvious: In nearly all the cases the column *Best* outperforms the column *Reset*. As it can be expected, in the cases where the load cost is not very high, the difference is even bigger. Thus, cheaper testing plans can be obtained when load operations are available.

Regarding the quality of the solutions found by RFD, we must analyze the differences between *RFD* and *B&B* rows. Let us recall that RFD was executed during only five minutes while the B&B strategy was running during one hour. Anyway, the results obtained by RFD are always better than those of B&B. In fact, though B&B can eventually find the optimal solution, the performance of RFD and B&B for similar execution times is incomparable: Even if we execute B&B for much longer times than RFD, solutions found by RFD clearly outperform those given by B&B.

Table 1. Summary of results

Method	Graph size	Sparse	Load cost	Best	Average	Variance	Reset
RFD	50	✓	20	1724	2611	411299	6494
B&B	50	✓	20	2036	-	-	13257
RFD	50	✓	100	2380	3499	121251	6248
B&B	50	✓	100	2895	-	-	7142
RFD	50	✓	1000	4062	4401	45120	3482
B&B	50	✓	1000	7306	-	-	8918
RFD	100	✓	20	3678	4118	51470	17569
B&B	100	✓	20	12670	-	-	14982
RFD	100	✓	100	4054	4669	276078	8775
B&B	100	✓	100	12830	-	-	14982
RFD	100	✓	1000	5429	5793	45082	5429
B&B	100	✓	1000	14630	-	-	14982
RFD	200	✓	20	5573	6756	530882	25266
B&B	200	✓	20	32819	-	-	69656
RFD	200	✓	100	7653	8260	73943	12670
B&B	200	✓	100	33219	-	-	69656
RFD	200	✓	1000	18198	19524	1168366	18198
B&B	200	✓	1000	37719	-	-	69656
RFD	50	x	20	265	288	164	296
B&B	50	x	20	566	-	-	566
RFD	50	x	100	244	270	141	244
B&B	50	x	100	580	-	-	580
RFD	50	x	1000	242	273	107	242
B&B	50	x	1000	580	-	-	580
RFD	100	x	20	246	278	616	246
B&B	100	x	20	607	-	-	607
RFD	100	x	100	245	284	1090	245
B&B	100	x	100	607	-	-	607
RFD	100	x	1000	242	262	86	242
B&B	100	x	1000	607	-	-	607
RFD	200	x	20	300	336	293	300
B&B	200	x	20	367	-	-	367
RFD	200	x	100	297	347	583	297
B&B	200	x	100	367	-	-	367
RFD	200	x	1000	277	336	685	277
B&B	200	x	1000	367	-	-	367

6   Conclusions

Finding optimal testing plans to reach some states or transitions of an FSM
at least once is an NP-hard problem if we consider that previously traversed

configurations can be saved/restored at some cost. We have presented a heuristic evolutionary method that obtains reasonable solutions and spends acceptable times. As it can be expected, saving/restoring configurations is a good option when the cost of such operations is low compared to the cost of the rest of transitions. Our experimental results show that, in fact, loading is a good choice even in scenarios where the cost of loading is not particularly low. Moreover, the results of our approach based on River Formation Dynamics show that this approach provides a good tradeoff between finding good results and not spending much computational time. In fact, these results confirm that RFD fits particularly well for problems consisting in forming a kind of covering tree.

As future work we wish to generalize our method to the case where *extended* finite state machines are considered. In particular, RFD adaptations considered in [8] show that RFD can deal with *variables* without necessarily unfolding FSM states into all combinations of *(variable value, state)*. Thus, the capability of our method to actually deal with EFSMs should be studied.

References

1. Brinksma, E., Tretmans, J.: Testing transition systems: An annotated bibliography. In: Cassez, F., Jard, C., Rozoy, B., Dermot, M. (eds.) MOVEP 2000. LNCS, vol. 2067, pp. 187–195. Springer, Heidelberg (2001)
2. de Jong, K.: Evolutionary computation: a unified approach. In: Genetic and Evolutionary Computation Conference, GECCO 2008, pp. 2245–2258. ACM Press, New York (2008)
3. Dorigo, M.: Ant Colony Optimization. MIT Press, Cambridge (2004)
4. Lee, D., Yannakakis, M.: Principles and methods of testing finite state machines: A survey. Proceedings of the IEEE 84(8), 1090–1123 (1996)
5. Petrenko, A.: Fault model-driven test derivation from finite state models: Annotated bibliography. In: Cassez, F., Jard, C., Rozoy, B., Dermot, M. (eds.) MOVEP 2000. LNCS, vol. 2067, pp. 196–205. Springer, Heidelberg (2001)
6. Rabanal, P., Rodríguez, I., Rubio, F.: Using river formation dynamics to design heuristic algorithms. In: Akl, S.G., Calude, C.S., Dinneen, M.J., Rozenberg, G., Wareham, H.T. (eds.) UC 2007. LNCS, vol. 4618, pp. 163–177. Springer, Heidelberg (2007)
7. Rabanal, P., Rodríguez, I., Rubio, F.: Finding minimum spanning/distances trees by using river formation dynamics. In: Dorigo, M., Birattari, M., Blum, C., Clerc, M., Stützle, T., Winfield, A.F.T. (eds.) ANTS 2008. LNCS, vol. 5217, pp. 60–71. Springer, Heidelberg (2008)
8. Rabanal, P., Rodríguez, I., Rubio, F.: Applying river formation dynamics to solve NP-complete problems. In: Nature-Inspired Algorithms for Optimisation. Studies in Computational Intelligence, vol. 193, pp. 333–368. Springer, Heidelberg (2009)
9. Rabanal, P., Rodríguez, I., Rubio, F.: A formal approach to heuristically test restorable systems (Extended version) (2009),
   http://kimba.mat.ucm.es/prabanal/
10. Rabanal, P., Rodríguez, I., Rubio, F.: Testing restorable systems by using RFD. In: IWANN 2009. LNCS, vol. 5517. Springer, Heidelberg (2009)
11. Rodríguez, I., Merayo, M.G., Núñez, M.: $\mathcal{HOTL}$: Hypotheses and observations testing logic. Journal of Logic and Algebraic Programming 74(2), 57–93 (2008)

Constrained Reachability of Process Rewrite Systems

Tayssir Touili

LIAFA, CNRA and Univ. Paris Diderot, France
Tayssir.Touili@liafa.jussieu.fr

Abstract. We consider the problem of analyzing multi-threaded programs with recursive calls, dynamic creation of parallel procedures, and communication. We model such programs by Process Rewrite Systems (PRS) which are sets of term rewriting rules. Terms in this framework represent program control structures. The semantics of PRS systems is defined modulo structural equivalences on terms expressing properties of the operators appearing in the terms (idle process, sequential composition, and asynchronous parallel composition).

We consider the problem of reachability analysis of PRSs under constraints on the execution actions. This problem is undecidable even for regular constraints. [LS98] showed that it becomes decidable for *decomposable* constraints for the PRS subclass PA if structural equivalences are not taken into account. In this work, we go further and show that for decomposable constraints, we can compute tree automata representations of the *constrained* reachability sets for the *whole* class of PRS modulo different structural equivalences. Our results can be used to solve program (data flow) analysis and verification problems that can be reduced to the constrained reachability analysis problem.

1 Introduction

Software model checking is an important and hard task. This is due to the complex features present in software such as data structures ranging over infinite domains, complex control structures due to mutual recursion, dynamic creation of parallel processes, etc. Thus, software model checking is a challenging problem.

Many program analysis and verification problems can be reduced to *forward/backward reachability analysis*, i.e., computing the set of all successors ($post^*$ image) or all predecessors (pre^* image) of a given set of configurations. We consider in this paper the reachability analysis problem of multi-threaded programs, i.e., programs with recursive calls, dynamic creation of parallel processes, and communication. Our work is carried out in the framework of term rewriting systems. We model programs as sets of term rewriting rules, and we develop tree-automata techniques allowing to compute reachability sets for various classes of such models.

More precisely, we model a program by a *Process Rewrite System* (PRS for short) [May98]. Such a system is a finite set of rules of the form $t \to t'$ where t and

M. Leucker and C. Morgan (Eds.): ICTAC 2009, LNCS 5684, pp. 307–321, 2009.

t' are terms built up from the idle process ("0"), a finite set of process variables (X), sequential composition ("·"), and asynchronous parallel composition ("||").

To model a program in this framework, process variables are used to represent control points in the program, rules of the form $X \to X_1 \cdot X_2$ represent sequential recursive calls, whereas rules of the form $X \to X_1 || X_2$ model dynamic creation of parallel processes. Moreover, communication between sequential processes and synchronization between parallel processes can be modeled using rules of the forms $X_1 \cdot X_2 \to X$ and $X_1 || X_2 \to X$. Hence, a term represents here the *control structure* of a program representing all processes running in parallel, the hierarchy between them, and their corresponding control stacks. Since the number of process variables is finite, the framework we consider allows the manipulation of data ranging over a finite domain. On the other hand, this framework allows to reason about programs with *unbounded control structures*.

Syntactical restrictions on PRS rules define a hierarchy of models: Pushdown systems and Petri nets correspond respectively to systems where only sequential or parallel composition is used. An interesting subclass of PRS is the so-called class of PAD systems where parallel composition may appear only in the right-hand-sides of the rules. This class subsumes both pushdown systems and the class of PA processes where all left-hand-sides of rules are process variables. These various classes of models correspond to different classes of programs: Pushdown systems model sequential recursive programs, PA systems correspond to programs with recursive sequential and parallel procedures but without communication, PAD extends the modeling power of PA by allowing communication between sequential recursive procedures (a procedure may deliver a result to its caller), and PRS allows also communication and synchronization between parallel procedures (the execution of a procedure may depend on the results delivered by several parallel procedures).

The standard semantics of PRSs (see [May98]) considers terms modulo a structural equivalence $\sim$ which expresses the fact that 0 is a neutral element of "·" and "||", that "·" is associative, and that "||" is associative and commutative. In [BT03], we showed that it can be desirable and useful to reason about terms modulo stronger structural equivalences, and that it may be sufficient to compute representatives of the reachability sets modulo the considered equivalences. Therefore, following [BT03], we consider the reachability problem of PRSs modulo the following equivalences: (1) term equality ($=$), (2) the relation $\sim_0$ which takes into account the neutrality of 0 w.r.t. "·" and "||", (3) the relation $\sim_s$ which, in addition, considers the associativity of "·", and (4) the equivalence $\sim$. To tackle the reachability problem for PRSs modulo these various structural equivalences, we represent *infinite* sets of process terms using tree automata since they present nice closure properties needed for program verification.

In [BT03], we showed that regular representatives of the reachability sets can be computed for the whole class of PRS for the equivalences $=, \sim_0$, and $\sim_s$; and that if the system is a PAD, then representatives of the reachability sets modulo $\sim$ can be computed. In this work, we go one step further and consider reachability *under constraints*. The problem is, given a (infinite) set of sequences of actions D, compute representatives of the set of terms reachable by the system after applying sequences of actions in D. Indeed, in program verification, it is interesting to determine the behavior of the program if it performs sequences of actions in a given form. Moreover, it was shown in [EK99] that data flow analysis necessitates reachability *under constraints*.

Unfortunately, even for the PRS subclass PA, and the trivial equivalence "=", this problem is undecidable if we consider regular constraints [LS98]. It becomes decidable for PA modulo "=" if we consider *decomposable* constraints [LS98] (a language is decomposable if it belongs to a finite set E of languages such that each member of E has a sequential and a parallel decomposition over E). In this work, we go further and extend this result to the whole class of PRS, and to all the equivalences. We show that modulo "=, $\sim_0$", and "$\sim_s$", we can compute regular representatives of the *constrained* reachability set for the whole class of PRS if the contraints are decomposable. For the equivalence "$\sim$", it is possible to compute representatives for the PRS subclass PAD.

We show that these results are important in program verification because all the constraints on the executed actions needed for data flow analysis and mentionned in [EK99] are decomposable. Furthermore, decomposable languages can describe interesting patterns under which it can be relevant to see the behavior of the program.

Related work. In [May98], Mayr considers the reachability problem between terms, i.e., given two terms t and t', determine whether t' is reachable from t. The problem we consider here is more general since we are interested in computing the set of all reachable configurations, or a representative of it modulo a structural equivalence, which allows to solve the term reachability problem. In [BT05], we propose a generic algorithm that computes *all* the reachable configurations (not only representatives) of some classes of PRS. There, we use a different class of tree automata. Reachability under constraints was not considered in [BT05].

In [BET03, BET05, Tou05, PST07], it was shown that reachability under constraints is useful to deal with synchronisation between parallel processes. These works as well as [RSJM05] do not compute the reachable configurations under a given execution constraint; they compute abstractions of the execution paths that lead from a set of configurations to another one. Our results can be used in these frameworks to compute the reachable configurations under a given *exact* (not abtract as in these works) constraint on the execution paths.

There are several other works about the reachability of multithreaded programs using different models (e.g. [BMOT05, ABT08]). Reachability under constraints was not considered in these works.

2   Terms and Tree Automata

An alphabet Σ is ranked if it is endowed with a mapping $rank : \Sigma \to \mathbb{N}$. For $k \geq 0$, Σ_k is the set of elements of rank k. Let $\mathcal{X}$ be a fixed denumerable set of variables $\{x_1, x_2, \ldots\}$. The set $T_\Sigma[\mathcal{X}]$ of terms over Σ and $\mathcal{X}$ is the smallest set that satisfies: (1) $\Sigma_0 \cup \mathcal{X} \subseteq T_\Sigma[\mathcal{X}]$; and (2) if $k \geq 1$, $f \in \Sigma_k$ and $t_1, \ldots, t_k \in T_\Sigma[\mathcal{X}]$, then $f(t_1, \ldots, t_k)$ is in $T_\Sigma[\mathcal{X}]$.

T_Σ stands for $T_\Sigma[\emptyset]$. Terms in T_Σ are called *ground terms*. A term in $T_\Sigma[\mathcal{X}]$ is *linear* if each variable occurs at most once. A *context* C is a linear term of $T_\Sigma[\mathcal{X}]$. Let $t_1, \ldots, t_n$ be terms of T_Σ, then $C[t_1, \ldots, t_n]$ denotes the term obtained by replacing in the context C the occurrence of the variable x_i by the term t_i, for each $1 \leq i \leq n$. To single out some occurrences of n subterms $t_1, \ldots, t_n$ into a given term t, we write $t = C[t_1, \ldots, t_n]$ for some context C.

To represent regular sets of terms, we use tree automata.

Definition 1. *A **finite tree automaton** is a tuple $\mathcal{A} = (Q, \Sigma, F, \delta)$ where Q is a finite set of states, Σ is a ranked alphabet, $F \subseteq Q$ is a set of final states, and δ is a set of rules of the form (1) $f(q_1, \ldots, q_n) \rightarrow q$, or (2) $a \rightarrow q$, or (3) $q \rightarrow q'$, where $a \in \Sigma_0$, $n \geq 0$, $f \in \Sigma_n$, and $q_1, \ldots, q_n, q, q' \in Q$.*

Let t be a ground term. A run of $\mathcal{A}$ on t is defined in a bottom-up manner as follows: first, the automaton annotates the leaves according to the rules (2), then it continues the annotation of the term t according to the rules (1) and (3): if the subterms $t_1, \ldots, t_n$ are annotated by states $q_1, \ldots, q_n$, and if the rule $f(q_1, \ldots, q_n) \rightarrow q$ is in δ then the term $f(t_1, \ldots, t_n)$ is annotated by q. A term t is accepted by a state $q \in Q$ if $\mathcal{A}$ reaches the root of t in q. Formally, the move relation $\rightarrow_\delta$ of $\mathcal{A}$ is defined as follows: let t and t' be two terms of $T_{\Sigma \cup Q}$, then $t \rightarrow_\delta t'$ iff there exist a context $C \in T_{\Sigma \cup Q}[\mathcal{X}]$, and (1) a rule $f(q_1, \ldots, q_n) \rightarrow q$ in δ such that $t = C[f(q_1, \ldots, q_n)]$ and $t' = C[q]$, or (2) a rule $a \rightarrow q$ in δ such that $t = C[a]$ and $t' = C[q]$, or (3) a rule $q \rightarrow q'$ in δ such that $t = C[q]$ and $t' = C[q']$. $\xrightarrow{*}_\delta$ is the reflexive-transitive closure of $\rightarrow_\delta$. The language accepted by a state $q \in Q$ is $L_q = \{t \in T_\Sigma \mid t \xrightarrow{*}_\delta q\}$. The language accepted (or recognized) by the automaton $\mathcal{A}$ is $\mathcal{L}(\mathcal{A}) = \bigcup\{L_q \mid q \in F\}$. A tree language is regular if it is accepted by a finite tree automaton.

Proposition 1. *[CDG+97] The class of regular tree languages is closed under union, intersection, and complementation. Moreover, it can be decided in linear time whether the language accepted by a finite tree automaton is empty.*

3   Process Rewrite Systems

3.1   Syntax

Let $Act = \{\epsilon, a, b, c, \ldots\}$ be a set of actions, where ϵ is a "silent" action. Let $Var = \{X, Y, \ldots\}$ be a set of process variables, and T_p be the set of process terms t defined by the following syntax:

$$t ::= 0 \mid X \mid t \cdot t \mid t \| t$$

Intuitively, 0 is the null process and "." (resp. "$\|$") denotes sequential composition (resp. asynchronous parallel composition). The set T_p can be seen as $T_{\Sigma_0 \cup \Sigma_2}$ where $\Sigma_0 = \{0\} \cup Var$ and $\Sigma_2 = \{., \|\}$. Thus, we can use tree automata to represent sets of process terms. We shall also use the usual infix notations to represent terms.

Definition 2 ([May98]). *A* Process Rewrite System *(PRS for short) is a finite set of rules of the form* $t_1 \xrightarrow{a} t_2$*, where* $t_1, t_2 \in T_p$*,* $t_1 \neq 0$*, and* $a \in Act$*. A* PAD *is a PRS where all the rules have as left hand sides sequential compositions of process variables like* $X \cdot Y \cdot Z$*. A* PA *is a PAD where all the rules have the form* $X \xrightarrow{a} t$*.*

Let R be a PRS, we denote by R^{-1} the PRS obtained by swapping the left hand sides and the right hand sides of the rules of R. We define $Sub(R)$ as the set of subterms of the left hand sides and the right hand sides of the rules of R.

3.2 Semantics

A PRS R induces a transition relation $\xrightarrow{a}_R$ over T_p defined by the following inference rules:

$$\frac{t_1 \xrightarrow{a} t_2 \in R}{t_1 \xrightarrow{a}_R t_2}; \quad \frac{t_1 \xrightarrow{a}_R t_1'}{t_1 || t_2 \xrightarrow{a}_R t_1' || t_2}; \quad \frac{t_1 \xrightarrow{a}_R t_1'}{t_1 \cdot t_2 \xrightarrow{a}_R t_1' \cdot t_2}; \quad \frac{t_2 \xrightarrow{a}_R t_2'}{t_1 || t_2 \xrightarrow{a}_R t_1 || t_2'}; \quad \frac{t_1 \sim_0 0 \ , \ t_2 \xrightarrow{a}_R t_2'}{t_1 \cdot t_2 \xrightarrow{a}_R t_1 \cdot t_2'}$$

where $\sim_0$ is an equivalence between process terms that identifies the terminated processes. It expresses the neutrality of the null process "0" w.r.t. "$||$", and ".":

A1: $t \cdot 0 \sim_0 0 \cdot t \sim_0 t || 0 \sim_0 0 || t \sim_0 t$

We consider the structural equivalence $\sim$ generated by the axioms A1 and the following axioms:

    A2: $(t \cdot t') \cdot t'' \sim t \cdot (t' \cdot t'')$: associativity of ".",
    A3: $t || t' \sim t' || t$: commutativity of "$||$",
    A4: $(t || t') || t'' \sim t || (t' || t'')$: associativity of '$||$'.

We denote by $\sim_s$ the equivalence induced by the axioms A1 and A2, and by $\sim_{||}$ the equivalence induced by the axioms A1, A3, and A4.

Observe that the last inference rule expresses that for a term $(t_1 \cdot t_2)$; t_2 can make moves only when $t_1 \sim_0 0$; i.e., only when t_1 has terminated its execution. Let $\equiv$ be an equivalence from the set $\{=, \sim_0, \sim_s, \sim_{||}, \sim\}$, where $=$ stands for the identity between terms. We denote by $[t]_\equiv$ the equivalence class modulo $\equiv$ of the process term t, i.e., $[t]_\equiv = \{t' \in T_p \mid t \equiv t'\}$. A language L is said to be compatible with the equivalence $\equiv$ if $[L]_\equiv = L$. We say that L' is a $\equiv$-representative of L if $[L']_\equiv = L$. Each equivalence $\equiv$ induces a transition relation $\xrightarrow{a}_{\equiv,R}$ defined as follows:

$$\forall t, t' \in T_p, t \xRightarrow{a}_{\equiv,R} t' \text{ iff } \exists u, u' \in T_p \text{ such that } t \equiv u, u \xrightarrow{a}_R u', \text{ and } u' \equiv t'$$

The relation $\xRightarrow{a}_{\equiv,R}$ is extended to sequences of actions in the usual way. Let $Post^*_{R,\equiv}(t) = \{t' \in T_p \mid \exists w \in Act^*, t \xRightarrow{w}_{\equiv,R} t'\}$, and $Pre^*_{R,\equiv}(t) = \{t' \in T_p \mid \exists w \in Act^*, t' \xRightarrow{w}_{\equiv,R} t\}$. Let $D \subseteq Act^*$. We denote by $Post^*_{R,\equiv}[D](t)$ the set $\{t' \in T_p \mid \exists w \in D \text{ such that } t \xRightarrow{w}_{R,\equiv} t'\}$. $Pre^*_{R,\equiv}[D](t)$ is defined in the same manner. All these definitions are extended to languages in the standard way.

In this paper, we suppose w.l.o.g. that the PRSs we are working with are in *normal form*, i.e., are such that $Sub(R)$ contains only elements of the form 0, X, $X\|Y$, or $X \cdot Y$. It can be shown that any PRS can be simulated by a PRS in this form by introducing some auxiliary variables [May98]. For example, the rule $X \xrightarrow{a} Y\|(Z\|W)$ can be replaced by $X \xrightarrow{\epsilon} Y\|X'$ and $X' \xrightarrow{a} Z\|W$.

3.3 Modeling of Multi-threaded Programs by PRSs

PRS subsumes several well-known classes of (infinite-state) models relevant in program modeling such as Prefix rewrite systems, BPA processes, Multiset rewrite systems, BPP, PA, and PAD processes [May98]. PRSs allow to model parallel programs with recursion as follows: We abstract each point of the program to a process variable. Thus, a process term t describes the control structure of the program. The process $t_1 \cdot t_2$ behaves like the process t_1 until it terminates and then behaves like t_2. The parallel execution of processes t_1 and t_2 is denoted by $t_1\|t_2$. The set Act contains the actions the different processes may perform. A rule $t_1 \xrightarrow{a} t_2$ indicates that the process t_1 can perform the action "a" and afterwards behave like t_2. A rule $t_1\|t_2 \xrightarrow{a} t$ refers to a pair of threads (t_1 and t_2) that synchronize and become process t. The creation of two processes t_1 and t_2 running in parallel is modeled by a rule $t \xrightarrow{a} t_1\|t_2$. A procedure call is represented by a rule of the form $t \xrightarrow{a} t_1 \cdot t_2$, where the process t calls the procedure t_1 and becomes process t_2. It becomes active again when t_1 terminates (this is due to the last inference rule of Subsection 3.2). Suppose the behavior of t_2 depends on the result of the computation t_1, this is represented by a finite number of rules $t_1^i \cdot t_2 \xrightarrow{a} t^i$, $1 \le i \le k$, for some constant k; meaning that t_1 is evaluated before passing control to t_2, if t_1 becomes t_1^i, then the caller becomes t^i and resumes its computation.

Let us consider a simple example of a multi-threaded program and show its corresponding PRS system. The JAVA code below corresponds to a typical concurrent server that launches a new thread to deal with each new client request. The number of launched threads is unbounded.

```
public void server() {
    Socket socket;
    while(true) {
        try{
            socket=serverSocket.accept();
        } catch (Exception e){
            System.err(e);
            continue;
        }
        Thread t=new thread(runnableService(socket));
        t.start();
    }
}
```

An instance of the procedure server() is represented by the process variable X, the instruction try is represented by the variable Y, and an instance of t.start() is represented by the variable Z. The variables T and F correspond to the booleans true and false meaning that the try instruction (represented by Y) succeeds or fails, respectively. The program is described by the following PRS rules (notice that this system is in fact a PAD):

- $X \rightarrow Y \cdot X$ (the procedure starts by executing Y),
- $Y \rightarrow T$ (Y returns true),
- $Y \rightarrow F$ (Y returns false),
- $T \cdot X \rightarrow X || Z$ (if Y returns true, then a new thread is launched),
- $F \rightarrow 0$ (otherwise, the request is ignored after failure).

4   Reachability under Constraints of PRS

In [EK99, BT03], it was shown that several problems of data flow analysis (such as the verification of safety properties) can be reduced to computing representatives of the sets $Post^*_{\cong}[D](L)$ and $Pre^*_{\cong}[D](L)$, where L is a tree language representing a regular (infinite) set of process terms, $\cong$ is an equivalence in $\{=, \sim_0, \sim_s, \sim\}$, and D is a (infinite) set of constraints in Act^*. In [BT03], we developed tree automata techniques to compute representatives of $Post^*_{\cong}(L)$ and $Pre^*_{\cong}(L)$ modulo the various structural equivalences mentionned above. In this work, we go further and tackle the problem of computing representatives of $Post^*_{\cong}[D](L)$ and $Pre^*_{\cong}[D](L)$ for a (infinite) set of sequences of actions $D \subseteq Act^*$. Unfortunately, this problem is undecidable even if we consider regular constraints (i.e., if D is a regular word language over Act^*) and without structural equivalences (i.e., if $\cong$ is $=$). This holds even for the subclass PA of PRS [LS98] (PA is the class where the left hand sides of the rules are process constants) . Lugiez and Schnoebelen [LS98] showed that this problem becomes decidable for PA if D is a *decomposable* language (a language is decomposable if it belongs to a finite set E of languages such that each member of E has a sequential and a parallel decomposition over E. We give the formal definition of decomposable languages in the next section.).

In this paper, we go further and show that we can compute $\cong$-representatives of the sets $Post^*_{\cong}[D](L)$ and $Pre^*_{\cong}[D](L)$ for $\cong \in \{=, \sim_0, \sim_s, \sim\}$ for the *whole* class of PRS if D is *decomposable*. Our results are important for program verification [EK99, BT03]. Indeed, all the constraint languages that are used in [EK99] for data flow analysis are decomposable (see the next section for a non exhaustive list of decomposable languages).

4.1   Decomposable Languages

We give in this section the definition of decomposable languages. Recall that for two given words x and y, the shuffle $x \amalg y$ is the set $\{x_1 y_1 \cdots x_n y_n \mid x = x_1 \cdots x_n, y = y_1 \cdots y_n\}$.

Definition 3 (Decomposable languages [LS98])

- $\{(D_1, D_1'), \ldots, (D_m, D_m')\}$ is a *(finite)* seq-decomposition *of D iff for every* $w, w' \in Act^*$ *we have:*

$$w.w' \in D \text{ iff } (w \in D_i, w' \in D_i' \text{ for some } 1 \le i \le m).$$

- $\{(D_1, D_1'), \ldots, (D_m, D_m')\}$ is a *(finite)* paral-decomposition *of D iff for every* $w, w' \in Act^*$ *we have:*

$$D \cap (w \amalg w') \neq \emptyset \text{ iff } (w \in D_i, w' \in D_i' \text{ for some } 1 \le i \le m).$$

- *A family* $\mathcal{D} = \{D_1, \ldots, D_n\}$ *of languages over Act is a* finite decomposition system *iff every* $D \in \mathcal{D}$ *has a seq-decomposition and a paral-decomposition only using D_i's from $\mathcal{D}$.*
- *D is* decomposable *if it belongs to a finite decomposition system.*

In the remaining, we will write $(D_1, D_2) \in_\| D$ (resp. $(D_1, D_2) \in. D$) if (D_1, D_2) appears in the paral-decomposition of D (resp. the seq-decomposition of D).

The following properties of decomposable languages were shown in [Sch99, GP03]: Any decomposable language is regular, the reverse does not hold. Decomposable languages form a class of regular languages closed under finite union, concatenation, and shuffle. Every commutative regular language is decomposable. Every language that is a finite union of products of commutative languages is decomposable. This includes the finite and cofinite[1] languages, and the languages of level 3/2 of Straubing's concatenation hierarchy of star-free sets (this corresponds to the class APC of [BMT01, BMT07]).

For example, let $Act = \{\epsilon, a, b\}$; it was shown in [GP03] that the following languages are decomposable, and their decomposition was provided: $(aab)^* \cup Act^*b(aa)^*abAct^*$, $Act^*b(aa)^*$, $(aa)^*abAct^*$, $Act^*b(aa)^*a$, $(aa)^*bAct^*$, $Act^*aAct^*bAct^*$, $Act^*bAct^*bAct^*$, $Act^*baAct^*abAct^*Act^*bAct^*aAct^*$, etc.

Thus, decomposable languages is an important class in program analysis. Indeed, it is interesting for program verification to know whether it is possible to reach some set of terms L' (representing, e.g., the bad configurations) from a set L (representing, e.g., the initial configurations) after repeating a given pattern of sequences of actions, such as e.g., $(aab)^* \cup Act^*b(aa)^*abAct^*$. Moreover, constrained reachability was shown to be useful for dataflow analysis in [EK99]. There, the constraints used are decomposable because they all belong to the class APC [BMT01, BMT07].

5 Constrained Reachability without Structural Equivalences

Through the rest of the paper, we fix a set of actions Act, a set of variables Var, and a PRS R over Var. We prove in this section that for any regular tree language L, $Post^*_{R,=}[D](L)$ and $Pre^*_{R,=}[D](L)$ are effectively regular if D is decomposable:

---

[1] A language is cofinite if it is the complement of a finite language.

Theorem 1. *Let L be a regular tree language and D a decomposable language. Then, finite automata that recognize $Post^*_{R,=}[D](L)$ and $Pre^*_{R,=}[D](L)$ can be effectively computed in polynomial time.*

In the rest of this section, we give the construction underlying this theorem. Let $Sub_r(R)$ be the set of all the subterms of the right hand sides of the rules of R. Let $Q_R = \{q_t \mid t \in Sub_r(R)\}$, and let δ_R be the following transition rules:

- $X \to q_X$, for every $X \in Sub_r(R)$,
- $||(q_X, q_Y) \to q_{X||Y}$, if $X||Y \in Sub_r(R)$,
- $\cdot(q_X, q_Y) \to q_{X \cdot Y}$, if $X \cdot Y \in Sub_r(R)$.

Then, it is clear that for every $t \in Sub_r(R)$, $L_{q_t} = \{t\}$.

Now, we are ready to give our construction. Let L be a regular language, and let $\mathcal{A} = (Q, \Sigma, F, \delta)$ be a finite tree automaton that recognizes L. Let $\mathcal{D}$ be a finite decomposition system. For every $D_0 \in \mathcal{D}$, we define the automaton $\mathcal{A}^*_R[D_0] = (Q_D, \Sigma, F_D, \delta_D)$ as follows:

- $Q_D = \{q, (q^{nil}, D), (q^T, D) \mid q \in Q \cup Q_R, D \in \mathcal{D}\}$. We denote by $\tilde{q}$ any element in $\{q^T, q^{nil}\}$.
- $F_D = \{(q^{nil}, D_0), (q^T, D_0) \mid q \in F\}$,
- δ_D is the smallest set of rules containing $\delta \cup \delta_R$ and such that for every $q_1, q_2, q \in Q \cup Q_R$:
  1. $q \to (q^T, D) \in \delta_D$ for every $q \in Q \cup Q_R$, $D \in \mathcal{D}$ such that $\epsilon \in D$.
  2. if $0 \xrightarrow{*}_\delta q$, then $0 \to (q^{nil}, D) \in \delta_D$, for every $D \in \mathcal{D}$ such that $\epsilon \in D$.
  3. if $t_1 \xrightarrow{a} t_2 \in R$, and there is a state $q \in Q \cup Q_R$ such that $t_1 \xrightarrow{*}_{\delta_D} (q^T, D)$, then for every $D_1, D_2, D', D'' \in \mathcal{D}$ such that $a \in D'$, $(D', D_1) \in D''$, and $(D, D'') \in D_2$:
     (a) $(q^T_{t_2}, D_1) \to (q^T, D_2) \in \delta_D$,
     (b) $(q^{nil}_{t_2}, D_1) \to (q^{nil}, D_2) \in \delta_D$,
  4. if $\cdot(q_1, q_2) \to q \in \delta \cup \delta_R$, then for every $D_1, D_2, D \in \mathcal{D}$ such that $(D_1, D_2) \in D$:
     (a) $\cdot((q^{nil}_1, D_1), (\tilde{q}_2, D_2)) \to (q^T, D) \in \delta_D$,
     (b) $\cdot((q^{nil}_1, D_1), (q^{nil}_2, D_2)) \to (q^{nil}, D) \in \delta_D$,
     (c) $\cdot((q^T_1, D), q_2) \to (q^T, D) \in \delta_D$,
  5. if $||(q_1, q_2) \to q \in \delta \cup \delta_R$, then for every $D_1, D_2, D \in \mathcal{D}$ such that $(D_1, D_2) \in_{||} D$:
     (a) $||((q^{nil}_1, D_1), (q^{nil}_2, D_2)) \to (q^{nil}, D) \in \delta_D$,
     (b) $||((\tilde{q}_1, D_1), (\tilde{q}_2, D_2)) \to (q^T, D) \in \delta_D$,
  6. if $q \to q' \in \delta \cup \delta_R$, then $(q^T, D) \to (q'^T, D) \in \delta_D$, and $(q^{nil}, D) \to (q'^{nil}, D) \in \delta_D$ for every $D \in \mathcal{D}$.

Note that the inference rules (3) construct a finite sequence of increasing sets of transitions $\delta^1_D \subset \delta^2_D \subset \dots \subset \delta^n_D$, where δ^{i+1}_D contains at most two transitions more that δ^i_D. This procedure terminates because there is a finite number of states in $Q \cup Q_R$ and a finite number of terms in $Sub_r(R)$.

The computed automaton satisfies the following:

Theorem 2. $\mathcal{A}_R^*[D_0]$ *recognizes* $Post_{R,=}^*[D_0](L)$.

To show that $Post_{R,=}^*[D_0](L)$ is accepted by $\mathcal{A}_R^*[D_0]$, it suffices to prove these two lemmas:

Lemma 1. *For every* $v \in T_p$ *and every* $q \in Q \cup Q_R$, *we have:*

- $v \xrightarrow{*}_{\delta_D} (q^T, D) \Rightarrow v \in Post_{R,=}^*[D](L_q),$
- $v \xrightarrow{*}_{\delta_D} (q^{nil}, D) \Rightarrow v \sim_0 0$ *and* $v \in Post_{R,=}^*[D](L_q).$

Lemma 2. *For every* $q \in Q \cup Q_R$, $u \in T_p$ *and* $D \in \mathcal{D}$,

$$\left(\exists w \in D \mid u \in Post_{R,=}^*[w](L_q)\right) \Rightarrow \left(u \xrightarrow{*}_{\delta_D} (q^T, D)\right).$$

These lemmas express that for every $q \in Q \cup Q_R$ and every $D \in \mathcal{D}$, $L_{(q^T,D)} = Post_{R,=}^*[D](L_q)$ and $L_{(q^{nil},D)} = Post_{R,=}^*[D](L_q) \cap \{u \in T_p \mid u \sim_0 0\}$. In particular this means that for every $t \in Sub_r(R)$, $L_{(q_t^T,D)} = Post_{R,=}^*[D](t)$ and $L_{(q_t^{nil},D)} = Post_{R,=}^*[D](t) \cap \{u \in T_p \mid u \sim_0 0\}$. The construction is based on the fact that:

- If $u_1 \in Post_{R,=}^*[D_1](t_1)$ and $u_2 \in Post_{R,=}^*[D_2](t_2)$, then $u_1 \| u_2 \in Post_{R,=}^*[D](t_1 \| t_2)$ for some D such that (D_1, D_2) appears in the paral-decomposition of D (rules (5)). Similarly, if $u_2 = t_2$ or $u_1 \sim_0 0$, then $u_1.u_2 \in Post_{R,=}^*[D](t_1 \cdot t_2)$ for some D such that (D_1, D_2) appears in the seq-decomposition of D (rules (4)).
- Let $u, t_1, t_2 \in T_p$, and $D'' \in \mathcal{D}$ be such that $t_1 \xrightarrow{a} t_2 \in R$ and $u \in Post_{R,=}^*[D''](t_2)$, then $u \in Post_{R,=}^*[D](t_1)$ for some $D, D' \in \mathcal{D}$ such that $a \in D'$ and (D', D'') appears in the seq-decomposition of D (rules (3)).

More precisely, the rules (3) mean that if $t_1 \in Post_{R,=}^*[D](L_q)$ and $t_1 \xrightarrow{a} t_2 \in R$, then $Post^*[D_1](t_2) \subseteq Post_{R,=}^*[D_2](L_q)$, where D_1, D_2 are such that there exist D', D'' such that $a \in D'$, $(D', D_1) \in D''$, and $(D, D'') \in D_2$. The rules (5) mean that if $\|(q_1, q_2) \to_\delta q$, $u_1 \in Post_{R,=}^*[D_1](L_{q_1})$, and $u_2 \in Post_{R,=}^*[D_2](L_{q_2})$, then $u_1 \| u_2 \in Post_{R,=}^*[D](L_q)$ for some D such that $(D_1, D_2) \in_\| D$. Rules (4) deal with transitions of the form $\cdot(q_1, q_2) \to_\delta q$. The states q and (q^{nil}, D) play an important role for these rules. Indeed, the rules (4) ensure that the right child of a "." node cannot be rewritten if the left child is not null, i.e., if the left child is not labeled by a state (q^{nil}, D).

A construction similar to the one above can be given for $Pre_{R,=}^*[D_0](L)$. It is based on the fact that $Pre_{R,=}^*[D_0](L) = Post_{R^{-1},=}^*[D_0](L)$.

5.1   Reachability Modulo $\sim_0$

Modulo $\sim_0$, every term t is equivalent to the terms $t \cdot 0$, $0 \cdot t$, $t \| 0$, $0 \| t$, $0 \cdot (t \cdot 0)$, $(0 \cdot 0) \cdot t$, $(0 \| 0) \cdot t$, ... etc. The previous construction can be adapted to perform reachability analysis modulo $\sim_0$. This can be done by (1) considering a special state q_{null} that recognizes all the null terms (all the terms which are equivalent to 0), (2) adding new rules that allow to have null terms recognized by q_{null} everywhere in the trees (for example, add rules of the form $||(q, q_{null}) \to q$, for every $q \in Q_D$), and (3) adding rules to simplify the rules of the computed automaton (for example $||(q_1, q_2) \to q$, or $\cdot(q_1, q_2) \to q$) in this way: if 0 is recognized by q_1, and the term u by q_2, then u should also be recognized by q (i.e., we add the rule $q_2 \to q$). These rules are added during the saturation process. We get then the following result:

Theorem 3. *Let L be a regular tree language and D a decomposable language. Then, finite automata that recognize $Post^*_{R, \sim_0}[D](L)$ and $Pre^*_{R, \sim_0}[D](L)$ can be effectively computed in polynomial time.*

6 Reachability Modulo $\sim_s$

Computing $post^*$- and pre^*-images modulo $\sim_s$ does not preserve regularity [GD89]. We show in this section that for any regular language L and any decomposable language D, we can effectively compute finite tree automata that recognize $\sim_s$-representatives of $Post^*_{R, \sim_s}[D](L)$ and $Pre^*_{R, \sim_s}[D](L)$.

The difference of this case with the previous ones comes from the fact that the rules of the form $X \cdot Y \to t$ can be applied non-locally, i.e., it can for example be applied to the terms $X \cdot (Y \cdot (Z \cdot T))$ and $X \cdot ((Y \cdot Z) \cdot T)$ since they are $\sim_s$-equivalent to $(X \cdot Y) \cdot (Z \cdot T)$. In fact, this rule can be applied to the subterms that have the form of the tree represented in the left side of Figure 1. Thus, if we want to produce a $\sim_s$-representative of the immediate successors of such a term by this rule, we can compute the term represented in the right side of Figure 1: we replace the occurrence of Y by t, and remove the X. We recall in the following the definition of a relation ζ_R introduced in [BT03] that performs this transformation, in addition to the other usual rules of R applied modulo $\sim_0$ (since the terms in Figure 1 considers simplified terms that do not consider 0's).

First, let us recall the notion of *seq-context*: Let $x \in \mathcal{X}$, a *seq-context* is a single-variable context $C[x]$ such that: (1) x is the leftmost leaf of C, and (2) all the ancestors of the variable x are labeled by ".".

ζ_R is the smallest transition relation over T_p that contains $\Rightarrow_{\sim_0, R}$ and such that for every rule $X \cdot Y \to t$ in R, and every seq-context C, $(X \cdot C[Y], C[t]) \in \zeta_R$. This transformation is depicted in Figure 1. Given a regular tree language L and a set of constraints D, $\zeta_R^*[D](L)$ is defined as previously.

For any set of constraints D, $\zeta_R^*[D](L)$ is a $\sim_s$-representative of $Post^*_{R, \sim_s}[D](L)$:

Proposition 2. *For every tree language L and set of constraints D, $Post^*_{R, \sim_s}[D](L) = [\zeta_R^*[D](L)]_{\sim_s}$ and $Pre^*_{R, \sim_s}[D](L) = [\zeta_{R^{-1}}^*[D](L)]_{\sim_s}$.*

We prove in this section the following:

Theorem 4. *Let L be a regular language and D be a decomposable language, then $\zeta_R^*[D](L)$ is effectively regular, and can be computed in polynomial time.*

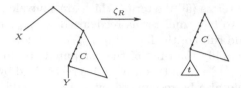

Fig. 1. Application of the rule $X \cdot Y \to t$ modulo $\sim_s$

Let L be a regular tree language. We suppose w.l.o.g. that L is compatible with $\sim_0$ (if this is not the case, we can make it compatible as explained in Section 5.1). Let $\mathcal{A} = (Q, \Sigma, F, \delta)$ be a tree automaton that recognizes L. Let $\mathcal{D}$ be a decomposable system, and let $D_0 \in \mathcal{D}$. We define the automaton $\mathcal{A}^*_{\varsigma_R}[D_0] = (\tilde{Q}_D, \Sigma, \tilde{F}_D, \tilde{\delta}_D)$ as follows:

- $\tilde{Q}_D = \{q, (q^T, D) \mid q \in Q \cup Q_R, D \in \mathcal{D}\} \cup \{((q, X), D) \mid q \in Q \cup Q_R, X \in Var, D \in \mathcal{D}\}$,
- $\tilde{F}_D = \{(q^T, D_0) \mid q \in F\}$,
- $\tilde{\delta}_D$ is the smallest set of rules containing $\delta \cup \delta_R$ and such that for every $q_1, q_2, q \in Q \cup Q_R$, for every $X, Y, X' \in Var$ such that $X \cdot Y \xrightarrow{a} t \in R$:

(α_1) $q \to (q^T, D) \in \tilde{\delta}_D$ for every $q \in Q \cup Q_R$ and $D \in \mathcal{D}$ s.t. $\epsilon \in D$,

(α_2) if $Y \xrightarrow{*}_{\tilde{\delta}_D} q$, then for every D_1, D_2, D' such that $a \in D'$, $(D', D_1) \in_. D_2$:

$$(q_t^T, D_1) \to ((q, X), D_2) \in \tilde{\delta}_D,$$

(α_3) if $t_1 \xrightarrow{b} t_2 \in R$, then for every D_1, D_2, D', D'' such that $b \in D'$, $(D', D_1) \in_. D''$, and $(D, D'') \in_. D_2$, if there is a state $q \in Q \cup Q_R$ such that:

    (a) $t_1 \xrightarrow{*}_{\tilde{\delta}_D} (q^T, D)$, then: $(q_{t_2}^T, D_1) \to (q^T, D_2) \in \tilde{\delta}_D$, or

    (b) $t_1 \xrightarrow{*}_{\tilde{\delta}_D} ((q, X), D)$, then: $(q_{t_2}^T, D_1) \to ((q, X), D_2) \in \tilde{\delta}_D$,

(α_4) if $\cdot(q_1, q_2) \to q \in \delta \cup \delta_R$, then for every D_1, D_2, D such that $(D_1, D_2) \in_.$ D:

    (a) $\cdot((q_1^T, D), q_2) \to (q^T, D) \in \tilde{\delta}_D$,

    (b) $\cdot\left(((q_1, X), D), q_2\right) \to ((q, X), D) \in \tilde{\delta}_D$,

    (c) if $0 \xrightarrow{*}_{\tilde{\delta}_D} ((q_1, X), D_1)$ then $(q_2^T, D_2) \to ((q, X), D) \in \tilde{\delta}_D$,

    (d) if $0 \xrightarrow{*}_{\tilde{\delta}_D} (q_1^T, D_1)$ then $(q_2^T, D_2) \to (q^T, D) \in \tilde{\delta}_D$,

    (e) if $X \xrightarrow{*}_{\tilde{\delta}_D} (q_1^T, D_1)$ then $((q_2, X), D_2) \to (q^T, D) \in \tilde{\delta}_D$,

    (f) if $X \xrightarrow{*}_{\tilde{\delta}_D} ((q_1, X'), D_1)$ then $((q_2, X), D_2) \to ((q, X'), D) \in \tilde{\delta}_D$,

(α_5) if $||(q_1, q_2) \to q \in \delta \cup \delta_R$, then for every D_1, D_2, D such that $(D_1, D_2) \in_{||}$ D:

    (a) $||((q_1^T, D_1), (q_2^T, D_2)) \to (q^T, D) \in \tilde{\delta}_D$,

    (b) if $0 \xrightarrow{*}_{\tilde{\delta}_D} (q_1^T, D_1)$ then $(q_2^T, D_2) \to (q^T, D) \in \tilde{\delta}_D$,

    (c) if $0 \xrightarrow{*}_{\tilde{\delta}_D} (q_2^T, D_2)$ then $(q_1^T, D_1) \to (q^T, D) \in \tilde{\delta}_D$,

(α_6) if $q \to q' \in \delta \cup \delta_R$, then for every $D \in \mathcal{D}$, $(q^T, D) \to (q'^T, D) \in \tilde{\delta}_D$, and $((q, X), D) \to ((q', X), D) \in \tilde{\delta}_D$,

Note that the inference rules (α_2), (α_3), (α_4), and (α_5) construct a finite sequence of increasing sets of transitions $\tilde{\delta}_D^1 \subset \tilde{\delta}_D^2 \subset \ldots \subset \tilde{\delta}_D^n$. It is finite because there is a finite number of states and of possible transitions.

Then, we can show that:

Lemma 3. *For every $v \in T_p$, $q \in Q \cup Q_R$, and $D \in \mathcal{D}$, we have:*

- $v \xrightarrow{*}_{\tilde{\delta}_D} (q^T, D) \Rightarrow v \in \zeta_R^*[D](L_q)$,
- $v \xrightarrow{*}_{\tilde{\delta}_D} ((q, X), D) \Rightarrow$ *there exists a seq-context C, a rule $X \cdot Y \xrightarrow{a} t$ s.t. $C[Y] \in L_q$ and $v \in \zeta_R^*[D''](C[t])$, for some D'' such that there exists $D', a \in D', (D', D'') \in D$.*

Lemma 4. *For every $q \in Q \cup Q_R$, $u \in T_p$, and $D \in \mathcal{D}$,*

- $(\exists w \in D \mid u \in \zeta_R^*[w](L_q)) \Rightarrow (u \xrightarrow{*}_{\tilde{\delta}_D} (q^T, D))$,
- $(\exists w \in D$, *a seq-context C, a rule $X \cdot Y \xrightarrow{a} t, C[Y] \in L_q, w = aw', u \in \zeta_R^*[w'](C[t]))$ then $u \xrightarrow{*}_{\tilde{\delta}_D} ((q, X), D)$.*

Thus, we get:

Theorem 5. $\mathcal{A}_{\zeta_R}^*[D_0]$ *recognizes* $\zeta_R^*[D_0](L)$.

Let us give the intuition behind the construction. The automaton needs to recognize the term t_1 that has the form described in the right side of Figure 1 as a successor of the term t_2 of the left side of the figure. To do so, when annotating the subterm t_1, the automaton singles out an occurrence of "t" (or more precisely of a successor of "t"), and guesses that it comes from the application of a rule of the form $X \cdot Y \to t$. This guess has to be validated afterwards when reaching the root of the seq-context C. More precisely, the idea is the same as previously when we do not consider structural equivalences: (q^T, D) recognizes the successors of L_q by ζ_R after applying sequences of actions in D. The rules $(\alpha_1) - (\alpha_6)$ that do not involve states of the form $((q, X), D)$ have the same meaning than the rules $(1) - (6)$ of the previous construction. New states $((q, X), D)$ are needed to perform the guesses. A term u is labelled with $((q, X), D)$ if there exist a seq-context C and a rule $X \cdot Y \xrightarrow{a} t$ in R such that $C[Y] \in L_q$, and this PRS rule has been applied to $\cdot(X, C[Y])$ to obtain $C[t]$ first, and then u after several rewritings $(u \in \zeta_R^*[D'](C[t])$ such that $\exists D_0 \in \mathcal{D}$ s.t. $a \in D_0$ and $(D_0, D') \in D)$. This means that if there is a transition rule of the automaton of the form $\cdot(q', q) \to q''$ such that $X \xrightarrow{*}_{\tilde{\delta}_D} (q'^T, D_1)$ (i.e. $X \in \zeta_R^*[D_1](L_{q'})$), then we can validate the guess and infer that $u \in \zeta_R^*[D_2](L_{q''})$ such that $(D_1, D) \in D_2$. This is expressed by rules $(\alpha_4 e)$. Moreover, if $X \xrightarrow{*}_{\tilde{\delta}} ((q', X'), D_1)$, meaning that X can be obtained from $L_{q'}$ with a sequence in D_1 if there is an X' which has been consumed from the left neighbourhood, then we can validate the guess X, and keep the guess X', i.e., we can annotate u with $((q', X'), D_2)$. This is expressed by rules $(\alpha_4 f)$.

The guesses are done by rules (α_2). Rules $(\alpha_4 b)$ ensure that the context C where the guess is made is a seq-context.

The rules (α_3) mean that if $t_1 \xrightarrow{a} t_2$ is a rule of R, and if t_1 is a successor of L_q, then so are all the successors of t_2. These rules keep track of the guesses. Observe that we do not need states of the form (q^{nil}, D). This is due to the fact that rules $(\alpha_4 c)$, $(\alpha_4 d)$, $(\alpha_5 b)$, and $(\alpha_5 c)$ take into account the neutrality of 0. For example, rules $(\alpha_4 d)$ express that if $\cdot (q_1, q_2) \to q$ is a rule of δ, and 0 is a successor of q_1, then $\cdot (0, u)$, where u is a successor of q_2 is a successor of q. Since $\cdot (0, u) \sim_0 u$, this means that u is a successor of q. Thus, the automaton needs only to consider u as a successor of state q, it does not need to recognize $\cdot (0, u)$. Note that we could not do this in the construction of Theorem 2, because there, equivalences were not considered, so u and $\cdot (0, u)$ need to be considered as two separate terms.

7   Constrained Reachability Modulo $\sim$

As in the case of $\sim_s$, computing $post^*$- and pre^*-images modulo $\sim$ does not preserve regularity. Our purpose is to compute $\sim$-representatives of the reachability sets $Post^*_{R,\sim}[D](L)$ and $Pre^*_{R,\sim}[D](L)$ for every regular language L and decomposable language D. We show that if R is a PAD, i.e., if the rules of R have only sequential compositions in their left hand sides, then, for any regular language L and decomposable language D, one can effectively construct a finite tree automaton that recognizes a $\sim$-representative of $Post^*_{R,\sim}[D](L)$. This is due to the previous construction and to the following proposition:

Proposition 3. *Let R be a PAD system, L a regular tree language, and D a set of action constraints. Then $Post^*_{R,\sim}[D](L) = [\zeta^*_R[D](L)]_\sim$, and if L is compatible with $\sim_{||}$ then $Pre^*_{R,\sim}[D](L) = [\zeta^*_{R^{-1}}[D](L)]_\sim$.*

In [BT03], we showed how to compute a counter tree automaton (0-CTA) with a decidable emptiness problem to recognize a $\sim$-representative of $Pre^*_{R,\sim}[D](L)$ if D is decomposable and R is a PAD (i.e., even if L is not compatible with $\sim_{||}$). This construction can be extended and combined with the construction underlying Theorems 5 and 4 to provide a $\sim$-representative of $Pre^*_{R,\sim}[D](L)$ if R is a PAD and D is decomposable. We do not give the details here because of lack of space.

References

[ABT08]   Atig, M.F., Bouajjani, A., Touili, T.: On the reachability analysis of acyclic networks of pushdown systems. In: van Breugel, F., Chechik, M. (eds.) CONCUR 2008. LNCS, vol. 5201, pp. 356–371. Springer, Heidelberg (2008)

[BET03]   Bouajjani, A., Esparza, J., Touili, T.: A generic approach to the static analysis of concurrent programs with procedures. In: POPL, pp. 62–73 (2003)

[BET05]   Bouajjani, A., Esparza, J., Touili, T.: Reachability analysis of synchronized
           pa systems. Electr. Notes Theor. Comput. Sci. 138(3), 153–178 (2005)
[BMOT05]   Bouajjani, A., Müller-Olm, M., Touili, T.: Regular symbolic analysis of
           dynamic networks of pushdown systems. In: Abadi, M., de Alfaro, L. (eds.)
           CONCUR 2005. LNCS, vol. 3653, pp. 473–487. Springer, Heidelberg (2005)
[BMT01]   Bouajjani, A., Muscholl, A., Touili, T.: Permutation Rewriting and Algo-
           rithmic Verification. In: LICS. IEEE, Los Alamitos (2001)
[BMT07]   Bouajjani, A., Muscholl, A., Touili, T.: Permutation rewriting and algo-
           rithmic verification. Inf. Comput. 205(2), 199–224 (2007)
[BT03]   Bouajjani, A., Touili, T.: Reachability analysis of process rewrite sys-
           tems. In: Pandya, P.K., Radhakrishnan, J. (eds.) FSTTCS 2003. LNCS,
           vol. 2914, pp. 74–87. Springer, Heidelberg (2003)
[BT05]   Bouajjani, A., Touili, T.: On computing reachability sets of process rewrite
           systems. In: Giesl, J. (ed.) RTA 2005. LNCS, vol. 3467, pp. 484–499.
           Springer, Heidelberg (2005)
[CDG+97]   Comon, H., Dauchet, M., Gilleron, R., Jacquemard, F., Lugiez, D.,
           Tison, S., Tommasi, M.: Tree automata techniques and applications (1997),
           http://www.grappa.univ-lille3.fr/tata
[EK99]   Esparza, J., Knoop, J.: An automata-theoretic approach to interprocedural
           data-flow analysis. In: Thomas, W. (ed.) FOSSACS 1999. LNCS, vol. 1578,
           pp. 14–30. Springer, Heidelberg (1999)
[GD89]   Gilleron, R., Deruyver, A.: The reachability problem for ground TRS and
           some extensions. In: TAPSOFT, pp. 227–243 (1989)
[GP03]   Gómez, A.C., Pin, J.-E.: On a conjecture of schnoebelen. In: Ésik, Z.,
           Fülöp, Z. (eds.) DLT 2003. LNCS, vol. 2710, pp. 35–54. Springer,
           Heidelberg (2003)
[LS98]   Lugiez, D., Schnoebelen, P.: The regular viewpoint on PA-processes. In:
           Sangiorgi, D., de Simone, R. (eds.) CONCUR 1998. LNCS, vol. 1466,
           pp. 50–66. Springer, Heidelberg (1998)
[May98]   Mayr, R.: Decidability and Complexity of Model Checking Problems for
           Infinite-State Systems. Phd. thesis, Munich University (1998)
[PST07]   Patin, G., Sighireanu, M., Touili, T.: Spade: Verification of multithreaded
           dynamic and recursive programs. In: Damm, W., Hermanns, H. (eds.) CAV
           2007. LNCS, vol. 4590, pp. 254–257. Springer, Heidelberg (2007)
[RSJM05]   Reps, T.W., Schwoon, S., Jha, S., Melski, D.: Weighted pushdown systems
           and their application to interprocedural dataflow analysis. Sci. Comput.
           Program. 58(1-2), 206–263 (2005)
[Sch99]   Schnoebelen, P.: Decomposable regular languages and the shuffle operator.
           EATCS Bull 67, 283–289 (1999)
[Tou05]   Touili, T.: Dealing with communication for dynamic multithreaded recur-
           sive programs. In: VISSAS, pp. 213–227 (2005)

Input-Output Model Programs

Margus Veanes and Nikolaj Bjørner

Microsoft Research, Redmond, WA, USA
{margus,nbjorner}@microsoft.com

Abstract. Model programs are used as high-level behavioral specifications typically representing abstract state machines. For modeling reactive systems, one uses input-output model programs, where the action vocabulary is divided between two conceptual players: the input player and the output player. The players share the action vocabulary and make moves that are labeled by actions according to their respective model programs. Conformance between the two model programs means that the output (input) player only makes output (input) moves that are allowed by the input (output) players model program. In a bounded game, the total number of moves is fixed. Here model programs use a background theory $\mathcal{T}$ containing linear arithmetic, sets, and tuples. We formulate the bounded game conformance checking problem, or BGC, as a theorem proving problem modulo $\mathcal{T}$ and analyze its complexity.

1 Introduction

Model programs are typically used to describe protocol-like behavior of software systems, with the underlying update semantics based on abstract state machines or ASMs [17]. At Microsoft, model programs are used for model-based testing of public application-level network protocols in the Windows organization, as an integral part of the protocol quality assurance process [16]. In such models, the action vocabulary is often divided into controllable and observable actions, reflecting the testers point of view, i.e., what actions are controllable by the tester versus what actions are observable by the tester. The central problem is to determine if an implementation *conforms* to a given specification. In the presence of controllable and observable actions, the problem can be described as a game conformance checking problem, where the tester executes controllable actions and the implementation responds with observable actions. Traditionally, model-based conformance testing is a black-box testing technique where the actual implementation code is assumed to be unknown to the tester.

In this paper we look at the game conformance checking problem from the symbolic (or static) analysis point of view. The implementation is not a "black box" but a "gray box". In other words, the implementation is also assumed to be given as a model program through some abstraction function.

The general game conformance checking problem is very hard but can be approximated in various ways. A natural approximation is to bound the number of steps or moves that the players make. This corresponds directly to the fact

M. Leucker and C. Morgan (Eds.): ICTAC 2009, LNCS 5684, pp. 322–335, 2009.

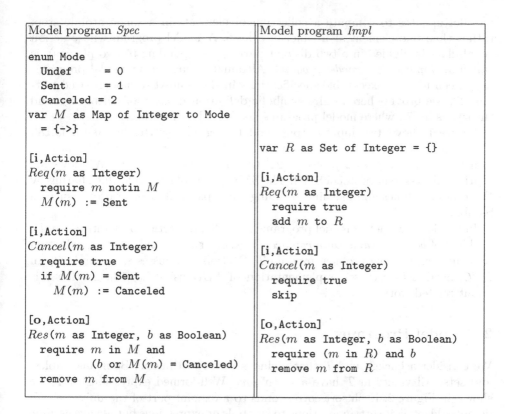

Model program *Spec*	Model program *Impl*

``
enum Mode
  Undef   = 0
  Sent   = 1
  Canceled = 2
var M as Map of Integer to Mode
  = {->}
 	
[i,Action]
Req(m as Integer)
  require m notin M
  M(m) := Sent
 	
[i,Action]
Cancel(m as Integer)
  require true
  if M(m) = Sent
    M(m) := Canceled
 	
[o,Action]
Res(m as Integer, b as Boolean)
  require m in M and
        (b or M(m) = Canceled)
  remove m from M
``
	``
	
	var R as Set of Integer = {}
	
	[i,Action]
	Req(m as Integer)
	  require true
	  add m to R
	
	[i,Action]
	Cancel(m as Integer)
	  require true
	  skip
	
	[o,Action]
	Res(m as Integer, b as Boolean)
	  require (m in R) and b
	  remove m from R
	``

Fig. 1. Here *Req* and *Cancel* are **i**-actions and *Res* is an **o**-action. The model program *Spec* specifies a request cancellation protocol. A request, identified by a message id m, can be Canceled at any time. A response must be associated to some pending request, where if b is false then the request must have been Canceled. The model program *Impl* describes a particular implementation that never cancels any requests, and responds to all requests in some arbitrary order.

that actual tests have a finite length. The problem we introduce and analyze in this paper is the *Bounded Game Conformance* problem of model programs, or BGC for short. We translate the problem into a theorem proving problem modulo a background theory that is most commonly needed in model programs, and analyze the complexity of the problem. For a class of model programs that are common in practice the problem is shown to be decidable. We also discuss a concrete analysis approach for BGC using a satisfiability modulo theories (SMT) based theorem prover Z3. The game conformance relation is based on alternating simulation [2]. We show that, under input enabledness, the **ioco** [23] conformance relation reduces to alternating simulation. It follows that symbolic bounded **ioco** checking can be reduced to BGC.

What differentiates model programs from traditional sequential programs is that model programs typically assume a rich background universe and often operate on a more abstract level, for example, they use set comprehensions and parallel updates to compute a collection of elements in a single atomic step, rather than one element at a time, in a loop. A model program whose action vocabulary is divided into two disjoint parts (corresponding to two players), is called an *input-output model program*. Although input-output model programs have been used as executable specifications in the context of model-based testing [27], we provide here a fully symbolic definition using a formal background theory, as in [7], where model programs need not be executable.

Figure 1 shows two input-output model programs written in AsmL [3,18]. The *Spec* model program in Figure 1 is an abstracted version of the cancellation feature in the SMB2 protocol [22] that is a successor of the Windows file sharing client-server protocol SMB. The SMB protocol is used for file sharing by Windows machines and machines running third party implementations, such as Samba.

In Section 2 we define model programs formally. In Section 3 we introduce the problem of *bounded game conformance checking* or *BGC* and show its reduction to a theorem proving problem modulo $\mathcal{T}$. Section 4 discusses the complexity of *BGC*. Section 5 discusses implementation of *BGC* using Z3 [13]. Section 6 is about related work.

2   Model Programs

We consider a background $\mathcal{T}$ that includes linear arithmetic, Booleans, tuples, and sets. All values in $\mathcal{T}$ have a given *sort*. Well-formed expressions of $\mathcal{T}$ are shown in Figure 2. Each sort corresponds to a disjoint part of the universe. We do not add explicit sort annotations to symbols or expressions but always assume that all expression are well-sorted. A value is *basic* if it is either a Boolean, an integer, or a tuple of basic values.

The expression $Ite(\varphi, t_1, t_2)$ equals t_1 if φ is true, and it equals t_2, otherwise. For each sort, there is a specific *Default* value in the background. In particular, for Booleans the value is *false*, for set sorts the value is $\emptyset$, for integers the value is 0 and for tuples the value is the tuple of defaults of the respective tuple elements.

The function *TheElementOf* maps every singleton set to the element in that set and maps every other set to *Default*. Note that *extensionality* of sets: $\forall v\, w\, (\forall y (y \in v \leftrightarrow y \in w) \rightarrow v = w)$, allows us to use set comprehensions as terms: the *comprehension term* $\{t(\bar{x}) \mid_{\bar{x}} \varphi(\bar{x})\}$ represents the set such that $\forall y (y \in \{t(\bar{x}) \mid_{\bar{x}} \varphi(\bar{x})\} \leftrightarrow \exists \bar{x}(t(\bar{x}) = y \wedge \varphi(\bar{x})))$.

Actions. There is a specific *action sort* $\mathbb{A}$, values of this sort are called *actions* and have the form $f(v_0, \ldots, v_{\mathrm{arity}(f)-1})$. *Default*$^{\mathbb{A}}$ has arity 0. Two actions are equal if and only if they have the same action symbol and their corresponding arguments are equal. An action $f(\bar{v})$ is called an *f-action*. Every action symbol f with arity $n > 0$, is associated with a unique *parameter variable* f_i for all i, $0 \le i < n$.[1]

---

[1] In AsmL one can of course use any formal parameter name, such as m in Figure 1, following standard conventions for method signatures.

$$T^\sigma \qquad\qquad ::= x^\sigma \mid Default^\sigma \mid Ite(T^\mathbb{B}, T^\sigma, T^\sigma) \mid TheElementOf(T^{\mathbb{S}(\sigma)}) \mid$$
$$\pi_i(T^{\sigma_0 \times \cdots \times \sigma_{i-1} \times \sigma \times \cdots \times \sigma_k})$$

$$T^{\sigma_0 \times \sigma_1 \times \cdots \times \sigma_k} ::= \langle T^{\sigma_0}, T^{\sigma_1}, \ldots, T^{\sigma_k} \rangle$$

$$T^\mathbb{Z} \qquad\qquad ::= k \mid T^\mathbb{Z} + T^\mathbb{Z} \mid k * T^\mathbb{Z}$$

$$T^\mathbb{B} \qquad\qquad ::= true \mid false \mid \neg T^\mathbb{B} \mid T^\mathbb{B} \wedge T^\mathbb{B} \mid T^\mathbb{B} \vee T^\mathbb{B} \mid T^\mathbb{B} \Rightarrow T^\mathbb{B} \mid \forall x\, T^\mathbb{B} \mid \exists x\, T^\mathbb{B} \mid$$
$$T^\sigma = T^\sigma \mid T^{\mathbb{S}(\sigma)} \subseteq T^{\mathbb{S}(\sigma)} \mid T^\sigma \in T^{\mathbb{S}(\sigma)} \mid T^\mathbb{Z} \leq T^\mathbb{Z}$$

$$T^{\mathbb{S}(\sigma)} \qquad\quad ::= \{T^\sigma \mid_{\bar{x}} T^\mathbb{B}\} \mid \emptyset^{\mathbb{S}(\sigma)} \mid T^{\mathbb{S}(\sigma)} \cup T^{\mathbb{S}(\sigma)} \mid T^{\mathbb{S}(\sigma)} \cap T^{\mathbb{S}(\sigma)} \mid T^{\mathbb{S}(\sigma)} \setminus T^{\mathbb{S}(\sigma)}$$

$$T^\mathbb{A} \qquad\qquad ::= f^{(\sigma_0, \ldots, \sigma_{n-1})}(T^{\sigma_0}, \ldots, T^{\sigma_{n-1}})$$

Fig. 2. Well-formed expressions in T. Sorts are shown explicitly here. An expression of sort σ is written T^σ. The sorts $\mathbb{Z}$ and $\mathbb{B}$ are for integers and Booleans, respectively, k stands for any integer constant, x^σ is a variable of sort σ. The sorts $\mathbb{Z}$ and $\mathbb{B}$ are *basic*, so is the *tuple sort* $\sigma_0 \times \cdots \times \sigma_k$, provided that each σ_i is basic. The *set sort* $\mathbb{S}(\sigma)$ is not basic and requires σ to be basic. All quantified variables are required to have basic sorts. The sort $\mathbb{A}$ is called the *action sort*, $f^{(\sigma_0, \ldots, \sigma_{n-1})}$ stands for an *action symbol* with fixed arity n and argument sorts $\sigma_0, \ldots, \sigma_{n-1}$, where each argument sort is a set sort or a basic sort. The sort $\mathbb{A}$ is *not* basic. The only atomic relation that can be used for $T^\mathbb{A}$ is equality. *Default*$^\mathbb{A}$ is a nullary action symbol. Boolean expressions are also called *formulas* in the context of T. In the paper, sort annotations are mostly omitted but are always assumed.

An *assignment* is a pair $x := t$ where x is a variable and t is a term (both having the same sort). An *update rule* is a finite set of assignments where the assigned variables are distinct. In the following definition, internal non-determinism of model programs (through choice variables [7]) is excluded, the initial state condition is omitted, and all state variables must be updated by each action. The last two restrictions are without loss of generality, and allow us to provide a simplified view of the definitions.

Definition 1 (Input-Output Model Program). *Input-output model program is a tuple* $P = (\Sigma, \Gamma^\mathrm{i}, \Gamma^\mathrm{o}, R)$, *where*

- Σ *is a finite set of variables called* state variables;
- Γ^i *is a finite set of* **i**-*action symbols*;
- Γ^o *is a finite set of* **o**-*action symbols*, $\Gamma^\mathrm{i} \cap \Gamma^\mathrm{o} = \emptyset$;
- R *is a collection* $\{R_f\}_{f \in \Gamma^\mathrm{i} \cup \Gamma^\mathrm{o}}$ *of action rules* $R_f = (\gamma, U)$, *where*
  - γ *is a formula called the* guard of f;
  - U *is an update rule* $\{x := t_x\}_{x \in \Sigma}$, *called the* update rule of f.

  All free variables in R_f *must be in* $\Sigma \cup \{f_i\}_{i < \mathrm{arity}(f)}$.

We often say *action* to also mean an action rule or an action symbol, if the intent is clear from the context. In the following, we say model program for input-output model program. The following special class of model programs is important when considering analysis.

Definition 2 (Basic Model Programs). A model program is *basic* if all parameter variables in it are basic.

Standard *ASM update rules* can be translated into update rules of model programs. A detailed translation from standard ASMs to model programs is given in [7]. In the general case, model programs also use *maps*, e.g., M is a map in *Spec* in Figure 1, that are used to represent dynamic functions of ASMs. In $\mathcal{T}$, maps are represented by their graphs as sets of pairs, see [7].

States. A *state* is a mapping of variables to values. Given a state S and an expression E, where S maps all the free variables in E to values, E^S is the *evaluation of E in S*. Given a state S and a formula φ, $S \models \varphi$ means that φ is true in S. A formula φ is *valid* (in $\mathcal{T}$) if φ is true in all states. *Since $\mathcal{T}$ is assumed to be the background theory we usually omit it, and assume that each state also has an implicit part that satisfies $\mathcal{T}$.* In the following let $P = (\Sigma, \Gamma^{\mathrm{i}}, \Gamma^{\mathrm{o}}, R)$ be a fixed model program.

Definition 3. An action $a = f(v_0, \ldots, v_{n-1})$ is *enabled* in a state S if $S' = S \cup \{f_i \mapsto v_i\}_{i<n}$ satisfies the guard of f. If a is enabled in S then a *causes a transition* from S to the state $S_1 = \{x \mapsto t_x^{S'}\}_{x \in \Sigma}$, denoted by $S \xrightarrow{a} S_1$.

An *input-output labeled transition system* or *LTS* for short is a tuple $(\mathbf{S}, S^0, L^{\mathrm{i}}, L^{\mathrm{o}}, T)$, where $\mathbf{S}$ is a set of *states*, $S^0 \in \mathbf{S}$ is an *initial state*, $L = L^{\mathrm{i}} \cup L^{\mathrm{o}}$ is a set of *labels*, where $L^{\mathrm{i}} \cap L^{\mathrm{o}} = \emptyset$, and $T \subseteq \mathbf{S} \times L \times \mathbf{S}$ is a *transition relation*.

Definition 4. $[\![P]\!]$ is the LTS $(\mathbf{S}, S^0, L^{\mathrm{i}}, L^{\mathrm{o}}, T)$; $S^0 = \{x \mapsto \mathit{Default}\}_{x \in \Sigma}$; L^{i} (L^{o}) is the set of all actions over Γ^{i} (Γ^{o}); T and $\mathbf{S}$ are the least sets such that, $S^0 \in \mathbf{S}$, and if $S \in \mathbf{S}$ and $S \xrightarrow{a} S_1$ then $S_1 \in \mathbf{S}$ and $(S, a, S_1) \in T$.

Given an action sequence $\alpha = (a_0, \ldots, a_{k-1})$ and transitions $S_i \xrightarrow{a_i} S_{i+1}$ for $0 \le i < k$, of an LTS, we write $S_0 \xrightarrow{\alpha} S_k$. If S_0 is the initial state then α is called a *trace* of the LTS. The set of all traces of $[\![P]\!]$ is denoted by *Traces*(P).

3   Bounded Game Conformance

The basic notion of conformance between two (input-output) model programs is based on the notion of *alternating simulation* between two LTSs. Definition 5 below is consistent with [11], and is based on [2]. The definition makes the assumption that the LTSs are *deterministic*, i.e., for any two transitions $S \xrightarrow{a} S'$ and $S \xrightarrow{a} S''$, $S' = S''$. Thus, LTSs are viewed here as *interface automata* [12] and the transition relation becomes a transition function. Note that $[\![P]\!]$ is deterministic for a model program P.[2] Let $M_i = (\mathbf{S}_i, S_i^0, L^{\mathrm{i}}, L^{\mathrm{o}}, T_i)$, for $i = 1, 2$, be deterministic LTSs. The intuition behind the following definition is that M_1 can only make outputs that M_2 can make, and M_2 can only make inputs that M_1 can make.

---

[2] This is not the case when choice variables are allowed in model programs.

Definition 5 ($\preceq$). $M_1 \preceq M_2$ iff there exists an alternating simulation ρ from M_1 to M_2 such that $(S_1^0, S_2^0) \in \rho$, where an *alternating simulation from M_1 to M_2* is a relation $\rho \subseteq \mathbf{S}_1 \times \mathbf{S}_2$ such that, for all $(S_1, S_2) \in \rho$:

- For all $a \in L^o$, if $S_1 \xrightarrow{a} S_1'$ then $S_2 \xrightarrow{a} S_2'$ and $(S_1', S_2') \in \rho$.
- For all $a \in L^i$, if $S_2 \xrightarrow{a} S_2'$ then $S_1 \xrightarrow{a} S_1'$ and $(S_1', S_2') \in \rho$.

Example 1. Consider the following two model programs, where $s^0 := \emptyset$ is the initial and only state, and *in* and *out* are nullary action symbols.

$$Spec_{trivial} = (\emptyset, \{in\}, \{out\}, \{(false, \emptyset)_{in}, (true, \emptyset)_{out}\})$$
$$Impl_{trivial} = (\emptyset, \{in\}, \{out\}, \{(true, \emptyset)_{in}, (false, \emptyset)_{out}\})$$
$$[\![Spec_{trivial}]\!] = (\{s^0\}, s^0, \{in\}, \{out\}, \{(s^0, out, s^0)\})$$
$$[\![Impl_{trivial}]\!] = (\{s^0\}, s^0, \{in\}, \{out\}, \{(s^0, in, s^0)\})$$

Clearly $[\![Impl_{trivial}]\!] \preceq [\![Spec_{trivial}]\!]$ and $[\![Spec_{trivial}]\!] \not\preceq [\![Impl_{trivial}]\!]$. $\boxtimes$

The following characterization of $\preceq$ in terms of traces, follows from Definition 5 and is used below.

Lemma 1. *$N \not\preceq M$ iff there exists a trace α that is a trace of both N and M, and there is an o-label (i-label) a such that (α, a) is a trace of N (M) but not a trace of M (N).*

For symbolic analysis, we are primarily interested in the approximations $\preceq_n$ of $\preceq$ where the depth $n \geq 0$ is bounded.

Definition 6 ($\preceq_n$). $M_1 \preceq_n M_2 \overset{\text{def}}{=} M_1 \preceq_n^{(S_1^0, S_2^0)} M_2$ where $M_1 \preceq_n^{(S_1, S_2)} M_2$ iff, either $n = 0$, or the following holds:

- For all $a \in L^o$, if $S_1 \xrightarrow{a} S_1'$ then $S_2 \xrightarrow{a} S_2'$ and $M_1 \preceq_{n-1}^{(S_1', S_2')} M_2$.
- For all $a \in L^i$, if $S_2 \xrightarrow{a} S_2'$ then $S_1 \xrightarrow{a} S_1'$ and $M_1 \preceq_{n-1}^{(S_1', S_2')} M_2$.

It follows easily from the definitions that $M_1 \preceq M_2$ iff $M_1 \preceq_n M_2$ for all $n \geq 0$.

Let P and Q be fixed model programs with the same action vocabularies.

Definition 7. *Q n-refines P, $Q \preceq_n P$, iff $[\![Q]\!] \preceq_n [\![P]\!]$.*

Intuitively, when P is a specification model program and Q is an implementation model program and $Q \preceq_n P$, then Q behaves as expected by P within n steps. Such bounded refinement (or a generalization of it with object-bindings) is used as the underlying notion of conformance in testing of reactive systems in [27], in particular, it is checked in the context of online testing [28]. The bound is due to the fact that tests are finite.

Example 2. Let *Impl* and *Spec* be as in Figure 1. One can show that *Impl* $\preceq_n$ *Spec* for all n and thus *Impl* $\preceq$ *Spec*. It is also the case that *Spec* $\preceq_1$ *Impl* but *Spec* $\not\preceq_2$ *Impl*; for example the trace $(Req(1), Req(1))$ is a trace of *Impl* but not a trace of *Spec*. $\boxtimes$

Definition 8 (BGC). *Bounded Game Conformance* problem or *BGC* is the problem of deciding if $Q \preceq_k P$.

In order to reduce BGC into a theorem proving problem, we construct a special formula from given P, Q and n, as defined in Definition 9. Given an expression E and a step number $i > 0$, we write $E[i]$ below for a copy of E where each (unbound) variable x in E has been uniquely renamed to a variable $x[i]$. We assume also that $E[0]$ is E. The intuition for the notation P_i and P_o below is that P_i is the "owner" of i-actions (P_i is the specification), and P_o is the "owner" of o-actions (P_o is the implementation).

Definition 9 (BGC Formula). Let P_i and P_o be model programs $(\overline{x_\star}, \Gamma^i, \Gamma^o, (\gamma_{f,\star}, U_{f,\star})_{f \in \Gamma^i \cup \Gamma^o})$, for $\star = P_i, P_o$. Assume that $\overline{x_{P_i}} \cap \overline{x_{P_o}} = \emptyset$.[3] Let $\widehat{i} = o$ and $\widehat{o} = i$. The *BGC formula* for P_i, P_o, and n is:

$$BGC(P_o, P_i, n) \overset{\text{def}}{=} (\overline{x_{P_o}} = \overline{Default} \wedge \overline{x_{P_i}} = \overline{Default}) \Rightarrow Ref(0, n)$$

$$Ref(n, n) \overset{\text{def}}{=} true$$

$$(i < n)\ Ref(i, n) \overset{\text{def}}{=} \bigwedge_{p \in \{i, o\}} \bigwedge_{f \in \Gamma^p} (act[i] = f(\overline{f[i]}) \Rightarrow \psi_1(i, n, p, f))$$

$$\psi_1(i, n, p, f) \overset{\text{def}}{=} \gamma_{f, P_p}[i] \Rightarrow (\gamma_{f, P_{\widehat{p}}}[i] \wedge \psi_2(i, n, p, f))$$

$$\psi_2(i, n, p, f) \overset{\text{def}}{=} \Big(\bigwedge_{x := t \in U_{f, P_p} \cup U_{f, P_{\widehat{p}}}} x[i+1] = t[i] \Big) \Rightarrow Ref(i+1, n)$$

where $\overline{f[i]} = f_0[i] \ldots f_{\text{arity}(f)-1}[i]$ are the parameter variables of action f for step i.[4] For each step number i, there is an additional variable $act[i]$ of sort $\mathbb{A}$ that records the selected action for step i.

Note that all parameter variables have distinct names in each step. The only connection between the steps happens via the state variables. Note also that the resulting formula is a universal formula, assuming that the guards and the update rules do not involve quantifiers (e.g. in comprehensions), i.e., in prenex form, all the quantifiers for the parameter variables are universal. This implies that the negation of the *BGC* formula is well suited for non-BGC checking of basic model programs (where the state variables can be eliminated) using satisfiability modulo $\mathcal{T}$. The sole purpose of the action variables is to enable easy extraction of the action sequence as a witness of the refinement violation.

The following theorem allows us to prove n-refinement by proving that the BGC formula is valid in $\mathcal{T}$.

Theorem 1. $BGC(P_o, P_i, n)$ *is valid in* $\mathcal{T}$ *iff* $P_o \preceq_n P_i$.

Proof (Sketch). The case $n = 0$ is trivial. Assume $n > 0$. Both directions are proved separately. For the direction ($\Longrightarrow$) we assume that $P_o \not\preceq_n P_i$ and get a

---

[3] Or just rename the state variables.
[4] Note that the parameter variables of f are shared between P_i and P_o.

shortest run of length $l \leq n$ where the last action is either a i-action that is enabled in P_i but not in P_o (or an o-action that is enabled in P_o but not in P_i). From this run we can construct a state that satisfies $\neg BGC(P_o, P_i, n)$, using the property that if $\neg BGC(P_o, P_i, l)$ is satisfiable then $\neg BGC(P_o, P_i, l')$ is also satisfiable, for $l' > l$ (because if $\gamma_{f,P_{\hat{p}}}[l]$ is false then so is $\gamma_{f,P_{\hat{p}}}[l] \wedge \psi_2$). The proof of ($\Longleftarrow$) is similar. $\boxtimes$

Relation to BMPC. There is an alternative way how $\preceq_n$ can be analyzed: by reducing $\npreceq_n$ to the BMPC problem [7]. *BMPC* is the problem: given a model program P, a reachability condition φ and step bound k, does there exist a trace α of length at most k such that $S_{[\![P]\!]}^0 \xrightarrow{\alpha} S$ and $S \models \varphi$.

For this reduction we use *product* of model programs. Let P_i, for $i = 1, 2$, be the model program $(\Sigma_i, \Gamma^i, \Gamma^o, \{(\gamma_{f,i}, U_{f,i})\}_{f \in \Gamma})$, where Σ_1 and Σ_2 are disjoint and $\Gamma = \Gamma^i \cup \Gamma^o$.

$$P_1 \otimes P_2 \stackrel{\text{def}}{=} (\Sigma_1 \cup \Sigma_2, \Gamma^i, \Gamma^o, \{(\gamma_{f,1} \wedge \gamma_{f,2}, U_{f,1} \cup U_{f,2})_{f \in \Gamma}\})$$

The following property holds for the product construction.

Lemma 2. $Traces(P_1 \otimes P_2) = Traces(P_1) \cap Traces(P_2)$.

Define the *game conformance invariant* as the following formula:

$$Inv_{\preceq}(P_1, P_2) \stackrel{\text{def}}{=} \forall (\bigwedge_{f \in \Gamma^o} (\gamma_{f,1} \Rightarrow \gamma_{f,2})) \wedge (\bigwedge_{f \in \Gamma^i} (\gamma_{f,2} \Rightarrow \gamma_{f,1}))$$

Theorem 2. $P_1 \npreceq_n P_2$ iff $\neg Inv_{\preceq}(P_1, P_2)$ is reachable in $P_1 \otimes P_2$ within n steps.

Proof. ($\Longrightarrow$) Assume $P_1 \npreceq_n P_2$. By Lemma 1 there is a trace α of length m of some $m < n$ such that $\alpha \in Traces(P_1)$ and $\alpha \in Traces(P_2)$ and there is either an output action a such that (α, a) is in $Traces(P_1)$ but not in $Traces(P_2)$ or an input action a such that (α, a) is in $Traces(P_2)$ but not in $Traces(P_1)$. It follows that $Inv_{\preceq}(P_1, P_2)$ must be false in the state reached by α. Moreover $\alpha \in Traces(P_1 \otimes P_2)$, by Lemma 2. Proof of ($\Longleftarrow$) is similar to ($\Longrightarrow$), by using Lemma 2 and Lemma 1. $\boxtimes$

Relation to **ioco**. A common notion of conformance that is used for testing reactive systems is **ioco** [23] that stands for input-output conformance. There are also several variations of **ioco**, discussed in [23], that are used for testing various extensions of reactive systems. Here we only look at basic **ioco** and consider traces that exclude *quiescence* δ.

The rationale behind excluding δ as a special action is that, in a model program, δ can be defined as a nullary o-action with an empty update rule[5] and a guard that is the negation of the existential closure of the conjunction of the guards of all the other o-actions. Thus, δ is enabled in a state S iff no other o-action is enabled in S and $S \xrightarrow{\delta} S$. Let P^δ denote a model program where δ is defined in this way.

---

[5] An empty update rule is equivalent to the trivial update rule $\{x := x\}_{x \in \Sigma}$.

Example 3. Consider the model program *Impl* in Figure 1, where *Res* is the only **o**-action. In $Impl^\delta$, δ has the guard $\neg \exists m\, b\, (m \in R \wedge b)$, that is equivalent to $R = \emptyset$. Similarly, in $Spec^\delta$, δ has the guard $M = \emptyset$.

An LTS M is *input-enabled* if in all states in M that are reachable from the initial state, all **i**-labels are enabled.[6] For example, *Impl* in Figure 1 is input-enabled. The following definition of **ioco** is consistent with the definition in [23] (provided that δ is defined as above).

Definition 10 (ioco). *Let M and N be LTSs over the same **i**-labels and **o**-labels. Assume N is input-enabled. N **ioco** M iff, for all traces α of M, if there is an **o**-label a such that (α, a) is a trace of N then (α, a) is a trace of M.*

The relationship between **ioco** and $\preceq$ has been somewhat unclear in the testing community (see for example the discussion in [28]). In our context, $\preceq$ is a generalization of **ioco**. The particular advantage of using $\preceq$ instead of **ioco** is that $\preceq$ is compositional. The definition of $\preceq$ can also be generalized to non-deterministic LTSs, in such a way that the theorem holds when P and Q include choice variables.

Theorem 3. *If $[\![Q]\!]$ is input-enabled then $[\![Q]\!]$ **ioco** $[\![P]\!] \Longleftrightarrow Q \preceq P$.*

Proof. By Lemma 1 and the assumption that $[\![Q]\!]$ is input-enabled. The assumption is needed for the direction $\Longrightarrow$.   ⊠

For the *bounded* version of **ioco** we restrict the length of the traces by a given bound n so that all traces in Definition 10 have a length that is at most n; denoted here by **ioco**$_n$. We get the following corollary of Theorem 1 and Theorem 3.

Corollary 1. *If $[\![Q]\!]$ is **i**-enabled then, $BGC(Q, P, n)$ is valid in $\mathcal{T}$ iff $[\![Q]\!]$ **ioco**$_n$ $[\![P]\!]$.*

4   Complexity of BGC

The general BGC problem over arbitrary model programs is highly undecidable. This follows from the well-known result that the validity problem of formulas in Presburger arithmetic with unary relations is Π_1^1-complete [1,19]. Using this result, it is enough to consider model programs that have one action with a single set-valued parameter and a linear arithmetic formula as the guard. To show inclusion in Π_1^1, one can use the same argument that is used in [7] to show that the BMPC problem is in Σ_1^1.

Corollary 2. *BGC is Π_1^1-complete.*

Even when all sets in the background are required to be finite the validity problem in $\mathcal{T}$ over finite sets is still co-re-complete [7].

---

[6] Such LTSs are called *input-output transition systems* in [23].

Corollary 3. *BGC over finite sets is co-re-complete.*

Even though the general BGC problem is undecidable, we are primarily concerned about practical applications. In most model programs, such as the ones in Figure 1, that are used to specify protocols (see also [21,30]), the actions typically only use *basic* parameters, i.e., parameters whose sort is not a set sort. In other words, our main target for analysis are *basic* model programs (recall Definition 2).

Theorem 4. *BGC of basic model programs is decidable. Moreover, the upper bound of the computational complexity is $2^{2^{2^{cn}}}$ and the lower bound is $2^{2^{cn}}$, where c is a constant and n is the size of the input (P, Q, k).*

Proof (Sketch). Consider the formula $\psi = BGC(Q, P, k)$. First, the formula ψ is translated into logic without sets but with unary relations, by replacing set variables with unary relations and by eliminating set comprehensions and set operations in the usual way, e.g., $t \in S$, where S is a set variable, becomes the atom $R_S(t)$, where R_S is a unary relation symbol. Let the resulting formula be φ. Next, introduce auxiliary predicates that define all the subformulas of φ, by applying the Tseitin transformation [24] to φ. Subsequently, eliminate those auxiliary predicates (as a form of de-Skolemization), by introducing additional quantifiers. (A similar elimination technique that can be used here follows from [15, p 129], see also [25]). The overall reduction implies that the computational complexity of BGC of basic model programs, regarding both the lower and the upper bound, is the same as that of Presburger arithmetic [15]. ☒

A naïve implementation of definition 9 could repeat the recursive calls to an exponential number of times. However, note that the results are all shared common sub-expressions.

From a practical perspective, the actual computational complexity of BGC over basic model programs problem depends on the quantifier alternation depth. In many problems the final formula is universal, because quantifiers are not used inside guards or update rules.

5   Implementation

We created a prototype for testing the Bounded Game Conformance formulas generated from definition 9[7]. The prototype uses the F# programmatic interface to the state-of-the art SMT solver Z3 [13] to represent Input-Output Model Programs as a collection of transition pairs. Each pair consists of a specification and an implementation transition and is tagged as either **i** or **o** to indicate which direction to check the alternating simulation. The data-types used in the model program are mapped directly to native Z3 theories. For example, the **Mode** enumeration type is mapped into a special case of algebraic data-types where enumerations are encoded as nullary constructors.

---

[7] See http://research.microsoft.com/en-us/people/nbjorner/ictac09.zip

The finite map M is represented as an array, and the theory of extensional arrays is used to handle the operations on M. Similarly, the set R is represented as an array that maps integers to Booleans. The operations, element-wise addition and removal required by Req and Res) are simply array updates. Z3 supports richer set operations as an extension to the theory of arrays, but this example does not make use of these. The prototype uses the fact that terms in Z3 are internally repre-

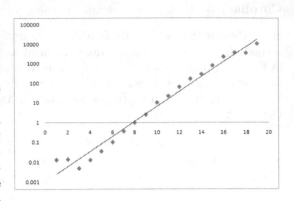

Fig. 3. Timing $BGC(P_o, P_i, n)$, $n = 1..19$

sented as shared directed acyclic graphs. In particular, the repeated occurrences of $Ref(i+1, n)$ represent the same formula. The formula is built only once, and reused in the different occurrences. The size of the resulting path formula is therefore proportional to the number of unfoldings n and to the size of the input model program.

On the other hand, the size of the input does not depend on the size of the state space. The potentially unbounded size of the state space is also not a factor when checking for bounded game conformance, but our techniques are sensitive to the number of paths in the unfoldings. Figure 3 shows the number of seconds it took Z3 to check for conformance for up to 19 unfoldings for our example in Figure 1. We observe that the time overhead grows exponen-

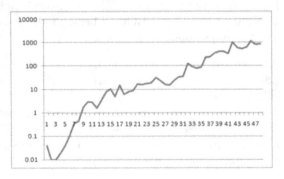

Fig. 4. Timing $Inv_{\preceq}(P_1, P_2)$, $n = 1..47$

tially with the number of unfoldings n (so linear in the number of paths that are checked). Not shown is the space overhead, which was very modest: space consumption during solving grew linearly with n, from 12 MB to around 20 MB. Figure 4 shows the similar timings required for checking the equivalent property $Inv_{\preceq}(P_1, P_2)$ for the BMPC formulation. The overhead of checking the invariant in this formulation is still exponential, but the growth is much slower and it is therefore possible to explore up to 47 unfoldings, with each check taking less than 20 minutes.

A more interesting use of bounded conformance checking is to detect bugs in the models used for either the specifications or implementations. We can *plant* a bug in our example from Figure 1 by changing the *Impl* transition *Res* to forget removing m from R. The bogus transition is therefore:

```
[o,Action]
Res(m as Integer, b as Boolean)
  require (m in R) and b
  skip
```

It takes Z3 well below a second to create a counter-example of length 3. Since the $BGC(P_o, P_i, n)$ formula contains equalities that track which actions are taken together with their parameters, it is easy to use Z3's model-producing facilities to extract the counter-example:

```
actions0 -> (req 1)
actions1 -> (res 1 true)
actions2 -> (res 1 true)
```

The counter-example says that the client request (*Req*) action is applied with input 1, followed by two server responses (*Res*) using the same parameter 1. The *Spec* model program is not enabled in response to this second action.

6 Related Work

BGC is related to the bounded model program checking problem or BMPC [7,26,29], that is a bounded path exploration problem of a given model program. BMPC is a generalization of bounded model checking to model programs. The technique of bounded model checking by using SAT solving was introduced in [4] and the extension to SMT was introduced in [14]. BMPC reduces to satisfiability modulo $\mathcal{T}$. BMPC can be reduced in polynomial time to BGC, providing the computational complexity bounds for BMPC, using Theorem 4, that are left open in [7]. Unlike BGC, the BCC [25] problem introduces k-depth quantifier alternation in the resulting formula, where k is the step bound. This is also the case for a generalization of BGC for non-deterministic model programs, in which case the reduction to BMPC, shown in Section 3, does not work. The resulting formula for a BMPC problem does not have quantifier alternation, even for non-deterministic model programs, since choice variables and parameter variables are treated equally.

Symbolic analysis of refinement relations through theorem proving are used in hardware [10,9]. Various refinement problems between specifications are also the topic of many analysis tools, where sets and maps are used as foundational data structures, such as ASMs, RAISE, Z, TLA+, B, see [5], where the techniques introduced here could be applied. In some cases, like in RAISE, the underlying logic is three-valued. In many of the formalisms, frame conditions need to be specified explicitly, and are not implicit as in the case of model programs or ASMs. In Alloy [20], the analysis is reduced to SAT, by finitizing the data types. In our case we bound the search depth rather than the size of the data types.

For implementation, we use the state of the art SMT solver Z3 [13], discussed in Section 5. Implementation of the reduction of BGC of basic input-output model programs to linear arithmetic, based on Theorem 4, is future work. In that context the reduction to Z3 can take advantage of built-in support for *Ite* terms, sets, algebraic data-types, and tuples. The background theory $\mathcal{T}$ can also be extended to include reals, that are natively supported in Z3. Our experiment indicated that Z3 could be used for modest bounded exploration. More interestingly, it posed an intriguing challenge for solvers like Z3 to better handle *diamond* structured formulas. One technique for handling *diamond* style formulas is explored in [6]. It uses a combination of abstract interpretation and constraint propagation to speed up the underlying constraint solving engine.

We see conformance from a game point of view, that view is inspired by [11]. The game view can also be used to formulate other problems related to input-output model programs, such as finding winning strategies to reach certain goal states. In the context of testing, a overview of using games is given in [31]. Game based testing approaches with finite model programs are also discussed in [8] using reachability games.

References

1. Alur, R., Henzinger, T.A.: A really temporal logic. In: Proc. 30th Symp. on Foundations of Computer Science, pp. 164–169 (1989)
2. Alur, R., Henzinger, T.A., Kupferman, O., Vardi, M.: Alternating refinement relations. In: Sangiorgi, D., de Simone, R. (eds.) CONCUR 1998. LNCS, vol. 1466, pp. 163–178. Springer, Heidelberg (1998)
3. AsmL, http://research.microsoft.com/fse/AsmL/
4. Biere, A., Cimatti, A., Clarke, E., Zhu, Y.: Symbolic model checking without BDDs. In: Cleaveland, W.R. (ed.) TACAS 1999. LNCS, vol. 1579, pp. 193–207. Springer, Heidelberg (1999)
5. Bjørner, D., Henson, M. (eds.): Logics of Specification Languages. Springer, Heidelberg (2008)
6. Bjørner, N., Dutertre, B., de Moura, L.: Accelerating Lemma Learning using Joins - DPPL(Join). In: Proceedings of short papers at LPAR 2008 (2008)
7. Bjørner, N., Gurevich, Y., Schulte, W., Veanes, M.: Symbolic bounded model checking of abstract state machines. Technical Report MSR-TR-2009-14, Microsoft Research (February 2009) (submitted to IJSI)
8. Blass, A., Gurevich, Y., Nachmanson, L., Veanes, M.: Play to test. Technical Report MSR-TR-2005-04, Microsoft Research (January 2005) Short version appears. In: Grieskamp, W., Weise, C. (eds.) FATES 2005. LNCS, vol. 3997, pp. 32–46. Springer, Heidelberg (2006)
9. Bryant, R.E., German, S.M., Velev, M.N.: Exploiting positive equality in a logic of equality with uninterpreted functions. In: Halbwachs, N., Peled, D.A. (eds.) CAV 1999. LNCS, vol. 1633, pp. 470–482. Springer, Heidelberg (1999)
10. Burch, J.R., Dill, D.L.: Automatic verification of pipelined microprocessor control. In: Dill, D.L. (ed.) CAV 1994. LNCS, vol. 818, pp. 68–80. Springer, Heidelberg (1994)
11. de Alfaro, L.: Game models for open systems. In: Dershowitz, N. (ed.) Verification: Theory and Practice. LNCS, vol. 2772, pp. 269–289. Springer, Heidelberg (2004)

12. de Alfaro, L., Henzinger, T.A.: Interface automata. In: ESEC/FSE, pp. 109–120. ACM Press, New York (2001)
13. de Moura, L., Bjørner, N.S.: Z3: An efficient SMT solver. In: Ramakrishnan, C.R., Rehof, J. (eds.) TACAS 2008. LNCS, vol. 4963, pp. 337–340. Springer, Heidelberg (2008)
14. de Moura, L., Rueß, H., Sorea, M.: Lazy theorem proving for bounded model checking over infinite domains. In: Voronkov, A. (ed.) CADE 2002. LNCS, vol. 2392, pp. 438–455. Springer, Heidelberg (2002)
15. Fisher, M.J., Rabin, M.O.: Super-exponential complexity of presburger arithmetic. In: Caviness, B.F., Johnson, J.R. (eds.) Quantifier Elimination and Cylindrical Algebraic Decomposition, pp. 122–135. Springer, Heidelberg (1998); Reprint from SIAM-AMS Proceedings, vol. VII, pp. 27–41 (1974)
16. Grieskamp, W., MacDonald, D., Kicillof, N., Nandan, A., Stobie, K., Wurden, F.: Model-based quality assurance of Windows protocol documentation. In: First International Conference on Software Testing, Verification and Validation, ICST, Lillehammer, Norway (April 2008)
17. Gurevich, Y.: Evolving Algebras 1993: Lipari Guide. In: Specification and Validation Methods, pp. 9–36. Oxford University Press, Oxford (1995)
18. Gurevich, Y., Rossman, B., Schulte, W.: Semantic essence of AsmL. Theor. Comput. Sci. 343(3), 370–412 (2005)
19. Halpern, J.Y.: Presburger arithmetic with unary predicates is Π_1^1 complete. Journal of Symbolic Logic 56, 637–642 (1991)
20. Jackson, D.: Software Abstractions. MIT Press, Cambridge (2006)
21. Jacky, J., Veanes, M., Campbell, C., Schulte, W.: Model-based Software Testing and Analysis with C#. Cambridge University Press, Cambridge (2008)
22. SMB2 (2008), http://msdn2.microsoft.com/en-us/library/cc246482.aspx
23. Tretmans, J.: Model based testing with labelled transition systems. In: Hierons, R.M., Bowen, J.P., Harman, M. (eds.) FORTEST. LNCS, vol. 4949, pp. 1–38. Springer, Heidelberg (2008)
24. Tseitin, G.S.: On the complexity of derivations in the propositional calculus. Studies in Mathematics and Mathematical Logic, Part II, 115–125 (1968)
25. Veanes, M., Bjørner, N.: Symbolic bounded conformance checking of model programs. Technical Report MSR-TR-2009-28, Microsoft Research (March 2009)
26. Veanes, M., Bjørner, N., Raschke, A.: An SMT approach to bounded reachability analysis of model programs. In: Suzuki, K., Higashino, T., Yasumoto, K., El-Fakih, K. (eds.) FORTE 2008. LNCS, vol. 5048, pp. 53–68. Springer, Heidelberg (2008)
27. Veanes, M., Campbell, C., Grieskamp, W., Schulte, W., Tillmann, N., Nachmanson, L.: Model-based testing of object-oriented reactive systems with Spec Explorer. In: Hierons, R.M., Bowen, J.P., Harman, M. (eds.) FORTEST. LNCS, vol. 4949, pp. 39–76. Springer, Heidelberg (2008)
28. Veanes, M., Campbell, C., Schulte, W., Tillmann, N.: Online testing with model programs. In: ESEC/FSE-13, pp. 273–282. ACM Press, New York (2005)
29. Veanes, M., Saabas, A.: On bounded reachability of programs with set comprehensions. In: Cervesato, I., Veith, H., Voronkov, A. (eds.) LPAR 2008. LNCS, vol. 5330, pp. 305–317. Springer, Heidelberg (2008)
30. Veanes, M., Saabas, A., Bjørner, N.: Bounded reachability of model programs. Technical Report MSR-TR-2008-81, Microsoft Research (May 2008)
31. Yannakakis, M.: Testing, optimization, and games. In: Proceedings of the Nineteenth Annual IEEE Symposium on Logic In Computer Science, LICS 2004, pp. 78–88. IEEE, Los Alamitos (2004)

IMITATOR: A Tool for Synthesizing Constraints on Timing Bounds of Timed Automata*

Étienne André

LSV – ENS de Cachan & CNRS, France

Abstract. We present here IMITATOR, a tool for synthesizing constraints on timing bounds (seen as parameters) in the framework of timed automata. Unlike classical synthesis methods, we take advantage of a given reference valuation of the parameters for which the system is known to behave properly. Our aim is to generate a constraint such that, under any valuation satisfying this constraint, the system is guaranteed to behave, in terms of alternating sequences of locations and actions, as under the reference valuation. This is useful for safely relaxing some values of the reference valuation, and optimizing timing bounds of the system. We have successfully applied our tool to various examples of asynchronous circuits and protocols.

1 Context

Timed automata [1] are finite control automata equipped with *clocks*, which are real-valued variables which increase uniformly. This model is useful for reasoning about real-time systems, because one can specify quantitatively the interval of time during which the transitions can occur, using timing bounds. However, the behavior of a system is very sensitive to the values of these bounds, and it is rather difficult to find their correct values. It is therefore interesting to reason *parametrically*, by considering that these bounds are unknown constants, or parameters, and try to synthesize a *constraint* (i.e., a conjunction of linear inequalities) on these parameters which will guarantee a correct behavior of the system. Such automata are called *parametric timed automata* (PTA) [2,11].

The synthesis of constraints for PTA has been mainly done by supposing given a set of "bad states" (see, e.g., [8,9]). The goal is to find a set of parameters for which the considered timed automaton does not reach any of these bad states. We call such a method a *bad-state oriented* method. By contrast, we present in this paper a tool based on a *good-state oriented* method.

2 Principle of IMITATOR

The tool IMITATOR (*Inverse Method for Inferring Time AbstracT behaviOR*) implements the algorithm *InverseMethod*, described in [4]. We assume given a

---

* This work is partially supported by the Agence Nationale de la Recherche, grant ANR-06-ARFU-005, and by Institut Farman (ENS Cachan).

M. Leucker and C. Morgan (Eds.): ICTAC 2009, LNCS 5684, pp. 336–342, 2009.

system modeled by a PTA $\mathcal{A}$. Whereas bad-state oriented methods consider a set of bad states, IMITATOR considers an initial tuple π_0 of values for the parameters, under which the system is known to behave properly. When the parameters are instantiated with π_0, the system is denoted by $\mathcal{A}[\pi_0]$. Under certain conditions, the algorithm *InverseMethod* generalizes this *good* behavior by computing a constraint K_0 which guarantees that, under any parameter valuation π satisfying K_0, the system behaves in the same manner: the behaviors of the timed automata $\mathcal{A}[\pi]$ and $\mathcal{A}[\pi_0]$ are *(time-abstract) equivalent*, i.e., the traces of execution viewed as alternating sequences of *locations* (or "control states") and actions are identical. This is written $\mathcal{A}[\pi] \equiv_{TA} \mathcal{A}[\pi_0]$. More formally, the algorithm *InverseMethod* solves the following *inverse problem* [4] for *acyclic* systems (i.e., with only finite traces) by computing a constraint K_0 such that:

1. $\pi_0 \models K_0$,
2. $\mathcal{A}[\pi] \equiv_{TA} \mathcal{A}[\pi_0]$, for any $\pi \models K_0$.

A practical application is to *optimize* (either decrease or increase) the value of some element of π_0, as long as it still satisfies K_0. This is of particular interest in the framework of digital circuits, in order to safely minimize some stabilization timings (typically "setup" or "hold").

The tool IMITATOR is available on its Web page[1].

3   General Structure

As depicted below, IMITATOR takes as inputs a PTA described in HyTECH syntax, and a reference valuation π_0. The aim of the program is to output a constraint K_0 on the parameters solving the inverse problem.

The algorithm *InverseMethod* on which IMITATOR relies can be summarized as follows. Starting with $K := True$, we iteratively compute a growing set of reachable symbolic states. A symbolic state of the system is a couple (q, C), where q is a location of the PTA, and C a constraint on the parameters[2]. When a π_0-*incompatible* state (q, C) is encountered (i.e., when $\pi_0 \not\models C$), K is refined as follows: a π_0-incompatible inequality J (i.e., such that $\pi_0 \not\models J$) is

---

[1] http://www.lsv.ens-cachan.fr/~andre/IMITATOR
[2] Strictly speaking, C is a constraint on the clock variables and the parameters, but the clock variables are omitted here for the sake of simplicity. See [4] for more details.

selected within C, and $\neg J$ is added to K. The procedure is then started again with this new K, and so on, until the whole set of reachable states ($Post^*$) is computed.

A simplified version of algorithm *InverseMethod* is given below, where the clock variables have been disregarded for the sake of simplicity. We denote by $Post^i_{\mathcal{A}(K)}(S)$ the set of symbolic states reachable from S in exactly i steps of $\mathcal{A}(K)$, and $\exists X : C$ denotes the elimination of clock variables in constraint C.

ALGORITHM *InverseMethod*($\mathcal{A}$, π_0)

Inputs	$\mathcal{A}$	: PTA of initial state s_0
	π_0	: Reference valuation of the parameters
Output	K_0	: Constraint on the parameters
Variables	i	: Current iteration
	K	: Current constraint on the parameters
	S	: Current set of symbolic states ($S = \bigcup_{j=0}^{i} Post^j_{\mathcal{A}(K)}(\{s_0\})$)

$i := 0$; $K := \textit{True}$; $S := \{s_0\}$

DO

    DO UNTIL there are no π_0-incompatible states in S

        Select a π_0-incompatible state (q, C) of S (i.e., s.t. $\pi_0 \not\models C$)

        Select a π_0-incompatible J in C (i.e., s.t. $\pi_0 \not\models J$)

        $K := K \wedge \neg J$; $S := \bigcup_{j=0}^{i} Post^j_{\mathcal{A}(K)}(\{(s_0)\})$

    OD

    IF $Post_{\mathcal{A}(K)}(S) = \emptyset$ **THEN RETURN** $K_0 := \bigcap_{(q,C) \in S}(\exists X : C)$

    FI

    $i := i + 1$; $S := S \cup Post_{\mathcal{A}(K)}(S)$

OD

This algorithm terminates and solves the inverse problem for acyclic systems. The acyclic class is interesting for hardware verification, e.g., when analyzing synchronous circuits over a fixed number (typically, 1 or 2) of clock cycles.

IMITATOR is a program written in Python, that drives HYTECH [10] for the computation of the *Post* operation. The Python program contains about 1500 lines of code, and it took about 4 man-months of work.

Remark. In order to handle cyclic examples, one modifies the algorithm by replacing, in the **IF** condition, $Post_{\mathcal{A}(K)}(S) = \emptyset$ by $Post_{\mathcal{A}(K)}(S) \subseteq S$. In that case, we ensure termination more often (see [4]). However, we do not guarantee any longer the identity of traces, but only the identity of reachable locations. This is interesting when $\mathcal{A}[\pi_0]$ is known to avoid a given bad location because, in this case, $\mathcal{A}[\pi]$ is also guaranteed to avoid this bad location, for any $\pi \models K_0$.

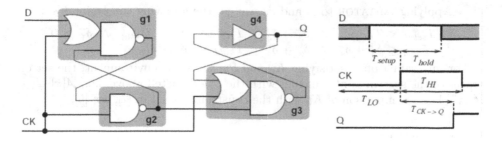

Fig. 1. Flip-flop circuit

4   An Illustrating Example

We consider an asynchronous "D flip-flop" circuit described in [7] and depicted on Fig. 1. It is composed of 4 gates (G_1, G_2, G_3 and G_4) interconnected in a cyclic way, and an environment involving two input signals D and CK. The global output signal is Q. Each gate G_i has a delay in the parametric interval $[\delta_i^-, \delta_i^+]$, with $\delta_i^- \leq \delta_i^+$. There are 4 other parameters (viz., $T_{HI}, T_{LO}, T_{setup}$, and T_{hold}) used to model the environment. Each gate is modeled by a PTA, as well as the environment. We consider an inertial model for gates, where any change of the input may lead to a change of the output (after some delay). The PTA $\mathcal{A}$ modeling the system results from the composition[3] of those 5 PTAs. The output signal of a gate G_i is named g_i (note that $Q = g_4$). The rising (resp. falling) edge of signal D is denoted by $D^\uparrow$ (resp. $D^\downarrow$) and similarly for signals $CK, Q, g_1, \ldots, g_4$. We consider the following instantiation π_0 of the parameters:

$$T_{HI} = 24 \qquad T_{LO} = 15 \qquad T_{setup} = 10 \qquad T_{hold} = 17 \qquad \delta_1^- = 7 \qquad \delta_1^+ = 7$$
$$\delta_2^- = 5 \qquad \delta_2^+ = 6 \qquad \delta_3^- = 8 \qquad \delta_3^+ = 10 \qquad \delta_4^- = 3 \qquad \delta_4^+ = 7$$

We consider an environment starting from $D = CK = Q = 0$ and $g_1 = g_2 = g_3 = 1$, with the following ordered sequence of actions for inputs D and CK: $D^\uparrow$, $CK^\uparrow$, $D^\downarrow$, $CK^\downarrow$, as depicted on Fig. 1 right. Therefore, we have the implicit constraint $T_{setup} \leq T_{LO} \wedge T_{hold} \leq T_{HI}$. For this environment and the instantiation π_0, the set of traces (alternating sequences of locations and actions) of the system is depicted below under the form of an oriented graph, where q_i, $1 \leq i \leq 9$, are locations of $\mathcal{A}$.

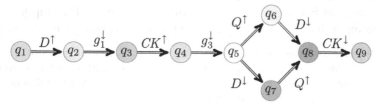

---

[3] The standard parallel composition of several PTAs is a PTA.

Applying IMITATOR to $\mathcal{A}$ and π_0, we get the following constraint $K_0{}^4$:

$$T_{setup} < T_{LO} \quad \wedge \quad \delta_3^+ + \delta_4^+ < T_{HI} \quad \wedge \quad \delta_1^+ < T_{setup} \quad \wedge \quad \delta_1^- > 0$$
$$\wedge \quad T_{hold} \leq \delta_3^+ + \delta_4^+ \quad \wedge \quad \delta_3^- + \delta_4^- \leq T_{hold} \quad \wedge \quad \delta_3^+ < T_{hold}$$

For any valuation π satisfying K_0 and for the same environment, the set of traces of the system $\mathcal{A}[\pi]$ coincides with the one depicted above, i.e., $\mathcal{A}[\pi] \equiv_{TA} \mathcal{A}[\pi_0]$. For a comparison of K_0 with the constraint found in [7], see [5].

5 Experiments

We applied the tool IMITATOR to various case studies from the literature, including a flip-flop circuit (described in Sect. 4), two protocols (root contention and CSMA/CD), as well as two real case studies: a portion of the memory circuit SPSMALL designed by ST-Microelectronics, and a distributed control system (SIMOP). All those experiments are detailed in [5]. The HYTECH source code of all the examples is available on IMITATOR webpage.

Example	# of PTAs	loc. per PTA	# of clocks	# of param.	# of iter.	$Post^*$	$\|K_0\|$	CPU time
Flip-flop [7]	5	[4, 16]	5	12	8	11	7	2 s
RCP [13]	5	[6, 11]	6	5	18	154	2	70 s
CSMA/CD [12,14]	3	[6, 7]	4	3	21	294	3	108 s
SPSMALL [6]	10	[3, 8]	10	22	31	31	23	78 mn
SIMOP [3]	5	[6, 16]	9	16	51	848	7	419 mn

The above table gives from left to right the name of the example, the number of PTAs composing the system $\mathcal{A}$, the lower and upper bounds on the number of locations per PTA, the numbers of clocks and parameters of $\mathcal{A}$, of iterations of the algorithm, of reached symbolic states, of inequalities in K_0 (after reduction), and the computation time on an Intel Quad Core 3 GHz with 3.2 Gb.

All these examples are acyclic[5], and thus guarantee the equality of traces, except SIMOP. In this latter case, we are only interested in avoiding a given bad location, and the equality of reachable locations is sufficient.

In the flip-flop and RCP examples, we took as π_0 an instance satisfying a constraint issued from a classical synthesis method of the literature. In this case, the constraint generated by our method may be the same as the constraint from the literature, but not necessarily: for example, in the case of the flip-flop circuit, K_0 is uncomparable with the original constraint of [7] (see [5] for details).

---

[4] It can be surprising that neither δ_2^- nor δ_2^+ appear in K_0. This constraint K_0 actually prevents G_2 from any change, as g_1 and CK are never both set to 1; therefore, g_2 always remains set to 1, and the delay of G_2 does not have any influence on the system for the considered environment.

[5] We considered an acyclic model for CSMA/CD and RCP by bounding the maximal number of collisions of messages.

In the CSMA/CD, SIMOP, VALMEM examples, the instantiation π_0 corresponds to typical data associated to the case study. In this case, the constraint K_0 allows us to optimize some values of the typical data π_0. This is useful, for example in order to safely relax some requirements on the environment of asynchronous circuits (see, e.g., [6]). In the SPSMALL case study, this allows us to safely optimize some nominal setup timing by 8 % (see [5]).

Running HyTech in a brute manner (fully parametric forward analysis) quickly leads to a saturation of the memory for most examples. One reason for which IMITATOR behaves well in practice is that the procedure drastically reduces the number of reachable states by quickly restraining K_0.

6   Final Remarks

Given a reference valuation π_0, IMITATOR solves the inverse problem for systems modeled by PTA with acyclic traces : it returns a constraint K_0 on the parameters guaranteeing that the sets of traces of $\mathcal{A}[\pi_0]$ and $\mathcal{A}[\pi]$ are identical, for any valuation π such that $\pi \models K_0$.

K_0 prevents all the bad behaviors (e.g. deadlocks), since it *imitates* the reference behavior of π_0, while constraints generated by classical methods may not prevent bad behaviors other than those specified by the bad states.

IMITATOR can be used in an *incremental* way as a complementary tool to enlarge constraints given by classical methods. For example, in the flip-flop case (see Sect. 4), the constraint, say Z, found in [7] is uncomparable with our constraint K_0. We can run IMITATOR once more with a reference valuation $\pi_1 \in Z \setminus K_0$. This gives a new constraint K_1, s.t. $K_0 \cup K_1$ is strictly larger than Z (see [5]).

Acknowledgments. I thank anonymous referees for their helpful comments.

References

1. Alur, R., Dill, D.L.: A theory of timed automata. TCS 126(2), 183–235 (1994)
2. Alur, R., Henzinger, T.A., Vardi, M.Y.: Parametric real-time reasoning. In: STOC 1993, pp. 592–601. ACM Press, New York (1993)
3. Amari, S., André, É., Chatain, T., De Smet, O., Denis, B., Encrenaz, E., Fribourg, L., Ruel, S.: Timed analysis of distributed control systems combining simulation and parametric model checking. Research report, LSV, ENS Cachan, France (2009)
4. André, É., Chatain, T., Encrenaz, E., Fribourg, L.: An inverse method for parametric timed automata. International Journal of Foundations of Computer Science (IJFCS) (to appear)
5. André, É., Encrenaz, E., Fribourg, L.: Synthesizing parametric constraints on various case studies using Imitator. Research report, Laboratoire Spécification et Vérification, ENS Cachan, France (June 2009)
6. Chevallier, R., Encrenaz-Tiphène, E., Fribourg, L., Xu, W.: Verification of the generic architecture of a memory circuit using parametric timed automata. In: Asarin, E., Bouyer, P. (eds.) FORMATS 2006. LNCS, vol. 4202, pp. 113–127. Springer, Heidelberg (2006)

7. Clarisó, R., Cortadella, J.: The octahedron abstract domain. In: Giacobazzi, R. (ed.) SAS 2004. LNCS, vol. 3148, pp. 312–327. Springer, Heidelberg (2004)

8. Clarke, E.M., Grumberg, O., Jha, S., Lu, Y., Veith, H.: Counterexample-guided abstraction refinement. In: Emerson, E.A., Sistla, A.P. (eds.) CAV 2000. LNCS, vol. 1855, pp. 154–169. Springer, Heidelberg (2000)

9. Frehse, G., Jha, S.K., Krogh, B.H.: A counterexample-guided approach to parameter synthesis for linear hybrid automata. In: Egerstedt, M., Mishra, B. (eds.) HSCC 2008. LNCS, vol. 4981, pp. 187–200. Springer, Heidelberg (2008)

10. Henzinger, T.A., Ho, P., Wong-Toi, H.: A user guide to HYTECH. In: Brinksma, E., Steffen, B., Cleaveland, W.R., Larsen, K.G., Margaria, T. (eds.) TACAS 1995. LNCS, vol. 1019, pp. 41–71. Springer, Heidelberg (1995)

11. Hune, T., Romijn, J., Stoelinga, M., Vaandrager, F.W.: Linear parametric model checking of timed automata. In: Margaria, T., Yi, W. (eds.) TACAS 2001. LNCS, vol. 2031, pp. 189–203. Springer, Heidelberg (2001)

12. Nicollin, X., Sifakis, J., Yovine, S.: Compiling real-time specifications into extended automata. IEEE Trans. on Software Engineering 18, 794–804 (1992)

13. Simons, D., Stoelinga, M.: Mechanical verification of the IEEE 1394a Root Contention Protocol using UPPAAL2k. International Journal on Software Tools for Technology Transfer 3(4), 469–485 (2001)

14. Wang, F.: Symbolic parametric safety analysis of linear hybrid systems with BDD-like data-structures. IEEE Trans. Softw. Eng. 31(1), 38–51 (2005)

GSPeeDI – A Verification Tool for Generalized Polygonal Hybrid Systems

Hallstein Asheim Hansen[1] and Gerardo Schneider[2]

[1] Buskerud University College, Kongsberg, Norway
Hallstein.Asheim.Hansen@hibu.no
[2] Dept. of Informatics, University of Oslo, Oslo, Norway
gerardo@ifi.uio.no

Abstract. The GSPeeDI tool implements a decision procedure for the reachability analysis of GSPDIs, planar hybrid systems whose dynamics is given by differential inclusions, and that are not restricted by the goodness assumption from previous work on the so-called SPDIs.

Unlike SPeeDI (a tool for reachability analysis of SPDIs) the underlying analysis of GSPeeDI is based on a breadth-first search algorithm, and it can handle more general systems.

1 Introduction

Hybrid systems combine dynamic and discrete behavior, and mathematical models can be defined for systems arising from real scenarios (e.g., a chemical plant) as well as for artificial constructions (e.g. by *hybridizing* a complex differential equation into connected piece-wise smaller equations). These systems are generally hard to analyze: most important verification problems are undecidable for non-trivial classes of hybrid systems. In this paper we deal with a class of planar hybrid systems whose dynamics is given by differential inclusions: *generalized polygonal hybrid systems* (GSPDIs). The reachability problem for GSPDI has been shown to be decidable [7].

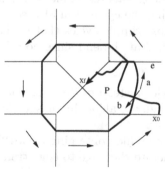

Fig. 1. GSPDI

A GSPDI is a pair $\mathcal{H} = \langle \mathbb{P}, \mathbb{F} \rangle$, where $\mathbb{P}$ is a finite partition of the plane (each $P \in \mathbb{P}$ being a convex polygon), called the *regions* of the GSPDI, and $\mathbb{F}$ is a function associating a pair of vectors to each polygon: $\mathbb{F}(P) = (\mathbf{a}_P, \mathbf{b}_P)$. In a GSPDI every point on the plane has its dynamics defined according to which polygon it belongs to: if $\mathbf{x} \in P$, then $\dot{\mathbf{x}} \in \angle_{\mathbf{a}_P}^{\mathbf{b}_P}$. The angle $\angle_{\mathbf{a}}^{\mathbf{b}}$ denotes a differential inclusion, meaning that the tangent vector at any point of a given trajectory must be a linear combination of vectors $\mathbf{a}$ and $\mathbf{b}$.

A complicating factor in the reachability analysis of GSPDIs is the presence of regions where the trajectory is allowed to enter and leave the region through

M. Leucker and C. Morgan (Eds.): ICTAC 2009, LNCS 5684, pp. 343–348, 2009.

the same edge, to slide along, or *bounce* off a given edge. For instance, in the example shown in Fig. 1 the dynamics of region P allows the trajectory to slide and bounce off the edge e. A region where no trajectory can enter and leave through the same edge is said to be *good*, and a GSPDI where all the regions are good is called an SPDI (we say that that SPDI satisfies the *goodness assumption*).

The tool GSPeeDI is the only tool we know of that implements a decision procedure to solve the reachability problem for this particular class of hybrid systems.

2 GSPeeDI

The tool GSPeeDI[1] is a collection of utilities to manipulate and reason mechanically about GSPDIs. It is implemented in 3000 lines of Python code.

The tool takes as input a GSPDI, together with a source and a target interval, on given edges. The tool operates on a graph whose nodes are the edges of the polygons (and not the polygons themselves) which are connected with directed arcs labelled with edge-to-edge one-dimensional successor functions over edge intervals. An *edge interval* represents an interval on a given edge. In order to check for reachability, we use a standard breadth-first search (BFS) model checking approach. We start from a set A containing an initial edge interval. Then we iteratively apply the possible transitions from the current set, adding the resulting edge intervals to A. The search ends if an edge interval from A contains the sought-after edge interval, or it ends when, if the sought-after edge interval cannot be reached, the fix-point is reached.

There are three kinds of possible transitions that one may take:

- Edge-to-edge transitions. The result of following the dynamics of a region, and represented as one step transition on the graph.
- 'Cycle' transitions. We only need to analyze simple cycles, which are then converted into *meta-transitions* in the graph. Using acceleration of such simple cycles we are able to compute all the edge intervals reachable by taking the cycle any number of times, without iterating the cycle in most cases.
- Sink transitions. We know how to identify those simple cycles that cannot be exited. These transitions will only be applied at the end since no other continuation is possible.

Using acceleration techniques for analyzing cycles instead of iterating them, we can sucessfully analyze large systems, even though the algorithm has a worst case complexity which is doubly exponential.

On the left of Fig. 2 we illustrate a typical input file containing a GSPDI composed of 8 regions. From this file we can generate the edge-to-edge transitions, and then create a picture of the GSPDI as shown in the upper right part of the figure. The lower right hand part shows a typical use scenario, where the imprecision is caused by a built-in floating point conversion routine in Python.

---

[1] http://heim.ifi.uio.no/hallstah/gspeedi/

Input file

```
# Points
P  1 1.5 1.5
P  2 2 2
P  3 1 2
P  4 1 1
P  5 2 1
P  6 3 2
P  7 2 3
P  8 1 3
P  9 0 2
P 10 0 1
P 11 1 0
P 12 2 0
P 13 3 1

# Regions

R 1 1 9 1 2 6 13 5
R 2 2 2 2 7 6
R 3 3 3 1 3 8 7 2
R 4 4 4 3 9 8
R 5 5a 5b 1 4 10 9 3
R 6 6 6 4 11 10
R 7 7 7 1 5 12 11 4
R 8 8 8 5 13 12

# Vectors

V 1 0 1
V 2 -1 1
V 3 -1 0
V 4 -1 -1
V 5b 0.2 -1
V 5a 0.1 -1
V 6 1 -1
V 7 1 0
V 8 1 1
V 9 -1.1 -1.1
```

Generated figure

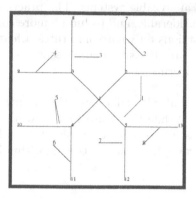

Session log

```
./search.py data/swimmer-g.graph '2->3~2-7' 0.5 '2->3~2-7' 0.2
Searching from:
N2->3~2-7   at   [[0.5, 0.5]]
to
N2->3~2-7   at   [[0.20000000000000001, 0.20000000000000001]]
True
```

In this example the search refers to a node in the graph, N2->3 2-7, which represents the edge 2-7. Since any edge may be traversed in both directions, we uniquely identify that we traverse the edge going from region 2 to region 3.

Fig. 2. Example

While the example contains only 8 regions, it has 84 simple edge cycles (including permutations). We may use various optimization techniques to reduce the search space, but even so, the number of possible paths reachable from a single edge may number in the thousands when we combine the cycles with edge-to-edge transitions.

3 Comparing and Contrasting with SPeeDI

A comparison with HyTech [3] is not meaningful since HyTech semi-decides more general hybrid systems than GSPeeDI, but it runs out of memory very quickly for very simple GSPDIs for which GSPeeDI gives an almost immediate answer due to acceleration. The obvious tool to compare GSPeeDI with is the tool SPeeDI [1], since GSPeeDI generalizes SPeeDI.

Our tool contains two major enhancements over SPeeDI, which justified a completely new implementation of reachability analysis for GSPDIs: We can analyze systems that are not restricted by the goodness assumption, and we do so using breadth-first (instead of depth-first) search.

Being able to analyze systems where the goodness asumption does not hold increases the number of analyzable systems. The practical implications for the design of the tool are considerable, and include a more complex vector/function library, and looser restrictions on what constitutes a feasible path of traversed edges and cycles. This in turn leads to a larger search space, so if all the regions are good, then SPeeDI performs much better, but SPeeDI cannot handle systems with non-good regions.

Another difference is that SPeeDI's algorithm is based on depth-first generation of feasible paths. While the depth-first algorithm may not necessarily generate the shortest possible counter example, it does have the advantage of generating the counter example as part of the algorithm itself.

4   Complexity

There are two main factors contributing to the run-time complexity of the tool. One is the computation of all the simple cycles in the directed GPSDI graph. The other is the execution of the breadth-first search algorithm. The latter has been shown to have a doubly exponential time complexity in the worst case. However, in practice we can apply a set of heuristics which reduce this complexity considerably, as explained below.

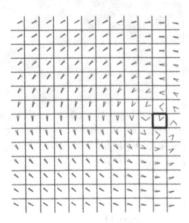

Fig. 3. Larger GSPDI example

Computing all simple cycles may be infeasible for large graphs: The number of simple cycles in a complete, directed graph with n nodes is exactly

$$\sum_{i=1}^{n-1} \binom{n}{n-i+1}(n-i)! \, .$$

For computing all simple cycles we have implemented the algorithm due to Tarjan [8], which has a time bound of $O((n+e)(c+1))$, where e is the number of edges and c the number of cycles in the graph. Clearly, the number of cycles is the factor determining the point at which a problem becomes infeasible.

Informal testing have shown that running an unmodified algorithm on examples with hundreds of nodes quickly becomes infeasible, both due to the execution time of the algorithm, and the number of (unpermutated) cycles.

Because of this the tool includes several domain specific optimizations to the algorithm. In particular we only investigate prefixes to cycles where:

- There actually are trajectories that make a complete cycle.
- The cycles will not be redundant. Cycles where the trajectories *bounce* off edges are not required to be analyzed.
- The generation of a cycle will not help analysis. This happens if a node represents an interval that may be reached in its entirety by any trajectory.

We will demonstrate the optimizations' effectiveness on a bigger example (partially shown in Fig. 3). The GSPDI contains 334 nodes (in the reachability graph). A run of the unmodified algorithm finds that the total number of cycles (without permutations) is 181398.

If we apply only the first optimization, we reduce that number to 1041 cycles. Adding the second optimization reduces the number to 112 cycles, and applying all three leaves us with 85 cycles. The optimizations cut off 811, 229, and 183 prefixes respectively.

So, for this particular example, we find that more than 99% of the possible cycles are redundant. Computing the number of permutations gives us a total of 1100 cycles subsequently used as meta-transitions in the breadth-first search.

The execution time of the program which generates the cycles is less than a minute on a low-end, modern CPU. On the same system a reachability search returning *false* (thus having computed the entire reach-set for a particular start-interval) finishes execution in slightly over ten seconds.

5   Discussion

We have presented a prototype tool for solving the reachability problem for generalized polygonal hybrid systems. The tool implements a BFS algorithm (as presented in [4]), following the theoretical results published in [7]. The algorithm is based on the analysis of a finite number of possible qualitative behaviors, including only simple loops which may be accelerated in most cases. Since the number of such behaviors may be extremely big, the tool uses several powerful heuristics that exploit the topological properties of planar trajectories for considerably reducing the set of actually explored paths on the reach-graph.

The main applications of GSPDIs is to over-approximate non-linear differential equations on the plane. Then we can apply GSPeeDI to perform reachability analysis. There is ongoing and future work in the area of automatically[2] partitioning the plane and generating GSPDIs based on such equations, based on whether properties such as Lipschitz continuity applies and can be exploited. This will allow for analysis of larger, real-world problems. The application of GSPeeDI to over-approximate planar differential equations could be combined with simulation techniques in order to further refine parts of the hybridized equation to make more precise analysis. This, together with the use of the phase portrait (see below) will produce less 'do not know' answers and increase the number of 'yes' and 'no' answers.

---

[2] A simple, ad-hoc application for automatic partitioning is distributed with the tool.

One line of future work is incorporating support for enhancements, optimizations and utilities currently available for SPeeDI, that have been already explored theoretically for SPDIs. This include the computation of the phase portrait of a system [2], which may allow both optimizations [6] and compositional parallelization [5] of the reachability analysis algorithm. Note that the implementation of such features will not add to the complexity of the tool as all the information needed to compute the phase portrait (invariance, viability and controllability kernels, and semi-separatrices) is already computed when analyzing simple cycles (see [5, 6] for more details).

We conjecture that the cycle generation and breadth-first search may mutually benefit from running in parallell and working with a shared state. There may, for example, be no need to generate cycles for sufficiently explored parts of the graph.

Acknowledgments. We would like to thank Gordon Pace for useful suggestions on how to improve the efficiency of the tool.

References

[1] Asarin, E., Pace, G., Schneider, G., Yovine, S.: SPeeDI: a verification tool for polygonal hybrid systems. In: Brinksma, E., Larsen, K.G. (eds.) CAV 2002. LNCS, vol. 2404, pp. 354–358. Springer, Heidelberg (2002)

[2] Asarin, E., Schneider, G., Yovine, S.: Towards computing phase portraits of polygonal differential inclusions. In: Tomlin, C.J., Greenstreet, M.R. (eds.) HSCC 2002. LNCS, vol. 2289, p. 49. Springer, Heidelberg (2002)

[3] Henzinger, T., Ho, P.-H., Wong-toi, H.: Hytech: A model checker for hybrid systems. Software Tools for Technology Transfer 1(1) (1997)

[4] Pace, G., Schneider, G.: Model checking polygonal differential inclusions using invariance kernels. In: Steffen, B., Levi, G. (eds.) VMCAI 2004. LNCS, vol. 2937, pp. 110–121. Springer, Heidelberg (2004)

[5] Pace, G., Schneider, G.: A compositional algorithm for parallel model checking of polygonal hybrid systems. In: Barkaoui, K., Cavalcanti, A., Cerone, A. (eds.) ICTAC 2006. LNCS, vol. 4281, pp. 168–182. Springer, Heidelberg (2006)

[6] Pace, G., Schneider, G.: Static analysis for state-space reduction of polygonal hybrid systems. In: Asarin, E., Bouyer, P. (eds.) FORMATS 2006. LNCS, vol. 4202, pp. 306–321. Springer, Heidelberg (2006)

[7] Pace, G.J., Schneider, G.: Relaxing goodness is still good. In: Fitzgerald, J.S., Haxthausen, A.E., Yenigun, H. (eds.) ICTAC 2008. LNCS, vol. 5160, pp. 274–289. Springer, Heidelberg (2008)

[8] Tarjan, R.E.: Enumeration of the elementary circuits of a directed graph. Technical report, Ithaca, NY, USA (1972)

Hierarchical Graph Rewriting as a Unifying Tool for Analyzing and Understanding Nondeterministic Systems

Kazunori Ueda, Takayuki Ayano, Taisuke Hori, Hiroki Iwasawa,
and Seiji Ogawa

Dept. of Computer Science and Engineering, Waseda University
3-4-1, Okubo, Shinjuku-ku, Tokyo 169-8555, Japan

Abstract. We have designed and implemented LMNtal (pronounced "elemental"), a language based on hierarchical graph rewriting that allows us to encode diverse computational models involving concurrency, mobility and multiset rewriting. Towards its novel applications, the system has recently evolved into a model checker that employs LMNtal as the modeling language and PLTL as the specification language. The strengths of our LMNtal model checker are its powerful data structure, highly nondeterministic computation it can express, and virtually no discrepancy between programming and modeling languages. Models expressed in Promela, MSR, and Coloured Petri Nets can be easily encoded into LMNtal. The visualizer of the LMNtal IDE turned out to be extremely useful in understanding models by state space browsing. The LMNtal IDE has been used to run and visualize diverse examples taken from the fields of model checking, concurrency and AI search.

1 Introduction

LMNtal [4] is a language model based on (a class of) hierarchical graph rewriting that uses point-to-point links to represent connectivity and membranes to represent hierarchy. LMNtal was designed to be a substrate language of various computational models, especially those addressing concurrency, mobility and multiset rewriting. As a graph/multiset rewriting language, it has close connections with Interaction Nets, Bigraphs, Chemical Abstract Machine and Constraint Handling Rules. Its outstanding feature is the ability to address the two fundamental structuring concepts, connectivity and hierarchy, which makes it promising as a modeling language as well as a programming language. The expressive power of the language was demonstrated through the encoding of various computational models including the ambient calculus [5] and the lambda calculus [6]. Although membranes were introduced to represent first-class multisets and to delimit the scope of rewrite rules, they turned out to play fundamental roles in the creation of and the operations on fresh local names as well [6].

Since its conception, the LMNtal project has focused on growing the unique computational model into a full-fledged programming language, and delivered

M. Leucker and C. Morgan (Eds.): ICTAC 2009, LNCS 5684, pp. 349–355, 2009.

a compiler-based implementation with a number of practical features [3]. The present paper reports our next-generation implementation that newly features state-space search and LTL model checking. Evolving LMNtal into model checking is motivated by the following observations:

- LMNtal allows straightforward translation from many modeling languages for computer-aided verification including state transition systems, multiset rewriting and process calculi.
- Models in those formalisms generally have a high degree of nondeterminism and demand a tool for understanding their properties and behavior.
- The computational model of LMNtal is turning out to be a suitable tool for describing a broad range of search problems.

An outstanding feature of our LMNtal model checker is that, unlike other modeling languages that are not offered as programming languages due to limited data types, any LMNtal program can readily be model-checked with virtually no restrictions. Of course, it is the responsibility of programmers to ensure the finiteness of models for the termination of model checking. Maude is another exception that allows model checking with inductive data types, but LMNtal goes one step forward by featuring hierarchical, cyclic graphs and comes with an IDE, an important tool described below.

Another key feature is that the IDE we have developed supports the *understanding of models—both with and without errors*—through the visualization of state spaces and execution paths, while most other model checkers are constructive only in bug catching. Rather than aiming for exploring huge state space, the LMNtal model checker and its IDE aim to explore two new directions of future programming languages and systems: (i) to provide a unified environment of execution and validation, and (ii) to offer fine-grained concurrency with a support for understanding its behavior. Since the performance of model checking critically depends on appropriate modeling, the LMNtal IDE can be used as a workbench for designing and analyzing models and hence is complementary to more specialized, high-performance model checkers.

2   LMNtal

We quickly overview LMNtal. LMNtal employs hierarchical graphs as its basic data structure, which consist of (i) atoms, (ii) links for 1-to-1 connection, and (iii) membranes that can enclose atoms and other membranes and can be crossed by links. Processes are graphs co-located with graph rewrite rules.

The syntax of LMNtal is given in Fig. 1, where two syntactic categories, *links* (denoted by X) and *names* (denoted by p), are presupposed. The name = is reserved for atomic processes for interconnecting two links.

A process P must observe the following *link condition*: Each link in P (excluding those links occurring in rules) may occur *at most twice*.

Intuitively, **0** is an inert process; $p(X_1, \ldots, X_m)$ $(m \geq 0)$ is an *atom* with m links; P, P is parallel composition called a *molecule*; $\{P\}$, a *cell*, is a process

$$
\begin{array}{rl}
\text{(Process)} & P ::= \mathbf{0} \mid p(X_1,\ldots,X_m) \mid P,P \mid \{P\} \mid T :\text{-} T \\
\text{(Process template)} & T ::= \mathbf{0} \mid p(X_1,\ldots,X_m) \mid T,T \mid \{T\} \mid T :\text{-} T \mid @p \mid \$p
\end{array}
$$

Fig. 1. Syntax of LMNtal (simplified)

```
v($v), h($h), u($u), d($d) :-
    $u=:=$h+$v, $d=:=$h-$v, $v1=$v+1 | queen($v,$h), v($v1).
v(1).    h(1), h(2), h(3), h(4), h(5).
u(2), u(3), u(4), u(5), u(6), u(7), u(8), u(9), u(10).
d(-4), d(-3), d(-2), d(-1), d(0), d(1), d(2), d(3), d(4).
```

Fig. 2. 5-queens

grouped by the membrane { }; and $T :\text{-} T$ is a rewrite rule for processes. Rewrite rules must observe several syntactic conditions (details omitted; see [4]) to ensure that reduction preserves the link condition. A *rule context*, $@p$, is to match a (possibly empty) multiset of rules within a cell, while a *process context*, $\$p$, is to match processes other than rules within a cell.

An abbreviation called a *term notation* allows an atom b without its final argument to occur as the kth argument of a, to mean that the kth argument of a and the final argument of b are interconnected. For instance, f(g(x)) is the same as f(A),g(B,A),x(B). A list with the elements A_i's can be written as $X = [A_1,\ldots,A_n]$, where X is the link to the list. Some atoms such as + are written as unary or binary operators. Parallel composition can be written both in comma-separated and period-terminated forms.

Numbers are unary atoms such as 8(X), where X is connected to the atom referring to it. Our extended syntax allows conditional rewrite rules such as

$$\texttt{p(X), \$n[X] :- int(\$n), \$n>0 | p(Y), \$n[Y], p(Z), \$n[Z]}$$

meaning that a graph consisting of a unary p and a positive integer will be duplicated, and LMNtal allows it to be abbreviated to p($n):- $n>0 | p($n),p($n).

Computation proceeds by rewriting processes using rules co-located in the same place of the nested membrane structure.

2.1 Two Quick Examples

LMNtal allows extremely concise encoding of typical examples in AI search.

The first, one-rule program (Fig. 2) finds a solution to the n-queens problem. Each queen "consumes" one <u>h</u>orizontal, one <u>v</u>ertical and two diagonal (<u>u</u>p and <u>d</u>own) rows given as initial resources. The program makes sense only with the newly implemented state-space search capability. Vertical rows are generated one at a time to reduce the search space. We can run the program either in the

```
P1=p([$h1|$t1]), P2=p([$h2|$t2]) :- $h1<$h2 |
    P1=p($t1), P2=p([$h1,$h2|$t2]).
poles(p([1,2,3,4,999]), p([999]), p([999])).
```

Fig. 3. Tower of Hanoi

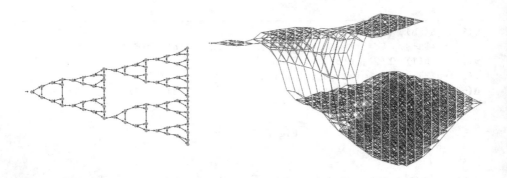

Fig. 4. Transition diagram visualized with StateViewer; the tower of Hanoi (left) and Church numeral exponentiation (right)

nondeterministic execution mode or in the model checking mode. In the latter case, states containing $v(n+1)$ are specified as accept states.

The next one-rule program (Fig. 3) explores the cyclic state space of the tower of Hanoi. The transition diagram automatically generated by StateViewer (Fig. 4, left) exhibits the recursive nature of the problem. The use of a multiset in the LHS of the rule absorbs structural symmetry and contributes to the brevity of the program.

3   Implementation

The LMNtal model checker (50,000 lines of code) builds upon a full-fledged implementation of LMNtal written in Java, which established the compilation technique of hierarchical graph rewriting and the intermediate instruction set.

The LMNtal model checker employs exactly the same compiler, which is a strength of our approach, but provides a new runtime in C with better performance and backtrack search. Properties to be checked are either given directly as Büchi automata, or are written in LTL and compiled into equivalent Büchi automata using LTL2BA. The meaning of propositional symbols in the claims are defined using the LMNtal syntax without the RHS. For instance, the property definition `f = p($x):-$x>0 |` defines the symbol f as "containing an atom p whose first argument is connected to a positive integer."

The model checker runtime receives (i) the intermediate code of the program, (ii) the intermediate code of the property definitions, and (iii) the Büchi

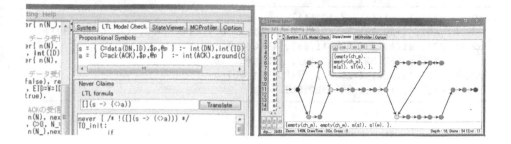

Fig. 5. LTL specification pane (left) and StateViewer (right)

automaton, and performs explicit-state LTL model checking. As a byproduct, the runtime also provides a nondeterministic execution mode that performs state-space search without property claims.

The challenge in implementing those new features was the checking algorithm of (hierarchical) graph isomorphism. Our algorithm first checks the hash values of hierarchical graphs and only when it collides, comparison based on exhaustive DFS is performed. The algorithm has enabled *model checking with graphs*, which benefits from the inherent symmetry reduction mechanism.

Integrated development environments are very important in verification because they greatly simplify the cumbersome procedure and the programs we verify are what we don't understand yet. Our publicly available LMNtalEditor[1] automates many of the steps necessary for verification. The panes of LMNtalEditor include the program editor, the system output pane, LTL specifier (Fig. 5, left), StateViewer (for nondeterministic execution), LTL StateViewer (for model checking), and the progress meter, the latter five of which are switchable.

StateViewer (Fig. 5, right) and LTL StateViewer render state transition diagrams and provide various functionalities for navigating and exploring them, including state search based on graph pattern matching. Coloring of states based on the number of transitions turned out to be very useful for finding special (e.g., final) states. Figure 4 (right) shows an automatically rendered state transition diagram (940 states) of the exponentiation of Church numerals (2^2) under our fine-grained encoding of the pure λ-calculus [6], which clearly indicates that there are two final states (representing the same λ-term with different graph representations) at different depths. Observations of this kind are a clue to finding interesting properties that are worth attempting to prove.

4   More Examples and Conclusion

LMNtal is simple but expressive enough to allow the translation of models expressed in other modeling languages.

---

[1] http://www.ueda.info.waseda.ac.jp/lmntal/

```
a0 :- n1(A0), a1(A1), {+A0,+A1}.
b0, n1(A0), {+A0,$a} :- n2(A1,B1), b1(A2,B2), {+A1,+A2,$a}, {+B1,+B2}.
n2(A0,B0), a1(A1), {+A0,+A1,$a}, {+B0,$b} :-
    n3(B1), a2(A2,B2), {+A2,$a}, {+B1,+B2,$b}.
n3(B0), b1(A0,B1), {+A0,$a}, {+B0,+B1,$b} :-
    b2(A1,B2), {+A1,$a}, {+B2,$b}.
```

Fig. 6. Simplified Needham-Schroeder protocol [1]

```
{ ch_m(empty), ch_w(empty), m, w.
  m :- m(s1).
  m(s1), ch_w(empty)   :- m(s2), ch_w(ini).
  m(s2), ch_m(ack)     :- m(s3), ch_m(empty).
  m(s3), timeout       :- m(s4).
  m(s4), ch_w(empty)   :- m(se), ch_w(shutup).
  m(s4), ch_w(empty)   :- m(s7), ch_w(dreq).
  m(s7), ch_m(data)    :- m(s8), ch_m(empty).
  m(s8), ch_w(empty)   :- m(s8), ch_w(data).
  m(s8), ch_w(empty)   :- m(se), ch_w(shutup).
  m(se), ch_m(shutup) :- m(sf), ch_m(empty).
  m(sf), ch_w(empty)   :- m(sg), ch_w(quiet).
  m(sg), ch_m(dead)    :- mEnd.

  % ... (similar for the partner process 'w') ...
}
{$p,@p}/ :- \+($p=(mEnd,wEnd,$q)) | {timeout,$p,@p}.
```

Fig. 7. Data transfer protocol (cf. the Promela version ([2], p.27))

MSR [1] is a multiset rewriting language with existential quantification (on the RHS) used for representing nonces. Figure 6 shows the simplified Needham-Schroeder protocol between the initiator **a** and the responder **b** though the channel **n**. In LMNtal, nonce creation is represented as the creation of a membrane, and references to nonces are represented as incident links to the membrane. The use of membranes to represent fresh local names and operations on them has played a crucial role in encoding diverse computational models.

Concurrent processes with shared variables and channels can also be translated into LMNtal. Figure 7 shows an example translated from a Promela model using channel communication, and Fig. 5 (right) shows the result of visualization. A channel with capacity n is represented as an n-ary atom whose empty slots are indicated by the atom `empty`.

To conclude, LMNtalEditor has provided a simple click-view-explore interface which significantly lowered the entry barrier to the world of verification and search. The tool is planned to feature abstraction and partial-order reduction to make the tool more powerful and scalable.

References

1. Cervesato, I., et al.: A Meta-notation for Protocol Analysis. In: Proc. CSFW 1999, pp. 55–69. IEEE Computer Society, Los Alamitos (1999)
2. Holzmann, G.: The SPIN Model Checker. Addison-Wesley, Reading (2004)
3. Murayama, K., et al.: Implementation of the Hierarchical Graph Rewriting Language LMNtal. Computer Software 25(2), 47–77 (2008)
4. Ueda, K., Kato, N.: LMNtal: A Language Model with Links and Membranes. In: Mauri, G., Păun, G., Jesús Pérez-Jímenez, M., Rozenberg, G., Salomaa, A. (eds.) WMC 2004. LNCS, vol. 3365, pp. 110–125. Springer, Heidelberg (2005)
5. Ueda, K.: Encoding Distributed Process Calculi into LMNtal. Electronic Notes in Theoretical Computer Science 209, 187–200 (2008)
6. Ueda, K.: Encoding the Pure Lambda Calculus into Hierarchical Graph Rewriting. In: Voronkov, A. (ed.) RTA 2008. LNCS, vol. 5117, pp. 392–408. Springer, Heidelberg (2008)

Author Index